Explanation of a Campsite Entry Caravan Europe 2012/2013

The town under which the campsite is listed, as shown on the relevant Sites Location Map at the end of each country's site entry pages

Distance and direction of the site from the centre of the town the site is listed under in kilometres (or metres), together with site's aspect

Site Location Map grid reference

Site open all year

GPS co-ordinates – latitude and longitude

Campsite name

Campsite address, including post code

Contact email address and website address

Description of the campsite and its facilities

Telephone and fax numbers including national code where applicable

Directions to the campsite

Comments and opinions of caravanners who have visited the site

Unspecified facilities for disabled guests

Charge per night in high season for car, caravan + 2 adults (in local currency) as at year of last report

The year in which the site was last reported on by a visitor

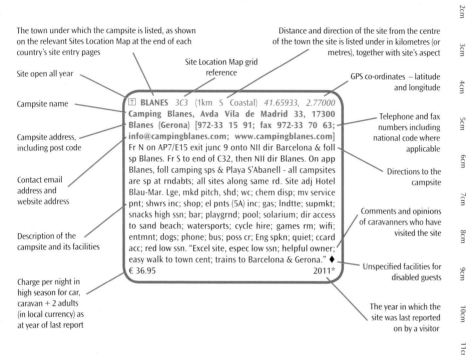

⊞ **BLANES** *3C3* (1km S Coastal) *41.65933, 2.77000*
Camping Blanes, Avda Vila de Madrid 33, 17300 Blanes (Gerona) [972-33 15 91; fax 972-33 70 63; info@campingblanes.com; www.campingblanes.com] Fr N on AP7/E15 exit junc 9 onto NII dir Barcelona & foll sp Blanes. Fr S to end of C32, then NII dir Blanes. On app Blanes, foll camping sps & Playa S'Abanell - all campsites are sp at rndabts; all sites along same rd. Site adj Hotel Blau-Mar. Lge, mkd pitch, shd; wc; chem disp; mv service pnt; shwrs inc; shop; el pnts (5A) inc; gas; lndtte; supmkt; snacks high ssn; bar; playgrnd; pool; solarium; dir access to sand beach; watersports; cycle hire; games rm; wifi; entmnt; dogs; phone; bus; poss cr; Eng spkn; quiet; ccard acc; red low ssn. "Excel site, espec low ssn; helpful owner; easy walk to town cent; trains to Barcelona & Gerona." ♦
€ 36.95   2011*

Popular Abbreviations
(for a full list of abbreviations please see page 11).

Site Description

sm: max 50 pitches	**med**: 51–150 pitches	**lge**: 151-500 pitches	**v lge**: 501+ pitches	**hdg**: hedged
mkd: marked	**sl**: sloping site	**pt sl**: sloping in parts	**terr**: terraced site	**shd**: plenty of shade
pt shd: part shaded	**unshd**: no shade	**hdstg**: some hard standing or gravel pitches		

Popular Abbreviations for Site Facilities

Adv bkg:	advanced booking accepted	**lndtte**:	washing machine(s) with or without tumble dryers
CCI or CCS:	Camping Card International or Camping Card Scandinavia accepted	**NH**:	suitable as a night halt;
chem disp:	dedicated chemical toilet disposal facilities	**quiet**:	peaceful, tranquil site
chem disp (wc):	no dedicated point; disposal via wc only	**rest**:	restaurant
CL-type:	very small, privately-owned, informal and usually basic, farm or country site	**shwrs**:	hot showers available at a fee
El pnts:	mains electric hook-ups	**shwrs inc**:	cost included in the site fee quoted
Eng spkn:	English spoken	**tradsmn**:	tradesmen call at the site, e.g. baker
entmnt:	entertainment (facilities or organised)	**SBS**	Site Booking Reference - Ref No. for a site included in the Caravan Club's network i.e. bookable through the Club
		ssn	season

Popular Generic Abbreviations

Adj: adjacent, nearby; **app**: approach, on approaching; **arr**: arrival, arriving **bef**: before **bet**: between **c'van**: caravan; **ccard acc**: Credit and/or debit cards accepted; **CChq acc**: Camping cheques accepted; **clsd**: closed **E**: East; **ent**: entrance/ entry to **excel**: excellent; **facs**: facilities; **foll**: follow; **fr**: from; **gd**: good; **inc**: included/inclusive; **L**: left; **M'van**: motorhome/ motor caravan; **narr**: narrow **N**: North; **o'fits**: outfits; **R**: right; **rec**: recommend/ed; **red**: reduced/reduction; **rte**: route **S**: South; **sp**: sign post/signposted; **strt**: straight, straight ahead **sw**: swimming **vg**: very good; **W**: West

Caravan Europe
Spain and Portugal

© The Caravan Club Limited 2012
Published by The Caravan Club Limited
East Grinstead House, East Grinstead
West Sussex RH19 1UA

General Enquiries: 01342 326944
Brochure Requests: 01342 327410
Travel Service Reservations: 01342 316101
Red Pennant Overseas
 Holiday Insurance: 01342 336633
Website: www.caravanclub.co.uk
Email: enquiries@caravanclub.co.uk

Editor: Rowena Sait
Email: rowena.sait@caravanclub.co.uk

Printed by Elanders Ltd
Newcastle-upon-Tyne
ISBN 978-0-9569510-1-4

Maps and distance charts generated from Collins Bartholomew
Digital Database

Maps © Collins Bartholomew Ltd 2011, reproduced by
permission of HarperCollins Publishers

Front cover photo: Portugal © iStockphoto.com/Rudi Lange
Below front cover images by Mrs Pauline Harrison; Mr Robert
Heaslewood; Mrs Susan Hatcher.

Contents

This free brochure brings you the best of Europe

Kopie, on the Lakes & Mountains Grand Tour

The Caravan Club has handpicked over 200 quality campsites throughout Europe, inspecting each one to make sure they deliver to the highest standards you expect.

This year we've added some terrific new sites for you to discover, from the foot of the Pyrénées to the beautiful Loire Valley.

Our ever-popular tours now include an amazing 33-night Grand Tour of Lakes & Mountains across Europe, a Celtic Grand Tour of Ireland & Brittany and a seven-night Champagne Tour of such famous names as Moët & Chandon and Tattinger.

There are escorted tours for those who've never travelled abroad before, GB Privilege motorhome-only tours, Atlantic Adventures, tours of the Dutch Bulbfields and so much more.

Download your free copy today or phone us to start enjoying the best of Europe.

THE CARAVAN CLUB

Find out more in our free 'Continental Caravanning' brochure available online at **www.caravanclub.co.uk/brochures** or call for your copy on **01342 327 410**

Welcome
to Caravan Europe 2012/2013

We are very pleased to be able to bring you the 2012/2013 edition of Caravan Europe, the dedicated guide to touring and campsites. This volume of the comprehensive handbook contains practical information with helpful hints and advice on touring and travelling in Spain and Portugal, as well as over 700 sites for you to choose from in these countries, the majority of which have been recommended by Caravan Club members.

Within Caravan Europe you will find campsites to suit all needs and requirements. Whether you're looking for a peaceful holiday in the countryside or mountains, or a lively resort by the sea or city, there really is something for everyone. What's more, every site entry has comments and reviews from fellow caravanners and tourers, giving you unique eyewitness accounts of each campsite.

In order to be able to include as many recommended campsites as possible we have continued to use our abbreviation list for site entries, which means you are able to choose from a wide variety of campsites across Spain and Portugal. We have included some of the most popular abbreviations on the bookmark page, so you can now always have these to hand whenever you check a site entry. You can also find the full list of abbreviations on page 11.

Caravan Europe has been put together to help you get the most out of your holiday and we hope that you find it a useful and enjoyable resource when planning your trip. Without you, the reader, Caravan Europe wouldn't be such an invaluable source of information. If you visit a campsite please fill in a site report form and share your experience with us. This will also give you automatic entry into our competition to win a Snooper Ventura Caravan Club Edition Sat Nav, the perfect satellite navigation system for anyone with a caravan.

We wish you a wonderful time on your travels and look forward to receiving your site reports!

Rowena Sait

Rowena Sait, Editor

Read on to discover
1000's of sites

www.caravanclub.co.uk

How to use this guide

Introduction

The information contained within Caravan Europe is presented in the following categories:

The Handbook

This includes general information about touring in Europe, such as legal requirements, advice and regulations. The Handbook chapters are at the front of the guide under the section headings:

Planning and Travelling

During Your Stay

These two sections are divided into chapters in alphabetical order, not necessarily the order of priority. Cross-references are given where additional information is provided in another chapter.

Country Introductions

Following on from the Handbook chapters you will find the Country Introductions chapter containing information, regulations and advice specific to each country. You should read the Country Introductions carefully in conjunction with the Handbook chapters before you set off on your holiday. Cross-references to other chapters are provided where appropriate.

Campsite Entries

After the Country Introduction you will find the campsite entries listed alphabetically according to the towns and villages in, or near to, where they are located. Where several campsites are shown in and around the same town they will be listed in clockwise order from the north.

To find a campsite all you need to do is look for the town or village of where you would like to stay in or nearby. If a campsite is not shown under the name of the particular town or village that you are searching for, then a cross-reference may indicate an alternative village or town under which it may be found in the guide. For example, for the town Castanares De La Rioja (Spain) the cross-reference will direct you to campsites listed under Haro.

To maintain consistency we have used local versions of town or city names.

In order to facilitate such a large number of campsites within Caravan Europe we have used abbreviations in the site entries. For a full and detailed list of these abbreviations please refer to

the chapter Explanation of a Campsite Entry. We have also included some of the most popular abbreviations used, as well as an explanation of a campsite entry, on the tear-out bookmark page for your convenience. Simply pull out the bookmark page at the front of Caravan Europe and you can then always have it to hand whenever you need to check a site entry in the guide.

Campsite Fees

Campsite entries show high season fees per night in Euros for a car, caravan, plus two adults, as at the year of the last report. In addition a deposit or booking fee may be charged, which might not be refundable. Prices given do not necessarily include electricity or showers, unless indicated, or local taxes. Outside of the main holiday season many sites offer discounts on the prices shown and also some sites may offer a reduction for longer stays.

Campsite fees may vary to the prices stated in the site entries. You are advised to always check fees when booking, or at least before pitching, as those shown in site entries should be used as a guide only.

that particular local area. With some exceptions sites are listed under towns up to approximately 15 kilometres away. The place names used as a central point are usually, but not always, the largest towns in each region; some may be only small villages.

Satellite Navigation

Most campsite entries in this guide now show a GPS (sat nav) reference. It is in the format 41.39277 (latitude north) and 2.17649 (longitude east), i.e. decimal degrees. Readings shown as -1.23456 indicate that the longitude position in question is west of the 0 degrees Greenwich meridian. This is important to bear in mind when inputting co-ordinates into your sat nav device for campsites in western France, most of Spain and Portugal. Readings given in other formats such as degrees + minutes + seconds or degrees + decimal minutes can be converted using www.cosports.com then click on GPS Lat/ Long Conversion, or simply use Google maps (http://maps.google.co.uk) and input a GPS reference in any format to locate a town, village or campsite.

Please be aware if you are using a sat nav device some routes may take you on roads that are narrow and/or are not suitable for caravans or large outfits.

The GPS co-ordinates given in this guide are derived from a number of reliable sources but it has not been possible to check them all individually. The Caravan Club cannot accept responsibility for any inaccuracies, errors or omissions or for their effects.

Sites Location Maps

Each town and village listed alphabetically in the site entry pages has a map grid reference number, e.g. 3B4 or C2. The map grid reference number is shown on each site entry. The maps can be found at the end of each country's site entry pages. The reference number will show you where each town or village is located. Place names are shown on the maps in two colours:

Red where there is a site open all year (or for at least approximately eleven months of the year)

Black where only seasonal sites which close in winter have been reported.

Please note: these maps are for general campsite location purposes only; a detailed road map or atlas is essential for route planning and touring.

Town names in capital letters (RED, BLACK or in ITALICS) correspond with towns listed on the Distance Chart.

The scale used for the Sites Location Maps means that it is not possible to pinpoint every town or village where a campsite exists. Where we cannot show an individual town or village on a Sites Location Map for reasons of space, we list it under another nearby town which then acts as a central point for campsites within

Site Report Forms

With the exception of campsites in The Club's Overseas Site Booking Service (SBS) network, The Caravan Club does not inspect sites listed in this guide. Virtually all of the site reports in Caravan Europe are submitted voluntarily by both members and non-members of The Caravan Club during the course of their own holidays.

> ## We rely on you, the users of this guide, to tell us about campsites you have visited

Sites which are not reported on for five to six years may be deleted from the guide. We therefore rely very much on you, the users of this guide, to tell us about campsites you have visited – old favourites as well as new discoveries.

You will find some site report forms towards the back of this guide which we hope you will complete and return to us by freepost. An abbreviated site report form is provided if you are reporting no changes (or only minor changes) to a site entry. Additional site report forms are available online and on request.

You can complete both the full and abbreviated versions of the site report forms on our website. Simply go to www.caravanclub.co.uk/europereport and either complete the form online or download blank forms to fill in later and post to The Caravan Club.

> ## Complete site report forms online – www.caravanclub.co.uk/europereport

For an explanation of the abbreviations that are used in the site entries, please refer to the chapter *Explanation of a Campsite Entry* or use the tear-out bookmark page at the front of the guide which shows some of the most popular abbreviations used.

Please submit reports as soon as possible. Information received by **mid September 2013** will be used wherever possible in the next edition of Caravan Europe. Reports received after that date are still very welcome and will be retained for entry in a subsequent edition. The editor is unable to respond individually to site reports submitted due to the large quantity that we receive.

Win a Sat Nav

If you submit site reports to the editor during 2012 and 2013 – whether by post, email or online – you will have your name entered into a prize draw to win the Snooper Ventura Caravan Club Edition Sat Nav (terms and conditions apply). Four runners up will also receive the latest editions of Caravan Europe.

The Snooper Ventura Caravan Club Edition Sat Nav will already have the GPS co-ordinates programmed in for the majority of campsites within the current edition of Caravan Europe as well as Club sites throughout the UK, allowing you to find sites around your present or future location at the touch of a button. It has been specifically designed for caravanners and will calculate routes that avoid obstacles such as narrow roads and low bridges, based on the size of your vehicle. The perfect equipment for anyone with a caravan or large motorhome!

Tips for Completing Site Reports

- If possible it is best to fill in a site report form while you are at the campsite or shortly after your stay. Once back at home it can be difficult to remember details of individual sites, especially if you visited several during your trip.

- When giving directions to a site, remember to include the direction of travel, e.g. 'from north on D137, turn left onto D794 signposted Combourg' or 'on N83 from Poligny turn right

snooper**ventura**
Caravan Club edition

at petrol station in village'. Wherever possible give road numbers, together with junction numbers and/or kilometre post numbers, where you exit from motorways or main roads. It is also helpful to mention useful landmarks such as bridges, roundabouts, traffic lights or prominent buildings, and to advise whether the site is signposted. If there are any roads that are difficult to access or narrow please also mention this in the report.

- When noting the compass direction of a site **this must be in the direction FROM THE TOWN the site is listed under TO THE SITE, and not the direction from the site to the town.** Distances are measured in a straight line and may differ significantly from the distance by road.

- If you are only amending a few details about a site there is no need to use the longer version form. You may prefer to use the abbreviated version but, in any event, do remember to give the campsite name and the town or village under which it is listed in the guide. Alternatively, use the online version of the form – www.caravanclub.co.uk/europereport

- If possible, give precise opening and closing dates, e.g. 1 April to 30 September. This information is particularly important for early and late season travellers.

The editor very much appreciates the time and trouble you take submitting reports on campsites that you have visited; without your valuable contributions it would be impossible to update this guide.

Every effort is made to ensure that information contained in this publication is accurate and that the details given in good faith in the site report forms are accurately reproduced or summarised. The Caravan Club Ltd has not checked these details by inspection or other investigation and cannot accept responsibility for the accuracy of these reports as provided by members and non-members, or for errors, omissions or their effects. In addition The Caravan Club Ltd cannot be held accountable for the quality, safety or operation of the sites concerned, or for the fact that conditions, facilities, management or prices may have changed since the last recorded visit. Any recommendations, additional comments or opinions have been contributed by caravanners and people staying on the site and are not generally those of The Caravan Club.

The inclusion of advertisements or other inserted material does not imply any form of approval or recognition, nor can The Caravan Club Ltd undertake any responsibility for checking the accuracy of advertising material.

Acknowledgements

The Caravan Club's thanks go to the AIT/FIA Information Centre (OTA), the Alliance Internationale de Tourisme (AIT), the Fédération International de Camping et de Caravaning (FICC) and to the national clubs and tourist offices of those countries who have assisted with this publication.

How to use this Guide

Explanation of a Campsite Entry

The town under which the campsite is listed, as shown on the relevant Sites Location Map at the end of each country's site entry pages

Site Location Map grid reference

Distance and direction of the site from the centre of the town the site is listed under in kilometres (or metres), together with site's aspect

Site open all year

GPS co-ordinates – latitude and longitude

Campsite name

⊞ BLANES *3C3* (1km S Coastal) *41.65933, 2.77000* Camping Blanes, Avda Vila de Madrid 33, 17300 Blanes (Gerona) [972-33 15 91; fax 972-33 70 63; info@campingblanes.com; www.campingblanes.com] Fr N on AP7/E15 exit junc 9 onto NII dir Barcelona & foll sp Blanes. Fr S to end of C32, then NII dir Blanes. On app Blanes, foll camping sps & Playa S'Abanell - all campsites are sp at rndabts; all sites along same rd. Site adj Hotel Blau-Mar. Lge, mkd pitch, shd; wc; chem disp; mv service pnt; shwrs inc; shop; el pnts (5A) inc; gas; lndtte; supmkt; snacks high ssn; bar; playgrnd; pool; solarium; dir access to sand beach; watersports; cycle hire; games rm; wifi; entmnt; dogs; phone; bus; poss cr; Eng spkn; quiet; ccard acc; red low ssn. "Excel site, espec low ssn; helpful owner; easy walk to town cent; trains to Barcelona & Gerona." ♦ € 36.95   2011*

Campsite address, including post code

Contact email address and website address

Description of the campsite and its facilities

Telephone and fax numbers including national code where applicable

Directions to the campsite

Comments and opinions of caravanners who have visited the site

Unspecified facilities for disabled guests

Charge per night in high season for car, caravan + 2 adults (in local currency) as at year of last report

The year in which the site was last reported on by a visitor

NOJA *1A4* (700m N Coastal) *43.49011, -3.53636* Camping Playa Joyel, Playa del Ris, 39180 Noja (Cantabria) [942-63 00 81; fax 942-63 12 94; playajoyel@ telefonica.net; www.playajoyel.com] Fr Santander or Bilbao foll sp A8/E70 (toll-free). Approx 15km E of Solares exit m'way junc 185 at Beranga onto CA147 N twd Noja & coast. On o'skirts of Noja turn L sp Playa del Ris, (sm brown sp) foll rd approx 1.5km to rndabt, site sp to L, 500m fr rndabt. Fr Santander take S10 for approx 8km, then join A8/E70. V lge, mkd pitch, pt sl, pt shd; wc; chem disp; mv service pnt; baby facs; shwrs inc; el pnts (6A) inc; gas; lndtte (inc dryer); supmkt; tradsmn; rest; snacks; bar; BBQ (gas/charcoal); playgrnd; pool; paddling pool; jacuzzi; direct access to sand beach adj; windsurfing; sailing; tennis; hairdresser; car wash; cash dispenser; wifi; entmnt; games/TV rm; 15% statics; no dogs; no c'vans/m'vans over 8m high ssn; phone; recep 0800-2200; poss v cr w/end & high ssn; Eng spkn; adv bkg; ccard acc; quiet at night; red low ssn/ snr citizens; CCI. "Well-organised site on sheltered bay; v busy high ssn; pleasant staff; gd, clean facs; superb pool & beach; some narr site rds with kerbs; midnight silence enforced; Wed mkt outside site; highly rec." ♦ 15 Apr-1 Oct. € 47.40 SBS - E05   2011*

Opening dates

Reference number for a site included in The Caravan Club's Site Booking Service network i.e. bookable through the Club

Site Description Abbreviations

Each site entry assumes the following unless stated otherwise:

Level ground, open grass pitches, drinking water on site, clean wc unless otherwise stated (own sanitation required if wc not listed), site is suitable for any length of stay within the dates shown.

aspect
urban – within a city or town, or on its outskirts
rural – within or on edge of a village or in open countryside
coastal – within one kilometre of the coast

size of site
sm – max 50 pitches
med – 51 to 150 pitches
lge – 151 to 500 pitches
v lge – 501+ pitches

pitches
hdg pitch – hedged pitches
mkd pitch – marked or numbered pitches
hdstg – some hard standing or gravel

levels
sl – sloping site
pt sl – sloping in parts
terr – terraced site

shade
shd – plenty of shade
pt shd – part shaded
unshd – no shade

Site Facilities Abbreviations

adv bkg
Advance booking accepted;
adv bkg rec – advance booking recommended

baby facs
Nursing room/bathroom for babies/children

beach
Beach for swimming nearby;
1km – distance to beach
sand beach – sandy beach
shgl beach – shingle beach

bus/metro/tram
Public transport within an easy walk of the site

CCI or CCS
Camping Card International or Camping Card Scandinavia accepted

chem disp
Dedicated chemical toilet disposal facilities;
chem disp (wc) – no dedicated point; disposal via wc only

CL-type
Very small, privately-owned, informal and usually basic, farm or country site similar to those in the Caravan Club's network of Certificated Locations

dogs
Dogs allowed on site with appropriate certification (a daily fee may be quoted and conditions may apply)

el pnts
Mains electric hook-ups available for a fee;
inc – cost included in site fee quoted
10A – amperage provided
conn fee – one-off charge for connection to metered electricity supply
rev pol – reversed polarity may be present

(see *Electricity and Gas* in the section *DURING YOUR STAY*)

Eng spkn
English spoken by campsite reception staff

entmnt
Entertainment facilities or organised entertainment for adults and/or children

fam bthrm
Bathroom for use by families with small children

gas
Supplies of bottled gas available on site or nearby

internet
Internet point for use by visitors to site;
wifi – wireless local area network available

lndtte
Washing machine(s) with or without tumble dryers, sometimes other equipment available, eg ironing boards;
lndtte (inc dryer) – washing machine(s) and tumble dryer(s)
lndry rm – laundry room with only basic clothes-washing facilities

Mairie
Town hall (France); will usually make municipal campsite reservations

mv service pnt
Special low level waste discharge point for motor caravans; fresh water tap and rinse facilities should also be available

NH

Suitable as a night halt

noisy

Noisy site with reasons given;
quiet – peaceful, tranquil site

open 1 Apr-15 Oct

Where no specific dates are given, opening
dates are assumed to be inclusive, ie Apr-Oct –
beginning April to end October (**NB: opening
dates may vary from those shown; check
in advance before making a long journey,
particularly when travelling out of the main
holiday season**)

phone

Public payphone on or adjacent to site

playgrnd

Children's playground

pool

Swimming pool (may be open high season only);
htd – heated pool
covrd – indoor pool or one with retractable cover

poss cr

During high season site may be crowded or
overcrowded and pitches cramped

red CCI/CCS

Reduction in fees on production of a Camping
Card International or Camping Card Scandinavia

rest

Restaurant;
bar – bar
BBQ – barbecues allowed (may be restricted to a
separate, designated area)
cooking facs – communal kitchen area
snacks – snack bar, cafeteria or takeaway

SBS

Site Booking Service (pitch reservation can be
made through the Caravan Club's Travel Service)

serviced pitch

Electric hook-ups and mains water inlet and grey
water waste outlet to pitch;
all – to all pitches
50% – percentage of pitches

shop(s)

Shop on site;
adj – shops next to site
500m – nearest shops
supmkt – supermarket
hypmkt – hypermarket
tradsmn – tradesmen call at the site, eg baker

shwrs

Hot showers available for a fee;
inc – cost included in site fee quoted

ssn

Season;
high ssn – peak holiday season
low ssn – out of peak season

50% statics

Percentage of static caravans/mobile homes/
chalets/fixed tents/cabins or long term seasonal
pitches on site, including those run by tour
operators

sw

Swimming nearby;
1km – nearest swimming
lake – in lake
rv – in river

TV

TV available for viewing by visitors (often in
the bar);
TV rm – separate TV room (often also a games
room)
cab/sat – cable or satellite connections to pitches

wc

Clean flushing toilets on site;
(cont) – continental type with floor-level hole
htd – sanitary block centrally heated in winter
own san – use of own sanitation facilities
recommended

Other Abbreviations

AIT	Alliance Internationale de Tourisme
a'bahn	Autobahn
a'pista	Autopista
a'route	Autoroute
a'strada	Autostrada
adj	Adjacent, nearby
alt	Alternative
app	Approach, on approaching
arr	Arrival, arriving
avail	Available
Ave	Avenue
bdge	Bridge
bef	Before
bet	Between
Blvd	Boulevard
C	Century, eg 16thC
c'van	Caravan
ccard acc	Credit and/or debit cards accepted (check with site for specific details)
CChq acc	Camping Cheques accepted
cent	Centre or central

clsd	Closed
conn	Connection
cont	Continue or continental (wc)
conv	Convenient
covrd	Covered
dep	Departure
diff	Difficult, with difficulty
dir	Direction
dist	Distance
dual c'way	Dual carriageway
E	East
ent	Entrance/entry to
espec	Especially
ess	Essential
excel	Excellent
facs	Facilities
FIA	Fédération Internationale de l'Automobile
FICC	Fédération Internationale de Camping & de Caravaning
FFCC	Fédération Française de Camping et de Caravaning
FKK/FNF	Naturist federation, ie naturist site
foll	Follow
fr	From
g'ge	Garage
gd	Good
grnd(s)	Ground(s)
hr(s)	Hour(s)
immac	Immaculate
immed	Immediate(ly)
inc	Included/inclusive
indus est	Industrial estate
INF	Naturist federation, ie naturist site
int'l	International
irreg	Irregular
junc	Junction
km	Kilometre
L	Left
LH	Left-hand
LS	Low season
ltd	Limited
mkd	Marked
mkt	Market
mob	Mobile (phone)
m'van	Motor caravan
m'way	Motorway
N	North
narr	Narrow
nr, nrby	Near, nearby
opp	Opposite
o'fits	Outfits
o'look(ing)	Overlook(ing)

o'night	Overnight
o'skts	Outskirts
PO	Post office
poss	Possible, possibly
pt	Part
R	Right
rd	Road or street
rec	Recommend/ed
recep	Reception
red	Reduced, reduction (for)
reg	Regular
req	Required
RH	Right-hand
rlwy	Railway line
rm	Room
rndabt	Roundabout
rte	Route
RV	Recreational vehicle, ie large motor caravan
rv/rvside	River/riverside
S	South
san facs	Sanitary facilities ie wc, showers, etc
snr citizens	Senior citizens
sep	Separate
sh	Short
sp	Sign post, signposted
sq	Square
ssn	Season
stn	Station
strt	Straight, straight ahead
sw	Swimming
thro	Through
TO	Tourist Office
tour ops	Tour operators
traff lts	Traffic lights
twd	Toward(s)
unrel	Unreliable
vg	Very good
vill	Village
W	West
w/end	Weekend
x-ing	Crossing
x-rds	Cross roads

Symbols Used

◆ Unspecified facilities for disabled guests check before arrival

⊞ Open all year

* Last year site report received (see Campsite Entries in Introduction)

Discover the overseas trave
goes the extra mile for you

You'll enjoy touring in Europe so much more with The Caravan Club

Even if you have toured Europe before, you'll find your holiday so much more enjoyable with The Club. You can rely on our help and expertise to make your time abroad truly carefree.

We can arrange everything: Continental site bookings, ferry crossings at great prices and the finest travel insurance, all handled with care and expertise.

With over 200 hand-picked sites across Europe, from France's famous wine regions or sun-kissed Spanish coastal gems to exploring the Swiss Alps, there's something for everyone.

"We called The Club's Travel Service and were immediately put at ease – they were really helpful and organised everything, including ferries, campsite, insurance – the lot!"

Alan Godfrey

service that

Relax, we can do it all for you:

- The best possible negotiated ferry fares
- Pitch bookings at over 200 Club-inspected sites
- Wide choice of Tours & Excursions from short breaks to Grand Tours
- Camping cheques, ideal for off-peak travel
- Unbeatable overseas holiday insurance
- Advice & information from our team of overseas advisors
- The indispensable Caravan Europe Guides
- Everything for new or experienced travellers abroad

Inset one: Les Saules (LOI), France
Inset two: Château de l'Epervière (LIZ), France

THE CARAVAN CLUB

Planning and Travelling

Caravanning and Touring Abroad – Practical Advice

You may be new to caravanning abroad, or perhaps it has been a while since you last toured in Europe. If so then this section of the handbook will offer you practical and useful advice, giving you the knowledge and confidence that you need to make the most of your trip and enjoy your holiday.

Travelling through Europe can be a daunting prospect. That's why the practical advice offered in this chapter has been put together, providing you with a summary of the comprehensive information contained elsewhere within the guide. Please be aware that laws, customs, regulations and advice differ in each country so you are recommended to make sure you are familiar with these for each country that you are planning to visit.

Before You Travel

Choosing Your Campsite

The great thing about touring is the freedom that it offers you. However, if you are new to travelling in Europe we would suggest that it might be wise not to be overly ambitious and to plan your trip carefully.

> **The great thing about touring is the freedom that it offers you**

There is a wide range of campsites available across Europe offering a choice of different facilities and amenities, but we would recommend that you stay in a campsite close to port on your first night of arrival. This will give you a little time to get used to driving on the right hand side of the road and you can then make a fresh start to your journey the next day, or spend a couple of days (or indeed your whole holiday) enjoying the campsite and surrounding area.

When choosing your campsite (or campsites) there are some important factors that you need to keep in mind. Firstly, the location, do you want to be by the sea or near to a city, or perhaps you have a specific interest such as museums or hiking?

You need to consider what facilities and amenities are available as well, both on the campsite and in the nearby area. If you have children then you may want to make sure there is a playground and entertainment on site, or maybe you would like a

good restaurant within easy walking distance. These are all important factors to consider before you decide on where to stay during your holiday in order to avoid disappointment.

You should also take into account the time of year you are planning on travelling. If you are going in low season then many facilities and amenities may be closed. If you are going in high season or during public holidays it is likely there will be a high number of traffic and tourists, therefore advanced booking is often recommended.

For further information to help you choose the right campsite for your holiday, please refer to the chapter *Continental Campsites*. This chapter includes useful information on campsites in Europe and also has a site booking letter, both in English and Spanish, for you to use when making a reservation.

Overseas Site Booking Service

For peace of mind you may prefer to use The Caravan Club's Overseas Site Booking Service which offers Club members pitch bookings on over 200 campsites throughout Europe. This gives you

Tunnel, is a matter of personal preference and convenience. The Channel Tunnel and crossings from Dover to Calais are quickest, but if you have a long drive from home to your departure port, you may prefer a longer crossing giving you the chance to relax for a few hours and enjoy a meal onboard. The chapter *Ferries and the Channel Tunnel* contains a list of ferry routes and additional information.

Make sure you know the overall length, as well as the height, of your vehicle(s), as vehicle decks on some ferries have areas where height is restricted, and this should be checked when making your booking.

The Club's website has a direct link through to a number of the most popular ferry operators' reservations systems and Club members can make their own reservations while still taking advantage of the Club's negotiated offers as well as the ferry companies' own early booking offers – see www.caravanclub.co.uk/overseas

Insurance

UK motor vehicle policies will usually give you the legal minimum of insurance for EU countries, however it is very important to check whether your comprehensive cover becomes third-party-only when you leave the UK. It may be necessary to pay an additional premium for comprehensive cover abroad.

Having insurance for your vehicles does not cover any other risks that may arise when you are on holiday, for example, emergency medical and hospital expenses, or loss or theft of personal belongings. The Caravan Club's Red Pennant Overseas Holiday Insurance gives you maximum protection against a variety of mishaps which might otherwise ruin your holiday and is tailor-made for the caravanner and motorhome tourer. This is backed by the Club's own helpline with multi-lingual staff available 24 hours a day, 365 days a year.

If you are going to leave your home unoccupied for any length of time, check your house and contents insurance policies regarding any limitations or regulations.

You will find further details, information and advice in the *Insurance chapter* or see www.caravanclub.co.uk/redpennant and www.caravanclub.co.uk/insurance

Documents

All members of your party must have a valid passport, including babies and children. The chapter *Documents* sets out the requirements and explains how to apply for a passport.

In some countries a passport must be carried at all times as a form of photographic identification. You should also keep a separate photocopy of your passport details and leave a copy of the personal details page with a relative or friend.

freedom and flexibility of travel while eliminating language problems, international deposit payments or waiting for replies by letter or email. Furthermore, you will have the reassurance of a confirmed pitch reservation and pitch fees paid in advance.

The Club's Continental Caravanning brochure (available from November every year) gives full details of the Overseas Site Booking Service and of the sites to which it applies, as well as information on the Club's range of package tours and excursions for caravanners. Campsite only bookings, which do not include a ferry crossing are subject to a £25.00 booking fee. Sites in the service may be booked via the Club's website, www.caravanclub.co.uk/overseas

All the sites in the Club's Overseas Site Booking Service are listed in this guide and are marked 'SBS' in their site entries. The Caravan Club cannot make advance reservations for any other campsites listed in this guide.

Choosing Your Ferry Crossing

There is a wide choice of ferry operators and routes available. The use of ferry crossings, or the Channel

You are best to carry a full valid photocard driving licence with paper counterpart. If you have an old style green license issued before 1991, which does not conform to EU standards or have a pictorial representation of what you are allowed to drive/tow, we would strongly recommend that you change this for a photo-card license or carry an International Driving Permit (IDP). Police overseas may have problems understanding the all green license, and subsequently you may be delayed on your journey if they have to wait for help in translating it. International Driving Permits (IDP's) can be obtained from selected Post Offices, The AA and the RAC.

Carry your vehicle's Vehicle Registration Certificate (V5C), insurance certificate and MOT road worthiness certificate, if applicable, together with a copy of your CRIS document (proof of ownership) in respect of your caravan.

For hired or leased vehicles (including company cars) you will not normally have the V5C and therefore will need to get a VE103 Vehicle on Hire Certificate from the vehicle owner instead.

See the **Documents chapter** in the section **PLANNING AND TRAVELLING** for full details.

Vehicles and Equipment

Ensure your car and caravan or motorhome are properly serviced and ready for the journey, paying particular attention to tyres and tyre pressures. Make sure caravan tyres are suited to the maximum weight of the caravan and the maximum permitted speed when travelling abroad - see the chapter **Motoring - Equipment** and, if you're a member of The Caravan Club, the Technical Information chapter of the Club's UK Sites Directory & Handbook.

Take a well-equipped spares and tool kit. Spare bulbs, a warning triangle (two are required in some countries), a reflective jacket/vest, fire extinguisher and a first-aid kit as these are legal requirements in many European countries. Nearside and offside extending mirrors are essential to give the best possible vision, together with a spare tyre/wheel for both car and caravan.

In many countries drivers who leave their vehicle when it is stationary on the carriageway must by law wear a reflective jacket or waistcoat, but it is sensible to do so in any country. A second jacket is a commonsense requirement for any passenger who also gets out of your vehicle to assist. Keep the jackets readily to hand inside your vehicle, not in the boot.

If headlights are likely to dazzle other road users, they must be adjusted to deflect to the right instead of the left using suitable beam deflectors or (in some cases) a built-in adjustment system.

Even if you are not planning to drive at night, you will need to switch your headlights on in tunnels or if visibility is poor. Some countries require dipped headlights to be used during daylight hours.

Bulbs are more likely to fail with constant use and therefore it is always recommended to carry spares, whether it is a legal requirement or not.

For a checklist of equipment please see page 25.

Towing

Before you tow make sure you know your car well and have the correct mirrors suitable for your car and caravan. Plan carefully to avoid roads that are too narrow or may have low bridges, and never stop where it is unsafe to do so, i.e. on bends, narrow roads, etc.

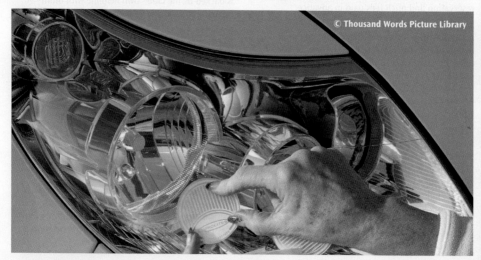

© Thousand Words Picture Library

Pull over safely to allow any build up of traffic behind you to pass wherever it is possible to do so and always keep a safe stopping distance between you and the vehicle in front. If you are overtaking or pulling across a main road allow yourself plenty of time to do this safely.

If you are new to towing, or if you would like to gain some valuable experience and knowledge, The Caravan Club runs 'Practical and Caravan Manoeuvring' courses, as well as 'Motorhome Manoeuvring' courses. These courses are open to both members and non-members of The Caravan Club and are designed to help you enjoy caravanning and touring more confidently.

For more information please visit www.caravanclub.co.uk/courses

Money

It is a good idea to carry a small amount of foreign currency, including loose change, for countries you are travelling through in case of emergencies, or when shopping. Many credit/debit cards issued in the UK will allow you to obtain cash from cash dispensers but it is best to check with your bank before you leave. Look for the same symbol on the machine as on your debit or credit card. Cash dispensers are often found in supermarkets as well as outside banks. The rate of exchange is often as good as anywhere else but there may be a charge.

Travellers' cheques are not widely accepted in some countries and credit cards issued by British banks may not be universally accepted, therefore it is wise to check before incurring expenditure. In some countries you may be asked to produce your passport for photographic identification purposes when paying by credit card.

See the chapter Money and the Country Introduction for further information.

On the Journey

Ferries and Eurotunnel

Report to the check-in desk at the ferry port or Eurotunnel terminal allowing plenty of time before the scheduled boarding time. As you approach the boarding area after passport control and Customs, staff will direct you to the waiting area or the boarding lane for your departure. As you are driving a 'high vehicle' you may be required to board first, or last. While waiting to board stay with your vehicle so that you can board immediately when instructed to do so. Virtually all ferries operate a 'drive on – drive off' system and you will not normally be required to perform any complicated manoeuvres, nor to reverse.

While waiting, turn off the 12V electricity supply to your fridge to prevent your battery going flat. Most fridges will stay adequately cool for several hours, as long as they are not opened. If necessary, place an ice pack or two (as used in cool boxes) in the fridge. You may be required to show that your gas supply has been turned off correctly.

Neither the ferry companies nor Eurotunnel permit you to carry spare petrol cans, empty or full, and Eurotunnel will not accept vehicles powered by LPG or dual-fuel vehicles. However Eurotunnel will accept vehicles fitted with LPG tanks for the purposes of heating, lighting, cooking or refrigeration, subject to certain conditions.

If your vehicle has been converted and is powered by LPG, some ferry companies require a certificate showing that the conversion has been carried out to the manufacturer's specification.

You will be instructed when to drive onto the ferry and, once on board, will be directed to the appropriate position. Treat ferry access ramps with caution, as they may be steep and/or uneven. Drive slowly as there may be a risk of grounding of any low point on the tow bar or caravan hitch. If your ground clearance is low, consider whether removing your stabiliser and/or jockey wheel would help.

Once boarded apply your car and caravan brakes. Vehicles are often parked close together and many passengers leaving their vehicles will be carrying bags for the crossing. It may, therefore, be wise to remove extended rear view mirrors as they may get knocked out of adjustment or damaged.

Make sure your car and caravan are secure and that, wherever possible, belongings are out of sight. Ensure that items on roof racks or cycle carriers are difficult to remove – a long cable lock may be useful.

Note the number of the deck you are parked on and the number of the staircase you use. You will not usually be permitted access to your vehicle during the crossing so take everything you require with you, including passports, tickets and boarding cards.

On ferry routes where you are permitted to transport pets, animals are usually required to remain in their owners' vehicles or in kennels on the car deck. On longer ferry crossings you can make arrangements at the onboard information desk for permission to visit your pet at suitable intervals.

See also **Pet Travel Scheme** under **Documents** in the section **PLANNING AND TRAVELLING**.

If you have booked cabins or seats go to the information desk immediately after boarding to claim them. Many ferries have a selection of restaurants and cafés, a shop, a children's play area, even a cinema, disco or casino to while away the time during the crossing. If you wish to use the main restaurant it may be advisable to make a reservation.

Listen carefully to onboard announcements, one of which will be important safety information at the time of departure. A further announcement will be made when it is time to return to your vehicle. Allow plenty of time to get down to the car deck. Don't start your engine until vehicles immediately in front of you start to move. Once off the ferry you may want to pull over into a parking area to allow the queue of traffic leaving the ferry to clear.

If you have made an advance booking on the Eurotunnel proceed to the signposted self check-in lanes. You will need to present the credit or debit card used when you made your booking. Having checked in you may, if you wish, visit the terminal to make any last minute purchases, etc, and then follow signs to passport control and customs. Your gas cylinder valves will be closed and sealed as a safety precaution and you will be asked to open the roof vents.

You will then join the waiting area allocated for your departure and will be directed onto the single-deck wagons of the train and told to park in gear with your brake on. You then stay in or around your vehicle for the 35 minute journey but will not be allowed to use your caravan until arrival. Useful information and music are supplied via the on-board radio station. On arrival, close the roof vent and release the caravan brake. When directed by the crew, drive off, remembering to drive on the right hand side of the road!

Motoring on the Continent

For comprehensive advice please see the chapters **Motoring Advice** and **Motoring Equipment** and the **Country Introduction chapters**. The following additional points may be helpful if you are feeling nervous about driving abroad.

Many roads are not as busy as those in the UK, but try to avoid rush hours in larger towns. There are fewer lorries on the roads at weekends and generally you will find that roads are quieter between 12pm and 2pm.

Don't attempt long distances in a single stint. Share the driving, if possible, and plan to break your journey overnight at a suitable campsite. There are thousands of sites listed in this guide, many of which are located near to motorways and main roads.

You are most likely to forget to drive on the right when pulling away from a parked position. It may be helpful to make yourself a sign and attach it to the dashboard to remind you to drive on the right. This can be removed before driving and replaced each time you stop. Alternatively, make a member of your party responsible for reminding the driver every time you start the car. Pay particular attention when turning left or when leaving a rest area, service station or campsite, and after passing through a one-way system.

Speed limit signs are in kilometres per hour - not miles per hour

Make sure the road ahead is clear before overtaking. Stay well behind the vehicle in front and, if possible, have someone with good judgement in the left-hand seat to give you the 'all clear'.

You will be charged tolls to use many European motorways. Credit cards are widely accepted as payment but not always. The Country Introduction chapters contain more details. Motorways provide convenient service stations and areas for a rest and a picnic en-route but, for your own safety, find an established campsite for an overnight stop.

Beware of STOP signs. You will encounter more of them than you find in the UK. Coming to a complete halt is compulsory in many European countries and failure to do so may result in a fine.

The maximum legal level of alcohol in the blood in most European countries is lower than that permitted in the UK. It is better not to drink at all when driving as penalties are severe.

If you are unfortunate enough to be involved in a road accident, take some photographs to back up the written description on your claim form.

During Your Stay

Arriving at the Campsite

Go to the campsite reception and fill in any registration forms required. A Camping Card International/Camping Card Scandinavia is recommended and usually accepted in lieu of handing over your passport.

If you have not booked in advance it is perfectly acceptable to ask to have a look around the campsite before deciding whether to stay or accept a particular pitch.

Pitches are usually available when the site re-opens after the lunch break and not normally before this time. Aim to arrive before 7pm or you may find the campsite reception closed; if this is the case you will probably find a member of staff on duty in the bar. It is essential to arrive before 10pm as the gates or barriers on most sites are closed for the night at this time. If you are delayed, remember to let the site know so that they will keep your pitch. When leaving, you will usually need to vacate your pitch by midday at the latest.

Many campsites offer various sporting activities, such as tennis, fishing, watersports, horseriding and bicycle hire, as well as entertainment programmes for children and/or adults in high season. Many also have a snack bar, restaurant and bar. Restrictions may apply to the use of barbecues because of the risk of fire; always check with site staff before lighting up.

Dogs are welcome on many campsites but some sites will not allow them during the high season (or at all), or will require them to be on a lead at all times. Check in advance. In popular tourist areas local regulations may ban dogs from beaches during the summer months.

If you have any complaints, take them up with site staff there and then. It is pointless complaining after the event, when something could have been done to improve matters at the time.

Food and Water

There is a limit to the amount of food which may be imported into other countries. In the light of animal health concerns in the UK in recent years, authorities abroad will understandably take a cautious approach and there is no guarantee that meat and dairy products, if found, will not be confiscated by Customs officers.

Be reasonable with the amount of food that you take with you and stick to basic items and/or children's special favourites. On occasion it may be difficult to obtain supplies of fresh milk, bread and cereals at campsite shops, particularly outside the summer season, so stock up before your arrival on site. It's often helpful to take your own supply of carrier bags and a cool box in hot weather.

Drinking water is normally clean and safe in countries covered in Caravan Europe, but you may find the taste different from your own local mains supply and prefer to drink bottled water.

Electricity and Gas

Calor Gas is not normally available on the Continent. Campingaz is widely available but you will need an adaptor to connect to a standard regulator. Alternatively carry sufficient gas for your stay, subject to the cross-Channel operator's regulations which may restrict you to three, two or even only one gas cylinder. Always check when making your booking.

Voltage on most sites is usually 220V or 230V nominal but may be lower. Most UK mains appliances are rated at 220V to 240V and usually work satisfactorily. Many sites have the European standard EN60309-2 connectors (formerly known as CEE17), into which you can plug your UK 3-pin connector and mains lead. However, on some sites you may need a continental 2-pin adaptor available from UK caravan accessory shops.

Caravanners may encounter the problem known as reverse polarity. This is where the site's 'live' line connects to the caravan's 'neutral' and vice versa and is due to different standards of plug and socket wiring that exist in other countries. The Club recommends checking the polarity immediately on connection, using a polarity tester, obtainable from a caravan accessory shop before you leave home.

The caravan mains electrical installation should not be used while a reversed polarity situation exists. Ask the site manager if you can use an alternative socket or bollard, as the problem may be restricted to that particular socket only. Frequent travellers to Europe who are electrically competent, often modify an adaptor to reverse the live and neutral connections. This can be tried in place of the standard connector, to see if the electricity supply then reverts to 'normal'. It is important that you are electrically competent or use an electrician to carry out the modification.

*See the chapter **Electricity and Gas** and **Country Introduction** for further information.*

Medical Matters

Before leaving home obtain a European Health Insurance Card (EHIC) which entitles you to emergency health care in the EU and some other countries. An EHIC is required for each individual family member, so allow enough time before your departure to obtain them. You can apply online on www.ehic.org.uk or by phoning 0845 6062030, or you can get an application form from a post office.

Specific advice on obtaining emergency medical treatment in the countries covered in this guide is summarised in the relevant country chapters and is also covered on the NHS website, www.nhs.uk/nhsengland/healthcareabroad. Alternatively obtain a copy of the Department of Health's leaflet, T7.1 Health Advice for Travellers which is downloadable from www.dh.gov.uk, email: dh@prolog.uk.com or call 08701 555455.

Check with your GP for the generic name of any prescription medicines you are taking. If you need more, or lose your supply, this will help a doctor or pharmacist to identify them. Keep receipts for any medication or treatment purchased abroad, plus the labels from the medicines, as these will be required if you make a claim on your travel insurance on returning home.

For further advice and information see the chapter Medical Matters.

Safety and Security

Safety is largely your own responsibility – taking sensible precautions and being aware of possible hazards won't spoil your holiday, but neglecting your safety and ignoring possible risks might.

The chapter entitled *Safety and Security* covers aspects of your own and your family's personal safety whilst on holiday. You are strongly advised to read this section carefully and follow the advice contained.

Other Information

Tourist Boards

Many European countries maintain tourist offices in the UK and they will supply you with information on their respective countries on request. In addition, a great deal of information can be obtained from the tourist board websites. Contact details of relevant tourist boards are given in the Country Introduction chapters.

Route Planning

It is wise to plan your route beforehand wherever possible. We have a route planning map chapter under the PLANNING AND TRAVELLING section for your reference.

Both the AA and RAC have useful websites offering a European route planning service with access for non-members: www.theaa.com and www.rac.co.uk. Please be aware that some routes may not be suitable for caravans or large vehicles.

Satellite Navigation

GPS co-ordinates are given for most site entries in this guide. Your sat nav is a valuable aid in finding a campsite, but it is important to realise that such systems are not perfect and they may take you on routes that are not suitable for caravans or large vehicles. It is wise, therefore, to use your sat nav in conjunction with an up to date map or atlas or use a sat nav that has been designed specifically for caravanners and motorhome owners such as the Snooper Ventura Caravan Club Edition.

For further advice see the chapter Motoring – Equipment.

Checklist

It is assumed that users of this guide are well aware of the domestic and personal items necessary for trips away and of the checks to be made to vehicles before setting off. The Caravan Club's Technical Office will supply a copy of a leaflet 'Things to Take' to Club members on request, or you can download it from www.caravanclub.co.uk

The checklist is intended as a reminder only and covers some of the necessary items:

Car

Extending mirrors
Fire extinguisher
First aid kit
Fuses
Headlight converters/deflectors
Jack and wheelbrace
Mobile phone charger
Nationality stickers – GB or IRL (car and caravan) if not included within number plate
Puncture kit (sealant)
Radiator hose
Reflective safety jacket(s)/vest(s)
Satellite navigation device
Snow chains (if possibility of using snow covered roads)
Spare bulbs
Spare key
Spare parts, e.g. fan belt
Spare wheel/tyre
Stabiliser

Tool kit
Tow ball cover
Tow rope
Warning triangle/s

Caravan

Awning and groundsheet

Bucket

Chemical toilet and fluid/sachets

Corner steady tool and pads

Electrical extension lead and adaptor(s)

Extra long motorhome water hose pipe

Fire extinguisher

Gas cylinders

Gas regulator (Campingaz) if planning to use Campingaz, or as a back-up in case other gas is not available

Gas adaptor and hoses (where regulator is fitted to the caravan) to suit 'local' gas cylinders

Hitch and/or wheel lock

Levelling blocks

Mains polarity tester

Nose weight gauge

Peg mallet

Spare bulbs, fuses and lengths of wire

Spare key

Spare 7-pin plug (12S plug is especially vulnerable to damage)

Spare water pump (submersible types are vulnerable to failure)

Spare wheel/tyre

Spirit level

Step and doormat

Water containers - waste/fresh

Water hoses – waste/fresh

Documents and Papers

Address book, contact telephone numbers

Camping Card International/Camping Card Scandinavia

Car/caravan/motorhome insurance certificates

Campsite booking confirmation(s)

Caravan Club membership card

Caravan Europe guide book/s

Copy of your CRIS document

Credit/debit cards, contact numbers in the event of loss

Valid driving licence (not provisional)

European Health Insurance Card (EHIC)

European Accident Statement

Ferry booking confirmation and timetable

Foreign currency

Holiday travel insurance documents (Red Pennant)

International Driving Permit (if applicable)

Letter of authorisation from vehicle owner (if applicable)

Maps and guides

MOT roadworthiness certificate (if applicable)

NHS medical card

Passport (plus photocopy of details page) and visas (if applicable)

Pet's passport and addresses of vets abroad

Phrase books

Telephone card

Travellers' cheques and/or travel money card

Vehicle Registration Certificate V5C

Technical Leaflets

The Caravan Club publishes technical leaflets for its members (some available to non-members) on a wide range of topics, many of which are relevant to caravanning abroad.

You are advised to request copies or see:

www.caravanclub.co.uk/expert-advice

Planning and Travelling
Continental Campsites

Introduction

There are thousands of excellent campsites throughout Europe belonging to local municipalities, families, companies or camping, touring and automobile clubs. Most sites are open to everyone but a few are reserved for their own members.

Compared with Caravan Club sites in the UK, pitches may be small and 80 square metres is not uncommon. Pitches may also be very close together, particularly in Germany and Italy where it is not uncommon to put your hand out of your caravan window and touch the caravan on the next pitch. This may present problems for large outfits and/or outfits with awnings. In the summer season it may also be difficult to put up awnings because of hard ground conditions in hot climates.

Generally the approaches and entrances to campsites are well signposted, but often only with a tent or caravan symbol or with the word 'Camping', rather than the site's full name.

There are usually sinks for washing up and laundry rooms containing washing machines and dryers. Many sites have a shop in high season, even if only for basic groceries, however some shops stock a wide variety of items. Often there is a restaurant or snack bar, Wi-Fi access, swimming pool and playground. Occasionally there may be a car wash, sauna, solarium, bureau de change, tourist information office and other facilities on site.

In the high season all campsite facilities are usually open and some sites offer organised entertainment for children and adults as well as local excursions. However, bear in mind that in the months of July and August, toilet and shower facilities and pitch areas will be under the greatest pressure.

Booking a Campsite

It is advisable to pre-book pitches during the high season. If you are planning a long stay then contact campsites early in the year. Some sites impose a minimum length of stay in order to guarantee their business. Usually there are one or two unreserved pitches available for overnight tourers.

Often it is possible to book directly via a campsite's website using a credit or debit card to pay a deposit if required. Otherwise you can write (enclosing a

© iStockphoto.com/Antony McAula

reply envelope or letters may be ignored) or email the campsite. A word of warning: **some campsites regard the deposit as a booking or admin fee and will not deduct the amount from your final bill.**

Site booking letters in English and Spanish are provided at the end of this chapter. Detachable response letters are also provided which should encourage site operators to reply. It is worth remembering that a site will very rarely reserve a special place for you. The acceptance of a reservation merely means you will be guaranteed a pitch; the best being allocated first or for repeat visitors. Not all campsites accept advance bookings.

If you do not book ahead you should plan to arrive no later than 4pm (even earlier at popular resorts) in order to secure a pitch, after that time sites fill up quickly. You also need to allow time to find another campsite if your first choice is fully booked.

Caravan Club Overseas Site Booking Service

The Caravan Club's Travel Service offers Club members an Overseas Site Booking Service (to which terms and conditions apply) to over 200 campsites throughout Europe. This service gives freedom and flexibility of travel but with the reassurance of a confirmed pitch reservation and pitch fees paid in sterling in advance. Full details of this service, plus information on special offers with ferry operators, tours & excursions programmes (some specifically aimed at motorhomes) and details of Red Pennant

Overseas Holiday Insurance appear in the Club's Continental Caravanning brochure – telephone 01342 327410 to request a copy, or visit www.caravanclub.co.uk/overseas

Booking a site through The Caravan Club gives you a price guarantee and no matter what happens to exchange rates, there will be no surcharges. Campsite only bookings, which do not include a ferry crossing, are subject to a £25.00 booking fee.

All Overseas Site Booking Service sites are listed in this guide and are marked 'SBS' in their site entries. Many of them can be booked via the Club's website, www.caravanclub.co.uk. **The Caravan Club cannot make advance reservations for any other campsites listed in this guide.**

Except in the case of those campsites included in the Club's pre-bookable Continental Caravanning network and marked SBS (Site Booking Service) at the end of their site entries, the Caravan Club has no contractual arrangements with any of the sites featured in this guide. Furthermore, even in the case of sites with which the Club is contracted, it has no direct control over day-to-day operations or administration. Only those sites marked SBS have been inspected by Caravan Club staff.

It is assumed by The Caravan Club Ltd, but not checked (except in the case of sites marked SBS), that all campsites fall under some form of local licensing, which may or may not take account of matters of safety and hygiene. Caravanners are responsible for checking such matters to their own satisfaction.

Sites Direct

In addition to the sites in the Site Booking Service network, Club members now have a greater choice of campsites available to book direct through the Club's website. The Club has implemented a link to enable

direct reservations within, for example, a particular region, or on sites with specific facilities. These sites (approximately 500) have not been inspected by Caravan Club representatives and all the information about them has been input by site owners themselves. Payment is direct to the site and any booking made through this channel is subject to the individual site's terms and conditions. For more information see www.caravanclub.co.uk/sitesdirect

Camping Cheques

The Caravan Club operates a low season scheme in association with Camping Cheques offering Club members flexible touring holidays. The scheme covers approximately 622 sites in 29 countries.

Camping Cheques are supplied through The Caravan Club as part of a package which includes return ferry fare and a minimum of seven Camping Cheques. Each Camping Cheque is valid for one night's low season stay for two people, including car and caravan/motorhome/trailer tent, electricity and one pet. Full details are contained in the Club's Continental Caravanning brochure.

Those sites which feature in the Camping Cheques scheme and which are listed in this guide are marked 'CChq' in their site entries.

Caravan Storage Abroad

The advantages of storing your caravan on a campsite in Europe are obvious, not least being the avoidance of the long tow to your destination, and a saving in ferry and fuel costs. Some campsites advertise a long-term storage facility or you may negotiate with a site which appeals to you.

However, there are pitfalls and understandably insurers in the UK are reluctant to insure a caravan which will be out of the country most of the time. There is also the question of invalidity of the manufacturer's warranty for caravans less than three years old if the supplying dealer does not carry out annual servicing.

See also Insurance *in the section* PLANNING AND TRAVELLING.

Electricity Supply

For your own safety you are strongly advised to read the chapter *Electricity and Gas* in the section *DURING YOUR STAY.*

Many campsites now include electricity and/or shower facilities in their 'per night' price and where possible this has been included in site entries. Where these are not included, a generous allowance should be made in your budget. It is not unknown for sites to charge up to the equivalent of £4 per night or more for electric hook-ups and £2 per shower. In winter sports areas, charges for electricity are generally higher in winter – the prices given in this guide are usually those charged during the summer months.

Facilities and Site Description

Campsite descriptions, facilities, directions, prices and other information are reported to the editor by users of this guide. Within individual site entries the comments (in inverted commas) are from people who have visited the site and it must be understood that people's tastes, opinions, priorities and expectations can differ greatly. Please also bear in mind that campsites change hands, opening dates and prices change and standards may rise or fall, depending on the season.

Facilities Out of Season

During the low season (this can be any time except July and early August) campsites may operate with limited facilities. Shops, swimming pools, bars and restaurants may be closed. A municipal site warden may visit in the morning and/or evening only to collect fees, which are sometimes reduced during the low season.

Sanitary Facilities

Facilities normally include toilet and shower blocks with shower cubicles, wash basins and razor sockets. Toilets are not always fitted with seats and do not always have toilet paper. The abbreviation 'wc' indicates the normal, pedestal type of toilet found in the UK. Some sites have footplate 'squatter' toilets and, where this is known, it is indicated by the abbreviation 'cont', i.e. continental.

It is recommended that you take your own universal flat plug (to fit all basin sizes) and toilet paper. During the low season it is not uncommon for only a few toilet and shower cubicles to be in use on a 'unisex' basis and they may not be cleaned as frequently as they are during the site's busy season. Hot water, other than for showers, may not be generally available.

In recent years many campsites have upgraded their sanitary facilities in line with visitors' expectations, but you may find that some are still unheated and may not offer items such as pegs on which to hang clothes/towels, or shelves for soap and shampoo. Rarely, there may be no shower curtains or shower cubicle doors and hence little or no privacy.

Waste Disposal

Site entries in this guide indicate (when known) where a campsite has a chemical disposal facility and/or a motorhome service point, which is assumed to include a waste (grey) water dump station and toilet cassette-emptying point.

Continental caravanners in general tend to prefer to use a site's toilet and shower facilities, together with its dishwashing and vegetable preparation areas, more than their British counterparts who prefer to use their own facilities in their caravan. Caravanners used to the level of facilities for the disposal of waste water on Caravan Club sites may well find that facilities on Continental campsites are not always of the same standard.

Chemical disposal points are occasionally difficult to locate and may be fixed at a high level requiring some strenuous lifting of cassettes in order to empty them. Disposal may simply be down a toilet – continental or otherwise. Wastemaster-style emptying points are not very common in Europe.

Formaldehyde chemical cleaning products are banned in many countries. It is recommended to always use formaldehyde free cleaning products that are kinder to the environment and the overwhelming proportion of current products are now formaldehyde free. In Germany the 'Blue Angel' (Blaue Engel) Standard, and in the Netherlands the 'Milieukeur' Standard, indicates that the product has particularly good 'green' credentials.

Rubbish bins are normally provided and at many campsites you will also find recycling bins. At some campsites, notably in Switzerland and Germany, you may have to purchase special plastic bags for the disposal of rubbish or pay a daily rubbish or environmental charge.

Finding a Campsite

Directions are given for all campsites listed in this guide and most also have GPS co-ordinates. Where known full street addresses are also given. The directions have been supplied by users of this guide and The Caravan Club is unable to check each one in detail for accuracy.

See the chapter **Motoring – Equipment** *in the section* **PLANNING AND TRAVELLING** *for more information on satellite navigation.*

Lunch Breaks

Some campsites close for a long lunch break, sometimes up to three hours, and occasionally there is no access for vehicles during this period. The time during which a site's entrance gate or barrier is closed may be reduced or extended according to the time of year. This may also apply to the overnight closure of gates and barriers. In addition, use of vehicles within the site may be restricted during certain hours to ensure a period of quiet. Check with individual campsites for their regulations.

Motorhomes – Overnight Stops

Towns and villages across Europe may provide dedicated overnight or short stay areas specifically for motorhomes, many of which have good security, electricity, water and waste facilities. These are known as 'Aires de Services', 'Stellplatz' or 'Aree di Sosta' and are usually well signposted with a motorhome pictogram.

Likewise, to cater for this growing market, many campsites in popular tourist areas have separate overnight areas of hardstanding with appropriate facilities often just outside the main campsite area. Fees are generally very reasonable.

A number of organisations publish guides listing thousands of these sites. Alternatively see www. campercontact.nl for details of thousands of sites for motorhomes in many countries in Europe.

For reasons of security The Caravan Club strongly advises against spending the night on petrol station service areas, ferry terminal car parks or isolated 'aires de repos' or 'aires de services' along motorways. *See the chapter* **Safety and Security** *in the section* **DURING YOUR STAY.**

Where known, information on the availability of public transport within easy reach of a campsite, as reported by caravanners, is given in the site entries in this guide.

Municipal Campsites

Municipal sites are found in towns and villages all over Europe, in particular in France, and in recent years many municipalities have improved standards on their sites while continuing to offer good value for money. However, on some municipal sites you may still find that sanitary facilities are basic and old-fashioned, even though they may be clean. Bookings for a municipal site can usually be made during office hours through the local town hall or, increasingly, the local tourist office.

Outside the high season you may find significant numbers of seasonal workers, market traders and itinerants resident on sites – sometimes in a separate, designated area. In most cases their presence does not cause other visitors any problem (other than early morning traffic noise as they leave for work) but where they are not welcome some sites refuse entry to caravans with twin-axles ('deux essieux' in French) or restrict entry by caravan height, weight or length, or charge a hefty additional fee. Check if any restrictions apply if booking in advance.

Recent visitors report that bona fide caravanners with twin-axle or over-height/weight/length caravans may be allowed entry, and/or may not be charged the higher published tariff, but this is negotiable with site staff at the time of arrival.

When approaching a town you may find that municipal sites are not always named and signposts may simply state 'Camping' or show a tent or caravan symbol.

Naturist Campsites

Details of a number of naturist sites are included in this guide and are shown with the word 'naturist' after their site name. Some, shown as 'part naturist' have separate areas for naturists. Visitors to naturist sites aged 16 and over usually (but not always) require an INF card or Naturist Licence and this is covered by membership of British Naturism (tel 01604 620361 or www.british-naturism.org.uk). Alternatively, holiday membership is available on arrival at any recognised naturist site (a passport-size photograph is required).

When looking for a site you will find that naturist campsites generally display the initials FNF, INF or FKK on their signs.

Opening Dates

Opening dates (where known) are given for campsites in this guide, many of which are open all year. Sometimes sites may close without notice for refurbishment work, because of a change of ownership or simply because of a lack of visitors or a period of bad weather.

Outside the high season it is always best to contact campsites in advance as some owners have a tendency to shut campsites when business is slack. Otherwise you may arrive to find the gates of an 'all year' campsite very firmly closed. Municipal campsites' published opening dates cannot always be relied on at the start and end of the season. It is advisable to phone ahead or arrive early enough to be able to find an alternative site if your first choice is closed.

Pets on Campsites

See also **Pet Travel Scheme** *under* **Documents** *and* **Holiday Insurance for Pets** *under* **Insurance** *in the section* **PLANNING AND TRAVELLING.**

Dogs are welcome on many campsites provided they conform to legislation and vaccination requirements, and are kept under control. Be prepared to present documentary evidence of vaccinations on arrival at a campsite.

Please be aware however that some countries authorities do not permit entry to certain breeds of dogs and some breeds will need to be muzzled and kept on a lead at all times. You are advised to contact the appropriate authorities of the countries that you plan to visit via their embassies in London before making travel arrangements for your dog.

Campsites usually have a daily charge for dogs. There may be limits on the number of dogs allowed, often one per pitch, or the type or breed accepted. Some campsites will not allow dogs at all or will require them to be on a lead at all times. Some campsites may also not allow dogs during the peak holiday season or will forbid you to leave your dog unattended in your caravan/motorhome, which can make going out for an evening meal or a day trip difficult. Dog owners must conform to site regulations concerning keeping dogs on a lead, dog-walking areas and fouling, and may find restricted areas within a site where dogs are not permitted.

In popular tourist areas local regulations may ban dogs from beaches during the summer.

Think very carefully before taking your pet abroad. Dogs used to the UK's temperate climate may find it difficult to cope with prolonged periods of hot weather. In addition, there are diseases transmitted by ticks, caterpillars, mosquitoes or sandflies, particularly in southern Europe, to which dogs from the UK have no natural resistance. Consult your vet about preventative treatment well in advance of your holiday. You need to be sure that your dog is healthy enough to travel and, if in any doubt, it may be in its best interests to leave it at home.

Visitors to southern Spain and Portugal, parts of central France and northern Italy, from mid-winter to late spring should be aware of the danger to dogs of pine processionary caterpillars. Dogs should be kept away from pine trees if possible or fitted with a muzzle that prevents the nose and mouth from touching the ground. This will also protect against poisoned bait sometimes used by farmers and hunters.

In the event that your pet is taken ill abroad a campsite will usually have information about local vets. Failing that, most countries have a telephone directory similar to the Yellow Pages, together with online versions such as www.pagesjaunes.fr.

Most European countries require dogs to wear a collar at all times identifying their owners. If your dog goes missing, report the matter to the local police and the local branch of that country's animal welfare organisation.

Prices

Campsite prices per night (for a car, caravan and two adults) are shown in local currencies. In EU member states where euros is not the official currency they are usually accepted for payment of campsite fees and other goods and services.

Payment of campsite fees should be made at least two hours before departure. Remember that if you stay on site after midday you may be charged for an extra day. Many campsites shown in this guide as accepting credit card payments may not do so for an overnight or short stay because of high transaction charges. Alternatively, a site will impose a minimum amount or will accept credit cards only in peak season. It is always advisable to check the form of payment required when you check in.

On arrival at a campsite which has an automatic barrier at the entrance you may be asked for a deposit, returnable on departure, for the use of a swipe card to operate the barrier. The amount will vary from site to site; €25 or €30 is usual.

Campsites may impose extra charges for the use of swimming pools and other leisure facilities, showers and laundrette facilities.

Registering on Arrival

On arrival at a campsite it is usual to have to register in accordance with local authority requirements, and to produce an identity document which the campsite office may retain during your stay. Most campsites now accept the Camping Card International (or Camping Card Scandinavia) instead of a passport and, where known, their site entries are marked CCI or CCS. CCIs are available to Caravan Club members at a cost of £6 by calling 01342 336633 or are free to members if you take out the Club's Red Pennant Overseas Holiday Insurance.

Alternatively, a photocopy of your passport may be acceptable and it is a good idea to carry a few copies with you to avoid depositing your passport and to speed up the check-in process.

Sites' Contact Details

Telephone numbers are given for most campsites listed in this guide together with fax numbers, website and email addresses where known.

The telephone numbers assume you are in the country concerned and the initial zero should be dialled, where applicable. If you are telephoning from outside the country concerned you should dial the international country code and the initial zero is omitted. For more details see the chapter *Keeping in Touch* and the *Country Introductions* chapter.

General Advice

Most campsites close from 10pm until 7am or 8am, however, late night arrival areas are sometimes provided for late travellers. Motorhomes in particular should check the gate/barrier closing time before going out for the evening in their vehicle. Check out time is usually between 10am and 12pm. Advise reception staff if you need to leave very early, for example, to catch a ferry.

If possible inspect the site and facilities before booking in. If your pitch is allocated at check-in ask to see it first to check the condition and access, as marked or hedged pitches can sometimes be difficult for large outfits. Riverside pitches can be delightful but keep an eye on the water level; in periods of heavy rain this may rise rapidly and the ground becomes boggy.

If the weather has been bad early in the season you may find that site staff have not been able, for example, to cut grass or hedges and prepare the site fully for visitors. At the end of the season grass pitches may be well worn and could be muddy or slippery after rain.

Often campsites have a daily discounted charge for children, however it is not unknown for site owners to charge the full adult daily rate for children from as young as three years old.

A tourist tax may be imposed by local authorities in some European countries. VAT may also be payable on top of your campsite fees. These charges are not usually included in the prices listed in this guide.

Speed limits on campsites are usually restricted to 10 km/h (6 mph). You may be asked to park your car in a separate area away from your caravan, particularly in the high season.

Some campsites ban the wearing of boxer shorts-style swimming trunks in pools on the grounds of hygiene. This rule may be strictly enforced.

The use of the term 'statics' in the campsite reports in this guide in many instances refers to long-term seasonal pitches, chalets, cottages, tour operators' fixed tents and cabins, as well as mobile homes.

Complaints

If you have a complaint take it up with site staff or owners at the time so that it can be dealt with promptly. It is pointless complaining after the event, when action to improve matters could have been taken at the time. In France, if your complaint cannot be settled directly with the campsite, and if you are sure you are within your rights, you may take the matter up with the Préfecture of the local authority in question.

The Caravan Club has no control or influence over day to day campsite operations or administration. Except in the case of a small number of sites in the Club's Overseas Site Booking Service with which it is contracted (marked SBS in site entries) and on which it has made a booking for you, it cannot intervene in any dispute you may have with a particular site.

Site Booking Letter – English

Date: Address (block caps)...…...................

....…

....

Tel No: (0044) ....

Fax No: (0044) ....…...........................……

Email ....…...............……...................

Dear Sir/Madam

I wish to make a reservation as follows:

Arriving (date and month)................ **Departing** (date and month)................ (........nights)

Adults   ....   **Children (+ ages)**   ....…......

Car	☐	**Caravan**	☐	**Motor Caravan**	☐	**Trailertent**	☐
Electrical Hook-up		☐		**Awning**	☐	**Extra tent**	☐

I look forward to an early reply and enclose an addressed envelope. When replying please advise all charges and deposit required. I look forward to meeting you and visiting your site.

Yours faithfully,

[Name in block capitals after signature]

Caravan Club Membership No.......................

✂ --

Reply

Date: Address...

....

....

Dear Mr/Mrs/Ms ....

Thank you for your reservation from .... to .... (........ nights).

- **YES, OK** – I am pleased to confirm your reservation (with/without electrical hook-up) and   look forward to welcoming you.
- **NO, SORRY** – I regret that the site is fully booked for the dates you request.

Yours sincerely

....

Site Booking Letter – Spanish

Fecha: Dirección (letra de imprenta)...……......

....……....

....

Nº de tel.: (0044) ....……....

Nº de fax: (0044) ....……...............................……

Email ....……..…….......…...……

Estimado Sr/Estimada Sra/Srta

Deseo realizar la siguiente reserva:

Llegada (fecha y mes) .... **Salida** (fecha y mes) .... (......... noches)

Adultos ....   **Niños** (+ edades) ....

Coche ☐   **Caravana** ☐   **Caravana de motor** ☐   **Tienda con remolque** ☐

Enganche eléctrico ☐   **Toldo** ☐   **Tienda adicional** ☐

Espero con interés recibir su confirmación y tengo el gusto de adjuntar un sobre con mi dirección. Cuando responda tenga la amabilidad de indicar todos los recargos y depósitos necesarios. Espero con ilusión conocerle y visitar su cámping.

Atentamente:

[Nombre en letra de imprenta después de la firma]

No de socio del Caravan Club ....

✂ --

Respuesta

Fecha: Dirección..

....

....

Estimado Sr/Estimada Sra/Srta

Agradecemos su reserva del .... al .... (.......... noches).

- **SI** – Tenemos el gusto de confirmar su reserva (con/sin enganche eléctrico) y esperamos con ilusión darle la bienvenida.
- **LO SENTIMOS** – Desafortunadamente le cámping está lleno durante las fechas que ha solicitado.

Atentamente:

....……..

Travelling to the UK from the European Union

On entry into the UK no tax or duty is payable on goods bought tax-paid in other EU countries which are for your own use and which have been transported by you. VAT and duty are included in the price of goods purchased and travellers can no longer buy duty-free or tax-free goods on journeys within the EU.

The following are guidance levels for the import of alcohol and tobacco into the UK but Customs do not enforce any absolute limits. However, if you bring in more than the following quantities Customs may suspect that they are for a commercial purpose and may ask questions and make checks. If you break the rules Customs may seize the goods – and the vehicle(s) used to transport them – and may not return them to you.

| 800 cigarettes |
| 400 cigarillos |
| 200 cigars |
| 1kg tobacco |
| 10 litres of spirits |
| 20 litres of fortified wine (e.g. port or sherry) |
| 90 litres of wine |
| 110 litres of beer |

No one under 17 years of age is entitled to the tobacco or alcohol allowances.

When entering the UK from another member state of the EU without having travelled to or through a non-EU country, you should use the blue Customs channel or exit reserved for EU travellers, provided your purchases are within the limits for imports from that country and you are not importing any restricted or prohibited goods, details of which are given later in this chapter.

Travelling to/from Non-EU Countries to/from the UK

Customs allowances for countries outside the EU apply to the following countries: Andorra, Croatia, Gibraltar, Norway and Switzerland.

You may purchase goods free of duty if travelling from the UK direct to a country outside the EU. Duty-free allowances for travellers returning to the UK (or entering any other EU country) from a non-EU country are generally as follows:

| 200 cigarettes, or 100 cigarillos, or 50 cigars, or 250gms tobacco |
| 1 litre of spirits or strong liqueurs over 22 per cent volume, or 2 litres of fortified wine, sparkling wine or any other alcoholic drink that's less than 22 per cent volume |
| 4 litres of still wine |
| 16 litres of beer |
| £390 worth of all other goods including perfume, gifts and souvenirs without having to pay tax and/ or duty (or £270 if you arrive by private plane or private boat for pleasure purposes) |

No one under 17 years is entitled to the tobacco or alcohol allowances.

When entering the UK from a non-EU country, or having travelled to or through a non-EU country, you should go through the red Customs channel or use the telephone at the Red Point if you have exceeded your Customs allowances, or if you are carrying any prohibited, restricted or commercial goods. Use the green Customs channel if you have 'nothing to declare'.

All dutiable items must be declared to Customs on entering the UK; failure to do so may mean that you forfeit them and your vehicle(s). Customs officers are legally entitled to examine your baggage and your vehicles and you are responsible for packing and unpacking. Whichever Customs channel you use, you may be stopped by a Customs officer and you and your vehicles may be searched.

If you are caught with goods that are prohibited or restricted, or goods in excess of your Customs allowances, you risk a heavy fine and possibly a prison sentence.

For further information contact HM Revenue & Customs National Advice Service on 0845 010 9000 (+44 2920 501 261 from outside the UK).

Travelling Within the European Union

While there are no limits on what travellers can buy and take with them when travelling between EU countries (provided the goods are for personal use and not for re-sale), the guidance levels are below:

800 cigarettes or 400 cigarillos or 200 cigars or 1kg tobacco

10 litres spirits over 22 per cent volume or 20 litres fortified wine not over 22 per cent volume

90 litres wine

110 litres beer

Boats

Virtually all boats of any size taken abroad must carry registration documents when leaving UK waters. Contact the Maritime and Coastguard Agency on 0870 6006505 or www.mcga.gov.uk for details. The Royal Yachting Association recommends that all boats have marine insurance and can provide details of the rules and regulations for taking a boat to countries bordering the Atlantic Ocean and the Baltic, Mediterranean and Black Seas – tel 0845 345 0400 or 023 8060 4100, www.rya.org.uk. Some countries require owners of certain types of vessels to have an International Certificate of Competence and information is contained in RYA publications.

If planning to take a boat abroad check with the appropriate tourist office before departure as rules and regulations for boat use vary from country to country. Third party insurance is compulsory in most European countries and is advisable elsewhere.

Currency

Any person entering or leaving the EU will have to declare the money that they are carrying if this amounts to €10,000 (or equivalent in other currencies)

or more. This includes cheques, travellers' cheques, money orders etc. This ruling does not apply to anyone travelling within the EU.

For further information contact HMRC Excise & Customs Helpline on 0845 010 9000.

Food and Plants

Travellers from within the EU may bring into the UK any fruit, vegetable or plant products without restriction as long as they are grown in the EU, are free from pests or disease and are for your own consumption. For food products Andorra, the Channel Islands, the Isle of Man, San Marino and Switzerland are treated as part of the EU.

From most countries outside the EU you are not allowed to bring into the UK any meat or dairy products. Other animal products may be severely restricted or banned and it is important that you declare any such products on entering the UK.

HM Revenue & Customs publish leaflets broadly setting out the rules, entitled 'Bringing Food Products into the UK' and 'Bringing Fruit, Vegetable and Plant Products into the UK'. These can be downloaded from their website or telephone the National Advice Service on 0845 010 9000.

Rules regarding food and plants can change at any time without notice. For up to date information please contact the Food and Environment Research Agency (Fera) on 0844 248 0071. If you are unsure about any item you are bringing in, or are simply unsure of the rules, you must go to the red Customs channel or use the phone provided at the Red Point to speak to a Customs officer.

In the light of animal health concerns in recent years in the UK, authorities abroad will understandably take a cautious approach to the import of foodstuffs. There is no guarantee that such products, if found, will not be confiscated by Customs officers.

Medicines

If you intend to take medicines with you when you go abroad you should obtain a copy of HMRC Notice 4, 'Taking Medicines With You When You Go Abroad', from HM Revenue & Customs National Advice Service on 0845 010 9000 or download it from www.hmrc.gov.uk. Alternatively contact the Drug Enforcement Policy Team, HM Revenue & Customs, New King's Beam House, 22 Upper Ground, London SE1 9PJ, tel 020 7865 5767.

There is no limit to the amount of medicines obtained without prescription, but medicines prescribed by your doctor may contain controlled drugs (i.e. subject to control under the Misuse of Drugs legislation) and you should check the allowances for these – in good time before you travel – in case you need to obtain a licence from the Home Office. In general, the permitted allowance for each drug is calculated on an average 15 days' dose.

Motor Vehicles and Caravans

Travellers between member states of the EU are entitled to import temporarily a motor vehicle, caravan or trailer into other member states without any Customs formalities.

Motor vehicles and caravans may be temporarily imported into non-EU countries generally for a maximum of six months in any twelve month period, provided they are not hired, sold or otherwise disposed of in that country.

Temporarily imported vehicles should not be left behind after the importer has left, should not be used by residents of the country visited and should not be left longer than the permitted period.

If you intend to stay longer than six months, take up employment or residence, or dispose of a vehicle you should seek advice well before your departure from the UK, for example from one of the motoring organisations.

Anyone temporarily importing into another country a vehicle – either hired or borrowed – which does not belong to them should carry a letter of authority from the vehicle owner and/or a VE103 Vehicle on Hire Certificate from the vehicle owner (this includes company cars).

See the chapter Documents in the section PLANNING AND TRAVELLING for further details.

Use of Caravan by Persons other than the Owner

Many caravan owners reduce the cost of a holiday by sharing their caravan with friends or relatives. Either the caravan is left on the Continent on a campsite

or it is handed over at the port. In making these arrangements it is important to consider the following:

- The total time the vehicle spends abroad must not exceed the permitted period for temporary importation.

- The owner of the caravan must provide the other person with a letter of authority. It is not permitted to accept a hire fee or reward.

- The number plate on the caravan must match the number plate on the tow car used.

- Both drivers' motor insurers must be informed if a caravan is being towed and any additional premium must be paid. If travelling to a country where an International Motor Insurance Certificate (Green Card) is required, both drivers' Certificates must be annotated to show that a caravan is being towed.

- If using The Caravan Club's Red Pennant Overseas Holiday Insurance, both drivers must be members of The Caravan Club and both must take out a Red Pennant policy.

See the chapter Insurance in the section PLANNING AND TRAVELLING.

© iStockphoto/Giorgio Magini

Personal Possessions

Generally speaking, visitors to countries within the EU are free to carry reasonable quantities of any personal articles, including valuable items such as jewellery, cameras, laptops, etc, required for the duration of their stay. It is sensible to carry sales receipts for new items, particularly of a foreign manufacture, in case you need to prove that tax has already been paid.

Visitors to non-EU countries may temporarily import personal items on condition that the articles are the personal property of the visitor and that they are not left behind when the importer leaves the country.

Prohibited and Restricted Goods

Just because something is on sale in another country does not mean it can be freely brought back to the UK. Regardless of where you are travelling from, the importation into the UK of some goods is restricted or banned, mainly to protect health and the environment. These include:

- Endangered animals or plants including live animals, birds and plants, ivory, skins, coral, hides, shells and goods made from them such as jewellery, shoes, bags and belts even though these items were openly on sale in the countries where you bought them.

- Controlled, unlicensed or dangerous drugs e.g. heroin, cocaine, cannabis, LSD, morphine, etc.

- Counterfeit or pirated goods such as watches, CDs and sports shirts; goods bearing a false indication of their place of manufacture or in breach of UK copyright.

- Offensive weapons such as firearms, flick knives, knuckledusters, push daggers or knives disguised as everyday objects.

- Pornographic material depicting extreme violence or featuring children such as DVDs, magazines, videos, books and software.

This list is by no means exhaustive; if in doubt contact HM Revenue & Customs National Advice Service for more information or, when returning to the UK, go through the red Customs channel or use the telephone at the Red Point and ask a Customs officer. It is your responsibility to make sure that you are not breaking the law.

Never attempt to mislead or hide anything from Customs officers; penalties are severe.

Documents

Camping Card International (CCI)

The Camping Card International (CCI) is a plastic credit card-sized identity card for campers and is valid worldwide (except in the USA and Canada). It is available to members of The Caravan Club and other clubs affiliated to the international organisations: the AIT, FIA and FICC.

A CCI may be deposited with campsite staff instead of a passport and is therefore essential in those countries where a passport must be carried at all times as a means of identification. A CCI is also recommended for other countries but it is not a legal document and campsite managers are within their rights to demand other means of identification. More than 1,100 campsites throughout Europe give a reduction to holders of a CCI, although this may not apply if you pay by credit card.

The CCI is provided automatically, free of charge, to Caravan Club members taking out the Club's Red Pennant Overseas Holiday Insurance, otherwise it costs £5.50 (2012). It provides extensive third party-liability cover and is valid for any personal injury and material damage you may cause while staying at a campsite, hotel or rented accommodation. Cover extends to the Club member and his/her passengers (maximum eleven people travelling together in the same private vehicle) and is valid for one year. The policy excludes any claims arising from accidents caused by any mechanically-propelled vehicle, i.e. a car. Full details of the terms and conditions and level of indemnity are provided with the card.

When leaving a campsite, make sure it is your card that is returned to you, and not one belonging to someone else.

See the Country Introductions for more information and www.campingcardinternational.com

Driving Licence & International Driving Permit (IDP)

Driving Licence

A full, valid driving licence should be carried at all times when driving abroad as you must produce it when asked to do so by the police and other authorities. Failure to do so may result in an immediate fine. If your driving licence is due to expire while you are away it can normally be renewed up to three months before the expiry date. If you need to renew your licence more than three months ahead of the expiry date contact the DVLA and they will advise you.

All European Union countries should recognise the pink EU-format paper driving licence introduced in the UK in 1990, subject to the minimum age requirements of the country concerned (normally 18 years in all the countries covered in this guide for a vehicle with a maximum weight of 3,500 kg and carrying not more than 8 people). However, there are exceptions in some European Countries and the Country Introductions in the relevant volumes of Caravan Europe contain details. It is strongly recommended that you upgrade your license to the current photocard license, which conforms to European Union standards.

Holders of an old-style green UK paper licence or a licence issued in Northern Ireland prior to 1991, which is not to EU format, should update it to a photocard licence before travelling in order to avoid any local difficulties with the authorities. Alternatively, obtain an International Driving Permit to accompany your UK licence. A photocard driving licence is also useful as a means of identification in other situations, e.g. when using a credit card, when the display of photographic identification may be required. Application forms are available from most post offices or apply online at www.direct.gov.uk

If you have a photocard driving licence, remember to carry both the plastic card and its paper counterpart.

Allow enough time for your application to be processed and do not apply if you plan to hire a car in the very near future. Selected post offices and DVLA local offices offer a premium checking service for photocard applications but the service is not available for online applications.

Driving licence – carry both the photocard and its paper counterpart

International Driving Permit (IDP)

If you hold a British photocard driving licence, no other form of photographic identification is required. If you plan to travel further afield then an IDP may still be required and you can obtain one over the counter at selected post offices (search on www.postoffice.co.uk or call 08457 223344) and from motoring organisations, namely the AA or the RAC, whether or not you are a member. An IDP costs £5.50 (2011) and is valid for a period of 12 months from the date of issue but may be post-dated up to three months.

To apply for an IDP you will need to be resident in Great Britain, have passed a driving test and be over 18 years of age. When driving abroad you should always carry your full national driving licence with you as well as your IDP.

European Health Insurance Card – Emergency Medical Benefits

For information on how to apply for a European Health Insurance Card (EHIC) and the medical care to which it entitles you, see the chapter *Medical Matters* in the section *DURING YOUR STAY*.

MOT Certificate

You are advised to carry your vehicle's MOT certificate of road worthiness (if applicable) when driving on the Continent as it may be required by the authorities if your vehicle is involved in an accident, or in the event of random vehicle checks. If your MOT certificate is due to expire while you are away you should have the vehicle tested before you leave home.

Passport

Many countries require you to carry your passport at all times and immigration authorities may, of course, check your passport on return to the UK. While abroad, it will help gain access to assistance from British Consular services and to banking services. Enter next-of-kin details in the back of your passport, keep a separate record of your passport details and leave a copy of it with a relative or friend at home.

The following information applies only to British citizens holding, or entitled to hold, a passport bearing the inscription 'United Kingdom of Great Britain and Northern Ireland'.

Applying for a Passport

Each person (including babies) must hold a valid passport. It is not now possible to add or include children on a parent's British passport. A standard British passport is valid for ten years, but if issued to children under 16 years of age it is valid for five years.

All new UK passports are now biometric passports, also known as ePassports, which feature additional security features including a microchip with the holder's unique biometric facial features. Existing passports will remain valid until their expiry date and holders will not be required to exchange them for biometric passports before then.

Full information and application forms are available from main post offices or from the Identity & Passport Service's website, www.direct.gov.uk where you can complete an online application. Allow at least six weeks for first-time passport applications, for which you will probably need to attend an interview at your nearest Identity and Passport Service (IPS) regional office once you have submitted your application – telephone the IPS helpline on 0300 2220000 to arrange one. Allow three weeks for a renewal application and at least one week for the replacement of a lost, stolen or damaged passport.

Main post offices offer a 'Check & Send' service for passport applications costing £8.17. To find your nearest 'Check & Send' post office call 08457 223344 or see www.postoffice.co.uk

Passport Validity

Most countries covered in this guide merely require you to carry a passport valid for the duration of your stay. However, in the event that your return home is delayed for any reason, and in order to avoid any local difficulties with immigration authorities, it is advisable to ensure that your passport is valid for at least six months after your planned return travel date. You can renew your passport up to nine months before expiry, without losing the validity of the current one.

Schengen Agreement

All the countries covered in all three volumes of Caravan Europe 2012/2013 – except Andorra and Croatia – are party to the Schengen Agreement, which allows people and vehicles to pass freely without border checks from country to country within the Schengen area. Where there are no longer any border checks you should still not attempt to cross land borders without a full, valid passport. It is likely that random identity checks will continue to be made for the foreseeable future in areas surrounding land borders.

The United Kingdom and Republic of Ireland do not fully participate in the Schengen Agreement.

Last but not least: your passport is a valuable document. It is expensive, time-consuming and inconvenient to replace and its loss or theft can lead to serious complications if your identity is later used fraudulently.

Pet Travel Scheme (PETS)

The Pet Travel Scheme (PETS) allows owners of dogs, cats and a number of other animals from qualifying European countries, to bring their pets into the UK (up to a limit of five per person) without quarantine, providing the animal has an EU pet passport. It also allows pets to travel from the UK to other EU qualifying countries. All of the countries covered in this guide are qualifying countries. However, the procedures to obtain the passport are lengthy and the regulations, out of necessity, are strict.

Be aware that some countries may not allow entry to certain types or breeds of dogs and may have rules relating to matters such as muzzling and transporting dogs in cars. You are advised to contact the appropriate authorities of the countries you plan to visit via their embassies in London before making travel arrangements for your dog. You should also check with your vet for the latest available information or call the PETS Helpline on 0870 2411710, email: quarantine@animalhealth.gsi.gov.uk.

More information is available from the website for the Department for Environment, Food & Rural Affairs (Defra), www.defra.gov.uk and you are advised to visit this website before you travel. Please note as of the 1st January 2012 rules for pets re-entering the UK have changed. Details are available on the Defra website.

The PETS scheme operates on a number of ferry routes between the Continent and the UK as well as on Eurotunnel services and Eurostar passenger trains from Calais to Folkestone. Some routes may only operate at certain times of the year; routes may change and new ones may be added – check with the PETS Helpline for the latest information.

Pets normally resident in the Channel Islands, Isle of Man and the Republic of Ireland can also enter the UK under the PETS scheme if they comply with the rules. Pets resident anywhere in the British Isles (including the Republic of Ireland) will continue to be able to travel freely within the British Isles and will not be subject to PETS rules. Owners of pets entering the Channel Islands or the Republic of Ireland from outside the British Isles should contact the appropriate authorities in those countries for advice on approved routes and other requirements.

It is against the law in the UK to possess certain types of dogs (unless an exemption certificate is held) and the introduction of PETS does not affect this ban.

For a list of vets near Continental ports, look in the local equivalent of the Yellow Pages telephone directory. Campsite owners or tourist offices located near Channel ports will be familiar with the requirements of British visitors and will probably be able to recommend a vet. Alternatively, the local British Consulate may be able to help, or the ferry company transporting your pet.

Adequate travel insurance for your pet is essential

Last but by no means least, adequate travel insurance for your pet is essential in the event of an accident abroad requiring veterinary treatment, emergency repatriation or long-term care if treatment lasts longer than your holiday. Travel insurance should also include liability cover in the event that your pet injures another animal or person or damages property whilst abroad. Contact The Caravan Club on 0800 0151396 or visit www.caravanclub.co.uk/petins for details of its Pet Insurance scheme, specially negotiated to take into account Club members' requirements both at home and abroad.

See *Holiday Insurance for Pets* under *Insurance* in the section *PLANNING AND TRAVELLING*.

Travelling with Children

Some countries require documentary evidence of parental responsibility from single parents travelling alone with children before allowing them to enter the country or, in some cases, before permitting children to leave the country. The authorities may want to see a birth certificate, a letter of consent from the other parent and some evidence as to your responsibility for the child.

If you are travelling with a minor under the age of 18 who is not your own, you must carry a letter of authorisation, naming the adult in charge of the child, from the child's parent or legal guardian.

For further information on exactly what will be required at immigration contact the Embassy or Consulate of the countries you intend to visit before your visit.

Vehicle Excise Licence

While driving abroad it is necessary to display a current UK vehicle excise licence (tax disc). If your vehicle's tax disc is due to expire while you are abroad you may apply to re-license the vehicle at a post office, by post, or in person at a DVLA local office, up to two months in advance. If you give a despatch address abroad the licence can be sent to you there.

Vehicle Registration Certificate (V5C)

You must always carry your Vehicle Registration Certificate (V5C) when taking your vehicle abroad. If you do not have one you should apply to a DVLA local office on form V62. If you need to travel abroad during this time you will need to apply for a Temporary Registration Certificate if you are not already recorded as the vehicle keeper.

Telephone DVLA Customer Enquiries on 0300 7906802 for more information.

Caravan – Proof of Ownership (CRIS)

In Britain and Ireland, unlike most other European countries, caravans are not formally registered in the same way as cars. This may not be fully understood by police and other authorities on the Continent. You are strongly advised, therefore, to carry a copy of your Caravan Registration Identification Scheme (CRIS) document.

Hired or Borrowed Vehicles

If using a borrowed vehicle you must obtain a letter of authority to use the vehicle from the registered owner. You should also carry the Vehicle Registration Certificate (V5C).

In the case of hired or leased vehicles, including company cars, when the user does not normally possess the V5C, ask the company which owns the vehicle to supply a Vehicle On Hire Certificate, form VE103, which is the only legal substitute for a V5C. See www.bvrla.co.uk or call them on 01494 434747 for more information.

If you are caught driving a hired vehicle abroad without this certificate you may be fined and/or the vehicle impounded.

Visas

British citizens holding a full UK passport do not require a visa for entry into any countries covered by this guide. EU countries may require a permit for stays of more than three months and you should contact the relevant country's UK embassy before you travel for information.

British subjects, British overseas citizens, British dependent territories citizens and citizens of other countries may need visas that are not required by British citizens. Again check with the authorities of the country you are due to visit at their UK embassy or consulate. Citizens of other countries should apply to their own embassy, consulate or High Commission for information.

Planning and Travelling
Ferries and the Channel Tunnel

Planning Your Trip

If travelling in July or August, or over peak weekends during school holidays, such as Easter and half-term, it is advisable to make a reservation as early as possible. Space for caravans on ferries is usually limited, especially during peak holiday periods. Off-peak crossings, which may offer savings, are usually filled very quickly.

When booking any ferry crossing, account must be taken of boats, bicycles, skylights and roof boxes in the overall height/length of your car and caravan or motorhome. Ferry operators require you to declare total dimensions. It is important, therefore, to report the dimensions of your outfit accurately when making a ferry booking, as vehicles which have been under-declared may be turned away at boarding.

Individual ferry companies may impose vehicle length or height restrictions according to the type of vessel in operation on that particular sailing or route. Always check when making your booking.

> **Report the dimensions of your outfit accurately when making a ferry booking**

Advise your booking agent at the time of making your ferry reservation of any disabled passengers. Ferry companies can then make the appropriate arrangements for anyone requiring assistance at ports or on board ships.

For residents of both Northern Ireland and the Republic of Ireland travelling to the Continent via the British mainland, Brittany Ferries, Irish Ferries and P & O Irish Sea offer special 'Landbridge' or 'Ferrylink' through-fares for combined crossings on the Irish Sea and the English Channel or North Sea.

The table on the following page shows current ferry routes from the UK to the Continent and Ireland. Some ferry routes may not be operational all year, and during peak holiday periods the transportation of caravans or motorhomes may be restricted. Current ferry timetables and tariffs can be obtained from The Caravan Club's Travel Service, from a travel agent or from ferry operators' websites.

Booking Your Ferry

The Caravan Club is an agent for most major ferry companies operating services to the Continent, Scandinavia, Ireland and the Isle of Wight, and each year provides thousands of Club members with a speedy and efficient booking service. Our Continental Caravanning brochure (available from November) and Winter Escapes brochure (available from July) feature a range of special offers with ferry operators – some of them exclusive to The Caravan Club. The brochure also includes full information on the Site Booking Service for campsites on the Continent, the Tours & Excursions programme, and Red Pennant Overseas Holiday Insurance. Telephone 01342 327410 to request a brochure or see www.caravanclub.co.uk/planning-your-trip/overseas-trips

During the course of the year, new special offers and promotions are negotiated and these are featured on the Travel Service News page of The Caravan Club Magazine and on the Club's website.

The Club's website has a direct link to a number of ferry operators' reservations systems allowing Club members to make their own reservations and still take advantage of the Club's negotiated offers and the ferry companies' own early booking offers. A credit card deposit is taken and the balance collected ten weeks before departure date. Some ferry operators are imposing fuel surcharges but these will be included in all fares quoted by The Caravan Club. Reservations may be made by telephoning The Caravan Club's Travel Service on 01342 316101 or on www.caravanclub.co.uk/planning-your-trip/overseas-trips

Route	Operator	Approximate Crossing Time	Maximum Frequency
Belgium			
Hull – Zeebrugge	P & O Ferries	12½ hrs	1 daily
Ramsgate – Ostend†	Transeuropa Ferries	4 hrs	5 daily
Denmark			
Harwich – Esbjerg	DFDS Seaways	18¼ hrs	3 per week
France			
Dover – Calais	P & O Ferries	1½ hrs	22 daily
Dover – Calais	SeaFrance	1½ hrs	17 daily
Dover – Dunkerque	DFDS Seaways	2 hrs	12 daily
Folkestone – Calais	Eurotunnel	35 mins	3 per hour
Newhaven – Dieppe	Transmanche Ferries	4 hrs	2 daily
Plymouth – Roscoff	Brittany Ferries	6 hrs	2 daily
Poole – Cherbourg	Brittany Ferries	2¼ hrs	1 daily
Poole – St Malo (via Channel Islands)	Condor Ferries	5 hrs	1 daily (May to Sep)
Portsmouth – Caen	Brittany Ferries	3¾ / 7½ hrs	4 daily
Portsmouth – Cherbourg	Brittany Ferries	3 / 4½ hrs	3 daily
Portsmouth – Cherbourg	Condor Ferries	5½ hrs	1 weekly (May to Sep)
Portsmouth – Le Havre	LD Lines	3¼ / 8 hrs	2 daily
Portsmouth – St Malo	Brittany Ferries	9 hrs	1 daily
Weymouth – St Malo (via Channel Islands)	Condor Ferries	9½ hrs	1 daily
Ireland – Northern			
Cairnryan/Troon – Larne	P & O Irish Sea	1 / 2 hrs	11 daily
Liverpool (Birkenhead) – Belfast	Stena Line	8 hrs	2 daily
Cairnryan – Belfast	Stena Line	2 / 3 hrs	7 daily
Ireland – Republic			
Cork – Roscoff†	Brittany Ferries	14 hrs	1 per week
Fishguard – Rosslare	Stena Line	2 / 3½ hrs	3 daily
Holyhead – Dublin	Irish Ferries	1¾ / 3¼ hrs	4 daily
Holyhead – Dublin	Stena Line	3¼ hrs	4 daily
Holyhead – Dun Loaghaire	Stena Line	2 hrs	2 daily
Liverpool – Dublin	P & O Irish Sea	8 hrs	2 daily
Liverpool (Birkenhead) – Dublin	Stena Line	7 hrs	2 daily
Pembroke – Rosslare	Irish Ferries	4 hrs	2 daily
Rosslare – Cherbourg†	Irish Ferries	19½ hrs	3 per week
Rosslare – Cherbourg†	Celtic Link Ferries	17 hrs	3 per week
Rosslare – Roscoff†	Irish Ferries	19½ hrs	4 per week
Swansea – Cork†	Fastnet Line	10 hrs	3 per week
Netherlands			
Harwich – Hook of Holland	Stena Line	6½ hrs	2 daily
Hull – Rotterdam	P & O Ferries	10¼ hrs	1 daily
Newcastle – Ijmuiden (Amsterdam)	DFDS Seaways	15½ hrs	1 daily
Spain			
Portsmouth – Bilbao	Brittany Ferries	24 hrs	2 per week
Portsmouth or Plymouth – Santander	Brittany Ferries	24 / 20 hrs	4 per week

† Not bookable through the Club's Travel Service.

Note: Services and routes correct at time of publication but subject to change.

Channel Tunnel

The Channel Tunnel operator, Eurotunnel, accepts cars, caravans and motorhomes (except those running on LPG and dual-fuel vehicles) on their service between Folkestone and Calais. While they accept traffic on a 'turn up and go' basis, they also offer a full reservation service for all departures with exact timings confirmed on booking.

All information was current at the time this guide was compiled in the autumn of 2011 and may be subject to change.

Gas - Safety Precautions and Regulations on Ferries and in the Channel Tunnel

UK based cross Channel ferry companies usually allow up to three gas cylinders per caravan, including the cylinder currently in use. However some, e.g. Brittany Ferries, DFDS Seaways, SeaFrance and Stena Line, restrict this to a maximum of two cylinders, which have to be securely fitted into your caravan. It is always advisable to check with the ferry company before setting out as regulations may change.

Cylinder valves should be fully closed and covered with a cap, if provided, and should remain closed during the crossing. Cylinders should be fixed securely in or on the caravan in the manner intended and in the position designated by your caravan's manufacturer. Ensure gas cookers and fridges are fully turned off. Gas cylinders must be declared at check-in and ships' crew may wish to inspect each cylinder for leakage before shipment. They will reject leaking or inadequately secured cylinders.

Eurotunnel will allow vehicles fitted with LPG tanks for the purposes of heating, lighting, cooking or refrigeration to use their service, but regulations stipulate that a total of no more than 47 kg of gas can be carried through the Channel Tunnel. Tanks must be switched off before boarding and must be less than 80% full; you will be asked to demonstrate this before you travel. **Vehicles powered by LPG or equipped with a dual-fuel system cannot be carried through the Channel Tunnel.**

Most ferry companies, however, are willing to accept LPG-powered vehicles provided they are advised at the time of booking. During the crossing the tank must be no more than 75% full and it must be turned off. In the case of vehicles converted to use LPG, some ferry companies also require a certificate showing that the conversion has been carried out to the manufacturer's specification.

The carriage of spare petrol cans, whether full or empty, is not permitted on ferries or through the Channel Tunnel.

It is your responsibility to check current safety precautions and regulations on ferries and channel tunnels before you travel.

Pets on Ferries and Eurotunnel

It is possible to transport your pet on a number of ferry routes to the Continent and Ireland, as well as on Eurotunnel services from Folkestone to Calais. At the time this guide was compiled the cost of return travel for a pet was between £30 and £50, depending on the route used. Advance booking is essential as restrictions apply to the number of animals allowed on any one departure. Make sure you understand the carrier's terms and conditions for transporting pets.

> **It's important to ensure that ferry staff know that your vehicle contains an animal**

On arrival at the port ensure that ferry staff know that your vehicle contains an animal. Once on board pets are normally required to remain in their owner's vehicle or in kennels on the car deck and, for safety reasons, access by pet owners to the vehicle decks while the ferry is at sea may be restricted. On longer ferry crossings you should make arrangements at the on-board information desk for permission to visit your pet at suitable intervals in order to check its well-being.

Information and advice on the welfare of animals before and during a journey is available on the website of the Department for Environment, Food and Rural Affairs (Defra), www.defra.gov.uk

See also Pet Travel Scheme under Documents and Holiday Insurance for Pets under Insurance in the section PLANNING AND TRAVELLING.

Caravan Club Sites Near Ports

Once you have chosen your ferry crossing and worked out your route to the port of departure you may like to consider an overnight stop at one of The Caravan Club sites listed in the table on the opposite page, especially if your journey to or from home involves a long drive.

Book online using the Club's UK Advance Booking Service at www.caravanclub.co.uk or call 01342 327490. Otherwise when sites are open, contact them direct.

Advance booking is recommended, particularly if you are planning to stay during July and August or over Bank Holidays.

Port	Nearest Club Site and Town	Tel No.
Cairnryan, Stranraer	New England Bay, Drummore	01776 860275
Dover, Folkestone, Channel Tunnel	Bearsted, Maidstone	01622 730018
	Black Horse Farm*, Folkestone	01303 892665
	Daleacres, Hythe	01303 267679
	Fairlight Wood, Hastings	01424 812333
Fishguard, Pembroke	Freshwater East, Pembroke	01646 672341
Harwich	Cambridge Cherry Hinton*, Cambridge	01223 244088
	Commons Wood*, Welwyn Garden City	01707 260786
	Round Plantation, Mildenhall	01638 713089
Holyhead	Penrhos, Benllech, Anglesey	01248 852617
Hull	Beechwood Grange, York	01904 424637
	Rowntree Park, York	01904 658997
Newcastle upon Tyne	Old Hartley, Whitley Bay	0191 237 0256
Newhaven	Sheepcote Valley*, Brighton	01273 626546
Plymouth	Plymouth Sound, Plymouth	01752 862325
Poole	Hunter's Moon*, Wareham	01929 556605
Portsmouth	Rookesbury Park, Fareham	01329 834085
Rosslare	River Valley, Wicklow	00353 (0)404 41647
Weymouth	Crossways, Dorchester	01305 852032

Site open all year

When seasonal Club sites near the ports are closed, the sites listed below may be useful overnight stops for early and late season travellers using cross-Channel or Irish Sea ports. Although they may not be 'on the doorstep' of the ports in question they are open all year or most of the year. All 'open all year' sites offer a limited supply of hardstanding pitches.

Port	Nearest Club Site and Town	Tel No.
Dover, Folkestone, Channel Tunnel	Abbey Wood, London	020 8311 7708
	Alderstead Heath, Redhill	01737 644629
	Amberley Fields, Crawley	01293 524834
	Crystal Palace, London	020 8778 7155
Fishguard, Pembroke, Swansea	Pembrey Country Park, Llanelli	01554 834369
Portsmouth	Abbey Wood, London	020 8311 7708
	Alderstead Heath, Redhill	01737 644629
	Amberley Fields, Crawley	01293 524834
	Crystal Palace, London	020 8778 7155

Alternatively, consider an overnight stay at a CL (Certificated Location) site within striking distance of your port of departure. Many CLs are open all year.

Full details of all these sites can be found in the latest edition of The Caravan Club's Sites Directory & Handbook and on the Club's website, www.caravanclub.co.uk

NB Amberley Fields, Commons Wood, Daleacres, Fairlight Wood, Hunter's Moon, Old Hartley, Rookesbury Park and Round Plantation are open to Caravan Club members only. Non-members are welcome at all the other Caravan Club sites listed above.

Car, Motorhome and Caravan Insurance

Insurance cover for your car, caravan, motorhome or trailer tent whilst travelling abroad is of the utmost importance. In addition, travel insurance, such as The Caravan Club's Red Pennant Overseas Holiday Insurance (available only to Club members), not only minimises duplication of cover offered by your motor and caravan insurance, but also covers other contingencies such as despatch of spare parts, medical and hospital fees, vehicle hire, vehicle recovery, etc.

See Holiday Insurance later in this section.

In order to be covered for a period abroad the following action is necessary:

• **Caravan** – Inform your caravan insurer/broker of the dates of your holiday and pay any additional premium required. The Caravan Club's 5Cs Caravan Insurance gives free foreign use cover for up to 182 days.

• **Car or Motorhome** – If your journey is outside the EU or EU Associated Countries (listed on the next page) inform your motor insurer/broker of the dates of your holiday, together with details of all the countries you will be visiting, and pay any additional premium. Also inform them if you are towing a caravan and ask them to include it on your Green Card if you need to carry one.

The Caravan Club's Car Insurance and Motorhome Insurance schemes extend to provide full policy cover for European Union or Associated Countries free of charge, provided the total period of foreign travel in any one annual period of insurance does not exceed 180 days for car insurance and 270 days for motorhome insurance. It may be possible to extend this period, although a charge will apply. The cover provided is the same as what a Club member enjoys in the UK, rather than just the minimum legal liability cover required by law in the countries that you are visiting.

Should you be delayed beyond the limits of your insurance you must, without fail, instruct your insurer/broker to maintain cover.

For full details of The Caravan Club's caravan insurance telephone 01342 336610 or for car and motorhome insurance products, telephone 0800 0284809 or visit our website, www.caravanclub.co.uk/insurance

Taking Your Car or Motorhome Abroad – Evidence of Insurance Cover (Green Card)

All countries require visiting motorists to have motor insurance cover for their legal liability to third parties. An International Motor Insurance Certificate, commonly known as a Green Card, is evidence of compliance with this requirement. However, motorists visiting EU and Associated Countries do not need a Green Card as, under EU legislation, a UK Motor Insurance Certificate is now accepted in all such countries as evidence that the obligatory motor insurance cover is in force.

Travellers outside of the EU and Associated Countries will need to obtain a Green Card document, for which insurers usually make a charge. If a Green Card is issued, your motor insurers should be asked to include reference on it to any caravan or trailer that you may be towing. If you do not have evidence of the obligatory insurance cover, you may have to pay for temporary insurance at a country's border.

Irrespective of whether a Green Card is required, it is advisable to notify your insurer/broker of your intention to travel outside of the UK and obtain confirmation that your policy has been extended to include use of the insured vehicle abroad, as your motor insurer may not automatically provide you

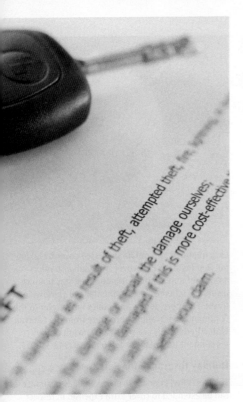

with full policy cover when abroad. You should ensure that your vehicle and motorhome policies provide adequate cover for your purposes, rather than the minimum cover that the country you are visiting obliges you to have.

European Accident Statement

You should also check with your motor insurer/broker to see if they provide a European Accident Statement to record details of any accident you may be involved in with your motor vehicle. Travelling with your Vehicle Registration Certificate, (V5C) or vehicle on hire certificate (VE103), MOT certificate (if applicable), certificate of motor insurance, copy of your CRIS document, European Accident Statement and valid UK pink EU-format paper driving licence or photocard driving licence should be sufficient in the event that you are stopped for a routine police check or following an accident whilst travelling within the EU or an Associated Country. These documents should never be left in your vehicle when it is unattended.

European Union and Associated Countries

European Union: Austria, Belgium, Bulgaria, Cyprus, Czech Republic, Denmark, Estonia, Finland, France, Germany, Greece, Hungary, Ireland, Italy, Latvia,

Lithuania, Luxembourg, Malta, Netherlands, Poland, Portugal, Romania, Slovakia, Slovenia, Spain, Sweden and the United Kingdom.

Associated EU Countries (i.e. non-EU signatories to the motor insurance Multilateral Guarantee Agreement): Andorra, Croatia, Iceland, Norway, Switzerland and Liechtenstein.

Although EU Countries, you may still wish to obtain a Green Card if visiting Bulgaria or Romania in order to avoid local difficulties which can sometimes arise in these countries. If you do not take a Green Card you should carry your certificate of motor insurance. If you plan to visit countries outside the EU and Associated Countries, and in particular central and eastern European countries, you should check that your motor insurer will provide the necessary extension of cover.

Croatia

If you are planning to visit Croatia and intend to drive through Bosnia and Herzegovina along the 20 km strip of coastline at Neum on the Dalmatian coastal highway to Dubrovnik you should obtain Green Card cover for Bosnia and Herzegovina. If you have difficulties obtaining such cover before departure contact the Club's Travel Service Information Officer for advice, email: travelserviceinfo@caravanclub.co.uk. Alternatively, temporary third-party insurance can be purchased at the country's main border posts, or in Split and other large cities. It is understood that it is not generally obtainable at the Neum border crossing itself.

For Club members insured under the Caravan Club's Car Insurance and Motor Caravan Insurance schemes full policy cover is available for the 20 km strip of coastline from Neum.

Caravans Stored Abroad

Caravan insurers will not normally insure caravans left on campsites or in storage abroad.

In these circumstances specialist policies are available from Towergate Bakers on 0800 4961516, www.tower gatebakers.co.uk, email bakers@towergate.co.uk or K Drewe Insurance, tel 0845 4085929, www.lookinsurance services.co.uk, email support@lookcaravans.co.uk

> **Insurers will not normally insure caravans left on campsite or in storage abroad**

Legal Costs Abroad

A driver who is taken to court following a road traffic accident in a European country runs the risk of being held liable for legal costs, even if cleared of any blame.

Motor insurance policies in the UK normally include cover for legal costs and expenses incurred (with insurer's consent) which arise from any incident that is covered under the terms and conditions of the policy. The Caravan Club's Car Insurance and Motorhome Insurance schemes incorporate such cover, together with optional additional legal expenses cover for recovering any other losses that are not included in your motor insurance policy. Similar optional legal expenses insurance is also offered as an addition to the Club's 5Cs Caravan Insurance scheme.

Holiday Travel Insurance

Having insured your vehicles, there are other risks to consider and it is essential to take out adequate travel insurance. The Caravan Club's Red Pennant Overseas Holiday Insurance is designed to provide as full a cover as possible at a reasonable fee. The Club's scheme is tailor-made for people with caravans, motorhomes or trailer tents and includes cover against the following:

Recovery of vehicles and passengers

Chauffeured recovery

Towing charges

Emergency labour costs

Spare parts location and despatch

Storage fees

Continuation of holiday travel, i.e. car hire, etc

Continuation of holiday accommodation, i.e. hotels, etc

Emergency medical and hospital expenses

Personal accident benefits

Legal expenses

Loss of deposits/cancellation cover

Emergency cash transfers

Personal effects and baggage insurance

Loss of cash or documents

Cost of telephone calls

If you are proposing to participate in dangerous sporting activities such as skiing, hang-gliding or mountaineering, check that your personal holiday insurance includes cover for such sports and that it also covers the cost of emergency mountain and helicopter rescue.

Look carefully at the exemptions to your insurance policy, including those relating to pre-existing medical conditions or the use of alcohol. Be sure to declare any pre-existing medical conditions to your insurer.

Club members can obtain increased cover by taking out Red Pennant **Plus** cover. The Club also offers a range of annual multi-trip and long stay holiday insurance schemes for Continental and worldwide travel. For more details and policy limits refer to the Continental Caravanning brochure from the Caravan Club. Alternatively see www.caravanclub.co.uk/redpennant for details or telephone 01342 336633.

Holiday Insurance for Pets

The Club's Red Pennant Overseas Holiday Insurance can be extended to cover extra expenses in respect of your pet that may arise as part of a claim for an incident normally covered under the Red Pennant policy, such as pet repatriation expenses. It does not, however, cover costs arising from an injury to, or the illness of your pet, or provide any legal liability cover to you as a pet owner.

For this you will require separate pet insurance, such as that offered by The Caravan Club, which covers treatment abroad, quarantine costs, emergency expenses, including boarding fees, as well as holiday cancellation costs. It also covers legal liability in the event of injury or damage caused by your pet.

Contact The Caravan Club on 0800 0151396 or see www.caravanclub.co.uk/petins for details of the Club's Pet Insurance scheme, specially negotiated to take into account Club members' requirements both at home and abroad.

> **See, www.caravanclub.co.uk/petins for details of our Pet Insurance scheme**

It is advisable, therefore, to ensure that you have adequate travel insurance for your pet in the event of an incident or illness abroad requiring veterinary treatment, emergency repatriation due to illness or long-term care in excess of the duration of your holiday.

Marine Insurance

Car Ferries

Vehicles driven by their owner are normally conveyed in accordance with the terms of the carrying companies' published by-laws or conditions, and if damage is sustained during loading, unloading or shipment, this must be reported at the time to the carrier's representative. Any claim arising from such damage must be notified in writing to the carrier concerned within three days of the incident. Nonetheless it is unwise to rely upon the carrier accepting liability for your claim so it would be prudent to have separate transit insurance.

The majority of motor policies provide transit insurance cover for vehicles during short sea crossings up to 65 hours normal duration – check this with your insurer/broker.

The Caravan Club's 5Cs Caravan Insurance policy automatically covers you for crossings of any length within the area covered by Red Pennant Overseas Holiday Insurance.

Boats

The Royal Yachting Association recommends that all boats have marine insurance. Third party insurance is compulsory for many countries, together with a translation of the insurance certificate into the appropriate language(s). Check with your insurer/broker before taking your boat abroad.

Medical Insurance

It is important to make sure your travel insurance also covers medical emergency expenses. Regardless of whether you have a European Health Insurance Card (EHIC), medical expenses can still be incurred so make sure your travel insurance policy will cover you.

The Caravan Club's Red Pennant cover is available to members. Please visit www.caravanclub.co.uk/redpennant for further information or telephone 01342 336633.

See the chapter Medical Matters in the section DURING YOUR STAY for further information.

Home Insurance

Most home insurers require advance notification if you are leaving your home unoccupied for 30 days or more. They often require that mains services (except electricity) are turned off, water drained down and that somebody visits the home once a week. Check your policy documents or speak to your insurer/broker.

The Caravan Club's Home Insurance policy provides full cover for up to 90 days when you are away from home (for instance when touring) and requires only common sense precautions for longer periods of unoccupancy.

Contact 0800 0284815 or see www.caravanclub.co.uk/homeins for details of our Home Insurance scheme, specially negotiated to suit the majority of Club members' requirements.

Personal Belongings

The majority of travellers are able to cover their valuables such as jewellery, watches, cameras, laptops, bicycles and, in some instances, small boats, under the All Risks section of their Householders' Comprehensive Policy. This includes The Caravan Club's Home Insurance scheme.

Vehicles Left Behind Abroad

If you are involved in an accident or breakdown whilst abroad which prevents you taking your vehicle home, you must ensure that your normal insurance cover is maintained to cover the period that the vehicle remains abroad, and that you are covered for the cost of recovering it to your home address.

You should remove all items of baggage and personal belongings from your vehicles before leaving them unattended. If this is not possible you should check with your insurer/broker to establish whether extended cover can be provided. In all circumstances, you must remove any valuables and items which might attract Customs duty, including wine, beer, spirits and cigarettes.

Planning and Travelling

International Holidays 2012 and 2013

International Holidays, Important Dates & UK Bank Holidays

2012				2013	
January	1	Sunday	New Year's Day	1	Tuesday
	2	Monday	Bank Holiday	-	-
	6	Friday	Epiphany	6	Sunday
February	22	Wednesday	Ash Wednesday	13	Wednesday
March	1	Thursday	St David's Day	1	Friday
	17	Saturday	St Patrick's Day	17	Sunday
	18	Sunday	Mother's Day	10	Sunday
	25	Sunday	British Summer Time Begins	31	Sunday
April	1	Sunday	Palm Sunday	24 Mar	Sunday
	6	Friday	Good Friday	29 Mar	Friday
	8	Sunday	Easter Day	31 Mar	Sunday
	9	Monday	Easter Monday	1	Monday
	23	Monday	St George's Day	23	Tuesday
May	7	Monday	May Bank Holiday	6	Monday
	17	Thursday	Ascension Day	9	Thursday
	27	May	Whit Sunday	19	Sunday
June	4	Monday	Spring Bank Holiday UK	27 May	Monday
	5	Tuesday	Queen's Diamond Jubilee (Bank Holiday)	-	-
	7	Thursday	Corpus Christi	30 May	Thursday
	17	Sunday	Father's Day	16	Sunday
July	20	Friday	1st Day of Ramadan*	9	Tuesday
August	15	Wednesday	Assumption	15	Thursday
	18	Saturday	Ramadan Ends*	7	Wednesday
	27	Monday	Bank Holiday UK	26	Monday
September	17	Monday	Jewish New Year (Rosh Hashanah)	5	Thursday
	26	Wednesday	Jewish Day of Atonement (Yom Kippur)	14	Saturday
October	28	Sunday	British Summer Time ends	27	Sunday
	31	Wednesday	Halloween	31	Thursday
November	1	Thursday	All Saints' Day	1	Friday
	11	Sunday	Remembrance Sunday	10	Sunday
	15	Thursday	Al Hijra – Islamic New Year	4	Monday
	30	Friday	St Andrew's Day	30	Saturday
December	25	Tuesday	Christmas Day	25	Wednesday
	26	Wednesday	St Stephen's Day; Boxing Day UK	26	Thursday

* Subject to the lunar calendar

NOTES   1) Outside the UK when a holiday falls on a Sunday it will not necessarily be observed the following day.

2) Public holidays in individual countries are listed in the relevant Country Introductions.

3) Dates listed here and in the Country Introduction Chapters are believed to be correct at time of publication, however please note some dates may not have officially been confirmed and may be subject to change.

Planning and Travelling
Money

Take your holiday money in a mixture of cash, credit and debit cards and travellers' cheques or pre-paid travel cards and keep them separately. Do not rely exclusively on only one method of payment.

*See **Customs** in the section **DURING YOUR STAY** for information about declaring the amount of cash you carry when entering or leaving the EU.*

Local Currency

It is not necessary to carry a large amount of cash but it is a good idea to take sufficient foreign currency for your immediate needs on arrival, including loose change if possible. Even if you intend to use credit and debit cards for most of your holiday spending, it makes sense to take some cash to tide you over until you are able to find a cash machine (ATM), and you may need change for parking meters or the use of supermarket trolleys.

You can change money at ports and on ferries but the rates offered do not generally represent the best value. The Post Office, many High Street banks, exchange offices and travel agents offer commission free foreign exchange, some will charge a flat fee and some offer a 'buy back' service. Most stock the more common currencies such as Euros, but it is wise to order in advance in case demand is heavy, or if you require an unusual currency.

> **Shop around and compare commission and exchange rates to make sure you get the best deal**

Currency can also be ordered by telephone or online for delivery to your home address on payment of a handling charge. Online providers such as the Post Office or Travelex and most of the High Street banks offer their customers an online ordering service which usually represents the best value. It can pay to shop around and compare commission and exchange rates, together with minimum charges.

If you pay for your currency with a credit or debit card the card issuer may charge a cash advance fee in addition to the commission and/or handling charge.

Banks and money exchanges in central and eastern Europe are not willing to accept Scottish and Northern Irish bank notes and may be reluctant to change any sterling which has been written on, is creased or worn, or is not in virtually mint condition.

Exchange rates (as at September 2011) are given in the Country Introductions in this guide. Up to date currency conversion rates can be obtained from your bank or national newspapers. Alternatively, www.oanda.com updates currency rates around the world daily and allows you to download a currency converter to your mobile phone.

Foreign Currency Bank Accounts

Frequent travellers or those who spend long periods abroad may find a euro bank account useful. Most such accounts impose no currency conversion charges for debit or credit card use and allow fee-free cash withdrawls at ATMs. Some banks may also allow you to spread your account across different currencies, depending on your circumstances. Your bank will advise you.

Travellers' Cheques

Travellers' cheques can be cashed in many countries, and are the safest way to carry large sums of money. They can be replaced quickly – usually within 24 hours – in the event of loss or theft. However, their popularity has declined in recent years and increasing numbers of foreign retailers and merchants are not accepting travellers' cheques, instead preferring debit/credit cards or cash. Recent visitors report difficulties in finding a bank that will cash them for non-account holders, and where they are accepted high commission charges may be incurred. Travellers' cheques may still be useful if you are travelling off the beaten track or in far-flung locations, but bear in mind that small bank branches may not offer foreign exchange services.

Commission is usually payable when you buy the cheques and/or when you cash them in. See the Country Introduction for more information.

Travel Money Cards

Travel money cards are issued by the Post Office, Travelex, Lloyds Bank and American Express amongst many others. For a comparison table see www.which-prepaid-card.co.uk

They are an increasingly popular and practical alternative to travellers' cheques as a pre-paid PIN protected travel money card offers the security of travellers' cheques, with the convenience of plastic. Load the card with the amount you need (in euros, sterling or US dollars) before leaving home, and then simply use cash machines to make withdrawals and/or present the card to pay for goods and services in shops and restaurants as you would a credit or debit card. You can obtain a second card so that another user can access the funds and you can also top the card up over the telephone or online while you are abroad.

These cards can be cheaper to use than credit or debit cards for both cash withdrawals and purchases as there are usually no loading or transaction fees to pay. In addition, because they are separate from your bank account, if the card is lost or stolen there is less risk of identity theft.

The Caravan Club has teamed up with Caxton FX to offer members a euro prepaid MasterCard travel money card. See www.caravanclub.co.uk/eurocard

Credit and Debit Cards

Credit and debit cards offer a convenient way of spending abroad. You can use a card to pay for goods and services wherever your card logo is displayed and also to obtain cash from ATMs using your PIN. ATMs usually offer an English language option once you insert your card.

For the use of cards abroad most banks impose a foreign currency conversion charge (typically 2.75% per transaction) which is usually the same for both credit and debit cards. If you use your credit card to withdraw cash there will be a further commission charge of up to 3% and you will be charged interest (possibly at a higher rate than normal) as soon as you withdraw the money.

In line with market practice, Barclaycard, which issues The Caravan Club's credit card, charges a 2.75% fee for all card transactions outside the UK. Cash withdrawals abroad are subject to a further 2% handling charge as in the UK. A £2 minimum fee applies with a maximum charge of £50 (information correct at time of publication).

> ## Contact your credit card issuer before you leave home to let them know you will be travelling abroad

Check the expiry date of your cards before you leave and memorise the PIN for each one. If you have several cards, take at least two in case you come across gaps in acceptance of certain cards, e.g. shops which accept only MasterCard or only VISA.

If you are planning an extended journey arrange for your credit or charge card account to be cleared each month by variable direct debit, ensuring that bills are paid on time and no interest is charged.

Credit and debit 'chip and PIN' cards issued by UK banks may not be universally accepted abroad and it is wise to check before incurring expenditure.

Contact your credit or debit card issuer before you leave home to let them know that you will be travelling abroad. In the battle against card fraud, card issuers are frequently likely to query transactions which they regard as unusual or suspicious. This may result in a cash withdrawal from an ATM being declined, or a retailer at the point of sale having to telephone for authorisation and/or confirmation of your details. Difficulties can occur if there is a language barrier or if the retailer is unwilling to bother with further checks. Your card may be declined or, worse still, temporarily stopped. In this instance you should insist that the retailer contacts the local authorisation centre but, in any event, it is a good idea to carry your card issuer's helpline number with you. You will also need this number to report the loss or theft of your card.

Dynamic Currency Conversion

When you pay with a credit or debit card, retailers may offer you the choice of currency for payment, e.g. a euro amount will be converted into sterling and then charged to your card account. You may be asked to sign an agreement to accept the conversion rate used and final amount charged and, having done so, there is no opportunity to change your mind or obtain a refund. This is known as a 'dynamic currency conversion' but the exchange rate used is unlikely to be as favourable as that used by your card issuer. You may also find retailers claiming that a sterling bill will automatically be generated when a UK-issued credit card is tendered and processed. If this is the case then you may prefer to pay by cash.

Some ATMs may give you the option to convert your withdrawal into sterling when you withdraw euros. It is often best to decline and opt to pay in the national currency.

Emergency Cash

If an emergency or robbery means that you need cash in a hurry, then friends or relatives at home can use the MoneyGram instant money transfer service available at post offices and branches of Thomas Cook.

This service, which does not necessarily require the sender to use a bank account or credit card, enables the transfer of money to over 233,000 money transfer agents around the world. Transfers take approximately ten minutes and charges are levied on a sliding scale.

> **As a last resort, contact the nearest British Embassy or Consulate for help**

Western Union operates a similar secure, worldwide service and has offices located in banks, post offices, travel agents, stations and shops. You can also transfer funds instantly by telephone on 0800 833833 or online at www.westernunion.co.uk

As a last resort, contact the nearest British Embassy or Consulate for help. The Foreign & Commonwealth Office in London can arrange for a relative or friend to deposit funds which will be authorised for payment by embassy staff. See individual Country Introductions for embassy and consulate addresses abroad.

Most travel insurance policies, including the Club's Red Pennant Overseas Holiday Insurance, will cover you for only a limited amount of lost or stolen cash (usually between £250 and £500) and you will probably have to wait until you return home for reimbursement.

The Euro

The Euro is the currency in use in many countries in Europe including Spain and Portugal. Each country's versions of banknotes and coins are valid in all the countries of the single currency euro zone.

Police have issued warnings that counterfeit euro notes are in circulation on the Continent. You should be aware and take all precautions to ensure that €10, €20 and €50 notes and €2 coins that you receive from sources other than banks and legitimate bureaux de change, are genuine.

Holiday Money Security

Treat your cards as carefully as you would cash. Use a money belt, if possible, to conceal cards and valuables and do not keep all your cash and cards in the same place. Split cash between members of your party. Memorise your PINs and never keep them with your credit/debit cards.

If you keep a wallet in your pocket, place a rubber band around it, as it is then more difficult for a pickpocket to slide the wallet out without your noticing.

To avoid credit or debit card 'cloning' or 'skimming' never let your card out of your sight. In restaurants follow the waiter to the till or insist that the card machine is brought to your table. This is particularly important as you may frequently find that a signature on a transaction slip is not checked against the signature on your card. If you do allow your card to be taken and it is gone for more than a minute, become suspicious.

If you suspect your card has been fraudulently used, or if your card is lost or stolen, or if a cash machine retains it, call the issuing bank immediately. All the major card companies and banks operate a 24-hour emergency helpline.

If you are unlucky enough to become a victim of fraud your bank should refund the money stolen, provided you have not been negligent or careless.

Keep your card's magnetic strip away from other cards and objects, especially if they are also magnetic. If the card is damaged in any way electronic terminals may not accept your transaction.

If you use travellers' cheques keep a separate note of their serial numbers in case of loss, and a record of where and when you cash them. If they are lost or stolen, contact the appropriate refund service immediately.

> **Carry your credit card issuer/bank's 24 hour UK helpline number with you in the event of loss or theft**

Carry your credit card issuer/bank's 24-hour UK helpline number with you. You might also want to consider joining a card protection plan so that in the event of loss or theft, one telephone call will cancel all your cards and arrange replacements.

Take care when using cash machines. If the machine is obstructed or poorly lit, avoid it. If someone near the machine is behaving suspiciously or makes you feel uneasy, find another one. If there is something unusual about the cash machine do not use it and report the matter to the bank or owner of the premises. Do not accept help from strangers and do not allow yourself to be distracted.

> **Always log off from internet banking upon completion of your session**

Be aware of your surroundings and if someone is watching you closely do not proceed with the transaction. Shield the screen and keyboard so that anyone waiting to use the machine cannot see you enter your PIN or transaction amount. Put your cash, card and receipt away immediately. Count your cash later and always keep your receipt to compare with your monthly statement.

If you bank over the internet and are using a computer in a public place such as a library or internet café, do not leave the PC unattended and ensure that no-one is watching what you type. Always log off from internet banking upon completion of your session to prevent the viewing of previous pages of your online session.

The cost of credit and debit card fraud is largely borne by banks and ultimately its customers, but the direct cost to cardholders should not be underestimated in terms of inconvenience and frustration, not to mention the time taken for incidents to be investigated and fraudently withdrawn funds to be returned to your account. There is the additional danger of identity theft.

Learn more about card fraud and preventative measures to combat it on www.cardwatch.org.uk

*See also **Security and Safety** in the section DURING YOUR STAY.*

Planning and Travelling
General Motoring Advice - Europe

Preparing For Your Journey

Adequate and careful preparation of your vehicles should be your first priority to ensure a safe and trouble free journey. Make sure your car and caravan, or motorhome, are properly serviced before you depart and take a well equipped spares kit and a spare wheel and tyre for your caravan to avoid any unnecessary disruptions to your holiday.

If you are a member of The Caravan Club re-read the Technical Information section of your UK Sites Directory & Handbook as it contains a wealth of information which is relevant to caravanning anywhere in the world.

Whether you are newcomers to caravanning or old hands, The Caravan Club offers a free advice service to Club members on technical and general caravanning matters, and also publishes information leaflets on a wide range of topics, all of which members can download from the Club's website. Alternatively, write to the Club's Technical Department or telephone for more details. For advice on issues specific to countries other than the UK, Club members should contact the Travel Service Information Officer, email: travelserviceinfo@caravanclub.co.uk

Documentation

Along with your driving licence always carry your Vehicle Registration Certificate (V5C) or the Vehicle on Hire Certificate (VE103), insurance certificate and MOT certificate (if applicable) when taking your vehicle abroad. You are also strongly advised to carry a copy of your Caravan Registration Identification Scheme (CRIS) document. You may be asked to show these documents when entering some countries.

If you are driving a hired or borrowed vehicle you must be in possession of a letter of authorisation from the owner, or a hire agreement.

See Documents in the section PLANNING AND TRAVELLING

Weight Limits

From both a legal and a safety point of view, it is essential not to exceed vehicle weight limits. European authorities are alert to the danger of over-weight vehicles and drivers are advised to carry with them documentation confirming their vehicle's maximum permitted laden weight. If your Vehicle Registration

Certificate (V5C) does not clearly state this, you will need to produce alternative certification, e.g. from a weighbridge.

If your vehicle(s) are pulled over by the police and you cannot produce this documentation you may have to accompany police to a weighbridge. Subsequently if your vehicle(s) are found to be overweight you will be liable to a fine and may have to jettison items. The Caravan Club, therefore, recommends a trip to a local weighbridge with your vehicle(s) fully laden before embarking on your holiday.

Some Final Checks

Experienced caravanners will be familiar with the checks necessary before setting off and the following list is a reminder:

- All car and caravan lights are working and sets of spare bulbs are packed
- The coupling is correctly seated on the towball and the breakaway cable is attached
- All windows, vents, hatches and doors are shut
- All on-board water systems are drained
- All mirrors are adjusted for maximum visibility
- Corner steadies are fully wound up and the brace is handy for your arrival on site
- Any fires or flames are extinguished and the gas cylinder tap is turned off. Fire extinguishers are fully charged and close at hand
- The over-run brake is working correctly
- The jockey wheel is raised and secured, the handbrake is released.

Driving On The Continent

Probably the main disincentive to driving abroad, particularly for caravanners, is the need to keep to the right-hand side of the road. However, for most people this proves to be no problem at all after the first hour or so. There are a few basic, but important, points to remember:

- Buy a good road map or atlas and plan ahead to use roads suitable for towing. See *Route Planning and GPS* in the chapter *Motoring – Equipment*.

- In your eagerness to reach your destination, don't attempt vast distances in a single stint. Share the driving, if possible, and plan to break your journey overnight at a suitable campsite. There are many sites listed in this guide and a lot of them are well situated near to motorways and main roads.

- Adjust all your mirrors for maximum rear-view observation. The vast majority of towed caravans – whatever the type of towing vehicle – will require extension mirrors to comply with legal requirements for an adequate rearwards view.

- Make sure the road ahead is clear before overtaking. Stay well behind the vehicle in front and, if possible, have someone with good judgement in the left-hand seat to give you the 'all clear'.

- If traffic builds up behind you, pull over safely and let it pass.

- Pay particular attention when turning left, when leaving a rest area/petrol station/campsite, or after passing through a one-way system, to ensure that you continue to drive on the right-hand side of the road.

- If your headlights are likely to dazzle other road users, adjust them to deflect to the right instead of the left, using suitable beam deflectors or (in some cases) a built-in adjustment system. Some lights can have the deflective part of the lens obscured with tape or a pre-cut adhesive mask, but check in your car's handbook if this is permitted or not. Some lights run too hot to be partially obscured in this way.

- When travelling, particularly in the height of the summer, it is wise to stop approximately every two hours (at the most) to stretch your legs and take a break.

- In case of a breakdown or accident, use hazard warning lights and warning triangle(s). Remember to wear a reflective jacket or waistcoat if you leave your vehicle.

Another disincentive for caravanners to travel abroad is the worry about roads and gradients in mountainous countries. Britain has steeper gradients on many of its main roads than many other European countries and traffic density is higher.

The chapter *Mountain Passes and Tunnels* under *PLANNING AND TRAVELLING* gives detailed advice on using mountain passes.

Another worry involves vehicle breakdown and language difficulties. The Caravan Club's comprehensive and competitively priced Red Pennant Overseas Holiday Insurance is geared to handle all these contingencies with multi-lingual staff available at the Club's headquarters 24 hours a day throughout the year – see www.caravanclub.co.uk/redpennant

Driving Offences

You are obliged to comply with the traffic rules and regulations of the countries you visit. Research shows that non-resident drivers are more likely to take risks and break the law due to their feeling of impunity. Cross-border enforcement of traffic laws is the subject of a European Directive which is being ratified by EU member states. This will bring an end to flagrant disregard of traffic rules and make them equally enforceable throughout the EU. In the meantime, a number of bi-lateral agreements already exist between European countries which means that there is no escaping penalty notices and demands for payment for motoring offences.

Make sure you are familiar with traffic laws in the countries you plan to visit, including speed limits and equipment you are legally required to carry. See the *Speed Limits* and *Essential Equipment* tables later in this guide and the additional information contained in the Country Introduction chapters.

Some foreign police officers can look rather intimidating to British visitors used to unarmed police. Needless to say, they expect you to be polite

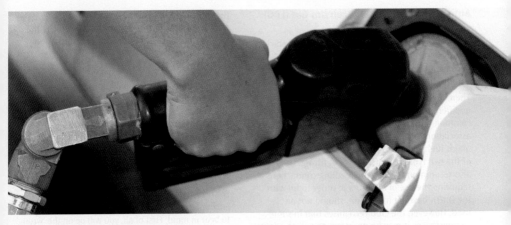

and show respect and, in return, they are generally helpful and may well be lenient to a visiting motorist. Never consider offering a bribe!

The authorities in many countries are hard on parking and speeding offenders. Visiting motorists should not be influenced by the speed at which locals drive; they often know where the speed traps are and can slow down in time to avoid being caught! In general, it is no use protesting if caught, as anyone who refuses to pay may have their vehicle impounded.

Be particularly careful if you have penalty points on your driving licence. If you commit an offence on the Continent which attracts penalty points, local police may well do checks on your licence to establish whether the addition of those points renders you liable to disqualification. If so you would then have to find other means to get yourself and your vehicle(s) home.

> Many police forces are authorised to carry out random breath tests

Drink-Driving

The maximum legal level of alcohol in the blood in most Continental countries is lower than that in the UK (in some it is zero), and many police forces are authorised to carry out random breath tests. It is wise to adopt the 'no drink when driving' rule at all times; offenders are heavily fined all over Europe and penalties can include confiscation of driving licence, vehicle(s) and even imprisonment. For more detailed information see the Country Introduction chapter.

On-the-Spot Fines

Many countries allow their police officers to issue fines which must be paid immediately, up to certain limits. The fine may be a deposit for a larger fine which will be issued to your home address. In most countries credit cards are not accepted in payment of on-the-spot fines and you may find yourself accompanied to the nearest cash machine. Always obtain a receipt for money handed over.

Fuel

During ferry crossings make sure your petrol tank is not over-full. Don't be tempted to carry spare petrol in cans; the ferry companies and Eurotunnel forbid this practice and even the carriage of empty cans is prohibited.

Grades of petrol sold on the Continent are comparable to those sold in the UK with the same familiar brands; 95 octane is frequently known as 'Essence' and 98 octane as 'Super'. Diesel is sometimes called 'Gasoil' and is normally available in all the countries covered in the Caravan Europe guides. The fuel prices given in the table at the end of this chapter were correct according to the latest information available in September 2011. Members of The Caravan Club can also check current fuel prices by visiting www.caravanclub.co.uk/overseasadvice

In sparsely populated regions it is a sensible precaution to travel with a full petrol tank and to keep it topped up. Similarly in remote rural areas in any country you may have difficulty finding a manned petrol station at night or on Sundays. Petrol stations offering a 24-hour service may involve an automated process which occasionally work only with locally issued credit cards.

See the Fuel Price Guide Table at the end of this chapter.

Automotive Liquified Petroleum Gas (LPG)

The increasing popularity of LPG – known as 'autogas' or GPL – and use of dual-fuelled vehicles means that the availability of automotive LPG has become an important issue for some drivers, and the Country Introductions provide more information.

There are different tank-filling openings in use in different countries. Pending the adoption of a common European filling system, UKLPG, the trade association for the LPG industry in the UK, and the major fuel suppliers recommend the use of either of the two types of Dutch bayonet fitting. UKLPG also recommends that vehicle-filling connections requiring the use of adaptors in order to fill with the Dutch bayonet filling gun, should not be used. However, the Club recognises that in some circumstances it may be necessary to use an adaptor and these are available from Autogas 2000 Ltd on 01845 523213, www.autogas.co.uk

Lead Replacement Petrol

Leaded petrol has been withdrawn from sale in many countries in Europe and, in general, is only available from petrol stations in the form of a bottled additive. Where lead replacement petrol is still available at the pump it is generally from the same pumps previously used for leaded petrol, i.e. red or black pumps, and may be labelled 'Super Plus', 'Super 98' or 'Super MLV', but it is advisable to check before filling up if this is not clear from information at the pump.

Low Emission Zones

Many cities in countries around Europe have introduced 'Low Emission Zones' (LEZ) in order to regulate vehicle pollution levels. Some schemes require you to buy a windscreen sticker, pay a fee or register your vehicle before entering the zone and you may need to show proof that your vehicle meets the required standard.

Before you travel visit the website www.lowemissionzones.eu for maps showing the location of the LEZ and for further information.

Motorhomes Towing Cars

A motorhome towing a small car using an A-frame or towing dolly is illegal in most European countries, although such units are sometimes encountered. Motorhome users wishing to tow a small car abroad should transport it on a braked trailer so that all four of the car's wheels are off the road.

Motorway Tolls

For British drivers who may never, or rarely, have encountered a toll booth, there are a couple of points to bear in mind. First of all, you will be on the 'wrong' side of the car for the collection of toll tickets at the start of the motorway section and payment of tolls at the end. If you are travelling without a front seat passenger, this can mean a big stretch or a walk round to the other side of the car. Most toll booths are solidly built and you should be careful of any high concrete kerbs when pulling up to them.

On entering a stretch of motorway you will usually have to stop at a barrier and take a ticket from a machine to allow the barrier to rise. Avoid the lanes dedicated to vehicles displaying electronic season tickets. You may encounter toll booths without automatic barriers where it is still necessary to take a ticket and, if you pass through without doing so, you may be fined. On some stretches of motorway there are no ticket machines as you enter and you simply pay a fixed sum when you exit.

Your toll ticket will indicate the time you entered the motorway. Be warned that in some countries electronic tills at exit booths calculate the distance a vehicle has travelled and the journey time. The police are automatically informed if speeding has taken place and fines are imposed.

Payment can be made by credit cards in most, but not all countries.

See the Country Introduction chapters for specific information.

Parking

Make sure you check local parking regulations, as fines may be imposed and unattended vehicles clamped or towed away. Look out for road markings and for short-term parking zones. It might be helpful to make a note of the words for the days of the week in the local language and the words for 'height', 'length', 'over' for example.

Ensure you are in possession of parking discs in towns where they are required. As a general rule, park on the right-hand side of the road in the direction of traffic flow, avoiding cycle and bus lanes and tram tracks. Vehicles should not cause an obstruction and should be adequately lit when parked at night.

The following are some signs that you may encounter.

| No parking on Monday, Wednesday, Friday or Sunday | No parking on Tuesday, Thursday or Saturday | Fortnightly parking on alternative sides |

| No parking from the 1st-15th of the month | No parking from the 16th-end of the month |

In parts of central Europe car theft may be a problem and you are advised to park only in officially designated, guarded car parks whenever possible.

Parking Facilities for the Disabled

The Blue Badge is recognised in most European countries and it allows disabled motorists to use the same parking concessions enjoyed by the citizens of the country you are visiting. Concessions differ from country to country, however, and it is important to know when and where you can and, more importantly, cannot park. If you are in any doubt about your rights, do not park.

Explanatory leaflets describing the concessions in countries inside and outside the EU are available from the Department for Transport's website, www.dft.gov.uk/transportforyou/access/bluebadge, or telephone 0300 1231102 to request copies. See also www.fiadisabledtravellers.com

Priority and Roundabouts

When driving on the Continent it is essential to be aware of other vehicles which may have priority over you, particularly when they join from the right into the road you are using. Road signs indicate priority or loss of priority and motorists must be sure that they understand the signs.

> **Never rely on being given right of way, even if you have priority**

Care should be taken at intersections and you should never rely on being given right of way, even if you have priority, especially in small towns and villages where local, often slow-moving, traffic will take right of way. Always give way to public service and military vehicles and to buses, trams and coaches.

In some countries in Europe priority at roundabouts is given to vehicles entering the roundabout (i.e. on the right) unless signposted on the contrary. This is a reversal of the UK rule and care is needed.

See the *Country Introduction Chapters* for more information.

Public Transport

In general in built-up areas be prepared to stop to allow a bus to pull out from a bus stop when the driver is signalling his intention to do so. Take particular care when school buses have stopped and passengers are getting on and off.

Overtaking trams in motion is normally only permitted on the right, unless on a one way street where you can overtake on the left if there is not enough space on the right. Do not overtake a tram near a tram stop. These may be in the centre of the road. When a tram or bus stops to allow passengers on and off, you should stop to allow them to cross to the pavement. Give way to trams which are turning across your carriageway.

Do not park so as to obstruct tram lines or force other drivers to do so; trams cannot steer round obstructions! Take care when crossing tram tracks, especially if the rails are wet, and be particularly careful when crossing them at shallow angles, on bends and at junctions.

Road Signs and Markings

Many road signs have the same general design in most countries in Europe making them fairly easily recognisable. Blue and green direction and marker signs are used to identify motorways and main roads but their use may be the opposite of that in the UK, i.e. motorways marked by green signs and main

roads by blue. This can be particularly confusing, for example when crossing from France where motorway signs are blue, into Switzerland or Italy where they are green.

Where text descriptions rather than symbols are used on information signs it can be helpful to make a note of a few basic words for flood, diversion, by-pass, etc. The country introductions lists a few such basic words and phrases in the local language for your reference.

You will often encounter STOP signs in situations which, in the UK, would probably be covered by a Give Way sign. Be particularly careful – coming to a complete halt is usually compulsory, even if local drivers seem unconcerned by it, and failure to do so may result in a fine. Be careful too in areas where maintenance of roads may be irregular and where white lines have been worn away.

A solid single or double white line in the middle of the carriageway always means no overtaking.

Direction signs in general may be confusing, giving only the name of a town on the way to a larger city, or simply the road number and no place name. They may be smaller than you expect and not particularly easy to spot.

Across the EU you will find that major routes have not only an individual road number, such as A6, but also a number beginning with an 'E' displayed on green and white signs. Routes running from east to west have even 'E' numbers, whereas routes running from north to south have odd 'E' numbers. This can be helpful when planning long-distance routes across international frontiers.

In some countries, particularly in Scandinavia and Belgium, through routes or motorways may only show the 'E' road numbers, so it would be advisable to make a note of them when planning your route. The E road system is not recognised in the UK and there are no such road signs.

Pedestrian Crossings

Stopping to allow pedestrians to cross at zebra crossings is not nearly as common a practice on the Continent as it is in the UK. Pedestrians often do not expect to cross until the road is clear and may be surprised if you stop to allow them to do so. Check your mirrors carefully when braking as other drivers behind you, not expecting to stop, may be taken by surprise. The result may be a rear-end shunt or, worse still, vehicles overtaking you at the crossing and putting pedestrians at risk.

Speed Limits

Remember speed limit signs are in kilometres per hour, not miles per hour. General speed limits are given in the table at the end of this chapter. Refer to the Country Introduction for detailed information.

Radar-detection devices, whether in use or not, are illegal in many countries on the Continent and should not be carried at all. If you have one in your vehicle remove it before leaving home.

Speed cameras are becoming more widespread throughout Europe but you should not expect them to be highly visible as they are in the UK. In many instances, for example on the German motorway network, they may be hidden or deliberately inconspicuous. The use of unmarked police cars using speed detection equipment is common. See the item *Radar/Speed Camera Detectors* in the chapter *Motoring – Equipment*.

Traffic Lights

Traffic lights may not be placed as conspicuously as they are in the UK, for instance they may be smaller, differently shaped or suspended across the road, with a smaller set on a post at the roadside. You may find that lights change directly from red to green, by-passing amber completely. Flashing amber lights generally indicate that you may proceed with caution if it is safe to do so but must give way to pedestrians and other vehicles.

> **Be cautious when approaching a green light, especially in fast-moving traffic**

A green filter light should be treated with caution as you may still have to give way to pedestrians who have a green light to cross the road.

You may find that drivers are not particularly well-disciplined about stopping as they approach a light as it turns red and if they are behind you in this situation, they will expect you to accelerate through the lights rather than brake hard to stop. Therefore be cautious when approaching a green light, especially if you are in a relatively fast-moving

stream of traffic. Similarly, be careful when pulling away from a green light and check left and right just in case a driver on the road crossing yours has jumped a red light.

Winter Driving

If you regularly caravan in wintry conditions a four-wheel drive car or all-terrain vehicle may be a good investment. An ABS braking system offers significant advantages as do other comforts such as heated seats and steering wheels.

Winter driving abroad requires extra preparation and caution, especially if you are heading for mountainous areas or to northern Europe. Major mountain passes are kept open in winter except in particularly extreme conditions. Otherwise keep to main roads wherever possible as they are more likely to be clear of snow and ice, and adjust your speed and driving technique to the road conditions. Scenic diversions are probably not a good idea in the depths of winter.

The law in some countries requires the fitting of winter tyres and/or the use of snow chains – see *Winter Tyres and Snow Chains* in the chapter *Motoring – Equipment*.

You can also visit www.caravanclub.co.uk/overseasadvice to access and download the Winter Equipment Requirements leaflet.

Fuel Price Guide

Prices per litre as at September 2011

Country	Unleaded			Diesel	
	Unleaded	Translation of Unleaded	Diesel	Diesel	Translation of Diesel
Andorra (EUR)	1.20 (95) 1.26 (98)	Sans plomb or sin plomo	1.09		Gazole or gasóleo
Austria (EUR)	1.40 (95) 1.53 (98)	Bleifrei	1.34		Diesel
Belgium (EUR)	1.65 (95) 1.68 (98)	Sans plomb or loodvrije	1.46		
Croatia (HRK)	9.88 (95) 10.24 (98)	Eurosuper or bez olova	8.92		Dizel
Czech Republic (CZK)	34.93 (95)	Natural or bez olova	34.27		Nafta
Denmark (DKK)	12.83 (95) 11.86 (98)	Blyfri	10.72		
Finland (EUR)	1.57 (95) 1.62 (98)	Lyijyton polttoaine	1.36		
France (EUR)	1.52 (95) 1.56 (98)	Essence sans plomb	1.34		Gazole
Germany (EUR)	1.58 (95) 1.61 (98)	Bleifrei	1.42		Diesel
Greece (EUR)	1.74 (95) 1.92 (98)	Amoliwdi wensina	1.52		Petreleo
Hungary (HUF)	391 (95)	Olommentes uzemanyag	379		Dizel or gázolaj
Italy (EUR)	1.60 (95) 1.75 (98)	Sensa piombo	1.56		Gasolio
Luxembourg (EUR)	1.32 (95) 1.36 (98)	Sans plomb	1.18		Gazole
Netherlands (EUR)	1.74 (95) 1.80 (98)	Loodvrije	1.40		Diesel or gasolie
Norway (NOK)	14.32 (95) 14.63 (98)	Blyfri bensin	13.43		Diesel
Poland (PLN)	5.18 (95) or 5.40 (98)	Bezolowiu	5.11		
Portugal (EUR)	1.59 (95) 1.65 (98)	Sem chumbo	1.37		Gasóleo or diesel
Slovakia (EUR)	1.38 (95)	Natural or olovnatych prisad	1.28		Nafta
Slovenia (EUR)	1.29 (95) 1.30 (98)	Brez svinca	1.24		
Spain (EUR)	1.35 (95) 1.46 (98)	Sin plomo	1.30		Gasóleo A or Gas-oil
Sweden (SEK)	14.38 (95) 14.78 (98)	Blyfri normal, premium	14.14		Diesel
Switzerland (CHF)	1.69 (95) 1.75 (98)	Bleifrei or sans plomb or sensa piomba	1.78		Diesel or gazole or gasolio
UK (GBP)	1.36 (95) 1.43 (98)		1.40		

Fuel prices courtesy of the AIT/FIA Information Centre (OTA) (September 2011)

Prices shown are in local currency, price per litre. The contents are belived to be correct at the date of publication but should be used for guideline purposes only. Differences in prices actually paid may be due to currency and oil price fluctuations as well as regional variations within countries.

For the most recent fuel prices please visit www.caravanclub.co.uk/overseasadvice

Speed Limits

Kilometres per hour (see Conversion Table below for equivalent miles per hour)

Country	Open Road			Motorways		
	Solo*	Towing	Motorhome (3,500-7,500kg)	Solo*	Towing	Motorhome (3,500-7,500kg)
Andorra	60-90	60-90	60-90	n/a	n/a	n/a
Austria	100	80***	70	100-130	100***	80
Belgium	90	90	90	120	120	90
Croatia	90-110	80	80	110-130	90	90
Czech Republic	80-90	80	80	130	80	80
Denmark	80-90	70	70	110-130	80	70
Finland	80-100	70-80	80	100-120 (100 for motorhome under 3,500kg)	80	80
France**	90-110	80-110**	80-100	110-130	90-130**	90-110
Germany	100	80	80	130	80	100
Greece	90-110 (80 for motorhome under 3,500kg)	80	80	130 (90 for motorhome under 3,500kg)	80	80
Hungary	90-110	70	70	130	80	80
Italy	90-110	70	80	130	80	100
Luxembourg	90	75	90	130	90	130
Netherlands	80-90	80-90***	80	120	90***	80
Norway	80	80	80	90-100	80	80
Poland	90-120	70-80	70-80	140	80	80
Portugal	90-100	70-80	70-90	120	100	100
Slovakia	90	90	80	130	90	80
Slovenia	90-100	80	80	130	80	80
Spain	90-100 (70-80 for motorhome under 3,500kg)	70-80	70-80	120 (90 for motorhome under 3,500kg)	80	90
Sweden ****	70-100	70-80	70-100	90-120	80	90-120
Switzerland	80-100	60-80	80	100-120	80	8+0

Converting Kilometres to Miles

km/h	20	30	40	50	60	70	80	90	100	110	120	130
mph	13	18	25	31	37	44	50	56	62	68	74	81

* Also including motorhomes under 3,500kg unless otherwise stated.
** Speed limits when towing a caravan/trailer in France is based on the gross train mass of your car/vehicle combination. If the gross train mass of the car/vehicle is over 3,500kg the speed limit is 90kph on motorways and 80-90kph on open roads. If the gross train mass of car/ vehicle is under 3,500kg the speed limit is 130kph on motorways and 90-110kph on open roads. To work out the gross train mass of your car/vehicle you need to add the fully laden weight of your car to your cars towing limit. For further information and for an example please visit www. caravanclub.co.uk/overseastravel. Please note in France speed limits are reduced in adverse weather.
*** If the combined weight of your car and caravan is over 3,500kg then the speed limit is the same as a motorhome over 3,500kg.
**** Speed limits vary greatly in Sweden and are dependent on the quality and safety of the road.

NOTES:
1) See Country Introductions in the relevant guides for further details, including special speed limits, where applicable.
2) Speed limits in built-up areas are generally much lower, and in some countries speed limits in residential areas may be as low as 20kph.
3) All information on this page is believed to be correct at the time of publication but may be subject to change. Speed limits often vary and some countries may trial new speed limits on certain roads and motorways. Check before you travel and always look for signs advising of speed limits on the journey. Please visit www.caravanclub.co.uk/overseasadvice to check the latest speed limits before you travel and for more detailed information and advice.

European Distances

Distances are shown in kilometres and are calculated from town/city centres along the most practical roads, although not necessarily taking the shortest route.

1km = 0.62 miles

Amsterdam	Athini (Athens)	Barcelona	Bergen	Berlin	Bilbao	Bordeaux	Bruxelles (Brussels)	Budapest	Calais	Dubrovnik	Firenze (Florence)	Frankfurt am Main	Genève (Geneva)	Göteborg (Gothenburg)	Hamburg	Helsinki	København (Copenhagen)	Lisboa (Lisbon)	Ljubljana	Luxembourg	Lyon	Madrid	Marseille
2836																							
1552	2090																						
1507	4017	2817																					
668	2584	1856	1320																				
1426	3422	613	2866	1974																			
1085	3240	566	2525	1632	338																		
211	2792	1365	1625	776	1235	893																	
1407	1510	1910	2179	852	2258	2061	1363																
368	2926	1381	1672	917	1196	866	195	1549															
2024	1265	2049	3204	1771	2381	2199	1970	787	2024														
1340	2115	1084	2476	1226	1432	1232	1185	929	1390	1074													
446	2396	1324	1537	538	1491	1149	401	970	595	1583	973												
909	2446	761	2120	1074	1109	678	721	1280	740	1405	604	588											
1043	3205	2354	791	656	2063	1162	1517	1316	2392	1851	1061	1644											
467	2780	1778	1050	284	1828	1486	585	1145	752	1967	1428	488	1071	584									
1204	2540	2388	1186	505	2525	2182	1316	2016	1893	1766	1101	1656	662	776									
780	2938	2091	1029	392	2141	1799	898	1253	1058	2125	1587	798	1381	241	321	795							
2269	4320	1241	3709	2817	883	1188	2077	3133	2061	3279	2307	2333	1983	3246	2669	3423	2982						
1239	1580	1451	2119	993	1778	1587	1191	429	1394	658	474	810	798	1262	1187	2023	1493	2640					
381	2637	1153	1655	766	1271	929	215	1184	409	1758	973	237	510	1192	625	1302	938	2113	974				
920	2559	634	2186	1224	982	531	733	1431	750	1518	695	691	151	1722	1146	1758	1459	1857	938	521			
1779	3760	618	3219	2326	394	697	1586	2510	1578	2719	1683	1842	1360	2755	2179	2913	2492	622	2038	1621	1234		
1231	2621	504	2496	1535	852	652	1044	1446	1057	1580	619	1003	439	2033	1456	2069	1769	1727	993	831	313	1104	
1040	2128	982	2165	1034	1330	995	885	944	1088	1087	296	673	318	1690	1117	1575	1427	2205	500	672	443	1581	509
834	1621	1347	1835	585	1696	1242	729	654	966	567	637	397	593	1209	786	490	946	2570	411	514	744	1947	1002
1807	2443	1551	2943	1693	1899	1699	1652	1396	1868	1675	466	1440	1071	2318	1895	1599	2054	2774	951	1439	1161	2150	1078
1049	993	2359	472	972	2409	2068	1167	1833	1620	1058	2167	1078	1661	320	592	907	557	3252	2055	1206	1727	2761	2039
501	946	1040	1941	1049	923	581	309	1487	287	1097	1133	575	504	1478	902	736	1215	1765	1243	354	459	1274	771
2076	2189	1131	3516	2624	690	994	1883	2907	1851	2671	2081	2139	1758	3052	2476	2311	2789	304	2429	1918	1631	571	1503
855	1753	1700	1659	338	1942	1600	890	514	1069	257	1020	497	918	997	625	431	734	2784	655	723	1067	2299	1380
1608	2244	1352	2744	1494	1700	1500	1453	1197	1668	1476	267	1241	872	2119	1696	1400	1855	2575	751	1240	962	1951	879
2483	4683	3844	2824	2129	3862	3519	2635	3038	2827	3870	3330	2530	3112	1528	2050	837	1745	4760	3269	2660	3214	4250	3625
977	1777	1510	1978	728	1858	1381	885	547	1127	632	629	540	732	1352	929	633	1089	2733	288	670	883	2110	1038
2305	2418	1010	3745	2856	920	1223	2112	2910	2100	2838	2084	2324	1761	3281	2705	2511	3018	400	2431	2152	1634	529	1506
1387	1126	2698	1009	1000	2748	2406	1505	1861	1662	1086	2195	1405	1988	481	928	1234	585	3590	2097	1545	2066	3100	2378
601	1277	1123	1751	752	1406	1065	432	1012	618	734	788	219	402	1276	702	406	1012	2249	773	219	490	1772	803
2350	511	2604	3531	2098	2936	2754	2306	1024	2491	779	1629	1910	1960	2719	2294	2054	2452	3834	1145	2151	2073	3274	2135
1200	1645	323	2640	1758	452	248	1007	1812	1101	1740	985	1225	662	2177	1600	1412	1913	1294	1347	1054	536	701	407
3041	5241	4402	1893	2687	4420	4077	3193	3596	3260	4428	3888	3088	3670	2570	2608	1367	2303	5316	3699	3218	3772	4808	4083
1899	2335	357	3164	2203	602	796	1711	2257	1717	2185	1430	1670	1107	2700	2124	1857	2437	970	1788	1499	981	347	852
1242	1928	1236	2311	1061	1584	1257	1137	692	1351	1043	255	829	580	1685	1262	966	1422	2459	240	925	705	1835	763
1223	2149	2339	1907	591	2531	2190	1332	670	1472	567	1502	1062	1557	1084	874	948	982	3374	1041	1289	1706	2883	2019
1151	1970	1793	1943	622	2147	1805	1107	243	1300	540	812	714	1024	1281	909	807	1017	3016	376	928	1174	2393	1321
1347	2166	1592	2348	999	1940	1614	1303	356	1476	917	611	910	936	1704	1299	1003	1441	2815	133	1087	1062	2192	1120
810	1418	1046	1914	837	1394	935	627	984	847	819	580	397	286	1438	865	569	1175	2269	717	414	436	1645	726

Luxembourg - Warszawa (Warsaw) = 1289 km

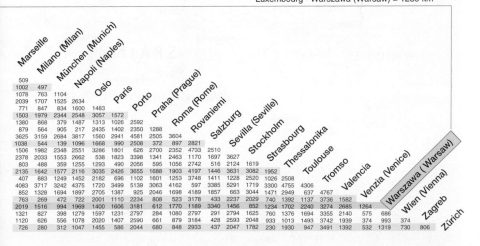

	Marseille	Milano (Milan)	München (Munich)	Napoli (Naples)	Oslo	Paris	Porto	Praha (Prague)	Roma (Rome)	Rovaniemi	Salzburg	Sevilla (Seville)	Stockholm	Strasbourg	Thessalonika	Toulouse	Tromso	Valencia	Venzia (Venice)	Warszawa (Warsaw)	Wien (Vienna)	Zagreb
Milano (Milan)	509																					
München (Munich)	1002	497																				
Napoli (Naples)	1078	763	1104																			
Oslo	2039	1707	1525	2634																		
Paris	771	847	834	1600	1483																	
Porto	1503	1979	2344	2548	3057	1572																
Praha (Prague)	1380	868	379	1487	1313	1026	2592															
Roma (Rome)	879	564	905	217	2435	1402	2350	1288														
Rovaniemi	3625	3159	2684	3817	1560	2941	4581	2505	3604													
Salzburg	1038	544	139	1096	1668	990	2508	372	897	2821												
Sevilla (Seville)	1506	1982	2348	2551	3286	1801	626	2700	2352	4733	2510											
Stockholm	2378	2033	1553	2662	538	1823	3398	1341	2463	1170	1697	3627										
Strasbourg	803	488	359	1255	1293	490	2056	595	1056	2742	516	2124	1619									
Thessalonika	2135	1642	1577	2116	3035	2426	3655	1688	1903	4197	1446	3631	3082	1952								
Toulouse	407	883	1249	1452	2182	696	1102	1601	1253	3748	1411	1228	2520	1026	2508							
Tromso	4083	3717	3242	4375	1720	3499	5139	3063	4162	597	3385	5291	1719	3300	4755	4306						
Valencia	852	1328	1694	1897	2705	1387	925	2046	1698	4189	1857	663	3044	1471	2949	637	4767					
Venzia (Venice)	763	269	472	722	2001	1110	2234	808	523	3178	433	2237	2029	740	1392	1137	3736	1582				
Warszawa (Warsaw)	2019	1516	994	1969	1400	1606	3181	612	1770	1189	3340	1456	852	1234	1702	2240	3274	2685	1264			
Wien (Vienna)	1321	827	398	1279	1597	1231	2797	284	1080	2797	291	2794	1625	760	1376	1694	3355	2140	575	686		
Zagreb	1120	626	556	1078	2020	1407	2590	661	879	3184	428	2593	2048	933	1013	1493	3742	1939	374	993	374	
Zürich	726	280	312	1047	1455	586	2044	680	848	2933	437	2047	1782	230	1930	947	3491	1392	532	1319	730	806

Route Planning

ATLANTIC
OCEAN

Legend:
- Motorways
- Major roads
- Main Roads
- ⊕ Major airports

ATLANTIC OCEAN

UNITED KINGDOM
Poole, Portsm
Plymouth, Weymouth, Newhav

English Chan

Guernsey, Cherbourg
Jersey, Le Havre
Roscoff, Cae
Brest
St Malo
Rennes

Nantes

Bay of Biscay
La Rochelle
Lim

Bordeaux

Ferrol
Santiago de Compostela
Vigo, Ourense, Oviedo, Gijón, Santander
León, Bilbao, Irun
Vitoria-Gasteiz, Pamplona
Braga, Logroño, ANDORR
Porto
Aveiro, Viseu, Valladolid
Zaragoza, Lleida, Man
Salamanca, Reus
PORTUGAL Coimbra
SPAIN
Leiria
MADRID, Alcalá de Henares
Talavera de la Reina, Toledo
LISBOA
Setúbal, Badajoz, Sagunto
Évora, Torrent, Valencia, Palma de
Puertollano, Albacete, Eivissa
Alcoy-Alcoi, Elda
Linares, Elche-Elx
Córdoba, Murcia
Sevilla, Lorca, Cartagena
Faro
El Puerto de Santa María, Jerez de la Frontera, Granada
San Fernando, Marbella, Málaga, Almería
Algeciras, GIBRALTAR
Tanger, Ceuta

Planning and Travelling

Motoring Equipment - Europe

Please note equipment requirements and regulations change frequently. To keep up to date with the latest equipment information please visit www.caravanclub.co.uk/overseasadvice

Bicycle and Motorbike Transportation

Regulations vary from country to country but as a general rule separate registration and insurance documents are required for a motorbike or scooter and these vehicles, as well as bicycles, must be carried on an approved carrier in such a way that they do not obscure rear windows, lights, reflectors or number plates. Vehicles should not be overloaded, i.e. exceed the maximum loaded weight recommended by your vehicle manufacturer.

© iStockPhoto.com/36clicks

Car Telephones

It is illegal to use a hand-held car phone or mobile phone while driving. Hands-free equipment should be fitted in your vehicle if you feel you must use the phone while travelling.

First Aid Kit

A first aid kit, in a strong dust-proof box, should be carried in case of an emergency. This is a legal requirement in several countries in Europe and is a must have item regardless.

See Essential Equipment Table at the end of this chapter and the chapter Medical Matters.

Fire Extinguisher

As a recommended safety precaution, an approved fire extinguisher should be carried in all vehicles. This is a legal requirement in several countries in Europe.

See *Essential Equipment Table* at the end of this chapter.

Glasses

It is a legal requirement in some countries for residents to carry a spare pair of glasses if they are needed for driving and it is recommended that visitors also comply. Elsewhere, if you do not have a spare pair, you may find it helpful to carry a copy of your prescription.

Lights

When driving on the Continent headlights need to be adjusted to deflect to the right, if they are likely to dazzle other road users, by means of suitable beam deflectors or (in some cases) a built-in adjustment system. Do not leave headlight conversion to the last minute as, in the case of some modern high-density discharge (HID), xenon or halogen-type lights, a dealer may need to make the necessary adjustment. Remember also to adjust headlights according to the load being carried and to compensate for the weight of the caravan on the back of your car.

Even if you do not intend to drive at night, it is important to ensure that your headlights will not dazzle others as you may need to use them in heavy rain or fog and in tunnels. If using tape or a pre-cut adhesive mask remember to remove it on your return home.

Dipped headlights should be used in poor weather conditions such as fog, snowfall or heavy rain and in a tunnel even if it is well lit. You may find police waiting at the end of a tunnel to check vehicles. In some countries the use of dipped headlights is compulsory at all times, day and night, and in others they must be used in built-up areas, on motorways or at certain times of the year.

Take a full set of spare light bulbs. This is a legal requirement in several countries.

See *Essential Equipment Table* at the end of this chapter.

Headlight-Flashing

On the Continent headlight-flashing is often used as a warning of approach or as an overtaking signal at night, and not, as is commonly the case in the UK, an indication that you are giving way, so use with great care in case it is misunderstood. When another driver flashes you, make sure of his intention before moving.

Hazard Warning Lights

Generally hazard warning lights should not be used in place of a warning triangle, but they may be used in addition to it.

Nationality Plate (GB/IRL)

A nationality plate of an authorised design must be fixed to the rear of both your car and caravan on a vertical or near-vertical surface. Checks are made and a fine may be imposed for failure to display a nationality plate correctly. These are provided free to members taking out The Caravan Club's Red Pennant Overseas Holiday Insurance – see www.caravanclub.co.uk/redpennant

Regulations allow the optional display on number plates of the Euro-Symbol which is a circle of stars on a blue background with an EU Member State's national identification letter(s) below – e.g. GB or IRL. On UK-registered vehicles whose number plates incorporate the Euro-Symbol, the display of an additional GB sticker on a vehicle is unnecessary when driving within the EU and Switzerland. However, it is still required when driving outside the EU even when number plates incorporate the Euro-Symbol, and it is still required for all vehicles without Euro-Symbol plates.

GB is the only permissible national identification code for cars registered in the UK. Registration plates displaying the GB Euro-Symbol must comply with the appropriate British Standard.

Radar/Speed Camera Detectors

The possession or use of a radar-detection device, whether in use or not, is illegal in many countries on the Continent and you should not carry one in your vehicle. Penalties include fines, vehicle confiscation or a driving ban. Some countries also ban the use of GPS satellite navigation devices which pinpoint the position of fixed speed cameras and you must, therefore, deactivate the relevant Points of Interest (PoI) function.

Rear View External Mirrors

In order to comply with local regulations and avoid the attention of local police forces, ensure that your vehicle's external mirrors are adjusted correctly to allow you to view both sides of your caravan or trailer – over its entire length – from behind the steering wheel. Some countries stipulate that mirrors should extend beyond the width of the caravan but should be removed or folded in when travelling solo, and this is common-sense advice for all countries.

Reflective Jackets/Waistcoats

Legislation has been introduced in many countries in Europe (see individual Country Introductions in relevant guides) requiring drivers to wear a reflective jacket or waistcoat if leaving a vehicle which is immobilised on the carriageway outside a built-up area. This is a commonsense requirement which will probably be extended to other countries and which should be observed wherever you drive. A second jacket is also recommended for a passenger who may need to assist in an emergency repair. Carry the jackets in the passenger compartment of your vehicle, rather than in the boot. The jackets should conform to at least European Standard EN471, Class 2 and are available from motor accessory shops and from the Club's shop – see www.caravanclub.co.uk/shop

Route Planning

An organisation called Keep Moving www.keepmoving.co.uk provides information on UK roads including routes to ferry ports, tel 09003 401100 or 401100 from a mobile phone. The Highway Agency has information for roads in England, including channel port access, visit www.trafficengland.com. Both the AA and RAC have useful websites offering a route planning service: www.theaa.com and www.rac.co.uk. Other websites offering a European routes service and/or traffic information include www.viamichelin.com and www.mappy.com which, amongst other things, provides city centre maps for major towns across Europe.

Detailed, large-scale maps or atlases of the countries you are visiting are essential. Navigating your way around other countries can be confusing, especially for the novice, and the more care you take planning your route, the more enjoyable your journey will be. Before setting out, study maps and distance charts.

If you propose travelling across mountain passes check whether the suggested route supplied by the route-planning website takes account of passes or tunnels where caravans are not permitted or recommended.

See the chapter *Mountain Passes and Tunnels*.

Satellite Navigation/GPS

Continental postcodes do not, on the whole, pinpoint a particular street or part of a street in the same way as the system in use in the UK. A French five-digit postcode, for example, can cover a very large area of many square kilometres.

GPS co-ordinates are given for most site entries in this guide and wherever possible full street addresses are given, enabling you to programme your sat nav as accurately as possible.

Your sat nav device is a valuable aid in finding a campsite in an area you are not familiar with, but it is important to realise that such equipment is not perfect. For example, sat nav routes are unlikely to allow for the fact that you are towing a caravan or driving a large motorhome. Use your common sense – if a road looks suspect, don't follow it.

It is probably wise therefore to use your sat nav in conjunction with the printed directions to campsites in this guide, which have been supplied by users of the guide based on their own experience of driving to the site, together with an up-to-date map or atlas. You may find it useful to identify a 'waypoint' (a nearby village, say) mentioned in these written directions and add it to your route definition when programming your sat nav to ensure you approach from a suitable direction. Please note the directions given in the site entries have not been provided by The Caravan Club but by users of Caravan Europe. The directions have not been checked in detail for accuracy, therefore always use in conjunction with an up to date map or atlas.

Update your sat nav device regularly and remember that, in spite of detailed directions and the use of a sat nav, local conditions such as road closures and roadworks may on occasion make finding your destination difficult.

*See the chapter **Introduction** in the section **HOW TO USE THIS GUIDE** for more information on satellite navigation.*

Seat Belts

The wearing of seat belts is compulsory in all the countries featured in this guide. On-the-spot fines will be incurred for failure to wear them and, in the event of an accident and insurance claim, compensation for injury may be reduced if seat belts are not worn.

As in the UK, legislation in many countries in Europe, requires all children up to a certain age or height to use a child restraint appropriate for their weight or size and, in addition, some countries' laws prohibit them from sitting in the front of a car.

Rear-facing baby seats must never be used in a seat protected by a frontal airbag unless the airbag has been deactivated.

Spares

Caravan Spares

On the Continent it is generally much more difficult to obtain spares for caravans than for cars and it will usually be necessary to obtain spares from a UK manufacturer or dealer before you travel.

Car Spares Kits

Some motor manufacturers can supply spares kits for a selected range of models; contact your dealer for details. The choice of spares will depend on the vehicle, how long you are likely to be away and your own level of competence in car maintenance, but the following is a list of basic items which should cover the most common causes of breakdown:

Radiator top hose • Fan belt • Fuses and bulbs • Windscreen wiper blade • Length of 12V electrical cable • Tools, torch and WD40 or equivalent water repellent/dispersant spray

Spare Wheel

Your local caravan dealer should be able to supply an appropriate spare wheel. If you have any difficulty in obtaining one, The Caravan Club's Technical Department will provide Club members with a list of suppliers' addresses on request.

Tyre legislation across Europe is more or less fully harmonised and, while the Club has no specific knowledge of laws on the Continent regarding the use of space-saver spare wheels, there should be no problems in using such a wheel provided its use is strictly in accordance with the manufacturer's instructions.

Towing Bracket

The vast majority of cars registered after 1 August 1998 are legally required to have a European Type approved towing bracket (complying with European Directive 94/20) carrying a plate giving its approval number and various technical details, including the maximum noseweight. The approval process includes strength testing to a higher value than provided in the previous British Standard, and confirmation of fitting to all the car manufacturer's approved mounting points. Your car dealer or specialist towing bracket fitter will be able to give further advice. Checks may be made by foreign police. From 29 April 2011 for brand new motorhome designs (launched on or after that date) and 29 April 2012 for existing designs (those already being built before 29 April 2011), all new motorhomes will need some form of type approval before they can be registered in the UK and as such can only be fitted with a type approved towing bracket. Note also that some manufacturers are type approving their vehicles ahead of these required dates, so check carefully with any vehicle built from 2009 onwards. This change will not affect older vehicles, which can continue to be fitted with non-approved towing brackets.

Tyres

Safe driving and handling when towing a caravan or trailer are very important and one major factor, which is frequently overlooked, is tyre condition. Your caravan tyres must be suitable for the highest speed at which you can legally tow, not for any lower speed at which you may choose to travel. Some older British caravans (usually over ten years old) may not meet this requirement and, if you are subject to a police check, this could result in an on-the-spot fine for each tyre, including the spare. Check your tyre specification before you leave and, if necessary, upgrade your tyres. The Caravan Club's technical advice leaflet 'Caravan Tyres and Wheels', available to members on the Club's website or by post, explains how to check if your tyres are suitable.

Most countries require a minimum tread depth of 1.6 mm over the central part of the whole tyre, but motoring organisations recommend at least 3 mm across the whole tyre. If you plan an extended trip and your tyres are likely to be more worn than this before you return home, replace them before you leave.

Tyre Pressure

Tyre pressure should be checked and adjusted when the tyres are cold; checking warm tyres will result in a higher pressure reading. The correct pressures will be found in your car handbook, but unless it states otherwise it is wise to add an extra four to six pounds per square inch to the rear tyres of a car when towing to improve handling and to carry the extra load on the hitch.

Make sure you know what pressure your caravan tyres should be. Some require a pressure much higher than that normally used for cars. Check your caravan handbook for details.

Tyre Sizes

It is worth noting that some sizes of radial tyre to fit the 13" wheels commonly used on older UK caravans are virtually impossible to find in stock at retailers abroad, e.g. 175R13C.

After a Puncture

The Caravan Club does not recommend the general use of liquid sealants for puncture repair. Such products should not be considered to achieve a permanent repair, and may indeed render the tyre irreparable. If sealant is used to allow the vehicle to be removed from a position of danger to one

of safety, the damaged tyre should be removed from the vehicle, repaired and replaced as soon as practically possible.

Following a caravan tyre puncture, especially on a single-axle caravan, it is advisable to have the opposite side (non-punctured) tyre removed from its wheel and checked inside and out for signs of damage resulting from overloading during the deflation of the punctured tyre. Failure to take this precaution may result in an increased risk of a second tyre deflation within a very short space of time.

Winter Tyres and Snow Chains

Winter tyres should be used in those countries with a severe winter climate and in some it is a legal requirement. Winter tyres are designed to minimise the hardening effect of low temperatures which in turn leads to less traction on the road, and to provide extra grip on snow and ice and in wet conditions. If you intend to make an extended winter trip or to travel regularly to where there may be snow or ice on the roads, it would be advisable to buy a set of winter tyres. Your local tyre dealer will be able to advise you.

Snow chains may be necessary on some roads in winter. They are compulsory in some countries during the winter where indicated by the appropriate road sign, when they must be fitted on at least two drive-wheels. They are not difficult to fit and it's a good idea to carry sturdy gloves to protect your hands when handling the chains in freezing conditions. For further information see the Country Introductions.

Polar Automotive Ltd sells and hires out snow chains (10% discount for Caravan Club members), tel 01892 519933 www.snowchains.com, email: polar@snowchains.com

Warning Triangles

In almost all European countries it is a legal requirement to use a warning triangle in the event of a breakdown or accident; some countries require two. It is strongly recommended that approved red warning triangles be carried as a matter of course.

A warning triangle should be placed on the road approximately 30 metres (100 metres on motorways) behind the broken down vehicle on the same side of the road. Always assemble the triangle before leaving your vehicle and walk with it so that the red, reflective surface is facing oncoming traffic. If a breakdown occurs round a blind corner, place the triangle in advance of the corner. Hazard warning lights may be used in conjunction with the triangle but they do not replace it.

See Essential Equipment Table at the end of this chapter.

Technical information compiled with the assistance of the Automobile Association.

Planning and Travelling

Essential Equipment in Europe

See also the information contained in the Handbook chapter and in the Country Introductions within the relevant Caravan Europe Volumes.
For up to date information on essential equipment requirements for countries in Europe please visit www.caravanclub.co.uk/overseasadvice

Country	Warning Triangle	Spare Bulbs	First Aid Kit	Reflective Jacket	Additional Equipment to be Carried/Used
Andorra	Yes (2)	Yes	Rec	Yes	Dipped headlights in poor daytime visibility. Winter tyres recommended; snow chains when road conditions or signs dictate.
Austria	Yes	Rec	Yes	Yes	Winter tyres from 1 Nov to 15 April.*
Belgium	Yes	Rec	Rec	Yes	Dipped headlights in poor daytime visibility.
Croatia	Yes (2 for vehicle with trailer)	Yes	Yes	Yes	Dipped headlights at all times from the last Sunday Oct to the last Sunday in Mar. Snow chains in winter months in certain regions is compulsory.*
Czech Rep	Yes	Yes	Yes	Yes	Dipped headlights at all times. Replacement fuses. Winter tyres or snow chains from 1 Nov to 31st March.*
Denmark	Yes	Rec	Rec	Rec	Dipped headlights at all times. On motorways use hazard warning lights when queues or danger ahead.
Finland	Yes	Rec	Rec	Yes	Dipped headlights at all times. Winter tyres Dec to Feb.*
France	Yes (2 rec)	Yes	Rec	Yes	Dipped headlights recommended at all times.
Germany	Yes	Rec	Rec	Rec	Dipped headlights recommended at all times. Winter tyres to be used in winter weather conditions.*
Greece	Yes	Rec	Yes	Rec	Fire extinguisher compulsory. Dipped headlights in towns at night and in poor daytime visibility.
Hungary	Yes	Rec	Yes	Yes	Dipped headlights at all times outside built-up areas and in built-up areas at night. Snow chains may be compulsory on some roads in winter conditions.*
Italy	Yes	Rec	Rec	Yes	Dipped headlights at all times outside built-up areas and in poor visibility. Snow chains from15 Oct to 15 April.*
Luxembourg	Yes	Rec	Rec	Yes	Dipped headlights at night and in daytime in bad weather.
Netherlands	Yes	Rec	Rec	Rec	Dipped headlights at night and in bad weather and recommended during the day.
Norway	Yes	Rec	Rec	Rec	Dipped headlights at all times. Winter tyres compulsory when snow or ice on the roads.*
Poland	Yes	Rec	Rec	Rec	Dipped headlights at all times.
Portugal	Yes	Rec	Rec	Yes	Dipped headlights in poor daytime visibility, in tunnels and in lanes where traffic flow is reversible.
Slovakia	Yes	Yes	Yes	Yes	Dipped headlights at all times. Winter tyres compulsory when compact snow or ice on the road.*
Slovenia	Yes (2 for vehicle with trailer)	Yes	Yes	Yes	Dipped headlights at all times. Hazard warning lights when reversing. Use winter tyres between 15 Nov and 15 March or carry snow chains.
Spain	Yes (2 Rec)	Rec	Rec	Yes	Dipped headlights at night and in tunnels and on 'special' roads (roadworks).
Sweden	Yes	Rec	Rec	Rec	Dipped headlights at all times. Winter tyres from 1 Dec to 31 March.
Switzerland (inc Liechtenstein)	Yes	Rec	Rec	Rec	Dipped headlights recommended at all times, compulsory in tunnels. Snow chains where indicated by signs.

NOTES:
1) All countries: seat belts (if fitted) must be worn by all passengers.
2) Rec: not compulsory for foreign-registered vehicles, but very strongly recommended
3) Headlamp converters, spare bulbs, fire extinguisher, first aid kit and reflective waistcoat are strongly recommended for all countries.
4) In some countries drivers who wear prescription glasses must carry a spare pair.
5) Please check information for any country before you travel as rules and regulations change. This information is to be used as a guide only and it is your responsibility to make sure you have the correct equipment.
   * For information and regulations on winter driving in these countries, please see the Country Introduction chapters in the relevant Caravan Europe guide.

Planning and Travelling

Mountain Passes and Tunnels

The mountain passes, rail and road tunnels listed in the tables are shown on the following maps. Numbers and letters against each pass or tunnel in the tables, correspond with the numbers and letters on the maps.

Please read the following advice carefully.

Advice for Drivers

Mountain Passes

The conditions and comments in the following tables assume an outfit with good power/weight ratio. Even those mountain passes and tunnels which do not carry a 'not recommended' or 'not permitted' warning may be challenging for any vehicle, more so for car and caravan outfits.

If in any doubt whatsoever, it is probably best to restrict yourself to those mountain passes which can be crossed by motorway. In any event, mountain passes should only be attempted by experienced drivers in cars with ample power and in good driving conditions; they should otherwise be avoided.

In the following table, where the entry states that caravans are not permitted or not recommended to use a pass, this generally – but not always – refers to towed caravans, and is based on advice originally supplied by the AA and/or local motoring organisations, but not checked by The Caravan Club. Motorhomes are seldom prohibited by such restrictions, but those which are relatively low powered or very large should find an alternative route. Always obey road signs at the foot of a pass, especially those referring to heavy vehicles, which may apply to some large motorhomes.

Do not attempt to cross passes at night or in bad weather. Before crossing, seek local advice if touring during periods when the weather is changeable or unreliable. Warning notices are usually posted at the foot of a pass if it is closed, or if chains or winter tyres must be used.

Caravanners are obviously particularly sensitive to gradients and traffic/road conditions on passes. Take great care when negotiating blind hairpins. The maximum gradient is usually on the inside of bends but exercise caution if it is necessary to pull out. Always engage a lower gear before taking a hairpin bend and give priority to vehicles ascending. Give priority to postal service vehicles – signposts usually show their routes. Do not go down hills in neutral gear.

Keep to the extreme right of the road and be prepared to reverse to give way to descending/ascending traffic.

On mountain roads it is not the gradient which taxes your car but the duration of the climb and the loss of power at high altitudes: approximately 10% at 915 metres (3,000 feet) and even more as you get higher. Turbo power restores much of the lost capacity.

To minimise the risk of the engine overheating, take high passes in the cool of the day, don't climb any faster than necessary and keep the engine pulling steadily. To prevent a radiator boiling, pull off the road safely, turn the heater and blower full on and switch off airconditioning. Keep an eye on water and oil levels. Never put cold water into a boiling radiator or it may crack. Check that the radiator is not obstructed by debris sucked up during the journey.

A long descent may result in overheating brakes; select the correct gear for the gradient and avoid excessive use of brakes. Note that even if using engine braking to control the outfit's speed, caravan brakes may activate due to the action of the overrun mechanism, causing them to overheat. Use lay-bys and lookout points to stop and allow brakes to cool.

In alpine areas snow prevents road repairs during the winter, resulting in road works during the summer, which may cause traffic delays. At times one-way traffic only may be permitted on some routes. Information will be posted at each end of the road.

Main roads crossing major passes are rarely totally unguarded; but minor passes may be unguarded or simply have stone pillars placed at close intervals. If you do not have a good head for heights consider a different route.

Leave the blade valve of your portable toilet open a fraction when travelling at altitude. This avoids pressure build-up in the holding tank. Similarly, a slightly open tap will avoid pressure build up in water pipes and fittings.

Tunnels

British drivers do not often encounter road tunnels but they are a common feature in Europe, for example, through mountain ranges. Tolls are usually charged for the use of major tunnels.

Ensure you have enough fuel before entering a tunnel. Emergency situations often involve vehicles stranded because of a lack of fuel.

When approaching a tunnel in bright sunshine, slow down to allow your eyes to adjust and look out for poorly-lit vehicles in front of you and for cyclists. Take sunglasses off before entering a tunnel and take care again when emerging into sunshine at the other end.

Signposts usually indicate a tunnel ahead and its length. Once inside, maintain a safe distance from the vehicle in front in case the driver brakes sharply. Minimum/maximum speed limits usually apply. Dipped headlights are usually required by law even in well-lit tunnels, so switch them on before you enter. Some tunnels may be poorly or totally unlit.

Snow chains, if used, must be removed before entering a tunnel in lay-bys provided for this purpose.

'No overtaking' signs must be strictly observed. Never cross central single or double lines. If overtaking is permitted in twin-tube tunnels, bear in mind that it is very easy to under-estimate distances and speed once inside. Watch out for puddles caused by dripping or infiltrating water.

In order to minimise the effects of exhaust fumes close all car windows and set the ventilator to circulate air, or operate the air conditioning system coupled with the recycled air option. If there is a traffic jam, switch your hazard warning lights on and stop a safe distance from the vehicle in front. Sound the horn only in a real emergency. Never change direction unless instructed to do so by tunnel staff or a police officer.

If you break down, try to reach the next lay-by and call for help from an emergency phone. If you cannot reach a lay-by, place your warning triangle at least 100 metres behind your vehicle. Passengers should leave the vehicle through doors on the right-hand side only. Modern tunnels have video surveillance systems to ensure prompt assistance in an emergency.

Mountain Pass Information

The dates of opening and closing given in the following tables are approximate and inclusive. Before attempting late afternoon or early morning journeys across borders, check their opening times as some borders close at night.

Gradients listed are the maximum which may be encountered on the pass and may be steeper at the inside of curves, particularly on older roads.

Gravel surfaces (such as dirt and stone chips) vary considerably; they can be dusty when dry and slippery when wet. Where known to exist, this type of surface has been noted.

In fine weather winter tyres or snow chains will only be required on very high passes, or for short periods in early or late summer. In winter conditions you will probably need to use them at altitudes exceeding 600 metres (approximately 2,000 feet).

Abbreviations

MHV	Maximum height of vehicle
MLV	Maximum length of vehicle
MWV	Maximum width of vehicle
MWR	Minimum width of road
OC	Occasionally closed between dates stated
UC	Usually closed between dates stated
UO	Usually open between dates stated, although a fall of snow may obstruct the road for 24-48 hours.

Mountain Passes and Tunnels Report Form

The Caravan Club welcomes up-to-date information on mountain passes and tunnels from caravanners who use them during the course of their holidays. Please use the Mountain Passes and Tunnels report forms at the back of the book and complete and return them as soon as possible after your journey.

Converting Gradients

20% = 1 in 5	11% = 1 in 9
16% = 1 in 6	10% = 1 in 10
14% = 1 in 7	8% = 1 in 12
12% = 1 in 8	6% = 1 in 16

Much of the information contained in the following tables was originally supplied by The Automobile Association and other motoring and tourist organisations. Additional updates and amendments have been supplied by caravanners who have themselves used the passes and tunnels. The Caravan Club has not checked the information contained in these tables and cannot accept responsibility for their accuracy, or for errors, omissions or their effects.

Major Mountain Passes – Pyrenees and Northern Spain

Before using any of these passes, PLEASE READ CAREFULLY THE ADVICE AT THE BEGINNING OF THIS CHAPTER

	Pass Height In Metres (Feet)	From To	Max Gradient	Conditions and Comments
❶	**Aubisque** (France) 1710 (5610)	Eaux Bonnes *Argelés-Gazost*	10%	UC mid Oct–Jun. MWR 3.5m (11'6") Very winding; continuous on D918 but easy ascent; descent including Col-d'Aubisque 1709m (5607 feet) and Col-du-Soulor 1450m (4757 feet); 8km (5 miles) of very narrow, rough, unguarded road with steep drop. **Not recommended for caravans**.
❷	**Bonaigua** (Spain) 2072 (6797)	Viella (Vielha) *Esterri-d'Aneu*	8.5%	UC Nov–Apr. MWR 4.3m (14'1") Twisting, narrow road (C28) with many hairpins and some precipitous drops. **Not recommended for caravans**. Alternative route to Lerida (Lleida) through Viella (Vielha) Tunnel is open all year. See *Pyrenean Road Tunnels* in this section.
❸	**Cabrejas** (Spain) 1167 (3829)	Tarancon *Cuenca*	14%	UO. On N400/A40. Sometimes blocked by snow for 24 hours. MWR 5m (16')
❹	**Col-d'Haltza and Col-de-Burdincurutcheta** (France) 782 (2565) and 1135 (3724)	St Jean-Pied-de-Port *Larrau*	11%	UO. A narrow road (D18/D19) leading to Iraty skiing area. Narrow with some tight hairpin bends; rarely has central white line and stretches are unguarded. Not for the faint-hearted. **Not recommended for caravans**.
❺	**Envalira** (France – Andorra) 2407 (7897)	Pas-de-la-Casa *Andorra*	12.5%	OC Nov–Apr. MWR 6m (19'8") Good road (N22/CG2) with wide bends on ascent and descent; fine views. MHV 3.5m (11'6") on N approach near l'Hospitalet. Early start rec in summer to avoid border delays. Envalira Tunnel (toll) reduces congestion and avoids highest part of pass. See *Pyrenean Road Tunnels* in this section.
❻	**Escudo** (Spain) 1011 (3317)	Santander *Burgos*	17%	UO. MWR probably 5m (16'5") Asphalt surface but many bends and steep gradients. **Not recommended in winter**. On N632; A67/N611 easier route.
❼	**Guadarrama** (Spain) 1511 (4957)	Guadarrama *San Rafael*	14%	UO. MWR 6m (19'8") On NVI to the NW of Madrid but may be avoided by using AP6 motorway from Villalba to San Rafael or Villacastin (toll).
❽	**Ibañeta (Roncevalles)** (France – Spain) 1057 (3468)	St Jean-Pied-de-Port *Pamplona*	10%	UO. MWR 4m (13'1") Slow and winding, scenic route on N135.
❾	**Manzanal** (Spain) 1221 (4005)	Madrid *La Coruña*	7%	UO. Sometimes blocked by snow for 24 hours. On A6.
❿	**Navacerrada** (Spain) 1860 (6102)	Madrid *Segovia*	17%	OC Nov–Mar. On M601/CL601. Sharp hairpins. Possible but **not recommended for caravans**.

	Pass Height In Metres (Feet)	From To	Max Gradient	Conditions and Comments
11	**Orduna** (Spain) 900 (2953)	Bilbao *Burgos*	15%	UO. On A625/BU556; sometimes blocked by snow for 24 hours. Avoid by using AP68 motorway.
12	**Pajares** (Spain) 1270 (4167)	Oviedo *Léon*	16%	UO. On N630; sometimes blocked by snow for 24 hours. **Not recommended for caravans.** Avoid by using AP66 motorway.
13	**Paramo-de-Masa** (Spain) 1050 (3445)	Santander *Burgos*	8%	UO. On N623; sometimes blocked by snow for 24 hours.
14	**Peyresourde** (France) 1563 (5128)	Arreau *Bagnères-de-Luchon*	10%	UO. MWR 4m (13'1") D618 somewhat narrow with several hairpin bends, though not difficult. **Not recommended for caravans.**
15	**Picos-de-Europa: Puerto-de-San Glorio, Puerto-de-Pontón, Puerto-de-Pandetrave** (Spain) 1609 (5279)	Unquera *Riaño*	12%	UO. MWR probably 4m (13'1") Desfiladero de la Hermida on N621 good condition. Puerto-de-San-Glorio steep with many hairpin bends. For confident drivers only.
		Riaño *Cangas-de-Onis*		Puerto-de-Ponton on N625, height 1280 metres (4200 feet). Best approach fr S as from N is very long uphill pull with many tight turns.
		Portilla-de-la-Reina *Santa Marina-de-Valdeón*		Puerto-de-Pandetrave, height 1562 metres (5124 feet) on LE245 not rec when towing as main street of Santa Marina steep & narrow.
16	**Piqueras** (Spain) 1710 (5610)	Logroño *Soria*	7%	UO. On N111; sometimes blocked by snow for 24 hours.
17	**Port** (France) 1249 (4098)	Tarascon-sur-Ariège *Massat*	10%	OC Nov-Mar. MWR 4m (13'1") A fairly easy, scenic road (D618), but narrow on some bends.
18	**Portet-d'Aspet** (France) 1069 (3507)	Audressein *Fronsac*	14%	UO. MWR 3.5m (11'6") Approached from W by the easy Col-des-Ares and Col-de-Buret; well-engineered but narrow road (D618); care needed on hairpin bends. **Not recommended for caravans.**
19	**Pourtalet** (France – Spain) 1792 (5879)	Laruns *Biescas*	10%	UC late Oct-early Jun. MWR 3.5m (11'6") A fairly easy, unguarded road, but narrow in places. Easier from Spain (A136), steeper in France (D934). **Not recommended for caravans.**
20	**Puymorens** (France) 1915 (6283)	Ax-les-Thermes *Bourg-Madame*	10%	OC Nov-Apr. MWR 5.5m (18') MHV 3.5m (11'6") A generally easy, modern tarmac road (N20). Parallel toll road tunnel available. See *Pyrenean Road Tunnels* in this section.

	Pass Height In Metres (Feet)	From To	Max Gradient	Conditions and Comments
21	Quillane (France) 1714 (5623)	Axat Mont-Louis	8.5%	OC Nov-Mar. MWR 5m (16'5") An easy, straightforward ascent and descent on D118.
22	Somosierra (Spain) 1444 (4738)	Madrid Burgos	10%	OC Mar-Dec. MWR 7m (23') On A1/E5; may be blocked following snowfalls. Snow-plough swept during winter months but wheel chains compulsory after snowfalls. Well-surfaced dual carriageway, tunnel at summit.
23	Somport (France – Spain) 1632 (5354)	Accous Jaca	10%	UO. MWR 3.5m (11'6") A favoured, old-established route; not particularly easy and narrow in places with many unguarded bends on French side (N134); excellent road on Spanish side (N330). Use of road tunnel advised – see *Pyrenean Road Tunnels* in this section. NB Visitors advise re-fuelling no later than Sabiñánigo when travelling south to north.
24	Toses (Tosas) (Spain) 1800 (5906)	Puigcerda Ribes-de-Freser	10%	UO MWR 5m (16'5") A fairly straightforward, but continuously winding, two-lane road (N152) with a good surface but many sharp bends; some unguarded edges. Difficult in winter.
25	Tourmalet (France) 2114 (6936)	Ste Marie-de-Campan Luz-St Sauveur	12.5%	UC Oct-mid Jun. MWR 4m (13'1") The highest French Pyrenean route (D918); approaches good, though winding, narrow in places and exacting over summit; sufficiently guarded. Rough surface & uneven edges on west side. **Not recommended for caravans.**
26	Urquiola (Spain) 713 (2340)	Durango (Bilbao) Vitoria/Gasteiz	16%	UO. Sometimes closed by snow for 24 hours. On BI623/A623. **Not recommended for caravans.**

Pyrenees and Northern Spain

Motorway
Motorway (Proposed)
Motorway Road Tunnel
Major/Main Roads
Minor Mountain Passes
(suitability for caravans not checked)
(3) Major Mountain Passes Suitable for Caravans
(10) Major Mountain Passes Unsuitable for Caravans
CC Major Road Tunnels

0   10   20   30   40   50 km

These maps should be used in conjunction with the information
in the Mountain Passes and Tunnels tables in this chapter.

2000m - +3000m
1000m - 2000m
100m - 1000m
0 - 100m

© Collins Bartholomew Ltd 2011

Conversion Tables

Length & Distance

Centimetres/Metres	Inches/Feet/Yards	Inches/Feet/Yards	Centimetres/Metres
1 cm	0.4 in	1 in	2.5 cm
10 cm	4 in	1 ft	30 cm
25 cm	10 in	3 ft/1 yd	90 cm
1 m	3 ft 3 in	10 yds	9 m
100 m	110 yds	100 yds	91 m
Kilometres	**Miles**	**Miles**	**Kilometres**
1	0.6	1	1.6
10	6.2	10	16.1
25	15.5	25	40.2
50	31.1	50	80.5
100	62.2	100	160.9

Kilometres to Miles

km/h	20	30	40	50	60	70	80	90	100	110	120	130
mph	13	18	25	31	37	44	50	56	62	68	74	81

Weight

Grams/Kilograms	Ounces/Pounds	Ounces/Pounds	GramsKilograms
10 gm	0.3 oz	1 oz	28 gm
100 gm	3.5 oz	8 oz	226 gm
1 kg	2 lb 3 oz	1 lb	453 gm
10 kg	22 lb	10 lb	4.54 kg
25 kg	55 lb	50 lb	22.65 kg

Capacity

Millilitres/Litres	Fluid Ounces/Pints/Gallon	Fluid Ounces/Pints/Gallon	Millilitres/Litres
10 ml	0.3 fl oz	1 fl oz	28 ml
100 ml	3.5 fl oz	20 fl oz/1 pint	560 ml
1 litre	1.8 pints	1 gallon	4.5 litres
10 litres	2.2 gallons	5 gallons	22.7 litres
50 litres	11 gallons	10 gallons	45.5 litres

Area

Hectares	Acres	Acres	Hectares
1	2.5	1	0.4
5	12.4	5	2
10	24.7	10	4
50	123.5	50	20.2

Tyre Pressures

Bar	PSI (lb/sq.in)	Bar	PSI (lb/sq.in)
1.00	15	3.05	44
1.50	22	3.50	51
2.00	29	4.15	60
2.50	36	4.75	69

Map Scales

Scale	Equivalent Distance	
1:100 000	1 cm = 1 km	1 in = 1¾ miles
1: 200 000	1 cm = 2 km	1 in = 3¼ miles
1: 400 000	1 cm = 4 km	1 in = 6¼ miles
1: 500 000	1 cm = 5 km	1 in = 8 miles
1: 750 000	1 cm = 7.5 km	1 in = 12 miles
1:1 000 000	1 cm = 10 km	1 in = 16 miles
1:1 250 000	1 cm = 12.5 km	1 in = 20 miles
1: 2 000 000	1 cm = 20 km	1 in = 32 miles

You'd have to go a long way to beat our ferry prices

We can make your trips to Europe much more rewarding in so many ways. We have over 200 hand-picked sites, chosen and checked by Club members. We also have dedicated overseas advisors to help you every step of the way.

But did you realise that The Caravan Club's travel service can save you money? We have negotiated special deals with all the major ferry operators that give you prices you'll find hard to beat even if you booked direct.

Book your ferry crossing and sites together with The Caravan Club and you're on your way to savings and a great holiday too.

Request a brochure or talk
to a dedicated overseas advisor
www.caravanclub.co.uk/continental
or call **01342 488 062**

THE
CARAVAN
CLUB

During Your Stay

Electricity and Gas in Europe

Electricity – General Advice

The nominal voltage for mains electricity has been 230 volts across the European Union for more than ten years, but varying degrees of 'acceptable tolerance' have resulted in significant variations in the actual voltage found. Harmonisation of voltage standards remains an on-going project. Most appliances sold in the UK are rated at 220-240 volts and usually work satisfactorily. However, some high-powered equipment, such as microwave ovens, may not function well and you are advised to consult the manufacturer's literature for further information.

Appliances which are 'CE' marked should work acceptably, as this marking indicates that the product has been designed to meet the requirements of relevant European directives.

The site entries in this guide contain information on minimum amperage supplied on campsites and the Country Introduction contains additional information (where known). Frequently you will be offered a choice of amperage and the following table gives an approximate idea of which appliances can be used (erring on the side of caution). You can work it out more accurately by noting the wattage of each appliance in your caravan. The kettle given is the caravan type, not a household kettle which usually has at least a 2000 watt element. Note that each caravan circuit also has a maximum amp rating which should not be exceeded.

Electrical Connections – EN60309-2 (CEE17)

Whilst there is a European Standard for connectors, namely EN60309-2 (formerly known as CEE17), this does not apply retrospectively and you may find some

Continental campsites where your UK 3-pin connector, which is to European Standard, will not fit. Accurate information is not easy to come by, but based on The Caravan Club's overseas sites booking service, approximately 80% of campsites in Europe do have some, or all, UK 3-pin hook-ups, leaving approximately 20% of campsites with only 2-pin hook ups. Therefore it is a good idea to carry a 2-pin adapter. See the relevant Caravan Europe titles and Country Introductions for more information.

Different types of connector may be found within one campsite, as well as within one country. If you find your CEE17 connector does not fit, ask campsite staff to borrow or hire an adaptor.

Even with a European Standard connection, a poor electrical supply is possible. The existence of the EN60309-2 (CEE17) standard should not be taken as an automatic sign of a modern system.

Amps	Wattage (Approx)	Fridge	Battery Charger	Air Conditioning	Colour TV	Water Heater	Kettle (750W)	Heater (1KW)
2	400	✓	✓					
4	800	✓	✓		✓	✓		
6	1200	✓	✓	*	✓	✓	✓	
8	1600	✓	✓	✓**	✓	✓	✓	✓**
10	2000	✓	✓	✓**	✓	✓	✓	✓**
16	3000	✓	✓	✓	✓	✓	✓	✓**

*   *Possible, depending on wattage of appliance in question*
**   *Not to be used at the same time as other high-wattage equipment*

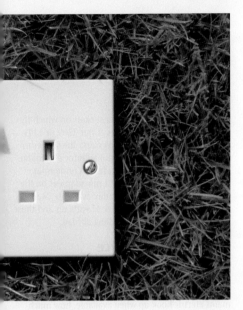

- Uncoil the connecting cable from the drum. **A coiled cable with current flowing through it may overheat.** Take your cable and insert the connector (female end) into the caravan inlet.
- Insert the plug (male end) into the site outlet socket.
- Switch caravan isolating switch to 'on'.
- Preferably insert a polarity tester into one of the 13-amp sockets in the caravan to check all connections are correctly wired. **Never leave it in the socket.** Some caravans have these devices built in as standard.

It is recommended that the supply is not used if the polarity is incorrect *(see **Reversed Polarity** overleaf)*.

WARNING

In case of doubt or, if after carrying out the above procedures the supply does not become available, or if the supply fails, consult the campsite operator or a qualified electrician.

Other Connections

French – 2-pin, plus earth socket. Adaptors available from UK caravan accessory shops.

German – 2-pin, plus 2 earth strips, found in Norway and Sweden and possibly still Germany.

Switzerland – 3-pin (but not the same shape as UK 3-pin). Adapters available to purchase in Switzerland. Most campsites using the Swiss 3-pin will have adaptors available for hire or to borrow.

If the campsite does not have a modern EN60309-2 (CEE17) supply, ask to see the electrical protection for the socket outlet. If there is a device marked with IDn = 30mA, then the risk is minimised.

Hooking Up to the Mains

Connection

Connection should always be made in the following order:

- Check your caravan isolating switch is at 'off'.

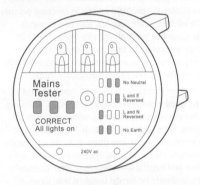

From time to time, you may come across mains supplies which differ in various ways from the common standards on most sites and your test equipment may not be able to confirm that such systems are satisfactory and safe to use. While it is likely that such systems will operate your electrical equipment adequately in most circumstances, it is possible that the protective measures in your equipment may not work effectively in the event of a fault.

Site Hooking Up Adaptor

(MAINS CONTINENTAL)

ADAPTATEUR DE PRISE AU SITE (SECTEUR)   CAMPINGPLATZ-ANSCHLUSS (NETZ)

EXTENSION LEAD TO CARAVAN
Câble de rallonge à la caravane
Verläengerungskabel zum wohnwagen

SITE OUTLET
Prise du site
Campingplatz-Steckdose

MAINS ADAPTOR
Adaptateur Secteur
Netzanschlußstacker

16 amp 230 volt AC

If your test equipment is not built into your caravan it should be readily available for everyday use.

To ensure your safety, the Club recommends that unless the system can be confirmed as safe, it should not be used.

Disconnection

• Switch your caravan isolating switch to 'off'.

• At the site supply socket withdraw the plug.

• Disconnect the cable from the caravan.

• Motorhomes – if leaving your pitch during the day, do not leave your mains cable plugged into the site supply, as this creates a hazard if the exposed live connections in the plug are touched or if the cable is not seen during grass-cutting.

Reversed Polarity

Even when the site connector is to European Standard EN60309-2 (CEE17), British caravanners are still likely to encounter the problem known as reversed polarity. This is where the site supply's 'live' line connects to the caravan's 'neutral' and vice versa. The Club strongly recommends that you always check the polarity immediately on connection, using a polarity tester available from caravan accessory shops.

The caravan mains electrical installation **should not be used** while reversed polarity exists. Try using another nearby socket instead, which may cure the problem. Frequent travellers to the Continent who are electrically competent often make up an adaptor themselves, clearly marked 'reversed polarity', with the live and neutral wires reversed. (The 'German' plug can simply be turned upside down, so no further adaptor is required.) If these steps do not rectify the reversed polarity, the site supply may be quite different from that used in the UK and we recommend, for your own safety, that you disconnect from the mains and **do not use the electrical supply.**

> **Always check the polarity immediately on connection**

Using a reversed polarity socket will probably not affect how an electrical appliance works BUT your protection in the event of a fault is greatly reduced. For example, a lamp socket may still be live as you touch it while replacing a blown bulb, even if the light switch is turned off.

Even when polarity is correct, it is always a wise precaution to check that a proper earth connection exists. A good indication of this can be achieved using a proprietary tester such as that shown on the previous page. However, there are earth faults that these simple devices are unable to identify and if there is any doubt about the integrity of the earth system, **DO NOT USE THE ELECTRICITY SUPPLY.**

Shaver Sockets

Most campsites provide shaver sockets on which the voltage is generally marked as either 220V or 110V. Using an incorrect voltage may cause the shaver to become hot or to fail. The 2-pin adaptor obtainable in the UK is sometimes too wide for Continental sockets. It is advisable to buy 2-pin adaptors on the Continent, where they are readily available. Many shavers will operate on a range of voltages and these are most suitable when travelling abroad.

Gas – General Advice

The rate of gas consumption is difficult to predict as it depends on many factors, including how many appliances you use in your outfit, whether you use a mains electric hook-up when available, how much you eat out and, of course, what the temperature is! As a rough guide plan to allow 0.45 kg of gas a day for normal summer usage.

With the exception of Campingaz, LPG cylinders normally available in the UK, e.g. Calor gas (both butane and propane), cannot be exchanged abroad. If possible, take sufficient gas with you for your holiday and bring back the empty cylinder(s). If additional capacity is required beyond what you would normally carry, check with cylinder suppliers to see if you can swap to a larger one (if there is room in your gas locker to carry it) or check if it is economic to carry a second cylinder. Note that ferry and tunnel operators may restrict the number of cylinders you are permitted to carry.

The wide availability of Campingaz means it is worth considering it as a fall-back if you run out of your 'normal' gas. However, prices vary widely from country to country, and maximum cylinder sizes are quite limited (2.75 kg of gas in a 907 cylinder), making it less practical for routine use in larger vehicles with several gas appliances. A Campingaz adapter is relatively inexpensive, though, and is widely available in the UK. It can be a prudent purchase prior to travelling, especially if taking a long holiday. It is also wise to hold a spare Calor gas cylinder in reserve in case you experience difficulty in finding a Campingaz supplier locally. With 130,000 stockists in 100 countries, however, these occasions should be rare, but prices may vary considerably from country to country. Alternatively, adaptors are available from Campingaz/Calor stockists to enable use of the normal Calor 4.5 kg regulator with a Campingaz cylinder.

If you are touring in winter or wherever cold weather conditions may be encountered, it is advisable to use propane gas instead of butane. BP Gaslight (propane) cylinders, which have been gaining in popularity in the UK, are available in several European countries. However, you cannot exchange cylinders bought in other European countries, nor bring ones back to other European countries for exchange. For news of further developments check the BP Gaslight website, www.bpgaslight.com

Take sufficient gas with you for your holiday

Many other brands of gas are available in different countries and, subject to the availability of suitable regulators, adapters and connecting hoses, as long as the cylinders fit in your gas locker these local brands can also be used with your outfit. If you regularly visit a country, it may well be worth buying a 'local' cylinder, as you can then exchange it in that country when necessary. If you are travelling across several countries this may not be a viable option.

The use of 30 mbar has been standardised for both butane and propane within the EU, replacing several different pressures previously used. On later model UK-specification caravans and motorhomes (2004 models and later) a 30 mbar regulator suited to both propane and butane use is fitted to the bulkhead of the gas locker. This is connected to the cylinder by means of a connecting hose (and sometimes an adaptor) to suit different brands or types of gas. Older outfits and some foreign-built ones may use a cylinder-mounted regulator, which may need to be changed to suit different brands or types of gas.

Hoses and adapters to suit the most common brands and types of gas are available in the UK from suppliers such as Gaslow (0845 4000 600 or www.gaslow.co.uk) or from good dealerships, and it may be easier to buy these before travelling, rather than rely on local availability when you are abroad.

WARNING

Refilling your own UK standard cylinder is prohibited by law in most countries, unless it is carried out at certain designated filling plants. Since these plants are few and far between, are generally highly mechanised and geared for cylinders of a particular size and shape, the process is usually not practical. Nevertheless, it is realised that many local dealers and site operators will fill your cylinders regardless of the prohibition. **The Caravan Club does not recommend the user-refilling of gas cylinders WHICH HAVE NOT BEEN SPECIFICALLY DESIGNED FOR THIS PURPOSE; there is real danger if cylinders are incorrectly filled.**

- Cylinders must never be over-filled under any circumstances.
- Regular servicing of gas appliances is important. A badly adjusted appliance can emit carbon monoxide, which could prove fatal. Check your vehicle or appliance handbook for service recommendations.
- Never use a hob or oven as a space heater.

*For information about the carriage of gas cylinders on ferries and in the Channel Tunnel, including safety precautions and regulations, see the chapter **Ferries and the Channel Tunnel** in the section **PLANNING AND TRAVELLING**.*

The Caravan Club publishes a range of technical leaflets for its members (some available to non-members) including detailed advice on the use of electricity and gas. You are advised to request copies or see www.caravanclub.co.uk/expert-advice

Keeping in Touch

Emails and the Internet

Wi-Fi hotspots are increasingly available on lots of campsites in Europe and many (but not all) offer Wi-Fi to their guests free of charge.

A Wi-Fi enabled laptop, tablet (such as an iPad) or a mobile 'smartphone' should enable the sending and receiving of emails, photos and video clips, together with website browsing, plus numerous other internet functions.

Alternatively there are internet cafés all over the world where you can log on to the internet and collect and send emails. You will be charged for the time you are logged on, however some public libraries in many countries offer free internet access.

WARNING:

Wi-Fi internet surfing abroad by means of a dongle (which uses a mobile phone network) is still prohibitively expensive, as is data roaming on internet enabled mobile phones. The reduction in international mobile phone roaming charges does not currently apply to data streaming.

Text Messages (SMS)

Using a mobile phone to send text messages is a cost-effective way of keeping in touch. There is a charge for sending texts but receiving them abroad is free.

A number of websites offer a free SMS text message service to mobile phones, e.g. www.cbfsms.com or www.sendsmsnow.com

International Direct Dial Calls

International access codes are given in the relevant Country Introduction chapters. To make an IDD call, first dial the international access code from the country you are in, followed by the local number you wish to reach including its area code (if applicable), e.g. from the UK to Portugal, dial 00351 – the international access code for Portugal

Most, but not all countries include an initial 0 in the area code. With the exception of Italy, where the 0 must be dialled, this initial 0 should not be dialled when calling from outside the country in question. Some countries' telephone numbers do not have area codes at all (e.g. Denmark, Luxembourg, Norway). If this is the case simply dial the international access

code and the number in full. The international access code to dial the UK from anywhere in the world is 0044.

International calls can be made from telephone boxes in most countries using coins or, more commonly, phonecards or credit cards, and often instructions are given in English.

Ring Tones

Ring tones vary from country to country and the UK's double ring is not necessarily used in other countries.

Global Telephone Cards

Rechargeable global telephone cards offer rates for international calls which are normally cheaper than credit card or local phonecard rates. Payment methods vary, but are usually by monthly direct debit from your credit card or bank account. Also widely available are pre-paid international phonecards available on-line or locally from post offices, newsagents, kiosks or shops. There are many websites selling international phonecards for use all over the world such as www.planetphonecards.com and www.thephonecardsite.com

Making Calls from your Laptop

If you download Skype to your laptop you can make free calls to other Skype users anywhere in the world using a Wi-Fi broadband connection. Rates for calls to

© iStockphoto.com/Lise Gagne

non-Skype users (landline or mobile phone) are also very competitively-priced. You will need a computer with a microphone and speakers, and a webcam is handy too. It is also possible to download Skype to an internet-enabled mobile phone to take advantage of the same low-cost calls – see www.skype.com

Radio and Television

Radio and Television Broadcasts

The BBC World Service broadcasts radio programmes 24 hours a day from a worldwide network of FM/AM/SW transmitters and you can listen on a number of platforms: online, via satellite or cable, DRM digital radio, internet radio or mobile phone. In addition, many local radio stations broadcast BBC World Service programmes in English on FM frequencies. You can find detailed information and programme schedules at www.bbc.co.uk/worldservice

Listeners in northern France can currently listen to BBC Radio 5 Live on either 693 or 909 kHz medium wave or BBC Radio 4 on 198 kHz long wave. Whereas analogue television signals will be switched off in the UK during 2012 no date has yet been fixed for the switch off of analogue radio signals.

BBC News Online is available on internet-enabled mobile phones, palmtop computers and other wireless handheld devices – text 81010 from your mobile phone or type www.bbc.co.uk/mobile into your browser for set-up information. Mobile phone network providers also have links to the BBC or Sky News from their own portals for breaking news and headlines.

Digital Terrestrial Television

As in the UK, television transmissions in most of Europe have been (or soon will be) converted to digital. The UK's high definition transmission technology may be more advanced than any currently implemented or planned in Europe. This means that digital televisions intended for use in the UK, whether for standard or high definition, might not be able to receive terrestrial signals in some countries.

Satellite Television

For English-language TV programmes the only realistic option is satellite, and satellite dishes are a common sight on campsites all over Europe. A satellite dish mounted on the caravan roof or clamped to a pole fixed to the drawbar, or one mounted on a foldable free-standing tripod, will provide good reception and minimal interference. Remember however that obstructions to the south east (such as tall trees or even mountains) or heavy rain, can interrupt the signals. A specialist dealer will be able to advise you on the best way of mounting your dish. You will also need a satellite receiver and ideally a satellite-finding meter. Many satellite channels are transmitted clear, or 'free-to-air', which means they can be received by any make of receiver, but others are encrypted and require the use of a Sky viewing card and digibox.

For the free-to-air channels, there is a choice of receivers including Sky, Freesat and generic makes. There is nothing to stop you taking a Sky digibox from home unless your Sky contract says you have to keep your Sky digibox connected to your phone line, in which case charges may apply. Alternatively you can take a Freesat receiver or a generic free-to-air receiver. There is also a camping kit which comprises a receiver, dish and stand, and 10m of cable all enclosed in a convenient plastic carrying case. They are available from caravan accessory shops and a variety of other outlets.

Freesat boxes are widely available on the high street, or you can buy a non-subscription Sky digibox from a number of online suppliers. To watch any encrypted channels, there is no option other than to use a Sky digibox, equipped with a viewing card. However, although it is not illegal to use a Sky viewing card outside the UK, it is against Sky's terms and conditions and it will be within their rights to cancel the card. The digibox itself is your own personal property and can be taken abroad without restriction. It will provide access to most free-to-air channels without having a viewing card in it. However, do note that if you intend to take a Sky+ box with you, it will not perform any of the record or playback functions without its designated Sky card. A Freesat+ recorder on the other hand has no such restrictions and can be used freely across Europe.

There are hundreds of English-language TV channels and national radio stations that can be received anywhere in the UK and, in some cases, large parts of Europe. The main entertainment channels such as BBC1, ITV1 and Channel 4 have for a number of years been more difficult to pick up in mainland Europe than others such as Channel 5. Unfortunately in 2012 these channels will be joined by others, including the Channel 5 family, due to the arrival of a new narrow-beam satellite. A 60cm dish will still suffice for most of France, Belgium and the Netherlands, as well as those parts of Germany, Switzerland and Spain that immediately border them, but as you travel further afield, you'll need a progressively larger dish to pick up the entertainment channels. On the plus side, those affected channels will no longer need a Sky viewing card, and users of Freesat and free-to-air receivers will have a greater choice of viewing. The news channels such as Sky News, BBC News and France 24 will almost certainly remain accessible across most of Europe.

As Caravan Europe went to press, the precise impact of the new satellite was still unknown. See the website www.satelliteforcaravans.co.uk (created and operated by a Caravan Club member) for the latest changes and developments, and for information on how to set up your equipment.

Television via a Laptop

With a modern laptop this is straightforward. In order to process the incoming signal the laptop must, as a minimum, be fitted with a TV tuner and a TV-in connector – basically an aerial socket. Some laptops have them built in, but if not you can obtain a plug-in USB adaptor. An alternative connection is the HDMI socket (High Definition Multimedia Interface) which is fitted to some of the more expensive laptops, for which you will need an HD digital receiver. For more information see www.radioandtelly.co.uk

Currently television programmes via BBC iPlayer are only available to users to download or stream in the UK . This is due to rights agreements, however the BBC are aware that there is a demand for an international version. Most radio programmes are available outside of the UK via BBC iPlayer as well as highlights from many BBC News programmes and BBC Sport video content. Check for updates before you travel www.bbc.co.uk/iplayer

Using Mobile Phones Abroad

Mobile phones have an international calling option called 'roaming,' which will automatically search for a local network when you switch your phone on, wherever you are in Europe. You should contact your service provider to obtain advice on the charges involved as these are partly set by the foreign networks you use and fluctuate with exchange rates. Most network providers offer added extras or 'bolt-ons' to your tariff to make the cost of calling to/from abroad cheaper.

There are no further formalities and the phone will work in exactly the same way as in the UK. When you arrive at your destination, your mobile will automatically select a network with the best service. You should also be able to access most of the features you use in the UK, including voicemail and pay-as-you-go top-up.

When calling UK landline or mobile phone numbers prefix the number with +44 and drop the initial 0 of the area code. Enter telephone numbers in your phone's memory in this way, and you will get through to those numbers when dialling from the memory, whether you are in the UK or abroad.

Because mobile phones will only work within range of a base station, reception in some remote rural areas may be patchy, but coverage is usually

excellent in main towns and near main roads and motorways. Approximate coverage maps can be obtained from many dealers.

If you are making calls to numbers within the country you are visiting, you only need to use the standard dialling code without the international code, rather like using your phone in the UK. To make a call to a country other than the UK from abroad, simply replace the +44 country code with the applicable country code, e.g. +351 for Portugal.

You should note that if you receive an incoming call while abroad, the international leg of the call will be charged to your mobile phone account because the caller has no way of knowing that they are making an international call. It is possible to bar or divert incoming calls when abroad and your service provider will supply a full list of options.

Mobile service providers have responded to pressure from the EU to reduce roaming charges but while mobile phone charges are coming down, sending and receiving video messages is still expensive – check with your network provider.

Global SIM Cards

As an alternative to paying your mobile service provider's roaming charges it is possible to buy a global SIM card which will enable your mobile phone to operate on a foreign mobile network more cheaply.

When you go abroad you simply replace the SIM card in your phone with the new card, remembering to leave a voicemail message on the old card telling callers that you have temporarily changed number. This service is offered by a number of network providers as well as companies such as www.roameo.co.uk, www.truphone.com and www.0044.co.uk

You may, however, find it simpler to buy a SIM card abroad but before doing this, check with your UK service provider to find out whether it has locked your phone against the use of a different SIM card and what, if anything, it will charge to unlock it. The website www.0044.co.uk has instructions on how to unlock mobile phones. If you plan to use a mobile phone a lot while abroad, e.g. to book campsites, restaurants, etc, then give some thought to buying a cheap 'pay-as-you-go' phone in the country you are visiting.

Hands-Free

Legislation in Europe forbids the use of mobile or car phones while driving except when using hands-free equipment. **If you are involved in an accident whilst driving and, at the same time, you were using a hand-held mobile phone, your insurance company may refuse to honour the claim.**

Internet & Wi-Fi-Enabled Phones

As technology advances VoIP (voice-over internet protocol) permits you to be contacted on and make calls from your usual mobile phone number while abroad. Part of your call is routed over the internet – see www.truphone.com for information about the latest mobile apps. You will need a Wi-Fi or 3G internet-enabled phone.

Mobile Internet Costs - Data Roaming

Please be aware that accessing the internet overseas via your mobile can be very expensive. It is recommended that you disable your internet access by switching 'data roaming' to off, in order to avoid a large mobile phone bill on your return. If you need to go online or check your email, find a free Wi-Fi hotspot. These are now often available on some campsites or in some cafes, bars and restaurants.

Finally.....

Make a note of your mobile phone's serial number, your own telephone number and the number of your provider's customer services and keep them in a safe place separate from your mobile phone.

Remember to pack your charger and travel adaptor. Charging packs, available from major mobile phone and other retailers, provide a power source to recharge your phone if you do not have access to a mains supply. Whichever network you use, check that you have the instructions for use abroad.

Medical Matters

This chapter offers advice and information on what to do before you travel, how to avoid the need for healthcare when you are away from home and what to do when you return.

Specific advice on obtaining emergency medical treatment in European countries is comprehensively covered country-by-country in the Healthcare Abroad section of the NHS Choices website, www.nhs.uk. Alternatively obtain a copy of the Department of Health's leaflet, T7.1 Health Advice for Travellers which is downloadable from www.dh.gov.uk, or call 020 7210 4850.

Very few countries offer such easy access to medical facilities as Britain. Obtaining medical treatment abroad may seem complicated to UK residents who are used to the NHS. Also in most countries around the world you will have to pay, often large amounts, for relatively minor treatment.

Before You Travel

If you have any pre-existing medical conditions it is wise to check with your GP that you are fit to travel. If your medical condition is complex then ask your doctor for a written summary of your medical problems and a list of medications currently used, together with other treatment details, and have it translated into the language of the country, or countries, that you are visiting. This is particularly important for travellers whose medical conditions require them to use controlled drugs or hypodermic syringes, in order to avoid any local difficulties with Customs.

See Customs Regulations in the section PLANNING AND TRAVELLING.

Check the health requirements for your destination; these may depend not only on the countries you are visiting, but which parts, at what time of the year and for how long. If you are travelling to an unusual destination, heading well off the beaten track, or if you simply want to be sure of receiving the most up-to-date advice, your first step should be to get a MASTA Travel Health Brief. This is designed to meet your specific travel health needs, helping you understand the travel health risks you may face together with any relevant vaccination, antimalarial and other protective advice. To obtain a MASTA Travel Health Brief free of charge simply log on to www.masta-travel-health.com

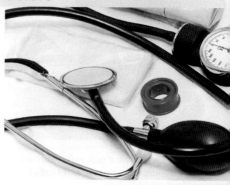

Always check that you have enough of your regular medications to last the duration of your holiday and carry a card giving your blood group and details of any allergies or dietary restrictions (a translation of these may be useful when visiting restaurants). Your doctor can normally prescribe only a limited quantity of medicines under the NHS so if you think you will run out of prescribed medicines whilst abroad, ask your doctor for the generic name of any drugs you use, as brand names may be different abroad. If you don't already know it, find out your blood group. In an emergency this may well ensure prompt treatment.

If you have any doubts about your teeth or plan to be away a long time, have a dental check-up before departure. An emergency dental kit is available from High Street chemists which will allow you temporarily to restore a crown, bridge or filling or to dress a broken tooth until you can get to a dentist.

A good website to check before you travel is www. nathnac.org/travel. This website gives general health and safety advice and reports of disease outbreaks, as well as highlighting potential health risks by country.

European Heath Insurance Card (EHIC)

Before leaving home apply for a European Health Insurance Card (EHIC). British residents who are temporarily visiting another EU member state, as well as Iceland, Liechtenstein, Norway or Switzerland, are entitled to receive state-provided emergency treatment during their stay on the same terms as residents of those countries. As well as treatment in the event of an emergency, this includes on-going medical care for a chronic disease or pre-existing illness, i.e. medication, blood tests and injections. The card shows name and date of birth and a personal identification number. It holds no electronic or clinical data.

Apply online for your EHIC on www.ehic.org.uk or by telephoning 0845 6062030 or by obtaining an application form from a post office. An EHIC is required by each individual family member, so allow enough time before your departure for applications to be processed. A child under 16 must be included in a parent or guardian's application as a dependant, and will receive his/her own card.

The EHIC is free of charge, is valid for up to five years and can be renewed up to six months before its expiry date. Before you travel remember to check that your EHIC is still valid.

> **Before you travel remember to check that your EHIC is still valid and allow enough time to apply**

Private treatment is generally not covered by your EHIC, and state-provided treatment may not cover everything that you would expect to receive free of charge from the NHS. If charges are made, these cannot be refunded by the British authorities but may be refundable under the terms of your holiday travel insurance policy.

An EHIC is not a substitute for travel insurance and **it is strongly recommended that you arrange full travel insurance before leaving home (see below) regardless of the cover provided by your EHIC.** Some insurance companies require you to have an EHIC and some will waive the policy excess if an EHIC has been used.

An EHIC issued in the UK is valid provided the holder remains ordinarily resident in the UK and eligible for NHS services. Restrictions may apply to nationals of other countries resident in the UK. For enquiries about applications see www.ehic.org.uk or call EHIC Enquiries on 0845 6062030. For other enquiries call 0845 6050707. If your EHIC is stolen or lost while you are abroad contact 0044 191 2127500 for help.

Residents of the Republic of Ireland, the Isle of Man and Channel Islands, should check with their own health authorities about reciprocal arrangements with other countries.

Holiday Travel Insurance

Despite the fact that you have an EHIC you may incur thousands of pounds of medical costs if you fall ill or have an accident, even in countries with which Britain has reciprocal health care arrangements. The cost of bringing a person back to the UK, in the event of illness or death, is **never** covered by reciprocal arrangements.

Therefore, separate additional travel insurance adequate for your destination is essential, such as The Caravan Club's Red Pennant Overseas Holiday Insurance, available to Club members – see www.caravanclub.co.uk/redpennant

First Aid

A first aid kit containing at least the basic requirements is an essential item and in some countries it is compulsory to carry one in your vehicle (see the *Essential Equipment Table* in the chapter *Motoring – Equipment*). Kits should contain items such as sterile pads, assorted dressings, bandages and plasters, hypo-allergenic tape, antiseptic wipes or cream, painkillers, gauze, cotton wool, scissors, finger stall, eye bath and tweezers. Add to that travel sickness remedies, a triangular bandage, medicated hand cleaner or wipes, a pair of light rubber gloves and a pocket mask in case you ever find yourself in a situation where you need to give mouth-to-mouth resuscitation. Also make sure you carry something for the treatment of upset stomachs, which often spoil more holidays than anything else.

> **A first aid kit is an essential item and it is compulsory to carry one in many countries**

It is always wise to carry a good first aid manual containing useful advice and instructions. The British Red Cross publishes a comprehensive First Aid Manual in conjunction with St John Ambulance and St Andrew's Ambulance Association, which is widely available. First aid essentials are also covered in a number of readily-available compact guide books.

Emergency Multilingual Phrasebook

The British Red Cross, with the advice of the Department of Health, produces an Emergency Multilingual Phrasebook covering the most common medical questions and terms. It is aimed primarily at health professionals but the document can be downloaded as separate pages in a number of European languages from the Department of Health's website. See www.dh.gov.uk/publications and use the search facility.

Vaccinations

The Department of Health advises long stay visitors to some eastern European countries to consider vaccination against hepatitis A. See the Country Introductions in the relevant edition of Caravan Europe for further information. Polio and tetanus booster injections are no longer routinely administered unless you are at particular risk – see www.nhs.uk

Tick-Borne Encephalitis (TBE) and Lyme Disease

Hikers and outdoor sports enthusiasts planning trips to forested, rural areas in some parts of central and eastern Europe, including many countries popular with tourists, such as (amongst others) Austria and Croatia, should seek medical advice well ahead of their planned departure date about preventative measures and immunisation against tick-borne encephalitis which is transmitted by the bite of an infected tick. TBE is a potentially serious and debilitating viral disease of the central nervous system, with the risk highest between spring and autumn when ticks are active in long grass, bushes and hedgerows in forested areas and in scrubland and areas where animals wander, including in and around campsites and at rural motorway rest areas. It is endemic in many countries in mainland Europe.

There is no vaccine against Lyme disease, an equally serious tick-borne infection, which, if left untreated, can attack the nervous system and joints. Early treatment with antibiotics will normally halt the progress of the disease, but you should be vigilant about checking yourself and your family for ticks and be aware of signs and symptoms of the disease.

If you think you might be at risk use an insect repellent containing DEET, wear long sleeves and long trousers, inspect the body for ticks after outdoor activity and remove with tweezers. Avoid unpasteurised dairy products in risk areas. See www.tickalert.org or telephone 01943 468010.

During Your Stay

Take your NHS medical card with you if visiting a non-EU country as you may be asked for it when seeking medical assistance. Some UK Primary Care Trusts will only issue medical cards on request.

If you require treatment in an EU country but do not have an EHIC, or are experiencing difficulties in getting your EHIC accepted, telephone the Department for Work & Pensions for assistance on the overseas healthcare team line 0044 (0)191 218 1999. The office is open from 8am to 5pm Monday to Friday and they will fax documents if necessary.

Claiming Refunds

If you are entitled to a refund from the authorities of the country in which you received treatment you should make a claim in that country either in person or by post before you return home. You must submit the original bills, prescriptions and receipts (keep photocopies for your records). The booklet T7.1 contains details of how to claim refunds, as does NHS Choices on www.nhs.uk/nhsengland/Healthcareabroad. If you cannot claim until your return home you should contact the Department for Work & Pensions on 0191 218 1999. The DWP will liaise with overseas authorities on your behalf to obtain a refund, which may take some time.

Accidents and Emergencies

If you are unfortunate enough to be involved in, or witness a road accident, or become involved in an emergency situation, firstly summon help early by any means available, giving the exact location of the accident or emergency and the number of casualties. Notify the police; most police officers have first aid training.

If you witnessed an accident the police may question you about it. Before leaving the scene, make a brief note and a rough sketch to indicate details of the time you arrived and left, the position of the vehicles and the injured, the surface of the road, camber, potholes, etc, the weather at the time of the accident, skid marks and their approximate length – in fact anything you feel might be relevant – then date it and sign it. Take photographs if possible. You may never be called on to use these notes, but if you are you have a written record made at the time, which could be of great value.

Calling the Emergency Services

The telephone numbers for police, fire brigade and ambulance services are given in each Country Introduction within each of the relevant Caravan Europe Guides. In all EU member states the number 112 can be used from landlines or mobile phones to call any of the emergency services. In most instances operators speak English.

> ### In all EU member states dial 112 to call any of the emergency services

Insect Bites

Most of the temperate parts of Europe have their fair share of nuisance insects such as mosquitoes and midges, particularly near lakes, and it is wise to use an insect repellant. A number of products are available including impregnated wrist and ankle bands and insect repellant sprays and coils. Covering exposed skin with long trousers and long-sleeved shirts is recommended after dark. Also see information earlier in this chapter about tick-borne encephalitis and Lyme disease.

Rabies

Rabies incidence across Europe has reduced in recent years, in large part due to EU-sponsored vaccination programmes. Apart from isolated incidents, rabies is now confined to a few member states in the east of the EU, principally Romania and Latvia.

Despite this, **DO NOT** bring any animals into the UK without first complying with the legal requirements. Always seek medical attention immediately if you get bitten by an animal. Rabies is an acute viral infection and can be fatal.

Swimming

Pollution of sea water at some Continental coastal resorts, including the Mediterranean, may still present a health hazard. Where the water quality may present risks, e.g. in rivers and lakes, as well as at the coast, or where it is simply unsafe to bathe, signs are usually erected, often accompanied by warning flags, which forbid bathing:

French: Défense de se baigner or Il est défendu de se baigner

Italian: Vietato bagnarsi or Evietato bagnarsi

Spanish: Prohibido bañarse or Se prohibe bañarse

Warning flags should always be taken very seriously – red is for danger, when you should not enter the water; usually yellow or orange means you may paddle at the water's edge, but may not swim. A green flag normally indicates that it is ok to swim. A chequered flag generally means that the lifeguard is temporarily absent. You should never go swimming alone and you should always make sure you know what each flag means and be aware of any risks before you decide to enter the water.

See Safety and Security in the next chapter for further information.

Sun Protection

Never under-estimate how ill careless exposure to the sun may make you. If you are not used to the heat it is very easy to fall victim to heat exhaustion or heat stroke. The symptoms include headache,

tiredness, weakness and thirst, leading to confusion, disorientation and, in very extreme cases, coma and death. Anyone showing signs of serious over-exposure to the sun should be placed indoors or in the shade, encouraged to sip water and kept cool by fanning or sponging down with cool water. Call a doctor if the patient becomes unconscious or delirious

Take sensible precautions: avoid sitting in the sun between 11am and 3pm; use a good quality sun-cream with high sun protection factor (SPF) and re-apply frequently; wear a sun hat and cover up with a cotton T-shirt when swimming; wear good quality sunglasses which filter UV rays, and finally take extra care at high altitude, especially in the snow and in windy conditions.

Children need extra protection as they burn easily, tend to stay out in the sun longer and are unaware of the dangers of over-exposure. Keep babies out of the sun at all times.

Water and Food

Water from mains supplies throughout Europe is generally good but the level of chemical treatment may make it unpalatable and you may prefer to use bottled water.

Food poisoning is a potential risk anywhere in the world, but in extremely hot conditions a common-sense approach is called for. Avoid food that has been kept warm for prolonged periods or left unrefrigerated for more than two to four hours. If the source is uncertain, do not eat unpasteurised dairy products, ice-cream, under-cooked meat, fish or shellfish, salads, raw vegetables or dishes containing mayonnaise.

Returning Home

If you become ill on your return home do not forget to tell your doctor that you have been abroad and which countries you have visited. Even if you have received medical treatment in another country, always consult your doctor if you have been bitten or scratched by an animal while on holiday.

If you were given any medicines in another country, it may not be legal to bring them back into the UK. If in doubt, declare them at Customs when you return.

If you develop an upset stomach while away or shortly afterwards and your work involves handling food, tell your employer immediately. If after returning home you develop flu-like symptoms, a fever or rash, contact your GP or NHS Direct.

Claim on your travel insurance as soon as possible for the cost of any medical treatment. Holders of an EHIC who have not been able to claim while abroad should put in a claim for a refund as soon as possible – see *Claiming Refunds* earlier in this chapter.

The European Union has strong and effective safety legislations. Nevertheless, safety is largely your own responsibility. Taking sensible precautions and being aware of possible hazards won't spoil your holiday, but a careless attitude might. The following advice will help you and your family have a safer and hopefully trouble-free holiday.

Cars and contents left at owners risk

Overnight Stops

The Caravan Club strongly recommends that overnight stops should always be at campsites and not at motorway service areas, ferry terminal car parks, petrol station forecourts or isolated 'aires de services' or 'aires de repos' on motorways where robberies, muggings and encounters with illegal immigrants are occasionally reported. If you ignore this advice and decide to use these areas for a rest during the day or overnight, then you are advised to take appropriate precautions, for example, shutting all windows, securing locks and making a thorough external check of your vehicle(s) before departing. Safeguard your property, e.g. handbags, while out of the caravan and beware of approaches by strangers.

Having said that, there is a wide network of 'Stellplätze', 'Aires de Services', 'Aree di Sosta' and 'Áreas de Servicio' in cities, towns and villages across Europe, many specifically for motorhomes, and many with good security and overnight facilities. It is rare that you will be the only vehicle staying on such areas, but avoid any that are isolated, take sensible precautions and trust your instincts. For example, if the area appears run down and there are groups of people hanging around who seem intimidating, then you are probably wise to move on.

Around the Campsite

The Caravan Club gives safety a high priority at its UK sites but visitors to the Continent sometimes find that campsites do not always come up to Club standards on electrical safety, hygiene and fire precautions.

Take a few minutes when you arrive on site to ensure that everyone, from the youngest upwards, understands where safety equipment is, how things work and where care is needed to avoid an accident. Once you've settled in, take a walk around the site to familiarise yourself with its layout and ensure that

your children are familiar with it and know where their caravan is. Even if you have visited the site before, layout and facilities may have changed.

Locate the nearest fire-fighting equipment and the nearest telephone box and emergency numbers.

Natural disasters are rare, but always think about what could happen. A combination of heavy rain and a riverside pitch could lead to flash flooding, for instance, so make yourself aware of site evacuation procedures.

Be aware of sources of electricity and cabling on and around your pitch. Advice about electrical hook-ups is given in detail in the chapter *Electricity and Gas* in the section *DURING YOUR STAY* – read it carefully.

A Club member has advised that, on occasion, site owners and/or farmers on whose land a site is situated, use poison to control rodents. Warning notices are not always posted and you are strongly advised to check if staying on a rural site and accompanied by your dog.

Common sense should tell you that you need to be careful if the site is close to a main road or alongside a river. Remind your children about the Green Cross Code and encourage them to use it. Adults and children alike need to remember that traffic is on the 'wrong' side of the road.

Incidents of theft from visitors to campsites are rare but when leaving your caravan unattended make sure you lock all doors and shut windows. Conceal valuables from sight and lock bicycles to a tree or to your caravan.

Children

If staying at a farm site, remember that the animals are not pets. Do not approach any animal without the farmer's permission and keep children supervised. Make sure they wash their hands after touching any farm animal. Do not approach or touch any animal which is behaving oddly or any wild animal which appears to be tame.

Watch out for children as you drive around the site and observe the speed limit (walking pace).

Children riding bikes should be made aware that there may be patches of sand or gravel around the site and these should be negotiated at a sensible speed. Bikes should not be ridden between or around tents or caravans.

Children's play areas are generally unsupervised. Check which installations are suitable for your children's ages and abilities and agree with them which ones they may use. Read and respect the displayed rules. Remember it is your responsibility to know where your children are at all times.

Be aware of any campsite rules concerning ball games or use of play equipment, such as roller blades and skateboards. Check the condition of bicycles which you intend to hire.

When your children attend organised activities, arrange when and where to meet afterwards.

Make sure that children are aware of any places where they should not go.

Never leave children alone inside a caravan.

Fire

Fires can be a dangerous hazard and it is important to follow a few basic safety rules. Any fire that starts will spread quickly if not properly dealt with. Follow these rules at all times:

- Never use portable paraffin or gas heaters inside your caravan. Gas heaters should only be fitted when air is taken from outside the caravan.
- Never search for a gas leak with a naked flame or change your gas cylinder inside the caravan. If you smell gas (or in the event of a fire starting), turn off the cylinder immediately, extinguish all naked flames and seek professional help.
- Never place clothing, tea towels or any other items over your cooker or heater to dry.
- Never leave a chip pan or saucepan unattended.
- Keep heaters and cookers clean and correctly adjusted.
- Know where the fire points and telephones are on site and know the site fire drill. Establish a

family fire drill. Make sure everyone knows how to call the emergency services.

- Where regulations permit the use of barbecues, take the following precautions to prevent fire:
  Never locate a barbecue near trees or hedges. Have a bucket of water to hand in case of sparks. Only use recommended fire-lighting materials. Do not leave a barbecue unattended when lit and dispose of hot ash safely.
  Do not let children play near a lit or recently extinguished barbecue.

Swimming Pools

Make the first visit to the pool area a 'family exploration' - not only to find out what is available, but also to identify features and check information which could be vital to your family's safety. Even if you have visited the site before, the layout may have changed, so check the following:

- Pool layout – identify shallow and deep ends and note the position of safety equipment. Check that poolside depth markings are accurate and whether there are any sudden changes of depth in the pool. The bottom of the pool should be clearly visible.
- Are there restrictions about diving and jumping into the pool? Are some surfaces slippery when wet? Ensure when diving into a pool that it is deep enough to do so safely.
- Check opening and closing times. For pools with a supervisor or lifeguard, note any times or dates when the pool is not supervised, e.g. lunch breaks or in low season. Read safety notices and rules posted around the pool. Check the location of any rescue equipment.
- Establish your own rules about parental supervision. Age and swimming ability are important considerations and at least one responsible adult who can swim should accompany and supervise children at the pool at all times. Remember that even a shallow paddling pool can present a danger to young children. Even if a lifeguard is present, you are responsible for your children and must watch them closely.
- Do not swim just after a meal, nor after drinking alcohol.

Water Slides

Take some time to watch other people using the slides so that you can see their speed and direction when entering the water. Find out the depth of water in the landing area. Ensure that your children understand the need to keep clear of the landing area.

Consider and agree with your children which slides they may use. Age or height restrictions may apply.

Check the supervision arrangements and hours of use; they may be different from the main pool times.

Check and follow any specific instructions on the proper use of each slide. The safest riding position is usually feet first, sitting down. Never allow your children to stand or climb on the slide.

Do not wear jewellery when using slides.

Beaches, Lakes and Rivers

Check for any warning signs or flags before you swim and ensure that you know what they mean. Check the depth of water before diving and avoid diving or jumping into murky water as submerged swimmers or objects may not be visible. Familiarise yourself with the location of safety apparatus and/ or lifeguards.

Children can drown in a very short time and in relatively small amounts of water. Supervise them at all times when they are in the water and ensure that they know where to find you on the beach.

Use only the designated areas for swimming, windsurfing, kayaking, jetskiing, etc. Always use life jackets where appropriate. Swim only in supervised areas whenever possible.

Familiarise yourself with tides, undertows, currents and wind strength and direction before you or your children swim in the sea. This applies in particular when using inflatables, windsurfing equipment, body boards, kayaks or sailing boats. Sudden changes of wave and weather conditions combined with fast tides and currents are particularly dangerous.

Establish whether there are submerged rocks or a steeply shelving shore which can take non-swimmers or weak swimmers by surprise. Be alert to the activities of windsurfers or jetskiers who may not be aware of the presence of swimmers.

On the Road

Do not leave valuable items on car seats or on view near windows in caravans, even if they are locked. Ensure that items on roof racks or cycle carriers are locked securely.

Beware of a 'snatch' through open car windows at traffic lights, filling stations, in traffic jams or at 'fake' traffic accidents. When driving through towns and cities keep your doors locked. Keep handbags, valuables and documents out of sight at all times.

In view of recent problems with stowaways in vehicles on cross-Channel ferries and trains, check that your outfit is free from unexpected guests at the last practical opportunity before boarding.

If flagged down by another motorist for whatever reason, take care that your own car is locked and windows closed while you check outside, even if someone is left inside. Be particularly careful on long, empty stretches of motorway and when you stop for fuel. Even if the people flagging you down appear to be officials (e.g. wearing yellow reflective jackets or

Nice © iStockPhoto.com/ValeryBareta

dark, 'uniform-type' clothing) show presence of mind and lock yourselves in immediately. They may appear to be friendly and helpful, but may be opportunistic thieves prepared to resort to violence. Have a mobile phone to hand and, if necessary, be seen to use it.

Road accidents are a significant risk in some countries where traffic laws may be inadequately enforced, roads may be poorly maintained, road signs and lighting inadequate, and driving standards poor. The traffic mix may be more complex with animal-drawn vehicles, pedestrians, bicycles, cars, lorries, and perhaps loose animals, all sharing the same space. In addition you will be driving on the 'wrong' side of the road and should, therefore, be especially vigilant at all times. Avoid driving at night on unlit roads.

Pursuing an insurance claim abroad can be difficult and it is essential if you are involved in an accident, to take all the other driver's details and complete a European Accident Statement supplied by your motor vehicle insurer.

It's a good idea to keep a fully-charged mobile phone with you in your car with the number of your breakdown organisation saved into it.

Personal Security

There is always the risk of being the victim of petty crime wherever you are in the world. As an obvious tourist you may be more vulnerable, but the number of incidents is very small and the fear of crime should not deter you from holidaying abroad.

The Foreign & Commonwealth Office produces a range of material to advise and inform British citizens travelling abroad about issues affecting their safety, including political unrest, lawlessness, violence, natural disasters, epidemics, anti-British demonstrations and aircraft safety. See the FCO's travel advice for all the countries covered by the Caravan Europe guides on www.fco.gov.uk or see BBC2 Ceefax, page 470.

Specific advice on personal security in countries covered in Caravan Europe are given in the Country Introduction chapters. The following points are a few general precautions to help ensure you have a safe and problem-free holiday:

- Leave valuables and jewellery at home. If you do take them, fit a small safe in your caravan and keep them in the safe or locked in the boot of your car. Do not leave money or documents, such as passports, in a car glovebox, or leave handbags and valuables on view. Do not leave bags in full view when sitting outside at cafés or restaurants. Do not leave valuables unattended on the beach.

- When walking be security-conscious. Avoid unlit streets at night, walk well away from the kerb and carry handbags or shoulder bags on the side away from the kerb. The less of a tourist you appear, the less of a target you are. Never read a map openly in the street or carry a camera over your shoulder.

- Carry only the minimum amount of cash. Distribute cash, travellers' cheques, credit cards and passports amongst your party; do not rely on one person to carry everything. Never carry a wallet in your back pocket. A tuck-away canvas wallet, moneybelt or 'bumbag' can be useful and waterproof versions are available. It is normally advisable not to resist violent theft.

- Do not use street money-changers; in some countries it is illegal.

- Keep a separate note of bank account and credit/debit card numbers and serial numbers of travellers' cheques. Join a card protection plan so that in the event of loss or theft, one telephone call will cancel all your cards and arrange replacements. Carry your credit card issuer/bank's 24-hour UK contact number with you.

- Keep a separate note of your holiday insurance reference number and emergency telephone number.

- Your passport is a valuable document; it is expensive and time-consuming to replace and its loss or theft can lead to serious complications if your identity is later used fraudulently. Keep a separate record of your passport details, preferably in the form of a certified copy of the details pages. Fill in the next-of-kin details in your passport. A photocopy of your birth certificate may also be useful.

- Many large cities have a drug problem with some addicts mugging and pickpocketing to fund their habit. Pickpockets often operate in groups, including children. Stay alert, especially in crowds, on trains, undergrounds and stations, near banks and foreign exchange offices, and when visiting well-known historical and tourist sites.

- Beware of bogus plain-clothes policemen who may ask to see your foreign currency or credit cards and passport. If approached, decline to show your money or to hand over your passport but ask for credentials and offer instead to go to the nearest police station.

- Laws vary from country to country and so does the treatment of offenders; find out something about local laws and customs and respect them. Behave and dress appropriately, particularly when visiting religious sites, markets and rural communities. Be aware of local attitudes to alcohol consumption. Do not get involved with drugs.

- Do respect Customs regulations. Smuggling is a serious offence and can carry heavy penalties. Do not carry parcels or luggage through Customs for other people and do not cross borders with people you do not know in your vehicle, such as hitchhikers. If you are in someone else's vehicle do not cross the border in it – get out and walk across; you do not know what might be in the vehicle. Do not drive vehicles across borders for other people.

- Hobbies such as birdwatching and train, plane and ship-spotting, combined with the use of cameras or binoculars, may be misunderstood (particularly near military installations) and you may risk arrest. If in doubt, don't.

- In the event of a natural disaster or if trouble flares up, contact family and friends to let them know that you are safe, even if you are nowhere near the problem area. Family and friends may not know exactly where you are and may worry if they think you are in danger.

The Risk of Terrorism

There is a global underlying risk of indiscriminate terrorist attacks, including in places frequented by foreign travellers, but it is important to remember that the overall risk of being involved in a terrorist incident is very low. Injury and death are far more likely through road accidents, swimming, alcohol-related occurrences or health problems.

Most precautions are simple common sense. Make sure you are aware of the political situation in the country you are visiting and keep an eye on the news. Report anything you think is suspicious to the local police. The FCO Travel Advice for each country within the Caravan Europe guides is summarised in the Country Introduction chapters, but situations can change so make a point of reading the FCO's advice before you travel and register for its email alerts, www.fco.gov.uk

British Consular Services Abroad

British Embassy and Consular staff offer practical advice, assistance and support to British travellers abroad. They can, for example, issue replacement passports, help Britons who have been the victims of crime, contact relatives and friends in the event of an accident, illness or death, provide information about transferring funds and provide details of local lawyers, doctors and interpreters. But there are limits to their powers and a British Consul cannot, for example, give legal advice, intervene in court proceedings, put up bail, pay for legal or medical bills, or for funerals or the repatriation of bodies, or undertake work more properly done by banks, motoring organisations and travel insurers.

Most British consulates operate an answerphone service outside office hours giving opening hours and arrangements for handling emergencies. If you require consular help outside office hours you may be charged a fee for calling out a Consular Officer. In countries outside the European Union where there are no British Consulates, you can get help from the embassies and consulates of other EU member states.

If you have anything stolen, e.g. money or passport, report it first to the local police and insist on a statement about the loss. You will need this in order to make a claim on your travel insurance. In the event of a fatal accident or death from whatever cause, get in touch with the nearest consulate at once.

If you commit a criminal offence you must expect to face the consequences. If you are charged with a serious offence, insist on the British Consul being informed. You will be contacted as soon as possible by a Consular Officer who can advise on local procedures, provide access to lawyers and insist that you are treated as well as nationals of the country which is holding you. However, they cannot get you released as a matter of course.

If you need help because something has happened to a friend or relative abroad contact the Consular Assistance Service on 020 7008 1500 (24 hours).

FCO's LOCATE Service

The FCO encourages ALL British nationals travelling abroad to register for this service, even for short trips. If a major catastrophe, crisis or natural disaster occurs the local British embassy or consulate will be able to contact you to check that you are all right and give advice, and if friends and family at home need to get in touch, you can be contacted easily. For more information see www.fco.gov.uk/locate

British and Irish Embassy and Consular Contact Details can be found in the Country Introduction chapters of the relevant Caravan Europe Guides.

Portugal

Country Introduction

Ponta da Piedade, A;garve

© *iStockPhoto.com/Karolina Grabara*

Population (approx): 10.6 million

Capital: Lisbon (population approx 2 million)

Area: 92,951 sq km (inc Azores and Madeira)

Bordered by: Spain

Terrain: Rolling plains in south; mountainous and forested north of River Tagus

Climate: Temperate climate with no extremes of temperature; wet winters in the north influenced by the Gulf Stream; elsewhere Mediterranean with hot, dry summers and short, mild winters

Coastline: 1,793km

Highest Point (mainland Portugal): Monte Torre 1,993m

Language: Portuguese

Local Time: GMT or BST, i.e. the same as the UK all year

Currency: Euros divided into 100 cents; £1 = €1.14, €1 = 87 pence (September 2011)

Telephoning: From the UK dial 00351 for Portugal. All numbers have 9 digits, including the area code which starts with a 2 and which must be dialled even for local calls. To call the UK from Portugal dial 0044, omitting the initial zero of the area code

Emergency numbers: Police 112; Fire brigade 112; Ambulance 112

Public Holidays 2012

Jan 1; Apr 6, 8, 25; May 1; Jun 7, 10 (Portugal Day); Aug 15; Oct 5 (Republic Day); Nov 1; Dec 1 (Independence Day), 8 (Immaculate Conception), 25.

Public Holidays 2013

Jan 1; Mar 29, 31; Apr 25; May 1, 30; Jun10 (Portugal Day); Aug 15; Oct 5 (Republic Day); Nov 1; Dec 1 (Independence Day), 8 (Immaculate Conception), 25.

Other holidays and saints' days are celebrated according to region. School summer holidays run from the end of June to the end of August

Tourist Office

PORTUGUESE TOURIST OFFICE
11 BELGRAVE SQUARE, LONDON SW1X 8PP
Tel: 0845 3551212
www.visitportugal.com   info@visitportugal.com

97

The following chapter should be read in conjunction with the important information contained in the Handbook chapters at the front of this guide.

Camping and Caravanning

There are more than 200 campsites in Portugal, and many of these are situated along the coast. Sites are rated from 1 to 4 stars. A Camping Card International (CCI) is recommended in lieu of a passport, and may entitle the holder to a reduction in price.

There are 21 privately owned campsites in the Orbitur chain. Caravanners can join the Orbitur Camping Club to obtain generous discounts off current rates. Senior citizens may join this Club free, otherwise the cost is €20. Membership can be arranged via any Orbitur site or on the Orbitur website. Their head office is at:

AVDA DA BOAVISTA 1681, 3° SALAS 5 A 8
P-4100-132 PORTO
Tel: 00351 22 6061360 Fax: 00351 22 6063590
www.orbitur.com
orbiturporto@orbitur.pt

Casual/wild camping is not permitted.

Motorhomes

A number of local authorities now provide dedicated short stay areas for motorhomes called 'Áreas de Serviçio'. It is rare that yours will be the only motorhome staying on such areas, but take sensible precautions and avoid any that are isolated. A 'Quick Stop' facility with reduced overnight prices is also available at all campsites in the Orbitur chain from 6.30pm to 9.30am.

Country Information

Cycling

In Lisbon there are cycle lanes in Campo Grande gardens, also from Torre de Belém to Cais do Sodré (7km) along the River Tagus, and between Cascais and Guincho. Elsewhere in the country there are few cycle lanes.

Transportation of Bicycles

Legislation stipulates that the exterior dimensions of a vehicle should not be exceeded and, in practice, this means that only caravans or motorhomes are allowed to carry bicycles/motorbikes at the rear of the vehicle. Bicycles may not extend beyond the width of the vehicle or more than 45cms from the back. However, bicycles may be transported on the roof of cars provided that an overall height of 4 metres is not exceeded. Cars carrying bicycles/motorbikes on the back may be subject to a fine.

If you are planning to travel from Spain to Portugal please note that slightly different regulations apply and these are set out in the Spain Country Introduction.

Electricity and Gas

Usually current on campsites varies between 6 and 15 amps. Plugs have two round pins. CEE connections are commonplace.

The full range of Campingaz cylinders is available.
See Electricity and Gas in the section DURING YOUR STAY.

Entry Formalities

Holders of British and Irish passports may visit Portugal for up to three months without a visa. For stays of over three months you will need to apply for a Registration Certificate from the local Camara Municipal (Town Hall) or from the nearest office of Servico de Estrangeiros e Fronteiras (immigration authority).

Regulations for Pets

See Pet Travel Scheme under Documents in the section PLANNING AND TRAVELLING.

Medical Services

For treatment of minor conditions go to a pharmacy (farmacia). Staff are generally well trained and are qualified to dispense drugs, which may only be available on prescription in Britain. In large towns there is usually at least one pharmacy whose staff speak English, and all have information posted on the door indicating the whereabouts of the nearest pharmacy open at night.

All municipalities have a health centre. State emergency health care and hospital treatment is free on production of a European Health Insurance Card (EHIC). You will have to pay for items such as X-rays, laboratory tests and prescribed medicines as well as dental treatment. Refunds can be claimed from local offices of the Administracão Regional de Saúde (regional health service).

For serious illness you can obtain the name of an English speaking doctor from the local police station or tourist office or from a British or American consulate. There is a private British hospital at Campo de Ourique, Rua Saraiva de Carvalho 49, 1269-098 Lisbon. Private treatment is expensive.

Normal precautions should be taken to avoid mosquito bites, including the use of insect repellents, especially at night.

You are strongly recommended to obtain comprehensive travel and medical insurance before travelling to Portugal, such as The Caravan Club's Red Pennant Overseas Holiday Insurance – see www.caravanclub.co.uk/redpennant

See Medical Matters in the section DURING YOUR STAY.

Opening Hours

Banks – Mon-Fri 8.30am-3pm; some banks in city centres are open until 6pm.

Museums – Tue-Sun 10am-5pm/6pm; closed Monday and may be closed from 12.30pm-2pm.

Post Offices – Mon-Fri 9am-6pm; may be closed for an hour for lunch.

Shops – Mon-Fri 9am-1pm & 3pm-7pm, Sat 9am-1pm; large supermarkets open Mon-Sun 9am/9.30am-10pm/11pm.

Safety and Security

The crime rate is comparatively low but pickpocketing, bag snatching and thefts from cars are common in major tourist areas. Be particularly vigilant on public transport, at crowded tourist sites and in public parks where it is wise to go in pairs. Keep car windows closed and doors locked while driving in urban areas at night. Pedestrians, particularly the elderly, are advised not to wear valuable jewellery or watches in public areas.

There has been an increase in reported cases of items stolen from vehicles in car parks. Thieves distract drivers by asking for directions, for example, or other information. Be cautious and alert if you are approached in this way in a car park. Do not leave valuables in an unattended car. Thieves often target foreign registered and hire cars.

Take care of your belongings at all times. Do not leave your bag on the chair beside you, under the table or hanging on your chair while you eat in a restaurant or café. Thieves often work in groups and create distractions with the aim of stealing.

Take extra care when crossing busy roads, especially late at night. This warning also applies to pedestrian crossings which are often badly lit and poorly marked.

Death by drowning occurs every year on Portuguese beaches. Warning flags should be taken very seriously. A red flag indicates danger and you should not enter the water when it is flying. If a yellow flag is flying you may paddle at the water's edge, but you may not swim. A green flag indicates that it is safe to swim, and a chequered flag means that the lifeguard is temporarily absent.

Do not swim from beaches which are not manned by lifeguards. The police are entitled to fine bathers who disobey warning flags.

During long, hot, dry periods forest fires occur frequently, especially in northern and central parts of the country. Take care when visiting or driving through woodland areas: ensure that cigarettes are extinguished properly, do not light barbecues, and do not leave empty bottles behind.

Both the Portuguese mainland and islands are susceptible to seismic activity. For more information and daily updates see the Portuguese Meteorological Office's website (English option), www.meteo.pt/pt/sismologia/actividade

Portugal shares with the rest of Europe an underlying threat from terrorism. Attacks could be indiscriminate and against civilian targets in public places including tourist sites.

See Safety and Security in the section DURING YOUR STAY.

British Embassy
RUA DE SÃO BERNARDO 33,
1249-082 LISBOA
Tel: 21 392 4000
www.ukinportugal.fco.gov.uk

There are also British Consulates/Honorary Consulates in Porto and Portimão.

Irish Embassy
VENIDA DA LIBERDADE No 200, 4th FLOOR
1250-147 LISBON
Tel: 213 308 200
www.embassyofireland.pt

Customs Regulations

Alcohol and Tobacco

For import allowances for alcohol and tobacco products see *Customs Regulations* in the section *PLANNING AND TRAVELLING*.

Documents

Driving Licence

All valid UK driving licences should be accepted in Portugal but holders of an older all green style licence are advised to update it to a photocard licence before travelling in order to avoid any local difficulties. Alternatively carry an International Driving Permit.

Passport

The Portuguese authorities stipulate that proof of identity bearing the holder's photograph and signature, e.g. a passport, should be carried at all times. Failure to do so may incur a fine.

Vehicle(s)

When driving you must carry your vehicle registration certificate (V5C), proof of insurance and MOT certificate (if applicable). There are heavy on the spot fines for those who fail to do so.

See Documents in the section PLANNING AND TRAVELLING.

Money

Travellers' cheques may be cashed in banks and are often accepted as a means of payment in shops, hotels and restaurants. Commission charges can be high.

The major credit cards are widely accepted and there are cash machines (Multibanco) throughout the country. A tax of €0.50 is added to credit card transactions.

Carry your credit card issuers'/banks' 24 hour UK contact numbers in case of loss or theft.

Motoring

Many Portuguese drive erratically and vigilance is advised. By comparison with the UK, the accident rate is high. Particular blackspots are the N125 along the south coast, especially in the busy holiday season, and the coast road between Lisbon and Cascais. In rural areas you may encounter horse drawn carts and flocks of sheep or goats. Otherwise there are no special difficulties in driving except in Lisbon and Porto, which are unlimited 'free-for-alls'.

Accident Procedures

The police must be called in the case of injury or significant material damage.

Alcohol

The maximum permitted level of alcohol is 50 milligrams in 100 millilitres of blood, i.e. lower than permitted in the UK (80 milligrams). It is advisable to adopt the 'no drink-driving' rule at all times.

Breakdown Service

The Automovel Club de Portugal (ACP) operates a 24 hour breakdown service covering all roads in mainland Portugal. Its vehicles are coloured red and white. Emergency telephones are located at 2km intervals on main roads and motorways. To contact the ACP breakdown service call +351 219 429113 from a mobile phone or 707 509510 from a landline.

The breakdown service comprises on the spot repairs taking up to a maximum of 45 minutes and, if necessary, the towing of vehicles. The charges for breakdown assistance and towing vary according to distance, time of day and day of the week, plus motorway tolls if applicable. Payment by credit card is accepted.

Alternatively, on motorways breakdown vehicles belonging to the motorway companies (their emergency numbers are displayed on boards along the motorways) and police patrols (GNR/Brigada de Trânsito) can assist motorists.

Essential Equipment

Reflective Jackets/Waistcoats

If your vehicle is immobilised on the carriageway you should wear a reflective jacket or waistcoat when getting out of your vehicle. This is a legal requirement for residents of Portugal and is recommended for visitors. Passengers who leave a vehicle, for example, to assist with a repair, should also wear one. Keep the jackets within easy reach inside your vehicle, not in the boot.

Warning Triangles

Use a warning triangle if, for any reason, a stationary vehicle is not visible for at least 100 metres. In addition, hazard warning lights must be used if a vehicle is causing an obstruction or danger to other road users.

Child Restraint System

Children under 12 years of age and less than 1.5m in height are not allowed to travel in the front passenger seat. They must be seated in a special child restraint system adapted to their size and weight in the rear of the vehicle, unless the vehicle only has two seats, or if the vehicle is not fitted with seat belts.

Children under the age of three years old can be seated in the front passenger seat as long as they are in a suitable rear facing child restraint system and the airbag has been deactivated.

See Motoring – Equipment in the section PLANNING AND TRAVELLING.

Fuel

Credit cards are accepted at most filling stations but a small extra charge may be added. There are no automatic petrol pumps.

LPG (gáz liquido) is widely available – see www.portugalmania.com/transports/gpl-portugal

See also Fuel under Motoring – Advice in the section PLANNING AND TRAVELLING.

Mountain Roads and Passes

There are no mountain passes or tunnels in Portugal. Roads through the Serra da Estrela near Guarda and Covilha may be temporarily obstructed for short periods after heavy snow but otherwise motorists will encounter no difficulties in winter.

Parking

In most cases vehicles must be parked facing in the same direction as moving traffic. Parking is very limited in the centre of main towns and cities and 'blue zone' parking schemes operate. Illegally parked vehicles may be towed away or clamped. Parking in Portuguese is 'estacionamento'.

See also Parking Facilities for the Disabled under Motoring – Advice in the section PLANNING AND TRAVELLING.

Priority

In general at intersections and road junctions, road users must give way to vehicles approaching from the right, unless signs indicate otherwise. At roundabouts vehicles already on the roundabout, i.e. on the left, have right of way.

Do not pass stationary trams at a tram stop until you are certain that all passengers have finished entering or leaving the tram and/or have reached the pavement at the side of the road.

Roads

Roads are surfaced with asphalt, concrete or stone setts. Main roads generally are well surfaced and may be three lanes wide, the middle lane being used for overtaking in either direction. Roads in the south of the country are generally in good condition, but, despite recent extensive road improvement schemes, some sections in the north may still be in a poor state. All roads, with the exception of motorways, should be treated with care; even a good section may suddenly deteriorate and potholes may be a hazard. Roads in many towns and villages are often cobbled and rough.

Drivers entering Portugal from Zamora in Spain will notice an apparently shorter route on the CL527/ N221 road via Mogadouro. Although this is actually the signposted route, the road surface is poor in places and this route is not recommended for trailer caravans. The recommended route is via the N122/IP4 to Bragança.

Road Signs and Markings

Road signs conform to international standards. Road markings are white or yellow. Signs on motorways (auto-estrada) are blue and on regional roads they are white with black lettering. Roads are classified as follows:

AE	Motorways
IP	Principal routes
IC	Complementary routes
EN	National roads
EM	Municipal roads
CM	Other municipal roads

Signs you might encounter are as follows:

Atalho – *Detour*

Entrada – *Entrance*

Estacão de gasolina – *Petrol station*

Estacão de policia – *Police station*

Estacionamento – *Parking*

Estrada con portagem – *Toll road*

Saida – *Exit*

Speed Limits

See Speed Limits Table under Motoring – Advice in the section PLANNING AND TRAVELLING.

Exceptions

Drivers must maintain a speed between 40 km/h (25 mph) and 60 km/h (37 mph) on the 25th April Bridge over the River Tagus in Lisbon. Speed limits are electronically controlled.

Visitors who have held a driving licence for less than one year must not exceed 90 km/h (56 mph) on any road subject to higher limits.

In built-up areas there is a speed limit of 50 km/h.

It is prohibited to use a radar detector or to have one installed in a vehicle. For maps showing the location of fixed speed cameras in and around major towns in Portugal see www.fixedspeedcamera.com

Towing

Motorhomes are permitted to tow a car on a four wheel trailer, i.e. with all four wheels off the ground. Towing a car on an A-frame (two back wheels on the ground) is not permitted.

Traffic Jams

Traffic jams are most likely to be encountered around the two major cities of Lisbon and Porto and on roads to the coast, such as the A1 Lisbon-Porto and the A2 Lisbon-Setúbal motorways, which are very busy on Friday evenings and Saturday mornings. The peak periods for holiday traffic are the last weekend in June and the first and last weekends in July and August.

Around Lisbon bottlenecks occur on the bridges across the River Tagus, the N6 to Cascais, the A1 to Vila Franca de Xira, the N8 to Loures and on the N10 from Setúbal via Almada.

Around Porto you may encounter traffic jams on the IC1 on the Arribada Bridge and at Vila Nova de Gaia, the A28/IC1 from Póvoa de Varzim and near Vila de Conde, and on the N13, N14 and the N15.

Major motorways are equipped with suspended signs which indicate the recommended route to take when there is traffic congestion.

Traffic Lights

There is no amber signal after the red. A flashing amber light indicates 'caution' and a flashing or constant red light indicates 'stop'. In Lisbon there are separate traffic lights in bus lanes.

Violation of Traffic Regulations

Speeding, illegal parking and other infringements of traffic regulations are heavily penalised.

You may incur a fine for crossing a continuous single or double white or yellow line in the centre of the road when overtaking or when executing a left turn into or off a main road, despite the lack of any other 'no left turn' signs. If necessary, drive on to a roundabout or junction to turn, or turn right as directed by arrows.

The police are authorised to impose on the spot fines and a receipt must be given. Most police vehicles are now equipped with portable credit card machines to facilitate immediate payment of fines.

Motorways

Motorway Tolls

Portugal has more than 2,600km of motorways (auto-estradas), with tolls (portagem) payable on most sections. Take care not to use the 'Via Verde' green lanes reserved for motorists who subscribe to the automatic payment system – be sure to go through a ticket booth lane where applicable, or one equipped with the new electronic toll system.

Dual carriageways (auto vias) are toll free and have a similar appearance to motoways, but speed limits are lower.

It is permitted to spend the night on a motorway rest or service area with a caravan, although The Caravan Club does not recommend this practice for security reasons. It should be noted that toll tickets are only valid for 12 hours and fines are incurred if this period of time is exceeded.

Vehicle are classified for tolls as follows:

Class 1	Vehicle with or without trailer with height from front axle less than 1.10m.
Class 2	Vehicle with 2 axles, with or without trailer, with height from front axle over 1.10m.
Class 3	Vehicle or vehicle combination with 3 axles, with height from front axle over 1.10m.
Class 4*	Vehicle or vehicle combination with 4 or more axles with height from front axle over 1.10m.

* Drivers of high vehicles of the Range Rover/Jeep variety, together with some MPVs, and towing a twin axle caravan pay Class 4 tolls.

New Electronic Tolls

A new electronic toll collecting system has been introduced on the following motorways in Portugal: A25, A28, A29, A41, A42 and parts of the A4 and A17. There are no longer manned toll booths on these roads; instead all tolls must be paid by means of a temporary electronic card (TD) available from some motorway service stations, post offices and Via Verde offices.

A deposit of €27 is payable when you hire the TD and this is refundable when you return it to any of the outlets mentioned above. If you use a debit card, toll costs will automatically be debited from your card. If you pay cash you will be required to preload the TD. For further information on payment see www. estradas.pt/portagensestrangeiros

On motorways where this system applies you will see a sign: 'Lanço Com Portagem' or 'Electronic Toll Only', together with details of the tolls charged. Drivers caught using these roads without a TD will incur a minimum fine of €25.

The toll roads A1 to A15 and A21 continue to have manned toll booths. Most, but not all, accept credit cards or cash.

For further information see www.estradas.pt/ portagensestrangeiros

Toll Bridges

25th April Bridge and Vasco da Gama Bridge

The 2km long 25th April Bridge in Lisbon crosses the River Tagus. Tolls are charged for vehicles travelling in a south-north direction only. Tolls also apply on the Vasco da Gama Bridge, north of Lisbon, but again only to vehicles travelling in a south-north direction. Overhead panels indicate the maximum permitted speed in each lane and, when in use, override other speed limit signs.

In case of breakdown, or if you need assistance, you should try to stop on one of the emergency hard shoulder areas and wait inside your vehicle until a patrol arrives. Switch on your hazard warning lights. Emergency telephones are placed at frequent internals. It is prohibited to carry out repairs, to push vehicles physically or to walk on the bridges. If you run out of petrol, you must wait for a patrol vehicle.

Touring

Some English is spoken in large cities and tourist areas. Elsewhere a knowledge of French could be useful.

A Lisboa Card valid for 24, 48 or 72 hours, entitles the holder to free unrestricted access to public transport, including trains to Cascais and Sintra, free entry to a number of museums, monuments and other places of interest in Lisbon and surrounding areas, and discounts in shops and places offering services to tourists. It is obtainable from tourist information offices, travel agents, some hotels and Carris ticket booths, or from www.europeancitycards.com

Portuguese cuisine is rich and varied and makes the most of abundant, locally grown produce; seafood is particularly good. The national speciality is bacalhau – dried, salted cod – for which there are 365 recipes, one for each day of the year. As well as port, many excellent and inexpensive wines are produced, both red and white, including the famous vinho verde (verde means young and fresh, not green!)

Do ensure when eating out that you understand exactly what you are paying for; appetisers put on the table are not free. Service is included in the bill, but it is customary to tip 5 to 10% of the total if you have received good service. Rules on smoking in restaurants and bars vary according to the size of the premises. The areas where clients are allowed to smoke are indicated by signs and there must be adequate ventilation.

Each town in Portugal devotes several days in the year to local celebrations which are invariably lively and colourful. Carnivals and festivals during the period before Lent, during Holy Week and during the grape harvest can be particularly spectacular.

Local Travel

A passenger and vehicle ferry crosses the River Sado estuary from Setúbal to Tróia and there are frequent ferry and catamaran services for cars and passengers across the River Tagus from various points in Lisbon including Belém and Cais do Sodré.

Both Lisbon and Porto have metro systems operating from 6am to 1am. For routes and fares information see www.metrolisboa.pt and www.metrodoporto.pt (English versions).

Throughout the country buses are cheap, regular and mostly on time, with every town connected. In Lisbon the extensive bus and tram network is operated by Carris, together with one lift and three funiculars which tackle the city's steepest hills. Buy single journey tickets on board from bus drivers or buy a rechargeable 'Sete Colinas' or Via Viagem card for use on buses and the metro.

In Porto buy a 'Euro' bus ticket, which can be charged with various amounts, from metro stations and transport offices. Validate tickets for each journey at machines on the buses. Also available is an 'Andante' ticket which is valid on the metro and on buses. Porto also has a passenger lift and a funicular so that you can avoid the steep walk to and from the riverside.

Taxis are usually cream in colour. In cities they charge a standard, metered fare; outside they may run on the meter or charge a flat rate and are entitled to charge for the return fare. Agree a price for your journey before setting off.

All place names used in the Site Entry listings which follow can be found in Michelin's Touring & Motoring Atlas for Spain & Portugal, scale 1:400,000 (1cm = 4km).

Portugal

SITES IN PORTUGAL

ALANDROAL *C3* (13km S Rural) *38.60645, -7.34674* **Camping Rosário, Monte das Mimosas, Rosário, 7250-999 Alandroal** [268 459566; info@campingrosario.com; www.camping rosario.com] Fr E exit IP7/A6 at Elvas W junc 9; at 3rd rndabt take exit sp Espanha, immed 1st R dir Juromenha & Redondo. Onto N373 until exit Rosário. Fr W exit IP7/A6 junc 8 at Borba onto N255 to Alandroal, then N373 E sp Elvas. After 1.5km turn R to Rosário & foll sp to site. Sm, hdstg, pt sl, pt shd; wc; chem disp; shwrs inc; el pnts (6A) €2.35; gas 2km; lndtte; shop 2km; tradsmn; rest; bar; playgrnd; pool; lake sw adj; boating; fishing; TV; no statics; dogs €1 (not acc Jul/Aug); Eng spkn; adv bkg; quiet; red long stay/low ssn; CCI. "Remote site being developed by enthusiastic young Dutch couple beside Alqueva Dam; excel touring base; ltd to 50 people max." 1 Mar-1 Oct. € 14.10   2009*

There aren't many sites open at this time of year. We'd better phone ahead to check the one we're heading for is open.

⊞ **ALBUFEIRA** *B4* (1.5km NE Urban) *37.10617, -8.25395* **Camping Albufeira, Estrada de Ferreiras, 8200-555 Albufeira** [289 587629; fax 289 587633; camping albufeira@mail.telepac.pt; www.campingalbufeira.net] Exit IP1/E1 sp Albufeira onto N125/N395 dir Albufeira; camp on L, sp. V lge, some mkd pitch, pt sl, pt shd, wc; chem disp; mv service pnt; shwrs inc; el pnts (10-12A) €3; gas; lndtte; shop; supmkt; rest; snacks; bar; playgrnd; 3 pools; sand beach 1.5km; tennis; sports park; cycle hire; games area; games rm; disco (soundproofed); wifi; entmnt; TV; 20% statics; dogs; phone; bus adj; car wash; cash machine; security patrols; poss v cr; Eng spkn; no adv bkg; quiet; ccard acc; red long stay/low ssn/CCI. "Friendly, secure site; excel pool area/rest/bar; some pitches lge enough for US RVs; pitches on lower part of site prone to flooding in heavy rain; conv beach & town; poss lge rallies during Jan-Apr; camp bus to town high ssn." ♦ € 24.10   2010*

⊞ **ALBUFEIRA** *B4* (10km W Urban) *37.11916, -8.35083* **Camping Canelas, Alcantarilha, 8365-908 Armação de Pêra** [282 312612; fax 282 314719; turismovel@mail. telepac.pt; www.camping-canelas.com] Fr Lagos take N125, turn R (S) at Alcantarilha twd Armação de Pêra, site in 1.5km on R. Fr IP1/A22 Algarve coastal m'way, take Alcantarilha exit & turn L on N125 into vill, turn R at rndabt. Site on R in 1.5km just bef 2nd rndabt. V lge, hdg pitch, pt sl, shd; wc; chem disp; mv service pnt; shwrs; el pnts (5-10A) €3-3.50; gas; lndtte; shop; tradsmn; rest high ssn; snacks; bar; BBQ; playgrnd; 3 solar htd pools; sand beach 1.5km; tennis; games area; games rm; entmnt; TV rm; 5% statics; dogs €2; bus; phone; poss cr; Eng spkn; red low ssn/long stay; CCI. "Spacious, shady, much improved site; v popular in winter; vg security at ent; excel cent for Algarve." ♦ € 19.00   2011*

See advertisement opposite

⊞ **ALBUFEIRA** *B4* (10.5km W Urban/Coastal) *37.10916, -8.35333* **Camping Armação de Pêra, 8365-184 Armação de Pêra** [282 312260; fax 282 315379; geral@camping-armacao-pera.com; www.camping-armacao-pera.com] Fr Lagos take N125 coast rd E. At Alcantarilha turn S onto N269-1 sp Armação de Pêra & Campismo. Site at 3rd rndabt in 2km on L. V lge, hdg pitch, pt sl, shd; wc; chem disp; mv service pnt; shwrs inc; el pnts (6-10A) €3-4; gas; lndtte (inc dryer); shop; rest; snacks; bar; playgrnd; pool & paddling pool; sand beach 500m; tennis; cycle hire; games area; games rm; internet; entmnt; TV rm; 25% statics; phone; bus adj; car wash; poss cr; Eng spkn; quiet; red low ssn; CCI. "Friendly, popular & attractive site; gd pool; min stay 3 days Oct-May; easy walk to town; interesting chapel of skulls at Alcantarilha; birdwatching in local lagoon; vg." ♦ € 20.50   2011*

See advertisement below

Camping Armação de Pêra - Algarve - Portugal
camping-armacao-pera.com tel. 282 312 260
geral@camping-armacao-pera.com fax 282 315 379

⊞ ALCACER DO SAL *B3* (1km NW Rural) *38.38027, -8.51583* Parque de Campismo Municipal de Alcácer do Sal, Olival do Outeiro, 7580-125 Alcácer do Sal [265 612303; fax 265 610079; cmalcacer@mail.telepac.pt] Heading S on A2/ IP1 turn L twd Alcácer do Sal on N5. Site on R 1km fr Alcácer do Sal. Sp at rndabt. Site behind supmkt. Sm, hdg/mkd pitch, pt sl, pt shd; wc; chem disp; mv service pnt; shwrs inc; el pnts (6-12A) €1.50; lndtte; shops 100m, rest, snacks & bar 50m; BBQ; playgrnd; pool, paddling pool adj; rv 1km; sand beach 24km; games area; internet; dogs; phone; bus 50m; clsd mid-Dec to mid-Jan; poss cr; Eng spkn; quiet; red low ssn; ccard acc; CCI. "Excel, clean facs; in rice growing area - major mosquito prob; historic town; spacious pitches; poss full in winter - rec phone ahead." ♦ € 10.40   2011*

⊞ ALCOBACA *B2* (N Urban) *39.5525, -8.97805* Campismo Municipal de Alcobaça, Avda Joaquim V Natividade, 2460-071 Alcobaça [262 582265] Turn W off A8/IC1at junc 21 onto N8 twd Alcobaça. Site on L on ent town, well sp. Med, hdg pitch, hdstg, pt sl, terr, shd; wc; chem disp; shwrs inc; el pnts (3-6A) €0.90-1.50; gas; lndtte; shop 100m, tradsmn; rest, snacks 200m; bar; playgrnd; pool 200m; TV; some statics; bus 250m; site clsd Jan; poss cr; Eng spkn; some rd noise; quiet; red low ssn/CCI. "Well-run, clean, tidy site; excel touring base; friendly staff; vg facs; Batalha & monastery worth a visit; fascinating Mon mkt nrby; pleasant sm town with gd rests; bus service to Lisbon." ♦ € 9.30   2008*

ALCOBACA *B2* (3km S Rural) *39.52611, -8.96583* Camping Silveira, Capuchos, 2460-479 Alcobaça [262 509573; silveira.capuchos@clix.pt; www.campingsilveira.com] S fr Alcobaça on N 8-6 sp Evora de Alcobaça. Site on L in 3km after Capuchos. Med, hdg pitch, pt shd; wc; shwrs inc; el pnts (6A) €1.50; gas; lndtte; shops 1.5km; rest, snacks, bar 1km; playgrnd; pool 3km; sand beach 10km; games rm; no statics; dogs free; bus 500m; Eng spkn; quiet; CCI. "Vg, wooded, CL-type site; friendly owner; gd views; excel facs; excel touring base." 1 May-30 Sep. € 13.00   2008*

⊞ ALJEZUR *B4* (3.5km N Rural) *37.33972, -8.81277* Camping Serrão, Herdade do Serrão, 8670-121 Aljezur [282 990220; fax 282 990229; info@parque-campismo-serrao.com; www.parque-campismo-serrao.com] Site off N120 sp Praia Amoreira & Campsite. Driving fr N 4km after Rogil turn by café on R on slight bend. Lge sp 200m bef turn. Driving fr S ignore 1st L turn sp Praia Amereira, 4km after Aljezur (camp sp 1.3km), turn on L by café. V lge, hdstg, shd; wc (some cont); chem disp; mv service pnt; shwrs inc; el pnts (6A) €2.60; lndtte; shop; tradsmn; rest; bar; playgrnd; pool; sand beach 3.5km; fishing; tennis; games area; cycle hire; entmnt; TV; some statics; dogs; phone; quiet; no adv bkg; ccard acc; red low ssn/long stay/CCI. "No mkd pitches, pitch between lines of trees; helpful owner; gd san facs; much quieter area than S coast; lovely beaches." ♦ € 22.50   2008*

ALVOR see Portimao *B4*

AMARANTE *C1* (1.5km NE Rural) *41.27805, -8.07027* Camping Penedo da Rainha, Rua Pedro Alveollos, Gatão, 4600-099 Amarante [255 437630; fax 255 437353; ccporto@sapo. pt] Fr IP4 Vila Real to Porto foll sp to Amarante & N15. On N15 cross bdge for Porto & immed take R slip rd. Foll sp thro junc & up rv to site. Lge, some hdstg, pt sl, terr, shd; wc; chem disp; mv service pnt; shwrs inc; el pnts (4A) €1.50; gas 2km; lndtte; shop in ssn & 2km; rest; snacks 100m; bar; playgrnd; sm pool & 3km; rv adj; fishing; canoeing; cycling; games rm; entmnt; TV; dogs; phone; bus to Porto fr Amarante; some Eng spkn; adv bkg; quiet; red low ssn/CCI. "Well-run site in steep woodland/parkland - take advice or survey rte bef driving to pitch; excel facs but some pitches far fr facs; few touring pitches; friendly, helpful recep; plenty of shade; conv Amarante old town & Douro Valley; Sat mkt." ♦ 1 Feb-30 Nov. € 12.50   2009*

⊞ **ARGANIL** *C2* (3km NE Rural) *40.2418, -8.06746* **Camp Municipal de Arganil, 3300-432 Sarzedo [235 205706; fax 235 200134; camping@mail.telepac.pt; www.cm-arganil. pt]** Fr Coimbra on N17 twd Guarda; after 50km turn S sp Arganil on N342-4; site on L in 4km in o'skts of Sarzedo bef rv bdge; avoid Góis to Arganil rd fr SW. Med, terr, shd; wc (some cont); mv service pnt; shwrs inc; el pnts (5-15A) €2.40; gas; lndtte; shop 100m; rest; snacks; bar; playgrnd; fishing & canoeing adj; ski in Serra da Estrela 50km Dec/Jan; TV; phone; Eng spkn; quiet; red low ssn/long stay/snr citizens; ccard acc; CCI. "Vg, well-run site; friendly owner; fine views; gd cent for touring." € 10.60   2007*

ARMACAO DE PERA see Albufeira *B4*

⊞ **AVEIRO** *B2* (6km SW Coastal) *40.59960, -8.74981* **Camping Costa Nova, Estrada da Vagueira, Quinta dos Patos, 3830-453 Ílhavo [234 393220; fax 234 394721; info@ campingcostanova.com; www.campingcostanova.com]** Site on Barra-Vagueira coast rd 1km on R after Costa Nova. V lge, mkd pitch, unshd; htd wc; chem disp; mv service pnt; shwrs inc; el pnts (2-6A) €2.40; gas; lndtte (inc dryer); shop; tradsmn; rest in ssn; snacks; bar; BBQ; playgrnd; pool 4km; sand beach; fishing; cycle hire; games area; games rm; internet; entmnt; TV rm; some statics; dogs €1.40; phone; poss cr; site clsd Jan; Eng spkn; adv bkg; quiet; ccard acc; red long stay; CCI. "Superb, peaceful site adj nature reserve; helpful staff; gd, modern facs; hot water to shwrs only; sm pitches; sep car park high ssn; vg." ♦ € 15.30   2010*

⊞ **AVEIRO** *B2* (10km W Coastal) *40.63861, -8.74500* **Parque de Campismo Praia da Barra, Rua Diogo Cão 125, Praia da Barra, 3830-772 Gafanha da Nazaré [tel/fax 234 369425; barra@cacampings.com; www.cacampings.com]** Fr Aveiro foll sp to Barra on A25/IP5; foll sp to site. Lge, mkd pitch, shd; wc (some cont); chem disp; mv service pnt; baby facs; shwrs inc; el pnts (6A) €2.50; gas; lndtte (inc dryer); shop; rest; bar; BBQ; playgrnd; pool 400m; sand beach 200m; cycle hire; games area; games rm; internet; entmnt; TV rm; 90% statics; dogs €1.60; phone; bus adj; recep open 0900-2200; Eng spkn; adv bkg; quiet; red low ssn; CCI. "Well-situated site with pitches in pine trees; old san facs." ♦ € 15.10   2010*

AVEIRO *B2* (8km NW Coastal/Rural) *40.70277, -8.7175* **Camping ORBITUR, N327, Km 20, 3800-901 São Jacinto [234 838284; fax 234 838122; infosjacinto@orbitur.pt; www.orbitur.pt]** Fr Porto take A29/IC1 S & exit sp Ovar onto N327. (Note long detour fr Aveiro itself by road - 30+ km.) Site in trees to N of São Jacinto. Lge, mkd pitch, hdstg, terr, shd; wc; chem disp; mv service pnt; baby facs; shwrs inc; el pnts (5-15A) €3-4 (poss rev pol); gas; lndtte; sm shop & 5km; tradsmn; rest; snacks; bar; BBQ; playgrnd; pool 5km; sand beach 2.5km; fishing; TV; some statics; dogs €1.50; phone; bus; car wash; Eng spkn; adv bkg; quiet; red low ssn/long stay/snr citizens; ccard acc; CCI. "Excel site; best in area; gd children's park; 15 min to (car) ferry; gd, clean san facs." ♦ 1 Jan-16 Oct. € 20.40   2011*

⊞ **AVIS** *C3* (1km SW Rural) *39.05638, -7.91138* **Parque de Campismo da Albufeira do Maranhão, Clube Náutico de Avis, Albufeira do Maranhão, 7480-999 Avis [242 412452; fax 242 410099; parque_campismo@cm-avis.pt; www. cm-avis.pt/parquecampismo]** Fr N exit A23/IP6 at Abrantes onto N2 dir Ponte de Sor, then N244 to Avis. Fr S exit A6/IP7 N at junc 7 Estremoz or junc 4 Montemor onto N4 to Arraiolos, then onto N370 to Pavia & Avis. Site sp. V lge, mkd pitch, terr, pt shd; wc; chem disp; mv service pnt; shwrs inc; el pnts (16A) €2.60; gas 1km; lndry rm; shop 1km; rest adj; snacks; bar; playgrnd; pool complex adj; lake fishing & shgl beach adj; watersports; tennis; games area; games rm; TV; dogs €1; bus 1km; Eng spkn; adv bkg; quiet; red long stay; CCI. "V pleasant site on lakeside; interesting, historic town; gd walking area." ♦ € 14.00   2009*

⊞ **BEJA** *C4* (500m S Urban) *38.00777, -7.86222* **Parque de Campismo Municipal de Beja, Avda Vasco da Gama, 7800-397 Beja [tel/fax 284 311911; cmb.dcd@iol.pt; www. cm-beja.pt]** Fr S (N122) take 1st exit strt into Beja. In 600m turn R at island then L in 100m into Avda Vasco da Gama & foll sp for site on R in 300m - narr ent. Fr N on N122 take by-pass round town then 1st L after Intermarche supmkt, then as above. Lge, hdstg, shd, gravel pitches; wc; chem disp; shwrs inc; el pnts (6A) €1.85; supmkt 500m; rest 500m; snacks 200m; bar adj; pool, tennis & football stadium adj; bus 300m; rlwy stn 1.5km; Eng spkn; poss noisy in ssn; red low ssn/CCI. "C'van storage facs; helpful staff; san facs old but clean; NH only." ♦ € 10.40   2011*

⊞ **BRAGA** *B1* (1km S Urban) *41.53831, -8.42208* **Parque Municipal da Ponte, São Lazaro, 4710 Braga [253 273355; fax 253 613387]** Fr Porto N14 N to Braga, then fr ring rd exit junc 2 onto N101 dir Guimarães. After Guimarães bear L for underpass sp hospital & other rtes. Site by old football stadium 200m on R (do not confuse with new stadium). Fr N drive thro city, foll sp Guimarães, bear L for underpass (no max height shown) sp hospital & other rtes. Sm, hdstg, pt sl, terr, pt shd; chem disp; wc; own san rec; shwrs inc; el pnts (16A) €1.65; gas; shop 200m; rest 500m; playgrnd; pool, tennis adj; no adv bkg; rd noise. "Not rec for disabled; terr pitches steep for vans, check site/pitch bef driving in; poss scruffy pitches & unclean shwrs; conv Porto, Gêres National Park; easy walk to city cent; NH only." € 12.00   2008*

BRAGANCA *D1* (6km N Rural) *41.84361, -6.74722* **Inatel Campismo de Bragança, Estrada de Rabal, 5300-671 Meixedo [tel/fax 273 329409; pc.braganca@inatel.pt]** Fr Bragança N for 6km on N103.7 twd Spanish border. Site on R, sp Inatel. Med, hdstg, pt sl, terr, pt shd; wc; chem disp; shwrs inc; el pnts (6A) inc; gas; lndry rm; shop & 6km; tradsmn; rest in ssn; snacks; bar; playgrnd; fishing; cycle hire; dogs; bus; poss cr; Eng spkn; quiet but barking dogs. "On S boundary of National Park; rv runs thro site; friendly staff; gd rest; vg facs but site a little scruffy (June 2010); lovely location by river." 1 Apr-30 Sep. € 18.65   2011*

PORTUGAL

BRAGANÇA *D1* (10km W Rural) *41.84879, -6.86120* **Cepo Verde Camping, Gondesende, 5300-561 Bragança [273 999371; fax 273 323577; cepoverde@bragancanet. pt; www.bragancanet.pt/cepoverde]** Fr IP4 fr W take N103 fr Bragança for 8km. Site sp fr IP4 ring rd. R off N103, foll lane & turn R at sp. NB Camping sp to rd 103-7 leads to different site (Sabor) N of city. Med, mkd pitch, hdstg, terr, pt shd; wc; chem disp; shwrs inc; el pnts (6A) €1.60 (poss rev pol & long lead poss req); lndtte; shop; rest; snacks; bar; playgrnd; pool; dogs; phone; bus 1km; Eng spkn; adv bkg; quiet; CCI. "Remote, friendly, v pleasant, scenic site adj Montesinho National Park; clean, modern facs; vg value." ♦ 1 Apr-30 Sep. € 12.60   2011*

BUDENS see Vila do Bispo *B4*

CABANAS TAVIRA see Tavira *C4*

⊞ **CALDAS DA RAINHA** *B3* (8km W Rural/Coastal) *39.43083, -9.20083* **Camping ORBITUR, Rua Maldonado Freitas, 2500-516 Foz do Arelho [262 978683; fax 262 978685; infofozarelho@orbitur.pt; www.orbitur.pt]** Take N360 fr Caldas da Raina twds Foz do Arelho. Site on L; well sp. Lge, mkd pitch, terr, shd; wc; chem disp; mv service pnt; shwrs; el pnts (5-15A) €3-4; gas; lndtte (inc dryer); shop; tradsmn; rest high ssn; snacks; bar; BBQ; playgrnd; htd pool high ssn; paddling pool; sand beach 2km; tennis; cycle hire; games rm; wifi; entmnt; cab/sat TV; 25% statics; dogs €1.50; car wash; Eng spkn; adv bkg; quiet; ccard acc; red low ssn; CCI. "Óbidos Lagoon nr; interesting walled town; attractive area; well-maintained, well-run site; excel san facs; excel touring base." ♦ € 24.60   2011*

I'll go online and tell the Club what we think of the campsites we've visited – www.caravanclub.co.uk/ europereport

⊞ **CAMINHA** *B1* (2km SW Coastal) *41.86611, -8.85888* **Camping ORBITUR-Caminha, Mata do Camarido, N13, Km 90, 4910-180 Caminha [258 921295; fax 258 921473; infocaminha@orbitur.pt; www.orbitur.pt]** Foll seafront rd N13/E1 fr Caminha dir Viana/Porto, at sp Foz do Minho turn R, site in approx 1km. Long o'fits take care at ent. Med, terr, shd; wc; mv service pnt; chem disp; shwrs inc; el pnts (5-15A) €3-4; gas; lndtte; shop (high ssn); rest (high ssn); snacks; bar; playgrnd; pool 2.5km; sand beach 150m; fishing; cycle hire; wifi; TV rm; 5% statics; dogs €1.50; Eng spkn; adv bkg; fairly quiet; ccard acc; red low ssn/long stay/ snr citizens; CCI. "Pleasant, woodland site; care in shwrs - turn cold water on 1st as hot poss scalding; Gerês National Park & Viana do Castelo worth visit; poss to cycle to Caminha; vg site, near attractive beach and short walk to pleasant town." ♦ € 25.60   2011*

⊞ **CAMPO MAIOR** *C3* (800m E Rural) *39.00833, -7.04833* **Parque de Campismo Rural Os Anjos, Estrada da Senhora da Saúde, 7370-150 Campo Maior [268 688138 or 965 236625 (mob); info@campingosanjos.com; www. campingosanjos.com]** Site sp fr Campo Maior on rd dir Vale de Albuquerque. Sm, some hdstg, terr, pt shd; wc; chem disp; baby facs; shwrs inc; el pnts (6A) €2.60; lndtte; shop in town; tradsmn; bar; communal BBQ; pool; lake sw, fishing & watersports 8km; games area; games rm; wifi; TV rm; no statics; dogs €1 (max 1); phone; Eng spkn; adv bkg (15 Nov-15 Feb open with adv bkg only); quiet; red low ssn/long stay; CCI. "Excel, peaceful site; v helpful, friendly, Dutch owners; gd touring base for unspoiled, diverse area; conv Spanish border, Badajoz & Elvas; Campo Maior beautiful, white town." ♦ € 14.60   2011*

CANDEMIL see Vila Nova de Cerveira *B1*

⊞ **CASCAIS** *A3* (5km NW Coastal/Urban) *38.72166, -9.46666* **Camping ORBITUR-Guincho, N247-6, Lugar de Areia, Guincho, 2750-053 Cascais [214 870450 or 857400; fax 214 857410; infoguincho@orbitur.pt; www.orbitur.pt]** Fr Lisbon take A5 W, at end m'way foll sp twd Cascais. At 1st rndabt turn R sp Birre & Campismo. Foll sp for 2.5km. Steep traff calming hump - care needed. V lge, some hdg/mkd pitch, terr, shd; wc; chem disp; mv service pnt; baby facs; shwrs inc; el pnts (6A) €3-4; gas; lndtte (inc dryer); supmkt & 500m; rest; snacks; bar; BBQ; playgrnd; pool; sand beach 800m; watersports & fishing 1km; tennis; cycle hire; horseriding 500m; golf 3km; games rm; wifi; entmnt; cab/sat TV; 50% statics; dogs on lead €1.50; phone; car wash; Eng spkn; adv bkg; some rd noise; ccard acc; red low ssn/long stay/snr citizens; CCI. "Sandy, wooded site behind dunes; v busy high ssn; poss diff lge o'fits due trees; steep rd to beach; gd san facs, poss stretched high ssn; gd value rest; vg low ssn; buses to Cascais for train to Lisbon." ♦ € 36.80 SBS - E10   2010*

CASTELO BRANCO *C2* (2.5km N Rural) *39.85777, -7.49361* **Camp Municipal Castelo Branco, 6000-113 Castelo Branco [272 322577; fax 272 322578; albigec@sm-castelobranco. pt]** Fr IP2 take Castelo Branco Norte, exit R on slip rd, L at 1st rndabt, site sp at 2nd rndabt. Turn L at T junc just bef Modelo supmkt, site 2km on L, well sp. Lge, pt sl, shd; wc; shwrs; chem disp; mv service pnt; el pnts (12A) €2.25; gas; lndtte; shop, rest, bar 2km; playgrnd; pool 4km; lake 500m; bus 100m; Eng spkn; quiet but some rd noise; CCI. "Useful NH on little used x-ing to Portugal; gd site but rds to it poor." 2 Jan-15 Nov. € 9.25   2009*

⊞ **CASTELO DE VIDE** *C3* (3km SW Rural) *39.39805, -7.48722* **Camping Quinta do Pomarinho, N246, Km 16.5, Castelo de Vide [965-755341 (mob); info@pomarinho.co.uk; www. pomarinho.com]** On N246 at km 16.5 by bus stop, turn into dirt track. Site in 500m. Sm, mkd pitch, hdstg, unshd; wc; chem disp; shwrs inc; el pnts (6-10A) €2.50-3.50; lndtte; shop 5km; tradsmn; pool; cycle hire; wifi; dogs; bus adj; Eng spkn; adv bkg; quiet. "On edge of Serra de São Mamede National Park; gd walking, fishing, birdwatching, cycling; vg." € 14.00   2009*

CASTRO DAIRE *B2* (6.4km S Rural) *40.8528, -7.9369* **Termas do Carvalhal, Termas do Carvalhal, Rua do Balneario, 3600-398 Castro Daire** [232 382342; geral@termasdocarvalhal.com; www.termasdocarvalhal.com] Head E on Largo de Sao Pedro, turn R onto R. do Comendador Oliveira Baptista, turn R N2, turn R Av. Central, turn L Av. De Ilidio Pessoa. Sm, pt sl, terr, pt sh; wc; chem disp; shwrs; el pts (15A) €1.16; shop; rest; bar; bus; quiet; NH; CCI. "Rustic site; san facs v clean; NH." April - October. € 10.35   2011*

⊞ **CELORICO DE BASTO** *C1* (500m NW Rural) *41.39026, -8.00581* **Parque de Campismo de Celorico de Basto, Adaufe-Gemeos, 4890-361 Celorico de Basto** [(255) 323340 or 964-064436 (mob); fax (255) 323341; geral@celoricode bastocamping.com; www.celoricodebastocamping.com] E fr Guimarães exit A7/IC5 S sp Vila Nune (bef x-ing rv). Foll sp Fermil & Celorico de Basto, site sp. Med, mkd pitch, some hdstg, shd; wc; chem disp; mv service pnt; shwrs inc; el pnts (6-16A) €2-3.20; gas; lndtte (inc dryer); shop; tradsmn; rest; bar; BBQ; playgrnd; pool 500m; rv sw & fishing adj; games area; wifi; entmnt; TV rm; some statics; dogs €1.80; phone; quiet; ccard acc; red long stay/CCI. "Peaceful, well-run site; gd facs; gd cycling & walking; vg." ♦ € 12.90   2009*

⊞ **CHAVES** *C1* (4km S Rural) *41.70166, -7.50055* **Camp Municipal Quinta do Rebentão, Vila Nova de Veiga, 5400-764 Chaves** [tel/fax 276 322733; cccchaves@sapo.pt] Fr o'skts Chaves take N2 S. After about 3km in vill of Vila Nova de Veiga turn E at sp thro new estate, site in about 500m. Med, hdstg, terr, pt shd; wc; chem disp; mv service pnt; shwrs inc; el pnts (6A) €1.50; gas 4km; lndry rm; shop 1km; rest; snacks; bar; BBQ; pool adj; rv sw & fishing 4km; cycle hire; dogs; phone; bus 800m; site clsd Dec; Eng spkn; adv bkg; red CCI. "Gd site in lovely valley but remote; helpful staff; facs block quite a hike fr some terr pitches; Chaves interesting, historical Roman town." ♦ € 12.50   2009*

⊞ **COIMBRA** *B2* (1km SE Urban) *40.18888, -8.39944* **Camping Municipal Parque de Campismo de Coimbra, Rua de Escola, Alto do Areeiro, Santo António dos Olivais, 3030-011 Coimbra** [tel/fax 239 086902; coimbra@cacampings.com; www.cacampings.com] Fr S on AP1/IP1 at junc 11 turn twd Lousa & in 1km turn twd Coimbra on IC2. In 9.5km turn R at rndabt onto Ponte Rainha, strt on at 3 rndabts along Avda Mendes Silva. Then turn R along Estrada des Beiras & cross rndabt to Rua de Escola. Or fr N17 dir Beira foll sp sports stadium/campismo. Fr N ent Coimbra on IC2, turn L onto ring rd & foll Campismo sps. V lge, terr, hdstg, pt sl, pt shd; htd wc; chem disp; mv service pnt; sauna; baby facs; shwrs inc; el pnts (20A) €2.70; gas; lndtte; shop; tradsmn; rest; snacks; bar; BBQ; playgrnd; pool adj; rv sw 300m; health club; tennis; cycle hire; games area; games rm; internet; TV rm; 10% statics; dogs €2.20; bus 100m; poss cr; Eng spkn; adv bkg; ccard acc; red long stay/low ssn/CCI. "Vg site & facs; v interesting, lively university town." ♦ € 16.10   2009*

⊞ **COIMBRAO** *B2* (NW Urban) *39.90027, -8.88805* **Camping Coimbrão, 185 Travessa do Gomes, 2425-452 Coimbrão** [tel/fax 244 606007; campingcoimbrao@web.de] Site down lane in vill cent. Care needed lge outfits, but site worth the effort. Sm, unshd; wc; chem disp; mv service pnt; shwrs inc; el pnts (6-10A) €2.20-3.30; lndtte (inc dryer); shop & snacks 300m; BBQ; playgrnd; pool; sw, fishing, canoeing 4km; wifi; TV; no dogs; bus 200m; Eng spkn; quiet; office open 0800-1200 & 1500-2200; red long stay/low ssn. "Excel site; helpful & friendly staff; gd touring base." ♦ € 12.70
2010*

CORTEGACA see Espinho *B1*

COSTA DE CAPARICA see Lisboa *B3*

When we get home I'm going to post all these site report forms to the Club for next year's guide. The deadline's mid September 2013

⊞ **COVILHA** *C2* (4km NW Rural) *40.28750, -7.52722* **Clube de Campismo do Pião, Rua 6 de Setembro 35, 356200-036 Covilhã** [tel/fax 275 314312; campismopiao@hotmail.com] App Covilhã, foll sp to cent, then sp to Penhas da Saúde/Seia; after 4km of gd but twisting climbing rd; site on L. Lge, terr, pt shd; wc; shwrs inc; el pnts (4-6A) €1.40; gas; shop; rest; snacks; bar; BBQ; playgrnd; pool; paddling pool; tennis; entmnt; TV; many statics; phone; bus adj; poss cr; Eng spkn; CCI. "Gd walking fr site; few touring pitches." ♦ € 11.30   2009*

DARQUE see Viana do Castelo *B1*

ELVAS *C3* (1.5km W Urban) *38.87305, -7.1800* **Parque de Campismo da Piedade, 7350-901 Elvas** [268 628997 or 622877; fax 268 620729] Exit IP7/E90 junc 9 or 12 & foll site sp dir Estremoz. Med, mkd pitch, hdstg, mostly sl, pt shd; wc; chem disp; shwrs inc; el pnts (16A) inc; gas; lndry rm; shop 200m; rest; snacks; bar; BBQ; playgrnd; dogs; phone; bus 500m; poss cr; CCI. "Attractive aqueduct & walls; Piedade church & relics adj; traditional shops; pleasant walk to town; v quiet site, even high ssn; adequate san facs; conv NH en rte Algarve." 1 Apr-15 Sep. € 16.50   2011*

ENTRE AMBOS OS RIOS see Ponte da Barca *B1*

⊞ **ERICEIRA** *B3* (1km N Coastal) *38.98055, -9.41861* **Camp Municipal Mil Regos, 2655-319 Ericeira** [261 862706; fax 261 866798; info@ericeiracamping.com; www.ericeira camping.com] On N247 coast rd, well sp N of Ericeira. V lge, pt sl, pt shd; wc (some cont); own san rec; shwrs inc; el pnts (10A) €3.50; gas; shop; rest; playgrnd; 2 pools adj; beach 200m; fishing; internet; entmnt; 75% statics; phone; bus adj; quiet. "Busy site with sea views; improvements in hand (2009); uneven, sl pitches." ♦ € 24.50   2009*

⊞ **ERMIDAS SADO** *B4* (7km NW Rural) *38.01805, -8.48500*
**Camping Monte Naturista O Barão (Naturist), Foros do
Barão, 7566-909 Ermidas-Sado [936710623 (mob); info@
montenaturista.com; www.montenaturista.com]** Fr A2 turn
W onto N121 thro Ermidas-Sado twd Santiago do Cacém. At
x-rds nr Arelãos turn R at bus stop (km 17.5) dir Barão. Site in
1km along unmade rd. Sm, mkd pitch, pt sl, pt shd; wc; chem
disp; mv service pnt; baby facs; fam bthrm; shwrs inc; el pnts
(6A) €3.20; lndry rm; shop 7.5km; tradsmn; meals on request;
bar; BBQ; pool; games area; wifi; TV; 10% statics; dogs €1;
bus 1.5km; Eng spkn; adv bkg; quiet; ccard acc; red long stay;
INF/CCI. "Gd, peaceful 'retreat-type' site in beautiful wooded
area; friendly atmosphere; spacious pitches - sun or shd." ♦
€ 15.80   2010*

⊞ **ESPINHO** *B1* (10km S Coastal) *40.9400, -8.65833* **Camping
Os Nortenhos, Praia de Cortegaça, 3885-278 Cortegaça
[256 752199; fax 256 755177; clube.nortenhos@netvisao.
pt; http://cccosnortenhos.cidadevirtual.pt]** Fr Espinho foll
rd thro Esmoriz twd Aveiro to Cortegaça vill. Turn R to beach
(Praia), site on L at beach. At T-junc with pedestrian precinct
in front turn L, take 2nd R then 2nd L. Other rtes difficult.
V lge, pt shd; wc (cont); shwrs; el pnts (6A); gas; shop; snacks;
bar; playgrnd; sand beach adj; entmnt; TV; 95% statics;
no dogs; phone; bus 500m; poss cr; quiet; ccard acc; CCI.
"Ltd tourer pitches & poss v cr high ssn; facs ltd at w/end;
conv Porto; guarded at ent; sun shelters over pitches." ♦
€ 7.00   2009*

ESTELA see Povoa De Varzim *B1*

⊞ **EVORA** *C3* (2km SW Urban) *38.55722, -7.92583* **Camping
ORBITUR, Estrada das Alcaçovas, Herdade Esparragosa,
7005-706 Évora [266 705190; fax 266 709830; infoevora@
orbitur.pt; www.orbitur.pt]** Fr N foll N18 & by-pass, then
foll sps for Lisbon rd at each rndabt or traff lts. Fr town cent
take N380 SW sp Alcaçovas, foll site sp, site in 2km. NB Narr
gate to site. Med, mkd pitch, hdstg, pt sl, pt shd; wc; chem
disp; mv service pnt; shwrs inc; el pnts (5-15A) €3-4 (long lead
poss req); gas; lndtte; shop; supmkt 500m; tradsmn; snacks;
bar; playgrnd; pool; paddling pool; tennis; games area; wifi;
TV rm; dogs €1.50; phone; car wash; bus; rlwy stn 2km; Eng
spkn; adv bkg; quiet; ccard acc; red low ssn/long stay/snr
citizens; red CCI. "Conv town cent, Évora World Heritage site
with wealth of monuments & prehistoric sites nrby; cycle path
to town; free car parks just outside town walls; poss flooding
some pitches after heavy rain." ♦ € 25.60 SBS - W17
                                                             2011*

⊞ **EVORAMONTE** *C3* (3km NE Rural) *38.79276, -7.68701*
**Camping Alentejo, Novo Horizonte, 7100-300 Evoramonte
[268 959283 or 936 799249 (mob); info@campingalentejo.
com; www.campingalentejo.com]** Fr E exit A6/E90 junc 7
Estremoz onto N18 dir Evora. Site in 8km at km 236. Sm, terr,
pt shd; wc; chem disp; mv service pnt; shwrs inc; el pnts (16A)
€8; lndry rm; tradsmn; BBQ; horseriding; wifi; no statics;pool;
dogs €1; bus adj; Eng spkn; adv bkg; quiet - some rd noise;
CCI. "Excel site; gd birdwatching, very friendly and helpful
owner." ♦ € 16.00   2011*

⊞ **FAO** *B1* (1km S Urban/Coastal) *41.50780, -8.77830* **Parque
de Campismo de Barcelos, Rua São João de Deus, 4740-380
Fão [253 981777; fax 253 817786; contacto@cccbarcelos.
com; www.cccbarcelos.com]** Exit A28/IC1 junc 8 fr S or junc
9 fr N onto N13 thro Fão twd coast. Site sp off rd M501. Sm,
pt shd; wc; chem disp; mv service pnt; baby facs; shwrs inc;
el pnts (3A) €3; gas; lndtte; shop, snacks, bar high ssn;
playgrnd; pool 5km; sand beach 800m; entmnt; TV; many
statics; no dogs; bus 800m; quiet. "Gd site; Barcelos mkt
Thurs." ♦ € 15.60   2009*

FERRAGUDO see Portimao *B4*

FERREIRA DO ZEZERE *B2* (1.5km E Rural) *39.70083, -8.27805*
**Camping Quinta da Cerejeira, 2240-333 Ferreira do Zêzere
[tel/fax 249 361756; info@cerejeira.com; www.cerejeira.
com]** Fr Serta (N) take N238 twd Tomar & turn E to Ferreira
do Zêzere. Thro Ferreira dir Vila de Rei, turn L at blue site
sp in 1km. Sm, terr, pt shd; wc; chem disp (wc); shwrs inc; el
pnts (6A) €2.25; gas 1.5km; lndtte; tradsmn; rest, snacks & bar
1.5km; BBQ; pool 1km; TV rm; bus 1.5km; Eng spkn; adv bkg;
red long stay; CCI. 1 Feb-30 Nov. € 12.75   2008*

⊞ **FIGUEIRA DA FOZ** *B2* (4km S Coastal/Urban) *40.11861,
-8.85666* **Camping ORBITUR-Gala, N109, Km 4, Gala,
3090-458 Figueira da Foz [233 431492; fax 233 431231;
infogala@orbitur.pt; www.orbitur.pt]** Fr Figueira da Foz
on N109 dir Leiria for 3.5km. After Gala site on R in approx
400m. Ignore sp on R 'Campismo' after long bdge. Lge, mkd
pitch, hdstg, terr, shd; wc; chem disp; mv service pnt; shwrs;
el pnts (6-10A) €3-4; gas; lndtte; shop; tradsmn; rest; snacks;
bar; BBQ; playgrnd; htd pool high ssn; paddling pool; sand
beach 400m; fishing 1km; tennis; games rm; wifi; entmnt; TV
rm; many statics; dogs €1.50; phone; car wash; Eng spkn; adv
bkg; red low ssn/long stay/snr citizens; ccard acc; CCI. "Gd,
renovated site adj busy rd; luxury san facs (furthest fr recep);
excel pool." ♦ € 29.00   2011*

FIGUEIRA DA FOZ *B2* (6km S Coastal) *40.14055, -8.86277*
**Camping Foz do Mondego, Cabedelo-Gala, 3080-661
Figueira da Foz [233 402740/2; fax 233 402749; foz.
mondego@fcmportugal.com; www.fcmportugal.com]**
Fr S on N109 turn L bef bdge sp Gala. Foll site sp. V lge, mkd
pitch; htd wc; chem disp; mv service pnt; baby facs; shwrs
inc; el pnts (2A) inc; gas; lndtte; shop 2km; rest; snacks;
bar; BBQ; playgrnd; sand beach adj; fishing; surfing; TV;
40% statics; dogs €0.50; phone; bus 1km; CCI. "Wonderful
sea views but indus est adj; NH only." ♦ 14 Jan-13 Nov.
€ 16.40   2009*

FOZ DO ARELHO see Caldas da Rainha *B3*

⊞ **FUNDAO** *C2* (3km SW Urban) *40.13276, -7.51205* **Camping
Quinta do Convento, 6234-909 Fundão [275 753118; fax
275 771368]** Fr N thro town cent; when almost thro town
take L fork at triangle dir Silvares; site 1km uphill on L - steep.
Site well sp fr A23. Med, hdstg, terr, shd; wc (some cont);
chem disp; mv service pnt; shwrs inc; el pnts (4-10A) €2;
lndtte; shop; rest; snacks; bar; playgrnd; pool; entmnt; TV;
bus 1.5km; adv bkg; quiet. "Guarded; no vehicle access after
2300; gd, friendly site with pleasant atmosphere; narr site rds
& pitches diff to access - rec arr early for easy pitching." ♦
€ 10.30   2007*

PORTUGAL

FUZETA see Olhao *C4*

GAFANHA DA NAZARE see Aveiro *B2*

⊞ **GERES** *C1* (1km N Rural) *41.76305, -8.19111* **Parque de Campismo de Cerdeira, Campo do Gerês, 4840-030 Terras do Bouro** [253 351005; fax 253 353315; info@ parquecerdeira.com; www.parquecerdeira.com] Fr N103 Braga-Chaves rd, 28km E of Braga turn N onto N304 at sp to Poussada. Cont N for 18km to Campo de Gerês. Site in 1km; well sp. V lge, shd; wc; chem disp; shwrs inc; el pnts (5-10A) €2.50-3.75; gas; lndry service; rest; bar; shop; playgrnd; lake sw; TV rm; cycle hire; fishing 2km; canoeing; few statics; no dogs; bus 500m; entmnt; poss cr; quiet; Eng spkn; ccard acc; CCI. "Beautiful scenery; unspoilt area; fascinating old vills nrby & gd walking; ltd facs low ssn." ♦ € 20.70   2008*

GERES *C1* (2km N Rural) *41.73777, -8.15805* **Vidoeiro Camping, Lugar do Vidoeiro, 4845-081 Gerês** [253 391289; aderepg@mail.telepac.pt; www.adere-pg.pt] NE fr Braga take N103 twds Chaves for 25km. 1km past Cerdeirinhas turn L twds Gerês onto N308. Site on L 2km after Caldos do Gerês. Steep rds with hairpins. Cross bdge & reservoir, foll camp sps. Lge, mkd pitch, hdstg, terr, pt shd; wc; chem disp; shwrs inc; el pnts (12A) €1.20; lndry rm; tradsmn; rest, bar 500m; BBQ; pool 500m, lake sw 500m; dogs €0.60; phone; quiet. "Attractive, wooded site in National Park; gd, clean facs; thermal spa in Gerês." ♦ 15 May-15 Oct. € 14.00   2009*

⊞ **GOIS** *C2* (1km S Rural) *40.15400, -8.11409* **Camp Municipal do Castelo, Castelo, 3330-309 Góis** [235 778585; fax 235 770129; reservas@goistur.com; www.goistur. com] Fr Coimbra take N17/N2 E to Góis, site sp to W of rv. Steep access rd. Med, terr, shd; wc (some cont); chem disp; baby facs; shwrs inc; el pnts (4-16A) €1.60-2.30; gas; lndry rm; shop; tradsmn; rest 150m; snacks; bar; BBQ; playgrnd; sand beach 15km; rv sw 500m; fishing; canoeing; tennis; cycle hire; entmnt; some chalets; dogs €1.40; bus 100m; poss cr; Eng spkn; adv bkg; quiet; red low ssn/CCI. "Quiet, clean site in beautiful wooded countryside; ltd pitches for lge o'fits; helpful owners; highly rec." ♦ € 12.40   2007*

⊞ **GOUVEIA** *C2* (6km NE Rural) *40.52083, -7.54149* **Camping Quinta das Cegonhas, Nabaínhos, 6290-122 Melo** [tel/fax 238 745886; cegonhas@cegonhas.com; www.cegonhas. com] Turn S at 114km post on N17 Seia-Celorico da Beira. Site sp thro Melo vill. Sm, pt shd; wc; chem disp; mv service pnt; shwrs; el pnts (4A) €2.20; lndtte; shop 300m; rest; snacks; bar; playgrnd; pool; entmnt; TV; dogs €0.75; bus 400m; Eng spkn; adv bkg; quiet; red long stay/low ssn; CCI. "Vg, well-run, busy site in grounds of vill manor house; friendly Dutch owners; beautiful location conv Torre & Serra da Estrella; gd walks; highly rec." ♦ € 16.55   2011*

⊞ **GUARDA** *C2* (500m SW Urban) *40.53861, -7.27944* **Camp Municipal da Guarda, Avda do Estádio Municipal, 6300-705 Guarda** [271 221200; fax 271 210025] Exit A23 junc 35 onto N18 to Guarda. Foll sp cent & sports centre. Site adj sports cent off rndabt. Med, hdstg, sl, shd; wc (some cont, own san rec); chem disp (wc); shwrs inc; el pnts (15A) €1.45; gas; lndry rm; shop; rest, snacks, bar high ssn; BBQ; playgrnd; pool 2km; TV; phone; bus adj; Eng spkn; poss noise fr rd & nrby nightclub; CCI. "Access to some pitches diff for c'vans, OK for m'vans; poss run down facs & site poss neglected low/mid ssn; walking dist to interesting town - highest in Portugal & poss v cold at night; music festival 1st week Sep." ♦ € 9.70   2009*

GUIMARAES *B1* (6km SE Rural) *41.42833, -8.26861* **Camping Parque da Penha, Penha-Costa, 4800-026 Guimarães** [tel/ fax 253 515912 or 253 515085; geral@turipenha.pt; www. turipenha.pt] Fr Guimarães sp Felgueiras. Turn R at sp for Nascente/Penha. Site sp. Lge, hdstg, pt sl, terr, shd; wc; shwrs inc; el pnts (6A) €1.80; gas; shop; rest adj; snacks; bar; playgrnd; pool; fishing; no statics; wifi; no dogs; phone; bus 200m, teleferic (cable car) 200m; car wash; poss cr; Eng spkn; adv bkg; poss noisy; CCI. "Excel staff; gd san facs; lower terrs not suitable lge o'fits; densely wooded hilltop site; conv Guimarães World Heritage site European City of Culture 2012; Cable car down to Guimaraes costs € 4.20 return." ♦ 1 Apr-30 Sep. € 10.40   2011*

⊞ **IDANHA A NOVA** *C2* (8km NE Rural) *39.95027, -7.18777* **Camping ORBITUR-Barragem de Idanha-a-Nova, N354-1, Km 8, Barragem de Idanha-a-Nova, 6060 Idanha-a-Nova** [277 202793; fax 277 202945; infoidanha@orbitur.pt; www.orbitur.pt] Exit IP2 at junc 25 sp Lardosa & foll sp Idanha-a-Nova on N18, then N233, N353. Thro Idanha & cross Rv Ponsul onto N354 to site. Avoid rte fr Castelo Branco via Ladoeiro as rd narr, steep & winding in places. Lge, mkd pitch, hdstg, terr, shd; wc; chem disp; mv service pnt; baby facs; shwrs inc; el pnts (6A) €3-4; gas; lndtte; shop; tradsmn; rest; snacks; bar; BBQ; playgrnd; htd pool; paddling pool; lake sw, fishing; watersports 150m; tennis; games rm; wifi; entmnt; cab/sat TV; 10% statics; dogs €1.50; phone; car wash; Eng spkn; adv bkg; quiet; red long stay/low ssn/snr citizens; ccard acc. "Uphill to town & supmkts; hot water to shwrs only; pitches poss diff - a mover req; level pitches at top of site; excel." ♦ € 29.40   2011*

ILHAVO see Aveiro *B2*

⊞ **LAGOS** *B4* (1km SW Urban/Coastal) *37.09469, -8.67218* **Parque de Campismo da Trindade, Rossio da Trindade, 8601-908 Lagos** [282 763893; fax 282 762885; info@ campingtrindade.com] Fr Faro on N125 app Lagos, foll sp for Centro; drive 1.5km along front past BP stn, up hill to traff lts; turn L & foll Campismo sp to L. Cont to traff island & foll to bottom of hill, ent on R. Site adj football stadium Sm, hdstg, terr, pt shd; wc; own san facs; chem disp; shwrs inc; el pnts (12A) €3.50; gas; lndtte (inc dryer); shop; rest; snacks; bar; playgrnd; pool 500m; sand beach 500m (steep steps); dogs €1; phone; poss cr; Eng spkn; rd noise; ccard acc; red long stay; CCI. "Gd beaches & cliff walks; clean san facs; gd size m'van pitches; conv walk into Lagos." ♦ € 16.70   2009*

⊞ **LAGOS** *B4* (4km W Rural/Coastal) *37.10095, -8.73220* **Camping Turiscampo, N125 Espiche, 8600-109 Luz-Lagos [282 789265; fax 282 788578; info@turiscampo.com or reservas@turiscampo.com; www.turiscampo.com]** Exit A22/IC4 junc 1 to Lagos then N125 fr Lagos dir Sagres, site 3km on R. Lge, hdg/mkd pitch, some hdstg, pt sl, terr, shd; htd wc; chem disp; mv service pnt; baby facs; shwrs inc; el pnts (6A) inc - extra for 10A; gas; lndtte (inc dryer); supmkt; tradsmn; rest; snacks; bar; BBQ; playgrnds; pool; paddling pool; solarium; sand beach 2km; fishing 2.5km; tennis 2km; cycle hire; games rm; games area; wifi; entmnt; TV rm; 25% statics; dogs €1.50; phone; bus to Lagos 100m; Eng spkn; adv bkg; quiet; ccard acc; red long stay/low ssn/CCI. "Superb, well-run, busy site; v popular for winter stays & rallies; all facs (inc excel pool) open all yr; gd san facs; helpful staff; lovely vill, beach & views; varied & interesting area, Luz worth visit." ♦ € 35.50 (CChq acc) 2011*

The opening dates and prices on this campsite have changed. I'll send a site report form to the Club for the next edition of the guide.

⊞ **LAGOS** *B4* (7km W Coastal/Urban) *37.10111, -8.71777* **Camping ORBITUR-Valverde, Estrada da Praia da Luz, Valverde, 8600-148 Lagos [214 857400 or 282 789211; fax 214 857410; infovalverde@orbitur.pt; www.orbitur.pt]** Foll coast rd N125 fr Lagos to Sagres for 3km. Turn L at traff lts sp Luz, site 2km on R, well sp. V lge, hdg/mkd pitch, hdstg, terr, pt shd; wc; chem disp; mv service pnt; baby facs; shwrs inc; el pnts (6A) €3.50-4.60; gas; lndtte (inc dryer); supmkt; tradsmn; rest; snacks; bar; BBQ: playgrnd; pool; paddling pool; sand beach 3km; tennis; sports facs; games area; games rm; wifi; entmnt; cab/sat TV; many statics; dogs €2; bus; car wash; Eng spkn; adv bkg; quiet; ccard acc; red low ssn/long stay/snr citizens/Orbitur card; CCI. "Well-run site on mildly sl grnd; v busy high ssn, spacious low ssn; friendly staff; modern, clean san facs; pitches on sandy grnd, access poss tight due trees; narr, busy rd to lovely beach/town; poss muddy in wet weather." ♦ € 38.30 SBS - E09 2011*

⊞ **LAMAS DE MOURO** *C1* (1km S Rural) *42.04166, -8.20833* **Camping Lamas de Mouro, 4960-170 Lamas de Mouro [251 465129; info@versana.pt; www.versana.pt]** Fr N202 at Melgaco foll sp Peneda National Park, site sp in Lamas de Mouro. Med, pt shd; wc; chem disp; mv service pnt; shwrs inc; el pnts (10A) €2.30; lndry rm; shop; tradsmn; rest; snacks; bar; cooking facs; playgrnd; natural pool; phone; bus 1km; poss cr; quiet; CCI. "Ideal for walking in National Park." € 14.80 2007*

LAVRA see Porto *B1*

⊞ **LISBOA** *B3* (10km SW Coastal) *38.65111, -9.23777* **Camping ORBITUR-Costa de Caparica, Ave Afonso de Albuquerque, Quinta de S. António, 2825-450 Costa de Caparica [212 901366 or 903894; fax 212 900661; infocaparica@orbitur.pt; www.orbitur.pt]** Take A2/IP7 S fr Lisbon; after Rv Tagus bdge turn W to Costa de Caparica. At end of rd turn N twd Trafaria, & site on L. Well sp fr a'strada. Lge, hdg/mkd pitch, terr, shd; wc; chem disp; mv service pnt; shwrs inc; el pnts (6A) €3; gas; lndtte (inc dryer); shop; tradsmn; rest; snacks; bar; BBQ; playgrnd; pool 800m; sand beach 1km; fishing; tennis; games rm; wifi; entmnt; TV; 25% statics; dogs €1.50; phone; car wash; bus to Lisbon; Eng spkn; adv bkg; some rd noise; ccard acc; red low ssn/long stay/snr citizens/Orbitur card; CCI. "Gd, clean, well run site; heavy traff into city; rec use free parking at Monument to the Discoveries & tram to city cent; ferry to Belém; ltd facs low ssn; pleasant, helpful staff." ♦ € 29.10 2011*

⊞ **LISBOA** *B3* (5km NW Urban) *38.72472, -9.20805* **Parque Municipal de Campismo de Monsanto, Estrada da Circunvalação, 1400-061 Lisboa [217628200; fax 217628299; info@lisboacamping.com; www.lisboacamping.com]** Fr W on A5 foll sp Parque Florestal de Monsanto/Buraca. Fr S on A2, cross toll bdge & foll sp for Sintra; join expressway, foll up hill; site well sp; stay in RH lane. Fr N on A1 pass airport, take Benfica exit & foll sp under m'way to site. Site sp fr all major rds. Avoid rush hours! V lge, mkd pitch, hdstg, pt sl, terr, pt shd; htd wc (cont); chem disp; mv service pnt; 80% serviced pitches; baby facs; fam bthrm; shwrs inc; el pnts (6-16A) inc; gas; lndtte; shop; tradsmn; rest; snacks; bar; playgrnd; pool; sand beach 10km; tennis; bank; post office; car wash; entmnt; TV rm; 5% statics; dogs free; frequent bus to city; rlwy station 3km; poss cr; Eng spkn; adv bkg; some rd noise; red low ssn; ccard acc; red CCI. "Well laid-out, spacious, guarded site in trees; ltd mv service pnt; take care hygiene at chem disp/clean water tap; facs poss badly maintained & stretched when site full; friendly, helpful staff; in high ssn some o'fits placed on sloping forest area (quiet); few pitches take awning; excel excursions booked at tourist office on site." ♦ € 30.00 2011*

LOURICAL *B2* (4km SW Rural) *39.99149, -8.78880* **Campismo O Tamanco, Rua do Louriçal, Casas Brancas, 3105-158 Louriçal [tel/fax 236 952551; campismo.o.tamanco@mail.telepac.pt; www.campismo-o-tamanco.com]** S on N109 fr Figuera da Foz S twds Leiria foll sp at rndabt Matos do Corrico onto N342 to Louriçal. Site 800m on L. Med, hdg/mkd pitch, pt shd; wc; chem disp; shwrs inc; el pnts inc (6-16A) €2.25-3.50; gas; lndtte; shop; tradsmn; rest; snacks; bar; pool; sand beach 12km; lake sw adj; cycle hire; entmnt; TV; dogs €0.60; bus 500m; poss cr; Eng spkn; adv bkg; rd noise; red low ssn/long stay; CCI. "Excel; friendly Dutch owners; chickens & ducks roaming site; superb mkt on Sun at Louriçal; a bit of real Portugal; gd touring base." 1 Feb-31 Oct. € 13.15 2007*

PORTUGAL

LUSO

⊞ **LUSO** B2 (1.5km S Rural) 40.38222, -8.38583 **Camping Luso, N336, Pampilhosa, Quinta do Vale do Jorge, 3050-246 Luso [231 930916; fax 231 930917; info@orbitur.pt]** S fr Luso on N336, sp. Lge, hdstg, pt sl, pt shd; wc; chem disp; mv service pnt; shwrs inc; el pnts (5-15A) €2.50; gas; lndtte; shop; tradsmn; rest; snacks; bar; playgrnd; pool 1km; sand beach 35km; tennis; games rm; TV rm; some statics; dogs €1.30; car wash; adv bkg; Eng spkn; quiet; red low ssn/long stay/snr citizens; ccard acc; CCI. "Excel site in wooded valley; vg san facs; some sm pitches unsuitable for c'vans + awnings; internet in vill; sh walk to interesting spa town; conv Coimbra." ♦ € 25.20   2011*

MARTINCHEL see Tomar B2

MEDAS GONDOMAR see Porto B1

MELO see Gouveia C2

⊞ **MIRA** B2 (3km W Rural) 40.44728, -8.75723 **Camping Vila Caia, Travessa Da Carreira Do Tiro, Lagoa 3070-176 Mira [231 451524; fax 231 451861; vlcaia@portugalmail.com; www.vilacaia.com]** S fr Aveiro on N109 for 29km; at Mira take N334 for 5km. Site sp on R 500m W of Lagoa de Mira. Lge, hdstg, pt shd; wc (some cont); chem disp; mv service pnt; shwrs inc; el pnts (4A) €3; gas; lndtte; shop; rest; snacks; bar; playgrnd; pool; paddling pool; sand beach 3km; fishing; tennis; cycle hire; entmnt; TV; some statics; dogs €1.30; phone; bus adj; site clsd Dec; Eng spkn; no adv bkg; quiet, but poss noisy entmnt high ssn; ccard acc; red low ssn; CCI. "Gd site." ♦ € 20.10   2011*

MIRA B2 (7km NW Coastal/Urban) 40.44472, -8.79888 **Camping ORBITUR-Mira, Estrada Florestal 1, Km 2, Dunas de Mira, 3070-792 Praia de Mira [231 471234; fax 231 472047; infomira@orbitur.pt; www.orbitur.pt]** Fr N109 in Mira turn W to Praia de Mira, foll site sp. Lge, hdg pitch, hdstg, shd; wc; chem disp; mv service pnt; shwrs inc; el pnts (5-15A) €3-4 (poss rev pol); gas; lndtte (inc dryer); shop (in ssn); tradsmn; rest, snacks, bar high ssn; playgrnd; pool 7km; sandy, surfing beach & dunes 800m; fishing; boating; wifi; entmnt; TV rm; 5% statics; dogs €1.50; phone; site clsd Dec; Eng spkn; adv bkg; poss noisy w/end; red low ssn/long stay/snr citizens; ccard acc; CCI. "Friendly, helpful staff; gd, clean, attractive site; excel surfing beach nr; suitable for cycling; nature reserve opp site." ♦ 1 Jan-16 Oct. € 26.70   2011*

MIRANDA DO DOURO D1 (500m W Rural) 41.49861, -6.28444 **Campismo Municipal Santa Lúzia, Rua do Parque de Campismo, 5210-190 Miranda do Douro [273 431273 or 430020; fax 273 431075; mirdouro@mail.telepac.pt; www.cm-mdouro.pt]** Fr Spain on ZA324/N221, cross dam & thro town, site well sp. Do not enter walled town. Lge, pt sl, terr, pt shd; wc; chem disp; shwrs inc; el pnts (5A) €1.50; shop, rest & 1km; snacks; bar; playgrnd; pool 300m; phone; bus 500m; Eng spkn; quiet; CCI. "Simple, peaceful site; interesting ent into N Portugal; old walled town; spectacular rv gorge; boat trips; unreliable opening dates." ♦ 1 Jun-30 Sep. € 9.50   2011*

⊞ **MIRANDELA** C1 (4km N Rural) 41.50690, -7.19685 **Camping Três Rios Maravilha, 5370-555 Mirandela [tel/fax 278 263177; clube.ccm@oninet.pt]** Fr IP4 take Mirandela N exit twd town. Foll camping sp at 1st rndabt. At 2nd rndabt take 1st exit, site on L in approx 2km, adj Rv Tuela. Site well sp. Lge, mkd pitch, pt shd; wc (some cont); chem disp; shwrs inc; el pnts (12-16A) €2 (poss rev pol); gas; lndtte; tradsmn; rest; snacks; bar; playgrnd; pool; canoeing; fishing; tennis; entmnt; TV; 60% statics; dogs; phone; bus, train 2km; Eng spkn; poss cr & noisy; red low ssn/CCI. "Pleasant situation by rv; busy site but quiet low ssn; friendly owner; attractive pool." ♦ € 14.00   2007*

MOGADOURO D1 (1km S Rural) 41.33527, -6.71861 **Parque de Campismo da Quinta da Agueira, Complexo Desportivo, 5200-244 Mogadouro [279 340230 or 936-989202 (mob); fax 279 341874; cameramogadouro@mail.telepac.pt]** Fr Miranda do Douro on N221 or fr Bragança on IP2 to Macedo then N216 to Mogadouro. Site sp adj sports complex. Lge, shd; wc; chem disp; mv service pnt; shwrs inc; el pnts (15A) €2; gas; lndry rm; shop 1km; rest 200m; snacks; bar; BBQ; playgrnd; pool adj; waterslide; beach 15km; tennis; car wash; entmnt; internet; TV; dogs €1.50; phone; bus 300m; Eng spkn; adv bkg; quiet. "In lovely area; gd touring base." ♦ 1 Apr-30 Sep. € 11.50   2009*

MONCARAPACHO see Olhao C4

⊞ **MONCHIQUE** B4 (6km S Rural) **Parque Rural Caldas de Monchique, Barracão 190, 8550-213 Monchique [282 911502; fax 282 911503; valedacarrasqueira@sapo.pt; www.valedacarrasqueira.com]** Fr S exit A22 N onto N266, site sp on R in 11km. Fr N on N266 dir Portimão, thro Monchique, site on L. Well sp. M'vans only. Sm, mkd pitch, hdstg, unshd; wc; chem disp; mv service pnt; all serviced pitches; shwrs inc; el pnts (16A); lndtte; bar; BBQ; pool; dogs; no adv bkg; Eng spkn; quiet. "Excel, peaceful, scenic, clean site; excel san facs; helpful staff; poss taking c'vans in future." € 15.00   2009*

MONTALEGRE C1 (10km S Rural) **Camping Penedones, 5470-235 Montalegre [276 510220; info@montalegre.com; www.montalegrehotel.com]** Fr N103 turn S at sp for Hotel Montalegre, site in 1km on lakeside. Well sp. Lge, some hdstg, pt shd; htd wc; chem disp; mv service pnt; shwrs inc; el pnts (6A) €2.10; lndry rm; rest; snacks; bar; playgrnd; lake sw; 10% statics; bus; quiet. "Beautiful situation; vg." 1 Apr-30 Sep. € 17.00   2010*

⊞ **MONTARGIL** B3 (5km N Rural) 39.10083, -8.14472 **Camping ORBITUR, Baragem de Montargil, N2, 7425-017 Montargil [242 901207; fax 242 901220; infomontargil@orbitur.pt; www.orbitur.pt]** Fr N251 Coruche to Vimiero rd, turn N on N2, over dam at Barragem de Montargil. Fr Ponte de Sor S on N2 until 3km fr Montargil. Site clearly sp bet rd & lake. Med, mkd pitch, hdstg, terr, pt shd; wc; chem disp; mv service pnt; shwrs inc; el pnts (6-10A) €3-4; gas; lndtte; shop & 3km; tradsmn; rest; snacks; bar; BBQ; playgrnd; pool; paddling pool; rv beach adj; boating; watersports; fishing; tennis; games rm; wifi; entmnt; cab/sat TV; 60% statics; dogs €1.50; phone; car wash; Eng spkn; adv bkg; some rd noise; ccard acc; red low ssn/long stay/snr citizens; CCI. "Friendly site in beautiful area." ♦ € 26.70   2011*

PORTUGAL

⊞ NAZARE *B2* (2km N Rural) *39.62036, -9.05630* **Camping Vale Paraíso, N242, 2450-138 Nazaré [262 561800; fax 262 561900; info@valeparaiso.com; www.valeparaiso.com]** Site thro pine reserve on N242 fr Nazaré to Leiria. V lge, mkd pitch, hdstg, terr, shd; wc (some cont); chem disp; mv service pnt; baby facs; shwrs inc; el pnts (4-10A) €3; gas; lndtte (inc dryer); supmkt; rest; snacks; bar; playgrnd; pools; paddling pool; sand beach 2km; lake 1km; fishing; games area; games rm; cycle hire; wifi; TV rm; 20% statics; dogs €2; bus; site clsd 19-26 Dec; Eng spkn; adv bkg; quiet; ccard acc; red low ssn/long stay; CCI. "Gd, clean site; well run; gd security; pitches vary in size & price, & divided by concrete walls; poss not suitable lge o'fits; bus outside gates to Nazare; exit down steep hill." ♦ € 22.85 (CChq acc) 2011*

NAZARE *B2* (2km E Rural) *39.59777, -9.05611* **Camping ORBITUR-Valado, Rua dos Combatentes do Ultramar 2, EN8, Km 5, Valado, 2450-148 Nazaré-Alcobaca [262 561111; fax 262 561137; infovalado@orbitur.pt; www.orbitur.pt]** Site on N of rd to Alcobaça & Valado (N8-4), opp Monte de São Bartolomeu. Lge, mkd pitch, terr, sl, shd; wc; chem disp; mv service pnt; shwrs inc; el pnts (6A) €3-4; gas; lndtte; shop & 2km; tradsmn;rest; snacks; bar; BBQ; playgrnd; pool; sand beach 1.8km; tennis; games rm; wifi; TV rm; 10% statics; dogs €1.50; phone; car wash; Eng spkn; adv bkg; red low ssn/long stay/snr citizens; ccard acc. "Pleasant site in pine trees; v soft sand - tractor avail; helpful manager; visits to Fátima, Alcobaça, Balhala rec." ♦ 1 Jan-16 Oct. € 25.60 2010*

⊞ ODECEIXE *B4* (1.5km NE Rural) *37.43826, -8.75596* **Camping São Miguel, 7630-592 São Miguel [282 947145; fax 282 947245; camping.sao.miguel@mail.telepac.pt; www.campingsaomiguel.com]** Fr N120 site ent 1.5km NE of Odeceixe. V lge, pt sl, shd; wc; chem disp; mv service pnt; shwrs inc; el pnts (6A) €2.75; gas; lndtte; shop, rest, snacks bar high ssn; BBQ; playgrnd; pool; paddling pool; sand beach 5km; tennis; games rm; TV; bus 500m; no dogs; phone; site clsd midnight-0800; adv bkg; quiet; red low ssn/long stay. "Gd, clean facs." ♦ € 25.50 2007*

⊞ ODEMIRA *B4* (7km W Rural) *37.60565, -8.73786* **Zmar Eco Camping Resort & Spa, Herdade A-de-Mateus, N393/1, San Salvador, 7630-011 Odemira [707 200626 or 283 690010; fax 283 690014; info@zmar.eu; www.zmar.eu]** Fr N on A2 take IC33 dir Sines. Just bef ent Sines take IC4 to Cercal (sp Sul Algarve) then foll N390/393 & turn R dir Zambujeira do Mar, site sp. Med, mkd pitch, hdstg, pt shd; wc; chem disp; mv service pnt; baby facs; fam bthrm; sauna; shwrs inc; private bthrms avail; el pnts (10A) inc; lndtte; shop; rest; snacks; bar; BBQ; cooking facs; playgrnd; 2 pools (1 htd, covrd); paddling pool; sand beach 7km; tennis; cycle hire; games area; wellness cent; fitness rm; wifi; excursions; entmnt; TV rm; 17% statics; Eng spkn; adv bkg; dogs €2.50; twin-axles acc (rec check in adv); quiet; red low ssn. "Superb new site 2009 (eco resort) with excel facs; in national park; vg touring base." ♦ € 40.00 (4 persons) (CChq acc) SBS - W14 2011*

⊞ ODIVELAS *B3* (3km NE Rural) *38.18361, -8.10361* **Camping Markádia, Barragem de Odivelas, 7920-999 Alvito [284 763141; fax 284 763102; markadia@hotmail.com; www.markadia.net]** Fr Ferreira do Alentejo on N2 N twd Torrão. After Odivelas turn R onto N257 twd Alvito & turn R twd Barragem de Odivels. Site in 7km, clearly sp. Med, hdstg, pt sl, pt shd; wc; chem disp; mv service pnt; shwrs inc; el pnts (16A) inc; gas; lndtte (inc dryer); shop; tradsmn; rest; snacks; bar; playgrnd; pool 50m; paddling pool; sand beach, lake sw 500m; boating; fishing; horseriding; tennis; no dogs Jul-Aug; phone; car wash; adv bkg; v quiet; red low ssn/CCI. "Beautiful, secluded site on banks of reservoir; spacious pitches; gd rest; site lighting low but san facs well lit; excel walking, cycling, birdwatching." ♦ € 24.30 2011*

⊞ OLHAO *C4* (10km NE Rural) **Camping Caravanas Algarve, Sitio da Cabeça Moncarapacho, 8700-618 Moncarapacho [289 791669]** Exit IP1/A22 sp Moncarapacho. In 2km turn L sp Fuzeta. At traff lts turn L & immed L opp supmkt in 1km. Turn R at site sp. Site on L. Sm, hdstg, pt sl, unshd; wc; chem disp; shwrs inc; el pnts (6A) inc; lndtte; shop, rest, snacks, bar 1.5km; sand beach 4km; 10% statics; dogs; poss cr; Eng spkn; adv bkg; quiet; 10% red CCI. "Situated on a farm in orange groves; pitches ltd in wet conditions; gd, modern san facs; gd security; Spanish border 35km; National Park Ria Formosa 4km." € 10.00 2008*

⊞ OLHAO *C4* (10km NE Rural) **Campismo Casa Rosa, 8700 Moncarapacho [289 794400; fax 289 792952; casarosa@sapo.pt; www.casarosa.com.pt]** Fr A22 (IP1) E twd Spain, leave at exit 15 Olhão/Moncarapacho. At rndabt take 2nd exit dir Moncarapacho. Cont past sp Moncarapacho Centro direction Olhão. In 1km at Lagoão, on L is Café Da Lagoão with its orange awning. Just past café is sp for Casa Rosa. Foll sp. Sm, hdstg, terr, unshd; htd wc; chem disp; shwrs inc; el pnts (6A) inc; gas 3km; lndtte; rest; pool; shgl beach 6km; rv sw 6km; sat TV; no dogs; Eng spkn; adv bkg; noise fr construction yard adj; CCI. "Excel CL-type site adj holiday apartments; adults only; helpful, friendly, Norwegian owners; evening meals avail; ideal for touring E Algarve; conv Spanish border; rec." ♦ € 13.00 2009*

⊞ OLHAO *C4* (1.5km E Rural) *37.03527, -7.82250* **Camping Olhão, Pinheiros do Marim, 8700-912 Olhão [289 700300; fax 289 700390 or 700391; parque.campismo@sbsi.pt; www.sbsi.pt]** Turn S twd coast fr N125 1.5km E of Olhão by filling stn. Clearly sp on S side of N125, adj Ria Formosa National Park. V lge, hdg/mkd pitch, pt sl, shd; wc; chem disp; mv service pnt; shwrs inc; el pnts (6A) €1.90; gas; lndtte inc dryers; supmkt; tradsmn; rest; bar; playgrnd; pool; paddling pool; beach 1.5km; tennis; games rm; games area; cycle hire; horseriding 1km; internet; TV; 75% statics; dogs €1.60; phone; bus adj; rlwy station 1.5km; sep car park for some pitches; car wash; security guard; Eng spkn; adv bkg; some rlwy noise; ccard acc; red long stay/low ssn; CCI. "Pleasant, helpful staff; excel pool; gd san facs; v popular long stay low ssn; many sm sandy pitches, some diff access for lge o'fits; gd for cycling, birdwatching; ferry to islands." ♦ € 17.20-19.50 2011*

See advertisement on next page

Camping Olhão

Open All Year

Tennis
Football
Bar
Swimming Pool
Restaurant
Bungalows
Mobile Homes

parque.campismo@sbsi.pt
Algarve - Portugal
www.sbsi.pt/camping
© 351 289 700 300

⊞ **OLHAO** *C4* (9km E Coastal/Urban) *37.05294, -7.74484*
**Parque Campismo de Fuzeta, 2 Rua do Liberdade, 8700-
019 Fuzeta [289 793459; fax 289 794034; camping@
jf-fuseta.pt]** Fr N125 Olhão-Tavira rd, turn S at traff lts at
Alfandanga sp Fuzeta & foll sp to site. Lge, some hdstg, pt
shd; wc; chem disp; shwrs €0.25; el pnts (6-10A) inc; gas;
lndtte; shop & 1km; rest adj; snacks; bar; BBQ; playgrnd adj;
sand beach adj; internet; 5% statics; dogs; phone; train 500m;
Eng spkn; no adv bkg; noise fr rd & adj bars; red long stay.
"Pleasant staff; popular with long-stay m'vanners; elec cables
run across site rds; poss flooding after heavy rain; clean
san facs; gd security; attractive area & fishing port." ♦
€ 16.70   2010*

⊞ **OLIVEIRA DE AZEMEIS** *B2* (1.5km E Rural) *40.8436,
-8.4664* **Camping La Salette, 3720-222 Oliveira de Azeméis
[256 674373]** Fr N1 turn E onto N224 to Vale de Cambra, foll
sp Parque La Salette. Med, shd; wc; shwrs €0.75; el pnts (6A)
€0.75 (poss rev pol); gas; lndtte; shop 100m; rest, snacks, bar
adj; BBQ; playgrnd 300m; pool adj; TV; phone; bus 200m;
quiet. "Picturesque area; friendly site; clean facs; gd NH." ♦
€ 8.50   2008*

⊞ **OLIVEIRA DO HOSPITAL** *C2* (9km SE Rural) *40.34647,
-7.80747* **Parque de Campisom de São Gião, 3400-570
São Gião [238 691154; fax 238 692451]** Fr N17 Guarda-
Coimbra rd turn S almost opp N230 rd to Oliveira do Hospital,
dir Sandomil. Site on R in about 3km over rv bdge. Lge,
shd; wc; chem disp; shwrs; el pnts (6A) €1.50; gas; lndtte;
shop; rest; snacks; bar; BBQ; playgrnd; pool 7km; fishing;
phone; 50% statics; no dogs; bus adj; quiet. "Facs basic but
clean; working water mill; app/exit long, steep, narr, lane."
€ 10.50   2009*

⊞ **OLIVEIRA DO HOSPITAL** *C2* (10km NW Rural) *40.40550,
-7.93100* **Camping Quinta das Oliveiras (Naturist), Rua de
Estrada Nova, Andorinha, 3405-498 Travanca de Lagos
[962 621287; fax 235 466007; campismo.nat@sapo.pt;
www.quinta-das-oliveiras.com]** Fr Oliveira do Hospital foll
N230 & N1314 to Travanca de Lagos. Then take N502 twd
Midões. After 2km turn R on N1313 to Andorinha. Site on R
1.5km after Andorinha. Sm, pt sl, terr, pt shd; wc; chem disp;
shwrs inc; el pnts (6A) €3.50; tradsmn; BBQ; playgrnd; pool;
dogs €2; poss cr; Eng spkn; adv bkg; quiet; red low ssn; INF
card. € 19.10   2009*

⊞ **ORTIGA** *C3* (1.5km SE Rural) *39.48277, -8.00305* **Parque
Campismo de Ortiga, Estrada da Barragem, 6120-525
Ortiga [241 573464; fax 241 573482; campismo@cm-
macao.pt]** Exit A23/IP6 junc 12 S to Ortiga. Thro Ortiga &
foll site sp for 1.5km. Site beside dam. Sm, mkd pitch, hdstg,
terr, pt shd; wc; chem disp; shwrs inc; el pnts (10A) €1.50;
lndtte; shop 1km; rest, snacks, bar adj; BBQ; playgrnd; lake
sw 100m; watersports; TV; 50% statics; dogs free; bus 1.5km;
poss cr; Eng spkn; quiet; red low ssn; CCI. "Lovely site in gd
position." ♦ € 10.80   2010*

⊞ **OURIQUE** *B4* (10km S Rural) *37.5675, -8.2644* **Camping
Serro da Bica, Horta da Bica, Aldeia de Palheiros, 7670-
202 Ourique [tel/fax 286 516750; info@serrodabica.com;
www.serrodabica.com]** Fr N of IC1 turn R at km post 679.4 &
foll sp to site. Fr S go past km post & do U-turn at turn off for
Castro da Cola, then as above. Sm, terr, pt shd; wc; chem disp;
shwrs inc; el pnts (10A) €2.50; gas; lndtte; tradsmn; bar; rv
nrby; wifi; no statics; bus 800m; Eng spkn; adv bkg; quiet; red
long stay; CCI. "Pretty site; gd walking; excel." € 13.00
                                                           2008*

PENACOVA *B2* (3km N Rural) *40.27916, -8.26805* **Camp
Municipal de Vila Nova, Rua dos Barqueiros, Vila Nova,
3360-204 Penacova [239 477946; fax 239 474857;
penaparque2@iol.pt]** IP3 fr Coimbra, exit junc 11, cross Rv
Mondego N of Penacova & foll to sp to Vila Nova & site. Med,
pt shd; wc; shwrs inc; el pnts (6A) €1; shop 50m; rest 150m;
snacks; bar; BBQ; playgrnd; rv sw 200m; fishing; cycle hire;
TV; no dogs; phone; bus 150m; Eng spkn; red CCI. "Open,
attractive site." 1 Apr-30 Sep. € 10.80   2011*

PENELA *B2* (500m SE Rural) *40.02501, -8.38900* **Parque
Municipal de Campismo de Panela, Rua do Convento
de Santo Antonio, 3230-284 Penela [239 569256; fax
239 569400]** Fr Coimbra S on IC2, L at Condeixa a Nova, IC3
dir Penela. Thro vill foll sp to site. Sm, hstg, pt sl, terr, pt shd;
wc; chem disp; shwrs €0.50; el pnts (6A) €0.50; shop, rest,
snacks, bar 200m; pool 500m; some statics; no dogs; bus adj;
some traff noise; CCI. "Attractive sm town; restful, clean, well-
maintained site." ♦ 1 Jun-30 Sep. € 4.50   2009*

⊞ **PENICHE** *B3* (3km E Coastal) *39.35388, -9.36111* **Camp Municipal de Peniche, Avda Monsenhor M Bastos, 2520-206 Peniche [262 789696; fax 262 789529; campismo-peniche@sapo.pt; www.cm-peniche.pt]** Site 2km E fr Lourinha after N114 (fr Obidos) joins N247; rd crosses bdge & site on R. V lge, terr, pt shd; wc; shwrs inc; el pnts (4A) €1.35; gas; lndtte; shop; rest; bar; playgrnd; pool adj; beach 200m; fishing; tennis; TV; 40% statics; phone; bus 500m; red low ssn; v quiet; ccard acc. "Friendly staff; interesting area; gd NH." ♦ € 11.20   2008*

⊞ **PENICHE** *B3* (1.5km NW Urban/Coastal) *39.36944, -9.39194* **Camping Peniche Praia, Estrada Marginal Norte, 2520 Peniche [262 783460; fax 262 789447; penichepraia@hotmail.com; www.penichepraia.pt]** Travel S on IP6 then take N114 sp Peniche; fr Lisbon N on N247 then N114 sp Peniche. Site on R on N114 1km bef Peniche. Med, hdg/mkd pitch, hdstg, unshd; wc; chem disp; mv service pnt; shwrs inc; el pnts (6A) inc; lndtte; shop 1.5km; tradsmn; rest, snacks, bar high ssn; BBQ; playgrnd; covrd pool; paddling pool; sand beach 1.5km; games rm; cycle hire; internet; entmnt; TV; 30% statics; phone; bus 2km; car wash; poss cr; Eng spkn; adv bkg rec; red long stay/low ssn/CCI. "Vg site in lovely location; some sm pitches; rec, espec low ssn." € 14.75   2008*

POCO REDONDO see Tomar *B2*

PONTE DA BARCA *B1* (11km E Rural) *41.82376, -8.31723* **Camping Entre-Ambos-os-Rios, Lugar da Igreja, Entre-Ambos-os-Rios, 4980-613 Ponte da Barca [258 588361; fax 258 452450; aderepg@mail.telepac.pt; www.adere-pg.pt]** N203 E fr Ponte da Barca, pass ent sp for vill. Site sp N twd Rv Lima, after 1st bdge. Lge, pt sl, shd; wc; shwrs inc; el pnts (6A) €1.20; gas; lndry rm; shop, rest 300m; snacks; bar; playgrnd; canoeing; fishing; entmnt; TV; dogs €0.60; phone; bus 100m; adv bkg; CCI. "Beautiful, clean, well-run site in pine trees; well situated for National Park." 15 May-30 Sep. € 12.50
                                                                 2010*

⊞ **PORTIMAO** *B4* (3km SE Coastal) *37.11301, -8.51096* **Camping Ferragudo, 8400-280 Ferragudo [282 461121; fax 282 461355; cclferragudo@clubecampismolisboa.pt; www.clubecampismolisboa.pt]** Leave N125 at sp Ferraguda, turn L at traff lts at end of Parchal vill onto N539. Foll sp to site. V lge, terr, pt shd; wc (some cont); mv service pnt; shwrs inc; el pnts (6A) inc; gas; lndry rm; shop; rest; snacks; bar; playgrnd; pool; sw & fishing 800m; entmnt; TV; 90% statics; no dogs; phone; bus 1km; v cr Jul/Aug; red low ssn; CCI. "Helpful staff; bus to Portimão at ent; shop/recep 1.5km fr pitches; unsuitable lge m'vans; housing bet site & beach." € 26.00   2010*

⊞ **PORTIMAO** *B4* (10km SW Rural) *37.13500, -8.59027* **Parque de Campismo da Dourada, 8500-053 Alvor [282 459178; fax 282 458002; campingdourada@hotmail.com]** Turn S at W end of N125 Portimão by-pass sp Alvor. Site on L in 4km bef ent town. V lge, pt sl, terr, shd; wc; chem disp; shwrs inc; el pnts (6A) €2.50; gas; lndtte; shop high ssn; rest; snacks; bar; playgrnd; pool; paddling pool; sand beach 1km; fishing; sports area; entmnt; TV rm; dogs €2; bus adj; poss noisy; red long stay/low ssn; CCI. "Friendly & helpful, family-run site; office poss unattended in winter, ltd facs & site untidy; excel rest; lovely town & beaches." ♦ € 19.00   2010*

⊞ **PORTIMAO** *B4* (7.5km NW Rural) *37.17286, -8.61323* **Camping Rural Chickenrun, Varzea do Farello, 8500-132 Mexilhoeira Grande [968 451636 (mob); chickenrun4077@aol.com; www.chickenrun.vpweb.co.uk]** W fr Portimão on A22, foll sp Mexilhoeira Grande & site. Site 1km N of Mexilhoeira Grande. Med, hdstg, pt shd; wc; chem disp; mv service pnt; shwrs; el pnts ((6A) €2.50; lndtte; tradsmn; snacks; bar; BBQ; pool; sand beach 8km; wifi; sat TV; dogs; bus 1km; Eng spkn; adv bkg; quiet; CCI. "Excel, rustic, peaceful setting amongst citrus & olive trees; helpful owners." ♦ € 7.00   2010*

⊞ **PORTO** *B1* (11km N Coastal) *41.2675, -8.71972* **Camping ORBITUR-Angeiras, Rua de Angeiras, Matosinhos, 4455-039 Lavra [229 270571 or 270634; fax 229 271178; infoangeiras@orbitur.pt; www.orbitur.pt]** Fr ICI/A28 take turn-off sp Lavra, site sp at end of slip rd. Site in approx 3km - app rd potholed & cobbled. Lge, pt sl, shd; wc (some cont); chem disp; mv service pnt; shwrs inc; el pnts (6A) €3-4 (check earth); gas; lndtte (inc dryer); shop; tradsmn; rest; snacks; bar; BBQ; playgrnd; pool; paddling pool; sand beach 400m; tennis; fishing; games area; games rm; wifi; entmnt; cab/sat TV; 70% statics; dogs €1.50; phone; bus to Porto at site ent; car wash; Eng spkn; adv bkg; red low ssn/long stay/snr citizens; ccard acc; CCI. "Friendly & helpful staff; clean, dated san facs; gd rest; gd pitches in trees at end of site but ltd space lge o'fits; fish & veg mkt in Matosinhos." ♦ € 26.70   2011*

⊞ **PORTO** *B1* (16km SE Rural) *41.03972, -8.42666* **Campidouro Parque de Medas, Lugar do Gavinho, 4515-397 Medas-Gondomar [224 760162; fax 224 769082; geral@campidouro.pt]** Take N12 dir Gondomar off A1. Almost immed take R exit sp Entre-os-Rios. At rndabt pick up N108 & in approx 14km. Sp for Medas on R, thro hamlet & forest for 3km & foll sp for site on R. Long, steep app. New concrete access/site rds. Lge, mkd pitch, hdstg, terr, pt shd; wc; chem disp; mv service pnt; serviced pitches; shwrs inc; el pnts (3-6A) €2.73 (poss rev pol); gas; lndtte; shop, rest (w/end only low ssn); bar; playgrnd; pool & paddling pool; rv sw, fishing, boating; tennis; games rm; entmnt; TV rm; 90% statics; phone; bus to Porto; poss cr; quiet; ccard acc; red CCI. "Beautiful site on Rv Douro; helpful owners; gd rest; clean facs; sm level area (poss cr by rv & pool) for tourers - poss noisy at night & waterlogged after heavy rain; bus to Porto rec as parking diff (ltd buses at w/end)." € 17.10   2008*

⊞ **PORTO** *B1* (6km SW Coastal) *41.11055, -8.66083* **Camping Marisol, Rua Alto das Chaquedas 82, Canidelo, 400-356 Vila Nova de Gaia [227 135942; fax 227 126351]** Fr Porto ring rd IC1 take N109 exit sp Espinho. In 1km take exit Madalena. Site sp on coast rd. Med, hdg pitch, pt shd; wc; chem disp; mv service pnt; shwrs inc; el pnts (6A) €2.50; gas; lndry rm; shop; rest; bar; BBQ; playgrnd; pool 800m; sand beach adj; games area; car wash; TV; 50% statics; dogs €1.80; bus 150m; poss cr; Eng spkn. "Conv for Porto; gd." ♦ € 13.50   2009*

PORTUGAL

⊞ **PORTO** *B1* (10km SW Coastal/Urban) *41.10777, -8.65611* **Camping ORBITUR-Madalena, Rua do Cerro 608, Praia da Madalena, 4405-736 Vila Nova de Gaia [227 122520 or 122524; fax 227 122534; infomadalena@orbitur.pt; www. orbitur.pt]** Fr Porto ring rd IC1/A44 take A29 exit dir Espinho. In 1km take exit slip rd sp Madalena opp Volvo agent. Watch for either 'Campismo' or 'Orbitur' sp to site along winding, cobbled rd. Lge, terr, pt sl, pt shd; wc (some cont); chem disp; mv service pnt; baby facs; shwrs inc; el pnts (6A) €3; gas; lndtte; shop; tradsmn; rest, snacks, bar in ssn; BBQ; playgrnd; pool; paddling pool; sand beach 250m; tennis; games area; games rm; wifi; entmnt; TV rm; 40% statics; dogs €1.50; phone; bus to Porto; car wash; Eng spkn; adv bkg; ccard acc; red low ssn/long stay/snr citizens; CCI. "Site in forest; restricted area for tourers; slight aircraft noise; some uneven pitches; poss ltd facs low ssn; excel bus to Porto cent fr site ent - do not take c'van into Porto." ♦ € 26.70   2011*

PORTO COVO see Sines *B4*

⊞ **POVOA DE VARZIM** *B1* (13km N Coastal) *41.46277, -8.77277* **Camping ORBITUR-Rio Alto, EN13, Km 13, Lugar do Rio Alto, Estela, 4570-275 Póvoa de Varzim [252 615699; fax 252 615599; inforioalto@orbitur.pt; www.orbitur.pt]** Fr A28 exit Póvoa onto N13 N; turn L 1km N of Estela at yellow Golf sp by hotel, in 2km (cobbles) turn R to camp ent. V lge, some hdg/mkd pitch, unshd; wc; chem disp; mv service pnt; baby facs; shwrs inc; el pnts (5-15A) €3-4; gas; lndtte (inc dryer); shop; tradsmn; rest; snacks; bar; BBQ; playgrnd; pool high ssn; sand beach 150m; tennis; games area; games rm; golf adj; wifi; entmnt; cab/sat TV; 50% static/ semi-statics; dogs €1.50; phone; bus 2km; car wash; poss cr; Eng spkn; adv bkg; poss cr; red low ssn/long stay/snr citizens; ccard acc; CCI. "Excel facs; helpful staff; vg rest on site; direct access to vg beach (steep sl); strong NW prevailing wind; excel touring base." ♦ € 29.00 SBS - W19   2011*

PRAIA DE MIRA see Mira *B2*

PRAIA DE QUIAIOS *B2* (2km W Coastal) *40.2200, -8.88666* **Camping ORBITUR, Praia de Quiaios, 3080-515 Quiaios [233 919995; fax 233 919996; infoquiaios@orbitur.pt; www.orbitur.pt]** Fr N109 turn W onto N109-8 dir Quiaios, foll sp 3km to Praia de Quiaios & site. Lge, some mkd pitch, pt shd; wc; chem disp; mv service pnt; shwrs inc; el pnts (10A) €3-4; gas; lndtte; supmkt; tradsmn; rest; snacks; bar; BBQ; playgrnd; pool 500m; sand beach 500m; tennis; cycle hire; games rm; TV; entmnt; 20% statics; dogs €1.50; phone; car wash; Eng spkn; adv bkg; quiet; ccard acc; red low ssn/snr citizens/long stay; CCI. "Interesting historical area; vg touring base; peaceful site; hot water to shwrs only; care needed some pitches due soft sand." ♦ 1 Jan-16 Oct. € 21.20   2010*

⊞ **QUARTEIRA** *C4* (2km N Coastal/Urban) *37.06722, -8.08666* **Camping ORBITUR-Quarteira, Estrada da Fonte Santa, Sá Carneira, 8125-618 Quarteira [289 302826 or 302821; fax 289 302822; infoquarteira@orbitur.pt; www.orbitur. pt]** Fr E & IP1/A22 take exit junc 12 at Loulé onto N396 to Quarteira; in 8.5km at rndabt by g'ge L along dual c'way. In 1km at traff lts fork R into site. No advance sp to site. V lge, mkd pitch, pt sl, terr, pt shd; wc; chem disp; mv service pnt; shwrs inc; el pnts (6A) €3-4 (long lead req some pitches); gas; lndtte (inc dryer); supmkt 200m; tradsmn; rest; snacks; bar; BBQ; playgrnd; pool; paddling pool; waterslide; sand beach 600m; tennis; games rm; wifi; entmnt; TV rm; 40% statics (tour ops); dogs €2; phone; bus 50m; car wash; Eng spkn; adv bkg; aircraft noise fr Faro; red low ssn/long stay/snr citizens; ccard acc; CCI. "Lovely site; popular winter long stay; narr site rds & tight turns; some o'hanging trees; some pitches diff lge o'fits; gd san facs; caterpillar problem Jan-Mar; easy walk to town; mkt Wed." ♦ € 30.10 SBS - W15   2010*

ROSARIO see Alandroal *C3*

⊞ **SAGRES** *B4* (2km W Coastal) *37.02305, -8.94555* **Camping ORBITUR, Cerro das Moitas, 8650-998 Vila de Sagres [282 624371; fax 282 624445; infosagres@orbitur.pt; www.orbitur.pt]** On N268 to Cape St Vincent; well sp. Lge, hdg/mkd pitch, hdstg, pt shd; wc; chem disp; mv service pnt; shwrs inc; el pnts (6-10A) €3-4; gas; lndtte (inc dryer); shop; rest; snacks; bar; BBQ; playgrnd; sand beach 2km; cycle hire; games rm; wifi; TV rm; dogs €1.50; car wash; Eng spkn; adv bkg; quiet; red long stay/low ssn/snr citizens; ccard acc. "Vg, clean, tidy site in pine trees; helpful staff; hot water to shwrs only; cliff walks." ♦ € 25.60   2010*

⊞ **SANTO ANTONIO DAS AREIAS** *C3* (1km SE Rural) *39.40992, -7.34075* **Camping Asseiceira, Asseiceira, 7330-204 Santo António das Areias [tel/fax 245 992940; gary-campingasseiceira@hotmail.com; www.campingasseiceira.com]** Fr N246-1 turn off sp Marvão/Santo António das Areias. Turn L to Santo António das Areias then 1st R on ent town then immed R again, up sm hill to rndabt. At rndabt turn R then at next rndabt cont straight on. There is a petrol stn on R, cont down hill for 400m. Site on L. Sm, pt sl, pt shd; wc; chem disp; shwrs inc; el pnts (16A) €4; gas 500m; shop, rest 3km; snacks; bar; pool; wifi; no statics; dogs €1; bus 1km; quiet; CCI. "Attractive area; peaceful, well-equipped, remote site among olive trees; clean, tidy; gd for walking, birdwatching; helpful, friendly, British owners; excel shower block on site recently rebuilt and maintained to a high standard; nr Spanish border; excel." ♦ € 15.00
2011*

SAO GIAO see Oliveira do Hospital *C2*

SAO JACINTO see Aveiro *B2*

⊞ **SAO MARCOS DA SERRA** *B4* (3km S Rural) *37.3350, -8.3467* **Campismo Rural Quinta Odelouca, Vale Grande de Baixo, CxP 644-S, 8375-215 São Marcos da Serra [282 361718; info@quintaodelouca.com; www.quintaodelouca.com]** Fr N (Ourique) on IC1 pass São Marcos da Serra & in approx 2.5km turn R & cross blue rlwy bdge. At bottom turn L & at cont until turn R for Vale Grande (paved rd changes to unmade). Foll sp to site. Fr S exit A22 junc 9 onto IC1 dir Ourique. Pass São Bartolomeu de Messines & at km 710.5 turn L & cross blue rlwy bdge, then as above. Sm, terr, pt shd; wc; chem disp; baby facs; shwrs inc; el pnts (10A) €2.10; lndtte; shop 3km; tradsmn; rest 2km; bar; BBQ; pool; lake sw; wifi; dogs €1; Eng spkn; adv bkg; quiet; CCI. "Helpful, friendly Dutch owners; phone ahead bet Nov & Feb; beautiful views; gd walks; vg." € 13.10
2009*

⊞ **SAO MARTINHO DO PORTO** *B2* (1.5km NE Coastal) *39.52280, -9.12310* **Parque de Campismo Colina do Sol, Serra dos Mangues, 2460-697 São Martinho do Porto [262 989764; fax 262 989763; parque.colina.sol@clix.pt; www.colinadosol.net]** Leave A8/IC1 SW at junc 21 onto N242 W to São Martinho, by-pass town on N242 dir Nazaré. Site on L. Lge, mkd pitch, hdstg, terr, pt shd; wc; chem disp; mv service pnt; shwrs inc; el pnts (6A) €2.75; gas; lndtte; shop high ssn; rest; snacks; bar; BBQ; playgrnd; pool; paddling pool; sand beach 2km; fishing; games area; games rm; TV; mobile homes/c'vans for hire; dogs €1; phone; bus 2km; site clsd at Xmas; poss cr; Eng spkn; adv bkg; quiet; ccard acc; CCI. "Gd touring base on attractive coastline; gd walking, cycling; vg san facs; excel site." ♦ € 20.60
2011*

See advertisement

⊞ **SAO PEDRO DE MOEL** *B2* (N Urban/Coastal) *39.75861, -9.02583* **Camping ORBITUR-São Pedro de Moel, Rua Volta do Sete, São Pedro de Moel, 2430 Marinha Grande [244 599168; fax 244 599148; infospedro@orbitur.pt; www.orbitur.pt]** Site at end of rd fr Marinha Grande to beach; turn R at 1st rndabt on ent vill. Site S of lighthouse. V lge, some hdg/mkd pitch, hdstg, pt terr, shd; wc; chem disp; mv service pnt; shwrs inc; el pnts (6A) €3-4 (poss rev pol); gas; lndtte; shop; tradsmn; rest; snacks; bar; BBQ; playgrnd; htd pool; paddling pool; waterslide; sand beach 500m (heavy surf); fishing; tennis; cycle hire; games rm; wifi; entmnt; cab/sat TV; some statics; dogs €1.50; phone; car wash; poss cr; Eng spkn; car low ssn/long stay/snr citizens; ccard acc; CCI. "Friendly, well-run, clean site in pine woods; easy walk to shops, rests; gd cycling to beaches; São Pedro smart resort; ltd facs low ssn site in attractive area and well run." ♦ € 28.60 SBS - W18
2011*

⊞ **SAO TEOTONIO** *B4* (7km W Coastal) *37.49497, -8.78667* **Camping Monte Carvalhal da Rocha, Praia do Carvalhal, Brejão, 7630-569 São Teotónio [282 947293; fax 282 947294; geral@montecarvalhalr-turismo.com; www.montecarvalhaldarocha.com]** Turn W off N120 dir Brejão & Carvalhal; site in 4.5km. Site sp. Med, shd; wc; shwrs inc; el pnts (16A) inc; gas; lndtte; shop, rest, snacks, bar high ssn; BBQ; playgrnd; sand beach 500m; fishing; cycle hire; TV; some statics; no dogs; phone; bus 2km; car wash; Eng spkn; adv bkg; quiet; ccard acc; red low ssn. "Beautiful area; friendly, helpful staff." € 26.00
2009*

SAO TEOTONIO *B4* (7km W Coastal) *37.52560, -8.77560* **Parque de Campismo da Zambujeira, Praia da Zambujeira, 7630-740 Zambujeira do Mar [283 961172; fax 283 961320; www.campingzambujeira.com.sapo.pt]** S on N120 twd Lagos, turn W when level with São Teotónio on unclassified rd to Zambujeira. Site on L in 7km, bef vill. V lge, pt sl, pt shd; wc; chem disp; mv service pnt; shwrs inc; el pnts (6-10A) €3; gas; shop, rest, snacks & bar high ssn; playgrnd; sand beach 1km; tennis; TV; dogs €4; phone; bus adj; Eng spkn; some rd noise; red low ssn/long stay. "Welcoming, friendly owners; in pleasant rural setting; hot water to shwrs only; sh walk to unspoilt vill with some shops & rest; cliff walks." Easter-31 Oct. € 24.50
2010*

SATAO *C2* (10km N Rural) *40.82280, -7.6961* **Camping Quinta Chave Grande, Casfreires, Ferreira d'Aves, 3560-043 Sátão [232 665552; fax 232 665352; chave-grande@sapo.pt; www.chavegrande.com]** Leave IP5 Salamanca-Viseu rd onto N229 to Sátão, site sp in Satão - beyond Lamas. Med, terr, pt shd; wc; chem disp; baby facs; shwrs inc; el pnts (6A) €3; gas; lndtte; shop 3km; tradsmn; rest 3km; snacks; bar; playgrnd; pool; paddling pool; tennis; games area; games rm; internet; TV; dogs €1.50; Eng spkn; quiet; red long stay. "Warm welcome fr friendly Dutch owners; gd facs; well organised BBQs - friendly atmosphere; gd touring base; gd walks fr site; excel." 15 Mar-31 Oct. € 17.00
2009*

田 **SERPA** C4 (1km W Urban) 37.94090, -7.60404 **Parque Municipal de Campismo Serpa, Rua da Eira São Pedro, 7830-303 Serpa [284 544290; fax 284 540109]** Fr IP8 take 1st sp for town; site well sp fr most directions - opp sw pool. Do not ent walled town. Med, pt sl, pt shd; wc; chem disp; shwrs inc; el pnts (6A) €1.25; gas; lndtte; shop 200m; rest, snacks, bar 50m; BBQ; daily mkt 500m; supmkt nr; pool adj; rv sw 5km; 20% statics; dogs; phone; adv bkg; some rd noise; no ccard acc; CCI. "Popular site; simple, high quality facs; interesting, historic town." ♦ € 7.75   2009*

田 **SESIMBRA** B3 (1km W Coastal) 38.43580, -9.11658 **Camp Municipal Forte do Cavalo, Porto de Abrigo, 2970 Sesimbra [212 288508; fax 212 288265; geral@cm-sesimbra.pt; www.cm-sesimbra.pt]** Fr Lisbon S on A2/IP7 turn S onto N378 to Sesimbra. Turn R immed after town ent sp Campismo & Porto. Fork R again sp Porto; L downhill at traff lts to avoid town cent. Turn R at sea front to site by lighthouse. Steep uphill app. V lge, pt sl, terr, shd; wc; shwrs inc; el pnts (6A) €2.15; gas; shop, rest 1km; snacks, bar 500m; BBQ; playgrnd; beach 800m; fishing; boating; no dogs; phone; bus 100m; poss cr; Eng spkn; no adv bkg; quiet; CCI. "Pitches ltd for tourers; gd views; lovely, unique fishing vill; castle worth visit; unreliable opening dates (poss not open until Jun) - phone ahead." € 13.35   2010*

田 **SETUBAL** B3 (4km W Coastal) 38.50299, -8.92909 **Parque de Campismo do Outão, Estrada de Rasca, 2900-182 Setúbal [265 238318; fax 265 228098]** Fr Setúbal take coast rd W twd Outão, site on L. V lge, mkd pitch, hdstg, pt shd; wc (some cont); chem disp; shwrs inc; el pnts (5A) inc; gas; shop; rest; bar; playgrnd; sand beach adj; 90% statics; dogs €1.50; poss cr; Eng spkn; some rd noise; ccard acc; red low ssn; red CCI. "Few pitches for tourers; hdstg not suitable for awning; vacant static pitches sm & have kerb." ♦ € 19.80   2010*

田 **TAVIRA** C4 (5km E Rural/Coastal) 37.14506, -7.60223 **Camping Ria Formosa, Quinta da Gomeira, 8800-591 Cabanas-Tavira [281 328887; fax 281 326087; info@ campingriaformosa.com; www.campingriaformosa.com]** Fr N125 turn S at Conceição dir 'Cabanas Tavira' & 'Campismo'. Cross rlwy line & turn L to site, sp. V lge, mkd pitch, hdstg, terr, pt shd; htd wc; chem disp; mv service pnt; baby facs; shwrs inc; el pnts (16A) €3; gas; lndtte (inc dryer); shop; tradsmn; rest; snacks; bar; BBQ; playgrnd; pool; paddling pool; cycle hire; sand beach 1.2km; games area; wifi; TV rm; dogs €2; bus 100m; train 100m; car wash; Eng spkn; adv bkg; quiet; ccard acc; red long stay/CCI. "Excel site; friendly, welcoming owner & staff; vg, modern san facs; various pitch sizes; cycle path to Tavira." ♦ € 19.60   2011*

田 **TOCHA** B2 (7.5km W Coastal) 40.32777, -8.84027 **Camping Praia da Tocha, Rua dos Pescadores, Nossa Sra da Tocha, Praia da Tocha, 3060-691 Tocha [231 447112; tocha@ cacampings.com; www.cacampings.com]** Fr N or S on N109, turn W onto N335 to Praia da Tocha, site sp. Med, pt shd; wc; chem disp; baby facs; shwrs; el pnts (4-6A) €1.85; gas; lndtte (inc dryer); shop, rest, snacks, bar high ssn; playgrnd; sand beach 200m; watersports; cycle hire; internet; TV rm; dogs €1.55; phone; bus adj; Eng spkn; adv bkg; quiet; CCI. "Well-maintained, pleasant site; helpful staff." ♦ € 11.80
2009*

田 **TOMAR** B2 (N Urban) 39.60694, -8.41027 **Campismo Parque Municipal, 2300-000 Tomar [249 329824; fax 249 322608; camping@cm-tomar.pt; www.cm-tomar.pt]** Fr S on N110 foll sp to town cent at far end of stadium. Fr N (Coimbra) on N110 turn R immed bef bdge. Site well sp fr all dirs. Med, mkd pitch, pt shd; htd wc; chem disp; mv service pnt; baby facs; shwrs inc; el pnts (10A) €1.40; lndry rm; tradsmn; shop, rest, snacks, bar in town; BBQ; playgrnd; pool adj; wifi; TV; no statics; dogs; phone adj; Eng spkn; adv bkg; quiet; red low ssn; ccard acc; CCI. "Useful base for touring Alcobaca, Batalha & historic monuments in Tomar; conv Fatima; Convento de Cristo worth visit; vg, popular, improved site; charming rvside town; easy access for lge vehicle, camp entry ticket gives free access to adj pool." € 16.00   2011*

I'll fill in a report online and let the Club know – www.caravanclub.co.uk/ europereport

This is a wonderful site.

TOMAR B2 (7km NE Rural) 39.63833, -8.33694 **Camping Pelinos, Casal das Aboboreiras, 2300-093 Tomar [249 301814; pelinos1@hotmail.com; www.campingpelinos.com]** N fr Tomar on N110, turn R to Calçadas at traff lts opp g'ge, foll site sp. Steep descent to site. Sm, terr, pt shd; wc; shwrs inc; el pnts (10A) €2; lndtte; rest; snacks; bar; BBQ (winter only); playgrnd; pool; lake sw, watersports, fishing 7km; TV; dogs; phone; bus 100m; Eng spkn; adv bkg; quiet; red low ssn; CCI. "Owner will assist taking o'fits in/out; vg." 15 Feb-15 Oct. € 11.50   2010*

田 **TOMAR** B2 (10km E Rural) 39.62538, -8.32166 **Camping Redondo, Rua do Casal Rei 6, 2300-035 Poço Redondo [tel/fax 249 376421; info@campingredondo.co.uk; www. campingredondo.com]** Fr N or S on N110, take IC3 for Tomar, then take exit at km97 Castelo do Bode/Tomar, dir Junceira. Foll site sp (red hearts) for 7km. Steep drop at site ent. Sm, pt sl, pt shd; wc; chem disp; mv service pnt; baby facs; shwrs inc; el pnts (6A) €2-2.30; lndtte; shop 2km; rest; snacks; bar; BBQ; playgrnd; pool; waterslide; lake beach 4.5km; sat TV; few statics; dogs €1; phone; bus; poss cr; Eng spkn; adv bkg; red low ssn; CCI. "Due steep drop at ent, site owner can tow c'vans out; peaceful site; friendly, helpful owners; excel walking area." € 13.60   2010*

TOMAR B2 (10km SE Rural) 39.53963, -8.31895 **Camping Castelo do Bode, 2200 Martinchel [241 849262; fax 241 849244; castelo.bode@fcmportugal.com]** S fr Tomar on N110, in approx 7km L onto N358-2 dir Barragem & Castelo do Bode. Site on L in 6km immed after dam; sh, steep app to ent. Med, mkd pitch, hdstg, terr, pt shd; wc (some cont); chem disp; shwrs inc; el pnts (6A) inc; supmkt 6km; tradsmn; rest, snacks 2km; bar; playgrnd; lake sw adj; boating; fishing; dogs €0.60; phone; bus to Tomar 1km; no adv bkg; quiet; CCI. "Site on edge of 60km long lake with excel watersports; old san facs, but clean; helpful staff; lge car park on ent Tomar - interesting town." ♦ 13 Jan-11 Nov. € 12.25   2011*

PORTUGAL

TRAVANCA DE LAGOS see Oliveira do Hospital *C2*

⊞ **VAGOS** *B2* (8km W Rural) *40.55805, -8.74527* **Camping ORBITUR-Vagueira, Rua do Parque de Campismo, 3840-254 Gafanha da Boa-Hora [234 797526; fax 234 797093; infovagueira@orbitur.pt; www.orbitur.pt]** Fr Aveiro take N109 S twd Figuera da Foz. Turn R in Vagos vill. After 6km along narr poor rd, site on R bef reaching Vagueira vill. V lge, mkd pitch, shd; wc; chem disp; mv service pnt; baby facs; shwrs inc; el pnts (6-16A) €3-4; gas; lndtte; supmkt, tradsmn, rest, bar high ssn; playgrnd; pool 1km; sand beach 1.5km; fishing 1km; tennis; games area; games rm; cycle hire; wifi; entmnt; 90% statics; dogs €1.50; Eng spkn; adv bkg; quiet; ccard acc; red low ssn/snr citizens; CCI. "V pleasant & well-run; friendly staff; poss diff access to pitches for lge o'fits; areas soft sand; gd touring base." ♦ € 21.20 (CChq acc) 2010*

VALHELHAS *C2* (1km W Rural) *40.40388, -7.40611* **Camp Municipal Rossio de Valhelhas, 6300-235 Valhelhas [275 487160; fax 275 487372; jfvalhelhas@clix.pt; www.valhelhas.com]** Fr Manteigas, site is on R of N232 on ent Valhelhas. Lge, shd; wc; shwrs inc; el pnts (5-10A) €1 (long lead req); lndry rm; shop 150m; rest 300m; snacks; bar; playgrnd; rv adj; fishing; games area; few statics; phone; bus 100m; poss cr; quiet; ccard not acc; CCI. "Pleasant, woodland site; conv for touring Serra da Estrela; rv dammed to make natural sw pool; friendly, helpful staff." 1 May-30 Sep. € 9.75 2008*

VALVERDE see Lagos *B4*

⊞ **VIANA DO CASTELO** *B1* (3km S Coastal) *41.67908, -8.82324* **Parque de Campismo Inatel do Cabedelo, Avda dos Trabalhadores, 4900-164 Darque [258 322042; fax 258 331502; pc.cabedelo@inatel.pt; www.inatel.pt]** Exit IC1 junc 11 to W sp Darque, Cabedelo, foll sp to site. Lge, mkd pitch, hdstg, pt sl, pt shd; wc (some cont); shwrs inc; el pnts (6A) inc; gas; lndtte; shop high ssn; tradsmn; snacks; bar; sand beach adj; entmnt; 30% statics; no dogs; phone; bus 100m; site clsd mid-Dec to mid-Jan; adv bkg; quiet; CCI. "V secure; gd for children; hourly ferry to Viana; spacious pitches under pines; poss poor facs low ssn & in need of refurb." ♦ € 12.50 2009*

⊞ **VIANA DO CASTELO** *B1* (2km SW Coastal/Urban) *41.67888, -8.82583* **Camping ORBITUR-Viana do Castelo, Rua Diogo Álvares, Cabedelo, 4935-161 Darque [258 322167; fax 258 321946; infoviana@orbitur.pt; www.orbitur.pt]** Exit IC1 junc 11 to W sp Darque, Cabedelo, foll sp to site in park. Lge, mkd pitch, pt sl, shd; wc; chem disp; mv service pnt; shwrs inc; el pnts (5-15A) €3-4; gas; lndtte; shop; tradsmn; rest; snacks; bar; BBQ; playgrnd; htd pool; lge sand beach adj; surfing; fishing; wifi; entmnt; TV; dogs €1.50; phone; car wash; Eng spkn; adv bkg; quiet; red low ssn/long stay/snr citizens; ccard acc; CCI. "Site in pine woods; friendly staff; gd facs; plenty of shade; major festival in Viana 3rd w/end in Aug; lge mkt in town Fri; sm passenger ferry over Rv Lima to town high ssn; Santa Luzia worth visit." ♦ € 29.10 2011*

VIEIRA DO MINHO *C1* (800m SE Urban) *41.63333, -8.13583* **Parque de Campismo de Cabreira, 4850 Vieira do Minho [253 648665; fax 253 648395; bina.vc@mail.telepac.pt; www.vieiraminhoturismo.com]** Take N103 E fr Braga for 30km; foll sp to Vieira Do Minho, site sp in Vieira. Lge, pt shd; wc; chem disp (wc); shwrs inc; el pnts (5A) €2.50; gas; lndtte; shop; rest; snacks; bar; playgrnd; 2 pools adj; rv adj; tennis; sports area; cycle hire; entmnt; phone; bus 1km; Eng spkn; quiet; CCI. "Gd, level grassy site; conv Gerês National Park." ♦ 1 Feb-31 Oct. € 14.50 2008*

⊞ **VILA DO BISPO** *B4* (8km SE Coastal/Rural) *37.07542, -8.83133* **Quinta dos Carriços (Part Naturist), Praia de Salema, 8650-196 Budens [282 695201; fax 282 695122; quintacarrico@oninet.pt; www.quintadoscarricos.com]** Take N125 out of Lagos twd Sagres. In approx 14km at sp Salema, turn L & again immed L twd Salema. Site on R 300m. Lge, pt terr (tractor avail), pt shd; htd wc; chem disp; mv service pnt; shwrs €0.75; el pnts (6-10A) €3.90 (metered for long stay); gas; lndtte; shop; rest; snacks; bar; playground; pool 1km; sand beach 1km; golf 1km; TV; 8% statics; dogs €2.45; phone; bus; Eng spkn; adv bkg (ess high ssn); noise fr adj quarry; ccard acc; red long stay/CCI. "Naturist section in sep valley; apartments avail on site; ltd pitches for lge o'fits; friendly Dutch owners; tractor avail to tow to terr; area of wild flowers in spring; beach 30 mins walk; buses pass ent for Lagos, beach & Sagres; excel." ♦ € 25.50 2011*

⊞ **VILA FLOR** *C1* (2.5km SW Rural) *41.29420, -7.17180* **Camp Municipal de Vila Flor, Barragem do Peneireiro, 5360-303 Vila Flor [278 512350; fax 278 512380; cm.vila.flor@mail.telepac.pt; www.cm-vilaflor.pt]** Site is off N215, sp fr all dirs. V bumpy app rd - 12km. V lge, terr, pt shd; wc; chem disp (wc); shwrs inc; el pnts (16A) €1.50; gas; lndry rm; shop; snacks; bar; BBQ; playgrnd; pool adj; tennis adj; TV rm; 10% statics; dogs; phone; clsd 2300-0700 (1800-0800 low ssn); poss v cr; adv bkg; noisy high ssn; CCI. "Friendly staff; access to pitches diff." ♦ € 9.40 2010*

VILA NOVA DE CACELA see Vila Real de Santo Antonio *C4*

⊞ **VILA NOVA DE CERVEIRA** *B1* (5km E Rural) *41.94362, -8.69365* **Parque de Campismo Convívio, Rua de Badão, 1 Bacelo, 4920-020 Candemil [251 794404; convivio@vodafone.pt; http://convivio.planetaclix.pt]** Fr Vila Nova de Cerveira dir Candemil on N13/N302, turn L at Bacelo, site sp. Sm, terr, pt shd; wc; chem disp; shwrs inc; el pnts (6A) €2.50; lndtte; shop 2km; tradsmn; rest 4km; snacks; bar; BBQ; htd pool; games rm; no statics; dogs €0.85; phone; bus/train 5km; poss cr; Eng spkn; adv bkg; quiet; red long stay; CCI. "No twin-axle c'vans acc; site open Oct-Mar for adv bkgs only." 1 Apr-1 Oct. € 13.00 2007*

VILA NOVA DE GAIA see Porto *B1*

⊞ **VILA NOVA DE MILFONTES** *B4* (1km N Coastal)
37.73194, -8.78277 **Camping Milfontes, 7645-300 Vila Nova de Milfontes [283 996140; fax 283 996104; geral@ parquemilfontes.com; www.campingmilfontes.com]** S fr Sines on N120/IC4 for 22km; turn R at Cercal on N390 SW for Milfontes on banks of Rio Mira; clear sp. V lge, hdg/mkd pitch, pt shd; wc; chem disp; mv service pnt; shwrs inc; el pnts (6A) €2 (long lead poss req); gas; lndtte; shop; supmkt & mkt 5 mins walk; rest, snacks, bar high ssn; playgrnd; sand beach 800m; TV; many statics; phone; bus 600m; poss cr; quiet; ccard acc; red CCI. "Pitching poss diff for lge o'fits due trees & statics; nr fishing vill at mouth Rv Mira with beaches & sailing on rv; pleasant site." ♦ € 18.00   2009*

We can fill in site report forms on the Club's website – www.caravanclub.co.uk/ europereport

VILA PRAIA DE ANCORA *B1* (7km S Coastal) *41.80255, -8.84821* **Parque de Campismo do Paço, 4910-024 Vila Praia de Âncora [tel/fax 258 912697; geral@campingpaco. com; www.campingpaco]** Fr N13 Caminha-Viana do Castelo, site sp 1km S of Âncora, km 81. Med, pt shd; wc; chem disp; mv service pnt; shwrs inc; el pnts (6A) €2.25; gas; lndtte; shop; tradsmn; rest; snacks; bar; BBQ; playgrnd; pool 1.5km; sand beach 1km; fishing; canoeing; games area; TV; phone; bus 600m; car wash; adv bkg; Eng spkn; quiet; ccard acc; red CCI. "Pleasant staff; excel san facs; vg touring base; gd beaches nr." 15 Apr-30 Sep. € 14.70   2007*

VILA REAL *C1* (500m NE Urban) *41.30361, -7.73694* **Camping Vila Real, Rua Dr Manuel Cardona, 5000-558 Vila Real [259 324724]** On IP4/E82 take Vila Real N exit & head S into town. Foll 'Centro' sp to Galp g'ge; at Galp g'ge rndabt, turn L & in 30m turn L again. Site at end of rd in 400m. Site sp fr all dirs. Lge, pt sl, terr, pt shd; wc; chem disp; baby facs; shwrs inc; el pnts (6A) €2; gas; sm shop adj; tradsmn; rest; snacks; bar; BBQ; playgrnd; pool complex adj; tennis; 10% statics; dogs; phone; bus 150m; poss cr; red CCI. "Conv upper Douro; gd facs ltd when site full; gd mkt in town; Lamego well worth a visit." ♦ 1 Mar-30 Nov. € 16.15   2011*

⊞ **VILA REAL DE SANTO ANTONIO** *C4* (3km W Coastal)
37.17972, -7.44361 **Parque Municipal de Campismo, 8900 Monte Gordo [281 510970; fax 281 510977; cmvrsa@ mail.telepac.pt]** Fr Faro on N125 turn R sp Monte Gordo. Site on sea front in 500m. Or fr Spain over bdge at border, exit junc 9 to Vila Real over rlwy line. Strt over rndabt & turn R at T-junc, site sp just bef ent town. V lge, pt sl, shd; wc (some cont); chem disp; shwrs inc; el pnts (10A) €1.90 (long cable poss req); gas; lndtte; shop & 1km; tradsmn; rest; snacks; bar; BBQ; playgrnd; sand beach 100m; canoeing; TV; 10% statics; dogs €3; phone; bus; train to Faro 3km; poss v cr; Eng spkn; no adv bkg; quiet; ccard acc; red low ssn/long stay/snr citizens; CCI. "V lge pitches but poss v overcr high ssn; many long stay c'vans; caution soft sand makes some pitches unreliable in wet; ground poss too soft for lge o'fits; san facs plentiful & clean; lovely area; gd security." ♦ € 13.50   2008*

⊞ **VILA REAL DE SANTO ANTONIO** *C4* (10km W Rural)
37.18649, -7.55003 **Camping Caliço Park, Sitio do Caliço, 8900-907 Vila Nova de Cacela [281 951195; fax 281 951977; transcampo@mail.telepac.pt]** On N side of N125 Vila Real to Faro rd. Sp on main rd & in Vila Nova de Cacela vill, visible fr rd. Lge, some hdstg, terr, pt sl, shd; wc; chem disp; shwrs inc; el pnts (6A) €2.80; gas; lndtte (inc dryer); shop; rest; snacks; bar; playgrnd; pool; sand beach 4km; cycle hire; wifi; many statics; dogs €1.60; phone; bus/ train 2km; Eng spkn; adv bkg; noisy in ssn & rd noise; ccard acc; red long stay/low ssn; CCI. "Friendly staff; not suitable for m'vans or tourers in wet conditions - ltd touring pitches & poss diff access; gd NH." € 17.15   2010*

VILAR DE MOUROS see Caminha *B1*

⊞ **VOUZELA** *C2* (2km E Rural) *40.71638, -8.09250* **Parque Campismo Municipal Vouzela, Monte da Senhora do Castelo, 3670-250 Vouzela [232 740020; fax 232 711513; parquecampismo@cm-vouzela.pt; www.cm-vouzela.pt]** Fr Vouzela foll N228; turn R sp Sra do Castelo. Site well sp fr town cent. Steep app. V lge, pt sl, terr, pt shd; wc; chem disp; mv service pnt; shwrs inc; el pnts (6-15A) €1.30; gas; lndry rm; shop; rest; snacks; bar; playgrnd; pool; tennis; cycle hire; entmnt; TV; 95% statics; dogs €1; phone; bus 3km; quiet except w/end; CCI. "Lovely location; poss diff to find pitch bet statics; access to higher terrs by steep hill." ♦ € 9.00   2008*

ZAMBUJEIRA DO MAR see Sao Teotonio *B4*

Distances are shown in kilometres and are calculated from town/city centres along the most practical roads, although not necessarily taking the shortest route. 1km = 0.62miles

Caravan Europe 1
Caravan Europe 2

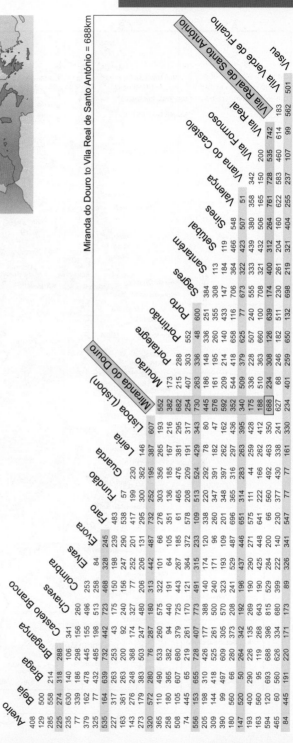

Miranda do Douro to Vila Real de Santo António = 688km

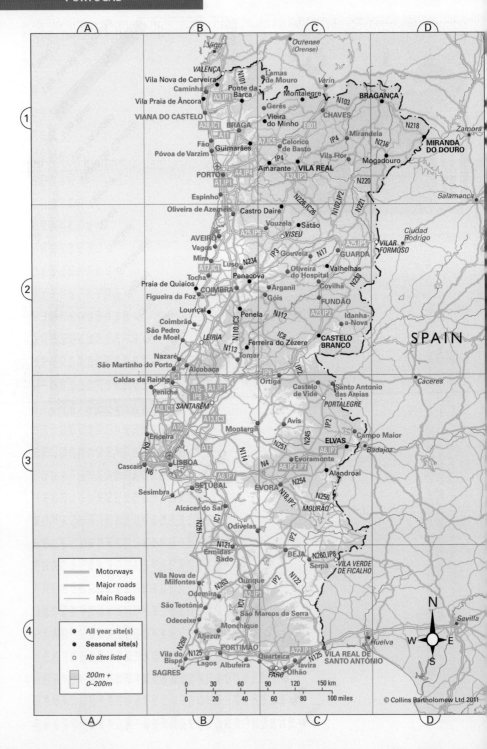

Vigo

VALENÇA
Vila Nova de Cerveira
Caminha
Vila Praia de Âncora
VIANA DO CASTELO
A28,IC1
Fão
Póvoa de Varzim
Guimarães
PORTO
A1,IP1
Espinho
Oliveira de Azeméis
AVEIRO
Vagos
Mira
Tocha
Praia de Quiaios
Figueira da Foz
Louriçal
Coimbrão
São Pedro
de Moel
Nazaré
São Martinho do Porto
Caldas da Rainha
Peniche
Ericeira
Cascais
Sesimbra
Alcácer do Sal
Vila Nova de
Milfontes
Odemira
São Teotónio
Odeceixe
Aljezur
Vila do
Bispo
SAGRES
Lagos

Ourense
(Orense)

Lamas
de Mouro
Ponte da
Barca
Montalegre
Gerés
Vieira
do Minho
A3,IP1
BRAGA
A11
A7,IC5
Celorico
de Basto
IP4
Amarante
VILA REAL
A24,IP3
N226,IC26

Verín
BRAGANÇA
N103
CHAVES
E801
IP4
Mirandela
Vila Flôr
N216
N218
MIRANDA
DO DOURO
Zamora

Mogadouro
N220
N102,IP2
N221
Salamanca

Castro Daire
Vouzela
Sátão
A25,IP5
VISEU
IP3
Gouveia
N17
Oliveira
do Hospital
Valhelhas
Arganil
Góis
Covilhã
FUNDÃO
A23,IP2
Idanha-
a-Nova

Ciudad
Rodrigo
A25,IP5
VILAR
FORMOSO
GUARDA
N233

SPAIN

A17,IC1
Luso
N234
Penacova
COIMBRA

Penela
N110,IC3
LEIRIA
N113
Ferreira do Zêzere
Tomar
IC8
N112

CASTELO
BRANCO

Alcobaça
IC1
A15-
IP6
A1,IP1
Ortiga
IP6
IP2

Castelo
de Vide
Santo Antonio
das Areias
PORTALEGRE

Cáceres

SANTARÉM
A8,IC1
A13,IC3
A10
A13
N114
Montargil
Avis
N251
N245
IP2
ELVAS
A6,IP7
Campo Maior
Badajoz

LISBOA
N6
SETÚBAL
A6,IP7
N4
Evoramonte
A6,IP2,IP7
Alandroal
ÉVORA
N18,IP2
N254
N256
MOURÃO

Odivelas
IC1
N261
N121
Ermidas-
Sado
BEJA
N260,IP8
Serpa
VILA VERDE
DE FICALHO

Sevilla

N263
Ourique
IP2
N122
A2,IP1
São Marcos da Serra
IC1
Monchique
N266
N125
PORTIMÃO
Quarteira
A22,IP1
N125
VILA REAL DE
SANTO ANTÓNIO
Albufeira
Tavira
FARO
Olhão
Huelva

Legend

	Motorways
	Major roads
	Main Roads

● All year site(s)
● Seasonal site(s)
○ No sites listed

200m +
0–200m

| 0 | 30 | 60 | 90 | 120 | 150 km |

| 0 | 20 | 40 | 60 | 80 | 100 miles |

© Collins Bartholomew Ltd 2011

N
W E
S

Spain

Country Introduction

© iStockPhoto.com/Ivan Bastien

Nerja, Andalucia

Population (approx): 46.1 million

Capital: Madrid (population approx 6.3 million)

Area: 510,000 sq km (inc Balearic & Canary Islands)

Bordered by: Andorra, France, Portugal

Terrain: High, rugged central plateau, mountains to north and south

Climate: Temperate climate; hot summers, cold winters in the interior; more moderate summers and cool winters along the northern and eastern coasts; very hot summers and mild/warm winters along the southern coast

Coastline: 4,964km

Highest Point (mainland Spain): Mulhacén (Granada) 3,478m

Languages: Castilian Spanish, Catalan, Galician, Basque

Local Time: GMT or BST + 1, i.e. 1 hour ahead of the UK all year

Currency: Euros divided into 100 cents; £1 = €1.14, €1 = 87 pence (September 2011)

Telephoning: From the UK dial 0034 for Spain.

All numbers have 9 digits, starting with 9, which incorporate the area code. Mobile phone numbers start with a 6. To call the UK from Spain dial 0044, omitting the initial zero of the area code. To call Gibraltar dial 00350

Emergency numbers: Police 112; Fire brigade 112; Ambulance (SAMUR) 112. Operators speak English. Civil Guard 062

Public Holidays 2012

Jan 2, 6; Apr 5, 6, 9; May 1; Jun 5; Oct 12 (National Holiday); Dec 6 (Constitution Day), 25, 26.

Public Holidays for 2013 not confirmed at date of publication.

Several other dates are celebrated for fiestas according to region. School summer holidays stretch from mid June to mid September.

Tourist Office

SPANISH TOURIST OFFICE
P.O. BOX 4009, LONDON W1A 6NB
Tel: 0845 9400180 (brochure requests) or 020 7486 8077
(Visits by appointment only)
www.spain.info/uk   info.londres@tourspain.es

The following introduction to Spain should be read in conjunction with the important information contained in the Handbook chapters at the front of this guide.

Camping and Caravanning

There are more than 1,200 campsites in Spain with something to suit all tastes – from some of the best and biggest holiday parks in Europe, to a wealth of attractive small sites offering a personal, friendly welcome. Most campsites are located near the Mediterranean, especially on the Costa Brava and Costa del Sol, as well as in the Pyrenees and other areas of tourist interest. Campsites are indicated by blue road signs. In general pitch sizes are small at about 80 square metres.

Recent visitors report that many popular coastal sites favoured for long winter stays may contain tightly packed pitches with long-term residents putting up large awnings, umbrellas and other secondary structures. Many sites allow pitches to be reserved from year to year, which can result in a tight knit community possibly biased to one nationality.

As a result the availability of pitches to short term tourists may be restricted to the smaller or less favoured areas of the site. If planning to stay on sites in the popular coastal areas between late spring and October, or in January and February, it is advisable to arrive early in the afternoon or to book in advance.

Although many sites claim to be open all year this cannot be relied on. It is common for many 'all year' sites to open only at weekends during the winter and facilities may be very limited. If planning a visit out of season, always check first.

A Camping Card International (CCI), while not compulsory, is recommended and is increasingly required when checking into sites. Failing that, provide reception staff with a photocopy of your passport for registration purposes rather than leave your passport for later collection. Senior citizens may be eligible for discounted prices at some sites on presentation of proof of age.

Motorhomes

A number of local authorities now provide dedicated or short stay areas for motorhomes called 'Áreas de Servicio'. For details see the websites www.lapaca.org (click on the motorhome symbol) or www.viajarenautocaravana.com for a list of regions/towns in Spain and Andorra which have at least one of these areas.

It is rare that yours will be the only motorhome staying on such areas, but take sensible precautions and avoid any that are isolated.

Some motorhome service points are situated in motorway service areas. Use these only as a last resort and do not be tempted to park overnight. The risk of a break-in is high.

Recent visitors to tourist areas on Spain's Mediterranean coast report that the parking of motorhomes on public roads and, in some instances, in public parking areas, may be prohibited in an effort to discourage 'wild camping'. Specific areas where visitors have encountered this problem include Alicante, Dénia, Palamós and the Murcian coast. Police are frequently in evidence moving parked motorhomes on and it is understood that a number of owners of motorhomes have been fined for parking on sections of the beach belonging to the local authority.

Country Information

Cycling

There are more than 1,800km of dedicated cycle paths in Spain, many of which follow disused railway tracks. Known as 'Vias Verdes' (Green Ways), they can be found mainly in northern Spain, in Andalucia, around Madrid and inland from the Costa Blanca. For more information see the website www.viasverdes.com or contact the Spanish Tourist Office.

There are cycle lanes in major cities and towns such as Barcelona, Bilbao, Córdoba, Madrid, Seville and Valencia. Madrid alone has over 100km of cycle lanes.

It is compulsory for all cyclists, regardless of age, to wear a safety helmet on all roads outside built-up areas. At night, in tunnels or in bad weather, bicycles must have front and rear lights and reflectors. Cyclists must also wear a reflective waistcoat or jacket while riding at night on roads outside built-up areas (to be visible from a distance of 150 metres) or when visibility is bad.

Strictly speaking, cyclists have right of way when motor vehicles wish to cross their path to turn left or right, but great care should always be taken. Do not proceed unless you are sure that a motorist is giving way.

Transportation of Bicycles

Spanish regulations stipulate that motor cycles or bicycles may be carried on the rear of a vehicle providing the rack to which the motorcycle or bicycle is fastened has been designed for the purpose. Lights, indicators, number plate and any signals made by the driver must not be obscured and the rack should not compromise the carrying vehicle's stability.

An overhanging load, such as bicycles, should not extend beyond the width of the vehicle but may exceed the length of the vehicle by up to 10% (up to 15% in the case of indivisible items). The load must be indicated by a 50cm x 50cm square panel with reflective red and white diagonal stripes. These panels may be purchased in the UK from motorhome or caravan dealers/accessory shops. There is currently no requirement for bicycle racks to be certified or pass a technical inspection.

If you are planning to travel from Spain to Portugal please note that slightly different official regulations apply. These are set out in the Portugal Country Introduction.

Electricity and Gas

The current on campsites should be a minimum of 4 amps but is usually more. Plugs have two round pins. Some campsites do not yet have CEE connections.

Campingaz is widely available in 901 and 907 cylinders. The Cepsa Company sells butane gas cylinders and regulators, which are available in large stores and petrol stations, and the Repsol Company sells butane cylinders at their petrol stations throughout the country. It is understood that Repsol and Cepsa depots will refill cylinders, but The Caravan Club does not recommend this practice.

French and Spanish butane and propane gas cylinders are understood to be widely available in Andorra.

See Electricity and Gas in the section DURING YOUR STAY.

Entry Formalities

Holders of valid British and Irish passports are permitted to stay up to three months without a visa. EU residents planning to stay longer are required to register in person at the Oficina de Extranjeros (Foreigners Office) in their province of residence or at a designated police station. You will be issued with a certificate confirming that the registration obligation has been fulfilled.

Regulations for Pets

See Pet Travel Scheme under Documents in the section PLANNING AND TRAVELLING.

Dogs must be kept on a lead in public places and in a car they should be isolated from the driver by means of bars or netting.

Medical Services

Basic emergency health care is available free from practitioners in the Spanish National Health Service on production of a European Health Insurance Card (EHIC). Some health centres offer both private and state provided health care and you should ensure that staff are aware which service you require. In some parts of the country you may have to travel some distance to attend a surgery or health clinic operating within the state health service. It is probably quicker and more convenient to use a private clinic, but the Spanish health service will not refund any private health care charges.

In an emergency go to the casualty department (urgencias) of any major public hospital. Urgent treatment is free in a public ward on production of an EHIC; for other treatment you will have to pay a proportion of the cost.

Medicines prescribed by health service practitioners can be obtained from a pharmacy (farmacia) and there will be a charge unless you are an EU pensioner. In all major towns there is a 24 hour pharmacy.

Dental treatment is not generally provided under the state system and you will have to pay for treatment.

The Department of Health has two offices in Spain to deal with health care enquiries from British nationals visiting or residing in Spain. These are at the British Consultate offices in Alicante and Málaga, telephone 965-21 60 22 or 952-35 23 00

You are strongly recommended to obtain comprehensive travel and medical insurance before travelling, such as The Caravan Club's Red Pennant Overseas Holiday Insurance – see www.caravanclub.co.uk/redpennant

Andorra

The EHIC is not accepted in Andorra and there are no reciprocal health care arrangements with Britain. You will have to pay the full cost of treatment.

See Medical Matters in the section DURING YOUR STAY.

Opening Hours

Banks – Mon-Fri 8.30am/9am-2pm/2.30pm, Sat 9am-1pm (many banks are closed on Saturdays during the summer months).

Museums – Tue-Sat 9am/10am-1pm/2pm & 3pm/4pm-6pm/8pm. Sun 9am/10am-2pm; closed Monday.

Post Offices – Mon-Fri 8.30am-2.30pm/2.30pm & 5pm-8pm/8.30pm, Sat 9am/9.30am-1pm/1.30pm.

Shops – Mon-Sat 9am/10am-1.30pm/2pm & 4pm/4.30pm-8pm/8.30pm; department stores and shopping centres do not close for lunch.

Safety and Security

Crime

Street crime exists in many Spanish towns and holiday resorts and is occasionally accompanied by violence. Keep all valuable personal items such as cameras or jewellery out of sight. The authorities have stepped up the police presence in tourist areas but nevertheless, you should remain alert at all times (including at airports, train and bus stations, and even in supermarkets and their car parks).

In Madrid particular care should be taken in the Puerto de Sol and surrounding streets, including the Plaza Mayor, Retiro Park and Lavapies, and on the metro. In Barcelona this advice also applies to the Ramblas, Monjuic, Plaza Catalunya, Port Vell and Olympic Port areas. Be wary of approaches by strangers either asking directions or offering any kind of help. These approaches are sometimes ploys to distract attention while they or their accomplices make off with valuables and/or take note of credit card numbers for future illegal use. Beware of muggers who use children or babies to distract your attention while you are being robbed.

The incidence of rape and sexual assault is very low; nevertheless attacks occur and are often carried out by other British nationals. Visitors are advised not to lower their personal security awareness because they are on holiday. You should also be alert to the availability and possible use of 'date rape' drugs. Purchase your own drinks and keep sight of them at all times to make sure they cannot be spiked.

A few incidents have been reported of visitors being approached by a bogus police officer asking to inspect wallets for fake euro notes, or to check their identity by keying their credit card PIN into an official looking piece of equipment carried by the officer. If in doubt ask to see a police officer's official identification, refuse to comply with the request and offer instead to go to the nearest police station.

Spanish police have set up an emergency number for holidaymakers with English speaking staff and offering round the clock assistance 902 10 2 112. An English speaking operator will take a statement about the incident, translate it into Spanish and fax or email it to the nearest police station. You still have to report in person to a police station if you have an accident, or have been robbed or swindled, and the helpline operator will advise you where to find the nearest one.

Motoring

Motorists travelling on motorways – particularly those north and south of Barcelona, in the Alicante region, on the M30, M40 and M50 Madrid ring roads and on the A4 and A5 – should be wary of approaches by bogus policemen in plain clothes travelling in unmarked cars. In all traffic related matters police officers will be in uniform. Unmarked vehicles will have a flashing electronic sign in the rear window reading 'Policía' or 'Guardia Civil' and will normally have blue flashing lights incorporated into their headlights, which are activated when the police stop you.

In non-traffic related matters police officers may be in plain clothes but you have the right to ask to see identification. Genuine officers may ask you to show them your documents but would not request that you hand over your bag or wallet. If in any doubt, converse through the car window and telephone the police on 112 or the Guardia Civil on 062 and ask them for confirmation that the registration number of the vehicle corresponds to an official police vehicle.

On the A7 motorway between the La Junquera and Tarragona toll stations be alert for 'highway pirates' who flag down foreign registered and hire cars (the latter have a distinctive number plate), especially those towing caravans. Motorists are sometimes targeted in service areas, followed and subsequently tricked into stopping on the hard shoulder of the motorway. The usual ploy is for the driver or passenger in a passing vehicle, which may be 'official-looking', to suggest by gesture that there is something seriously wrong with a rear wheel or exhaust pipe (a tyre having been punctured earlier, for example, at a petrol station). The Club has received reports of the involvement of a second vehicle whose occupants also indicate a problem at the rear of your vehicle and gesture that you should pull over onto the hard shoulder. If flagged down by other motorists or a motorcyclist in this way, be extremely wary. Within the Barcelona urban area thieves may also employ the 'punctured tyre' tactic at traffic lights.

In instances such as this, the Spanish Tourist Office advises you not to pull over but to wait until you reach a service area or toll station. If you do get out of your car when flagged down take care it is locked while you check outside, even if someone is left inside. Car keys should never be left in the ignition. Be suspicious when parked in lay-bys or picnic areas, of approaches by other motorists asking for help.

General

Spain shares with the rest of Europe an underlying threat from terrorism. Attacks could be indiscriminate and against civilian targets in public places including tourist areas.

The Basque terrorist organisation, ETA, has been less active in recent years and on 20 October 2011 announced a "definitive cessation of armed activity." However you should always be vigilant and follow the instructions of local police and other authorities. British nationals are not a specific target for ETA terrorism but attacks could happen in places frequented by tourists.

Coast guards operate a beach flag system to indicate the general safety of beaches for swimming: red – danger / do not enter the water; yellow – take precautions; green – all clear. Coast guards operate on most of the popular beaches, so if in doubt, always ask. During the summer months stinging jellyfish frequent Mediterranean coastal waters.

There is a high risk of forest fires during the hottest months and you should avoid camping in areas with limited escape routes. Take care to avoid actions that could cause a fire, e.g. careless disposal of cigarette ends. It is possible that the Spanish government will introduce a total prohibition on the lighting of fires (including barbecues) in forest areas throughout Spain.

Respect Spanish laws and customs. Parents should be aware that Spanish law defines anyone under the age of 18 as a minor, subject to parental control or adult supervision. Any unaccompanied minor coming to the attention of the local authorities for whatever reason is deemed to be vulnerable under the law and faces being taken into a minors centre for protection until a parent or suitable guardian can be found.

Andorra

For Consular help while in Andorra contact the British Consulate-General in Barcelona – see below.

See Safety and Security in the section DURING YOUR STAY.

British Embassy & Consulate-General

TORRE ESPACIO, PASEO DE LA CASTELLANA 259D
28046 MADRID
Tel: 917 14 63 00
http://ukinspain.fco.gov.uk/en/

British Consulate-General

AVDA DIAGONAL 477-13, 08036 BARCELONA
Tel: 902 109 356

There are also British Consulates in Bilbao, Alicante and Málaga.

Irish Embassy

IRELAND HOUSE, PASEO DE LA CASTELLANA 46-4
28046 MADRID
Tel: 914 36 40 93
www.embassyofireland.es

There are also Irish Honorary Consulates in Alicante, Barcelona, Bilbao, El Ferrol, Málaga and Seville.

Customs Regulations

Alcohol and Tobacco

For import allowances for alcohol and tobacco products see *Customs Regulations* in the section *PLANNING AND TRAVELLING.*

Under Spanish law the number of cigarettes which may be exported from Spain is set at eight hundred. Anything above this amount is regarded as a trade transaction which must be accompanied by the required documentation. If travellers are apprehended with more than 800 cigarettes but without the necessary paperwork, they face seizure of the cigarettes and a large fine.

Caravans and Motorhomes

A vehicle or vehicle combination exceeding 12 metres in length must display two yellow reflectors at the rear of the towed vehicle – see information under *Essential Equipment* later in this chapter.

Documents

Driving Licence

The British EU format pink driving licence is recognised in Spain. Holders of the old style all green driving licence are advised to replace it with a photocard version. Alternatively, the old style licence may be accompanied by an International Driving Permit available from the AA, Green Flag or the RAC.

Passport

Visitors must be able to show some form of identity if requested to do so by the police and you should carry your passport at all times.

Vehicle(s)

When driving in Spain it is compulsory at all times to carry your driving licence, vehicle registration certificate (V5C), insurance certificate and MOT certificate (if applicable). Vehicles imported by a person other than the owner must have a letter of authority from the owner.

See also Documents and Insurance in the section PLANNING AND TRAVELLING.

Money

All bank branches offer foreign currency exchange, as do many hotels and travel agents. Travellers' cheques are accepted as a means of payment in hotels, shops and restaurants but recent visitors continue to report difficulties cashing euro travellers' cheques and you should not rely on them for your immediate cash needs.

The major credit cards are widely accepted as a means of payment in shops, restaurants and petrol stations. Smaller retail outlets in non commercial areas may not accept payments by credit card – check before buying. When shopping carry your passport or photocard driving licence if paying with a credit card as you will almost certainly be asked for photographic proof of identity.

Carry your credit card issuers'/banks' 24 hour UK contact numbers in case of loss or theft of your cards.

Keep a supply of loose change as you could be asked for it frequently in shops and at kiosks.

Motoring

Drivers should take particular care as driving standards can be erratic, e.g. excessive speed and dangerous overtaking, and the accident rate is higher than in the UK. Pedestrians should take particular care when crossing roads (even at zebra crossings) or walking along unlit roads at night.

Accidents

The Central Traffic Department runs an assistance service for victims of traffic accidents linked to an emergency telephone network along motorways and some roads. Motorists in need of help should ask for 'auxilio en carretera' (road assistance). The special ambulances used are connected by radio to hospitals participating in the scheme.

It is not necessary to call the emergency services in case of light injuries. A European Accident Statement should be completed and signed by both parties and, if conditions allow, photos of the vehicles and the location should be taken. If one of the drivers involved does not want to give his/her details, the other should call the police or Guardia Civil.

Alcohol

The maximum permitted level of alcohol is 50 milligrams in 100 millilitres of blood, i.e. less than in the UK (80 milligrams) and it reduces to 30 milligrams for drivers with less than two years experience, drivers of vehicles with more than 8 passenger seats and for drivers of vehicles over 3,500kg. After a traffic accident all road users involved have to undergo a breath test. Penalties for refusing a test or exceeding the legal limit are severe and may include immobilisation of vehicles, a large fine and suspension of your driving licence. This limit applies to cyclists as well as drivers of private vehicles.

Breakdown Service

The motoring organisation, Real Automóvil Club de España (RACE), operates a breakdown service and assistance may be obtained 24 hours a day by telephoning the national centre in Madrid on 915 94 93 47. After hearing a message in Spanish press the number 1 to access the control room where English is spoken.

RACE's breakdown vehicles are blue and yellow and display the words 'RACE Asistencia' on the sides. This service provides on the spot minor repairs and towing to the nearest garage. Charges vary according to type of vehicle and time of day, but payment for road assistance must be made in cash.

Essential Equipment

Lights

Dipped headlights should be used on all roads at night and in tunnels. Bulbs are more likely to fail with constant use and you are recommended to carry spares.

Dipped headlights must be used at all times on 'special' roads, e.g. temporary routes created at the time of road works such as the hard shoulder, or in a contra-flow lane.

Headlight flashing is only allowed to warn other road users about an accident or a road hazard, or to let the vehicle in front know that you intend to overtake.

Reflective Jacket/Waistcoat

If your vehicle is immobilised on the carriageway outside a built-up area at night, or in poor visibility, you must wear a reflective jacket or waistcoat when getting out of your vehicle. This rule also applies to passengers who may leave the vehicle, for example, to assist with a repair.

Reflectors/Marker Boards for Caravans

Any vehicle or vehicle combination, i.e. car plus caravan over 12 metres in length, must display at the rear of the towed vehicle two aluminium boards. These must have a yellow centre with a red outline, must be reflective and comply with ECE70 standards. These must be positioned between 50cm and 150cm off the ground and must be 500mm x 250mm or 565mm x 200mm in size. Alternatively a single horizontal reflector may be used measuring 1300mm x 250mm or 1130mm x 200mm.

To buy these aluminium marker boards (under Spanish regulations stickers are not acceptable) contact www.hgvdirect.co.uk, tel 0845 6860008. Contact your local dealer or caravan manufacturer for advice on fitting them to your caravan.

Warning Triangles

Foreign registered vehicles are recommended to carry two triangles (as required by Spanish drivers) in order to avoid any local difficulties which may arise. Warning triangles should be placed 50 metres behind and in front of broken down vehicles.

Child Restraint System

Children under the age of 12 years old and under the height of 1.35m must use a suitable child restraint system adapted for their size and weight (this does not apply in taxis in urban areas). Children measuring more than 1.35m in height may use an adult seatbelt.

See also Motoring – Equipment in the section PLANNING AND TRAVELLING.

Fuel

Credit cards are accepted at most petrol stations, but you should be prepared to pay cash if necessary in remote areas.

LPG (Autogas) can be purchased from some Repsol filling stations. Details of approximately 33 sales outlets throughout mainland Spain can be found on www.spainautogas.com

See also *Fuel under Motoring – Advice* in the section
PLANNING AND TRAVELLING.

Mountain Passes and Tunnels

Some passes are occasionally blocked in winter
following heavy falls of snow. Check locally for
information on road conditions.

See *Mountain Passes and Tunnels* in the section *PLANNING
AND TRAVELLING.*

Parking

Parking regulations vary depending on the area of
a city or town, the time of day, the day of the week,
and whether the date is odd or even. In many towns
parking is permitted on one side of the street for the
first half of the month and on the other side for the
second half of the month. Signs marked '1-15' or '16-
31' indicate these restrictions.

Yellow road markings indicate parking restrictions.
Parking should be in the same direction as the traffic
flow in one way streets or on the right hand side when
there is two way traffic. Illegally parked vehicles may
be towed away or clamped but, despite this, you will
frequently encounter double and triple parking.

In large cities parking meters have been largely
replaced by ticket machines and these are often
located in areas known as 'zona azul', i.e. blue zones.
The maximum period of parking is usually one and
a half hours between 8am and 9pm. In the centre of
some towns there is a 'zona O.R.A.' where parking is
permitted for up to 90 minutes against tickets bought
in tobacconists and other retail outlets.

In many small towns and villages it is advisable to
park on the edge of town and walk to the centre,
as many towns can be difficult to navigate due to
narrow, congested streets.

See also *Parking Facilities for the Disabled under Motoring
– Advice* in the section *PLANNING AND TRAVELLING.*

Pedestrians

Jaywalking is not permitted. Pedestrians may not cross
a road unless a traffic light is at red against the traffic,
or a policeman gives permission. Offenders may be
fined.

Priority and Overtaking

As a general rule traffic coming from the right has
priority at intersections. When entering a main road
from a secondary road drivers must give way to traffic
from both directions. Traffic already on a roundabout
(i.e. from the left) has priority over traffic joining it.
Trams and emergency vehicles have priority at all times
over other road users and you must not pass trams
that are stationary while letting passengers on or off.

Motorists must give way to cyclists on a cycle lane,
cycle crossing or other specially designated cycle track.
They must also give way to cyclists when turning left
or right.

You must use your indicators when overtaking.
If a vehicle comes up behind you signalling that it
wants to overtake and if the road ahead is clear, you
must use your right indicator to acknowledge the
situation.

Roads

There are approximately 14,000km of highways and
dual carriageways. Roads marked AP (autopista) are
generally toll roads and roads marked A (autovía) or
N (nacional) are dual carriageways with motorway
characteristics – but not necessarily with a central
reservation – and are toll-free. In recent years some
major national roads have been upgraded to Autovías
and, therefore, have two identifying codes or have
changed codes, e.g. the N-I from Madrid to Irún near
the French border is now known as the A1 or Autovía
del Norte. Autovías are often as fast as autopistas and
are generally more scenic.

Roads managed by regional or local authorites are
prefixed with the various identification letters such as
C, CV, GR, L or T.

All national roads and roads of interest to tourists are
generally in good condition, are well signposted, and
driving is normally straightforward. Hills often tend
to be longer and steeper than in parts of the UK and
some of the coastal roads are very winding, so traffic
flows at the speed of the slowest lorry.

As far as accidents are concerned the N340 coast
road, especially between Málaga and Fuengirola, is
notorious, as are the Madrid ring roads, and special
vigilance is necessary.

Road humps are making an appearance on Spanish
roads and recent visitors report that they may be high,
putting low stabilisers at risk.

Andorra

The main road to Barcelona from Andorra is the
C14/C1412/N141b via Ponts and Calaf. It has a good
surface and avoids any high passes. The N260 along
the south side of Andorra via Puigcerda and La Seo de
Urgel also has a good surface.

Road Signs and Markings

Road signs conform to international standards. Lines
and markings are white. Place names may appear both
in standard (Castilian) Spanish and in a local form, e.g.
Gerona/Girona, San Sebastián/Donostia, Jávea/Xàbio,
and road atlases and maps usually show both.

SPAIN

You may encounter the following signs:

Carretera de peaje – *Toll road*

Ceda el paso – *Give way*

Cuidado – *Caution*

Curva peligrosa – *Dangerous bend*

Despacio – *Slow*

Desviación – *Detour*

Dirección única – *One-way street*

Embotellamiento – *Traffic jam*

Estacionamiento prohibido – *No parking*

Estrechamiento – *Narrow lane*

Gravillas – *Loose chippings/gravel*

Inicio – *Start*

Obras – *Roadworks*

Paso prohibido – *No entry*

Peligro – *Danger*

Prioridad – *Right of way*

Salida – *Exit*

Todas direcciones – *All directions*

Many non motorway roads have a continuous white line on the near (verge) side of the carriageway. Any narrow lane between this line and the side of the carriageway is intended primarily for pedestrians and cyclists and not for use as a hard shoulder.

A continuous line also indicates 'no stopping' even if it is possible to park entirely off the road and it should be treated as a double white line and not crossed except in a serious emergency. If your vehicle breaks down on a road where there is a continuous white line along the verge, it should not be left unattended as this is illegal and an on the spot fine may be levied.

Many road junctions have a continuous white centre line along the main road. This line must not be crossed to execute a left turn, despite the lack of any other 'no left turn' signs. If necessary, drive on to a 'cambio de sentido' (change of direction) sign to turn.

Turning permitted   Change direction only as shown

Traffic police are keen to enforce both the above regulations.

Watch out for traffic lights which may be mounted high above the road and hard to spot. The international three colour traffic light system is used in Spain. Green, amber and red arrows are used on traffic lights at some intersections.

Speed Limits

See Speed Limits Table under Motoring – Advice in the section PLANNING AND TRAVELLING.

In built-up areas speed is limited to 50 km/h (31 mph) except where signs indicate a lower limit. Reduce your speed to 20 km/h (13 mph) in residential areas. On motorways and dual carriageways in built-up areas, speed is limited to 80 km/h (50 mph) except where indicated by signs.

Outside built-up areas motorhomes of any weight are limited to 90 km/h (56 mph) on motorways and dual carriageways, to 80 km/h (50 mph) on other main roads with more than one lane in each direction, and to 70 km/h (44 mph) on secondary roads.

It is prohibited to own, transport or use radar detectors. For the location of fixed speed cameras in Spain see www.fixedspeedcamera.com. Drivers are not allowed to make signals to warn other drivers of the presence of police, e.g. headlight flashing.

Foreign Registered Vehicles

When a radar camera detects a foreign registered vehicle exceeding the speed limit, a picture of the vehicle and its number plate will be sent not only to the relevant traffic department, but also to the nearest Guardia Civil mobile patrol. The patrol will then stop the speeding vehicle and impose an on the spot fine which non-residents must pay immediately, otherwise the vehicle will be confiscated until the fine is paid.

This is to prevent offenders flouting the law and avoiding paying their fines, as pursuing them is proving costly and complicated for the Spanish authorities.

Towing

Motorhomes are prohibited from towing a car unless the car is on a special towing trailer with all four wheels off the ground.

Any towing combination in excess of 10 metres in length must keep at least 50 metres from the vehicle in front except in built-up areas, on roads where overtaking is prohibited, or where there are several lanes in the same direction.

Traffic Jams

Roads around the large cities such as Madrid, Barcelona, Zaragoza, Valencia and Seville are extremely busy on Friday afternoons when residents leave for the mountains or coast, and again on Sunday evenings when they return. The coastal roads along the Costa Brava and the Costa Dorada may also be congested. The coast road south of Torrevieja is frequently heavily congested as a result of extensive holiday home construction.

Summer holidays extend from mid June to mid September and the busiest periods are the last weekend in July, the first weekend in August and the period around the Assumption holiday in mid August.

Traffic jams occur on the busy AP7 from the French border to Barcelona during the peak summer holiday period. An alternative route now exists from Malgrat de Mar along the coast to Barcelona using the C32 where tolls are lower than on the AP7.

The Autovía de la Cataluña Central (C25) provides a rapid east-west link between Gerona and Lleida via Vic, Manresa and Tàrrega. There is fast access from Madrid to La Coruña in the far north-west via the A6/AP6.

Information on road conditions, traffic delays, etc can be found (in English) on http://infocar.dgt.es/etraffic

Violation of Traffic Regulations

The police are empowered to impose on the spot fines. Visiting motorists must pay immediately otherwise a vehicle will be confiscated until the fine is paid. An official receipt should be obtained. An appeal may be made within 15 days and there are instructions on the back of the receipt in English. RACE can provide legal advice – tel 902 40 45 45.

Motorways

The Spanish motorway system has been subject to considerable expansion in recent years with more motorways under construction or planned. The main sections are along the Mediterranean coast, across the north of the country and around Madrid. Tolls are charged on most autopistas but many sections are toll-free, as are autovias. Exits on autopistas are numbered consecutively from Madrid. Exits on autovias are numbered according to the kilometre point from Madrid.

Many different companies operate within the motorway network, each setting their own tolls which may vary according to the time of day and classification of vehicles. For an overview of the motorway network (in English) see www.aseta.es. This website has links to the numerous motorway companies where you will be able to view routes and tolls (generally shown in Spanish only).
Tolls are payable in cash or by credit card.

Avoid signposted 'Via T' lanes showing a circular sign with a white capital T on a blue background where toll collection is by electronic device only. Square 'Via

T' signs are displayed above mixed lanes where other forms of payment are also accepted.

Rest areas with parking facilities, petrol stations and restaurants or cafés are strategically placed and are well signposted. Emergency telephones are located at 2km intervals.

Motorway signs near Barcelona are confusing. To avoid the city traffic when heading south, follow signs for Barcelona, but the moment signs for Tarragona appear follow these and ignore Barcelona signs.

Touring

One of Spain's greatest attractions is undoubtedly its cuisine. Spanish cooking is rich and varied with many regional specialities and traditional dishes which have achieved worldwide fame, such as paella, gazpacho and tapas. Seafood in particular is excellent and plentiful. A fixed price menu or 'menú del dia' invariably offers good value. Service is generally included in restaurant bills but a tip of approximately €1 per person up to 10% of the bill is appropriate if you have received good service. Smoking is not allowed in inddor public places, including bars, restaurants and cafés.

Spain is one of the world's top wine producers, enjoying a great variety of high quality wines of which cava, rioja and sherry are probably the best known. Local beer is low in alcohol content and is generally drunk as an aperitif to accompany tapas.

Perhaps due to the benign climate and long hours of sunshine, Spaniards tend to get up later and stay out later at night than their European neighbours. Out of the main tourist season and in 'non-touristy' areas it may be difficult to find a restaurant open in the evening before 9pm.

Taking a siesta is still common practice, although it is now usual for businesses to stay open during the traditional siesta hours.

Spain's many different cultural and regional influences are responsible for the variety and originality of fiestas held each year. Over 200 have been classified as 'of interest to tourists' while others have gained international fame, such as La Tomatina mass tomato throwing battle held each year in August in Buñol near Valencia. A full list of fiestas can be obtained from the Spanish Tourist Office, www.spain.info/uk or from provincial tourist offices. In addition, every year each town celebrates its local Saint's Day which is always a very happy and colourful occasion.

The Madrid Card, valid for one, two or three days, gives free use of public transport, free entry to various attractions and museums, including the Prado, Reina Sofia and Thyssen-Bornemisza collection, as well as free tours and discounts at restaurants and shows.

You can buy the card from www.madridcard.com or by visiting the City Tourist Office in Plaza Mayor, or on Madrid Visión tour buses. Similar generous discounts can be obtained with the Barcelona Card, valid from two to five days, which can be purchased from tourist offices or online at www.barcelonaturisme.com. Other tourist cards are available in Burgos, Córdoba, Seville and Zaragoza.

The region of Valencia and the Balearic Islands are prone to severe storms and torrential rainfall between September and November and are probably best avoided at that time. Monitor national and regional weather on www.wmo.int

Gibraltar

For information on Gibraltar contact:

GIBRALTAR GOVERNMENT TOURIST OFFICE
150 STRAND, LONDON WC2R 1JA
Tel: 020 7836 0777
www.gibraltar.gi or www.gibraltar.gov.uk   info@gibraltar.gov.uk

There are no campsites on the Rock, the nearest being at San Roque and La Línea de la Concepción in Spain. The only direct access to Gibraltar from Spain is via the border at La Línea which is open 24 hours a day. You may cross on foot and it is also possible to take cars or motorhomes to Gibraltar.

A valid British passport is required for all British nationals visiting Gibraltar. Nationals of other countries should check entry requirements with the Gibraltar Government Tourist Office.

There is currently no charge for visitors to enter Gibraltar but Spanish border checks can cause delays and you should be prepared for long queues. As roads in the town are extremely narrow and bridges low, it is advisable to park on the outskirts. Visitors advise against leaving vehicles on the Spanish side of the border owing to the high risk of break-ins.

An attraction to taking the car into Gibraltar includes English style supermarkets and a wide variety of competitively priced goods free of VAT. The currency is sterling and British notes and coins circulate alongside Gibraltar pounds and pence, but note that Gibraltar notes and coins are not accepted in the UK. Scottish and Northern Irish notes are not generally accepted in Gibraltar. Euros are accepted but the exchange rate may not be favourable.

Disabled visitors to Gibraltar may obtain a temporary parking permit from the police station on production of evidence confirming their disability. This permit allows parking for up to two hours (between 8am and 10pm) in parking places reserved for disabled people.

Violence or street crime is rare but there have been reports of people walking from La Línea to Gibraltar at night being attacked and robbed.

If you need emergency medical attention while on a visit to Gibraltar, treatment at primary healthcare centres is free to UK passport holders under the local medical scheme. Non UK nationals need a European Health Insurance Card (EHIC). You are not eligible for free treatment if you go to Gibraltar specifically to be treated for a condition which arose elsewhere, e.g in Spain.

Local Travel

Madrid boasts an extensive and efficient public transport network including a metro system, suburban railways and bus routes. You can purchase a pack of ten tickets which offer better value than single tickets. In addition, tourist travel passes for use on all public transport are available from metro stations, tourist offices and travel agencies and are valid for one to seven days – you will need to present your passport when buying them. Single tickets must be validated before travel. For more information see www.ctm-madrid.es.

Metro systems also operate in Barcelona, Bilbao, Seville and Valencia and a few cities operate tram services including La Coruña, Valencia, Barcelona and Bilbao. The Valencia service links Alicante, Benidorm and Dénia.

Various operators run year round ferry services from Spain to North Africa, the Balearic Islands and the Canary Islands. All enquiries should be made through their UK agent:

SOUTHERN FERRIES
30 CHURTON STREET, VICTORIA, LONDON SW1V 2LP
Tel: 0844 8157785, Fax: 0844 815 7795
www.southernferries.co.uk mail@southernferries.co.uk

All place names used in the Site Entry listings which follow can be found in Michelin's Tourist & Motoring Atlas for Spain & Portugal, scale 1:400,000 (1cm = 4km).

ABEJAR *3C1* (800m NW Rural) *41.81645, -2.78869* **Camping El Concurso, Ctra Abejar-Molinos de Duero s/n, Km 1, N234, 42146 Abejar (Soria)** [975-37 33 61; fax 975-37 33 96; info@campingelconcurso.com; www.campingelconcurso.com] N234 W fr Soria to Abejar. Turn onto rd CL117 dir Molinos de Duero, site on L. Lge, mkd pitch, pt sl, pt shd; wc; chem disp; mv service pnt; shwrs inc; el pnts (5A) inc; gas; lndtte; shop & 500m; tradsmn; rest; snacks; bar; BBQ; playgrnd; pool; paddling pool; lake 2km; some statics; dogs; phone; poss cr & noisy in ssn; ccard acc; CCI. "Nr lake & National Park; v beautiful; gd san facs; not suitable m'van due slope." ♦ Easter-12 Oct. € 19.50   2009*

⊞ **ABIZANDA** *3B2* (5km N Rural) *42.28087, 0.19740* **Fundación Ligüerre de Cinca, Ctra A138, Km 28, 22393 Abizanda (Huesca)** [974-50 08 00; fax 974-50 08 30; info@liguerredecinca.com; www.liguerredecinca.com] A138 N fr Barbastro, site sp at km 29, or S fr Ainsa site sp at km 27, 18km S of Ainsa. Med, hdg/mkd pitch, terr, shd; wc; chem disp; shwrs inc; baby rm; el pnts (10A) inc; gas; lndtte; shop, rest, snacks, bar high ssn; playgrnd; pool; lake sw 1km; watersports; tennis; cycle hire; games rm; horseriding; car wash; 10% statics; dogs; phone; poss cr; Eng spkn; adv bkg; quiet; ccard acc; red long stay; CCI. "Excel facs, ltd low ssn; highly rec; site in 2 parts sep by ravine, bottom terr muddy in wet; trees may be diff for lge o'fits; helpful staff; lovely site; nearest shops at Ainsa; conv Ordesa & Monte Perdido National Park." € 29.00   2010*

⊞ **AGER** *3B2* (300m W Rural) *42.00277, 0.76472* **Camping Val d'Àger, Calle Afores s/n, 25691 Ager (Lleida)** [973-45 52 00; fax 973-45 52 02; iniciatives@valldager.com; www.campingvalldager.com/] Fr C13 turn W onto L904/C12 twd L'Ametlla & Àger. Cross Rv Noguera, site sp on L. Med, terr, pt shd; wc; chem disp; shwrs inc; el pnts €5.70; lndtte; shop & 800m; rest; snacks; bar; BBQ; playgrnd; pool high ssn; paddling pool; games area; games rm; wifi; some statics; dogs €3.60; adv bkg; quiet. "Mountain views; high o'fits rec to park nr recep (due trees); vg, peaceful site." ♦ € 22.10   2009*

⊞ **AGUILAR DE CAMPOO** *1B4* (27.8km SW Rural) *42.58977, - 4.33260* **Camping Fuente De Los Caños, Fuente Los Canos,34400 Herrera De Pisuerga (Palencia)** [639- 81 34 69] From N take A67 take exit marked Herrera de Pisuerga a Olmos de Ojeda/P-227, turn R onto Av de Eusebio Salvador Merino, turn R onto Lugar de la Fuente los Canos, site will be on the L. Sm site; pt shd; chem disp; wc; shwr; el pnts (3A); river adj; lndry rm; playgrnd; pool; fishing; cycle hire; walking. "Suitable for a NH." € 18.90   2011*

⊞ **AGUILAR DE CAMPOO** *1B4* (3km W Rural) *42.78694, -4.30222* **Monte Royal Camping, Ave Virgen del Llano, s/n, 34800 Aguilar de Campóo (Palencia)** [979-18 10 07] App site fr S on N611 fr Palencia. At Aguilar de Campóo turn W at S end of rv bdge at S end of town. Site on L in 3km; sp at edge of reservoir. Fr N take 3rd exit fr rndabt on N611. Do not tow thro town. Lge, mkd pitch, pt sl, shd; wc; chem disp (wc); baby facs; shwrs €0.60; el pnts (6A) inc; gas; lndtte; shops 3km; rest in ssn; bar; playgrnd; sand beach nr lake; watersports; horseriding; fishing; TV; 20% statics; dogs; phone; ccard acc; CCI. "Useful, peaceful NH 2 hrs fr Santander; ltd/basic facs low ssn & poss stretched high ssn - in need of maintenance (2010); barking dogs poss problem; friendly staff; gd walking, cycling & birdwatching in National Park; unreliable opening dates low ssn." ♦ € 20.60   2011*

There aren't many sites open at this time of year. We'd better phone ahead to check the one we're heading for is open.

⊞ **AGUILAS** *4G1* (4km NE Rural) *37.42638, -1.55083* **Camping Águilas, Ctra Cabo Cope, Los Geráneos, 30880 Águilas (Murcia)** [968-41 92 05; fax 968-41 92 82; info@campingaguilas.es; www.campingaguilas.es] Fr A7 N of Lorca take C3211 dir Águilas. On joining N332 turn L & foll sp L to Calabardina/Cabo Cope; site on L within 3km. Med, mkd pitch, hdstg, pt shd; wc; chem disp; mv service pnt; shwrs inc; el pnts (10A) €5; gas; lndtte; shop high ssn; rest; snacks; bar; playgrnd; pool; sand beach 4km; tennis; wifi; 30% statics; dogs €1; phone; site poss clsd last 2 weeks May & Sep; Eng spkn; adv bkg; quiet; red low ssn/long stay; ccard acc; red low ssn; CCI. "All pitches shaded with trees or netting; clean facs; helpful staff; popular winter long stay; excel." € 39.00   2010*

⊞ **AGUILAS** *4G1* (2km SW Coastal) *37.3925, -1.61111* **Camping Bellavista, Ctra de Vera, Km 3, 30880 Águilas (Murcia)** [tel/fax 968-44 91 51; info@campingbellavista.com; www.campingbellavista.com] Site on N332 Águilas to Vera rd on R at top of sh, steep hill, 100m after R turn to El Cocon. Well marked by flags. Fr S by N332 on L 400m after fuel stn, after v sharp corner. Sm, hdg pitch, hdstg, pt sl, pt shd; wc; chem disp; mv service pnt; shwrs inc; el pnts (10A) €5.20 or metered; gas; lndtte (inc dryer); sm shop; tradsmn; rest adj; snacks; BBQ; playgrnd; pool; sand beach 300m; cycle hire; wifi; some statics; dogs €2.50; poss cr; Eng spkn; adv bkg; quiet; ccard acc; red long stay/low ssn; CCI. "Gd autumn/winter stay; clean, tidy site with excel facs; ltd pitches for lge o'fits; helpful owner; fine views; rd noise at 1 end; excel town & vg beaches." € 24.45   2010*

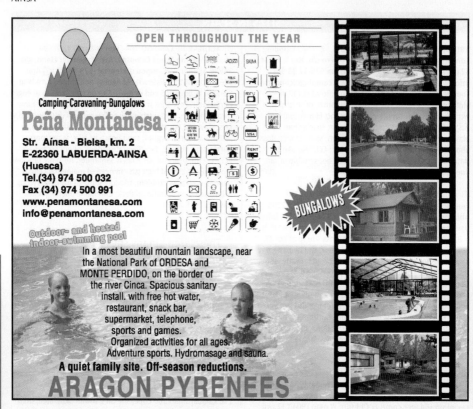
SPAIN

AINSA *3B2* (2.5km N Rural) *42.43555, 0.13583* **Camping Peña Montañesa**, Ctra Ainsa-Bielsa, Km 2.3, 22360 Labuerda (Huesca) [974-50 00 32; fax 974-50 09 91; info@penamontanesa.com; www.penamontanesa.com] E fr Huesca on N240 for approx 50km, turn N onto N123 just after Barbastro twd Ainsa. In 8km turn onto A138 N for Ainsa & Bielsa. Or fr Bielsa Tunnel to A138 S to Ainsa & Bielsa, site sp. NB: Bielsa Tunnel sometimes clsd bet Oct & Easter due to weather. Lge, mkd pitch, shd; htd wc; chem disp; mv service pnt; baby facs; sauna; shwrs inc; el pnts (6-10A) inc; gas; lndtte (inc dryer); supmkt; rest; snacks; bar; BBQ (gas/elec only); playgrnd; htd pools (1 covrd); lake sw 2km; fishing; canoeing; tennis; cycle hire; horseriding; games area; games rm; wifi; entmnt; TV; 30% statics; dogs €4.25; no c'vans/m'vans over 10m; phone; adv bkg; quiet, poss some noise fr local festival mid-Aug; ccard acc; red low ssn; CCI. "Situated by fast-flowing rv; very friendly staff; Eng spkn; gd, clean san facs; pitching poss diff due trees; nr beautiful medieval town of Ainsa & Ordesa National Park; excel." ♦ € 32.00 SBS - E12   2011*

See advertisement

AINSA *3B2* (10km N Rural) *42.50916, 0.12777* **Camping Valle de Añisclo**, Ctra Añisclo, Km 2, 22363 Puyarruego (Huesca) [974-50 50 96; info@valleanisclo.com; www.staragon.com/campingvalleanisclo/] N fr Ainsa on A138, at Escalona turn L onto HU631 dir Puyarruego. In 2km cross bdge, site on R at ent to vill. Med, mkd pitch, pt sl, pt shd; htd wc; chem disp; mv service pnt; baby facs; shwrs inc; el pnts (6A) €4.50; lndtte; shop; rest; snacks; bar; playgrnd; rv adj; wifi; dogs €1.65; phone; Eng spkn; adv bkg; quiet; red low ssn. "Excellent walking & birdwatching - nightingales; helpful owners; excel." Easter-15 Oct. € 18.50   2010*

AINSA *3B2* (1km E Rural) *42.41944, 0.15111* **Camping Ainsa**, Ctra Ainsa-Campo, 22330 Ainsa (Huesca) [tel/fax 974-50 02 60; info@campingainsa.com; www.campingainsa.com] Fr Ainsa take N260 E dir Pueyo de Araguás, cross rv bdge, site sp L in 200m. Foll lane to site. Sm, terr, pt shd; wc; baby facs; shwrs inc; el pnts €4.75; gas; lndtte; shop 1km; rest, snacks bar high ssn; playgrnd; pool; games rm; wifi; TV; 50% statics; dogs €2.20; phone; poss cr; some noise mornings; ccard acc; red low ssn; CCI. "Pleasant, welcoming, well-maintained site; fine view of old city & some pitches mountain views; vg san facs; not suitable lge o'fits; gd pool." Holy Week-30 Oct. € 22.25   2009*

⊞ **AINSA** *3B2* (6km NW Rural) *42.43004, 0.07881* **Camping Boltaña, Ctra N260, Km 442, Ctra Margudgued, 22340 Boltaña (Huesca)** [974-50 23 47; fax 974-50 20 23; info@ campingboltana.com; www.campingboltana.com] Fr Ainsa head twd Boltaña, turn L over rv & foll sp. Site is 2km E of Boltaña, final 300m on single track rd. Med, mkd pitch, pt sl, terr, pt shd; htd wc; chem disp; mv service pnt; baby facs; shwrs inc; el pnts (4-10A) €6.40; gas; lndtte (inc dryer); shop & 2km; tradsmn; rest; snacks; bar; playgrnd; pool; paddling pool; fishing 600m; tennis 1km; cycle hire; horseriding 500m; games area; cycle hire; adventure sports; wifi; 30% statics; dogs €3.25; phone; clsd 15 Dec-15 Jan; crs; Eng spkn; adv bkg; poss noisy; ccard acc; red low ssn. "Conv Ordesa National Park; poss diff for disabled travellers; san facs stretched high ssn; friendly, helpful staff; Ainsa old town worth visit; excel." ♦ € 29.00 (CChq acc)   2010*

ALBANYA *3B3* (W Rural) *42.30630, 2.70970* **Camping Bassegoda Park, Camí Camp de l'Illa, 17733 Albanyà (Gerona)** [972-54 20 20; fax 972-54 20 21; info@bassegoda park.com; www.bassegodapark.com] Fr France exit AP7/ E15 junc 3 onto GI510 to Albanyà. At end of rd turn R, site on rvside. Fr S exit AP7 junc 4 dir Terrades, then Albanyà. App poss diff for lge o'fits Med, hdg pitch, hdstg, pt shd; htd wc; chem disp; mv waste; baby facs; shwrs inc; el pnts (10A) €6.75; lndtte (inc dryer); shop; tradsmn; rest; snacks; bar; BBQ; playgrnd; pool; fishing; trekking; hill walking; mountain biking; cycle hire; games area; games rm; wifi; entmnt; TV rm; 8% statics; dogs €4.75 (1 only); phone; Eng spkn; adv bkg; quiet; ccard add; red low ssn/snr citizens/CCI. "Excel site surrounded by woods, rvs & streams; excel san facs, espec for disabled; well worth a detour." ♦ 1 Mar-11 Dec. € 28.65   2010*

ALBARRACIN *3D1* (2km E Rural) *40.41228, -1.42788* **Camp Municipal Ciudad de Albarracín, Camino de Gea s/n, 44100 Albarracín (Teruel)** [tel/fax 978-71 01 97 or 657-49 84 33 (mob); campingalbarracin5@hotmail.com; www.campingalbarracin.com] Fr Teruel take A1512 to Albarracín. Go thro vill, foll camping sps. Med, pt sl, pt shd; wc; chem disp; baby facs; shwrs inc; el pnts (16A) inc; gas; lndtte; shop & adj; tradsmn; snacks; bar; BBQ; playgrnd; pool adj in ssn; wifi; some statics; dogs; phone; poss cr; adv bkg; quiet; ccard acc; CCI. "Gd site; immac san facs; narr pitches poss diff for lge o'fits; sports cent adj; gd touring base & gd walking fr site; rec." 15 Mar-3 Nov. € 19.25   2011*

ALBERCA, LA *1D3* (2km N Rural) *40.50915, -6.12312* **Camping Al-Bereka, Ctra Salamanca-La Alberca, Km 75.6, 37624 La Alberca (Salamanca)** [923-41 51 95; www.albereka.com] Fr Salamanca S on N630/E803 take C515 to Mogarraz, then SA202 to La Alberca. Site on L at km 75.6 bef vill. Rte fr Ciudad Real OK but bumpy in places. Med, mkd pitch, terr, shd; wc; chem disp; shwrs inc; el pnts (3-6A) €3.50; lndtte; shop; rest; snacks; bar; BBQ; playgrnd; pool; paddling pool; TV; some statics; dogs; quiet; ccard acc; CCI. "Gd, quiet site; helpful owner; beautiful countryside; La Alberca medieval vill with abbey." ♦ 15 Mar-31 Oct. € 21.40   2009*

ALBERCA, LA *1D3* (6km N Rural) *40.52112, -6.13756* **Camping Sierra de Francia, Ctra Salamanca-La Alberca, Km 73, 37623 El Caserito (Salamanca)** [923-45 40 81; fax 923-45 40 01; info@campingsierradefrancia.com; www. campingsierradefrancia.com] Fr Cuidad Rodrigo take C515. Turn R at El Cabaco, site on L in approx 2km. Med, hdg/mkd pitch, shd; wc; shwrs; mv service pnt; el pnts (3-6A) €3.75; gas; lndtte; shop; rest; bar; BBQ; playgrnd; pool; paddling pool; cycle hire; horseriding; wifi; some statics; dogs free; quiet; ccard acc. "Conv 'living history' vill of La Alberca & Monasterio San Juan de la Peña; excel views." ♦ Holy Week-15 Sep. € 18.40   2009*

⊞ **ALCALA DE LOS GAZULES** *2H3* (4km E Rural) *36.46403, -5.66482* **Camping Los Gazules, Ctra de Patrite, Km 4, 11180 Alcalá de los Gazules (Cádiz)** [956-42 04 86; fax 956-42 03 88; camping@losgazules.e.telefonica.net; www. campinglosgazules.com] Fr N exit A381 at 1st junc to Alcalá, proceed thro town to 1st rndabt & turn L onto A375/A2304 dir Ubriqu, site sp strt ahead in 1km onto CA2115 dir Patrite on v sharp L. Fr S exit A381 at 1st sp for Acalá. At rndabt turn R onto A375/A2304 dir Ubrique. Then as above. Med, mkd pitch, pt sl, pt shd; wc; chem disp (wc); mv service pnt; shwrs inc; el pnts (10A) €5.25 (poss rev pol); lndtte; shop; rest; bar; playgrnd; pool; cycle hire; TV rm; 90% statics; dog €2; phone; adv bkg; red long stay/low ssn; CCI. "Well-maintained, upgraded site; take care canopy frames; sm pitches & tight turns & kerbs on site; friendly, helpful staff; ltd facs low ssn; ltd touring pitches; attractive town with v narr streets, leave car in park at bottom & walk; gd walking, birdwatching." € 46.00   2010*

ALCANAR *3D2* (3km N Coastal) *40.59500, 0.56998* **Camping Los Alfaques, 43530 Alcanar Platja (Tarragona)** [977-74 05 61; fax 977-74 25 95; info@alfaques.com; www. alfaques.com] Fr N exit AP7 junc 41 onto N340 thro Amposta, site sp on N340 approx 2km S of Sant Carles de la Ràpita. Lge, mkd pitch, pt sl, shd; wc; chem disp (wc); shwrs inc; el pnts (5A) €5; gas; lndtte; shop & 2km; rest; snacks; bar; playgrnd; pool 200m; steep, shgl beach adj; fishing; internet; entmnt; 30% statics; dogs €3; phone; rd noise. "Sm, cr pitches - seafront pitches rec; conv ancient town of Morella; no twin-axles; NH only." 1 Apr-30 Sep. € 26.00   2008*

ALCANTARA *2E2* (4km NW Rural) *39.74126, -6.89520* **Camping Puente de Alcántara, Ctra EX117, Km 36, Finca Los Cabezos, 10980 Alcántara (Cáceres)** [927-39 09 47; recepcion@campingalcantara.com; www. campingalcantara.com] W fr Alcántara to Roman bdge over Rv Tagus. Turn R at camping sp over cattle grid. Med, pt sl, unshd; wc; chem disp; shwrs inc; el pnts (5A) €4; gas; lndtte; shop; snacks; bar; playgrnd; pool; watersports; tennis; adv bkg; quiet; ccard acc; CCI. "Nice views; attractive vill with many storks; gd birdwatching area; friendly owner; ltd facs low ssn." ♦ 15 Mar-30 Sep. € 18.00   2008*

SPAIN

⊞ **ALCARAZ** *4F1* (6km E Rural) *38.67301, -2.40462*
**Camping Sierra de Peñascosa, Ctra Peñascosa-
Bogarra, Km 1, 02313 Peñascosa (Albacete) [967-
38 25 21; info@campingsierrapenascosa.com; www.
campingsierrapenascosa.com]** Fr N322 turn E bet km posts
279 & 280 sp Peñascosa. In vill foll site sp for 1km beyond
vill. Gravel access track & narr ent. Sm, mkd pitch, hdstg, terr,
shd; wc; chem disp; shwrs; el pnts (6A) €4; gas; lndtte; shop;
rest high ssn; snacks; bar; playgrnd; pool; cycle hire; dogs €2;
open w/end in winter; v quiet; ccard acc; CCI. "Not suitable
lge o'fits or faint-hearted; pitches sm, uneven & amongst
trees - care needed when manoeuvring; historical sites nr." ♦
€ 21.00   2009*

⊞ **ALCOSSEBRE** *3D2* (2.5km NE Coastal/Rural) *40.27016,
0.30646* **Camping Ribamar, Partida Ribamar s/n, 12579
Alcossebre (Castellón) [964-76 11 63; fax 964-76 14 84;
info@campingribamar.com; www.campingribamar.com]**
Exit AP7 at junc 44 into N340 & foll sp to Alcossebre, then
dir Sierra de Irta & Las Fuentes. Turn in dir of sea & foll sp
to site in 2km - pt rough rd. Med, hdg/mkd pitch, hdstg, pt
sl, terr, pt shd; wc; chem disp; mv service pnt; baby facs;
shwrs inc; el pnts (10A) €4.40 (metered for long stay); gas;
lndtte (inc dryer); shop; tradsmn; supmkt 2km; rest; bar;
playgrnd; pool; sand beach 100m; paddling pool; tennis;
games area; games rm; wifi; entmnt; TV rm; 25% statics;
dogs €1.70; poss cr; Eng spkn; adv bkg; quiet; red long stay/
low ssn; CCI. "Excel, refurbished tidy site in 'natural park';
warm welcome; realistic pitch sizes; variable prices; excel
san facs; beware caterpillars in spring - poss dangerous for
dogs." ♦ € 42.50 SBS - W04   2011*

See advertisement opposite (above)

⊞ **ALCOSSEBRE** *3D2* (2.5km S Coastal) *40.22138, 0.26888*
**Camping Playa Tropicana, 12579 Alcossebre (Castellón)
[964-41 24 63; fax 964 41 28 05; info@playatropicana.
com; www.playatropicana.com]** Fr AP7 exit junc 44 onto
N340 dir Barcelona. After 3km at km 1018 turn on CV142 twd
Alcossebre. Just bef ent town turn R sp 'Platjes Capicorb', turn
R at beach in 2.5km, site on R. Lge, mkd pitch, pt terr, pt shd;
htd wc; chem disp; baby facs; some serviced pitches; shwrs
inc; el pnts (10A) €4.50; gas; lndtte; supmkt; rest; snacks; bar;
playgrnd; pool; sand beach adj; watersports; cycle & kayak
hire; games area; beauty salon; cinema rm; wifi; entmnt; TV;
car wash; 10% statics; no dogs; poss cr; Eng spkn; adv bkg
rec high ssn; quiet; ccard acc; red low ssn/long stay & special
offers; various pitch prices. "Excel facs & security; superb
well-run site; vg low ssn; poss rallies Jan-Apr; management v
helpful; poss flooding after heavy rain; pitch access poss diff
lge o'fits due narr access rds & high kerbs; take fly swat!" ♦
€ 63.00   2010*

⊞ **ALGAMITAS** *2G3* (3km SW Rural) *37.01934, -5.17440*
**Camping El Peñon, Ctra Algámitas-Pruna, Km 3, 41661
Algámitas (Sevilla) [955-85 53 00; info@campingalgamitas.
com]** Fr A92 turn S at junc 41 (Arahal) to Morón de la Frontera
on A8125. Fr Morón take A406 & A363 dir Pruna. At 1st
rndabt at ent Pruna turn L onto SE9225 to Algámitas. Site on
L in approx 10km - steep app rd. Sm, hdg/mkd pitch, hdstg,
pt shd; wc; chem disp (wc); mv service pnt; shwrs inc; el
pnts (16A) €3.32; gas; lndtte (inc dryer); shop 3km; rest; bar;
BBQ; playgrnd; pool; games area; 50% statics; dogs; site clsd
13-24 Nov; adv bkg; quiet; cc acc; CCI. "Conv Seville, Ronda
& white vills; walking, hiking & horseriding fr site; excel rest;
excel, clean san facs; vg site - worth effort to find." ♦
€ 15.10   2009*

⊞ **ALHAMA DE MURCIA** *4F1* (6km NW Rural) *37.88888,
-1.49333* **Camping Sierra Espuña, El Berro, 30848
Alhama de Murcia (Murcia) [968-66 80 38; fax 968-
66 80 79; camping@campingsierraespuna.com; www.
campingsierraespuna.com]** Exit A7 junc 627 or 631 to
Alhama de Murcia & take C3315 sp Gebas & Mula. Ignore
1st sp to site & after Gebas foll sp to site sp El Berro, site on
edge of vill. 15km by rd fr Alhama - narr, twisty & steep in
parts, diff for lge o'fits & m'vans over 7.5m. Med, hdstg, terr,
pt shd; wc; chem disp; baby facs; shwrs; el pnts (6A) €4.28
(poss rev pol); gas; lndtte; shop 200m; rest in vill; snacks;
bar; playgrnd; pool; tennis; minigolf; organised activities;
wifi; 30% statics; dogs €2.14; phone; adv bkg; quiet but
poss noise w/end; red long stay; ccard acc; CCI. "In Sierra
Espuña National Park on edge of unspoilt vill; gd walking,
climbing, mountain biking area; friendly staff; highly rec." ♦
€ 17.20   2009*

⊞ **ALHAURIN DE LA TORRE** *2H4* (4km W Rural) *36.65174,
-4.61064* **Camping Malaga Monte Parc, 29130 Alhaurín de
la Torre (Málaga) [tel/fax 951-29 60 28; info@malaga
monteparc.com; www.malagamonteparc.com]** W fr Málaga
on AP7 or N340 take exit for Churriana/Alhaurín de la Torre.
Thro Alhaurín de la Torre take A404 W sp Alhaurín el Grande,
site on R, sp. Sm, hdg/mkd pitch, hdstg, pt sl, shd; htd wc
(cont); chem disp; shwrs inc; el pnts (6A) inc; lndtte; shop
4km; rest; snacks; bar; BBQ; pool; golf nrby; wifi; TV; some
statics; dogs €1.70; bus 200m; Eng spkn; adv bkg; quiet; ccard
acc; red low ssn; CCI. "Vg site; well-appointed, clean san facs;
friendly Welsh owner." ♦ € 24.70   2009*

⊞ **ALICANTE** *4F2* (10km NE Coastal) *38.41333, -0.40556*
**Camping Bon Sol, Camino Real de Villajoyosa 35, Playa
Muchavista, 03560 El Campello (Alicante) [tel/fax 965-
94 13 83; bonsol@infonegocio.com; www.infonegocio.
com/bonsol]** Exit AP7 N of Alicante at junc 67 onto N332 sp
Playa San Juan; on reaching coast rd turn N twds El Campello;
site sp. Sm, mkd pitch, hdstg, pt shd, all serviced pitches; wc;
chem disp; shwrs; el pnts (4A) €4.50; lndtte; shop; rest; bar;
sand beach; 50% statics; adv bkg; ccard acc; red long stay/low
ssn; CCI. "Diff ent for long o'fits; helpful staff; noisy at w/end;
poss cold shwrs; vg." ♦ € 31.50   2011*

⊞ **ALICANTE** *4F2* (10km NE Coastal) *38.43638, -0.3887*
Camping Costa Blanca, Calle Convento 143, 03560
El Campello (Alicante) [tel/fax 965-63 06 70; info@
campingcostablanca.com; www.campingcostablanca.com]
Exit AP7/E15 junc 67 onto N332, site visible on L at turn for
El Campello. Med, hdg pitch, hdstg, shd; htd wc; chem disp;
mv service pnt; shwrs inc; baby facs; el pnts (6A) €4.30; gas;
lndtte; shop; rest; snacks; bar; playgrnd; pool; waterslides;
sand beach 500m; watersports; tennis 800m; horseriding
1km; golf 3km; TV cab/sat; 80% statics; dogs free; train 1km;
sep car park; poss cr; adv bkg; some noise fr rlwy; red long
stay; CCI. "Pleasant site nr archaeological site & fishmkt;
modern facs; friendly, helpful staff; not suitable RVs & lge
o'fits due narr access to pitches; pitches sm & low canvas
awnings; gd security; v popular low ssn." ♦ € 28.10
2008*

⊞ **ALLARIZ** *1B2* (1.5km W Rural) *42.18443, -7.81811*
Camping Os Invernadeiros, Ctra Allariz-Celanova, Km 3,
32660 Allariz (Ourense) [988-44 01 26; fax 988-44 20 06;
reatur@allariz.com] Well sp off N525 Orense-Xinzo rd &
fr A52. Steep descent to site off rd OU300. Height limit 2.85m
adj reception - use gate to R. Sm, pt shd; wc; shwrs inc; el
pnts €4; gas; lndtte; shop; snacks; bar; playgrnd; pool 1.5km;
horseriding; cycle hire; some statics; dogs €2; bus 1.8km; Eng
spkn; quiet; red long stay; ccard acc; CCI. "Vg; steep slope into
site, level exit is available; site combined with horseriding
stable; rv walk adj." € 21.00
2011*

ALMAYATE see Torre del Mar *2H4*

⊞ **ALMERIA** *4G1* (23km SE Coastal/Rural) *36.80187,
-2.24471* Camping Cabo de Gata, Ctra Cabo de Gata s/n,
Cortijo Ferrón, 04150 Cabo de Gata (Almería) [950-
16 04 43; fax 950-52 00 03; info@campingcabodegata.
com; www.campingcabodegata.com] Exit m'way
N340/344/E15 junc 460 or 467 sp Cabo de Gata, foll sp to
site. Lge, hdg/mkd pitch, shd; wc; chem disp; baby facs;
shwrs inc; el pnts (6-16A) €4.60; gas; lndtte; supmkt high
ssn; tradsmn; rest; snacks; bar; BBQ; playgrnd; pool; diving
cent; sand beach 900m; tennis; games area; games rm;
excursions; cycle hire; wifi; TV; some statics; dogs €2.80;
bus 1km; Eng spkn; adv bkg; quiet; ccard acc; red long
stay/low ssn/CCI. "M'vans with solar panels/TV aerials take
care sun shades; gd cycling, birdwatching esp flamingos;
popular at w/end; isolated, dry area of Spain with many
interesting features; warm winters; excel site." ♦ € 24.85
SBS - W10
2011*

See advertisement below

⊞ **ALMERIA** *4G1* (4km W Coastal) *36.82560, -2.51685*
Camping La Garrofa, Ctra N340a, Km 435.4, 04002 Almería [tel/fax 950-23 57 70; info@lagarrofa.com; www.lagarrofa. com] Site sp on coast rd bet Almería & Aguadulce. Med, mkd pitch, pt sl, shd; wc; chem disp; mv service pnt; shwrs inc; el pnts (6-10A) €4.30-4.90; gas; lndtte; shop; rest; snacks; bar; playgrnd; shgl beach adj; games area; wifi; 10% statics; dogs €2.40; phone; bus adj; sep car park; quiet; red low ssn/ long stay; CCI. "V pleasant site adj eucalyptus grove; helpful staff; modern, clean facs; sm pitches, not rec lge o'fits; vg." ♦ € 20.50   2009*

⊞ **ALMERIA** *4G1* (10km W Coastal) *36.79738, -2.59128*
Camping Roquetas, Ctra Los Parrales s/n, 04740 Roquetas de Mar (Almería) [950-34 38 09; fax 950-34 25 25; info@ campingroquetas.com; www.campingroquetas.com] Fr A7 take exit 429; ahead at rndabt A391 sp Roquetas. Turn L at rndabt sp camping & foll sp to site. V lge, pt shd; wc; chem disp; mv service pnt; shwrs inc; el pnts (10-15A) €6.35-7.45; gas; lndtte; shop; snacks; bar; 2 pools; paddling pool; shgl beach 400m; tennis; TV rm; 10% statics; dogs €2.25; phone; bus 1km; Eng spkn; adv bkg rec high ssn; quiet; ccard acc; red low ssn/long stay/CCI. "Double-size pitches in winter; helpful staff; gd clean facs; tidy site but poss dusty; artificial shade; many long term visitors in winter." ♦ € 25.60   2009*

⊞ **ALMUNECAR** *2H4* (6km W Coastal) *36.73954, -3.75358*
Nuevo Camping La Herradura, Paseo Andrés Segovia s/n (Peña Parda), 18690 La Herradura (Granada) [958-64 06 34; fax 958-64 06 42; laherradura@neuvocamping.com; www. nuevocamping.com] Turn S off N340 sp La Herradura & foll rd to seafront. Turn R to end of beach rd. Site not well sp. Avoid town cent due narr rds. Med, mkd pitch, pt terr, pt shd; wc; chem disp; mv service pnt; serviced pitches; shwrs inc; el pnts (5A) €3.50; gas 500m; lndtte; shop, rest, snacks, bar adj; playgrnd; shgl beach adj; 20% statics; dogs €1.50; phone; bus 300m; poss v cr; adv bkg; quiet; red low ssn/long stay; CCI. "Friendly, attractive site in avocado orchard; mountain views some pitches; height restriction lge m'vans; some sm pitches - v tight to manoeuvre; vg san facs but ltd low ssn; popular winter long stay." ♦ € 22.00   2010*

⊞ **ALTEA** *4F2* (4km S Coastal) *38.57751, -0.06440* **Camping Cap-Blanch, Playa de Albir, 03530 Altea (Alicante)** [965-84 59 46; fax 965-84 45 56; capblanch@ctv.es; www. camping-capblanch.com] Exit AP7/E15 junc 64 Altea-Collosa onto N332, site bet Altea & Benidorm, dir Albir. 'No entry' sps on prom rd do not apply to access to site. Lge, pt shd, hdstg; wc; chem disp; mv service pnt; baby facs; shwrs inc; el pnts (5-10A) €3.50; gas; shop 100m; lndtte (inc dryer); rest; bar; playgrnd; shgl beach adj; watersports; tennis; golf 5km; wifi; TV; some statics; carwash; poss cr; Eng spkn; no adv bkg; quiet; ccard acc; red low ssn/long stay. "V cr in winter with long stay campers; lge pitches; Altea mkt Tues; buses to Benidorm & Altea; handy for lovely beach; most pitches hdstg on pebbles." ♦ € 25.00   2011*

⊞ **AMETLLA DE MAR, L'** *3C2* (2.5km S Coastal) *40.86493, 0.77860* **Camping L'Ametlla Village Platja, Paratge Stes Creus s/n, 43860 L'Ametlla de Mar (Tarragona)** [977-26 77 84; fax 977-26 78 68; info@campingametlla. com; www.campingametlla.com] Exit AP7 junc 39, fork R as soon as cross m'way. Foll site sp for 3km - 1 v sharp, steep bend. Lge, hdg/mkd pitch, hdstg, terr, pt shd; htd wc; chem disp; mv service pnt; baby facs; shwrs inc; el pnts (5A) inc; gas; lndtte; shop high ssn; rest; snacks; bar; BBQ; playgrnd; pool; paddling pool; shgl beach 400m; diving cent; games area; games rm; fitness rm; cycle hire; wifi; entmnt; TV rm; some statics; dogs free; phone; Eng spkn; adv bkg; some rd & rlwy noise; ccard acc; red low ssn/long stay; CCI. "Conv Port Aventura & Ebro Delta National Park; excel site & facs." ♦ € 36.50   2011*

⊞ **ARANDA DE DUERO** *1C4* (3km N Rural) *41.70138, -3.68666* **Camping Costajan, Ctra A1/E5, Km 164-165, 09400 Aranda de Duero (Burgos)** [947-50 20 70; fax 947-51 13 54; campingcostajan@camping-costajan.com] Sp on A1/ E5 Madrid-Burgos rd, N'bound exit km 164 Aranda Norte, S'bound exit km 165 & foll sp to Aranda & site 500m on R. Med, pt sl, shd; wc; chem disp; mv service pnt; shwrs inc; el pnts (10A) €5 (poss rev pol &/or no earth); gas; lndtte; shop; tradsmn; supmkt 3km; rest high ssn; snacks; bar; BBQ; playgrnd; pool high ssn; tennis; games area; wifi; 10% statics; dogs €2; phone; bus 2km; Eng spkn; adv bkg; quiet, but some traff noise; red low ssn but ltd facs; CCI. "Lovely site under pine trees; poultry farm adj; diff pitch access due trees & sandy soil; friendly, helpful owner; site poss clsd low ssn - phone ahead to check; many facs clsd low ssn & gate clsd o'night until 0800; recep poss open evening only low ssn; excel facs for disabled; poss cold/tepid shwrs low ssn; gd winter NH." € 22.40   2011*

⊞ **ARANJUEZ** *1D4* (1.5km NE Rural) *40.04222, -3.59944* **Camping International Aranjuez, Calle Soto del Rebollo s/n, 28300 Aranjuez (Madrid)** [918-91 13 95; fax 918-92 04 06; info@campingaranjuez.com; www. campingaranjuez.com] Fr N (Madrid) turn off A4 exit 37 onto M305. After ent town turn L bef rv, after petrol stn on R. Take L lane & watch for site sp on L, also mkd M305 Madrid. Site in 500m on R. (If missed cont around cobbled rndabt & back twd Madrid.) Fr S turn off A4 for Aranjuez & foll Palacio Real sp. Join M305 & foll sp for Madrid & camping site. Site on Rv Tajo. Warning: rd surface rolls, take it slowly on app to site & ent gate tight. Med, hdg/mkd pitch, pt sl, unshd; htd wc; chem disp; mv service pnt; some serviced pitches; baby facs; shwrs inc; el pnts (16A) €4 (poss no earth, rev pol); gas; lndtte (inc dryer); shop; hypmkt 3km; rest; snacks; bar; playgrnd; pool & paddling pool; rv fishing; canoe & cycle hire; games area; wifi; entmnt; some statics; dogs free; phone; quiet; ccard acc; red low ssn/long stay; CCI. "Well-maintained site; gd san facs; gd value; some lge pitches - access poss diff due trees; some uneven pitches - care req when pitching; pleasant town - World Heritage site; conv Royal Palace & gardens & Madrid by train; vg." ♦ € 30.00   2011*

See advertisement

SPAIN

ARBON 1A3 (S Rural) 43.48141, -6.70376 Camping La Cascada, 33718 Arbón (Asturias) [985-62 50 81; camping lacascada@hotmail.com] Approx 20km W of Luarca on N634, turn S onto AS25 for approx 10km. Immed bef town of Navía, site sp. Winding rd. Med, sl, pt shd; wc; chem disp (wc); shwrs inc; el pnts (3-4A) €2.70; gas; shop & 1km; snacks; bar; BBQ; playgrnd; pool; sand beach 12km; 15% statics; dogs; phone; bus 1km; Eng spkn; adv bkg; quiet; CCI. "V friendly, family-run site in beautiful area; excel info fr local tourist office." Easter-15 Sep. € 14.00   2008*

⊞ ARCOS DE LA FRONTERA 2G3 (1km E Rural) 36.75222, -5.78722 Camping Lago de Arcos, 11630 Arcos de la Frontera (Cádiz) [956-70 83 33; fax 956-70 80 00; lagodearcos@campings.net] Exit A382 junc 29 S to Arcos A372. Turn L at sp El Santiscal & site, site on R. Med, pt shd; wc; shwrs inc; el pnts (5A) €3.53; gas; lndtte; sm shop; snacks; bar; playgrnd; pool high ssn; dogs; phone; poss cr; quiet; ccard acc; CCI. "Noisy at Easter due Running Bull Festival; unkempt low ssn & poss itinerants; phone to check open in low ssn; busy w/end; friendly staff; most pitches have canopy frames; sh walk to lake." ♦ € 17.61   2008*

⊞ ARENAS DEL REY 2G4 (5km N Rural) 36.99439, -3.88064 Camping Los Bermejales, Km 360, Embalse Los Bermejales, 18129 Arenas del Rey (Granada) [958-35 91 90; fax 958-35 93 36; camping@losbermejales.com; www.losbermejales.com] On A44/E902 S fr Granada, exit at junc 139 dir La Malahá onto A385. In approx 10km, turn L onto A338 dir Alhama de Granada & foll sp for site. Fr A92 foll sp Alhama de Granada, then Embalse Los Bermejales. Med, mkd pitch, hdstg, terr, pt shd; wc; chem disp; mv service pnt; shwrs inc; el pnts (9A) €2.67; gas; lndtte; shop; rest; snacks; bar; BBQ; playgrnd; pool; lake sw & sand/shgl beach adj; fishing (licence req); pedalos; tennis; TV rm; 50% statics; dogs; phone; poss cr high ssn; little Eng spkn; adv bkg; quiet. "Ideal base for touring Granada; Roman baths 12km at Alhama de Granada; vg disabled facs." ♦ € 16.70   2011*

ARENAS, LAS 1A4 (1km E Rural) 43.30083, -4.80500 Camping Naranjo de Bulnes, Ctra Cangas de Onís-Panes, Km 32.5, 33554 Arenas de Cabrales (Asturias) [tel/fax 985-84 65 78; campingnaranjodebulnes@yahoo.es] Fr Unquera on N634, take N621 S to Panes, AS114 23km to Las Arenas. Site E of vill of Las Arenas de Cabrales, both sides of rd. V lge, mkd pitch, pt sl, pt terr, pt shd; wc; chem disp; baby facs; shwrs inc; el pnts (10A) €3.50 (poss rev pol); gas; lndtte; shop; rest; snacks; bar; playgrnd; internet; TV rm; bus 100m; poss cr; rd noise; ccard acc. "Beautifully-situated site by rv; delightful vill; attractive, rustic-style san facs - hot water to shwrs only; wcs up steps; poss poor security; conv Picos de Europa; mountain-climbing school; excursions; walking; excel cheese festival last Sun in Aug." 2 Mar-4 Nov. € 25.60   2011*

ARIJA 1A4 (1km N Rural) 43.00064, -3.94492 Camping Playa de Arija, Avda Gran Via, 09570 Arija (Burgos) [942-77 33 00; fax 942-77 32 72; dptocomercial@campingplayadearija.com; www.campingplayadearija.com] Fr W on A67 at Reinosa along S side of Embalse del Ebro. Go thro Arija & take 1st L after x-ing bdge. Go under rlwy bdge, site well sp on peninsula N of vill on lakeside. Or fr E on N623 turn W onto BU642 to Arija & turn R to peninsula & site. NB Rd fr W under repair 2009 & in poor condition. Lge, unshd; wc; chem disp; mv service pnt; baby facs; shwrs inc; el pnts (5A) €3; lndtte; shop; rest; bar; BBQ; playgrnd; lake sw & beach; watersports; games area; 10% statics; dogs; phone; bus 1km; quiet; CCI. "Gd new site; gd birdwatching; low ssn phone ahead for site opening times." Easter-15 Sep. € 17.50   2009*

⊞ ARNES 3C2 (1km NE Rural) 40.9186, 0.2678 Camping Els Ports, Ctra Tortosa T330, Km 2, 43597 Arnes (Tarragona) [tel/fax 977-43 55 60; elsports@hotmail.com] Exit AP7 at junc Tortosa onto C12 sp Gandesa. Turn W onto T333 at El Pinell de Brai, then T330 to site. Med, pt shd; htd wc; shwrs inc; el pnts €4.20; lndtte; rest; bar; pool; paddling pool; games area; cycle hire; horseriding 3km; entmnt; TV rm; some statics; no dogs; phone; bus 1km; quiet; ccard acc. "Nr nature reserve & many sports activities; excel walking/mountain cycling; basic san facs; poss smells fr adj pig units (2009); rock pegs req." ♦ € 18.40   2009*

SPAIN

AURITZ *3A1* (3km SW Rural) *42.97302, -1.35248* **Camping Urrobi, Ctra Pamplona-Valcarlos, Km 42, 31694 Espinal-Aurizberri (Navarra)** [tel/fax 948-76 02 00; info@ campingurrobi.com; www.campingurrobi.com] NE fr Pamplona on N135 twd Valcarlos thro Erro; 1.5km after Auritzberri (Espinal) turn R on N172. Site on N172 at junc with N135 opp picnic area. Med, pt shd; wc; chem disp; mv service pnt; shwrs inc; el pnts (5A) €4.90; gas; lndtte; shop; tradsmn; supmkt 1.5km; rest; snacks; bar; BBQ; playgrnd; pool; rv adj; tennis; cycle hire; horseriding; wifi; 20% statics; phone; Eng spkn; adv bkg; quiet; ccard acc; CCI. "Excel, busy site & facs; solar htd water - hot water to shwrs only; walks in surrounding hills; ltd facs low ssn; poss youth groups." ♦ 1 Apr-31 Oct. € 20.00   2010*

AVIN see Cangas de Onis *1A3*

⊞ **AYERBE** *3B2* (1km NE Rural) *42.28211, -0.67536* **Camping La Banera, Ctra Loarre Km.1, 22800 Ayerbe (Huesca)** [tel/ fax 974-38 02 42; labanera@gmail.com] Take A132 NW fr Huesca dir Pamplona. Turn R at 1st x-rds at ent to Ayerbe sp Loarre & Camping. Site 1km on R on A1206. Med, mkd pitch, terr, pt shd; wc; chem disp (wc); baby facs; fam bthrm; shwrs inc; el pnts (6A) €2.50; gas; lndtte; shop 1km; rest; snacks; bar; cooking facs; TV rm; dogs; some Eng spkn; adv bkg; quiet; ccard acc; red long stay; CCI. "Friendly, pleasant, well-maintained, peaceful, family-run site; facs clean; pitches poss muddy after rain; helpful owners; wonderful views; close to Loarre Castle; care req by high o'fits as many low trees." ♦ € 12.50   2010*

⊞ **AYERBE** *3B2* (10km NE Rural) *42.31989, -0.61848* **Camping Castillo de Loarre, Ctra del Castillo s/n, 22809 Loarre (Huesca)** [tel/fax 974-38 27 22; info@campingloarre.com; www.campingloarre.com] NW on A132 fr Huesca, turn R at ent to Ayerbe to Loare sp Castillo de Loarre. Pass 1st site on R (La Banera) & foll sp to castle past Loarre vill on L; site on L. App rd steep & twisting. Med, pt sl, pt shd; wc; chem disp; shwrs inc; el pnts (6A) €4.50; gas; lndtte; shop; tradsmn; rest; snacks; bar; playgrnd; sm pool; cycle hire; 10% statics; dogs; phone; site clsd Feb; poss cr; Eng spkn; quiet; ccard acc; CCI. "Elevated site in almond grove; superb scenery & views, esp fr pitches on far L of site; excel birdwatching - many vultures/ eagles; site open w/end in winter; busy high ssn & w/ends; pitching poss diff lge o'fits due low trees; worth the journey." ♦ € 16.00   2010*

BAIONA *1B2* (5km NE Urban/Coastal) *42.13861, -8.80916* **Camping Playa América, Ctra Vigo-Baiona, Km 9.250, 36350 Nigrán (Pontevedra)** [986-36 54 03 or 986-36 71 61; fax 986 36 54 04; oficina@campingplayaamerica.com; www.campingplayaamerica.com] Sp on rd PO552 fr all dirs (Vigo/Baiona) nr beach. Med, mkd pitch, pt shd; wc; chem disp; mv service pnt; baby facs; shwrs inc; el pnts (6A) €4.50; gas; lndtte; shop; tradsmn; rest; snacks; bar; BBQ; playgrnd; pool; paddling pool; sand beach 300m; cycle hire; 60% statics; dogs; bus 500m; poss cr; Eng spkn; adv bkg; CCI. "Friendly staff; pleasant, wooded site; gd." ♦ 16 Mar-15 Oct. € 24.60   2008*

⊞ **BAIONA** *1B2* (1km E Coastal) *42.11416, -8.82611* **Camping Bayona Playa, Ctra Vigo-Baiona, Km 19, Sabarís, 36393 Baiona (Pontevedra)** [986-35 00 35; fax 986- 35 29 52; campingbayona@campingbayona.com; www. campingbayona.com] Fr Vigo on PO552 sp Baiona. Or fr A57 exit Baiona & foll sp Vigo & site sp. Lge, mkd pitch, pt shd; wc; chem disp; mv service pnt; shwrs inc; el pnts (3A) €4.80; gas; lndtte; shop; rest; snacks; bar; playgrnd; pool; waterslide; sand beach adj; 50% statics; dogs; phone; poss cr; adv bkg (ess high ssn); quiet; red low ssn/long stay; CCI. "Area of o'stndg natural beauty with sea on 3 sides; well-organised site; excel, clean san facs; avoid access w/end as v busy; ltd facs low ssn; tight access to sm pitches high ssn; gd cycle track to town; replica of ship 'La Pinta' in harbour." ♦ € 28.40   2011*

BAIONA *1B2* (7km S Coastal) *42.08642, -8.89129* **Camping Mougás (Naturist), As Mariñas 20B, Ctra Baiona-A Guarda, Km 156, 36309 Mougás (Pontevedra)** [986-38 50 11; fax 986-38 29 90; campingmougas@campingmougas.com] Fr Baiona take coastal rd PO552 S; site sp. Med, pt shd; wc; chem disp; shwrs; el pnts €4.65; lndtte; supmkt; rest; snacks; bar; BBQ; playgrnd; pool; fishing; tennis; games rn; entmnt; some statics; phone; ccard acc; red low ssn; CCI. "Excel staff; lovely site on rocky coast; gd for watching sunsets; gd NH." ♦ Holy Week-15 Sep. € 25.00   2008*

⊞ **BALAGUER** *3C2* (8km N Rural) *41.86030, 0.83250* **Camping La Noguera, Partida de la Solana s/n, 25615 Sant Llorenç de Montgai (Lleida)** [973-42 03 34; fax 973-42 02 12; jaume@campinglanoguera.com; www.campinglanoguera. com] Fr Lleida, take N11 ring rd & exit at km 467 onto C13 NE dir Andorra & Balaguer. Head for Balaguer town cent, cross rv & turn R onto LV9047 dir Gerb. Site on L in 8km thro Gerb. App fr Camarasa not rec. Lge, mkd pitch, hdstg, terr, pt shd; wc; chem disp; mv service pnt; baby facs; shwrs inc; el pnts (6A) €5.15; gas; lndtte; supmkt; tradsmn; rest; snacks; bar; BBQ; playgrnd; pool; games area; TV rm; 80% statics; dogs €3.50; phone; poss cr; Eng spkn; adv bkg; quiet; ccard acc; red long stay; CCI. "Next to lake & nature reserve; gd cycling; poss diff lge o'fits." ♦ € 20.60   2008*

BANOS DE FORTUNA see Fortuna *4F1*

BANOS DE MONTEMAYOR see Béjar *1D3*

⊞ **BANYOLES** *3B3* (2km W Rural) *42.12071, 2.74690* **Camping Caravaning El Llac, Ctra Circumvalació de l'Estany s/n, 17834 Porqueres (Gerona)** [tel/fax 972-57 03 05; info@ campingllac.com; www.campingllac.com] Exit AP7 junc 6 to Banyoles. Go strt thro town (do not use by-pass) & exit town at end of lake in 1.6km. Use R-hand layby to turn L sp Porqueres. Site on R in 2.5km. Lge, mkd pitch, pt shd; chem disp; htd wc; shwrs; el pnts €4.60; lndtte; shop; snacks; bar; pool; lake sw; wifi; 80% statics; dogs €2.30; bus 1km; site clsd mid-Dec to mid-Jan; poss cr; quiet but noisy rest/disco adj in high ssn; red long stay/low ssn. "Immac, ltd facs low ssn & stretched high ssn; sm pitches bet trees; pleasant walk around lake to town; site muddy when wet." ♦ € 22.10   2009*

BARBATE see Vejer de la Frontera *2H3*

BARCELONA See sites listed under El Masnou, Gavà and Sitges.

BARREIROS/REINANTE see Foz *1A2*

⊞ **BEAS DE GRANADA** *2G4* (750m N Rural) *37.22416, -3.48805* **Camping Alto de Viñuelas, Ctra de Beas de Granada s/n, 18184 Beas de Granada (Granada) [958-54 60 23; fax 958-54 53 57; info@campingaltodevinuelas. com; www.campingaltodevinuelas.com]** E fr Granada on A92, exit junc 256 & foll sp to Beas de Granada. Site well sp on L in 1.5km Sm, mkd pitch, terr, pt shd; htd wc; chem disp; mv service pnt; shwrs inc; el pnts (5A) €3.50; lndtte (inc dryer); shop; rest; snacks; bar; BBQ; playgrnd; pool; wifi; 10% statics; dogs; bus to Granada at gate; Eng spkn; red long stay; CCI. "In beautiful area; views fr all pitches; 4X4 trip to adj natural park; gd; conv for night halt." € 33.00   2011*

⊞ **BECERREA** *1B2* (15km E Rural) *42.86138, -7.12000* **Camping Os Ancares, Ctra NV1, Liber, 27664 Mosteiro-Cervantes (Lugo) [tel/fax 982-36 45 56; www.camping osancares.com]** Fr A6 exit Becerreá S onto LU722 sp Navia de Suarna. After 10km in Liber turn R onto LU723 sp Doiras, site in 7km just beyond Mosteiro hamlet; site sp. Site ent steep & narr - diff lge o'fits & lge m'vans. Med, terr, shd; wc; shwrs inc; el pnts (6A) €3; gas; lndry rm; rest; snacks; bar; playgrnd; pool; fishing; horseriding; some statics; dogs €1; poss cr; quiet; CCI. "Isolated, scenic site; gd rest & san facs; ltd facs low ssn; low trees some pitches; gd walking." € 14.20
2008*

BEGUR *3B3* (1.5km S Rural) *41.94040, 3.19890* **Camping Begur, Ctra d'Esclanyà, Km 2, 17255 Begur (Gerona) [972-62 32 01; fax 972-62 45 66; info@campingbegur. com; www.campingbegur.com]** Exit AP7/E15 junc 6 Gerona onto C66 dir La Bisbal & Palamós. At x-rds to Pals turn L dir Begur then turn R twd Esclanyà, site on R, clearly sp. Slope to site ent. Lge, mkd pitch, hdstg, shd; wc; chem disp; mv service pnt; baby facs; serviced pitches; shwrs inc; el pnts (10A) inc; lndtte; supmkt; rest; snacks; bar; BBQ; playgrnd; pool; paddling pool; sand/shgl beach 2km; tennis; cycle hire; games area; games rm; gym; wifi; entmnt; 14% statics; dogs €6.50; phone; bus adj; Eng spkn; adv bkg; red long stay/snr citizens/CCI. "Excel, peaceful site; narr site rds poss diff lge o'fits; adj castle & magnificent views; excel touring base." ♦ 15 Apr-25 Sep. € 42.90   2010*

BEJAR *1D3* (6km S Rural) *40.36344, -5.74918* **Camping Cinco Castaños, Ctra de la Sierra s/n, 37710 Candelario (Salamanca) [923-41 32 04; fax 923-41 32 82; profetur@ candelariohotel.com; www.candelariohotel.com]** Fr Béjar foll sp Candelario on C515/SA220, site sp on N side of vill. Steep bends & narr app rd. Sm, mkd pitch, pt sl, pt shd; htd wc; chem disp (wc); baby facs; shwrs inc; el pnts (6A) €3.15; gas; lndtte; shop 500m; rest; bar; playgrnd; pool high ssn; no dogs; bus 500m; phone; quiet; CCI. "Mountain vill; friendly owner; no facs in winter; no lge o'fits as steep site." ♦ Holy Week-15 Oct. € 18.50   2011*

⊞ **BEJAR** *1D3* (15km SW Rural) *40.28560, -5.88182* **Camping Las Cañadas, Ctra N630, Km 432, 10750 Baños de Montemayor (Cáceres) [927-48 11 26; fax 927-48 13 14; info@campinglascanadas.com; www.campinglascanadas. com]** Fr S turn off A630 m'way at 437km stone to Heruns then take old N630 twd Béjar. Site at 432km stone, behind 'Hervas Peil' (leather goods shop). Fr N exit A66 junc 427 thro Baños for 3km to site at km432 on R. Lge, mkd pitch, pt sl; shd (net shdg); htd wc; chem disp; mv service pnt; baby facs; shwrs inc; el pnts (5A) €4; gas; lndtte; shop; rest; snacks; bar; playgrnd; pool; paddling pool; fishing; tennis; cycle hire; games area; TV rm; 60% statics; dogs; poss cr; Eng spkn; quiet but rd noise; ccard acc; red long stay/low ssn; CCI. "Gd san facs but poss cold shwrs; high vehicles take care o'hanging trees; gd walking country; NH/sh stay." ♦ € 17.35 (CChq acc)   2009*

⊞ **BELLVER DE CERDANYA** *3B3* (2km E Rural) *42.37163, 1.80674* **Camping Bellver, Ctra N260, Km 193.7, 17539 Isòvol (Gerona) [973-51 02 39; fax 973-51 07 19; camping bellver@campingbellver.com; www.campingbellver.com]** On N260 fr Puigcerdà to Bellver; site on L, well sp. Lge, mkd pitch, shd; htd wc; chem disp (wc); shwrs inc; el pnts (5A) €3.50; gas; lndtte; rest; snacks; bar; playgrnd; pool; 90% statics; dogs; phone; poss cr; Eng spkn; quiet; ccard acc; CCI. "Friendly, helpful staff; lovely pitches along rv; san facs immac; v quiet low ssn; gd NH for Andorra." € 19.20   2011*

⊞ **BELLVER DE CERDANYA** *3B3* (1km W Rural) *42.37110, 1.73625* **Camping La Cerdanya, Ctra N260, Km 200, 25727 Prullans (Lleida) [973-51 02 62; fax 973-51 06 72; cerdanya@prullans.net; www.prullans.net/camping]** Fr Andorra frontier on N260, site sp. Lge, mkd pitch, shd; wc; baby facs; mv service pnt; shwrs inc; el pnts (4A) €5.15; gas; lndtte; shop; rest; snacks; playgrnd; pool; paddling pool; games area; internet; entmnt; 80% statics; dogs €3.45; phone; bus 1km; poss cr; adv bkg; quiet; red long stay; ccard acc. ♦ € 20.60   2011*

BELLVER DE CERDANYA *3B3* (1km W Rural) *42.37299, 1.76042* **Camping Solana del Segre, Ctra N260, Km 198, 25720 Bellver de Cerdanya (Lleida) [973-51 03 10; fax 973-51 06 98; info@solanadelsegre.com; www.solanadelsegre. com]** Take N260 fr Puigcerdà to Seo de Urgell, site at km 198 after Bellver de Cerdanya on L. Lge, pt sl, pt shd; wc; chem disp; shwrs inc; baby facs; el pnts (5A) €4.20; lndtte; shop; rest (w/end only low ssn); snacks; bar; BBQ; playgrnd; pool; games area; games rm; wifi; entmnt; 80% statics; dogs €5; phone; bus 500m; poss cr; adv bkg; quiet; ccard acc; red low ssn. "Steep site rds & exit fr site to main rd; poss diff for cars under 2L; conv NH nr Cadí Tunnel." ♦ 1 Jul-31 Aug. € 37.00
2008*

BENABARRE *3B2* (500m N Urban) *42.1103, 0.4811* **Camping Benabarre, 22580 Benabarre (Huesca) [974-54 35 72; fax 974-54 34 32; aytobenabarre@aragon.es]** Fr N230 S, turn L after 2nd camping sp over bdge & into vill. Ignore brown camping sp (part of riding cent). Med, some hdstg, pt shd; wc; shwrs inc; el pnts (10A) inc; shops 500m; bar; pool; tennis; no statics; bus 600m; phone; quiet. "Excel, friendly, simple site; gd facs; gd value for money; v quiet low ssn; warden calls 1700; mkt on Fri; lovely vill with excel chocolate shop; conv Graus & mountains - a real find." 1 Apr-30 Sep. € 14.00
2008*

SPAIN

BENAMAHOMA see Ubrique *2H3*

⊞ **BENASQUE** *3B2* (3km N Rural) *42.62420, 0.54478* **Camping Aneto, 22440 Benasque (Huesca) [974-55 11 41; fax 974-55 16 63; info@campinganeto.com; www.campinganeto.com]** Fr Vielha N230 then N260 to Castejón de Sos, foll sp to Benasque, site on L in 3km. Med, pt sl, pt shd; wc; chem disp; shwrs inc; el pnts (10A) €4.60; gas; lndtte; shop in ssn & 3km; tradsmn; rest in ssn; snacks; bar; BBQ; playgrnd; sw 3km; trekking; poss cr; Eng spkn; 75% statics; site clsd Nov; phone; quiet; ccard acc; CCI. "Friendly owners; access to pitches poss diff lge o'fits; unspoilt countryside; stunning app via gorges fr S; gd walking, wildflowers." € 25.00   2008*

⊞ **BENICARLO** *3D2* (1.5km NE Urban/Coastal) *40.42611, 0.43777* **Camping La Alegría del Mar, Ctra N340, Km 1046, Calle Playa Norte, 12580 Benicarló (Castellón) [964-47 08 71; info@campingalegria.com; www.campingalegria.com]** Sp off main N340 app Benicarló. Take slip rd mkd Service, go under underpass, turn R on exit & cont twd town, then turn at camp sp by Peugeot dealers. Sm, mkd pitch, pt shd; htd wc; shwrs; el pnts (4-6A) €4.70; gas; lndtte; shop 500m; rest; snacks; bar; playgrnd; sm pool; beach adj; games rm; wifi; some statics; dogs; phone; bus 800m; poss cr; quiet but rd noise at night & poss cockerels!; red long stay/low ssn; ccard acc. "British owners; access to pitches variable, poss diff in ssn; vg, clean san facs; Xmas & New Year packages; phone ahead to reserve pitch; excel." € 22.00   2009*

⊞ **BENICASSIM** *3D2* (500m NE Coastal) *40.05709, 0.07429* **Camping Bonterra Park, Avda de Barcelona 47, 12560 Benicàssim (Castellón) [964-30 00 07; fax 964 10 06 69; info@bonterrapark.com; www.bonterrapark.com]** Fr N exit AP7 junc 45 onto N340 dir Benicàssim. In approx 7km turn R to Benicàssim/Centro Urba; strt ahead to traff lts, then turn L, site on L 500m after going under rlwy bdge. Lge, mkd pitch, hdstg, pt sl, shd; htd wc; chem disp; mv service pnt; some serviced pitches; baby facs; shwrs inc; el pnts (6-10) inc; gas; lndtte (inc dryer); shop; rest; snacks; bar; BBQ; playgrnd; 2 pools (1 covrd & htd); paddling pool; sand beach 300m; tennis; cycle hire; gym; entmnt; games area; wifi; games/TV rm; 15% statics; dogs €2.24 (not acc Jul/Aug); no c'vans/m'vans over 10m; phone; train; sep car park; Eng spkn; adv bkg; rd noise; ccard acc; red long stay/low ssn/CCI. "Fabulous site in perfect location; excel cycle tracks & public transport; lovely beach; reasonable sized pitches; well-kept & well-run; clean modern san facs; access to some pitches poss diff due to trees; sun shades some pitches; winter festival 3rd wk Jan; Harley Davidson rallies Jan & Sep, check in adv; highly rec." ♦ € 59.15 SBS - E19   2011*

See advertisement

⊞ **BENICASSIM** *3D2* (4.5km NW Coastal) *40.05908, 0.08515* **Camping Azahar, Ptda Villaroig s/n, 12560 Benicàssim (Castellón) [964-30 31 96; fax 964-30 25 12; info@ campingazahar.es; www.campingazahar.es]** Fr AP7 junc 45 take N340 twd València; in 5km L at top of hill (do not turn R to go-karting); foll sp. Turn R under rlwy bdge opp Hotel Voramar. Lge, mkd pitch, pt sl, terr, unshd; htd wc; chem disp; mv service pnt; baby facs; shwrs inc; el pnts (4-6A) €2.90 (long leads poss req); gas; lndtte; rest; snacks; bar; playgrnd; pool; sand beach 300m across rd; tennis at hotel; cycle hire; 25% statics; dogs €4.07; phone; bus adj; poss cr high ssn; Eng spkn; bus adj; adv bkg; ccard acc; red long stay/low ssn/snr citizens; CCI. "Popular site, esp in winter; poss noisy high ssn; access poss diff for m'vans & lge o'fits; poss uneven pitches; organised events; gd walking & cycling; gd touring base." ♦ € 28.42   2010*

⊞ **BENIDORM** *4F2* (1km N Coastal) *38.5514, -0.09628* **Camping Arena Blanca, Avda Dr Severo Ochoa 44, 03503 Benidorm (Alicante) [965-86 18 89; fax 965-86 11 07; info@camping-arenablanca.es; www.camping-arenablanca.es]** Fr AP7 exit junc 65 onto N332 dir Playa Levante. Site sp. Med, terr, pt shd; wc; chem disp; some serviced pitches; shwrs inc; el pnts (16A) €3; gas; lndtte; supmkt; rest; snacks; bar; playgrnd; pool; paddling pool; sand beach 1km; cash machine; sat TV conn all pitches; 30% statics; dogs free; phone; bus 200m; adv bkg; quiet; ccard acc; red long stay/red CCI. ♦ € 27.00   2008*

⊞ **BENIDORM** *4F2* (2km N Coastal) *38.56926, -0.09328* **Camping Almafrá, Partida de Cabut 25, 03503 Benidorm (Alicante) [tel/fax 965-88 90 75; info@campingalmafra.es; www.campingalmafra.es]** Exit AP7 junc 65 onto N332 N. Foll sp Alfaz del Pi, site. Lge, mkd pitch, unshd; htd wc; sauna; baby facs; sauna; private san facs avail; shwrs inc; el pnts (16A); lndtte (inc dryer); shop; rest; snacks; bar; BBQ; playgrnd; 2 htd pools (1 covrd); paddling pool; jacuzzi; tennis; wellness/fitness cent; games area; gym; wifi; entmnt; sat TV; 30% statics; no dogs; adv bkg; quiet; red long stay/low ssn/CCI. ♦ (CChq acc)   2010*

⊞ **BENIDORM** *4F2* (1.5km NE Urban) *38.54833, -0.09851* **Camping El Raco, Avda Dr Severo Ochoa s19, Racó de Loix, 03500 Benidorm (Alicante) [965-86 85 52; fax 965-86 85 44; info@campingraco.com; www.campingraco.com]** Turn off A7 m'way at junc 65 then L onto A332; take turning sp Benidorm Levante Beach; ignore others; L at 1st traff lghts; strt on at next traff lts, El Raco turn on R. Lge, hdg/mkd pitch, hdstg, pt sl, pt shd; wc; chem disp; 50% serviced pitches; baby facs; shwrs inc; el pnts (10A) €4; gas; lndtte (inc dryer); shop; rest; snacks; bar; BBQ; playgrnd; 2 pools (1 htd, covrd); beach 1.5km; games area; wifi; TV; 30% statics; bus; poss v cr in winter; quiet; red low ssn; CCI. "Excel site; popular winter long stay but strictly applied rules about leaving c'van unoccupied; el pnts metered for long stay." ♦ € 26.50   2010*

OPEN THROUGHOUT THE YEAR

SPECIAL FEES IN WINTER SEASON

WOODEN BUNGALOWS & CHALETS

AT 300 m FROM THE BEACH

Avda. Barcelona, 47 - 12560 Benicàssim - Castellón (Spain)
T. +34 964 300 007 - F. +34 964 300 008 - info@bonterrapark.com - www.bonterrapark.com

⊞ **BENIDORM** *4F2* (3km NE Urban) *38.56024, -0.09844* Camping Benisol, Avda de la Comunidad Valenciana s/n, 03500 Benidorm (Alicante) [965-85 16 73; fax 965-86 08 95; campingbenisol@yahoo.es; www.camping benisol.com] Exit AP7/E15 junc 65 onto N332. Foll sp Benidorm, Playa Levante (avoid by-pass). Dangerous rd on ent to sit; site ent easy to miss. Lge, hdg pitch, hdstg, shd; wc; chem disp; serviced pitches; shwrs inc; el pnts (4-6A) €2.80; gas; lndtte; shop & rest (high ssn); snacks; bar; playgrnd; pool (hgh ssn); sand beach 4km; TV; 85% statics; dogs; phone; bus to Benidorm; poss cr; Eng spkn; adv bkg with dep; some rd noise; red long stay/low ssn; CCI. "Helpful staff; well-run, clean site; many permanent residents." ♦ € 27.20   2011*

⊞ **BENIDORM** *4F2* (3km NE Coastal) *38.54438, -0.10325* Camping La Torreta, Avda Dr Severo Ochoa 11, 03500 Benidorm (Alicante) [965-85 46 68; fax 965-80 26 53; campinglatorreta@gmail.com] Exit AP7/E15 junc 65 onto N332. Foll sp Playa Levante, site sp. Lge, mkd pitch, hdstg, pt sl, terr, pt shd (bamboo shades); wc (some cont); chem disp; mv service pnt; shwrs inc; el pnts (10A) €3.40; gas; lndtte (inc dryer); shop; rest; snacks; bar; playgrnd; pool; paddling pool; sand beach 1km; wifi; 10% statics; dogs; bus; no adv bkg; quiet; red long stay; CCI. "Take care siting if heavy rain; some pitches v sm; popular with long stay winter visitors." ♦ € 29.00   2010*

⊞ **BENIDORM** *4F2* (1km E Coastal) *38.5449, -0.10696* Camping Villasol, Avda Bernat de Sarriá 13, 03500 Benidorm (Alicante) [965-85 04 22; fax 966-80 64 20; info@camping-villasol.com; www.camping-villasol.com] Leave AP7 at junc 65 onto N332 dir Alicante; take exit into Benidorm sp Levante. Turn L at traff lts just past Camping Titus, then in 200m R at lts into Avda Albir. Site on R in 1km. Care - dip at ent, poss grounding. V lge, mkd pitch, hdstg, shd; htd wc; chem disp; baby facs; shwrs inc; el pnts (5A) €4.28; lndtte; supmkt; rest; snacks; bar; playgrnd; 2 pools (1 htd, covrd); sand beach 300m; games area; wifi; sat TV all pitches; medical service; currency exchange; 5% statics; no dogs; phone; adv bkg; Eng spkn; quiet; ccard acc; red low ssn/long stay. "Excel, well-kept site especially in winter; some sm pitches; friendly staff." ♦ € 34.55   2008*

⊞ **BERCEO** *1B4* (200m SE Rural) *42.33565, -2.85335* Camping Berceo, El Molino s/n, 26327 Berceo (La Rioja) [941-37 32 27; fax 941-37 32 01; camping.berceo@fer.es] Fr E on N120 foll sp Tricio, San Millan de la Cogolla on LR136/LR206. Fr W foll sp Villar de Torre & San Millan. In Berceo foll sp sw pools & site. Med, hdg/mkd pitch, hdstg, pt sl, shd; htd wc; chem disp; baby facs; fam bthrm; shwrs inc; el pnts (7A) €4.70; lndtte (inc dryer); shop; tradsmn; rest; snacks; bar; playgrnd; pool; paddling pool; cycle hire; wifi; TV; 50% statics; phone; bus 200m; adv bkg; quiet; red long stay; CCI. "Excel base for Rioja vineyards; gd site." ♦ € 30.65   2010*

BESALU *3B3* (2km E Rural) *42.20952, 2.73682* **Camping Masia Can Coromines, Ctra N260, Km 60, 17851 Maià del Montcal (Gerona) [tel/fax 972-59 11 08; coromines@grn. es; www.cancoromines.com]** NW fr Gerona on C66 to Besalú. Turn R sp Figueras (N260) for 2.5km. At 60km sp turn into driveway on L opp fountain for approx 300m. Narr app & ent. Site is 1km W of Maià. Narr site ent poss diff lge o'fits. Sm, pt shd; wc; serviced pitch; shwrs €0.50; el pnts (10-15A) €3; gas; lndtte; shop 2.5km; rest high ssn; snacks; bar; playgrnd; pool; cycle hire; internet; some statics; dogs €2.90; Eng spkn; adv bkg; quiet with some rd noise; ccard acc; CCI. "Friendly, family-run site in beautiful area; gd walks; facs poss stretched when site full." ♦ 1 Apr-4 Nov. € 20.40   2011*

BIELSA *3B2* (7km W Rural) *42.65176, 0.14076* **Camping Pineta, Ctra del Parador, Km 7, 22350 Bielsa (Huesca) [974-50 10 89; fax 974-50 11 84; info@campingpineta. com; www.campingpineta.com]** Fr A138 in Beilsa turn W & foll sp for Parador Monte Perdido & Valle de Pineta. Site on L after 8km (ignore previous campsite off rd). Lge, terr, pt sl, pt shd; wc; chem disp; mv service pnt; baby facs; shwrs inc; el pnts (6A) €4.50 (poss rev pol); gas; lndtte (inc dryer); shop & 8km; rest; snacks; bar; BBQ; playgrnd; pool; games area; cycle hire; some statics; phone; ccard acc; CCI. "Well-maintained site; clean facs; glorious location in National Park." Easter-10 Dec. € 20.05   2009*

⊞ **BIESCAS** *3B2* (1km SE Rural) *42.61944, -0.30416* **Camping Gavín, Ctra N260, Km 502.5, 22639 Gavín (Huesca) [974-48 50 90 or 659-47 95 51; fax 974-48 50 17; info@ campinggavin.com; www.campinggavin.com]** Take N330/ A23/E7 N fr Huesca twd Sabiñánigo then N260 twd Biescas & Valle de Tena (do not take 1st sp Biescas fr Huesca). Bear R on N260 at g'ge on app to Biescas & foll sp Gavín & site, well sp. Site is at km 502.5 fr Huesca, bet Biescas & Gavín. Lge, mkd pitch, terr, pt shd; htd wc; chem disp; mv service pnt; baby facs; fam bthrm; shwrs inc; el pnts (10A) inc; gas; lndtte (inc dryer); shop; tradsmn; rest; snacks; bar; playgrnd; pool; tennis; cycle hire in National Park; wifi; TV rm; 40% statics; dogs inc; phone; bus 1km; adv bkg; quiet; CCI. "Wonderful, scenic site nr Ordesa National Park; poss diff access to pitches for lge o'fits & m'vans; superb htd san facs; Eng spkn; immac kept site; excel." ♦ € 37.36 (CChq acc)   2011*

⊞ **BILBAO** *1A4* (14km N Coastal) *43.38916, -2.98444* **Camping Sopelana, Ctra Bilbao-Plentzia, Km 18, Playa Atxabiribil 30, 48600 Sopelana (Vizcaya) [946-76 19 81; fax 944-21 50 10; recepcion@campingsopelana.com; www. campingsopelana.com]** In Bilbao cross rv by m'way bdge sp to airport, foll 637/634 N twd & Plentzia. Cont thro Sopelana & foll sp on L. Med, hdg pitch, sl, terr; wc (some cont); own san; chem disp; mv service pnt; baby facs; shwrs; el pnts (10A) €3.50; gas; lndtte; shop, rest (w'end only low ssn); snacks; bar; playgrnd; pool; sand beach 200m; 70% statics; metro 2km; poss cr; Eng spkn; adv bkg ess high ssn; quiet but noise fr disco adj; red long stay; CCI. "Poss stong sea winds; ltd space for tourers; pitches sm, poss flooded after heavy rain & poss diff due narr, steep site rds; ltd facs low ssn & poss v unclean; poss no hot water for shwrs; helpful manager; site used by local workers; poor security in city cent/Guggenheim car park; poss clsd low ssn - phone ahead to check; NH/sh stay only." ♦ € 25.50   2009*

BILBAO *1A4* (3km NW Urban) *43.27600, -2.96700* **Camp Municipal Caravaning Bilbao, Ribera de Zorrozaurre 2, 48014 Bilbao (Vizcaya) [944-79 57 60; informacion@ bilbaoturismo.bilbao.net; www.bilbao.net/bilbaoturismo]** Exit A8 junc 117; foll sps to Plaza Sagrado Corazón; at rndabt (with column) take exit at 11 o'clock to Euskalduna Bdge across rv; at next rndabt take last exit along rv. Site in 1.6km. Lock-up g'ge on R. NB A drive thro busy city cent with only occasional yellow sps 'Caravannes Parking'. Rec download Michelin map bef travel. Sm, hdstg, shd; htd wc; chem disp; mv service pnt; shwrs inc; el pnts inc; bus adj to metro; some rd & rlwy noise; max stay 3 days. "Unconventional site v conv for Bilbao; gd san facs; lock-up g'ge facs for 10-15 o'fits; gd." 15 Jul-15 Sep. € 10.00   2008*

BLANES *3C3* (1km S Coastal) *41.65944, 2.77972* **Camping Bella Terra, Avda Vila de Madrid 35-40, 17300 Blanes (Gerona) [972-34 80 17 or 972-34 80 23; fax 972-34 82 75; info@campingbellaterra.com; www.campingbellaterra. com]** Exit A7 junc 9 via Lloret or junc 10 via Tordera. On app Blanes, all campsites are sp at rndabts; all sites along same rd. V lge, mkd pitch, hdstg, pt sl, shd; wc; chem disp; mv service pnt; baby facs; shwrs inc; el pnts (5A) inc; gas; lndtte (inc dryer); shop; tradsmn; rest; snacks; bar; BBQ; playgrnd; pools; sand beach adj; tennis; games area; games rm; cycle hire; wifi; entmnt; TV rm; 15% statics; dogs €4.50; Eng spkn; quiet; ccard acc; red long stay/low ssn/CCI. "Split site - 1 side has pool, 1 side adj beach; pitches on pool side lger; vg site with excel facs." ♦ 27 Mar-26 Sep. € 42.40   2010*

⊞ **BLANES** *3C3* (1km S Coastal) *41.65933, 2.77000* **Camping Blanes, Avda Vila de Madrid 33, 17300 Blanes (Gerona) [972-33 15 91; fax 972-33 70 63; info@campingblanes. com; www.campingblanes.com]** Fr N on AP7/E15 exit junc 9 onto NII dir Barcelona & foll sp Blanes. Fr S to end of C32, then NII dir Blanes. On app Blanes, foll camping sps & Playa S'Abanell - all campsites are sp at rndabts; all sites along same rd. Site adj Hotel Blau-Mar. Lge, mkd pitch, shd; wc; chem disp; mv service pnt; shwrs inc; shop; el pnts (5A) inc; gas; lndtte; supmkt; snacks high ssn; bar; playgrnd; pool; solarium; dir access to sand beach; watersports; cycle hire; games rm; wifi; entmnt; dogs; phone; bus; poss cr; Eng spkn; quiet; ccard acc; red low ssn. "Excel site, espec low ssn; helpful owner; easy walk to town cent; trains to Barcelona & Gerona." ♦ € 36.95   2011*

See advertisement opposite (above)

BLANES *3C3* (1km S Coastal) *41.6550, 2.77861* **Camping El Pinar Beach, Avda Villa de Madrid s/n, 17300 Blanes (Gerona) [972-33 10 83; fax 972-33 11 00; camping@ elpinarbeach.com; www.elpinarbeach.com]** Exit AP7/ E15 junc 9 dir Malgrat. On app Blanes, all campsites are sp at rndabts; all sites along same rd. V lge, mkd pitch, shd; wc; chem disp; mv service pnt; baby facs; shwrs inc; el pnts (5A) inc; lndtte; shop; rest; snacks; bar; BBQ; playgrnd; pool; paddling pool; sand beach adj; games area; entmnt; excursions; internet; TV; 10% statics; dogs €2; phone; adv bkg; ccard acc; red long stay/low ssn/CCI. "V pleasant site; gd facs; lovely beach; lots to do." ♦ 27 Mar-26 Sep. € 36.00   2010*

⊞ **BLANES** *3C3* (1km S Coastal) *41.66408, 2.78249* **Camping S'Abanell, Avda Villa de Madrid 7-9, 17300 Blanes (Gerona)** [972-33 18 09; fax 972-35 05 06; info@sabanell.com; www.sabanell.com] Take coast rd S fr cent Blanes. Site well sp on L in 1km. Lge, mkd pitch, pt sl, shd; wc; chem disp; serviced pitches; shwrs; el pnts (6A) €3; gas; lndtte; shop; rest; snacks; bar; sand beach adj; 5% statics; dogs €1; phone; site clsd 25 Dec-6 Jan; poss cr; adv bkg; rd noise; red low ssn/ snr citizens; CCI. "Friendly, helpful staff; lge o'fits may need manhandling due pitch layout." € 32.90   2008*

⊞ **BLANES** *3C3* (1.5km SW Urban/Coastal) *41.66305, 2.78083* **Camping La Masia, Calle Cristòfor Colon 44, 17300 Blanes (Gerona)** [972-33 10 13; fax 972-33 31 28; info@ campinglamasia.com; www.campinglamasia.com] Fr A7 exit junc 9 sp Lloret de Mar, then Blanes. At Blanes foll sp Blanes Sur (Playa) & Campings, site immed past Camping S'Abanell, well sp. V lge, hdstg, pt shd; htd wc; chem disp; mv service pnt; 25% serviced pitches; sauna; steam rm; baby facs; shwrs inc; el pnts (3-5A) inc; lndtte (inc dryer); shop; rest; snacks; bar; playgrnd; 2 pools (1 htd, covrd); paddling pool; sand beach nrby; watersports; tennis 500m; weights rm; wellness cent; games area; games rm; wifi; entmnt; TV rm; 90% statics; dogs; site clsd mid-Dec to mid-Jan; poss cr; Eng spkn; adv bkg; poss noisy at w/ends; red long stay/low ssn; CCI. "Well-maintained site; excel, clean facs; helpful staff." ♦ € 38.50 (CChq acc)   2009*

BLANES *3C3* (1.5km SW Coastal) *41.66206, 2.78046* **Camping Solmar, Calle Cristòfor Colom 48, 17300 Blanes (Gerona)** [972-34 80 34; fax 972-34 82 83; campingsolmar@ campingsolmar.com; www.campingsolmar.com] Fr N on AP7/E15 exit junc 9 onto NII dir Barcelona & foll sp Blanes. Fr S to end of C32, then NII dir Blanes. On app Blanes, foll camping sps. Lge, hdg/mkd pitch, shd; wc; chem disp; mv service pnt; baby facs; shwrs inc; el pnts (6A) inc; lndtte (inc dryer); shop; rest; snacks; bar; BBQ; playgrnd; 2 pools; paddling pool; sand beach 150m; tennis; games area; games rm; wifi; entmnt; some statics; dogs free; bus 100m; adv bkg; quiet; ccard acc; red long stay/low ssn/CCI. "Excel site & facs." ♦ 2 Apr-12 Oct. € 39.45   2011*

See advertisement below

BOCA DE HUERGANO see Riaño *1A3*

⊞ **BOCAIRENT** *4F2* (9km E Rural) *38.75332, -0.54957* **Camping Mariola, Ctra Bocairent-Alcoi, Km 9, 46880 Bocairent (València)** [962-13 51 60; fax 962-13 50 31; info@campingmariola.com; www.campingmariola.com] Fr N330 turn E at Villena onto CV81. N of Banyeres & bef Bocairent turn E sp Alcoi up narr, steep hill with some diff turns & sheer drops; site sp. Lge, hdstg, pt shd; htd wc (cont); mv service pnt; shwrs inc; el pnts (6A) €4; lndtte; shop; rest; snacks; bar; BBQ; cooking facs; playgrnd; pool; paddling pool; games area; internet; 50% statics; phone; ccard acc; CCI. "In Mariola mountains; gd walking." € 17.55   2011*

SPAIN

BOLTANA see Ainsa *3B2*

BONANSA see Pont de Suert *3B2*

⊞ **BOSSOST** *3B2* (3km SE Rural) *42.74921, 0.70071* **Camping Prado Verde, Ctra de Lleida a Francia, N230, Km 173, 25551 Era Bordeta/La Bordeta de Vilamòs (Lleida) [tel/fax 973-64 71 72; info@campingpradoverde.es; www.campingpradoverde.es]** On N230 at km 173 on banks of Rv Garona. Med, shd; htd wc; mv service pnt; baby facs; shwrs; el pnts (6A) €5.50; lndtte (inc dryer); shop & 3km; rest; snacks; bar; playgrnd; pool; paddling pool; fishing; cycle hire; wifi; TV; some statics; dogs; bus; quiet; ccard acc; CCI. "V pleasant NH." € 22.00   2010*

BOSSOST *3B2* (4km S Rural) *42.75122, 0.69677* **Camping Bedura Park, Ctra N230, Km 174.5, 25551 Era Bordeta (Lleida) [tel/fax 973-64 82 93; info@bedurapark.com; www.bedurapark.com]** Fr N on N230, R over rv behind Camping Forcanada. Fr S on N230, 10km fr Viela, L turn over rv. Site is 12km fr French border. Med, mkd pitch, terr, pt shd; wc; chem disp; baby facs; shwrs; el pnts (5A) €4.25; gas; lndtte; shop; rest; BBQ; playgrnd; htd pool; fishing; cycle hire; 20% statics; no dogs; phone; bus 200m; poss cr; Eng spkn; adv bkg; CCI. "Skiing, walking in area; excel." ♦ Holy Week-30 Sep. € 28.50   2008*

I'll go online and tell the Club what we think of the campsites we've visited – www.caravanclub.co.uk/europereport

BROTO *3B2* (1.2km W Rural) *42.59779, -0.13072* **Camping Oto, Afueras s/n, 22370 Oto-Broto (Huesca) [974-48 60 75; fax 974-48 63 47; info@campingoto.com; www.campingoto.com]** On N260 foll camp sp on N o'skts of Broto. Diff app thro vill but poss. Lge, pt sl, pt shd; wc; chem disp; baby facs; shwrs inc; el pnts (10A) €3.80 (poss no earth); gas; lndtte; shop; snacks; bar; BBQ; playgrnd; pool; paddling pool; entmnt; adv bkg; quiet; ccard acc. "Excel, clean san facs; excel bar & café; friendly owner; pitches below pool rec; some noise fr adj youth site; conv Ordesa National Park." 6 Mar-14 Oct. € 16.70   2008*

⊞ **BROTO** *3B2* (6km W Rural) *42.61576, -0.15432* **Camping Viu, Ctra N260, Biescas-Ordesa, Km 484.2, 22378 Viu de Linás (Huesca) [974-48 63 01; fax 974-48 63 73; info@campingviu.com; www.campingviu.com]** Lies on N260, 4km W of Broto. Fr Broto, N for 2km on rd 135; turn W twd Biesca at junc with Torla rd; site approx 4km on R. Med, sl, pt shd; htd wc; chem disp; mv service pnt; shwrs inc; el pnts (5-8A) €4.20; gas; lndtte; shop; rest; BBQ; playgrnd; games rm; cycle hire; horseriding; walking, skiing & climbing adj; car wash; phone; adv bkg; quiet; ccard acc; CCI. "Friendly owners; gd home cooking; fine views; highly rec; clean, modern san facs; poss not suitable for lge o'fits." € 17.40   2011*

BURGO DE OSMA, EL *1C4* (17km N Rural) *41.7292, -3.0481* **Camping Cañón del Rió Lobos, Ctra El Burgo de Osma-San Leonardo, 42317 Ucero (Soria) [tel/fax 975-36 35 65]** On SO 920 17km N fr El Burgo de Osma or S fr San Leonardo de Yagüe. Site 1km N of Ucero. Care needed over narr bdge in vill cent. Med, hdg/mkd pitch, hdstg & grass, shd; wc; chem disp; mv service pnt; shwrs inc; el pnts (6A) €4.85; lndtte; rest; snacks; bar; BBQ; playgrnd; pool; no dogs; quiet; no ccard acc; CCI. "Sm pitches/tight turning - help avail; heart of canyon of Rv Lobos; v pretty location; gd base walking, cycling, climbing; bird watchers' paradise; poss w/end only until beginning Jun." Easter-30 Sep. € 22.50   2008*

BURGOS () **Camping -Motel Pecon del Conde,**   2011*

⊞ **BURGOS** *1B4* (2.5km E Rural) *42.34111, -3.65777* **Camp Municipal Fuentes Blancas, Ctra Cartuja Miraflores, Km 3.5, 09193 Burgos [tel/fax 947-48 60 16; info@campingburgos.com; www.campingburgos.com]** E or W on A1 exit junc 238 & cont twd Burgos. Strt over 1st rndabt, then turn R sp Cortes. Look for yellow sps to site. Lge, mkd pitch, shd; some htd wc; chem disp; mv service pnt; baby facs; shwrs inc; el pnts (6A) inc; gas; lndtte; shop high ssn & 3km; rest; snacks; bar; playgrnd; pool high ssn; games area; wifi; 10% statics; dogs €2.17; phone; bus at gate; poss cr; Eng spkn; quiet; ccard acc; CCI. "Clean facs but refurb req (2010); neat, roomy, well-maintained site adj woodland; some sm pitches; ltd facs low ssn; poss v muddy in wet; easy access town car parks or cycle/rv walk; Burgos lovely town; gd NH." € 22.60   2011*

CABO DE GATA see Almería *4G1*

⊞ **CABRERA, LA** *1D4* (1km SW Rural) *40.85797, -3.61580* **Camping Pico de la Miel, Ctra N1, Km 58, Finca Prado Nuevo, 28751 La Cabrera (Madrid) [918-68 80 82 or 918-68 95 07; fax 918-68 85 41; pico-miel@picomiel.com; www.picodelamiel.com]** Fr Madrid on A1/E5, exit junc 57 sp La Cabrera. Turn L at rndabt, site sp. Lge, mkd pitch, pt sl, pt shd; htd wc; chem disp; shwrs inc; el pnts (10A) €4.45; gas; lndtte (inc dryer); shop high ssn; supmkt 1km; rest, snacks; bar high ssn & w/end; playgrnd; Olympic-size pool; paddling pool; sailing; fishing; windsurfing; tennis; games area; squash; mountain-climbing; car wash; 75% statics; dogs; phone; v cr high ssn & w/end; some Eng spkn; adv bkg; quiet; ccard acc; red long stay/low ssn/CCI. "Attractive walking country; conv Madrid; ltd touring area not v attractive; some pitches have low sun shades; excel san facs; ltd facs low ssn." ♦ € 24.00   2011*

CABRERA, LA *1D4* (15km SW Rural) *40.80821, -3.69106* **Camping Piscis, Ctra Guadalix de la Sierra a Navalafuente, Km 3, 28729 Navalafuente (Madrid) [918-43 22 68; fax 918-43 22 53; campiscis@campiscis.com; www.campiscis.com]** Fr A1/E5 exit junc 50 onto M608 dir Guidalix de la Sierra, foll sp to Navalafuente & site. Lge, hdg pitch, hdstg, pt sl, pt shd; wc; chem disp; shwrs €0.30; el pnts (5A) €4.85 (long lead req); gas; lndtte; shop 6km; rest; snacks; bar; playgrnd; pool; paddling pool; watersports 10km; tennis; games area; 75% statics; quiet; adv bkg; Eng spkn; ccard acc; red low ssn; CCI. "Mountain views; walking; bus to Madrid daily outside gate; spacious pitches but uneven; rough site rds." ♦ 15 Jun-15 Sep. € 24.20   2010*

SPAIN

⊞ **CACERES** *2E3* (4km NW Urban) *39.48861, -6.41277* **Camp Municipal Ciudad de Cáceres, Ctra N630, Km 549.5, 10080 Cáceres [tel/fax 927-23 31 00; info@campingcaceres. com; www.campingcaceres.com]** Fr Cáceres ring rd take N630 dir Salamanca. At 1st rndbt turn R sp Via de Servicio with camping symbol. Foll sp 500m to site. Or fr N exit A66 junc 545 onto N630 twd Cáceres. At 2nd rndabt turn L sp Via de Servicio, site on L adj football stadium. Med, mkd pitch, hdstg, terr, unshd; wc; chem disp; mv service pnt; individ san facs each pitch; shwrs inc; el pnts (10-16A) €4.50; gas; lndtte; shop; rest; snacks; bar; BBQ; playgrnd; pool high ssn; paddling pool; games area; wifi; TV; 15% statics; dogs; bus 500m over footbdge; Eng spkn; adv bkg; distant noise fr indus est nrby; ccard acc; red low ssn/CCI. "Vg, well-run site; excel facs; vg value rest; gd for disabled access; good bus service to and from interesting old town with many historical bldgs." € 30.00   2011*

CADAQUES *3B3* (1km N Coastal) *42.29172, 3.28260* **Camping Cadaqués, Ctra Port Lligat 17, 17488 Cadaqués (Gerona) [972-25 81 26; fax 972-15 93 83; info@campingcadaques. com]** At ent to town, turn L at rdbt (3rd exit)sp thro narr streets, site in about 1.5km on L. NB App to Cadaqués on busy, narr mountain rds, not suitable lge o'fits. If raining, roads only towable with 4x4. Lge, mkd pitch, hdstg, sl, pt shd; wc; chem disp; shwrs; el pnts (5A) €5.15; gas; lndtte; shop; rest; snacks; bar; playgrnd; pool; paddling pool; shgl beach 600m; no dogs; sep car park; poss cr; Eng spkn; no adv bkg; quiet; ccard acc. "Cadaqués home of Salvador Dali; sm pitches; medical facs high ssn; san facs poss poor low ssn; next to motorway so poss noisy but good for en-route stop." Easter-17 Sep. € 30.00   2011*

CADAVEDO see Luarca *1A3*

⊞ **CALATAYUD** *3C1* (15km N Rural) *41.44666, -1.55805* **Camping Saviñan Parc, Ctra El Frasno-Mores, Km 7, 50299 Saviñan (Zaragoza) [tel/fax 976-82 54 23]** Exit A2/E90 (Zaragoza-Madrid) at km 255 to T-junc. Turn R to Saviñan for 6km, foll sps to site 1km S. Lge, hdstg, terr, pt shd; wc; chem disp; mv service pnt; shwrs inc; el pnts (6-10A) €4.20; gas; lndtte; shop; playgrnd; pool high ssn; tennis; horseriding; 50% statics; dogs €2.70; phone; site clsd Jan; quiet; ccard acc; CCI. "Beautiful scenery & views; some sm narr pitches; rec identify pitch location to avoid stop/start on hill; terr pitches have steep, unfenced edges; many pitches with sunscreen frames & diff to manoeuvre long o'fits; modern facs block but cold in winter & poss stretched high ssn; hot water to some shwrs only; gates poss clsd low ssn - use intercom; site poss clsd Feb." € 22.00   2011*

CALATAYUD *3C1* (3km E Rural) *41.36247, -1.60505* **Camping Calatayud, Ctra Madrid-Barcelona, Km 239, 50300 Calatayud (Zaragoza) [976-88 05 92; fax 976-36 07 76; rsanramon237@msn.com]** Fr W exit A2 sp Calatayud; site on S side of old N11 (parallel to new dual c'way) at km stone 239a. Med, pt shd; wc; chem disp; shwrs; el pnts (5-10A) €5.35 (poss rev pol); gas; lndtte; snacks; shop 2km; pool; dogs; some rd noise; ccard acc; CCI. "Site area bleak; clean, refurbished san facs & pool; easy to manoeuvre twin-axles; interesting town; much improved NH." 15 Mar-30 Oct. € 21.40   2009*

⊞ **CALDES DE MONTBUI** *3C3* (2km N Rural) *41.6442, 2.1564* **Camping El Pasqualet, Ctra Sant Sebastià de Montmajor, Km 0.3, 08140 Caldes de Montbui (Barcelona) [938-65 46 95; fax 938-65 38 96; elpasqualet@elpasqualet.com; www.elpasqualet.com]** N fr Caldes on C59 dir Montmajor, site sp on L off rd BV1243. Med, terr, pt shd; wc; chem disp; mv service pnt; baby facs; shwrs inc; el pnts (4A) €6.90; gas; lndtte (inc dryer); shop 2km; tradsmn; rest; snacks; bar; playgrnd; pool; games area; TV rm; 80% statics; dogs €2.60; bus 2km; site clsd mid-Dec to mid-Jan; poss cr; adv bkg; quiet. "Beautiful area; ltd touring pitches; facs poss stretched high ssn." ♦ € 26.40   2010*

CALELLA *3C3* (2km NE Coastal) *41.61774, 2.67680* **Camping Caballo de Mar, Passeig Maritim s/n, 08397 Pineda de Mar (Barcelona) [937-67 17 06; fax 937-67 16 15; info@ caballodemar.com; www.caballodemar.com]** Fr N exit AP7 junc 9 & immed turn R onto NII dir Barcelona. Foll sp Pineda de Mar & turn L twd Paseo Maritimo. Fr S on C32 exit 122 dir Pineda de Mar & foll dir Paseo Maritimo. Lge, mkd pitch, shd; wc; chem disp; baby facs; shwrs inc; el pnts (3-6A) €3.40-4.40; gas; lndtte; shop; tradsmn; rest; snacks; bar; BBQ; playgrnd; pool; sand beach adj; games area; games rm; entmnt; internet; 10% statics; dogs €2.20; rlwy stn 2km (Barcelona 30 mins); Eng spkn; adv bkg; quiet; ccard acc; red long stay/CCI. "Excursions arranged; gd touring base & conv Barcelona; gd, modern facs; excel." ♦ 31 Mar-30 Sep. € 25.60   2011*

⊞ **CALELLA** *3C3* (1km S Coastal) *41.60722, 2.63973* **Camping Botànic Bona Vista Kim, Ctra N11, Km 665.8, 08370 Calella de la Costa (Barcelona) [937-69 24 88; fax 937-69 58 04; info@botanic-bonavista.net; www.botanic-bonavista.net]** A19/C32 exit sp Calella onto NII coast rd, site is sp S of Calella on R. Care needed on busy rd & sp almost on top of turning (adj Camp Roca Grossa). Lge, mkd pitch, hdstg, terr, pt shd; shwrs inc; wc; chem disp; mv service pnt; sauna; shwrs inc; el pnts (6A) €7.80 (rev pol); lndtte; supmkt; rest; snacks; bar; BBQ/picnic area; playgrnd; pool; paddling pool; sand beach adj; solarium; jacuzzi; TV; 20% statics; dogs €5.90; phone; poss cr; Eng spkn; adv bkg; some rd noise; ccard acc; CCI. "Steep access rd to site - owner prefers to tow c'vans with 4x4; poss diff v lge m'vans; all pitches have sea view; friendly owner; clean facs; train to Barcelona fr St Pol (2km)." ♦ € 30.80   2010*

CALELLA *3C3* (1km SW Coastal) *41.60635, 2.63890* **Camping Roca Grossa, Ctra N-11, Km 665, 08370 Calella (Barcelona) [937-69 12 97; fax 937-66 15 56; rocagrossa@rocagrossa. com; www.rocagrossa.com]** Situated off rd N11 at km stone 665, site sp. V steep access rd to site. Lge, sl, terr, shd; wc; chem disp; mv service pnt; shwrs inc; el pnts (6A) €6; gas; lndtte; shop & rest at ent; snacks; bar; games rm; TV rm; pool; playgrnd; beach adj; windsurfing; tennis; statics; phone; dogs €4.20; adv bkg; Eng spkn; ccard acc. "V friendly, family-run site; steep - tractor pull avail - but level pitches; clean modern facs; excel pool & playgrnd on top of hill; scenic drive to Tossa de Mar; conv for Barcelona." 1 Apr-30 Sep. € 28.40   2010*

SPAIN

⊞ **CALLOSA D'EN SARRIA** *4F2* (6km NE Rural) *38.65450, -0.09246* **Camping Fonts d'Algar, Ptda Segarra, 03510 Callosa d'en Sarrià (Alicante)** [639-52 03 65 or 699-11 26 88 (mob); campingalgar@hotmail.com; www.campingfontsdalgar.co.uk] Exit A7 junc 64 & take CV755 NW dir Alcoi to Collosa. In Callosa take CV715 N & in 2km turn R at sp Fonts d'Algar. Steep, narr rd bef site on R. Med, hdstg, terr, unshd; wc; chem disp; shwrs inc; el pnts (5-16A) €4.50; shop & shop 6km; rest; snacks; bar; BBQ; sand beach 15km; entmnt; some statics; dogs; Eng spkn; quiet. "Mountain views; cactus garden & waterfalls nr; site being improved (2010)." € 23.00   2010*

CALONGE see Playa de Aro *3B3*

⊞ **CALPE** *4F2* (1km N Urban/Coastal) *38.6542, 0.0681* **Camping La Merced, Ctra de la Cometa, 03710 Calpe (Alicante)** [965-83 00 97] Exit A7/E15 at junc 63 & foll sp Calpe Norte down hill to traff lts & turn L. Foll dual c'way round Calpe, past Peñón de Ifach. Pass Cmp Levante on L, at next rndabt turn L, site on R in 400m. Med, mkd pitch, hdstg, pt terr, shd; htd wc; chem disp; mv service pnt; shwrs inc; el pnts (10A) €3.50 (poss long cable req); gas; lndtte; shop; supmkt 400m; rest 150m; snacks; bar; BBQ; sand beach 400m; TV rm; 10% statics; dogs €2.50; phone; bus 50m; poss cr; Eng spkn; adv bkg; poss noisy; red long stay/low ssn; CCI. "Gd san facs but dated; improved site; log fire in bar in winter; fair site; unkempt low ssn." ♦ € 25.60   2008*

⊞ **CALPE** *4F2* (1km N Urban/Coastal) *38.64781, 0.07172* **Camping Levante, Avda de la Marina s/n, 03710 Calpe (Alicante)** [tel/fax 965-83 22 72; info@campinglevantecalpe.com; www.campinglevantecalpe.com] Fr N332 (Alicante-València) take slip rd sp Calpe. Foll dual c'way round Calpe past Peñón-de-Ifach. Pass site on L, cont to rndabt & back to site. Sm, hdstg, shd; wc; chem disp; shwrs inc; el pnts (6A) inc; lndtte; shop; rest; snacks; bar; sand beach 100m; 10% statics; dogs; bus; Eng spkn; adv bkg; quiet; ccard acc; red long stay; CCI. "Well-run, clean, tidy site; liable to flood after heavy rain; pleasant town & promenade." € 25.20   2008*

⊞ **CALPE** *4F2* (300m NE Urban/Coastal) *38.64488, 0.05604* **Camping CalpeMar, Calle Eslovenia 3, 03710 Calpe (Alicante)** [tel/fax 965-87 55 76; info@campingcalpemar.com; www.campingcalpemar.com] Exit AP7/E15 junc 63 onto N332 & foll sp, take slip rd sp Calpe Norte & foll dual c'way CV746 round Calpe twd Peñón d'Ifach. At rndabt nr police stn with metal statues turn L, then L at next rndabt, over next rndabt, site 200m on R. Med, hdg/mkd pitch, hdstg, unshd; htd wc; chem disp; baby facs; all serviced pitches; shwrs inc; el pnts (10A) inc (metered for long stay); lndtte (inc dryer); ice; shop 500m; tradsmn; rest; snacks; bar; BBQ; playgrnd; pool; sand beach 300m; games area; games rm; entmnt; Spanish lessons; car wash; dog wash; wifi; TV rm; 3% statics; dogs free; phone; extra large pitches avail at additional charge; bus adj; sep car park; Eng spkn; adv bkg; quiet; ccard acc; red long stay/low ssn; CCI. "High standard site; well-kept & laid out; gd security; excel." ♦ € 38.00   2011*

See advertisement below

⊞ **CAMARASA** *3B2* (23km N Rural) *42.00416, 0.86583* **Camping Zodiac, Ctra C13, Km 66, La Baronia de Sant Oisme, 25621 Camarasa (Lleida)** [tel/fax 973-45 50 03; zodiac@campingzodiac.com; www.campingzodiac.com] Fr C13 Lleida to Balaguer. N of Balaguer take C13 & foll sp for Camarasa, then dir Tremp & site. Steep, winding but scenic app rd. Med, hdstg, pt sl, terr, pt shd; wc; chem disp; baby facs; shwrs; el pnts (5A) €4.60; shop; lndtte; rest; snacks; bar; playgrnd; pool; rv sw adj; tennis; TV; 90% statics; phone; Eng spkn; quiet; ccard acc. "Site on reservoir; poss untidy, shabby low ssn; some sm pitches diff due trees; excel views & walks; Terradets Pass 2km." ♦ € 18.80   2011*

CAMBRILS See also sites listed under Salou.

⊞ **CAMBRILS** *3C2* (1km N Rural) *41.07928, 1.06661* **Camping Àmfora d'Arcs, Ctra N340, Km 1145, 43391 Vinyols i Els Arcs (Tarragona)** [977-36 12 11; fax 977-79 50 75; info@amforadarcs.com; www.amforadarcs.com] Exit AP7 junc 37 onto N340 E & watch for km sps, site bet 1145 & 1146km. Lge, hdg pitch, hdstg, pt shd; wc; chem disp; shwrs inc; el pnts (5A) inc; gas; lndtte; supmkt opp; rest high ssn; bar; playgrnd; pool; beach 1.5km; 60% statics; dogs €4.50; phone; bus 300m; site poss clsd Xmas; poss cr; Eng spkn; adv bkg; noisy espec at w/end; ccard acc; red long stay/low ssn; CCI. "Sm pitches." € 34.50   2009*

SPAIN

CAMBRILS 3C2 (1.5km N Urban/Coastal) 41.06500, 1.08361 **Camping Playa Cambrils Don Camilo, Carrer Oleastrum 2, Ctra Cambrils-Salou, Km 1.5, 43850 Cambrils (Tarragona)** [977-36 14 90; fax 977-36 49 88; camping@playacambrils.com; www.playacambrils.com] Exit A7 junc 37 dir Cambrils & N340. Turn L onto N340 then R dir port then L onto coast rd. Site sp on L at rndabt after rv bdge 100m bef watch tower on R, approx 2km fr port. V lge, hdg/mkd pitch, shd; wc; chem disp; baby facs; shwrs inc; el pnts (5A) inc; gas; lndtte (inc dryer); supmkt; rest; snacks; bar; playgrnd; htd pool; paddling pool; sand beach adj; tennis; games rm; boat hire; cycle hire; watersports; entmnt; children's club; cinema; wifi; TV rm; 25% statics; bus 200m; cash machine; doctor; 24-hour security; dogs €4.35; Eng spkn; adv bkg ess high ssn; some rd & rlwy noise; ccard acc; red long ssn/low ssn/CCI. "Helpful, friendly staff; sports activities avail; Port Aventura 5km; vg site." ♦ 15 Mar-12 Oct. € 43.35 (CChq acc) 2011*

See advertisement above

CAMBRILS 3C2 (5km N Rural) 41.11132, 1.04558 **Vinyols Camp, Camí de Berenys s/n, 43391 Vinyols i Els Arcs** [977-85 04 09; fax 977-76 84 49; info@vinyolscamp.com; www.vinyolscamp.com] Exit AP7 junc 37 N onto T312 dir Montbrió del Camp for 4km. Turn R at rndabt onto T314 dir Vinyols; site at ent to vill. Med, pt shd; el pnts (4A); shop 200m; rest; snacks; bar; pool; paddling pool; sand beach 5km; internet; entmnt; some statics; dogs €2.50; adv bkg; quiet. "Peaceful, ecological, farm site." 7 Mar-2 Nov. € 17.20 2008*

⊞ **CAMBRILS** 3C2 (S Urban/Coastal) 41.06550, 1.04460 **Camping La Llosa, Ctra N340, Km 1143, 43850 Cambrils (Tarragona)** [977-36 26 15; fax 977-79 11 80; info@camping-lallosa.com; www.camping-lallosa.com] Exit A7/E15 at junc 37 & join N340 S. Head S into Cambrils (ignore L turn to cent) & at island turn R. Site sp on L within 100m. Fr N exit junc 35 onto N340. Strt over at x-rds, then L over rlwy bdge at end of rd, strt to site. V lge, hdstg, shd; wc; shwrs inc; el pnts (5A) €5; gas; lndtte; shop; rest; snacks; bar; playgrnd; pool; sand beach; entmnt high ssn; car wash; 50% statics; dogs €2.50; phone; bus 500m; poss cr; Eng spkn; some rd & rlwy noise; ccard acc; red long ssn/low ssn. "Interesting fishing port; gd facs; excel pool; gd supmkt nrby; poss diff siting for m'vans due low trees; excel winter NH." ♦ € 28.10 2011*

CAMBRILS 3C2 (2km S Coastal) 41.05533, 1.02333 **Camping Joan, Urbanització La Dorada, Passeig Marítim 88, 43850 Cambrils (Tarragona)** [977-36 46 04; fax 977-79 42 14; info@campingjoan.com; www.campingjoan.com] Exit AP7 junc 37 onto N340, S dir València. Turn off at km 1.141 & Hotel Daurada, foll site sp. Lge, hdg/mkd pitch, hdstg, terr, shd; htd wc; chem disp; mv service pnt; baby facs; shwrs inc; el pnts (5A) €4.40; gas; lndtte; supmkt; rest; snacks; bar; BBQ; playgrnd; pool & paddling pool; sand beach adj; watersports; fishing; cycle hire; games area; games rm; wifi; entmnt; sat TV; 16% statics; dogs €3.10; phone; currency exchange; car wash; Eng spkn; adv bkg; quiet; red low ssn/long stay/CCI. "Conv Port Aventura; gd family site; v clean san facs; friendly welcome; some sm pitches; gd beach; vg." ♦ 27 Mar-5 Nov. € 29.95 2009*

CAMBRILS 3C2 (5km SW Coastal) 41.04694, 1.00361 **Camping Oasis Mar, Ctra de València N340, Km 1139, 43892 Montroig (Tarragona)** [977-17 95 95; fax 977-17 95 16; info@oasismar.com; www.oasismar.com] Fr AP7 exit 37; N340 Tarragona-València rd, at Montroig, km 1139. Lge, mkd pitch, pt shd; wc; chem disp; shwrs inc; baby facs; el pnts (5A) €5; gas; lndtte; shop; rest; snacks; bar; BBQ; playgrnd; pool; sand beach adj; watersports; 30% statics; dogs €5.08 Eng spkn; red long stay/low ssn. "Excel site by super beach; friendly, helpful owners; gd facs; busy at w/end when statics occupied; vg." 1 Mar-31 Oct. € 30.00 2009*

CAMBRILS 3C2 (7km SW Coastal) 41.04011, 0.98061 **Camping Els Prats - Marius, Ctra N340, Km 1137, Montroig del Camp, 43892 Miami Playa (Tarragona)** [977-81 00 27; fax 977-17 09 01; info@campingelsprats.com; www.campingelsprats.com] Exit AP7 junc 37 onto N340 twds València. At km 1137 turn dir Camping Marius, under rlwy bdge & turn R to site. Lge, mkd pitch, shd; wc; chem disp; mv service pnt; baby facs; shwrs; el pnts (5A) €4.50; lndtte; shop; rest; snacks; bar; playgrnd; pool; sand beach adj; watersports; games area; tennis 100m; horseriding 3km; golf 6km; cycle hire; entmnt; TV; 20% statics; dogs €2.50 (not acc end Jun-mid Aug); adv bkg; quiet; ccard acc. "Pleasant, well-run, family site." ♦ 6 Mar-12 Oct. € 32.00 2008*

CAMBRILS *3C2* (8km SW Coastal) *41.03333, 0.96777* **Playa Montroig Camping Resort, N340, Km1.136, 43300 Montroig (Tarragona) [977-81 06 37; fax 977-81 14 11; info@playamontroig.com; www.playamontroig.com]** Exit AP7 junc 37, W onto N340. Site has own dir access onto N340 bet Cambrils & L'Hospitalet de L'Infant, well sp fr Cambrils. V lge, mkd pitch, pt sl, shd; htd wc; chem disp; mv service pnt; serviced pitches; baby facs; shwrs inc; el pnts (10A) inc; gas; lndtte; supmkt; rest; snacks; bars; playgrnd; 3 htd pools; sand beach adj; tennis; games area; games rm; skateboard track; many sports; cycle hire; golf 3km; cash machine; doctor; wifi; entmnt; 30% statics; no dogs; phone; Eng spkn; adv bkg; some rd & rlwy noise; ccard acc; red snr citizens/low ssn/CCI. "Magnificent, clean, secure site; private, swept beach; some sm pitches & low branches; 4 grades pitch/price; highly rec." ♦ 1 Apr-30 Oct. € 68.00   2011*

CAMBRILS *3C2* (8km W Coastal) *41.03807, 0.97478* **Kawan Village Camping La Torre del Sol, Ctra N340, Km 1.136, Miami-Playa, 43300 Montroig Del Camp (Tarragona) [977-81 04 86; fax 977-81 13 06; info@latorredelsol.com; www.latorredelsol.com]** Leave A7 València/Barcelona m'way at junc 37 & foll sp Cambrils. After 1.5km join N340 coast rd S for 6km. Watch for site sp 4km bef Miami Playa. Fr S exit AP7 junc 38, foll sp Cambrils on N340. Site on R 4km after Miami Playa. Site ent narr, alt ent avail for lge o'fits. V lge, hdg/mkd pitch, shd; wc; chem disp; mv service pnt; baby facs; sauna; shwrs inc; el pnts (6A) inc (10A avail); gas; lndtte (inc dryer); supmkt; tradsmn; rest; snacks; bar; BBQ; playgrnd; 2 htd pools; paddling pool; whirlpool; jacuzzi; direct access private sand beach; tennis; squash; cycle hire; gym; skateboard zone; golf 4km; cinema; disco; games rm; wifi; entmnt; TV; 40% statics; no dogs; poss v cr; Eng spkn; adv bkg; quiet, but some rd/rlwy noise & disco; ccard acc; red low ssn. "Attractive well-guarded site for all ages; sandy pitches; gd, clean san facs; steps to facs for disabled; access to pitches poss diff lge o'fits due trees & narr rds; radios/TVs to be used inside vans only; conv Port Aventura, Aquaparc, Aquopolis; highly rec, can't praise site enough; excel; ♦ 15 Mar-31 Oct. € 52.00 (CChq acc) SBS - E14   2011*

⊞ **CAMPELL** *4E2* (1km S Rural) *38.77672, -0.10529* **Camping Vall de Laguar, Carrer Sant Antoni 24, 03791 La Vall de Laguar (Alicante) [965-57 74 90 or 699-77 35 09; info@campinglaguar.com; www.campinglaguar.com]** Exit A7 junc 62 sp Ondara. Turn L to Orba onto CV733 dir Benimaurell & foll sp to Vall de Laguar. In Campell vill (narr rds) fork L & foll site sp uphill (narr rd). Steep ent to site. Lge o'fits ignore sp in vill & turn R to Fleix vill. In Fleix turn L to main rd, downhill to site sp at hairpin. Diff app. Med, mkd pitch, hdstg, terr, pt shd; htd wc; chem disp; shwrs inc; el pnts (5-10A) €2.75; gas; lndtte; shop 500m; rest; snacks; bar; BBQ; pool; sand beach 18km; 50% statics; dogs €1.30; phone; Eng spkn; adv bkg; quiet; ccard acc; red low ssn/long stay; CCI. "Sm pitches diff for lge o'fits; m'vans 7.50m max; excel home-cooked food in rest; ideal site for walkers; mountain views; friendly owners live on site; excel but rec sm o'fits & m'vans only." ♦ € 21.50   2009*

CAMPELLO, EL see Alicante *4F2*

⊞ **CAMPRODON** *3B3* (2km S Rural) *42.29010, 2.36230* **Camping Vall de Camprodón, Les Planes d'en Xenturri, Ctra Ripoll-Camprodón, C38, Km 7.5, 17867 Camprodón [972-74 05 07; fax 972-13 06 32; info@valldecamprodon.net; www.valldecamprodon.net]** Fr Gerona W on C66/C26 to Sant Pau de Segúries. Turn N onto C38 to Camprodón, site sp. Access over bdge weight limit 3,5000 kg. Lge, mkd pitch, pt shd; htd wc; mv service pnt; baby facs; shwrs; el pnts (4-10) €4.20-9.10 (poss rev pol); lndtte (inc dryer); shop; rest; snacks; bar; BBQ; playgrnd; pool; paddling pool; rv fishing; tennis; games area; horseriding; wifi; entmnt; TV; 90% statics; dogs €5; bus 200m; o'night m'van area (no san facs); adv bkg; quiet. "Camprodón attractive vill; lovely scenery; peaceful site; helpful staff; ltd facs low ssn." ♦ € 31.40 (CChq acc)   2011*

CANDAS see Gijon *1A3*

CANDELARIO see Béjar *1D3*

CANET DE MAR *3C3* (E Coastal) *41.59086, 2.59195* **Camping Globo Rojo, Ctra N11, Km 660.9, 08360 Canet de Mar (Barcelona) [tel/fax 937-94 11 43; camping@globo-rojo.com; www.globo-rojo.com]** On N11 500m N of Canet de Mar. Site clearly sp on L. Gd access. Med, hdg/mkd pitch, hdstg, shd; wc; chem disp; baby facs; shwrs; el pnts (10A) €6; gas; lndtte; shop; tradsmn; rest; snacks; bar; BBQ; playgrnd; pool; paddling pool; shgl beach & watersports adj; tennis; games area; horseriding 2km; cycle hire; internet; TV rm; 80% statics; dogs €5.50; phone; sep car park; Eng spkn; adv bkg; rd noise; ccard acc; red low ssn/CCI. "Excel facs; friendly, family-run site; busy w/end; slightly run down area; conv Barcelona by train (40km)." ♦ 1 Apr-30 Sep. € 42.00   2010*

⊞ **CANGAS DE ONIS** *1A3* (16km E Rural) *43.33527, -4.94777* **Camping Picos de Europa, Ctra Cangas de Onís-Cabrales, Km 17, 33556 Avín (Asturias) [985-84 40 70; fax 985-84 42 40; info@picos-europa.com; www.picos-europa.com]** N625 fr Arriondas to Cangas, then AS114 dir Panes for approx 16km. Go thro Avín vill, site on R at 17km marker - sp fr both dirs. Med, hdg/mkd pitch, terr, pt shd; wc; chem disp; baby facs; shwrs inc; el pnts (6A) €3.80; gas; lndtte (inc dryer); shop; rest; snacks; bar; pool; beach 20km; horseriding; canoeing on local rvs; some statics; phone; poss cr; Eng spkn; adv bkg; some rd noise & goat bells; ccard acc; CCI. "Owners v helpful; beautiful, busy, well-run site; vg value rest; modern san facs; poss diff access due narr site rds & cr; some sm pitches - lge o'fits may need 2; conv local caves, mountains, National Park, beaches; vg rest." € 20.00   2010*

CANGAS DE ONIS *1A3* (3km SE Rural) *43.34715, -5.08362* Camping Covadonga, 33589 Soto de Cangas (Asturias) [tel/fax 985-94 00 97; info@camping-covadonga.com; www.camping-covadonga.com] N625 fr Arriondas to Cangas de Onis, then AS114 twds Covadonga & Panes, cont thro town sp Covadonga. At rndabt take 2nd exit sp Cabrales, site on R in 100m. Access tight. Med, mkd pitch, pt shd; wc; chem disp; shwrs; el pnts (10A) €3.50 (no earth); lndtte (inc dryer); shop; supmkt in town; rest; snacks; bar; bus adj; poss cr; adv bkg; quiet, but slight rd noise; red long stay; CCI. "Sm pitches; take care with access; site rds narr; 17 uneven steps to san facs; conv for Picos de Europa." Holy Week & 15 Jun-30 Sep. € 21.20   2009*

CAPMANY see Figueres *3B3*

CARAVIA ALTA see Colunga *1A3*

CARBALLINO *1B2* (1.5km W Rural) Camp Municipal Arenteiro, Parque Etnográfico do Arenteiro s/n, 32500 O Carballiño (Ourense) [988-27 38 09; camping@carballino. org; www.campingarenteiro.carballino.org] N fr Ourense on N541, just beyond km 29, turn L at Godas do Rio at site sp. Site in 1km on L. Sm, mkd pitch, shd; wc; chem disp; mv service pnt; shwrs inc; el pnts (10A) €2.50; lndry rm; shop & 1.5km; rest; snacks; bar; BBQ; playgrnd; dogs; Eng spkn; quiet; red CCI. "In Ribeiro wine area among well-wooded mountains; vg mkd walks; highly rec." ♦ Holy Week & 1 May-30 Sep. € 12.50   2010*

⊞ **CARBALLO** *1A2* (6km N Coastal) *43.29556, -8.65528* Camping Baldayo, Rebordelos, 15684 Carballo (La Coruña) [981-73 95 29] On AC552 fr La Coruña dir Carballo, turn R approx 3km bef Carballo sp Noicela 8km. Then R sp Caión, next L & site sp when app dunes. App fr Arteijo diff for lge vans. Sm, pt sl, terr, pt shd; wc; chem disp; shwrs; el pnts €1.50; lndtte; shop; snacks; bar; playgrnd; sand beach 500m; 95% statics; no dogs; phone; poss cr; quiet. "Sm pitches & narr camp rds poss diff lge o'fits; poss unkempt low ssn." € 15.20   2008*

CARBALLO *1A2* (10km N Coastal) *43.29305, -8.62239* Camping As Nevedas, Ctra Carballo-Caión, Km.8,5, Noicela, 15100 Carballo (La Coruña) [tel/fax 981-73 95 52; info@ asnevedas.com; www.asnevedas.com] On AC552 fr La Coruña dir Carballo, turn R approx 3km bef Carballo sp Noicela 8km. Site on L in vill. Sm, hdg pitch, pt sl, pt shd; wc; chem disp (wc); serviced pitch; shwrs inc; el pnts (5A) €2.60; gas; lndtte; shop; tradsmn; rest; bar; BBQ; playgrnd; pool; sand beach 2km; golf 2km; 20% statics; dogs; bus fr ent; phone; poss cr; Eng spkn; adv bkg; quiet; red long stay; ccard acc; CCI. "Santiago de Compostela 45km; water amusement park 15km; friendly staff; facs slightly run-down low ssn; mkt Sun Carballo; excel." 1 Apr-29 Sep. € 17.94   2008*

CARCHUNA see Motril *2H4*

CARIDAD, LA (EL FRANCO) *1A3* (1km SE Coastal) *43.54795, -6.80701* Camping Playa de Castelló, Ctra N634, Santander-La Coruña, Km 532, 33758 La Caridad (El Franca) (Asturias) [985-47 82 77; camping_castello@hotmail.com] On N634/ E70 Santander dir La Coruña, turn N at km 532. Site in 200m fr N634, sp fr each direction. Sm, mkd pitch, pt shd; wc; chem disp; baby facs; shwrs inc; el pnts (2-5A) €3; gas; lndtte; shop; tradsmn, bar high ssn only; BBQ; playgrnd; shgl beach 800m; internet; some statics; dogs €1; bus 200m; Eng spkn; adv bkg; quiet; red long stay/CCI. "A green oasis with character; gd." Holy Week & 1 Jun-30 Sep. € 17.00   2010*

⊞ **CARIDAD, LA (EL FRANCO)** *1A3* (2.7km W Rural) Camping A Grandella, Ctra N634, Km 536.9 (Desvío San Juan de Prendonés), 33746 Valdepares (Asturias) [661-35 28 70 (mob); camping@campingagrandella.com; www.camping agrandella.com] Sp fr N634/E70. Med, pt shd; wc; chem disp; shwrs inc; el pnts €3.50; lndtte; snacks; bar; playgrnd; bus 200m; some statics; dogs €1; site clsd mid-Dec to mid-Jan; quiet. "Attractive little site; well-situated." € 18.00   2010*

⊞ **CARLOTA, LA** *2G3* (1km NE Rural) *37.68321, -4.91891* Camping Carlos III, Ctra de Madrid-Cádiz Km 430.5, 14100 La Carlota (Córdoba) [957-30 03 38; fax 957-30 06 97; camping@campingcarlosiii.com; www.campingcarlosiii. com] Approx 25km SW fr Córdoba on A4/E5, exit at km 432 turning L under autovia. Turn L at rndabt on main rd, site well sp on L in 800m. Lge, mkd pitch, hdstg, pt sl, pt shd; htd wc (some cont); chem disp; shwrs inc; el pnts (5-10A) €4; gas; lndtte; shop; rest; bar; BBQ; playgrnd; pool; horseriding; 30% statics; dogs; phone; Eng spkn; adv bkg; ccard acc; red long stay; CCI. "V efficient, well-run site; less cr than Córdoba municipal site; excel pool; gd; clean facs; if pitched under mulberry trees, poss staining fr berries; bus to Córdoba every 2 hrs."♦ € 20.85   2010*

⊞ **CARRION DE LOS CONDES** *1B4* (W Rural) *42.33694, -4.60638* Camping El Edén, Ctra Vigo-Logroño, Km 200, 34120 Carrión de los Condes (Palencia) [979-88 11 52] Exit A231 to Carrión, turn L immed onto N120 sp Burgos & ent town fr NE. Site sp E & W ents to town off N120 adj Rv Carrión at El Plantio. App poorly sp down narr rds to rv. Suggest park nr Café España & check rte on foot. Med, mkd pitch, pt shd; wc; shwrs; mv service pnt; el pnts (5A) €3.50; gas; lndtte; rest; bar; playgrnd; dogs; bus 500m; ccard acc. "Pleasant walk to town; basic rvside site; recep in bar/rest; site open w/ends only low ssn; fair NH." ♦ € 14.90   2008*

⊞ **CARTAGENA** *4G1* (10km SW Coastal/Rural) *37.58611, -1.0675* Camping Naturista El Portús (Naturist), 30393 Cartagena (Murcia) [968-55 30 52; fax 968-55 30 53; elportus@elportus.com; www.elportus.com] Fr N332 Cartagena to Mazarrón rd take E20 to Canteras. In Canteras turn R onto E22 sp Isla Plana & in 500m turn L onto E21 sp Galifa/El Portús. In 2km at rndabt, site ent on L. Lge, mkd pitch; some hdstg, pt shd; wc; chem disp; mv service pnt; shwrs inc; el pnts (6A) inc; gas; lndtte (inc dryer); shop; rest; snacks; bar; playgrnd; htd, covrd pool & paddling pool; shgl beach adj; tennis; games area; gym; spa; golf 15km; internet; entmnt; 30% statics; dogs €4.80; phone; bus 1km; poss cr; Eng spkn; ccard acc; red low ssn/long stay; INF card req. "Restful low ssn; gd situation; many long-stay winter visitors; helpful staff; random pitching & poss untidy site; Cartagena interesting old town." ♦ € 40.80   2009*

CÀMPING masnou ✿ ✿ ✿

C/ Mas Nou, 7 · 17486 Castelló d'Empúries · Costa Brava · (Girona) Spain
T. +34 972 45 41 75 · Fax +34 972 45 43 58 · info@campingmasnou.com **www.campingmasnou.com**

CASPE *3C2* (12km NE Rural) *41.28883, 0.05733* **Lake Caspe Camping, Ctra N211, Km 286.7, 50700 Caspe (Zaragoza)** [976-63 41 74 or 689-99 64 30 (mob); fax 976-63 41 87; lakecaspe@lakecaspe.com; www.lakecaspe.com] Fr E leave AP2 or N11 at Fraga & foll N211 dir Caspe to site. Fr W take N232 fr Zaragoza then A1404 & A221 E thro Caspe to site in 16km on L at km 286.7, sp. Med, hdg/mkd pitch, hdstg, pt shd; wc; chem disp; baby facs; shwrs inc; el pnts (5-10A) €5.60; gas; lndtte; shop; rest; snacks; bar; playgrnd; pool high ssn; fishing; sailing; 10% statics; dogs €3.75; phone; poss cr; Eng spkn; adv bkg; quiet; CCI. "Gd, well-run, scenic site but isolated (come prepared); avoid on public hols; site rds gravelled but muddy after rain; sm pitches nr lake; gd watersports; mosquitoes." 1Mar-11 Nov. € 21.60   2011*

CASTANARES DE LA RIOJA see Haro *1B4*

CASTELLBO see Seo de Urgel *3B3*

CASTELLO D'EMPURIES *3B3* (4km NE Rural) *42.26460, 3.10160* **Camping Mas Nou, Ctra Mas Nou 7, Km 38, 17486 Castelló d'Empúries (Gerona)** [972-45 41 75; fax 972-45 43 58; info@campingmasnou.com; www.camping masnou.com] On m'way A7 exit 3 if coming fr France & exit 4 fr Barcelona dir Roses (E) C260. Site on L at ent to Empuriabrava - use rndabt to turn. Lge, shd, mkd pitch; htd wc; chem disp; mv service point; baby facs; shwrs inc; el pnts (10A) €4.90; lndtte (inc dryer); shops 200m; rest; snacks; bar; BBQ; playgrnd; pool; beach 2.5km; tennis; games area; wifi; entmnt; TV; 5% statics; dogs €2.35; phone; Eng spkn; red long stay/low ssn; ccard acc; CCI. "Aqua Park 4km, Dali Museum 10km; gd touring base; helpful staff; well-run site; excel, clean san facs; sports activities & children's club; gd cycling; excel." ♦ 31 Mar-30 Sep. € 38.70 (CChq acc)

2011*

See advertisement above

CASTELLO D'EMPURIES *3B3* (4km SE Coastal) *42.20725, 3.10026* **Camping Nautic Almatá, Aiguamolls de l'Empordà, 17486 Castelló d'Empúries (Gerona)** [972-45 44 77; fax 972-45 46 86; info@almata.com; www.almata.com] Fr A7 m'way exit 3; foll sp to Roses. After 12km turn S for Sant Pere Pescador & site on L in 5km. Site clearly sp on rd Castelló d'Empúries-Sant Pere Pescador. Lge, pt shd; wc; chem disp; shwrs inc; el pnts (10A) inc; rest; gas; shop; lndtte; playgrnd; pool; sand beach adj; sailing school; tennis; games area; horseriding; cycle hire; TV; disco bar on beach; entmnt; dogs €6.40; poss cr; adv bkg; quiet; red low ssn. "Excel, clean facs; ample pitches; sports facs inc in price; helpful staff; direct access to nature reserve; waterside pitches rec." ♦ 16 May-20 Sep. € 59.00   2011*

CASTELLO D'EMPURIES *3B3* (1km S Coastal) *42.25563, 3.13791* **Camping Castell Mar, Ctra Roses-Figueres, Km 40.5, Playa de la Rubina, 17486 Castelló d'Empúries (Gerona)** [972-45 08 22; fax 972-45 23 30; cmar@ campingparks.com; www.campingparks.com] Exit A7 at junc 3 sp Figueres; turn L onto C260 sp Roses, after traff lts cont twd Roses, turn R down side of rest La Llar for 1.5km, foll sp Playa de la Rubina. Lge, hdg/mkd pitch, pt shd; wc; chem disp; serviced pitches; baby facs; shwrs inc; el pnts (10A) inc; gas; lndtte (inc dryer); shop; tradsmn; rest; snacks; bar; BBQ; playgrnd; pool; paddling pool; sand beach 100m; games rm; entmnt; sat TV; 30% statics; dogs; phone; Eng spkn; adv bkg; quiet; red low ssn; CCI. "Pitches poss unsuitable lge o'fits; gd location; excel for families." ♦ 22 May-19 Sep. € 59.00   2011*

See advertisement opposite

CASTELLO D'EMPURIES *3B3* (5km S Coastal) *42.23735, 3.12121* **Camping-Caravaning Laguna, Platja Can Turias, 17486 Castelló d'Empúries (Gerona)** [972-45 05 53; fax 972-45 07 99; info@campinglaguna.com; www. campinglaguna.com] Exit AP7 junc 4 dir Roses. After 12km at rndabt take 3rd exit, site sp. Site in 4km; rough app track. V lge, mkd pitch, pt shd; wc; chem disp; mv service pnt; some serviced pitches (inc gas); baby facs; shwrs inc; el pnts (5A) inc; gas; lndtte; supmkt; rest; snacks; bar; playgrnd; htd pool; sand beach; sailing; watersports; tennis; games area; multisports area; cycle hire; horseriding; wifi; entmnt; 4% statics; dogs €2; Eng spkn; adv bkg; quiet; red snr citizens/ long stay/low ssn; ccard acc; CCI. "Clean, modern san facs; gd birdwatching; excel." ♦ 5 Apr-31 Oct. € 49.70   2010*

CAMPiNG
CASTELL MAR
CASTELLÓ D'EMPURIES
(Costa Brava)
CP 17486, ESPAÑA
Tel. +34 972 45 08 22
Fax +34 972 45 23 30
cmar@campingparks.com
GPS 42°15'10.93"N / 3° 7'48.36"E

CAMPiNG ①
CASTELL MONTGRi
Ctra. de Torroella a l'Estartit. Km 4,7
L'ESTARTIT (Costa Brava)
CP 17258, ESPAÑA
Tel. +34 972 75 16 30
Fax +34 972 75 09 06
cmontgri@campingparks.com
GPS 42°15'19.74"N / 3° 8'14.28"E

www.campingparks.com

CASTRO URDIALES *1A4* (1km N Coastal) *43.39000, -3.24194* **Camping de Castro, Barrio Campijo, 39700 Castro Urdiales (Cantabria)** [942-86 74 23; fax 942-63 07 25; info@camping.castro.com] Fr Bilbao turn off A8 at 2nd Castro Urdiales sp, km 151. Camp sp on R by bullring. V narr, steep lanes to site - no passing places, great care req. Lge, pt sl, pt terr, unshd; wc; shwrs inc; el pnts (6A) €3; lndtte; shop; rest; bar; playgrnd; pool; sand beach 1km; 90% statics; dogs; phone; bus; poss cr; Eng spkn; adv bkg; quiet; CCI. "Gd, clean facs; conv NH for ferries; ltd touring pitches." ♦ Easter & 1 Jun-30 Sep. € 19.50   2008*

CASTROJERIZ *1B4* (1km NE Rural) *42.29194, -4.13361* **Camping Camino de Santiago, Calle Virgen del Manzano s/n, 09110 Castrojeriz (Burgos)** [947-37 72 55 or 658-96 67 43 (mob); fax 947-37 72 56; info@campingcamino.com; www.campingcamino.com] Exit A62/E80 junc 40 dir Los Balbases, Vallunquera & Castrojeriz - narr, uneven rd. In 16 km ent Castrojeriz, site well sp off BU404 under ruined castle. Med, hdg/mkd pitch, pt sl, shd; wc (some cont); chem disp (wc); shwrs inc; el pnts (5-10A) €4 (poss no earth); lndtte (inc dryer); shop 1km; rest; snacks; bar; games area; games rm; internet; TV rm; dogs €2; bus 200m; some Eng spkn; quiet; CCI. "Lovely site; helpful owner; pilgrims' refuge on site; some diff sm pitches; vg." ♦ 1 Mar-30 Nov. € 20.00   2010*

CASTROPOL see Ribadeo *1A2*

CAZORLA *2F4* (6km E Rural) *37.9059, -2.93597* **Camping Puente de las Herrerías, El Vadillo del Castril, 23470 Cazorla (Jaén)** [953-72 70 90; info@puentedelasherrerias.com; www.puentedelasherrerias.com] Fr Cazorla foll sp for Parador & then Puente de la Herrerías. Driving distance 25km fr Cazorla on narr rd with many bends & two passes - not rec trailer c'vans. Lge, pt shd; wc; shwrs; el pnts (16A) €3.10; gas; shop; rest; snacks; bar; playgrnd; pool; horseriding; cycle hire; phone; quiet. "Stunning scenery in National Park." Easter-15 Oct. € 20.64   2008*

CAZORLA *2F4* (2km SW Rural) *37.90444, -3.01416* **Camping San Isicio, Camino de San Isicio s/n, 23470 Cazorla (Jaén)** [tel/fax 953-72 12 80; campingcortijo@hotmail.com] Fr W on A319, turn R bef Cazorla, foll sp. Sm, pt shd; wc; shwrs; el pnts €2.50; playgrnd; pool; dogs free; quiet. "Perched on steep hill; towing service for c'vans but really only suitable sm m'vans; ltd facs but a lovely site." 1 Mar-1 Nov. € 16.60   2008*

CEE *1A1* (6km NW Coastal) *42.94555, -9.21861* **Camping Ruta Finisterre, Ctra La Coruña-Finisterre, Km 6, Playa de Estorde, 15270 Cée (La Coruña)** [tel/fax 981-74 63 02; www.rutafinisterre.com] Foll sp thro Cée & Corcubión on rd AC445 twd Finisterre; site easily seen on R of rd (no thro rd). Lge, mkd pitch, terr, shd; wc; chem disp; shwrs inc; el pnts (10A) €4; gas; lndtte; shop & 1km; rest; snacks; bar; playgrnd; sand beach 100m; dogs €3.70; phone; bus adj; poss cr; Eng spkn; adv bkg; some rd noise; ccard acc; CCI. "Family-run site in pine trees - check access to pitch & el pnts bef positioning; gd, clean facs; 5km to Finisterre; clean beach adj; peaceful." ♦ Holy Week & 1 Jun-10 Sep. € 22.90   2010*

CERVERA DE PISUERGA *1B4* (500m W Rural) *42.87135, -4.50332* **Camping Fuentes Carrionas, La Bárcena s/n, 34840 Cervera de Pisuerga (Palencia)** [979-87 04 24; fax 979-12 30 76; campingfuentescarrionas@hotmail.com] Fr Aguilar de Campóo on CL626 pass thro Cervera foll sp CL627 Potes. Site sp on L bef rv bdge. Med, mkd pitch, pt shd; wc; chem disp; shwrs inc; el pnts €3.50; lndtte; shop 500m; rest 500m; bar; tennis; games area; 80% statics; bus 100m; quiet; CCI. "Gd walking in nature reserve; conv Casa del Osos bear info cent." ♦ Holy Week-30 Sep. € 20.60   2009*

⊞ **CHILCHES** *4E2* (1km S Coastal) *39.75722, -0.16333* **Camping Mediterráneo, Avda Mare Nostrum s/n, 12592 Chilches (Castellón)** [tel/fax 964-58 32 18; informacion@mediterraneocamping.com] Exit AP7 junc 49 onto N340 S, exit junc 947-948 twds Chilches. Fr Chilches take CV2280 to coast & turn S, site sp. Lge, mkd pitch, hdstg, shd; wc; chem disp; shwrs inc; el pnts inc; gas; lndtte; shop; tradsmn; rest; snacks; bar; playgrnd; pool; sand beach 500m; solarium; TV rm; some statics; dogs; phone; bus 1km; poss cr; adv bkg; ccard acc; red long stay/CCI. ♦ € 32.10   2008*

SPAIN

SPAIN

⊞ **CIUDAD RODRIGO** *1D3* (1km SW Rural) *40.59206, -6.53445* Camping La Pesquera, Ctra Cáceres-Arrabal, Km 424, Huerta La Toma, 37500 Ciudad Rodrigo (Salamanca) [tel/fax 923-48 13 48; campinglapesquera@hotmail.com; www. campinglapesquera.com] Fr Salamanca on A62/E80 exit junc 332. Look for tent sp on R & turn R, then 1st L & foll round until site on rvside. Med, mkd pitch, pt shd; wc; shwrs inc; el pnts (6A) inc; lndtte; shop; snacks; rv sw, fishing adj; wifi; TV; dogs free; phone; poss cr; no adv bkg; quiet; ccard acc; CCI. "Medieval walled city worth visit - easy walk over Roman bdge; gd san facs; gd, improved site. Friendly nice small site, good for NH very gd site." ♦ € 22.50   2011*

⊞ **CLARIANA** *3B3* (4km NE Rural) *41.95878, 1.60361* Camping La Ribera, Pantà de Sant Ponç, 25290 Clariana de Cardener (Lleida) [tel/fax 973-48 25 52; info@ campinglaribera.com; www.campinglaribera.com] Fr Solsona S on C55, turn L onto C26 at km 71. Go 2.7km, site sp immed bef Sant Ponç Dam. Lge, mkd pitch, hdstg, pt shd; wc; chem disp; baby facs; shwrs; el pnts (4-10A) €3.30-6.60; lndtte; shop; snacks; bar; playgrnd; pool; paddling pool; lake sw & beach 500m; tennis; games area; TV; 95% statics; dogs; bus 2.5km; phone; quiet. "Excel facs; gd site; narr pitches." ♦ € 26.60   2008*

COLERA see Llançà *3B3*

COLOMBRES see Unquera *1A4*

COLUNGA *1A3* (1km N Coastal) *43.49972, -5.26527* Camping Costa Verde, Playa La Griega de Colunga, 33320 Colunga (Asturias) [tel/fax 985-85 63 73] N632 coast rd, fr E turn R twd Lastres in cent of Colunga; site 1km on R. Med, mkd pitch, unshd; wc; chem disp; mv service pnt; baby facs; shwrs; el pnts (5A) €3.50 - €5.20 (poss rev pol); gas; lndtte; shop; rest; bar; BBQ; playgrnd; sand beach 500m; games area; cycle hire; 50% statics; dogs €3; bus 500m; adv bkg; quiet but some rd noise; ccard acc; CCI. "Beautiful sandy beach; lovely views to mountains & sea; poss noise some fr rd & resident static owners; some site access rds used for winter storage; gd, plentiful facs; ltd hot water low ssn; friendly, welcoming staff; pleasant town." Easter & 1 Jun-30 Sep. € 19.25   2011*

COLUNGA *1A3* (8km E Coastal) *43.47160, -5.18434* Camping Arenal de Moris, Ctra de la Playa s/n, 33344 Caravia Alta (Asturias) [985-85 30 97; fax 985-85 31 37; camoris@ desdeasturias.com; www.arenaldemoris.com] Fr E70/A8 exit junc 337 onto N632 to Caravia Alta, site clearly sp. Lge, mkd pitch, terr, pt shd; wc; chem disp; shwrs inc; el pnts (5A) €4.50; lndtte; shop; rest; snacks; bar; playgrnd; pool; sand beach 500m; tennis; 10% statics; bus 1.5km; adv bkg; quiet but rd noise; ccard acc; CCI. "Lovely views to mountains & sea; well-kept, well-run site; excel, clean san facs." Easter-20 Sep. € 24.00   2009*

COMA RUGA see Vendrell, El *3C3*

COMILLAS *1A4* (1km E Coastal) *43.38583, -4.28444* **Camping de Comillas, 39520 Comillas (Cantabria) [942-72 00 74; fax 942-21 52 06; info@campingcomillas.com; www. campingcomillas.com]** Site on coast rd CA131 at E end of Comillas by-pass. App fr Santillana or San Vicente avoids town cent & narr streets. Lge, hdg/mkd pitch, pt sl, pt shd; wc; chem disp; shwrs inc; el pnts (5A) €3.85; lndtte (inc dryer); shop; tradsmn; rest 1km; snacks; bar; playgrnd; sand beach 800m; TV; dogs; phone; poss cr; adv bkg; quiet; CCI. "Clean, ltd facs low ssn (hot water to shwrs only); vg site in gd position with views; easy walk to interesting town; gd beach across rd; helpful owner; vg." Holy Week & 1 Jun-30 Sep. € 25.20
2010*

COMILLAS *1A4* (3km E Rural) *43.38328, -4.24689* **Camping El Helguero, 39527 Ruiloba (Cantabria) [942-72 21 24; fax 942-72 10 20; campingelhelguero.com; www. campingelhelguero.com]** Exit A8 junc 249 dir Comillas onto CA135 to km 7. Turn dir Ruiloba onto CA359 & thro Ruiloba & La Iglesia, fork R uphill. Site sp. Lge, mkd pitch, pt sl, pt shd; htd wc; chem disp; mv service pnt; baby facs; shwrs inc; el pnts (6A) €4.35; lndtte (inc dryer); shop, rest, snacks, bar in ssn; playgrnd; pool; paddling pool; sand beach 3km; tennis 300m; cycle hire; wifi; many statics; dogs; night security; poss v cr high ssn; Eng spkn; poss noisy high ssn; ccard acc; CCI. "Attractive site; gd touring cent; clean facs but some in need of refurb; helpful staff; sm pitches poss muddy in wet." ♦ 1 Apr-30 Sep. € 24.05 (CChq acc) 2010*

⊞ COMILLAS *1A4* (3km W Rural/Coastal) *43.3858, -4.3361* **Camping Rodero, Ctra Comillas-St Vicente, Km 5, 39528 Oyambre (Cantabria) [942-72 20 40; fax 942-72 26 29; info@campingrodero.es; www.campingrodero.es]** Exit A8 dir San Vicente de la Barquera, cross bdge over estuary & take R fork nr km27.5. Site just off C131 bet San Vicente & Comillas, sp. Lge, mkd pitch, pt sl, terr, pt shd; wc; chem disp; mv service pnt; shwrs inc; el pnts (6A) €3; gas; lndtte; shop; tradsmn; rest; snacks; bar; playgrnd; pool; sand beach 200m; games area; wifi; 10% statics; no dogs; phone; bus 200m; poss v cr; adv bkg; ccard acc; CCI. "Lovely views; friendly owners; site noisy but happy - owner puts Dutch/British in quieter part; sm pitches; poss run down low ssn & prob clsd in winter - phone ahead to check." ♦ € 29.00 2009*

⊞ CONIL DE LA FRONTERA *2H3* (3km N Coastal) *36.30206, -6.13082* **Camping Cala del Aceite (Naturist), Ctra del Puerto Pesquero, Km 4, 11140 Conil de la Frontera (Cádiz) [956-44 29 50; fax 956-44 09 72; info@caladelaceite.com; www.caladelaceite.com]** Exit A48 junc 26 dir Conil. In 2km at rndabt foll sp Puerto Pesquero along CA3208 & CA4202. Site sp. V lge, mkd pitch, pt shd; wc; chem disp;sauna; shwrs inc; el pnts (10A) €5.50; gas; lndtte; supmkt; rest; snacks; bar; playgrnd; pool; beach 500m; jacuzzi & steam room; separate naturist area on site; dogs €3; phone; poss cr; Eng spkn; adv bkg; quiet; red long stay; CCI. "Friendly, helpful staff; interesting region; gd cliff-top walking; lge pitches; long stay winter offers; gd, modern san facs." ♦ Holy Week-31 Oct. € 30.60 2011*

⊞ CONIL DE LA FRONTERA *2H3* (3km NE Rural) *36.31061, -6.11276* **Camping Roche, Carril de Pilahito s/n, N340km 19.2, 11149 Conil de la Frontera (Cádiz) [956-44 22 16; fax 956-44 30 02; info@campingroche.com; www. campingroche.com]** Exit A48 junc 15 Conil Norte. Site sp on N340 dir Algeciras. Lge, mkd pitch, hdstg, pt shd; wc; chem disp; mv service pnt; el pnts (10A) €5; lndtte; shop; rest; snacks; bar; BBQ low ssn; playgrnd; pool; paddling pool; sand beach 2.5km; tennis; games area; games rm; TV; 20% statics; dogs €3.75; Eng spkn; adv bkg; quiet; red low ssn/long stay; special monthly rates. "V pleasant, peaceful site in pine woods; all-weather pitches; friendly, helpful staff; clean san facs; superb beaches nr." ♦ € 28.00
2011*

See advertisement

⊞ CONIL DE LA FRONTERA *2H3* (1.3km NW Rural/Coastal) *36.29340, -6.09626* **Camping La Rosaleda, Ctra del Pradillo, Km 1.3, 11140 Conil de la Frontera (Cádiz) [956-44 33 27; fax 956-44 33 85; info@campinglarosaleda.com; www. campinglarosaleda.com]** Exit A48 junc 26 dir Conil. In 2km at rndabt foll sp Puerto Pesquero along CA3208. Site sp on R. Lge, mkd pitch, some hdstg, pt sl, terr, pt shd; wc; chem disp; mv service pnt; shwrs inc; el pnts (5-10A) inc; gas; lndtte; shop & 1.3km; tradsmn; rest; snacks; bar; playgrnd; pool; sand beach 1.3km; entmnt; internet; 10% statics; no dogs 15 Jun-15 Sep, otherwise in sep area €5; phone; car wash; Eng spkn; adv bkg; quiet; red low ssn/long stay; CCI. "Well-run site; friendly, helpful staff; gd social atmosphere; poss noisy w/end; sm pitches not suitable lge o'fits but double-length pitches avail; poss itinerants; pitches soft/muddy when wet; lge rally on site in winter; gd walking & cycling; sea views; historical, interesting area; conv Seville, Cádiz, Jerez, day trips Morocco." ♦ € 38.50 2010*

⊞ CORDOBA *2F3* (8km N Rural) *37.96138, -4.81361* **Camping Los Villares, Ctra Los Villares, Km 7.5, 14071 Córdoba (Córdoba) [957-33 01 45; fax 957-33 14 55; campingvillares@latinmail.com]** Best app fr N on N432: turn W onto CP45 1km N of Cerro Muriano at km 254. Site on R after approx 7km shortly after golf club. Last 5-6km of app rd v narr & steep, well-engineered. Badly sp, easy to miss. Or fr city cent foll sp for Parador until past municipal site on R. Shortly after, turn L onto CP45 & foll sp Parque Forestal Los Villares, then as above. Sm, hdstg, sl, shd; wc; chem disp; shwrs inc; el pnts (15A) €4.30 (poss rev pol); gas; lndry rm; shop; rest & bar (high ssn); some statics; no dogs; bus 1km; quiet; red long stay; CCI. "In nature reserve; peaceful; cooler than Córdoba city with beautiful walks, views & wildlife; sm, close pitches; basic facs (v ltd & poss unclean low ssn); mainly sl site in trees; strictly run; take care electrics; poss no drinking water/hot water." ♦ € 17.70 2009*

⊞ **CORDOBA** *2F3* (1km NW Urban) *37.90063, -4.7875* **Camp Municipal El Brillante, Avda del Brillante 50, 14012 Córdoba** [957-40 38 36; fax 957-28 21 65; elbrillante@ campings.net; www.campingelbrillante.com] Fr N1V take Badejoz turning N432. Take rd Córdoba N & foll sp to Parador. Turn R into Paseo del Brilliante which leads into Avda del Brilliante; white grilleblock wall surrounds site. Alt, foll sp for 'Macdonalds Brilliante.' Site on R 400m beyond Macdonalds on main rd going uphill away fr town cent. Site poorly sp. Med, hdg/mkd pitch, hdstg, pt shd; wc; chem disp; mv service pnt; serviced pitches; shwrs inc; el pnts (6-10A) €5 (poss no earth); gas; lndtte (inc dryer); shop; tradsmn; hypmkt nrby; rest, snacks high ssn; bar; playgrnd; pool adj in ssn; dogs free; phone; bus adj; poss cr; Eng spkn; no adv bkg; quiet but traff noise & barking dogs off site; ccard not acc; CCI. "Well-run, busy, clean site; rec arr bef 1500; friendly staff; sun shades over pitches; easy walk/gd bus to town; poss cramped pitches - diff lge o'fits; poss itinerants low ssn (noisy); gd for wheelchair users; highly rec." ♦ € 32.00   2011*

CORUNA, A see Coruña, La *1A2*

CORUNA, LA *1A2* (5km E Coastal) *43.34305, -8.35722* **Camping Bastiagueiro, Playa de Bastiagueiro, 15110 Oleiros (La Coruña)** [981-61 48 78; fax 981-26 60 08] Exit La Coruña by NVI twd Betanzos. After bdge, take AC173 sp Santa Cruz. At 3rd rndabt, take 3rd exit sp Camping. In 100m, turn R up narr rd. Site on R in 150m. Sm, pt shd; wc (some cont); chem disp; shwrs inc; el pnts (6A) €4; gas; lndtte; shop; snacks; bar; playgrnd; sand beach 500m; dogs; phone; bus 300m; o'night area for m'vans; poss cr; adv bkg; quiet; CCI. "Friendly owners; lovely views of beach; care req thro narr ent gate, sharp turn & steep exit; poss feral cats on site & facs poss unclean in winter; some refurb needed." Easter & 1 Jun-30 Sep. € 20.00   2010*

The opening dates and prices on this campsite have changed. I'll send a site report form to the Club for the next edition of the guide.

CORUNA, LA *1A2* (9km E Rural) *43.34806, -8.33592* **Camping Los Manzanos, Olieros, 15179 Santa Cruz (La Coruña)** [981-61 48 25; info@camping-losmanzanos.com; www. camping-losmanzanos.com] App La Coruña fr E on NVI, bef bdge take AC173 sp Santa Cruz. Turn R at 2nd traff lts in Santa Cruz cent (by petrol stn), foll sp, site on L. Fr AP9/E1 exit junc 3, turn R onto NVI dir Lugo. Take L fork dir Santa Cruz/ La Coruña, then foll sp Meiras. Site sp. Lge, pt shd; wc; chem disp; shwrs; el pnts (6A) €4.80; gas; lndtte (inc dryer); shop; rest; snacks; bar; playgrnd; pool; TV; 10% statics; dogs free; phone; adv bkg (day bef arr only); ccard acc; CCI. "Lovely site; steep slope into site, level exit is available; helpful owners; hilly 1km walk to Santa Cruz for bus to La Coruña or park at Torre de Hércules (lighthouse) & take tram; conv for Santiago de Compostela; excel." Easter-30 Sep. € 25.60   2011*

⊞ **COTORIOS** *4F1* (500m Rural) *38.04807, -2.85128* **Camping Chopera, Cazorla-Cotoríos, Km 21, Santiago Pontones, 23478 Cotoríos (Jaén)** [tel/fax 953-71 30 05] Fr Jaén-Albacete rd N322 turn onto A1305, nr Villanueva del Arzobispo, sp El Tranco. In 26km at app to El Tranco lake (sh distance after exit fr tunnel), turn R & cross over embankment. Cotoríos at km 52-53, approx 25km on shore of lake & Río Guadalquivir. Warning, if towing c'van, do not app via Cazorla as rds are tortuous. Only app & return fr Villanueva as rd well surfaced, but still some steep sections. Med, shd; wc; shwrs; el pnts (16A) €3; lndtte; gas; shop; snacks; bar; playgrnd; rv adj; dogs; phone; car wash; ccard acc; red low ssn. "In cent of beautiful National Park; lots of wildlife." ♦ € 15.55   2008*

⊞ **COTORIOS** *4F1* (2km E Rural) *38.05255, -2.83996* **Camping Llanos de Arance, Ctra Sierra de Cazorla/Beas de Segura, Km 22, 23478 Cotoríos (Jaén)** [953-71 31 39; fax 953-71 30 36; arancell@inicia.es; www.llanosdearance.com] Fr Jaén-Albacete rd N322 turn E onto A1305 N of Villanueva del Arzobispo sp El Tranco. In 26km to El Tranco lake, turn R & cross over embankment. Cotoríos at km stone 53, approx 25km on shore of lake & Río Guadalaquivir. App fr Cazorla or Beas definitely not rec if towing. Lge, shd; wc; shwrs; el pnts (5A) €3.21; gas; shops 1.5km; rest; snacks; bar; BBQ; playgrnd; pool; 2% statics; no dogs; phone; poss cr; quiet; ccard acc; red low ssn; CCI. "Lovely site; excel walks & bird life, boar & wild life in Cazorla National Park." € 17.75   2008*

⊞ **COVARRUBIAS** *1B4* (500m E Rural) *42.05944, -3.51527* **Camping Covarrubias, Ctra Hortigüela, 09346 Covarrubias (Burgos)** [947-40 64 17; fax 983-29 58 41; proatur@ proatur.com; www.proatur.com] Take N1/E5 or N234 S fr Burgos, turn onto BU905 after approx 35km. Site sp on BU905. Med, mkd pitch, pt sl, pt shd; wc; shwrs; el pnts (12A) €3.42; gas; lndtte; shop 500m; rest; bar; playgrnd; pool & paddling pool; 50% statics; phone; poss cr; ccard acc. "Ltd facs low ssn; pitches poss muddy after rain; charming vill; poss vultures!" € 19.35   2008*

CREIXELL *3C3* (Coastal) *41.16338, 1.45878* **Camping La Plana, Ctra N340, Km 1182, 43839 Creixell (Tarragona)** [977-80 03 04; fax 977-66 36 63] Site sp at Creixell off N340. Med, hdstg, shd; wc; chem disp; shwrs inc; el pnts inc; gas; lndtte; shop; rest; snacks; bar; sand beach adj; poss cr; Eng spkn; adv bkg; some rlwy noise. "Vg, v clean site; v helpful & pleasant owners." 1 May-30 Sep. € 21.00   2011*

CREIXELL *3C3* (Coastal) *41.16390, 1.44682* **Camping La Sirena Dorada, Ctra N340, Km 1181, 43839 Creixell (Tarragona)** [977-80 13 03; fax 977-80 12 15; info@sirenadorada. com; www.sirenadorada.com] Fr N exit AP7 at junc 31, foll N340 sp Tarragona, site 200m past Roman arch on L. Fr S exit junc 32 onto N340 to Creixall. Lge, pt shd; wc; shwrs inc; mv service pnt; el pnts (5A) €5.40; gas; lndtte; shop; rest; bar; playgrnd; pool; waterslide; sand beach 200m; games area; wifi; entmnt; 15% statics; poss cr; adv bkg; quiet; CCI. "Unreliable opening dates - low ssn phone to check open." ♦ 1 Mar-1 Nov. € 32.50   2008*

CREIXELL *3C3* (1km S Coastal) *41.15714, 1.44137* **Camping Gavina Platja, Ctra N340, Km 1181, Platja Creixell, 43839 Creixell de Mar (Tarragona)** [977-80 15 03; fax 977-80 05 27; info@gavina.net; www.gavina.net] Exit AP7 junc 31 (Coma-Ruga) onto N340 dir Tarragona. At km 1181 turn R twd Playa de Creixel via undergnd passage. Site 1km S of Creixell, adj beach - foll sp Creixell Platja. Lge, mkd pitch, pt shd; wc; chem disp; baby facs; fam bthrm; shwrs inc; el pnts (6A) €4.50; gas; lndtte; shop; rest; snacks; bar; playgrnd; sand beach adj; watersports; tennis; wifi; entmnt; 20% statics; dogs; poss cr; adv bkg rec Jul/Aug; some train noise; ccard acc; red long stay; CCI. "Rest o'looks beach; Port Aventura 20km." ♦ 4 Apr-31 Oct. € 34.50 (CChq acc)   2009*

CREVILLENT see Elche *4F2*

⊞ **CUBILLAS DE SANTA MARTA** *1C4* (4km S Rural) *41.80511, -4.58776* **Camping Cubillas, Ctra N620, Km 102, 47290 Cubillas de Santa Marta (Valladolid)** [983-58 50 02; fax 983-58 50 16; info@campingcubillas.com; www.campingcubillas.com] A62 Valladolid-Palencia, turn W at km 102. Site on L. Lge, some hdg/mkd pitch, pt sl, unshd; wc; chem disp; mv service pnt; shwrs inc; el pnts (6-10A) €4-5.80; gas; lndtte; sm shop; tradsmn; rest; snacks & bar in ssn; BBQ; playgrnd; pool; entmnt; 50% statics; dogs €2; phone; site clsd 18 Dec-10 Jan; Eng spkn; ccard acc; red long stay/low ssn; CCI. "Ltd space for tourers; conv visit Palencia & Valladolid; rd & m'way, rlwy & disco noise at w/end until v late; v ltd facs low ssn; NH only." ♦ € 24.65   2011*

CUDILLERO *1A3* (2.5km SE Rural) *43.55416, -6.12944* **Camping Cudillero, Ctra Playa de Aguilar, Aronces, 33150 El Pito (Asturias)** [tel/fax 985-59 06 63; info@campingcudillero.com; www.campingcudillero.com] Exit N632 (E70) sp El Pito. Turn L at rndabt sp Cudillero & in 300m at end of wall turn R at site sp, cont for 1km, site on L. Do not app thro Cudillero; streets v narr & steep; much traffic. Med, hdg/mkd pitch, pt shd; wc; chem disp; baby facs; shwrs inc; el pnts (3-5A) €4.05; gas; lndtte; shop; snacks high ssn; bar; playgrnd; htd pool; sand beach 1.2km; games area; entmnt high ssn; wifi; TV; no statics; dogs €2.15; phone; bus 1km; adv bkg; quiet; CCI. "Excel, well-maintained, well laid-out site; some generous pitches; gd san facs; steep walk to beach & vill." ♦ Holy Week & 1 May-18 Sep. € 24.20   2011*

CUDILLERO *1A3* (2km S Rural) *43.55555, -6.13777* **Camping L'Amuravela, El Pito, 33150 Cudillero (Asturias)** [tel/fax 985-59 09 95; camping@lamuravela.com; www.lamuravela.com] Exit N632 (E70) sp El Pito. Turn L at rndabt sp Cudillero & in approx 1km turn R at site sp. Do not app thro Cudillero; streets v narr & steep; much traffic. Med, mkd pitch, pt sl, unshd; wc; chem disp; mv service pnt; shwrs inc; el pnts €4.10; gas; shop; snacks; bar; pool; paddling pool; sand beach 2km; 50% statics (sep area); dogs €1; poss cr; ccard acc high ssn. "Pleasant, well-maintained site; gd clean facs; hillside walks into Cudillero, attractive fishing vill with gd fish rests; red facs low ssn & poss only open w/ends; surroundings excellent." Holy Week & 1 Jun-30 Sep. € 24.60   2011*

CUENCA *3D1* (8km N Rural) *40.12694, -2.14194* **Camping Cuenca, Ctra Cuenca-Tragacete, Km 7, 16147 Cuenca** [tel/fax 969-23 16 56; info@campingcuenca.com; www.campingcuenca.com] Fr Madrid take N400/A40 dir Cuenca & exit sp 'Ciudad Encantada' & Valdecabras on CM2110. In 7.5km turn R onto CM2105, site on R in 1.5km. Foll sp 'Nalimiento des Rio Jucar'. Lge, pt sl, pt terr, pt shd; wc; chem disp; mv service pnt; shwrs inc; el pnts (6-10A) €4; gas; lndtte; shop; snacks; bar; playgrnd; pool high ssn; jacuzzi; tennis; games area; 15% statics; dogs €1; phone; poss cr esp Easter w/end; Eng spkn; adv bkg; quiet; CCI. "Pleasant, well-kept, green site; gd touring cent; friendly, helpful staff; excel san facs but ltd low ssn; interesting rock formations at Ciudad Encantada." ♦ 19 Mar-11 Oct. € 20.80   2010*

CUEVAS DEL ALMANZORA see Garrucha *4G1*

CULLERA see Sueca *4E2*

DEBA *3A1* (6km E Coastal) *43.29436, -2.32853* **Camping Itxaspe, N634, Km 38, 20829 Itziar (Guipúzkoa)** [tel/fax 943-19 93 77; itxaspe@hotmail.es; www.campingitxaspe.com] Exit A8 junc 13 dir Deba; at main rd turn L up hill, in 400m at x-rds turn L, site in 2km - narr, winding rd. NB Do not go into Itziar vill. Sm, mkd pitch, pt sl, pt shd; wc; chem disp; baby facs; shwrs; el pnts (5A) €4; gas; shop; rest; bar adj; BBQ; playgrnd; pool; solarium; shgl beach 4km; wifi; some statics; bus 2km; adv bkg; quiet; red low ssn; CCI. "Excel site; helpful owner; w/ends busy; sea views." ♦ 1 Apr-30 Sep. € 23.80   2011*

DEBA *3A1* (5km W Coastal) *43.30577, -2.37789* **Camping Aitzeta, Ctra Deba-Guernica, Km. 3.5, C6212, 20930 Mutriku (Guipúzkoa)** [943-60 33 56; fax 943-60 31 06; www.campingseuskadi.com/aitzeta] On N634 San Sebastián-Bilbao rd thro Deba & on o'skts turn R over rv sp Mutriku. Site on L after 3km on narr & winding rd up short steep climb. Med, mkd pitch, terr, pt shd; wc; chem disp (wc); shwrs inc; el pnts (4A) €3; gas; lndry rm; sm shop; rest 300m; snacks; bar; playgrnd; sand beach 1km; dogs; bus 500m; phone; quiet; CCI. "Easy reach of Bilbao ferry; sea views; gd, well-run, clean site; not suitable lge o'fits; ltd pitches for tourers; helpful staff; walk to town." ♦ 1 May-30 Sep. € 21.00   2010*

⊞ **DEBA** *3A1* (7km W Rural) *43.31340, -2.39459* **Camping Santa Elena, Ctra Deba-Gernika, Km 5, 20830 Mutriku (Guipúzkoa)** [tel/fax 943-60 39 82; www.campingseuskadi.com/santaelena] On N634 San Sebastián-Bilbao rd, thro Deba on o'skts turn R over rv bdge, thro Mutriku & at end of town slowly under narr bdge, 30m after turn R sp Galdonamendi, 2km up hill. Med, sl, terr, shd; wc; shwrs; el pnts €3.50; lndtte; shop; rest; playgrnd; sand beach 4km; 80% statics; phone; poss cr w/end; adv bkg; quiet. "Blocks ess for levelling; gd views; sm pitches & narr site rds." € 21.50   2008*

DELTEBRE *3D2* (8km E Coastal) *40.72041, 0.84849* **Camping L'Aube, Afores s/n, 43580 Deltebre (Tarragona)** [977-26 70 66; fax 977-26 75 05; campinglaube@hotmail.com; www.campinglaube.com] Exit AP7 junc 40 or 41 onto N340 dir Deltebre. Fr Deltebre foll T340 sp Riumar for 8km. At info kiosk branch R, site sp 1km on R. Lge, mkd pitch, hdstg, pt shd; wc; chem disp; mv service pnt; shwrs inc; el pnts (3-10A) €2.80-5; lndtte; shop; rest; bar; snacks; pool; playgrnd; phone; sand beach adj; 40% statics; poss cr low ssn; red long stay; CCI. "At edge of Ebro Delta National Park; excel birdwatching; ltd facs in winter." ♦ 1 Mar-31 Oct. € 16.00   2011*

DELTEBRE *3D2* (10km SE Coastal) *40.65681, 0.77971* **Camping Eucaliptus, Playa Eucaliptus s/n, 43870 Amposta (Tarragona)** [tel/fax 977-47 90 46; eucaliptus@campingeucaliptus.com; www.campingeucaliptus.com] Exit AP7/E15 at junc 41. Foll sp to Amposta but do not go into town. Take sp for Els Muntells on TV3405 then Eucaliptus beach. Site on R 100m fr beach. Lge, mkd pitch, pt shd; wc; chem disp; shwrs; el pnts (5A) €4.30; gas; lndtte; shops; rest; snacks; bar; BBQ area; playgrnd; pool; paddling pool; sand beach adj; fishing; watersports; cycling; entmnt; 40% statics; dogs €2.40; poss cr; adv bkg; noisy w/end & high ssn; red long stay; CCI. "Vg, well-run, peaceful site; gd facs; gd bar/rest; excel birdwatching; poss mosquito prob." ♦ Holy Week-27 Sep. € 24.10   2009*

DENIA *4E2* (2km SE Coastal) *38.83203, 0.13895* **Camping Tolosa, Camí d´Urios 32, Les Rotes, 03700 Dénia (Alicante)** [965-78 72 94; info@campingtolosa.com; www.campingtolosa.com] Fr E end of Dénia Harbour take Jávea/Les Rotes rd. In approx 2km keep L at fork exit Jávea rd on R. In approx 1km site app clearly sp on L; site 300m twd sea. Med, mkd pitch, hdstg, pt shd; wc; chem disp; shwrs inc; el pnts (6A) €3; gas; shop; supmkt adj; bar; BBQ; shgl beach adj; 40% statics; dogs; phone; bus 300m; poss cr; quiet; red long stay. "Well-managed site; pleasant staff; sm pitches." Holy Week & 1 Apr-30 Sep. € 26.00   2008*

⊞ **DENIA** *4E2* (3.5km SE Coastal) *38.82968, 0.14767* **Camping Los Pinos, Ctra Dénia-Les Rotes, Km 3, Les Rotes, 03700 Dénia (Alicante)** [tel/fax 965-78 26 98; lospinosdenia@gmail.com] Fr N332 foll sp to Dénia then dir Les Rotes/Jávea, site sp. Narr access rd poss diff lge o'fits. Med, mkd pitch, pt shd; wc; chem disp; shwrs inc; el pnts (6-10A) €3.20; gas; lndtte; shop adj; tradsmn; BBQ; cooking facs; playgrnd; shgl beach adj; internet; TV rm; 25% statics; dogs €3; phone; bus 100m; poss cr; Eng spkn; adv bkg; quiet; red long stays/low ssn; ccard acc; CCI. "Friendly, well-run, clean, tidy site but san facs a little 'tired' (Mar 09); excel value; access some pitches poss diff due trees - not suitable lge o'fits or m'vans; many long-stay winter residents; cycle path into Dénia; social rm with log fire; naturist beach 1km, private but rocky shore." ♦ € 25.40   2009*

⊞ **DENIA** *4E2* (9km W Rural/Coastal) *38.86750, -0.01615* **Camping Los Llanos, Partida Deveses 32, 03700 Dénia (Alicante)** [965-75 51 88 or 649-45 51 58; fax 965-75 54 25; losllanos@losllanos.net; www.losllanos.net] Exit AP7 junc 62 dir Dénia onto CV725. At lge rndabt turn L & foll sp to site along N332a. Med, pt shd; wc; chem disp; mv service pnt; shwrs inc; el pnts (10A) €3.50; lndtte; shop & 2km; rest 500m; snacks; bar; playgrnd; pool; paddling pool; sand beach 150m; wifi; 30% statics; dogs €2; phone; bus 100m; poss cr; adv bkg; quiet; ccard acc; red long stay. "Pleasant site; gd, modern san facs; gd touring base; friendly, helpful staff; vg." € 25.00   2009*

⊞ **DOS HERMANAS** *2G3* (1km W Urban) *37.27756, -5.93642* **Camping Villsom, Ctra Sevilla/Cádiz A4, Km 554.8, 41700 Dos Hermanas (Sevilla)** [tel/fax 954-72 08 28; campingvillsom@hotmail.com] Fr AP4/E5 Sevilla-Cádiz, exit junc 553 on SE3205 dir Dos Hermanas Centro, site on L immed bef L fork & bdge for Dos Hermanas. Lge, hdg/mkd pitch, hdstg, pt sl, pt shd; wc (some cont); chem disp; shwrs inc; el pnts (8A) €3.30 (poss no earth); gas; lndtte; sm shop; hypmkt 1km; snacks in ssn; bar; playgrnd; pool in ssn; wifi; bus to Seville 300m (over bdge & rndabt); site clsd 25 Dec-9 Jan; poss cr; Eng spkn; adv bkg; rd noise; ccard acc; CCI. "Adv bkg rec Holy Week; sm pitches - poss diff access lge o'fits; helpful staff; clean, tidy, well-run site; vg, san facs, ltd low ssn; height barrier at Carrefour hypmkt - ent via deliveries." € 31.90   2011*

⊞ **ELCHE** *4F2* (7km S Rural) *38.17770, -0.80876* **Marjal Costa Blanca Eco Camping Resort, 03330 Crevillent** [965-48 49 45; camping@marjalcostablanca.com; www.marjalcostablanca.com] Fr A7/E15 merge onto AP7 (sp Murcia), take exit 730; site sp fr exit. V lge, hdg/mkd pitch, hdstg, pt shd; wc; chem disp; baby facs; shwrs; serviced pitches; el pnts (16A) inc; gas; lndtte (inc dryer); supmkt; rests; snacks; bar; BBQ area; playgrnd; htd pool complex; wellness cent with fitness studio, htd pools, saunas, physiotherapy & spa; lake sw; tennis; car wash; hairdresser; doctor's surgery; games area; games rm; entmnt; wifi; TV; statics; tour ops; dogs €2.20; ccard acc; lge pitches extra charge; red low ssn. "Superb site; gd security." ♦ € 40.00 SBS - W05   2011*

⊞ **ELCHE** *4F2* (10km SW Urban) *38.24055, -0.81194* **Camping Las Palmeras, Ctra Murcia-Alicante, Km 45.3, 03330 Crevillent (Alicante)** [965-40 01 88 or 966-68 06 30; fax 966-68 06 64; laspalmeras@laspalmeras-sl.com; www.laspalmeras-sl.com] Exit A7 junc 726/77 onto N340 to Crevillent. Immed bef traff lts take slip rd into restaurant parking/service area. Site on R, access rd down side of rest. Med, mkd pitch, hdstg, pt shd; wc; chem disp; shwrs inc; el pnts (6A) inc; lndtte; supmkt adj; rest; snacks; bar; pool; paddling pool; 10% statics; dogs free; ccard acc; CCI. "Useful NH; report to recep in hotel; helpful staff; gd cent for touring Murcia; gd rest in hotel; gd, modern san facs; excel." € 45.00   2011*

SPAIN

ERRATZU *3A1* (E Rural) *43.18055, -1.45166* **Camping Baztan, Ctra Francia s/n, 31714 Erratzu (Navarra)** [948-45 31 33; fax 948-45 30 85; campingbaztan@campingbaztan.com; www. campingbaztan.com] Fr N121B km 62 marker take NA2600 sp Erratzu. In vill strt on at staggered x-rds & foll sp dir France, site on R outside vill 100m after Y junc. App rd thro vill narr with tight turns. Med, hdg/mkd pitch, shd; wc; chem disp; shwrs inc; el pnts inc; lndtte; shop; rest; playgrnd; pool; dogs €4; poss cr; adv bkg; quiet; ccard acc. "Site manned w/end only low ssn; gd walking; lovely scenery." ♦ 9 Apr-31 Oct. € 33.10   2008*

⊞ **ESCALA, L'** *3B3* (2km SE Coastal) *42.11048, 3.16378* **Camping Cala Montgó, Avda Montgó s/n, 17130 L'Escala (Gerona)** [972-77 08 66; fax 972-77 43 40; calamontgo@ betsa.es; www.betsa.es] Exit AP7 junc 4 Figueres onto C31 dir L'Escala & Montgó to site. V lge, pt sl, pt shd; wc; chem disp; baby facs; shwrs inc; el pnts (5A) €4.10; gas; lndtte; shop; tradsmn; rest; bar; playgrnd; pool; paddling pool; sand beach 200m; fishing; sports area; cycle hire; 30% statics; dogs; poss cr; adv bkg; quiet; ccard not acc; red low ssn; CCI. "Nr trad fishing vill; facs ltd/run down; quiet low ssn; exposed, poss windy & dusty site." ♦ € 36.00   2009*

ESCALA, L' *3B3* (500m S Urban/Coastal) *42.1211, 3.1346* **Camping L'Escala, Camí Ample 21, 17130 L'Escala (Gerona)** [972-77 00 84; fax 972-77 00 08; info@campinglescala. com; www.campinglescala.com] Exit AP7 junc 5 onto GI623 dir L'Escala; at o'skts of L'Escala, at 1st rndabt (with yellow sign GI623 on top of rd direction sp) turn L dir L'Escala & Ruïnes Empúries; at 2nd rndabt go str on dir L'Escala-Riells, then foll site sp. Do not app thro town. Med, hdg/mkd pitch, pt shd; wc; chem disp; all serviced pitches; baby facs; shwrs inc; el pnts (6A) inc; gas; lndtte; supmkt; tradsmn; rest 100m; snacks; bar; BBQ; playgrnd; beach 300m; TV; 20% statics; no dogs; phone; car wash; poss cr; Eng spkn; adv bkg; quiet; red low ssn; CCI. "Access to sm pitches poss diff lge o'fits; helpful, friendly staff; vg, modern san facs; Empúrias ruins 5km; vg." ♦ 27 Mar-26 Sep. € 41.00   2010*

ESCALA, L' *3B3* (1km S Coastal) *42.1134, 3.1443* **Camping Maite, Avda Montó, Playa de Riells, 17130 L'Escala (Gerona)** [tel/fax 972-77 05 44; www.campingmaite.com] Exit A7 junc 5 dir L'Escala. Thro town dir Riells to rndabt with supmkts on each corner, turn R to site. Lge, mkd pitch, some terr, shd; wc; chem disp; mv service pnt; shwrs inc; el pnts (6A) €4.30; gas; shop adj; rest; bar; playgrnd; beach 200m; TV; bus 1km; adv bkg; red long stay; ccard acc; CCI. "Well-run site; quiet oasis in busy resort; steep site rds; some pitches narr access." ♦ 1 Jun-15 Sep. € 20.80   2011*

ESCALA, L' *3B3* (2km S Coastal) *42.11027, 3.16555* **Camping Illa Mateua, Ave Montgó 260, 17130 L'Escala (Gerona)** [972-77 02 00 or 77 17 95; fax 972-77 20 31; info@ campingillamateua.com; www.campingillamateua.com] On N11 thro Figueras, approx 3km on L sp C31 L'Escala; in town foll sp for Montgó & Paradis. Lge, terr, pt shd; wc; chem disp; mv service pnt; baby facs; shwrs inc; el pnts (5A) inc; gas; lndtte; shop; rest; bar; playgrnd; 2 pools; sand beach adj; watersports; tennis; games area; entmnt; 5% statics; dogs €3.60; Eng spkn; adv bkg ess high ssn; quiet; red low ssn/ long stay; CCI. "V well-run site; spacious pitches; excel san facs; gd beach; no depth marking in pool." ♦ 15 Mar-10 Oct. € 46.60   2011*

ESCALA, L' *3B3* (3km S Coastal) *42.10512, 3.15843* **Camping Neus, Cala Montgó, 17130 L'Escala (Gerona)** [972-77 04 03 or 972-20 86 67; fax 972-77 27 51 or 972-22 24 09; info@ campingneus.com; www.campingneus.com] Exit AP7 junc 5 twd L'Escala then turn R twd Cala Montgó & foll sp. Med, mkd pitch, pt sl, pt terr, shd; wc; chem disp; mv service pnt; baby facs; shwrs inc; el pnts (6A) €4; gas; lndtte; shop; snacks; bar; playgrnd; pool; paddling pool; sand beach 850m; fishing; tennis; car wash; internet; entmnt; TV rm; 15% statics; dogs €2; phone; bus 500m; Eng spkn; adv bkg; quiet; ccard acc; red low ssn/long stay; CCI. "Pleasant, clean site in pine forest; gd san facs; lge pitches; vg." 28 May-19 Sep. € 39.00   2009*

⊞ **ESCORIAL, EL** *1D4* (6km NE Rural) *40.62630, -4.09970*
**Camping-Caravaning El Escorial, Ctra Guadarrama a
El Escorial, Km 3.5, 28280 El Escorial (Madrid)** [918-
90 24 12 or 902-01 49 00; fax 918-96 10 62; info@
campingelescorial.com; www.campingelescorial.com]
Exit AP6 NW of Madrid junc 47 El Escorial/Guadarrama,
onto M505 & foll sp to El Escorial, site on L at km stone
3,500 - long o'fits rec cont to rndabt (1km) to turn & app
site on R. V lge, mkd pitch, some hdstg, pt shd; htd wc;
chem disp; baby facs; shwrs inc; el pnts (5A) inc (long cable
rec); gas; lndtte; shop, rest, snacks & bar in ssn & w/end;
BBQ; hypmkt 5km; BBQ; playgrnd; 3 pools high ssn; tennis;
horseriding 7km; games rm; cash machine; wifi; entmnt;
TV; 25% statics (sep area); dogs free; c'vans/m'vans over
8m must reserve lge pitch with elec, water & drainage; adv
bkg; some Eng spkn; poss cr & noisy at w/end; ccard acc.
"Excel, busy site; mountain views; helpful staff; clean facs;
gd security; sm pitches poss diff due trees; o'head canopies
poss diff for tall o'fits; facs ltd low ssn; trains & buses to
Madrid nr; Valle de Los Caídos & Palace at El Escorial well
worth visit; easy parking in town for m'vans if go in early;
mkt Wed." ♦ € 34.25 SBS - E13   2011*

See advertisement on previous page

ESCULLOS, LOS see Nijar *4G1*

ESPINAL see Auritz *3A1*

⊞ **ESPONELLA** *3B3* (500m N Rural) *42.1817, 2.7949* **Camping
Esponellà, Ctra Banyoles-Figueres, Km 8, 17832 Esponellà
(Gerona)** [972-59 70 74; fax 972-59 71 32; informa@
campingesponella.com; www.campingesponella.com]
Heading S fr French frontier, turn R (W) at Figueras on N260.
After 13km turn L at junc to Banyoles, site in 6.5km. Fr S foll
C66 N fr Gerona, then in 17km turn R twds Figueres. Lge, hdg
pitch, pt shd; htd wc (some cont); chem disp; shwrs inc; rest;
el pnts (5A) €4.70 (check earth); lndtte; shop; rest; bar; BBQ;
playgrnd; 2 htd covrd pools; tennis; games area; cycle hire;
rv fishing; horseriding; entmnt; 40% statics; dogs €2; quiet;
red long stay/CCI. "Excel facs but ltd low ssn; v busy w/end;
lovely site but poss not suitable lge o'fits due trees; gd walks."
€ 28.15   2008*

ESPOT *3B2* (500m SE Rural) *42.95916, 1.14916* **Camping Sol
I Neu, Ctra Sant Maurici s/n, 25597 Espot (Lleida)** [973-
62 40 01; fax 973-62 41 07; camping@solineu.com; www.
solineu.com] N fr Sort on C13 turn L to Espot on rd LV5004,
site on L in approx 6.5km by rvside. Med, mkd pitch, pt shd;
wc; chem disp; baby facs; shwrs inc; el pnts (6-10A) €5.15;
gas; lndtte; shop, bar high ssn; playgrnd; pool; paddling pool;
TV; dogs €3.60; quiet; ccard acc; CCI. "Excel facs; beautiful site
nr National Park (Landrover taxis avail - no private vehicles
allowed in Park); suitable sm o'fits only; poss unreliable
opening dates." 1 Jul-31 Aug. € 23.70   2008*

ESPOT *3B2* (1km W Rural) *42.58527, 1.0750* **Camping
Voraparc, Ctra Sant Maurici s/n, Prat del Vedat, 25597
Espot (Lleida)** [973-62 41 08 or 973-25 23 24; fax 973-
62 41 43; info@voraparc.com; www.voraparc.com] Fr Sort
N on C13 N. At sp turn L for Espot, go thro vill then turn R for
National Park. Site in 1.5km on R. Well sp. Med, mkd pitch,
pt sl, shd; wc; chem disp (wc); mv service pnt; baby facs;
shwrs inc; el pnts (6A) €4.25 (poss rev pol); gas; lndtte; shop;
tradsmn; snacks; bar; BBQ; playgrnd; htd pool; watersports
nrby; walks; cycle hire; TV/games rm; no statics; dogs; phone;
bus 1km; Eng spkn; adv bkg; quiet; red long stay; ccard acc;
CCI. "Friendly owners; clean facs; access rd narr & needs care;
National Park in walking/cycling distance; gd birdwatching;
excel." ♦ Holy Week & 1 May-30 Sep. € 20.60   2008*

ESTARTIT L' *3B3* (W Coastal) *42.05333, 3.19277* **Camping
Rifort, Ctra de Torroella s/n, Km 5.5, 17258 L'Estartit
(Gerona)** [972-75 04 06; fax 972-75 17 22; campingrifort@
campingrifort.com; www.campingrifort.com] Site on
rndabt at ent to L'Estartit. Med, hdg/mkd pitch, terr, pt shd;
wc; chem disp; mv service pnt; shwrs; baby facs; el pnts
€4.15; gas; lndtte; shop 500m; snacks; bar; pool; sand beach
500m; tennis 150m; watersports; internet; some statics;
dogs €2.15; phone; bus adj; Eng spkn; adv bkg; noise fr adj
main rd & entmnt; red low ssn; ccard acc. "Family-run; excel,
immac facs." ♦ 7 Apr-12 Oct. € 22.10   2008*

ESTARTIT, L' *3B3* (500m Urban/Coastal) *42.04808, 3.1871*
**Camping La Sirena, Calle La Platera s/n, 17258 L'Estartit
(Gerona)** [972-75 15 42; fax 972-75 09 44; info@camping-
lasirena.com; www.camping-lasirena.com] Fr Torroella
foll sp to L'Estartit on rd GI641. On o'skts of vill turn R at Els
Jocs amusements, site on L 200m. Lge, pt shd; wc; chem
disp; baby facs; shwrs inc; el pnts (6-10A) €5 (poss long lead
req); gas; lndtte (inc dryer); shop; rest; snacks; bar; BBQ;
playgrnd; htd pool; paddling pool; sand beach adj; scuba
diving; internet; money exchange; car wash; TV; 10% statics;
dogs €2.50; bus adj; Eng spkn; quiet; red long stay/low ssn;
CCI. "Sm pitches, diff lge o'fits; poss long walk to beach; v
ltd facs low ssn; gd value boat trips; nature reserve adj." ♦
Easter-12 Oct. € 26.00   2009*

ESTARTIT, L' *3B3* (1km S Coastal) *42.04972, 3.18416* **Camping
El Molino, Camino del Ter, 17258 L'Estartit (Gerona)**
[tel/fax 972-75 06 29] Fr N11 junc 5, take rd to L'Escala. Foll
sp to Torroella de Montgri, then L'Estartit. Ent town & foll
sp, site on rd GI 641. V lge, hdg pitch, pt sl, pt shd; wc; mv
service pnt; shwrs; el pnts (6A) €3.60; gas; lndtte; supmkt high
ssn & 2km; rest; bar; playgrnd; sand beach 1km; games rm;
internet; bus 1km; poss cr; adv bkg. "Site in 2 parts - 1 in shd,
1 at beach unshd; gd facs; quiet location outside busy town."
1 Apr-30 Sep. € 22.00   2010*

SPAIN

T. +34 972 751 805
info@campinglesmedes.com

WWW.CAMPINGLESMEDES.COM

- Family campsite OPEN ALL YEAR ROUND in the heart of nature, and just 800 metres from the beach
- In a superb natural and cultural setting
- Modern facilities: heated indoor swimming pool, solarium, sauna...
- Good times assured for all the family
- Water sports, bicycle hire...

lesmedes c à m p i n g

G P S 42° 02' 33" N / 3° 11' 00" E

17258 – L'ESTARTIT – Catalunya – COSTA BRAVA – Spain

⊞ **ESTARTIT, L'** 3B3 (2km S Coastal) 42.04250, 3.18333 **Camping Les Medes, Paratge Camp de l'Arbre s/n, 17258 L'Estartit** (Gerona) [972-75 18 05; fax 972-75 04 13; info@campinglesmedes.com; www.campinglesmedes.com] Fr Torroella foll sp to L'Estartit. In vill turn R at town name sp (sp Urb Estartit Oeste), foll rd for 1.5km, turn R, site well sp. Lge, mkd pitch, shd; htd wc; chem disp; mv service pnt; serviced pitches; baby facs; sauna; shwrs inc; el pnts (6A) €4.60; gas; lndtte; shop; rest; snacks; bar; playgrnd; htd indoor/outdoor pools; sand beach 800m; watersports; solarium; tennis; games area; horseriding 400m; cycle hire; car wash; games rm; wifi; entmnt; TV; 7% statics; no dogs high ssn otherwise €2.60; phone; site clsd Nov; poss cr; Eng spkn; adv bkg; quiet; red long stay/low ssn (pay on arrival); CCI. "Excel, popular, family-run & well organised site; helpful staff; gd clean facs & constant hot water; gd for children; no twin-axle vans high ssn - by arrangement low ssn; conv National Park; well mkd foot & cycle paths." ♦ € 35.90   2011*

See advertisement above

I'll fill in a report online and let the Club know – www.caravanclub.co.uk/europereport

This is a wonderful site.

ESTARTIT, L' 3B3 (W Coastal) 42.05670, 3.19785 **Camping Estartit, Calle Villa Primevera 12, 17258 L'Estartit** (Gerona) [972-75 19 09; fax 972-75 09 91; www.campingestartit.com] Exit AP7 junc 6 onto C66, then take G642 dir Torroella de Montgri & L'Estartit; fork L on ent L'Estartit, foll site sps. Med, pt sl, shd; htd wc; chem disp; baby facs; shwrs ; el pnts (6A) €3.73; gas; lndtte; shop; rest adj; snacks; bar; playgrnd; htd pool; paddling pool; sand beach 400m; entmnt; 15% statics; no dogs 20/6-20/8; phone; poss cr; Eng spkn; red long stay. "Friendly staff; 100m fr vill cent; gd security; gd walks adj nature reserve; bar/rest & night club adj; facs poss stretched high ssn." 1 Apr-30 Sep. € 23.90   2011*

ESTARTIT, L' 3B3 (1km W Coastal) 42.05035, 3.18023 **Camping Castell Montgri, Ctra de Torroella, Km 4.7, 17258 L'Estartit** (Gerona) [972-75 16 30; fax 972-75 09 06; cmontgri@campingparks.com; www.campingparks.com] Exit A7 junc 5 onto GI 623 dir L'Escala. Foll sp on rd C252 fr Torroella de Montgri to L'Estartit. Site on L clearly sp. V lge, hdg pitch, terr, hdstg, shd; wc; mv service pnt; chem disp; baby facs; shwrs inc; el pnts (10A) inc; gas; lndtte (inc dryer); shop; rest; snacks; bar; playgrnd; 3 pools; waterslide; beach 1km; tennis; games area; watersports; wifi; entmnt; TV; car wash; money exchange; 30% statics; dogs free; phone; poss cr; adv bkg; red long stay/low ssn. "Gd views; help given to get to pitch; excel site." ♦ 12 May-30 Sep. € 62.00   2011*

See advertisement on page 153

ESTARTIT, L' 3B3 (1km W Coastal) 42.04907, 3.18385 **Camping L'Empordà, Ctra Torroella-L'Estartit, Km 4.8, 17258 L'Estartit** (Gerona) [972-75 06 49; fax 972-75 14 30; info@campingemporda.com; www.campingemporda.com] Exit AP7 junc 5 onto GI623 dir L'Escala. Bef L'Escala turn S onto C31 dir Torroella de Montgri, then at Torroella take rd GI641 dir L'Estartit. Site bet L'Estartit & Torroella, opp Castell Montgri. Lge, hdg/mkd pitch, pt shd; wc; chem disp; shwrs inc; baby facs; el pnts (6A) €4.70; gas; lndtte; shop; bar; playgrnd; pool; paddling pool; sand beach 1km; tennis; entmnt; organised walks; wifi; TV; dogs €2.80; phone; bus 70m; car wash; poss cr; adv bkg; quiet; red low ssn/long stay; CCI. "Family-run, pleasant & helpful; easy walking dist town cent; lge pitches." ♦ 2 Apr-12 Oct. € 25.90   2011*

⊞ **ESTELLA** 3B1 (2km S Rural) 42.65695, -2.01761 **Camping Lizarra, Paraje de Ordoiz s/n, 31200 Estella** (Navarra) [948-55 17 33; fax 948-55 47 55; info@campinglizarra.com; www.campinglizarra.com] N111 Pamplona to Logroño. Leave N111 sp Estella, turn R at T-junc, bear R at traff lts & turn R immed after rd tunnel, site sp. Pass factory, site on L in 1.5km. Well sp thro town. Lge, mkd pitch, wide terr, pt sl, unshd; htd wc; chem disp; mv service pnt; baby facs; shwrs inc; el pnts (6A) inc; gas; lndtte; shop high ssn; rest; snacks; bar; BBQ; playgrnd; pool; 80% w/end statics; phone; bus at w/end; site clsd mid-Dec to early Jan; poss cr; Eng spkn; noisy; ccard acc; CCI. "Poss school parties; no hdstg; poss muddy when wet; interesting old town; excel birdwatching in hills; on rte Camino de Compostella; unreliable opening low ssn." ♦ € 25.25   2011*

⊞ **ESTEPAR** *1B4* (2km NE Rural) *42.29233, -3.85097* **Camping Cabia, Ctra Burgos-Valladolid, Km 15.2, 09192 Cabia/Cavia (Burgos)** [947-41 20 78] Site 15km SW of Burgos on N side of A62/E80, adj Hotel Rio Cabia. Ent via Campsa petrol stn, W'bound exit 17, E'bound exit 16, cross over & re-join m'way. Ignore camp sp at exit 18 (1-way). Med, pt shd; wc; chem disp; shwrs inc; el pnts (6A) inc; shops 15km & basic supplies fr rest; rest; bar; playgrnd; few statics; dogs; constant rd noise; ccard acc; CCI. "Friendly, helpful owner; gd rest; conv for m'way for Portugal but poorly sp fr W; poss v muddy in winter; refurbed san facs; NH only." € 14.00   2010*

⊞ **ESTEPONA** *2H3* (7km E Coastal) *36.45436, -5.08105* **Camping Parque Tropical, Ctra N340, Km 162, 29680 Estepona (Málaga)** [tel/fax 952-79 36 18; parquetropical camping@hotmail.com; www.campingparquetropical.com] On N side of N340 at km 162, 200m off main rd. Med, hdg/ mkd pitch, terr, pt shd; wc; chem disp; mv service pnt; serviced pitch; shwrs inc; el pnts (10A) €4; gas; lndtte; shop; rest; snacks; bar; sm playgrnd; htd, covrd pool; sand/ shgl beach 1km; golf, horseriding nrby; wildlife park 1km; 10% statics; dogs €2; phone; bus 400m; poss cr; Eng spkn; adv bkg; rd noise; red low ssn/long stay; CCI. "Site run down (Feb 09); facs in need of update; helpful owners." ♦ € 27.00   2009*

ETXARRI ARANATZ *3B1* (2km N Rural) *42.91255, -2.07919* **Camping Etxarri, Parase Dambolintxulo, 31820 Etxarri-Aranatz (Navarra)** [tel/fax 948-46 05 37; info@ campingetxarri.com; www.campingetxarri.com] Fr N exit A15 at junc 112 to join A10 W dir Vitoria/Gasteiz. Exit at junc 19 onto NA120; go thro Etxarri vill, turn L & cross bdge, then take rd over rlwy. Turn L, site sp. Med, hdg pitch, pt shd; wc; chem disp; shwrs inc; el pnts (6A) €5.50; gas; lndtte; shop; rest; bar; BBQ; pool; playgrnd; sports area; archery; horseriding; cycling; wifi; entmnt; 90% statics; dogs €2.15; phone; poss cr; Eng spkn; ccard acc; red low ssn; CCI. "Gd, wooded site; gd walks; interesting area; helpful owner; conv NH to/fr Pyrenees; youth hostel & resident workers on site - site poss scruffy but san facs gd; various pitch sizes & shapes, some diff lge o'fits; NH only." 4 Mar-31 Dec. € 20.85
                    2010*

EUSA see Pamplona *3B1*

FARGA DE MOLES, LA see Seo de Urgel *3B3*

⊞ **FIGUERES** *3B3* (1km N Urban) *42.28311, 2.94978* **Camping Pous, Ctra N11A, Km 8.5, 17600 Figueres (Gerona)** [972-67 54 96; fax 972-67 50 57; hostalandrol@wanadoo.es] Fr N exit AP7/E15 at junc 3 & join N11. Then foll N11A S twd Figueres. Site on L in 2km, ent adj Hostal Androl. From S exit junc 4 onto NII to N of town. At rndabt (access to AP7 junc 3) foll NII S, then as above. Site recep in hotel. No access to N11A fr junc 4. Med, mkd pitch, pt sl, shd; wc; chem disp; shwrs inc; el pnts (10A) €3; shop 1km; rest; snacks; bar; playgrnd; few statics; dogs €3; bus adj; Eng spkn; quiet with some rd noise; ccard acc. "Gd, clean site but san facs slightly run down & ltd/unisex low ssn; easy access; pleasant owner; excel rest; 30 min walk to town (busy main rd, no pavements) & Dali museum; 18km fr Roses on coast." ♦ € 25.00
                    2010*

⊞ **FIGUERES** *3B3* (12km N Rural) *42.37305, 2.91305* **Camping Les Pedres, Calle Vendador s/n, 17750 Capmany (Gerona)** [972-54 91 92 or 686 01 12 23 (mob); recep@ campinglespedres.com; www.campinglespedres.net] S fr French border on N11, turn L sp Capmany, L again in 2km at site sp & foll site sp. Med, mkd pitch, pt sl, pt shd; htd wc; chem disp; shwrs inc; el pnts (6-10A) €4.15; lndry rm; shop 1km; rest; snacks; bar; pool; sand beach 25km; 20% statics; dogs; phone; Eng spkn; adv bkg; quiet; ccard acc; red low ssn; CCI. "Helpful Dutch owner; lovely views; gd touring & walking cent; gd winter NH." ♦ € 24.15   2010*

FIGUERES *3B3* (8km NE Rural) *42.33902, 3.06758* **Camping Vell Empordà, Ctra Roses-La Jonquera s/n, 17780 Garriguella (Gerona)** [972-53 02 00 or 972-57 06 31 (LS); fax 972-55 23 43; vellemporda@vellemporda.com; www. vellemporda.com] On A7/E11 exit junc 3 onto N260 NE dir Llançà. Nr km 26 marker, turn R sp Garriguella, then L at T-junc N twd Garriguella. Site on R shortly bef vill. Lge, hdg/ mkd pitch, hdstg, terr, shd; htd wc; chem disp; mv service pnt; baby facs; shwrs inc; el pnts (6-10A) inc; gas; lndtte; shop; rest; snacks; bar; BBQ; playgrnd; pool; paddling pool; sand beach 6km; games area; games rm; entmnt; internet; TV; 20% statics; dogs €4.50; phone; Eng spkn; adv bkg; quiet; ccard acc; red long stay/low ssn; CCI. "Conv N Costa Brava away fr cr beaches & sites; 20 mins to sea at Llançà; o'hanging trees poss diff high vehicles; excel." ♦ 1 Feb-15 Dec. € 35.40   2011*

See advertisement

⊞ **FIGUERES** *3B3* (15km NW Rural) *42.31444, 2.77638* **Camping La Fradera, Pedramala, 17732 Sant Llorenç de la Muga (Gerona)** [tel/fax 972-54 20 54; camping.fradera@ teleline.es; www.terra.es/personal2/camping.fradera] Fr cent Figueres take N260 W dir Olot. After 1km turn R at mini-rndabt (supmkt on L), pass police stn to rd junc, strt on & cross over A7 m'way & pass thro Llers & Terrades to Sant Llorenç. Site 1km past vill on L. Med, mkd pitch, pt shd; wc; chem disp; shwrs inc; el pnts (6A) €2.67; lndtte; shop 2km; tradsmn; snacks; rest in vill; playgrnd; htd pool; rv sw 1km; few statics; poss cr; Eng spkn; adv bkg; quiet; ccard acc; red long stay. "Vg site in delightful vill in foothills of Pyrenees; fiesta 2nd w/end Aug; pleasant staff; gates clsd low ssn - phone owner." ♦ € 19.26   2011*

FORNELLS DE LA SELVA see Gerona *3B3*

⊞ **FORTUNA** *4F1* (3km N Rural) *38.20562, -1.10712* **Camping Fuente, Camino de la Bocamina s/n, 30709 Baños de Fortuna (Murcia)** [968-68 51 25; info@campingfuente.com; www.campingfuente.com] Fr Murcia on A7/E15 turn L onto C3223 sp Fortuna. After 19km turn onto A21 & foll sp Baños de Fortuna, then sp 'Complejo Hotelero La Fuente'. Avoid towing thro vill, if poss. Med, mkd pitch, hdstg, pt sl, unshd; htd wc; chem disp; private san facs some pitches; shwrs; el pnts (10-16A) €2.16 or metered; gas; lndtte (inc dryer); shop; tradsmn; rest; snacks; bar; BBQ; playgrnd; htd pool, spa, jacuzzi; wifi; some statics; dogs €1.08; phone; bus 200m; adv bkg; ccard acc; red long stay; CCI. "Gd san facs; excel pool & rest; secure o'flow parking area; many long-stay winter visitors - adv bkg rec; ltd recep hrs low ssn; poss sulphurous smell fr thermal baths." ♦ € 16.74 SBS - W03   2010*

CÀMPING VELL EMPORDÀ

Ctra. Roses - La Jonquera s/n
E-17780 GARRIGUELLA
(Girona) COSTA BRAVA

Tel (winter) (34) 972 57 06 31
Tel. (34) 972 53 02 00 - Fax (34) 972 55 23 43
www.vellemporda.com • vellemporda@vellemporda.com

⊞ **FORTUNA** *4F1* (3km N Rural) *38.20666, -1.11194* **Camping Las Palmeras**, 30709 Baños de Fortuna (Murcia) [tel/fax 968-68 60 95] Exit A7 junc 83 Fortuna; cont on C3223 thro Fortuna to Los Baños; turn R & foll sp. Concealed R turn on crest at beg of vill. Med, mkd pitch, pt shd; wc; chem disp (wc); shwrs; el pnts (6-10A) €2.20-3 or metered; gas; lndtte; shops 300m; tradsmn; rest; snacks; bar; natural hot water mineral pool 200m; some statics; dogs €0.54; poss cr; quiet; adv bkg acc; red long stay; ccard acc; CCI. "Gd value, friendly site; gd, modern san facs; gd rest; lge pitches; poss tatty statics; thermal baths also at Archena (15km)." ♦
€ 11.88   2010*

⊞ **FOZ** *1A2* (7km E Coastal) *43.55416, -7.17000* **Camping Playa Reinante Anosa Casa, Estrada da Costa 42, 27279 Barreiros/Reinante** (Lugo) [tel/fax 982-13 40 05; info@ campinganosacasa.com; www.campinganosacasa.com] E fr Barreiros on N634, exit rd at Reinante opp Hotel Casa Amadora, turn R at beach, site on R. Sm, unshd; wc; chem disp; shwrs €1; el pnts €4.50; gas; lndtte; shop, rest, snacks, bar 500m; BBQ; sand beach adj; wifi; 10% statics; dogs €5; bus/train 900m; quiet. "Owners & location make up for basic facs in need of upgrading; excel coastal walking fr site." ♦
€ 18.00   2009*

⊞ **FOZ** *1A2* (8km E Coastal) **Camping Benquerencia, 27792 Benquerencia-Barreiros** (Lugo) [982-12 44 50 or 679-15 87 88 (mob); contactol@campingbenquerencia.com; www.campingbenquerencia.com] Fr junc of N642 & N634 S of Foz; E twd Ribadeo; in 1km past Barreiros at km stone 566 turn L at site sp. Site on R in 1.5km. Med, mkd pitch, pt sl, pt shd; wc; shwrs inc; el pnts (6A) €3.50; gas; lndtte; shop in ssn & 2km; rest; bar; playgrnd; sand beach 400m; tennis; games area; phone; quiet; ccard acc; CCI. "Hot water to shwrs only; NH only." € 18.50   2009*

FOZ *1A2* (2.5km NW Coastal/Rural) *43.58678, -7.28356* **Camping San Rafael, Playa de Peizas, 27789 Foz** (Lugo) [tel/fax 982-13 22 18; info@campingsanrafael.com; www. campingsanrafael.com] N fr Foz on N642, site sp on R. Med, pt sl, unshd; wc; chem disp; mv service pnt; shwrs inc; el pnts (5A) €4.50; gas; lndtte; shop; tradsmn; rest; snacks; bar; sand beach adj; games area; wifi; dogs €1; bus 200m; poss cr; adv bkg; quiet; 15% red long stay; ccard acc; CCI. "Peaceful, spacious site; basic facs; hot water to shwrs only; take care electrics; pay night bef departure." 1 Apr-30 Sep. € 17.55   2009*

⊞ **FRAGA** *3C2* (1km SE Urban) *41.51738, 0.35553* **Camping Fraga, Calle Major 22, Km 437, Ptda Vincanet s/n, 22520 Fraga** (Huesca) [974-34 52 12; info@campingfraga.com; www.campingfraga.com] Fr W pass thro Fraga town on N11. After about 500m turn Rat mini rbdt into indus est just past petrol stn. Turn R again in indus est, foll site sp. Fr E turn L into indus est at mini rbdt just bef petrol stn. NB steep app poss v diff lge o'fits. Sm, mkd pitch, hdstg, terr, pt shd; wc; chem disp; mv service pnt; shwrs inc; el pnts (6A) €3.20 (rev pol & poss long lead req); lndtte; hypmkt 1km; tradsmn; rest; snacks; bar; playgrnd; pool; TV rm; some statics; dogs €2.70; phone; bus 1km; poss cr; adv bkg; red low ssn; CCI. "Conv NH bet Zaragoza & Tarragona; unspoilt town in beautiful area; rec not to hook-up if in transit - ltd reliable el pnts; chem disps placed between pitches; NH only." ♦ € 22.70
2011*

FRANCA, LA *1A4* (1km NW Coastal) *43.39250, -4.57722* **Camping Las Hortensias, Ctra N634, Km 286, 33590 Colombres/Ribadedeva** (Asturias) [985-41 24 42; fax 985-41 21 53; lashortensias@campinglashortensias.com; www.campinglashortensias.com] Fr N634 on leaving vill of La Franca, at km286 foll sp 'Playa de la Franca' & cont past 1st site & thro car park to end of rd. Med, mkd pitch, pt sl, pt terr, pt shd; wc; chem disp; baby facs; shwrs inc; el pnts (6-10A) €5; gas; lndtte; shop; rest; snacks, bar adj; playgrnd; sand beach adj; tennis; cycle hire; phone; dogs (but not on beach) €5; bus 800m; poss cr; Eng spkn; adv bkg; ccard acc; red low ssn/CCI. "Beautiful location nr scenic beach; sea views fr top terr pitches; vg." 5 Jun-30 Sep. € 28.50
2011*

See advertisement on next page

FRESNEDA, LA *3C2* (2.5km SW Rural) *40.90705, 0.06166* **Camping La Fresneda, Partida Vall del Pi, 44596 La Fresneda** (Teruel) [978-85 40 85; info@campinglafresneda. com; www.campinglafresneda.com] Fr Alcañiz S on N232 dir Morella, in 15km turn L onto A231 thro Valjunquera to La Fresneda; cont thro vill; in 2.5km turn R onto site rd. Site sp fr vill. Sm, hdg/mkd pitch, terr, pt shd; wc; chem disp; baby facs; shwrs inc; el pnts (6A) inc; gas 2.5km; lndtte; tradsmn; rest; snacks; bar; plunge pool; wifi; no dogs; phone; poss cr; Eng spkn; quiet; ccard acc; red long stay; CCI. "Narr site rds; poss diff lge o'fits; various pitch sizes; gd." ♦ 15 Mar-15 Oct. € 22.47   2010*

SPAIN

CAMPING "LAS HORTENSIAS"
Playa de la Franca · E-33590 Ribadedeva (Asturias-Spain)
Tel. 985.41.24.42 · Fax. 985.41.21.53
wwww.campinglashortensias.com

Turn off at km 286 of the N-634 Santander – Oviedo (Playa de la Franca) and continue 500 m.

First cat. holiday site with excellent installations. Situated at fine sandy beach of La Franca at 30 min. of the Picos de Europa and 60 min. from Santander and Oviedo. In quiet and safe surroundings. The site is built in terraces and with asphalt paths. Tennis courts. Ideal also for sports fishing and excursions to beautiful regions.

FRIAS *1B4* (3km NW Rural) *42.77097, -3.29686* **Camping Friás,** Ctra Quintana-Martin, 09211 Galíndez-Friás (Burgos) [947-35 71 98; fax 947-35 71 99; info@campingfrias.com; www.campingfrias.com] Fr AP1 take N232 & N629 NW to Trespaderne. Turn sharp R (dir Miranda) & E for 10km. Foll site sp at Friás. Site on R in 3km bef rv bdge. Med, mkd pitch, pt shd; wc; chem disp; mv service pnt; shwrs €0.60; el pnts (5A) €3.50; shop; rest; bar; 3 pools; rv adj; fishing; archery; cycle hire; 95% statics; dogs €3; phone; poss cr w/end; quiet; ccard acc. "Open w/end only in winter, but phone ahead to check; sh stay/NH only; interesting vill with castle & Roman bdge." 1 Apr-30 Sep. € 20.50   2008*

⊞ **FUENGIROLA** *2H4* (2km SW Coastal) *36.5207, 4.6306* **Camping Fuengirola,** Ctra Cádiz-Málaga Km 207, 29640 Fuengirola (Málaga) [tel/fax 952-47 41 08] On R of N340 Málaga-Algeciras rd opp hotel immed at km stone 207. Go slowly down service stn exit (if missed, next rndabt is 2km). Lge, shd; wc; chem disp; serviced pitches; shwrs inc; el pnts (6A) €2.75; gas; lndtte; shop; rest; bar; playgrnd; pool; sand beach adj; watersports; TV; adv bkg; Eng spkn; some rd noise; red long stay; ccard acc; CCI. "Sea views; clean facs; helpful staff; take care tree sap - can eat into lacquer finish of cars!" € 29.00   2008*

⊞ **FUENGIROLA** *2H4* (9km W Coastal) *36.48943, -4.71813* **Camping Los Jarales,** Ctra N340, Km 197 Calahonda, 29650 Mijas-Costa (Málaga) [tel/fax 952-93 00 03; www.campinglosjarales.com] Fr Fuengirola take N340 W twd Marbella, turn at km 197 stone; site located to N of rd. Lge, mkd pitch, hdstg, pt sl, pt shd; wc; chem disp; serviced pitch; shwrs inc; el pnts (5A) €3.25; gas; lndtte; shop adj; rest; snacks; bar; playgrnd; pool; sand beach 400m; tennis; TV; no dogs; bus adj; poss cr; Eng spkn; adv bkg; rd noise; red long stay/CCI. "Well-run site; buses to Marbella & Fuengirola." ◆ € 21.43   2011*

⊞ **FUENTE DE PIEDRA** *2G4* (700m S Rural) *37.12905, -4.73315* **Camping Fuente de Pedra,** Calle Campillos 88-90, 29520 Fuente de Piedra (Málaga) [952-73 52 94; fax 952-73 54 61; info@camping-rural.com; www.camping-rural.com] Turn off A92 at km 132 sp Fuente de Piedra. Sp fr vill cent. Or to avoid town turn N fr A384 just W of turn for Bobadilla Estación, sp Sierra de Yeguas. In 2km turn R into nature reserve, cont for approx 3km, site on L at end of town. Sm, mkd pitch, hdstg, pt sl, terr, pt shd; wc; shwrs inc; el pnts (10A) €5; gas; lndry rm; shop; rest; snacks; bar; BBQ; playgrnd; pool in ssn; internet; 25% chalets; dogs €3; phone; bus 500m; Eng spkn; poss noise fr adj public pool; ccard acc; red long stay/low ssn/CCI. "Mostly sm, narr pitches, but some avail for o'fits up to 7m; gd rest; san facs dated & poss stretched; adj lge lake with flamingoes; gd." ◆ € 22.00   2009*

FUENTE DE SAN ESTEBAN, LA *1D3* (1km E Rural) *40.79128, -6.24384* **Camping El Cruce,** Ctra A62, Km 291 (E80), 37200 La Fuente de San Esteban (Salamanca) [923-44 01 30; campingelcruce@yahoo.es] On A62/E80 (Salamanca-Portugal) rd stone 291 immed behind hotel on S side of rd. Fr E watch for sp 'Cambio de Sentido' to cross main rd. Med, pt shd; wc; chem disp; shwrs; el pnts (6A) €3 (poss no earth); rest adj; snacks; bar; playgrnd; wifi; Eng spkn; some rd noise; ccard acc; CCI. "Conv NH/sh stay en rte Portugal; friendly." ◆ 1 May-30 Sep. € 16.00   2009*

⊞ **FUENTEHERIDOS** *2F3* (600m SW Rural) *37.9050, -6.6742* **Camping El Madroñal,** Ctra Fuenteheridos-Castaño del Robledo, Km 0.6, 21292 Fuenteheridos (Huelva) [959-50 12 01; castillo@campingelmadronal.com; www.campingelmadronal.com] Fr Zafra S on N435n turn L onto N433 sp Aracena, ignore first R to Fuenteheridos vill, camp sp R at next x-rd 500m on R. At rndabt take 2nd exit. Avoid Fuenteheridos vill - narr rds. Med, mkd pitch, pt sl, pt shd; wc; chem disp; shwrs; el pnts €3.20; gas; lndry rm; shop & 600m; snacks; bar high ssn; BBQ; 2 pools; cycle hire; horseriding; 80% statics; dogs; phone; bus 1km; car wash; quiet; CCI. "Tranquil site in National Park of Sierra de Aracena; pitches among chestnut trees - poss diff lge o'fits or m'vans & poss sl & uneven; o'hanging trees on site rds." € 14.20   2008*

GALENDE see Puebla de Sanabria *1B3*

⊞ **GALLARDOS, LOS** *4G1* (4km N Rural) *37.18448, -1.92408* **Camping Los Gallardos, 04280 Los Gallardos (Almería) [950-52 83 24; fax 950-46 95 96; reception@campinglosgallardos.com; www.campinglosgallardos.com]** Fr N leave A7/E15 at junc 525; foll sp to Los Gallardos; pass under a'route after 800m; turn L into site ent. Med, mkd pitch, hdstg, pt shd; wc; chem disp; serviced pitch; mv service pnt; shwrs inc; el pnts (10A) €3; gas; lndtte; supmkt; rest (clsd Thurs); snacks; bar; pool; sand beach 10km; 2 grass bowling greens; golf; tennis adj; dogs €2.25; 40% statics; poss v cr; m'way noise; adv bkg; reds long stay/low ssn; ccard acc; CCI. "British owned; 90% British clientele low ssn; gd social atmosphere; sep drinking water supply nr recep; prone to flooding wet weather." ♦ € 17.60   2011*

We can fill in site report forms on the Club's website – www.caravanclub.co.uk/europereport

⊞ **GANDIA** *4E2* (2km N Coastal) *38.98613, -0.16352* **Camping L'Alqueria, Avda del Grau s/n; 46730 Grao de Gandía (València) [962-84 04 70; fax 962-84 10 63; lalqueria@lalqueria.com; www.lalqueria.com]** Fr N on A7/AP7 exit 60 onto N332 dir Grao de Gandía. Site sp on rd bet Gandía & seafront. Lge, mkd pitch, hdstg, pt sl, pt shd; htd wc; chem disp; mv service pnt; baby facs; shwrs inc; el pnts (10A) €5.94; gas; lndtte; shop; rest adj; snacks; bar; playgrnd; htd, covrd pool; jacuzzi; sand beach 1km; games area; cycle hire; wifi; entmnt; 30% statics inc disabled accessible; sm dogs (under 10kg) €1.90; phone; bus; adv bkg; quiet; ccard acc; red long stay/snr citizens; CCI. "Pleasant site; helpful family owners; lovely pool; easy walk to town & stn; excel beach nrby; bus & train to Valencia." ♦ € 35.95   2010*

⊞ **GARGANTILLA DEL LOZOYA** *1C4* (2km SW Rural) *40.9503, -3.7294* **Camping Monte Holiday, Ctra C604, Km 8.8, 28739 Gargantilla del Lozoya (Madrid) [918-69 50 65; fax 918-69 52 78; monteholiday@monteholiday.com; www.monteholiday.com]** Fr N on A1/E5 Burgos-Madrid rd turn R on M604 at km stone 69 sp Rascafría; in 8km turn R immed after rlwy bdge & then L up track in 300m, foll site sp. Do not ent vill. Lge, terr, pt sl, pt shd; wc; chem disp; mv service pnt; baby facs; shwrs inc; el pnts (7A) €4.30 (poss rev pol); lndtte (inc dryer); shop 6km; rest; bar; pool; wifi; 80% statics; bus 500m; phone; little Eng spkn; adv bkg; quiet; ccard acc; red CCI. "Interesting, friendly site; vg san facs; gd views; easy to find; some facs clsd low ssn; lovely area but site isolated in winter & poss heavy snow; conv NH fr m'way & for Madrid & Segovia; excel wooded site & v rural but well worth the short drive fr the N1 E5". ♦ € 25.60 (CChq acc)   2011*

GARRIGUELLA see Figueres *3B3*

⊞ **GARRUCHA** *4G1* (6km N Coastal) *37.23785, -1.79911* **Camping Cuevas Mar, Ctra Garrucha-Villaricos s/n, 04618 Palomares-Cuevas de Almanzora (Almería) [tel/fax 950-46 73 82; www.campingcuevasmar.com]** Exit A7 at junc 537 sp Cuevas del Almanzora & take A1200 sp Vera. In 2km turn L onto AL7101 (ALP118) sp Palomares & take 2nd exit at rndabt immed bef Palomares, site on L in 1.5km. Fr S exit A7 at junc 520, by-pass Garrucha, site on L in 6km. Med, hdg/mkd pitch, hdstg, pt shd; wc; chem disp; mv service pnt; baby facs; shwrs inc; el pnts (6A) €4.20; gas 3km; lndtte (inc dryer); shop; tradsmn; rest 500m; bar; BBQ; playgrnd; pool; jacuzzi; sand/shgl beach 350m; wifi; 10% statics; dogs €2; bus adj; poss cr; adv bkg; red low ssn/long stay; CCI. "Immac, well-maintained site; lge pitches; friendly owner; vg san facs; only 1 tap for drinking water; cycle track adj; beautiful coastline; mosquito problem; Fri mkt Garrucha; popular long stay site." ♦ € 33.20   2011*

GATA *1D3* (4km W Rural) *40.21145, -6.64208* **Camping Sierra de Gata, Ctra EX109 a Gata, Km 4.100, 10860 Gata (Cáceres) [927-67 21 68; fax 927-67 22 11; cgata@turiex.com; www.turiex.com/cgata]** Foll sp Gata fr rd EX109/C526, site sp on unmkd rd on rvside. Med, shd; wc; chem disp; shwrs; el pnts (5-10A) €4.25; gas; lndtte; shop; rest 100m; snacks; bar; playgrnd; pool; fishing; paddling pool; tennis; games area; cycle hire; entmnt; TV; statics; dogs €2; phone; quiet. "Peaceful, family-run site in beautiful area." ♦ 15 Feb-14 Dec. € 17.00   2008*

GAVA *3C3* (5km S Coastal) *41.27245, 2.04250* **Camping Tres Estrellas, C31, Km 186.2, 08850 Gavà (Barcelona) [936-33 06 37; fax 936-33 15 25; fina@camping3estrellas.com; www.camping3estrellas.com]** Fr S take C31 (Castelldefels to Barcelona), exit 13. Site at km 186.2 300m past rd bdge. Fr N foll Barcelona airport sp, then C31 junc 13 Gavà-Mar slip rd immed under rd bdge. Cross m'way, turn R then R again to join m'way heading N for 400m. Lge, mkd pitch, pt sl, pt shd; htd wc; chem disp; mv service pnt; baby facs; shwrs inc; el pnts (6A) €5.40 (poss rev pol &/or no earth); gas; lndtte (inc dryer); shop; rest; snacks; bar; BBQ; playgrnd; htd pool; sand beach adj; tennis; internet; entmnt; TV; 20% statics; dogs €5.40; phone; bus to Barcelona 400m; poss cr; Eng spkn; adv bkg; aircraft & rd noise & w/e noise fr disco nrby; ccard acc; red snr citizens/CCI. "20 min by bus to Barcelona cent; poss smells fr stagnant stream in corner of site; poss mosquitoes." ♦ 15 Mar-15 Oct. € 40.10 (CChq acc)   2011*

GERONA *3B3* (8km S Rural) *41.9224, 2.82864* **Camping Can Toni Manescal, Ctra de la Barceloneta, 17458 Fornells de la Selva (Gerona) [972-47 61 17; fax 972-47 67 35; campinggirona@campinggirona.com; www.campinggirona.com]** Fr N leave AP7 at junc 7 onto N11 dir Barcelona. In 2km turn L to Fornells de la Selva; in vill turn L at church (sp); over rv; in 1km bear R & site on L in 400m. NB Narr rd in Fornells vill will not poss lge o'fits. Sm, mkd pitch, pt sl, pt shd; wc; chem disp; baby facs; shwrs inc; el pnts (5A) inc (poss long lead req); gas; lndtte; shop, rest 2km; snacks, bar 4km; playgrnd; pool; sand beach 23km; dogs; bus 1.5km; train nr; Eng spkn; adv bkg; quiet; ccard acc; CCI. "Pleasant, open site on farm; gd base for lovely medieval city Gerona - foll bus stn sp for gd, secure m'van parking; welcoming & helpful owners; lge pitches; ltd san facs; excel cycle path into Gerona, along old rlwy line; Gerona mid-May flower festival rec; gd touring base away fr cr coastal sites." 1 Jun-30 Sep. € 23.00   2009*

SPAIN

GETAFE see Madrid *1D4*

⊞ **GIJON** *1A3* (4km E Rural) *43.51365, -5.59896* **Camping Deva-Gijón, Parroquia de Deva, 33394 Deva (Asturias)** [985-13 38 48; fax 985-13 38 89; info@campingdeva-gijon.com; www.campingdeva-gijon.com] Exit A8 junc 382 N. Site nr km marker 65 - foll sp carefully. Lge, mkd pitch; pt sl, terr, pt shd; serviced pitches; wc; chem disp; shwrs inc; el pnts (16A) €3.30; lndtte; shop, rest, snacks in ssn; bar; pool & paddling pool; sand beach 4km; tennis; cycle hire; golf 3km; internet; 50% statics; bus nr; car wash; sep car park; poss cr; noisy visitors & nr rd; ccard acc €40 min; CCI. "Gd touring base for 2 National Parks; facs ltd low ssn & v open san facs not rec winter." ♦ ₤ 23.60   2008*

⊞ **GIJON** *1A3* (9.5km NW Coastal) *43.58343, -5.75713* **Camping Perlora, Ctra Candás, Km 12, Perán, 33491 Candás (Asturias)** [tel/fax 985-87 00 48; recepcion@campingperlora.com; www.campingperlora.com] Exit A8 junc 404 dir Candás (take care staggered junc). In 9km at rndabt turn R sp Perlora (AS118). At sea turn L sp Candás, site on R. Avoid Sat mkt day. Med, mkd pitch, pt sl, terr, unshd; wc; chem disp; some serviced pitches; shwrs inc; el pnts (5A) €3.50; gas; lndtte (inc dryer); shop; rest; playgrnd; sand beach 1km; tennis; watersports; fishing; wifi; 80% statics; dogs free; phone; bus adj; poss cr; Eng spkn; quiet; ccard not acc; red long stay. "Excel; helpful staff; attractive, well-kept site on dramatic headland; ltd space for tourers; superb san facs, ltd low ssn; easy walk to Candás." ♦ ₤ 18.60   2010*

GIJON *1A3* (13km NW Coastal) *43.57575, -5.74530* **Camping Buenavista, Ctra Dormon-Perlora s/n, Carreño, 33491 Perlora (Asturias)** [tel/fax 985-87 17 93; buenavista@campingbuenavista.com; www.campingbuenavista.com] Fr Gijón take AS19 sp Tremañes & foll rd for approx 5km. On sharp L bend take exit on R (Avilés) & immed L onto AS239 sp Candás/Perlora, site sp. Med, terr, pt shd; wc; chem disp; shwrs; el pnts inc; gas; lndtte; shop; rest; snacks; bar; playgrnd; sand beach 500m; 70% statics; bus 200m; site open w/end only out of ssn & clsd Dec & Jan; poss cr; noisy; CCI. "Oviedo historic town worth a visit; quite steep pull-out, need gd power/weight ratio." 15 Jun-15 Sep. € 22.70   2011*

GIRONELLA *3B3* (500m S Rural) *42.01378, 1.87849* **Camping Gironella, Ctra C16/E9, Km 86.750 Entrada Sud Gironella, 08680 Gironella (Barcelona)** [938-25 15 29; fax 938-22 97 37; informacio@campinggironella.com; www.campinggironella.cat] Site is bet Berga & Puig-reig on C16/E9. Well sp. Med, hdg/mkd pitch, hdstg, pt shd; wc; chem disp; serviced pitch; baby facs; shwrs inc; el pnts (3-10A) €2.75-7; gas; lndtte; shop; tradsmn; rest; snacks; bar; playgrnd; htd pool; games rm; entmnt; TV rm; 90% statics; dogs €1; phone; bus 600m; poss cr; Eng spkn; adv bkg; quiet; CCI. "Pleasant site; friendly staff; ltd touring pitches (phone ahead); conv NH." ♦ Holy Week, 1 Jul-15 Sep & w/e low ssn. € 18.00   2011*

GORLIZ *1A4* (700m N Coastal) *43.41782, -2.93626* **Camping Arrien, Uresarantze Bidea, 48630 Gorliz (Bizkaia)** [946-77 19 11; fax 946-77 44 80; recepcion@campinggorliz.com; www.campinggorliz.com] Fr Bilbao foll m'way to Getxo, then 637/634 thro Sopelana & Plentzia to Gorliz. In Gorliz turn L at 1st rndabt, pass tourist office on R, then R at next rndabt, strt over next, site on L adj sports cent/running track. Not sp locally. Lge, pt sl, pt shd; wc; chem disp; shwrs inc; el pnts (3-5A) €4.20; lndtte; gas; shop; rest; snacks; bar; BBQ; playgrnd; sand beach 700m; 60% statics; dogs €1; phone; bus 150m; poss cr; Eng spkn; ccard acc; red long stay/CCI. "Useful base for Bilbao & ferry (approx 1hr); bus to Plentzia every 20 mins, fr there can get metro to Bilbao; friendly, helpful staff; poss shortage of hot water." 1 Mar-31 Oct. € 27.10   2011*

GRANADA *2G4* (4km N Rural) *37.24194, -3.63333* **Camping Granada, Cerro de la Cruz s/n, 18210 Peligros (Granada)** [tel/fax 958-34 05 48; pruizlopez1953@yahoo.es] S on A44 fr Jaén twd Granada; take exit 121 & foll sp Peligros. Turn L at rndabt after 1km by Spar shop, site access rd 300m on R. Single track access 1km. Med, hdstg, terr, pt shd; wc; chem disp; shwrs inc; el pnts (5A) €4.32; gas; lndtte; shop; rest; bar; playgrnd; pool; tennis; dogs €1.30; bus 1km; poss cr; some Eng spkn; adv bkg; quiet; ccard acc; CCI. "Friendly, helpful owners; well-run site in olive grove; vg facs; superb views; gd access for m'vans but poss diff for v lge o'fits; pitches poss uneven & muddy after rain; site rds & access steep; conv Alhambra - book tickets at recep." ♦ Holy Week & 1 Jul-30 Sep. € 24.62   2009*

GRANADA *2G4* (4km N Urban) *37.19832, -3.61166* **Camping Motel Sierra Nevada, Avda de Madrid 107, 18014 Granada** [958-15 00 62; fax 958-15 09 54; campingmotel@terra.es; www.campingsierranevada.com] App Granada S-bound on A44 & exit at junc 123, foll dir Granada. Site on R in 1.5km just beyond bus stn & opp El Campo supmkt, well sp. Lge, shd; wc; chem disp; mv service pnt; baby facs; shwrs inc; el pnts (6A) €4.20; gas; lndtte (inc dryer); supmkt opp; rest; snacks; BBQ; playgrnd; 2 pools adj; sports facs; wifi; dogs; bus to city cent 500m; poss cr (arr early); Eng spkn; noisy at w/end; ccard acc; CCI. "V helpful staff; excel san facs, but poss ltd low ssn; motel rms avail; can book Alhambra tickets at recep (24 hrs notice); conv city." ♦ 1 Mar-31 Oct. € 25.60   2011*

GRANADA *2G4* (9km E Rural) *37.16083, -3.45555* **Camping Cubillas, Ctra Bailén-Motril, Km 115, 18220 Albolote (Granada)** [958-45 34 08] Exit A44/E902 junc 116 dir El Chaparral, site sp. Sm, mkd pitch, pt sl, pt shd; wc; chem disp; mv service pnt; shwrs inc; el pnts (5-10A) €2.50; gas; shop; snacks; bar; lake sw; playgrnd; boating & fishing adj; dogs; quiet; 10% red long stay & CCI. "Useful NH for Granada; some birdwatching; friendly staff; ltd facs low ssn." ♦ 9 May-13 Dec. € 17.20   2009*

⊞ **GRANADA** *2G4* (13km E Rural) *37.16085, -3.45388* **Camping Las Lomas, 11 Ctra de Güejar-Sierra, Km 6.5, 18160 Güejar-Sierra (Granada)** [958-48 47 42; fax 958-48 40 00; info@campinglaslomas.com; www.campinglaslomas.com] Fr A44 exit onto by-pass 'Ronda Sur', then exit onto A395 sp Sierra Nevada. In approx 4km exit sp Cenes, turn under A395 to T-junc & turn R sp Güejar-Sierra, Embalse de Canales. After approx 3km turn L at sp Güejar-Sierra & site. Site on R 6.5km up winding mountain rd. Med, hdg/mkd pitch, terr, pt shd; htd wc; chem disp; mv service pnt; baby facs; fam bthrm; shwrs inc; el pnts (10A) €4 (poss no earth/rev pol); gas; lndtte (inc dryer); shop; rest; snacks; bar; playgrnd; pool; paddling pool; waterskiing nrby; wifi; dogs free; bus adj; poss cr; Eng spkn; adv bkg ess; quiet; red long stay; ccard acc; CCI. "Helpful, friendly owners; well-run site; conv Granada (bus at gate); access poss diff for lge o'fits; excel san facs; gd shop & rest; beautiful mountain scenery; excel site." ♦ € 27.00   2010*

⊞ **GRANADA** *2G4* (3km SE Urban) *37.12444, -3.58611* **Camping Reina Isabel, Calle de Laurel de la Reina, 18140 La Zubia (Granada)** [958-59 00 41; fax 958-59 11 91; info@ reinaisabelcamping.com; www.reinaisabelcamping.com] Exit A44 nr Granada at junc sp Ronda Sur, dir Sierra Nevada, Alhambra, then exit 2 sp La Zubia. Foll site sp approx 1.2km on R; narr ent set back fr rd. Med, hdg pitch, hdstg, pt shd; htd wc; chem disp; mv service pnt; baby facs; shwrs inc; el pnts (5A)poss rev pol €4.20; gas; lndtte; shop; supmkt 1km; tradsmn; snacks; bar; pool high ssn; internet; TV; dogs free; phone; bus to Granada cent; Eng spkn; poss cr; adv bkg rec at all times; quiet except during festival in May; ccard acc; red long stay/low ssn; red CCI. "Well-run, busy site; poss shwrs v hot/cold - warn children; helpful staff; ltd touring pitches & sm; poss student groups; conv Alhambra (order tickets at site), shwr block not heated." ♦ € 24.80   2011*

⊞ **GRANADA** *2G4* (12km S Rural) *37.06785, -3.65176* **Camping Suspiro del Moro, 107 Avda de Madrid, 18630 Otura (Granada)** [tel/fax 958-55 54 11; info@camping suspirodelmoro.com; www.campingsuspirodelmoro.com] On A44/E902 dir Motril, exit junc 139. Foll camp sp fr W side of rndabt; site visible at top of slight rise on W side of A44, 1km S of Otura. Med, mkd pitch, hdstg, shd; wc; chem disp; mv service pnt; shwrs inc; el pnts (5A) €3 (poss no earth); gas; lndry rm; shop; snacks & rest in ssn; bar; playgrnd; lge pool; tennis; games area; 10% statics; phone; bus to Granada adj; Eng spkn; rd noise & noisy rest at w/end; red low ssn; ccard acc; CCI. "Decent site; reasonable pitches; quiet low ssn; clean facs but inadequate for site this size." ♦ € 19.10   2011*

⊞ **GRANADA** *2G4* (10km W Rural) *37.19150, -3.65444* **Camping Maria Eugenia, Avda Andalucia 190, Santa Fé, 18014 Granada** [958-20 06 06; fax 958-20 63 17; campingmariaeugenia@gmail.com; www.campingmaria eugenia.com] On A329/A92G fr Granada dir Antequera.Fr W exit A92 junc 230 dir Granada. By-pass Santa Fé, site on R in 3km, nr airport - sps last minutes only. Sm, mkd pitch, pt shd; wc; chem disp; mv service pnt; shwrs inc; el pnts (10-16A) €3.60-4.60; lndtte; shop; rest; snacks; bar; BBQ; pool; TV; 30% statics; dogs; phone; bus fr site ent; poss cr; rd noise. "Friendly, family-run site; unkempt low ssn; conv Granada, bus adj; NH only." € 19.60   2008*

⊞ **GRAUS** *3B2* (6km S Rural) *42.13069, 0.30980* **Camping Bellavista & Subenuix, Embalse de Barasona, Ctra Graus N123, Km 23, 22435 La Puebla de Castro (Huesca)** [974-54 51 13; fax 974 34 70 71; info@hotelcamping bellavista.com; www.hotelcampingbellavista.com] Fr E on N230/N123 ignore 1st sp for Graus. Cont to 2nd sp 'El Grado/ Graus' & turn R. Site on L in 1km adj hotel. Med, mkd pitch, terr, pt shd; htd wc; chem disp; shwrs inc; el pnts (10A) €4.50; gas; lndtte; shop; rest; snacks; bar; playgrnd; pool; lake sw adj; watersports; boat hire; fishing; tennis; horseriding; wifi; entmnt; TV rm; 50% statics; dogs €1; phone; Eng spkn; adv bkg; noisy at w/end; red low ssn; ccard acc; CCI. "Helpful staff; sm pitches; excel rest; beautiful position above lake with sandy beach; mountain views; gd NH." € 18.60   2011*

GRAUS *3B2* (5km SW Rural) *42.13130, 0.30871* **Camping Lago Barasona, Ctra Barbastro-Graus, N123A, Km 25, 22435 La Puebla de Castro (Huesca)** [974-54 51 48 or 974-24 69 06; fax 974-54 52 28; info@lagobarasona.com; www.lagobarasona.com] Fr E on N123, ignore 1st sp for Graus. Cont to 2nd sp 'El Grado/Graus/Benasque' & turn R. Site on L in 2km. Lge, hdg/mkd pitch, hdstg, sl, terr, shd; htd wc; chem disp; mv service pnt; baby facs; shwrs inc; el pnts (6A) inc; gas; lndtte (inc dryer); shop; tradsmn; rest; snacks; bar; BBQ; playgrnd; 2 pools; paddling pool; lake beach & sw 100m; watersports; sailing; tennis; fitness rm; horseriding 1km; wifi; entmnt; TV rm; 15% statics; dogs €3; Eng spkn; adv bkg; quiet; ccard acc; red long stay; CCI. "Excel, well-equipped site; lge pitches; helpful staff; adj reservoir water levels likely to drop; highly rec." ♦ 1 Mar-12 Dec. € 36.80 (CChq acc)   2011*

GUADALUPE *2E3* (1.5km S Rural) *39.44232, -5.31708* **Camping Las Villuercas, Ctra Villanueva-Huerta del Río, Km 2, 10140 Guadalupe (Cáceres)** [927-36 71 39; fax 927-36 70 28] Exit A5/E90 at junc 178 onto EX118 to Guadalupe. Do not ent town. Site sp on R at rndabt at foot of hill. Med, shd; wc; shwrs; el pnts €2.50 (poss no earth/rev pol); lndtte; shop; rest; bar; playgrnd; pool; tennis; ccard acc. "Vg; helpful owners; ltd facs low ssn; some pitches sm & poss not avail in wet weather; nr famous monastery." 1 Mar-15 Dec. € 12.50   2011*

⊞ **GUARDA, A** *1B2* (2km E Coastal) *41.89876, -8.84703* **Camping Santa Tecla, Ctra Tui-La Guardía, Salcidos, 36780 A Guarda (Pontevedra)** [986-61 30 11; fax 986-61 30 63; campingstatecla@telefonica.net; www.campingsantatecla. com] S fr Vigo on PO552 coast rd. Site well sp thro A Guarda. Lge, mkd pitch, pt shd; wc; chem disp; mv service pnt; shwrs; el pnts €3.70; gas; lndtte; shop; rest; bar; playgrnd; pool; rv sw adj; games area; dogs; bus 1km; Eng spkn; quiet; red low ssn. "Views across estuary to Portugal; 2km fr ferry; excel san facs; ltd facs low ssn; unreliable opening low ssn - poss w/end only - phone ahead." ♦ € 22.50   2008*

⊞ **GUARDAMAR DEL SEGURA** *4F2* (2km N Rural/Coastal) *38.10916, -0.65472* **Camping Marjal, Ctra N332, Km 73.4, 03140 Guardamar del Segura (Alicante) [966-72 70 70; fax 966-72 66 95; camping@marjal.com; www.camping marjal.com]** Fr N exit A7 junc 72 sp Aeropuerto/Santa Pola; in 5km turn R onto N332 sp Santa Pola/Cartagena, U-turn at km 73.4, site sp on R at km 73.5. Fr S exit AP7 at junc 740 onto CV91 twd Guardamar. In 9km join N332 twd Alicante, site on R at next rndabt. Lge, hdg/mkd pitch, hdstg, pt shd; all serviced pitches; wc; chem disp; baby facs; sauna; shwrs inc; el pnts (16A) €3 or metered; gas; lndtte (inc dryer); supmkt; rest; snacks & bar; BBQ; playgrnd; 2 htd pools (1 covrd); tropical water park; sand beaches 1km (inc naturist); lake sw 15km; tennis; sports cent; cycle hire; wifi; entmnt; TV rm; 18% statics; dogs €2.20; phone; recep 0800-2300; adv bkg rec; Eng spkn; quiet; red long stay/low ssn; ccard acc; CCI. "Gd facs; friendly, helpful staff; excel family entmnt & activities; well sign-posted; large shower cubicles; excel"
♦ € 65.00 SBS - W07   2011*

See advertisement

GUARDAMAR DEL SEGURA *4F2* (1km S Coastal) *38.07298, -0.65294* **Camping Palm-Mar, 03140 Guardamar del Segura (Alicante) [tel/fax 965-72 88 56; admin@campingpalmmar. es; www.campingpalmmar.es]** Foll site sp fr N332 at x-rds, twds sea. Med, hdg/mkd pitch, pt shd; wc; chem disp; mv service pnt; baby facs; shwrs inc; el pnts (3A) €5; lndtte; shop; rest; snacks; bar; BBQ; playgrnd; sand beach adj; internet; TV rm; 20% statics; dogs; bus adj; no adv bkg; quiet; red long stay." 1 Jun-30 Sep. € 30.00   2008*

GUARDIOLA DE BERGUEDA *3B3* (3.5km SW Rural) *42.21602, 1.83705* **Camping El Berguedà, Ctra B400, Km 3.5, 08694 Guardiola de Berguedà (Barcelona) [938-22 74 32; campingberguda@gmail.com; www.campingberguda. com]** On C16 S take B400 W dir Saldes. Site is approx 10km S of Cadí Tunnel. Med, mkd pitch, some hdstg, terr, pt shd; wc; chem disp; baby facs; shwrs; el pnts (6A) €3.90 (poss rev pol); gas; lndtte; shop; tradsmn; rest; snacks; bar; BBQ; playgrnd; pool; paddling pool; games area; games rm; TV; some statics; phone; dogs; Eng spkn; quiet; CCI. "Helpful staff; vg san facs; beautiful, remote situation; gd walking; poss open w/ends in winter" ♦ Easter-30 Nov. € 18.20   2008*

GUEJAR SIERRA see Granada *2G4*

GUITIRIZ *1A2* (1km N Rural) **Camping El Mesón, 27305 Guitiriz (Lugo) [982-37 32 88]** On A6 NW fr Lugo, exit km 535 sp Guitiriz, site sp. Sm, pt sl, pt shd; wc; chem disp (wc); shwrs inc; el pnts (6A) €3.30; gas; supmkt 1km; rest; bar; playgrnd; pool 6km; rv sw 500m; phone; bus adj; quiet. 15 Jun-15 Sep. € 15.00   2008*

⊞ **HARO** *1B4* (600m N Urban) *42.57900, -2.85153* **Camping de Haro, Avda Miranda 1, 26200 Haro (La Rioja) [941-31 27 37; fax 941-31 20 68; campingdeharo@ fer.es; www.campingdeharo.com]** Fr N or S on N124 take exit sp A68 Vitoria/Logrono & Haro. In 500m at rndabt take 1st exit, under rlwy bdge, cont to site on R immed bef rv bdge. Fr AP68 exit junc 9 to town; at 2nd rndabt turn L onto LR111 (sp Logroño). Immed after rv bdge turn sharp L & foll site sp. Avoid cont into town cent. Med, hdg/mkd pitch, pt shd; htd wc; chem disp; mv service pnt; shwrs inc (am only in winter); el pnts (5-6A) €3.85; gas; lndtte (inc dryer); shop & 600m; snacks; bar; BBQ; playgrnd; htd pool high ssn; wifi; 70% statics; dogs €2.40; phone; bus 800m; car wash; site clsd 9 Dec-13 Jan; poss cr; Eng spkn; adv bkg; quiet (not w/ end), some rv noise; red low ssn; ccard acc; CCI. "Clean, tidy site - peaceful low ssn; friendly owner; some sm pitches & diff turns; excel facs; statics busy at w/ends; conv Rioja 'bodegas' & Bilbao & Santander ferries; conv NH reception closed 1300-1500 no entry then due to security barrier" ♦ € 19.80 (CChq acc)   2011*

⊞ **HARO** *1B4* (10km SW Rural) *42.53017, -2.92173* **Camping De La Rioja, Ctra de Haro/Santo Domingo de la Calzada, Km 8.5, 26240 Castañares de la Rioja (La Rioja) [941-30 01 74; fax 941-30 01 56; info@campingdelarioja.com]** Exit AP68 junc 9, take rd twd Santo Domingo de la Calzada. Foll by-pass round Casalarreina, site on R nr rvside just past vill on rd LR111. Lge, hdg pitch, pt shd; htd wc; chem disp; shwrs; el pnts (4A) €3.90 (poss rev pol); gas; lndtte (inc dryer); sm shop; rest; snacks; bar; pool high ssn; tennis; cycle hire; entmnt; dogs; clsd 10 Dec-8 Jan; 90% statics; dogs; bus adj; site clsd 9 Dec-11 Jan; poss cr; adv bkg; noisy high ssn; ccard acc. "Fair site but fairly isolated; basic san facs but clean; ltd facs in winter; sm pitches; conv for Rioja wine cents; Bilbao ferry." € 26.80   2009*

⊞ **HECHO** *3B1* (8km N Rural) *42.7878, -0.7300* **Camping Borda Bisáltico, Ctra Gabardito, Km 2, 22720 Hecho (Huesca) [974-37 53 88; info@bordabisaltico.com; www. bordabisaltico.com]** Fr Jaca W on N240 dir Pamplona, after 25km at Puente La Reina turn R onto A176 then take HU210. Foll sp. Site in 8km. Take care, 1.5km narr, winding, potholed rd. Med, sl, terr, pt shd; wc; chem disp; mv service pnt; baby facs; shwrs inc; el pnts (3A) €4; gas; lndtte; tradsmn; rest; bar; no statics; site clsd 2-30 Nov; dogs; phone; bus; quiet; CCI. "Well-organised site; friendly owners; beautiful views; excel, modern san facs; gd walking, climbing, birdwatching; poss erratic elec supply (generator) & pitches not level; phone ahead to check open low ssn; excel." € 17.50   2008*

⊞ **HECHO** *3B1* (1km S Rural) *42.73222, -0.75305* **Camping Valle de Hecho, Ctra Puente La Reina-Hecho s/n, 22720 Hecho (Huesca) [974-37 53 61; fax 976-27 78 42; camping hecho@campinghecho.com; www.campinghecho.com]** Leave Jaca W on N240. After 25km turn N on A176 at Puente La Reina de Jaca. Site on W of rd, o'skts of Hecho/Echo. Med, mkd pitch, pt sl, pt shd; htd wc; chem disp; mv service pnt; shwrs inc; el pnts (5-15A) €4.20; gas; lndtte; shop; rest; snacks; bar; playgrnd; pool; games area; 50% statics; dogs; phone; bus 200m; quiet; ccard acc; CCI. "Pleasant site in foothills of Pyrenees; excel, clean facs but poss inadequate hot water; gd birdwatching area; Hecho fascinating vill; shop & bar poss clsd low ssn except w/end; v ltd facs low ssn; not suitable lge o'fites." € 22.35   2010*

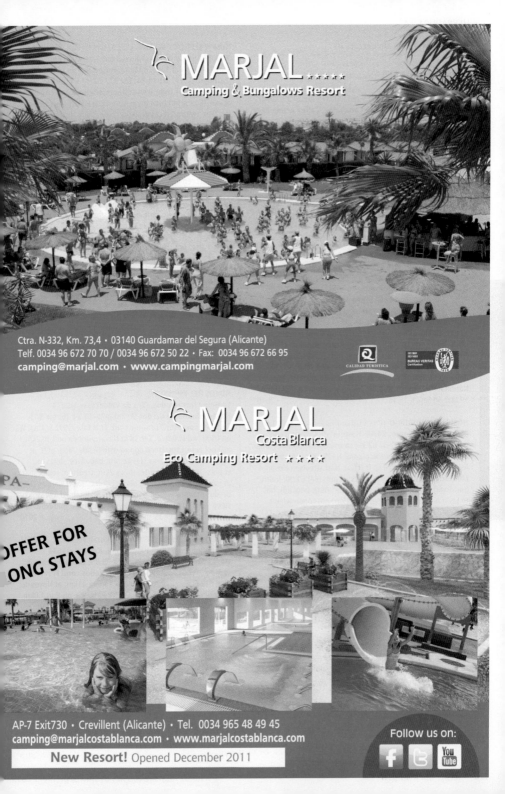

HERRADURA, LA see Almuñécar *2H4*

HONDARRIBIA see Irun *3A1*

⊞ **HORCAJO DE LOS MONTES** *2E4* (200m E Rural) *39.32440, -4.6358* **Camping Mirador de Cabañeros, Calle Cañada Real Segoviana s/n, 13110 Horcajo de los Montes (Ciudad Real) [926-77 54 39; fax 926-77 50 03; info@campingcabaneros. com; www.campingcabaneros.com]** At km 53 off CM4103 Horcajo-Alcoba rd, 200m fr vill. CM4106 to Horcajo fr NW poor in parts. Med, mkd pitch, hdstg, terr, pt shd; htd wc; chem disp; mv service pnt; baby facs; shwrs; el pnts (6A) €4.20; gas; shop 500m; rest; bar; BBQ; playgrnd; pool; rv sw 12km; games area; games rm; tennis 500m; cycle hire; entmnt; TV; 10% statics; dogs €2; phone; adv bkg rec high ssn; quiet; red long stay/low ssn; ccard acc; CCI. "Beside Cabañeros National Park; beautiful views." ♦ € 20.30   2011*

HORNOS *4F1* (9km SW Rural) *38.18666, -2.77277* **Camping Montillana Rural, Ctra Tranco-Hornos A319, km 78.5, 23292 Hornos de Segura (Jaén) [953-12 61 94 or 680-15 21 10 (mob); www.campingmontillana.com]** Fr N on N322 take A310 then A317 S then A319 dir Tranco & Cazorla. Site nr km 78.5, ent by 1st turning. Fr S on N322 take A6202 N of Villaneuva del Arzobispo. In 26km at Tranco turn L onto A319 & nr km 78.5 ent by 1st turning up slight hill. Sm, mkd pitch, hdstg, terr, pt shd; wc; chem disp; shwrs inc; el pnts (10A) €3.20; lndtte; shop; tradsmn; rest; snacks; bar; pool; lake adj; 5% statics; dogs; phone; some Eng spkn; adv bkg; quiet; CCI. "Beautiful area; conv Segura de la Sierra, Cazorla National Park; much wildlife; friendly, helpful staff; gd site." 19 Mar-30 Sep. € 15.44   2010*

HOSPITAL DE ORBIGO *1B3* (N Urban) *42.4664, -5.8836* **Camp Municipal Don Suero, 24286 Hospital de Órbigo (León) [987-36 10 18; fax 987-38 82 36; camping@hospitaldeorbigo. com; www.hospitaldeorbigo.com]** N120 rd fr León to Astorga, km 30. Site well sp fr N120. Narr streets in Hospital. Med, hdg pitch, pt shd; wc; shwrs; el pnts (6A) €1.90; lndtte (inc dryer); shop, bar high ssn; rest adj; BBQ; pool adj; bus to León nr; 50% statics; dogs; bus 1km; poss open w/end only mid Apr-May; phone; poss cr; Eng spkn; ccard acc; CCI. "Statics v busy w/ends, facs stretched; poss noisy; phone ahead to check site open if travelling close to opening/closing dates." ♦ Holy Week-30 Sep. € 14.40   2009*

⊞ **HOSPITALET DE L'INFANT, L'** *3C2* (2km S Coastal) *40.97750, 0.90361* **Camping Cala d'Oques, Via Augusta s/n, 43890 L'Hospitalet de l'Infant (Tarragona) [977-82 32 54; fax 977-82 06 91; info@caladoques.com; www.caladoques. com]** Exit AP7 junc 38 onto N340. Take rd sp L'Hospitalet de l'Infant at km 1128. Lge, terr, shd; htd wc; mv service pnt; baby facs; shwrs; el pnts (10A) €4.95; gas; lndtte; shop; rest; bar; playgrnd; sand/shgl beach adj (naturist beaches nr); wifi; entmnt; dogs €3.40; poss cr; Eng spkn; some rlwy & rd noise; ltd facs low ssn; red snr citizens/long stay/low ssn; CCI. "Friendly, relaxing site; clean, modern san facs; well kept site; vg rest; sea views; poss v windy; conv Aquapolis & Port Aventura; mkd mountain walks; vg NH & longer stay." € 38.00   2011*

⊞ **HOSPITALET DE L'INFANT, L'** *3C2* (2km S Coastal) *40.97722, 0.90083* **Camping El Templo del Sol (Naturist), Polígon 14-15, Playa del Torn, 43890 L'Hospitalet de l'Infant (Tarragona) [977-82 34 34; fax 977-82 34 64; info@ eltemplodelsol.com; www.eltemplodelsol.com]** Leave A7 at exit 38 or N340 twds town cent. Turn R (S) along coast rd for 2km. Ignore 1st camp sp on L, site 200m further on L. Lge, hdg/mkd pitch, pt sl, pt shd; wc; chem disp; serviced pitch; shwrs inc; el pnts (6A) inc; gas; lndtte; shop; rest; snacks; bar; playgrnd; pools; solar-energy park; jacuzzi; official naturist sand/shgl beach adj; cinema/theatre; TV rm; 5% statics; poss cr; Eng spkn; adv bkg (dep); some rlwy noise rear of site; ccard acc; red long stay/low ssn; INF card. "Excel naturist site; no dogs, radios or TV on pitches; lge private wash/shwr rms; pitches v tight - take care o'hanging branches; conv Port Aventura; mosquito problem; poss strong winds - take care with awnings." ♦ 1 Apr-22 Oct. € 43.35   2009*

⊞ **HOSPITALET DE L'INFANT, L'** *3C2* (8km S Coastal) *40.94024, 0.85688* **Camping La Masia, Playa de l'Almadrava, Km 1121, N340, 43890 L'Hospitalet de l'Infant (Tarragona) [977-82 31 02 or 82 05 88; fax 977-82 33 54]** Site sp on sea side of N340 at km 1121. Med, hdstg, sl, terr, pt shd; wc; chem disp (wc); jaccuzi; baby facs; sauna; shwrs inc; el pnts (5A) €4; lndtte; shop; rest; bar; BBQ; playgrnd; pool; beach adj; gym; tennis; games area; squash; minigolf; cycle hire; horseriding 5km; golf 6km; entmnt; games/TV rm; internet; 80% statics; phone; site clsd Jan; poss cr; rlwy noise. "Not rec lge o'fits due poss diff access to pitches." ♦ € 31.50   2008*

HOYOS DEL ESPINO *1D3* (4km E Rural) *40.34313, -5.13131* **Camping Navagredos, Ctra de Valdecasas, 05635 Navarredonda de Gredos (Ávila) [920-20 74 76; fax 983-29 58 41; proatur@proatur.com]** Fr N take N502 S. Then W on C500 twd El Barco. Site sp in Navarredonda on L in 2km, just bef petrol stn. Steep app rd with bends. Med, pt sl, pt shd; wc; chem disp; mv service pnt; baby facs; shwrs inc; el pnts (10A) €3.90; lndtte; shops 2km; tradsmn; rest & snacks in ssn; bar; BBQ; internet; phone; quiet. "Excel walking in Gredos mountains; some facs poorly maintained low ssn; steep slope to san facs; site open w/ends until mid-Nov." ♦ Easter-12 Oct. € 17.35   2010*

HOYOS DEL ESPINO *1D3* (1.5km S Rural) *40.34055, -5.17527* **Camping Gredos, Ctra Plataforma, Km.1.8, 05634 Hoyos del Espino (Ávila) [920-20 75 85; campingredos@ campingredos.com; www.campingredos.com]** Fr N110 turn E at El Barco onto AV941 for approx 41km; at Hoyos del Espino turn S twd Plataforma de Gredos. Site on R in 1.8km. Or fr N502 turn W onto AV941 dir Parador de Gredos to Hoyos del Espino, then as above. Sm, pt sl, pt shd; wc; chem disp; shwrs inc; el pnts €2.90; gas; lndtte; shop 1km; snacks; playgrnd; rv sw adj; cycle hire; horseriding; adv bkg; quiet; CCI. "Lovely mountain scenery." ♦ Holy Week & 1 May-1 Oct. € 12.20   2011*

HUESCA 3B2 (1.5km SW Urban) 42.13725, -0.41900 **Camping San Jorge, Calle Ricardo del Arco s/n, 22004 Huesca** [tel/fax 974-22 74 16; contacto@campingsanjorge.com; www.campingsanjorge.com] Exit A23 S of town at km 568 & head N twd town cent. Site well sp adj municipal pool & leisure facs. Med, shd; wc; chem disp (wc); shwrs inc; el pnts (10A) €4; lndtte; shop; snacks; bar; 2 pools; internet; dogs; bus 300m; ccard acc; CCI. "Grassy pitches poss flooded after heavy rain; san facs gd but poss stretched high ssn; vg pool; friendly; conv town cent; gd supmkt 250m; gd NH." 15 Mar-15 Oct. € 18.48   2011*

There aren't many sites open at this time of year. We'd better phone ahead to check the one we're heading for is open.

⊞ **HUMILLADERO** 2G4 (500m S Rural) 37.10750, -4.69611 **Camping La Sierrecilla, Avda de Clara Campoamor s/n, 29531 Humilladero (Málaga)** [951-19 90 90 or 693-82 81 99 (mob); fax 952-83 43 73; info@lasierrecilla.com; www.campinglasierrecilla.com] Exit A92 junc 138 onto A7280 twd Humilladero. At vill ent turn L at 1st rndabt, site visible. Med, mkd pitch, terr, hdstg, pt sl, pt shd; htd wc; chem disp; mv service pnt; fam bathrm; baby facs; serviced pitches; shwrs inc; el pnts (16A) €3.50; lndtte; shop 1km; rest; snacks; bar; BBQ; playgrnd; htd pool; paddling pool; wifi; entmnt; 10% statics; dogs €1.50; Eng spkn; adv bkg; quiet; CCI. "Excel new site; gd modern, san facs; vg touring base; gd walking; horseriding, caving, archery high ssn; Fuentepiedra lagoon nrby; new trees planted, still need a year or so to give much shade, but attractive none the less." ♦ € 18.00 (CChq acc)   2011*

⊞ **IRUN** 3A1 (2km N Rural) 43.36638, -1.80436 **Camping Jaizkibel, Ctra Guadalupe Km 22, 20280 Hondarribia (Guipúzcoa)** [943-64 16 79; fax 943-64 26 53; jaizkibel@campingseuskadi.com; www.campingseuskadi.com/jaizkibel] Fr Hondarribia/Fuenterrabia inner ring rd foll sp to site below old town wall. Do not ent town. Med, hdg pitch, pt hdstg, terr, pt shd; wc; baby facs; shwrs; el pnts (6A) inc (check earth); lndtte; tradsmn; rest; bar; BBQ; playgrnd; sand beach 1.5km; tennis; wifi; 90% statics; no dogs; phone; bus 1km; Eng spkn; adv bkg; quiet; red low ssn; ccard acc; CCI. "Easy 20 mins walk to historic town; scenic area; gd walking; gd touring base but ltd space for tourers; clean facs; gd rest & bar." € 29.00   2010*

⊞ **IRUN** 3A1 (3km S Rural) 43.31540, -1.87419 **Camping Oliden, Ctra NI Madrid-Irún, Km 470, 20180 Oiartzun (Guipúzcoa)** [943-49 07 28; oliden@campingseuskadi.com] On S side of N1 at E end of vill. Lge, pt sl, pt shd; wc; chem disp; mv service pnt; shwrs; el pnts (5A) €3.53; lndtte (inc dryer); shops adj; rest; bar; playgrnd; pool in ssn; beach 10km; bus 200m; some statics; rlwy & factory noise; red CCI. "Steps to shwrs, diff access for disabled; grass pitches v wet low ssn; NH only." € 17.80   2009*

⊞ **ISABA** 3B1 (13km E Rural) 42.86607, -0.81195 **Camping Zuriza, Ctra Anso-Zuriza, Km 14, 22728 Ansó (Huesca)** [tel/fax 974-37 01 96; campingzuriza@valledeanso.com; http://campingzuriza.valledeanso.com] On NA1370 N fr Isaba, turn R in 4km onto NA2000 to Zuriza. Foll sp to site. Fr Ansó, take HUV2024 N to Zuriza. Foll sp to site; narr, rough rd not rec for underpowered o'fits. Lge, pt sl, pt shd; wc; some serviced pitches; shwrs inc; el pnts €4.80; lndtte; shop; tradsmn; rest; bar; playgrnd; 50% statics; phone; quiet; ccard acc; CCI. "Beautiful, remote valley; no vill at Zuriza, nearest vills Isaba & Ansó; no direct route to France; superb location for walking." € 18.00   2010*

ISLA 1A4 (4km SW Rural) 43.46446, -3.60773 **Camping Los Molinos de Bareyo, 39170 Bareyo (Cantabria)** [942-67 05 69; losmolinosdebareyo@ceoecant.es; www.campingonline.com/molinosdebareyo/] Exit A8 at km 185 & foll sp for Beranga, Noja. Bef Noja at rndabt take L for Ajo, site sp on L up hill. Do not confuse with Cmp Los Molinos in Noja. V lge, mkd pitch, terr, pt shd; htd wc; chem disp; shwrs inc; el pnts (3A) €3.60; lndtte; shop; rest; snacks; bar; BBQ; playgrnd; htd pool; sand beach 4km; tennis; games area; TV rm; 60% statics; dogs; phone; bus 1km; site clsd mid Dec-end Jan; poss cr; Eng spkn; adv bkg; CCI. "Vg site on hill with views of coast; lively but not o'crowded high ssn." ♦ 1 Jun-30 Sep. € 22.50   2010*

ISLA 1A4 (1km NW Coastal) 43.50261, -3.54351 **Camping Playa de Isla, Calle Ardanal 1, 39195 Isla (Cantabria)** [tel/fax 942-67 93 61; consultas@playadeisla.com; www.playadeisla.com] Turn off A8/E70 at km 185 Beranga sp Noja & Isla. Foll sp Isla. In town to beach, site sp to L. Then in 100m keep R along narr seafront lane (main rd bends L) for 1km (rd looks like dead end). Med, mkd pitch, pt sl, terr, pt shd; wc; chem disp; shwrs inc; el pnts (3A) €4.50; gas; lndtte; shop & 1km; snacks; bar; playgrnd; sand beach adj; 90% statics; no dogs; phone; bus 1km; poss cr; quiet; ccard acc; CCI. "Beautiful situation; ltd touring pitches; busy at w/end." Easter-30 Sep. € 28.25   2009*

⊞ **ISLA CRISTINA** 2G2 (1.5km E Coastal) 37.19976, -7.30075 **Camping Giralda, Ctra La Antilla, Km 1.5, 21410 Isla Cristina** [959-34 33 18; fax 959-34 32 84; recepcion@campinggiralda.com; www.campinggiralda.com] Exit A49 sp Isla Cristina & go thro town heading E (speed bumps in town). Or exit A49 at km 117 sp Lepe. In Lepe turn S on H4116 to La Antilla, then R on coast rd to Isla Cristina & site. V lge, mkd/hdstg/sandy pitches; shd, wc; chem disp; mv service pnt; baby facs; shwrs inc; el pnts €5.90; gas; lndtte; shop; rest; snacks; bar; playgrnd; pool high ssn; paddling pool; sand beach nrby; windsurfing; TV rm; 20% statics; dogs €2.60; poss cr, even low ssn; Eng spkn; red long stay/low ssn; ccard acc. "Helpful staff; some pitches uneven & muddy in wet weather; unkempt low ssn; san facs OK, irreg cleaning low ssn; diff for lge o'fits; narr site rds, some high kerbs; gd winter stay." ♦ € 25.70   2008*

ISLA CRISTINA

⊞ **ISLA CRISTINA** *2G2* (4km E Coastal) *37.20555, -7.26722*
**Camping Playa Taray, Ctra La Antilla-Isla Cristina, Km
9, 21430 La Redondela (Huelva)** [959-34 11 02; fax 959-
34 11 96; www.campingtaray.com] Fr W exit A49 sp Isla
Cristina & go thro town heading E. Fr E exit A49 at km 117 sp
Lepe. In Lepe turn S on H4116 to La Antilla, then R on coast rd
to Isla Cristina & site. Lge, pt shd; wc; mv service pnt; shwrs;
el pnts (10) €4.28; gas; lndtte; shop; bar; rest; playrnd; sand
beach adj; some statics; phone; dogs; bus; quiet; ccard acc;
red long stay/low ssn; CCI. "Gd birdwatching, cycling; less
cr than other sites in area in winter; poss untidy low ssn &
ltd facs; poss diff for lge o'fits; friendly, helpful owner." ♦
€ 19.10   2011*

⊞ **ISLA CRISTINA** *2G2* (7km E Coastal) *37.20796, -7.25222*
**Camping Luz, Ctra La Antilla-Isla Cristina, Km 5, 21410
Isla Cristina (Huelva)** [959-34 11 42; fax 059-48 64 54]
Fr W exit A49 sp Isla Cristina & go thro town heading E. Fr E
exit A49 at km 117 sp Lepe. In Lepe turn S on H4116 to La
Antilla, then R on coast rd to Isla Cristina & site. Med, pt sl, pt
shd; wc; shwrs inc; el pnts (5A) inc; gas; lndtte; shop & 3km;
tradsmn; rest; snacks; bar; BBQ; playgrnd; pool; beach 200m;
40% statics; dogs; phone; bus 50m; poss cr; rd noise/noisy
at w/end; red long stay; CCI. "V friendly staff, well-managed;
vg shwrs; ltd facs low ssn; uneven pitches; poss diff for lge
o'fits." € 35.00 (3 persons)   2008*

ISLA PLANA see Puerto de Mazarrón *4G1*

ISLARES see Oriñón *1A4*

ITZIAR see Deba *3A1*

⊞ **IZNATE** *2G4* (1km NE Rural) *36.78449, -4.17442* **Camping
Rural Iznate, Ctra Iznate-Benamocarra s/n, 29792 Iznate
(Málaga)** [tel/fax 952-53 56 13; info@campingiznate.com;
www.campingiznate.com] Exit A7/E15 junc 265 dir Cajiz &
Iznate. Med, mkd pitch, hdstg, unshd; wc; chem disp; shwrs;
el pnts (5-16A) €3-3.50 (poss no earth); gas; lndtte; shop;
rest; snacks; bar; pool; shgl beach 8km; wifi; some statics;
dogs €2.10; bus adj; Eng spkn; quiet; red long stay/low ssn.
"Beautiful scenery & mountain villages; conv Vélez-Málaga
& Torre del Mar; pleasant owners; many ssnl static c'vans -
scruffy low ssn." € 17.70   2010*

⊞ **JACA** *3B2* (2km W Urban) *42.56416, -0.57027* **Camping
Victoria, Avda de la Victoria 34, 22700 Jaca (Huesca)**
[974-35 70 08; fax 974-35 70 09; victoria@campings.
net; www.campingvictoria.es] Fr Jaca cent take N240 dir
Pamplona, site on R. Med, mkd pitch, pt shd; wc; chem disp;
mv service pnt; shwrs inc; el pnts (10A) €5; lndtte; snacks;
bar; BBQ; playgrnd; htd pool high ssn; 80% statics; dogs; bus
adj; quiet. "Basic facs, but clean & well-maintained; friendly
staff; conv NH/sh stay Somport Pass." € 22.00   2011*

⊞ **JARANDILLA DE LA VERA** *1D3* (2km W Rural) *40.12723,
-5.69318* **Camping Yuste, Ctra EX203, Km 47, 10440
Aldeanueva de la Vera (Cáceres)** [927-57 26 59] Fr Plasencia
head E on EX203 following sp for Parador, site at km stone
47 in Aldeanueva de la Vera. Clearly sp down narr rd. Med,
pt sl, pt shd; wc; shwrs; el pnts (5A) inc; gas; lndry rm; shop;
rest; snacks; bar; BBQ; pool; rv fishing; tennis; games rm; TV;
bus 500m; phone; quiet. "Simple, well-maintained, attractive
site." 15 Mar-15 Sep. € 24.80   2010*

⊞ **JAVEA/XABIA** *4E2* (1km S Rural) *38.78333, 0.17294*
**Camping Jávea, Camí de la Fontana 10, 03730 Jávea
(Alicante)** [965-79 10 70; fax 966-46 05 07; info@camping
javea.es; www.camping-javea.com] Exit N332 for Jávea on
A132, cont in dir Port on CV734. At rndabt & Lidl supmkt,
take slip rd to R immed after rv bdge sp Arenal Platjas &
Cap de la Nau. Strt on at next rndabt to site sp & slip rd
100m sp Autocine. If you miss slip rd go back fr next rndabt.
Lge, mkd pitch, pt shd; wc; chem disp; baby facs; shwrs inc;
el pnts (8A) €4.56 (long lead rec); gas; lndtte; shop 500m;
tradsmn; rest; snacks; bar; BBQ; playgrnd; pool; paddling
pool; sand beach 1.5km; tennis; games area; internet;
15% statics; dogs €2; adv bkg; quiet; red low ssn/long stay;
ccard acc; CCI. "Excel site & rest; variable pitch sizes/prices;
some lge pitches - lge o'fits rec phone ahead; gd, clean san
facs; mountain views; helpful staff; m'vans beware low
trees; gd cycling." ♦ € 27.16   2011*

See advertisement

⊞ **JAVEA/XABIA** *4E2* (3km S Coastal) *38.77058, 0.18207*
**Camping El Naranjal, Cami dels Morers 15, 03730 Jávea
(Alicante)** [965-79 29 89; fax 966-46 02 56; delfi@
campingelnaranjal.com; www.campingelnaranjal.com]
Exit A7 junc 62 or 63 onto N332 València/Alicante rd. Exit at
Gata de Gorgos to Jávea. Foll sp Camping Jávea/Camping El
Naranjal. Access rd by tennis club, foll sp. Med, mkd pitch,
hdstg, pt shd; htd wc; chem disp; mv service pnt; baby facs;
shwrs inc; el pnts (10A) €4.05 (poss rev pol); gas; lndtte (inc
dryer); shop; tradsmn; rest; snacks; bar; BBQ; playgrnd;
pool; paddling pool; sand beach 500m; tennis 300m; cycle
hire; games rm; golf 3km; wifi; TV rm; 35% statics; dogs free;
phone; bus 500m; adv bkg; Eng spkn; quiet; ccard acc; red
long stay/low ssn/CCI. "Gd scenery & beach; pitches poss tight
lge o'fits; excel rest; immac facs; tourist info - tickets sold;
rec." t € 26.00   2010*

⊞ **JIMENA DE LA FRONTERA** *2H3* (NW Rural) *36.44299,
-5.45985* **Camping Los Alcornocales, Ctra CC3331/A369,
11330 Jimena de la Frontera (Cádiz)** [956-64 00 60; fax
956-64 12 90; alcornocales@terra.es] Site sp fr A369 Ronda
to Algeciras rd. Rec app fr N onto C3331, turn L at camping
sp at top of bank, site on R in 100m. Do not enter Jimena -
narr rds. Med, hdg/mkd pitch, pt sl, terr, shd; wc; chem disp;
shwrs inc; el pnts €3.85; gas; lndtte; shop; rest; bar; cycle
hire; excursions; 90% statics; dogs; phone; adv bkg; quiet;
ccard acc; red CCI. "Friendly owner; site poss unkempt & ltd
facs low ssn; unsuitable lge o'fits; conv Gibraltar; 5 mins walk
to attractive hill town; wonderful flora, fauna & scenery in
National Park." ♦ € 17.37   2008*

LABUERDA see Ainsa *3B2*

Campingjávea

Swimming pool (25 x12,5m) and children's pool with 1.000m2, grassy ground. Palm trees, etc.sites up to 80m2,well shaded and sunny sites for winter stays. Installations with hot water and heating. Bar-restaurant (only in Easter week and summer). Children's playground, sport grounds, social room, car washing, washing machine, etc. Te. (money nd cards), fax, post, safe, credit cardsadmitted - Visa & Master.

In Javea-Xabia, one of the most beautibul places of the Valencian Comunity, at 40 km of Benidorm and Terra Mítica, 90 km from Alicante and 110 km from Valencia. Motorway AP-7. Easy reaching by Liverpool-street.

Open throughout the year. Very low fees for long stays in winter.

Cami de la Fontana 10 · Aptdo.83 · E-03730 · Jávea/Xàbia · Alicante (Spain) · GPS: 00 10' 19'' O · 38 47' 00'' N
Tel. (0034) 965.79.10.70 · Fax (0034) 966.46.05.07 · info@camping-javea.com · www.camping-javea.com · www.campingjavea.es

LAREDO *1A4* (500m W Urban/Coastal) *43.40888, -3.43277* **Camping Carlos V, Avnda Los Derechos Humanos 15, Ctra Residencial Playa, 39770 Laredo (Cantabria)** [tel/fax 942-60 55 93] Leave A8 at junc 172 to Laredo, foll yellow camping sp, site on W side of town. Med, mkd pitch, pt shd; wc; mv service pnt; baby facs; shwrs inc; el pnts €2.60; gas; lndtte; shop & 100m; rest; bar; playgrnd; sand beach 200m; dogs €2.14; bus 100m; poss cr; noisy; CCI. "Well sheltered & lively resort; sm area for tourers; gd, clean, modern facs." 6 May-30 Sep. € 25.14   2009*

LAREDO *1A4* (2km W Coastal) *43.41441, -3.44800* **Camping Laredo, Calle Rep de Filipinas s/n, 39770 Laredo (Cantabria)** [942-60 50 35; fax 942-61 31 80; info@campinglaredo.com; www.campinglaredo.com] Fr A8 exit junc 172 sp Laredo; cont N at rndabt into Laredo Playa, L at traff lts & foll sp hospital & site. Lge, mkd pitch, pt shd; wc; chem disp; mv service pnt; baby facs; shwrs; el pnts (6A) €3.25; gas; lndtte; shop (high ssn) snacks; bar; playgrnd; pool (caps essential); sand beach 500m; cycle hire; horseriding; TV; 20% statics; no dogs; phone; bus 300m; poss cr; noisy; adv bkg; red CCI. Holy Week & 1 Jun-15 Sep. € 23.60   2008*

LAREDO *1A4* (2km W Coastal) *43.41176, -3.45329* **Camping Playa del Regatón, El Sable 8, 39770 Laredo (Cantabria)** [tel/fax 942-60 69 95; info@campingplayaregaton.com; www.campingplayaregaton.com] Fr W leave A8 junc 172, under m'way to rndabt & take exit sp Calle Rep Colombia. In 800m turn L at traff lts, in further 800m turn L onto tarmac rd to end, passing other sites. Fr E leave at junc 172, at 1st rndabt take 2nd exit sp Centro Comercial N634 Colindres. At next rndabt take exit Calle Rep Colombia, then as above. Lge, mkd pitch; pt shd; wc; chem disp; mv service pnt; shwrs inc; el pnts (6A) €4.30; gas; lndtte; shop; rest; bar; sand beach adj & 3km; horseriding mr; wifi; 75% statics; no dogs; bus 600m; Eng spkn; adv bkg; quiet; ccard acc; red long stay/CCI. "Clean site; sep area for tourers; wash up facs (cold water) every pitch; gd, modern facs; gd NH/sh stay (check opening times of office for el pnt release)." ♦ 1 Apr-25 Sep. € 30.05   2011*

⊞ **LASPAULES** *3B2* (Rural) *42.47149, 0.59917* **Camping Laspaúles, Ctra N260, Km 369, 22471 Laspaúles (Huesca)** [974-55 33 20; camping@laspaules.com; www.laspaules.com] Approx 20km NW Pont de Suert, in cent of vill adj rv. Med, pt shd; wc; baby facs; shwrs; el pnts (6A) €4.90; gas; lndry rm; shop & in vill; tradsmn; snacks; bar; playgrnd; pool; paddling pool; TV; some statics; quiet; ccard acc; red long stay/low ssn; CCI. "V pleasant; pitches well back fr rd." € 19.60   2008*

⊞ **LEKEITIO** *3A1* (3km S Coastal) *43.35071, -2.49260* **Camping Leagi, Calle Barrio Leagi s/n, 48289 Mendexa (Vizcaya)** [tel/fax 946-84 23 52; leagi@campingleagi.com; www.campingleagi.com] Fr San Sebastian leave A8/N634 at Deba twd Ondarroa. At Ondarroa do not turn into town, but cont on BI633 beyond Berriatua, then turn R onto BI3405 to Lekeitio. Fr Bilbao leave A8/N634 at Durango & foll BI633 twd Ondarroa. Turn L after Markina onto BI3405 to Lekeitio - do not go via Ondarroa. Steep climb to site & v steep tarmac ent to site. Only suitable for o'fits with v high power/weight ratio. Med, mkd pitch, pt sl, unshd; wc; chem disp; mv service pnt; serviced pitch; shwrs inc; el pnts (5A) €3.90 (rev pol); lndtte; shop; rest; snacks; bar; playgrnd; sand beach 1km; many statics; dogs; bus 1.5km; cr & noisy high ssn; ccard acc (over €50); CCI. "Ltd facs low ssn; tractor tow avail up to site ent; beautiful scenery; excel local beach; lovely town; gd views; gd walking." € 26.40   2010*

LEKUNBERRI *3A1* (500m SE Rural) *43.00043, -1.88831* **Aralar Camping, Plazaola 9, 31870 Lekunberri (Navarra)** [tel/fax 948-50 40 11 or 948-50 40 49; info@campingaralar.com; www.campingaralar.com] Exit fr AP15 at junc 124 dir Lukunberri & foll sp for site. Site on R after v sharp downhill turn. Med, all hdstg, pt sl, terr, pt shd; htd wc; chem disp; shwrs inc; el pnts (5A) €4.65; gas; lndtte; shop; rest; snacks; bar; playgrnd; pool; cycle hire; horseriding; TV; dogs €2.95; 70% statics; phone; some Eng spkn; quiet; ccard acc. "Beautiful scenery & mountain walks; only 14 sm touring pitches; avoid Pamplona mid-Aug during bull-run; site also open at w/end & long w/end all year except Jan/Feb." Holy Week & 1 Jun-30 Sep. € 22.50   2009*

LEON *1B3* (3km SE Urban) *42.5900, -5.5331* **Camping Ciudad de León, Ctra N601, 24195 Golpejar de la Sobarriba** [tel/fax 987-26 90 86; camping_leon@yahoo.es; www.vivaleon.com/campingleon.htm] SE fr León on N601 twds Valladolid, L at top of hill at rndabt & Opel g'ge & foll site sp Golpejar de la Sobarriba; 500m after radio masts turn R at site sp. Narr track to site ent. Sm, pt sl, shd; wc; chem disp; shwrs inc; el pnts inc (4A) €3.60; gas; lndtte; shop; rest; snacks; bar; playgrnd; pool; paddling pool; tennis; cycle hire; dogs €1.50; bus 200m; quiet; adv bkg; poss cr; Eng spkn; CCI. "Clean, pleasant site; helpful, welcoming staff; access some sm pitches poss diff; easy access to León." ♦ 1 Jun-20 Sep. € 18.60   2011*

LEON *1B3* (12km SW Urban) *42.51250, -5.77472* **Camping Camino de Santiago, Ctra N120, Km 324.4, 24392 Villadangos del Páramo (León)** [tel/fax 987-68 02 53; info@campingcaminodesantiago.com; www.campingcaminodesantiago.com] Access fr N120 to W of vill, site sp on R (take care fast, o'taking traff). Fr E turn L in town & foll sp to site. Lge, mkd pitch, pt shd; wc; chem disp; mv service pnt; baby facs; shwrs inc; el pnts €3.75; gas; lndtte; shop; rest; snacks; bar; pool; wifi; 50% statics; dogs; phone; bus 300m; poss cr; adv bkg; rd noise; ccard acc; red long stay; CCI. "Poss no hot water low ssn; facs tired; pleasant, helpful staff; mosquitoes; vill church worth visit; gd NH." ♦ Easter-28 Sep. € 18.20   2009*

⊞ **LINEA DE LA CONCEPCION, LA** *2H3* (S Urban/Coastal) *36.19167, -5.3350* **Camping Sureuropa, Camino de Sobrevela s/n, 11300 La Línea de la Concepción (Cádiz)** [956-64 35 87; fax 956-64 30 59; info@campingsureuropa.com; www.campingsureuropa.com] Fr S on E5/N340 onto N351 coast rd. Just bef Gibraltar turn R up lane, in 200m turn L into site. Fr N on AP7, exit junc 124 onto A383 dir La Línea; foll sp Santa Margarita thro to beach. Foll rd to R along sea front, site in approx 1km - no advance sp. App rd to site off coast rd poss floods after heavy rain. Med, hdg/mkd pitch, hdstg, pt shd; wc; chem disp (wc); shwrs inc; el pnts €3.50; lndtte; bar; sand beach 500m; sports club adj; some statics; clsd 21 Dec-7 Jan; no dogs; phone; bus 1.5km; site clsd 20 Dec-7 Jan; poss cr; Eng spkn; adv bkg; quiet but noise fr adj sports club; no ccard acc; CCI. "Clean, flat, pretty site (gd for disabled); vg, modern san facs; sm pitches & tight site rds poss diff twin-axles & l'ge o'fits; ideal for Gibraltar 4km; stay ltd to 4 days." ♦ € 17.00   2010*

LLAFRANC see Palafrugell *3B3*

⊞ **LLANCA** *3B3* (500m N Coastal) *42.37083, 3.15388* **Camping L'Ombra, Ctra Bisbal-Portbou, Km 16.5, 17490 Llançà (Gerona)** [tel/fax 972-12 02 61; campinglombra@terra.es] Fr Figueres on N260 dir Portbou, site on L 500m N of traff lts at Llançà turn off. Med, mkd pitch, pt sl, pt shd; wc; chem disp; shwrs inc; el pnts €4; lndtte; shop; supmkt 1km; bar; playgrnd; beach 1km; internet; 75% statics; dogs €1.50; bus 500m; train 1km; quiet; red low ssn. "Useful winter base for coastal towns when other sites clsd." € 27.00   2008*

LLANCA *3B3* (4km N Coastal) *42.40320, 3.14580* **Camping Caravaning Sant Miquel, Pozo 22, 17469 Colera (Gerona)** [tel/fax 972-38 90 18; info@campingsantmiquel.com; www.campingsantmiquel.com] Take main rd fr Portbou to Cadaqués. After 7km turn L into Colera vill, then 1st R over bdge, turn L into site in 200m, well sp. Lge, mkd pitch, pt shd; wc; chem disp; shwrs inc; el pnts (6-10A) €4.45; gas; lndtte; shop; rest; snacks; bar; playgrnd; htd pool; shgl beach 1km; watersports; diving; cycle hire; entmnt; TV rm; 10% statics; dogs €2; poss cr; Eng spkn; adv bkg; quiet; ccard acc; CCI. "Friendly site; gd rest & pool; poss v cr high ssn with students; conv local fishing ports & Dali Museum." ♦ 1 Apr-30 Sep. € 21.10   2008*

LLANES *1A4* (8km E Coastal) *43.39948, -4.65350* **Camping La Paz, Ctra N634, Km 292, 33597 Playa de Vidiago (Asturias)** [tel/fax 985-41 12 35; delfin@campinglapaz.com; www.campinglapaz.eu] Take Fr A8/N634/E70 turn R at sp to site bet km stone 292 & 293 bef Vidiago.Site access via narr 1km lane. Stop bef bdge & park on R, staff will tow to pitch. Narr site ent & steep access to pitches. Lge, mkd pitch, terr, shd; wc; chem disp; mv service pnt; baby facs; shwrs inc; el pnts (9A) €4.82 (poss rev pol); gas; lndtte (inc dryer); shop; rest; bar; BBQ; playgrnd; sand beach adj; fishing; watersports; horseriding; mountain sports; golf 4km; games rm; wifi; TV; no statics; dogs €2.51; phone; poss cr w/end; Eng spkn; adv bkg; quiet; ccard acc; CCI. "Exceptionally helpful owner & staff; sm pitches; gd, modern san facs; excel views; cliff top rest; superb beaches in area." ♦ Easter-30 Sep. € 42.00   2011*

See advertisement

LLANES *1A4* (2km W Coastal) *43.42500, -4.78944* **Camping Las Conchas de Póo, Ctra General, 33509 Póo de Llanes (Asturias)** [tel/fax 985-40 22 90] Exit A8/E70 at Llanes West junc 307 & foll sp. Site on rd AS263. Med, sl, terr, pt shd; wc; chem disp; baby facs; shwrs inc; el pnts (5A) €3.20; lndtte (inc dryer); shop; rest; bar; playgrnd; sand beach adj; 50% statics; dogs; bus adj; phone; bus; quiet. "Pleasant site; footpath to lovely beach." 1 Jun-30 Sep. € 17.40   2009*

LLANES *1A4* (5km W Coastal) *43.43471, -4.81810* **Camping Playa de Troenzo, Ctra de Celerio-Barro, 33595 Celorio (Asturias)** [985-40 16 72; fax 985-74 07 23; troenzo@telepolis.com] Fr E take E70/A8 past Llanes & exit at junc 307 to Celorio. At T-junc with AS263 turn L dir Celorio & Llanes. Turn L on N9 (Celorio) thro vill & foll sp to Barro. Site on R after 500m (after Maria Elena site). Lge, terr, pt shd; wc; chem disp; mv service pnt; shwrs inc; el pnts (6A) €2.51; gas; lndtte; shop; rest; snacks; bar; playgrnd; sand beach 400m; 90% statics; dogs; phone; poss cr; Eng spkn; adv bkg; CCI. "Lovely, old town; most pitches sm; for pitches with sea views go thro statics to end of site; gd, modern facs; gd rests in town; nr harbour." 16 Feb-19 Dec. € 19.10   2011*

1ªCat.

CAMPING LA PAZ

Playa de Vidiago
E-33597 Llanes (Asturias)
Km. 292 - CN 634 - E70
Tel./Fax (34) 985 41 12 35
Individual pitches on terraces at
different levels. Beside the mountains
"Picos de Europa". Ideal to enjoy
spanisch festivals, traditional food
and folk in a mountain scenery.

OPEN FROM EASTER TILL 15.10

QUIET AND FRIENDLY ENVIRONMENT

www.campinglapaz.com ~ delfin@campinglapaz.com

LLAVORSI *3B2* (8km N Rural) *42.56004, 1.22810* **Camping Del Cardós,** Ctra Llavorsí-Tavascan, Km 85, 25570 Ribera de Cardós (Lleida) [973-62 31 12; fax 973-62 31 83; info@ campingdelcardos.com; www.campingdelcardos.com] Take L504 fr Llavorsi dir Ribera de Cardós for 9km; site on R on ent vill. Med, mkd pitch, pt shd; wc; chem disp; mv service pnt; shwrs; el pnts (4-6A) €5.30; gas; lndtte (inc dryer); shop; tradsmn; rest; playgrnd; pool; 2 paddling pools; fishing; games area; TV rm; 5% statics; dogs €3.60; Eng spkn; quiet; CCI. "By side of rv, v quiet low ssn; excel." 1 Apr-20 Oct. € 24.00 2009*

⊞ **LLAVORSI** *3B2* (9km N Rural) *42.56890, 1.23040* **Camping La Borda del Pubill,** Ctra de Tavescan, Km 9.5, 25570 Ribera de Cardós (Lleida) [973-62 30 80; fax 973-62 30 28; info@campinglabordadelpubill.com; www. campinglabordadelpubill.com] Fr France on A64 exit junc 17 at Montréjeau & head twd Spanish border. At Vielha turn E onto C28/C1412 to Llavorsí, then L504 to Ribera. Fr S take N260 fr Tremp to Llavorsí, then L504 to site. Lge, pt shd; htd wc; baby facs; shwrs; el pnts €5.30; gas; lndtte; shop, rest high ssn; snacks; bar; playgrnd; htd pool; paddling pool; rv sw & fishing; kayaking; trekking; adventure sports; quad bike hire; horseriding; skiing 30km; games area; games rm; TV; 10% statics; dogs €3; phone; car wash; adv bkg; quiet; ccard acc. "In beautiful area; excel walking; gd rest." ♦ € 24.10 2009*

LLORET DE MAR *3B3* (1km S Coastal) *41.6973, 2.8217* **Camping Tucan,** Ctra Blanes-Lloret, 17310 Lloret de Mar (Gerona) [972-36 99 65; fax 972-36 00 79; info@ campingtucan.com; www.campingtucan.com] Fr N exit AP7 junc 9 onto C35 twd Sant Feliu then C63 on R sp Lloret de Mar. Fr S take last exit fr C32 & foll sp Lloret de Mar, site on L, sp. Lge, mkd pitch, terr, shd; wc; chem disp; baby facs; shwrs inc; el pnts (3-6A) €3.40-4.40; gas; lndtte; shop; rest; snacks; bar; BBQ; playgrnd; pool; paddling pool; sand beach 600m; games area; golf 500m; entmnt; internet; TV rm; 25% statics; dogs €2; phone; bus; car wash; Eng spkn; adv bkg; quiet; ccard acc; red long stay/ snr citizens/CCI. "Well-appointed site; friendly staff." ♦ 1 Apr-30 Sep. € 27.80 2011*

⊞ **LLORET DE MAR** *3B3* (1km SW Coastal) *41.6984, 2.8265* **Camping Santa Elena-Ciutat,** Ctra Blanes/Lloret, 17310 Lloret de Mar (Gerona) [972-36 40 09; fax 972-36 79 54; santaelana@betsa.es; www.betsa.es] Exit A7 junc 9 dir Lloret. In Lloret take Blanes rd, site sp at km 10.5 on rd GI 682. V lge, pt sl; wc; baby facs; shwrs; el pnts (5A) €3.90; gas; lndtte; shop; rest; snacks; bar; playgrnd; pool; paddling pool; shgl beach 600m; games area; phone; cash machine; poss cr; Eng spkn; quiet low ssn; red facs low ssn; CCI. "Ideal for teenagers." ♦ € 34.60 2011*

⊞ **LOBOS, LOS** *4G1* (2km NE Rural) **Camping Hierbabuena,** Los Lobos, 04610 Cuevas del Almanzora (Almería) [tel/ fax 950-16 86 97 or 629-68 81 53 (mob)] S fr Lorca on A7; at Cuevas del Almanzora turn L onto A332 to Los Lobos - do not ent vill; 400m after junc with A1201 (dir El Largo & Pulpí) turn L & foll gravel rd to site in 1km. Sm, mkd pitch, hdstg, pt shd; htd wc; chem disp; baby facs; shwrs inc; el pnts (6-10A) inc; gas (Spanish only); lndtte; supmkt & rest 5km; snacks & bar 500m; BBQ; playgrnd; sand beach 5km; 75% statics (sep area); dogs free; Eng spkn; adv bkg; quiet; ccard not acc; red long stay. "Gd for long winter stay; friendly British owners; lge pitches; pretty & interesting area; excel choice of beaches; gd walking, cycling & sightseeing; vg security; excel." ♦ € 25.45 2009*

⊞ **LOGRONO** *3B1* (500m N Urban) *42.47187, -2.45164* **Camping La Playa,** Avda de la Playa 6, 26006 Logroño (La Rioja) [941-25 22 53; fax 941-25 86 61; info@camping laplaya.com; www.campinglaplaya.com] Leave Logroño by bdge 'Puente de Piedra' on N111, then turn L at rndabt into Camino de las Norias. Site well sp in town & fr N111, adj sports cent Las Norias, on N side of Rv Ebro. Med, hdg pitch, shd; wc; mv service pnt; shwrs inc; el pnts (5A) €4.80; gas; lndtte (inc dryer); shop; snacks, bar in ssn; playgrnd; pool; rv sw adj; tennis; 80% statics; dogs €2; red CCI. "Sh walk to town cent; ltd facs low ssn & site poss clsd; vg." ♦ € 25.00 2011*

⊞ **LOGRONO** *3B1* (10km W Rural) *42.41613, -2.55169*
**Camping Navarrete, Ctra La Navarrete-Entrena, Km 1.5,
26370 Navarrete (La Rioja)** [941-44 01 69; fax 941-44 06 39;
campingnavarrete@fer.es; www.campingnavarrete.com]
Fr AP68 exit junc 11, at end slip rd turn L onto LR137 to
Navarette. Foll sp thro town for Entrena (S) on LR137 dir
Entrena. Site 1km on R. Lge, mkd pitch, pt shd; wc; chem disp;
mv service pnt; baby facs; shwrs inc; el pnts (6A) €4.40; gas;
lndtte; shop; snacks; bar; BBQ; playgrnd; pool & paddling pool;
tennis; horseriding; car wash; wifi; 95% statics; dogs €2.40; site
clsd 10 Dec-12 Jan; bus 1.3km; Eng spkn; noisy at w/end; ccard
acc; red low ssn/long stay. "Professionally run, clean, tidy site;
excel san facs; helpful staff; some sm pitches; Bilbao ferry 2 hrs
via m'way; interesting area; highly rec." € 22.00   2011*

I'll go online and tell the
Club what we think of the
campsites we've visited –
www.caravanclub.co.uk/
europereport

⊞ **LORCA** *4G1* (8km W Rural) *37.62861, -1.74888* **Camping La
Torrecilla, Ctra Granada-LaTorrecilla, 30817 Lorca (Murcia)**
[tel/fax 968-44 21 96; campinglatorrecilla@hotmail.
com] Leave A7/E15 at junc 585. In 1km turn L, site well sp.
Med, mkd pitch, hdstg, pt sl, pt shd; htd wc; chem disp; mv
service pnt; shwrs inc; el pnts (6A) €3.21; gas; lndtte; shop
2km; tradsmn; rest; snacks; bar; BBQ; playgrnd; pool; tennis;
games area; TV rm; 95% statics; dogs; phone; bus 1km; poss
cr; Eng spkn; quiet; ccard acc; red long stay. "Ltd touring
pitches & el pts; friendly, helpful staff; excel pool; vg san
facs." ♦ € 14.30   2009*

⊞ **LUARCA** *1A3* (1km NE Coastal) *43.54914, -6.52426*
**Camping Los Cantiles, Ctra N634, Km 502.7, 33700 Luarca
(Asturias)** [tel/fax 985-64 09 38; cantiles@campingloscantiles.
com; www.campingloscantiles.com] On A8 exit junc 467
(sp Luarca/Barcia/Almuña), At rndabt foll sp to Luarca, after
petrol stn turn R, foll sp to site. Not rec to ent town fr W.
Not rec to foll SatN as may take you up v steep & narr rd. On
leaving site, retrace to main rd - do not tow thro Luarca. Med,
hdg pitch, pt shd; wc; chem disp; baby facs; shwrs inc; el pnts
inc (3-6A) €2-2.50; gas; lndtte; shop; tradsmn; rest high ssn;
snacks; bar; pool 300m; shgl beach at foot of cliff; dogs €1;
phone; poss cr; Eng spkn; adv bkg; quiet; red long stay; CCI.
"Site on cliff top; some narr site rds; pitches soft after rain;
steep climb down to beach; 30 min walk to interesting town
& port." ♦ € 18.50   2011*

⊞ **LUARCA** *1A3* (12km E Rural/Coastal) *43.54898, -6.38420*
**Camping La Regalina, Ctra de la Playa s/n, 33788 Cadavedo
(Asturias)** [tel/fax 985-64 50 56; info@laregalina.com]
Fr N632 dir Cadavedo, km126. Site well sp. Med, pt shd;
wc; chem disp; shwrs inc; el pnts (5-8A) €2.30; gas; shop;
rest; snacks; bar; pool; beach 1km; TV; 10% statics; dogs
€3; phone; bus 600m; adv bkg; quiet; red long ssn;
red long stay. "Scenic area; pretty vill; ltd facs low ssn; gd."
€ 21.10   2009*

LUARCA *1A3* (2km W Coastal) *43.55116, -6.55310* **Camping
Playa de Taurán, 33700 Luarca (Asturias)** [tel/fax 985-
64 12 72 or 619-88 43 06 (mob); tauran@campingtauran.
com; www.campingtauran.com] Exit A8/N634 junc 471 sp
Luarca, El Chano. Cont 3.5km on long, narr, rough access rd.
Rd thro Luarca unsuitable for c'vans. Med, some hdg pitch,
pt sl, pt shd; wc; chem disp; mv service pnt; baby facs; shwrs
inc; el pnts (10A) €3.50; gas; lndtte; shop; tradsmn; rest;
snacks; bar; BBQ; pool; paddling pool; shgl beach 200m; sand
beach 2km; cycle hire; phone; dogs €1; quiet; red long stays.
"Sea & mountain views; off beaten track; conv fishing & hill
vills; peaceful, restful, attractive, well-kept site; steep access
to beach; excel." 1 Apr-30 Sep. € 18.50   2010*

LUMBIER *3B1* (500m W Rural) *42.6500, -1.3119* **Camping
Iturbero, Ctra N240 Pamplona-Huesca, 31440 Lumbier
(Navarra)** [948-88 04 05; fax 948-88 04 14; iturbero@
campingiturbero.com; www.campingiturbero.com]
SE fr Pamplona on N240 twds Yesa Reservoir. In 30km L on
NA150 twds Lumbier. In 3.5km immed bef Lumbier turn R
at rndabt then over bdge, 1st L to site, adj sw pool. Well sp
fr N240. Med, hdg/mkd pitch, some hdstg, pt shd; wc; chem
disp; mv service pnt; shwrs inc; el pnts (5A) €4.95; gas; lndtte;
shop 1km; rest; snacks; bar; BBQ; playgrnd; pool 100m;
tennis; hang-gliding; 25% statics; dogs; bus 1km; quiet; CCI.
"Beautiful, well-kept site; clean, basic facs; excel touring base;
open w/end only Dec-Easter (poss fr Sep) but clsd 19 Dec-19
Feb; eagles & vultures in gorge & seen fr site; helpful staff;
Lumbier lovely sm town." Holy Week-8 Dec. € 22.30
                                                    2008*

⊞ **LUMBRALES** *1C3* (6km NE Rural) *40.95750, -6.65611*
**Camping La Hojita, Ctra de Fregeneda, Km 89, 37240
Lumbrales (Salamanca)** [923-16 92 68 or 655-91 95 80 (mob);
camping_la_hojita@hotmail.com; www.campinglahojita.
com] Fr Salamanca or fr Portuguese border, site sp on CL517.
Sm, mkd pitch, shd; wc; chem disp; mv service pnt; baby facs;
shwrs inc; el pnts (10A) €3.15; lndtte; shop 2km; rest; snacks;
bar; BBQ; playgrnd; pool; some statics; Eng spkn; quiet; red
long stay. "Excel, tranquil site." 1 Apr-1 Nov. € 18.00
                                                    2009*

MACANET DE CABRENYS *3B3* (1km S Rural) *42.37314, 2.75419*
**Camping Maçanet de Cabrenys, Mas Roquet s/n, 17720
Maçanet de Cabrenys (Gerona)** [667-77 66 48 (mob); info@
campingmassanet.com; www.campingmassanet.com]
Fr N, exit AP7 junc 2 at La Jonquera onto N-II dir Figueres; at
km 767 turn R onto GI-502/GI-503 dir Maçanet de Cabrenys;
turn L 500m bef vill; site sp. Or fr S, exit AP7 junc 4 at Figueres
onto N-II dir France; at km 766 turn L onto GI-502 dir Maçanet
de Cabrenys; then as above. Sm, mkd pitch, some hdstg, sl,
terr, pt shd; htd wc; chem disp; mv service pnt; baby facs;
shwrs; el pnts (10A) €4.80; gas; lndtte; sm shop & 2km;
tradsmn; ltd rest; snacks; bar; BBQ; playgrnd; pool; cycle
hire; cycle rtes fr site; games rm; wifi; TV; some statics; dogs
€4; Eng spkn; quiet; adv bkg; ccard acc; red low ssn; CCI. ♦
1 Mar-31 Dec. € 26.65 (CChq acc)   2010*

⊞ **MADRID** *1D4* (8km NE Urban) *40.45361, -3.60333* **Camping Osuna, Calle de los Jardines de Aranjuez, Avda de Logroño s/n, 28042 Madrid [917-41 05 10; fax 913-20 63 65; camping.osuna.madrid@microgest.es]** Fr M40, travelling S clockwise (anti-clockwise fr N or E) exit junc 8 at Canillejas sp 'Avda de Logroño'. Turn L under m'way, then R under rlwy, immed after turn R at traff lts. Site on L corner - white painted wall. Travelling N, leave M40 at junc 7 (no turn off at junc 8) sp Avda 25 Sep, U-turn at km 7, head S to junc 8, then as above. Med, hdg/mkd pitch, pt sl, pt shd; wc; chem disp; shwrs inc; el pnts (5A) €4.85 (long lead rec); lndtte; shop 600m; playgrnd; metro to town 600m; 10% statics; dogs free; phone; poss cr; rd & aircraft noise; Eng spkn; red low ssn; CCI. "Sm pitches poss diff lge o'fits; poss neglected low ssn & facs tired (June 2010); poss itinerants; conv city cent." ♦ € 25.40   2010*

⊞ **MADRID** *1D4* (13km S Urban) *40.31805, -3.68888* **Camping Alpha, Ctra de Andalucía N-IV, Km 12.4, 28906 Getafe (Madrid) [916-95 80 69; fax 916-83 16 59; info@campingalpha.com; www.campingalpha.com]** Fr S on A4/E5 twd Madrid, leave at km 12B to W dir Ocaña & foll sp. Fr N on A4/E5 at km 13B to change dir back onto A4; then exit 12B sp 'Polígono Industrial Los Olivos' to site. Lge, hdstg, hdg pitch, pt shd; wc; chem disp; mv service pnt; shwrs inc; el pnts (15A) €5.90 (poss no earth); lndtte; shop; rest; snacks; bar; playgrnd; pool high ssn; tennis; games area; 20% statics; dogs; phone; poss cr; Eng spkn; adv bkg; ccard acc; red CCI. "Lorry depot adj; poss vehicle movements 24 hrs but minimal noise; bus & metro to Madrid 30-40 mins; vg, clean facs; helpful staff; NH or sh stay." € 27.95   2011*

See advertisement below

⊞ **MADRIGAL DE LA VERA** *1D3* (500m E Rural) *40.14864, -5.35769* **Camping Alardos, Ctra Madrigal-Candeleda, 10480 Madrigal de la Vera (Cáceres) [tel/fax 927-56 50 66; mirceavd@hotmail.com; www.campingalardos.es]** Fr Jarandilla take EX203 E to Madrigal. Site sp in vill nr rv bdge. Med, mkd pitch, pt shd; wc; chem disp; shwrs inc; el pnts (6-10A) €4; lndtte; shop & 1km; rest; snacks; bar; BBQ; playgrnd; pool; rv sw adj; TV; 10% statics; no dogs; phone; poss cr Jul/Aug; Eng spkn; adv bkg; ccard not acc. "Friendly owners; superb site; ltd facs low ssn; beautiful scenery; excel touring area; ancient Celtic settlement at El Raso 5km." € 23.30   2009*

⊞ **MALGRAT DE MAR** *3C3* (500m SW Coastal) *41.63161, 2.72061* **Camping Bon Repós, Pg Maritim s/n, 08398 Santa Susanna (Barcelona) [937-67 84 75; fax 937-76 85 26; info@campingbonrepos.com; www.campingbonrepos.com]** App fr Gerona on rd N11, site sp. Track leaves on L of N11; foll camp sp for 680m & turn R at sea-front T-junc. Cont thro Santa Susanna, down underpass & turn L in middle, app rd to site on beach behind rlwy stn; sp. NB Heavy rain may cause flooding of underpass; alt exit max 2.5m height. V lge, shd; wc; chem disp; baby facs; shwrs inc; el pnts (5A) €9; gas; lndtte; supmkt; rest; bar; playgrnd; 2 pools; beach adj; watersports; tennis; entmnt; 10% statics; dogs €2.50; train to Barcelona 400m; poss cr; poss noisy; ccard acc; red low ssn. "Some sm pitches & some on water's edge; vg site." ♦ € 37.50   2008*

⊞ **MAMOLA, LA** *2H4* (500m W Coastal) *36.74062, -3.29976* **Camping Castillo de Baños, Castillo de Baños, 18750 La Mamola (Granada) [958-82 95 28; fax 958-82 97 68; info@campingcastillo.com; www.campingcastillo.com]** Fr E on A7/E15 exit km 360.4 sp Camping/Rest El Paraiso/Castillo de Baños, site on L after rest at ent to vill. Fr W exit km 359.3. Lge, mkd pitch, hdstg, pt shd; wc; chem disp; mv service pnt; shwrs inc; el pnts (5A) €4; gas; lndtte (inc dryer); shop; tradsmn; rest; snacks; bar; playgrnd; pool; private shgl beach adj; fishing; cycle hire; entmnt; internet; Eng spkn; dogs €2.50; bus 200m; adv bkg; ccard acc; quiet; red low ssn/CCI. "Poss rallies low ssn." ♦ € 23.50   2010*

⊞ **MANGA DEL MAR MENOR, LA** *4G2* (27.7km E Urban) *37.6244, -0.7447* **Caravaning La Manga, Autovia Cartagena - La Manga, exit 11, E-30370 La Manga del Mar Menor [968-56 30 19; lamanga@caravaning.es; www.caravaning.es]** Take Autovia CT-32 fr Cartagena to La Manga; take exit 800B twds El Algar/Murcia; keep L, merge onto Autovia MU312; cont to foll MU-312; cont onto Ctra a La Manga & cont onto Av Gran Via; site clearly sp. Lge, hdg, hdstg; pt shd; wc; chem disp; mv service pnt; serviced pitches; baby facs; shwrs inc; el pnts (10A) inc; lndtte (inc dryer); supmkt; rest; snacks; bar; BBQ; playgrnd; pools; beach; gym; sauna; jacuzzi; outdoor fitness course; tennis; watersports; cycle hire & horseridng nrby; games rm; entmnt; wifi; some statics; dogs €1.25; Eng spkn; adv bkg; bus to Murcia and Cartagena; recep open 24 hrs; ccard acc. "Open air cinema & children's programme high ssn; lovely location & gd for golfers; Mar Menor well worth visiting; v gd rest; helpful staff." € 29.50   2011*

See advertisement on next page

SPAIN

⊞ **MANGA DEL MAR MENOR, LA** 4G2 (2km W Coastal) 37.62455, -0.74300 **Camping La Manga, Ctra El Algar/Cabo de Palos, Km 12, 30386 La Manga del Mar Menor (Murcia)** [968-56 30 14 or 56 30 19; fax 968-56 34 26; lamanga@ caravaning.es; www.caravaning.es] Leave MU312 junc 11 sp Playa Honda; over dual c'way then turn R. Site sp fr La Manga. Ent visible beside dual c'way with flags flying. V lge, hdg/ mkd pitch, hdstg, pt shd; htd wc; chem disp; mv service pnt; sauna; serviced pitches; shwrs inc; el pnts (10A) metered; gas; lndtte (inc dryer); supmkt; rest; snacks; bar; BBQ; playgrnd; 2 pools (1 htd, covrd); paddling pool; direct access sand beach; fishing; watersports; windsurfing; horseriding; jacuzzi; gym; tennis; cinema; games rm; wifi; entmnt; cab TV/TV rm; 30% statics; dogs €1.40; no c'vans/m'vans over 12m; phone; poss cr; Eng spkn; adv bkg ess; ccard acc; red long stay/low ssn. "Immac, busy, popular site; Mar Menor shallow & warm lagoon; gd for families; some narr site rds & trees - rec park in car park on arr & walk to find pitch; gd walking; mountain biking; bird sanctuary; poss lge rallies on site Dec-Mar; excel." ♦ € 29.50 (CChq acc) SBS - E16   2011*

⊞ **MANZANARES EL REAL** 1D4 (8km NE Rural) 40.74278, -3.81583 **Camping La Fresneda, Ctra M608, Km 19.5, 28791 Soto del Real (Madrid)** [tel/fax 918-47 65 23] Fr AP6/NV1 turn NE at Collado-Villalba onto M608 to Cerceda & Manzanares el Real. Foll rd round lake to Soto del Real, site sp at km 19.5. Med, shd; wc; chem disp; baby facs; shwrs €0.15; el pnts (6A) €3.50; gas; lndtte; shop; snacks; bar; playgrnd; pool; tennis; dogs €3; phone; rd noise; ccard acc. ♦ € 24.00   2009*

⊞ **MANZANARES EL REAL** 1D4 (3km NW Rural) 40.74165, -3.87509 **Camping El Ortigal, Montañeros 19, La Pedriza, 28410 Manzanares el Real (Madrid)** [918-53 01 20] Fr AP6/ NV1 turn NE at Collado-Villalba onto M608 to Cerceda & Manzanares el Real. In 6km take L sp to Manzanares, cross rv & immed L. Sp at this junc; site further 3km - speed humps. Not many sp to site or Pedriza. Lge, pt sl; wc; shwrs; el pnts (10A) €3.85 (poss rev pol); gas; shop; rest; bar; playgrnd; 99% statics/chalets; phone; red low ssn. "Sm area for tourers - rec arr early; warm welcome; san facs dated; attractive country & views; excel walking in adj National Park." ♦ € 25.70   2008*

⊞ **MARBELLA** 2H3 (7km E Coastal) 36.50259, -4.80413 **Camping La Buganvilla, Ctra N340, Km 188.8, 29600 Marbella (Málaga)** [952-83 19 73 or 952-83 19 74; fax 952-83 19 74; info@campingbuganvilla.com; www. campingbuganvilla.com] E fr Marbella for 6km on N340/E15 twds Málaga. Pass site & cross over m'way at Elviria & foll site sp. Fr Málaga exit R off autovia immed after 189km marker. Lge, terr, shd; wc; chem disp; shwrs; el pnts (10A) €4.80; gas; lndtte; shop & 250m; rest; bar & sun terr; playgrnd; pool; sand beach 350m; games rm; wifi; TV; phone; dogs €4 (not acc Jul/Aug); Eng spkn; adv bkg; poss noisy at w/end; red long stay/snr citizens; ccard acc; CCI. "Relaxed, conv site; helpful staff; excel beach." ♦ € 28.50   2009*

The opening dates and
prices on this campsite
have changed.
I'll send a site report
form to the Club for the
next edition of the guide.

⊞ **MARBELLA** 2H3 (10km E Coastal) 36.49111, -4.76416 **Camping Marbella Playa, Ctra N340, Km 192.8, 29600 Marbella (Málaga)** [952-83 39 98; fax 952-83 39 99; recepcion@campingmarbella.com; www.campingmarbella. com] Fr Marbella on A7/N340 coast rd (not AP7/E15 toll m'way) & site is on R bef 193 km stone & just bef pedestrian bdge over A7/N340, sp 'to beach'. Fr Málaga U-turn on m'way as follows: pass 192km mark & immed take R slip rd to Elviria to turn L over bdge, back onto A7/N340. Turn R bef next bdge. Lge, mkd pitch, hdstg, pt shd; wc; chem disp; mv service pnt; baby facs; shwrs; el pnts (10A) €4; gas; lndry service; supmkt; rest; snacks; bar; BBQ; playgrnd; pool; sand beach adj; watersports; tennis 50m; wifi; TV; dogs; phone; bus nr; poss v cr; rd noise; ccard acc; red low ssn/long stay/snr citizens/ CCI. "Pitches tight; clean facs but tired; gd supmkt; friendly, helpful manager; gd base Costa del Sol; noisy peak ssn & w/ends, espec Sat nights." ♦ € 26.00   2010*

⊞ **MARBELLA** *2H3* (12km E Coastal) *36.48881, -4.74294*
Kawan Village Cabopino, Ctra N340/A7, Km 194.7, 29600
Marbella (Málaga) [tel/fax 952-83 43 73 or 952-85 01 06;
info@campingcabopino.com; www.campingcabopino.
com] Fr E site is on N side of N340/A7; turn R at km 195
'Salida Cabopino' past petrol stn, site on R at rndabt. Fr W
on A7 turn R at 'Salida Cabopino' km 194.7, go over bdge to
rndabt, site strt over. NB Do not take sm exit fr A7 immed
at 1st Cabopino sp. Lge, mkd pitch, pt sl, pt shd; wc; chem
disp; mv service pnt; baby facs; shwrs inc; el pnts (10A) inc
(poss long lead req); lndtte (inc dryer); shop; rest; snacks; bar;
BBQ (gas/elec); playgrnd; 2 pools (1 covrd); sand beach/dunes
200m; watersports; marina 300m; games area; archery; golf
driving range; wifi; games/TV rm; 50% statics; dogs €1.75;
no c'vans/m'vans over 11m high ssn; bus 100m; Eng spkn; rd
noise & lge groups w/enders; ccard acc; red low ssn; CCI. "V
pleasant site set in pine woodland; busy, particularly w/end;
sm pitches, poss diff access lge o'fits; blocks req some pitches;
gd, clean san facs." ♦ € 35.80 (CChq acc) SBS - E21   2011*

⊞ **MARIA** *4G1* (8km W Rural) *37.70823, -2.23609* **Camping
Sierra de María**, Ctra María a Orce, Km 7, Paraje La Piza,
04838 María (Málaga) [950-16 70 45 or 660-26 64 74 (mob);
fax 950-48 54 16; info@campingsierrademaria.com; www.
campingsierrademaria.com] Exit A92 at junc 408 to Vélez
Rubio, Vélez Blanco & María. Foll A317 to María & cont dir
Huéscar & Orce. Site on R. Med, mkd pitch, pt sl, pt shd;
wc; chem disp; shwrs; el pnts (6-10A) €3.75; shop high ssn;
rest; bar; cycle hire; horseriding; some statics; dogs; adv
bkg; quiet; ccard acc; CCI. "Lovely, peaceful, ecological site
in mountains; much wildlife; variable pitch sizes; facs poss
stretched high ssn; v cold in winter." ♦ € 16.20   2011*

⊞ **MARINA, LA** *4F2* (1.5km S Coastal) *38.12972, -0.65000*
Camping Internacional La Marina, Ctra N332a, Km 76,
03194 La Marina (Alicante) [965-41 92 00; fax 965-41 91 10;
info@campinglamarina.com; www.campinglamarina.
com] Fr N332 S of La Marina turn E twd sea at rndabt
onto Camino del Cementerio. At next rndabt turn S onto
N332a & foll site sp along Avda de l'Alegría. V lge, hdg/
mkd pitch, hdstg, terr, shd; htd wc; chem disp; mv service
pnt; 50% serviced pitches; baby facs; fam bthrm; sauna;
solarium; shwrs inc; el pnts (10A) €3.21; gas; lndtte (inc
dryer); supmkt; rest; snacks; bars; playgrnd; 2 pools (1 htd/
covrd); waterslides; sand beach 500m; fishing; watersports;
tennis; games area; games rm; fitness cent; entmnt; disco;
wifi; TV rm; 10% statics; dogs €2.14; phone; bus 50m; car
wash; security; Eng spkn; adv bkg; ccard acc; various pitch
sizes/prices; red long stay/low ssn; CCI. "Popular winter site
- almost full late Feb; v busy w/end; clean, high quality facs;
bus fr gate; gd security; gd rest." ♦ € 59.40   2011*

See advertisement below

SPAIN

⊞ **MASNOU, EL** *3C3* (750m W Coastal) *41.4753, 2.3033*
**Camping Masnou, Ctra NII, Km 633, Carrer de Camil Fabra
33, 08320 El Masnou (Barcelona) [tel/fax 935-55 15 03;
masnou@campingsonline.es]** App site fr N on N11. Pass El
Masnou rlwy station on L & go strt on at traff lts. Site on R
on N11 after km 633. Not clearly sp. Med, pt sl, shd; wc; mv
service pnt; shwrs inc; el pnts €5.88; shop, snacks, bar high
ssn; BBQ; playgrnd; pool high ssn; sand beach opp; internet;
dogs; phone; bus 300m; train to Barcelona nr; poss v cr; Eng
spkn; rd & rlwy noise; ccard acc; CCI. "Blocks of flats either
side of site; gd pitches, no awnings; some sm pitches, poss
shared; facs vg, though poss stretched when site busy; no
restriction on NH vehicle movements; well-run, friendly site
but a little 'tired'; gd service low ssn." ♦ € 33.70   2010*

⊞ **MATARO** *3C3* (3km E Coastal) *41.55060, 2.48330* **Camping
Barcelona, Ctra NII, Km 650, 08304 Mataró (Barcelona)
[937-90 47 20; fax 937-41 02 82; info@campingbarcelona.
com; www.campingbarcelona.com]** Exit AP7 onto C60 sp
Mataró. Turn N onto NII dir Gerona. Site sp on L after rndabt.
Lge, mkd pitch, hdstg, shd; wc; chem disp; mv service pnt;
baby facs; shwrs inc; el pnts (6A) €5.50; gas; lndtte; shop;
rest; snacks; bar; playgrnd; pool; paddling pool; sand beach
1.5km; games area; games rm; animal fare; wifi; entmnt; TV;
5% statics; dogs €4; shuttle bus to beach & town; Eng spkn;
adv bkg; rd noise; ccard acc; red long stay/low ssn; CCI. "Conv
Barcelona 28km; pleasant site; friendly, welcoming staff." ♦
4 Mar-1 Nov. € 46.80   2010*

⊞ **MAZAGON** *2G2* (10km E Coastal) *37.09855, -6.72650*
**Camping Doñana Playa, Ctra San Juan del Puerto-
Matalascañas, Km 34.6, 21130 Mazagón (Huelva)
[959-53 62 81; fax 959-53 63 13; info@campingdonana.
com; www.campingdonana.com]** Fr A49 exit junc 48 at
Bullullos del Condado onto A483 sp El Rocio, Matalascañas.
At coast turn R sp Mazagón, site on L in 16km. V lge, mkd
pitch, hdstg, pt shd; wc; chem disp; shwrs inc; el pnts (6A)
€5.20; shop; rest; snacks; bar; playgrnd; pool; sand beach
300m; watersports; games area; cycle hire; entmnt;
some statics; dogs €4.10; bus 500m; site clsd 14 Dec-14 Jan;
adv bkg; quiet but v noisy Fri/Sat nights; red low ssn; CCI.
"Pleasant site amongst pine trees but lack of site care low ssn;
basic san facs, ltd low ssn; lge pitches but poss soft sand." ♦
€ 30.40   2009*

MENDEXA see Lekeitio *3A1*

⊞ **MENDIGORRIA** *3B1* (500m SW Rural) *42.62416, -1.84277*
**Camping El Molino, Ctra Larraga, 31150 Mendigorría
(Navarra) [948-34 06 04; fax 948-34 00 82; info@
campingelmolino; www.campingelmolino.com]**
Fr Pamplona on N111 turn L at 25km in Puente la Reina onto
NA601 sp Mendigorría. Site sp thro vill dir Larraga. Med, some
mkd pitch, pt shd; wc; chem disp; serviced pitches; baby
facs; shwrs inc; el pnts (6A) inc; gas; lndtte (inc dryer); shop;
tradsmn; rest; snacks; bar; BBQ; playgrnd; pool; paddling
pool; waterslide; canoe hire; tennis; games area; wifi; TV;
statics (sep area); dogs; phone; poss cr at w/end; clsd 23
Dec-14 Jan & poss Mon-Thurs fr Nov to Feb, phone ahead
to check; adv bkg; poss v noisy at w/end; ccard acc; CCI. "Gd
clean san facs; solar water heating - water poss only warm; vg
leisure facs; v ltd facs low ssn; for early am dep low ssn, pay
night bef & obtain barrier key; friendly, helpful staff; lovely
medieval vill." ♦ € 25.50   2011*

MEQUINENZA *3C2* (Urban) *41.37833, 0.30555* **Camp
Municipal Octogesa, Ctra Alcanyís-Fraga s/n, Km 314, 50170
Mequinenza (Zaragoza) [974-46 44 31; fax 974-46 50 31;
rai@fuibol.net; www.fuibol.net]** Exit AP2 junc
4 onto N211 S. On ent Mequinenza just past wooded area on
L, turn L thro break in service rd, site well sp. Tight ent poss
unsuitable lge o'fits. Med, hdg/mkd pitch, terr, pt shd; wc;
chem disp (wc); shwrs inc; el pnts (6A) €3.90; lndtte; shop
1km; rest; snacks; bar; BBQ; playgrnd; 2 pools high ssn;
tennis; dogs; phone; Eng spkn; adv bkg; quiet but noise fr arr
of fishing parties; ccard acc; CCI. "Site part of complex on
bank of Rv Segre; base for fishing trips - equipment supplied;
sm pitches unsuitable lge o'fits; NH only." 15 Feb-15 Nov.
€ 17.70   2009*

⊞ **MERIDA** *2E3* (2km SE Urban) *38.93558, -6.30426* **Camping
Mérida, Avda de la Reina Sofia s/n, 06800 Mérida (Badajoz)
[924-30 34 53; fax 924-30 03 98; proexcam@jet.es; www.
pagina.de/campingmerida]** Fr E on A5/E90 exit junc 333/334
to Mérida, site on L in 2km. Fr W on A5/E90 exit junc 346,
site sp. Fr N exit A66/E803 at junc 617 onto A5 E. Leave at
junc 334, site on L in 1km twd Mérida. Fr S on A66-E803 app
Mérida, foll Cáceres sp onto bypass to E; at lge rndabt turn
R sp Madrid; site on R after 2km. Med, mkd pitch, pt sl, pt
shd; wc; chem disp; shwrs inc; el pnts (6A) €3.20 (long lead
poss req & poss rev pol); gas; lndtte; ltd shop high ssn &
3km; hypmkt 6km; rest; snacks; bar; pool; paddling pool;
TV; some statics; dogs; phone; no bus; quiet but some rd
noise; CCI. "Roman remains & National Museum of Roman
Art worth visit; poss diff lge o'fits manoeuvring onto pitch due
trees & soft ground after rain; gd seafood rest; ltd facs low
ssn; conv NH; warden calls to collect fees, new san facs." ♦
€ 17.50   2011*

⊞ **MIAJADAS** *2E3* (10km SW Rural) *39.09599, -6.01333*
**Camping-Restaurant El 301, Ctra Madrid-Lisbon, Km 301,
10100 Miajadas (Cáceres) [927-34 79 14; camping301@
hotmail.com]** Leave A5/E90 just bef km stone 301 & foll sp
'Via de Servicio' with rest & camping symbols; site in 500m.
Med, pt shd; wc; chem disp; shwrs inc; el pnts (8A) €4 (poss no
earth); gas; lndtte; shop; rest; snacks; bar; playgrnd; pool; TV;
phone; m'way noise & dogs; ccard acc; CCI. "Well-maintained,
clean site; grass pitches; OK wheelchair users but steps to
pool; gd NH." € 16.20   2010*

MIJAS COSTA see Fuengirola *2H4*

⊞ **MIRANDA DEL CASTANAR** *1D3* (500m S Rural) *40.47527,
-5.99833* **Camping El Burro Blanco, Camino de las Norias
s/n, 37660 Miranda del Castañar (Salamanca) [tel/fax 923-
16 11 00; elbb@infonegocio; www.elburroblanco.net]**
Fr Ciudad Rodrigo take SA220 to El Cabaco then foll sp for
2km to Miranda del Castañar. In 2km turn L onto concrete/
dirt rd for 700m. Site on R. Sm, mkd pitch, terr, pt shd; wc;
chem disp; shwrs inc; el pnts (2-10A) €1.50-4.80; lndtte; shop,
rest, snacks 1km; tradsmn; bar; pool; no statics; dogs; phone
1km; Eng spkn; quiet; 10% red 3+ days; CCI. "Nice scenery, set
in oak wood; medieval hill-top town 500m; tight ent to some
pitches, manhandling req; excel." 1 Apr-1 Oct. € 18.80
2008*

SPAIN

MOANA *1B2* (3km W Coastal) *42.26991, -8.75202* **Camping Tiran, Ctra Cangas-Moaña, Km 3, 36957 Moaña (Pontevedra) [986-31 01 50; fax 986-44 72 04]** Exit AP9 junc 146 & foll sp Moaña/Cangas. Site beyond Moaña. Med, hdg pitch, terr, pt shd; wc; shwrs inc; el pnts (6A) inc; lndry rm; shop; tradsmn; rest; snacks; bar; playgrnd; beach adj; TV; 80% statics; no dogs; phone; adv bkg; quiet. "Site on v steep hill - only suitable m'vans & single-axle c'vans with powerful tow car; gd touring base S Galicia." 3 Apr-5 Oct. € 25.00   2008*

MOIXENT *4E2* (12km N Rural) *38.96488, -0.79917* **Camping Sierra Natura (Naturist), Finca El Tejarico, Ctra Moixent-Navalón, Km 11.5, 46810 Enguera (València) [962-25 30 26; fax 962-25 30 20; info@sierranatura.com; www.sierranatura.com]** Exit A35 fr N exit junc 23 or junc 23 fr S onto CV589 sp Navalón. At 11.5km turn R sp Sierra Natura - gd rd surface but narr & some steep, tight hairpin bends (owners arrange convoys on request). Fr E on N340 exit junc 18 (do not take junc 14). Sm, pt sl, pt shd; wc; chem disp; baby facs; sauna; shwrs inc; el pnts (10A) €5.20; lndry rm; shop & 12 km; rest; snacks; bar; playgrnd; pool; 10% statics; dogs €4.55; phone; poss cr; Eng spkn; adv bkg; quiet; red long stay. "Tranquil, family-run site in remote area; unusual architecture; stunning mountain scenery; nature walks on site; excel pool & rest complex." ♦ 1 Mar-30 Oct. € 19.16   2011*

⊞ **MOJACAR** *4G1* (3.5km S Coastal) *37.12656, -1.83250* **Camping El Cantal di Mojácar, Ctra Garrucha-Carboneras, 04638 Mojácar (Almería) [950-47 82 04; fax 950-47 83 34]** Fr N on coast rd AL5105, site on R 800m after Parador, opp 25km sp.Or exit A7 junc 520 sp Mojácar Parador. Foll Parador sps by-passing Mojácar, to site. Med, hdstg, pt shd; wc; chem disp; mv service pnt; shwrs inc; el pnts (15A) €3; gas; lndry rm; shop 500m; tradsmn; shops adj; rest; snacks; bar adj; BBQ; sand beach adj; 5% statics; dogs; phone; bus; poss v cr; some rd noise; red long stay/low ssn; CCI. "Pitches quite lge, not mkd; lge o'fits rec use pitches at front of site; busy site." ♦ € 22.20   2009*

⊞ **MOJACAR** *4G1* (9km S Rural) *37.06536, -1.86864* **Camping Sopalmo, Sopalmo, 04638 Mojácar (Almería) [950-47 84 13; fax 950-47 30 02; info@campingsopalmoelcortijillo.com; www.campingsopalmoelcortijillo.com]** Exit A7/E15 at junc 520 onto AL6111 sp Mojácar. Fr Mojácar turn S onto A1203/AL5105 dir Carboneras, site sp on W of rd about 1km S of El Agua del Medio. Sm, mkd pitch, hdstg, pt shd; wc; chem disp (wc); shwrs; el pnts (15A) €3; gas; lndtte; sm shop (high ssn); tradsmn; rest; snacks 6km; bar; shgl beach 1.7km; internet; 10% statics; dogs €1; Eng spkn; adv bkg; some rd noise; ccard not acc; red low ssn; CCI. "Clean, pleasant, popular site; remote & peaceful; friendly owner; gd walking in National Park." ♦ € 19.70   2008*

⊞ **MOJACAR** *4G1* (4km SW Coastal) *37.08888, -1.85599* **Camping Cueva Negra, Camino Lotaza, 2, 04638 Mojácar (Almería) [950-47 58 55; fax 950-47 57 11; info@ campingcuevanegra.es; www.campingcuevanegra.es]** Leave N340/E15 at junc 520 for AL151 twd Mojácar Playa. Turn R onto coastal rd. Site 500m fr Hotel Marina on R. App rd diff lge o'fits.m'vans due grounding. Take care dip at site ent. Med, hdg/mkd pitch, all hdstg, terr, unshd; wc; chem disp; mv service pnt; shwrs inc; el pnts (22A) €3.30; gas; lndtte; shop; tradsmn; rest; snacks; bar; covrd pool; jacuzzi; sand beach adj; entmnt; TV; 5% statics; dogs €1.90; poss cr; adv bkg; quiet; red 30+ days; CCI. "Well-kept, beautifully laid-out site; clean san facs but some basic; pleasant atmosphere; gd touring base; facs stretched when site full." ♦ € 28.60
2011*

⊞ **MOJACAR** *4G1* (500m W Rural) *37.14083, -1.85916* **Camping El Quinto, Ctra Mojácar-Turre, 04638 Mojácar (Almería) [950-47 87 04; fax 950-47 21 48; camping elquinto@hotmail.com]** Fr A7/E15 exit 520 sp Turre & Mojácar. Site on R in approx 13km at bottom of Mojácar vill. Sm, hdg/mkd pitch, hdstg, pt shd; wc; chem disp; mv service pnt; shwrs inc; el pnts (6-10A) €3.21; gas; lndtte; shop; tradsmn; rest 3km; snacks; bar; BBQ; playgrnd; pool; sand beach 3km; dogs €1; phone; poss cr; Eng spkn; adv bkg; quiet but some rd noise; red long stay; CCI. "Neat, tidy site; mkt Wed; close National Park; excel beaches; metered 6A elect for long winter stay; popular in winter, poss cr & facs stretched; security barrier; poss mosquitoes; drinking water ltd to 5L a time." ♦ € 20.50   2011*

⊞ **MOJACAR** *4G1* (5km W Rural) *37.16394, -1.89361* **Canada Camping, 04639 Turre (Almería) [627-76 39 08 (mob); canadacampingmojacar@yahoo.co.uk]** Exit A7/E15 at junc 525 & foll sp Los Gallardos on N340A. After approx 3km turn L at sp Turre & Garrucha onto A370. In 3.5km slow down at green sp 'Kapunda' & turn R in 300m at sp 'Casa Bruns'. Site in 100m - bumpy access. Sm, hdg/mkd pitch, hdstg, unshd; wc; chem disp; mv service pnt; shwrs inc; el pnts (6A) €3.50; lndry rm; shop, rest, snacks, bar 4km; BBQ; no statics; dogs; adv bkg; quiet - some rd noise. "Gd, British-owned, adults-only site; friendly atmosphere; lge pitches; mountain views." € 10.00   2010*

⊞ **MONASTERIO DE RODILLA** *1B4* (800m NE Rural) *42.4604, -3.4581* **Camping Picon del Conde, Ctra N1 Madrid-Irún, Km 263, 09292 Monasterio de Rodilla (Burgos) [tel/fax 947-59 43 55; info@picondelconde.com; www.picondelconde.com]** Fr A1 join N1 at exit 2 or 3, site is on N1 at km marker 263 - behind motel. Easy to miss in heavy traff. Med, hdg/mkd pitch, shd; htd wc; chem disp; shwrs inc; el pnts (5A) €3.60; gas; lndry rm; shop; rest; snacks; bar; playgrnd; pool; 75% statics; dogs; phone; rd noise; ccard acc; CCI. "Ltd facs low ssn; poss migrant workers; caution el pnts; new grnd floor san facs 2009; site muddy in wet weather; friendly staff; 2 hrs drive fr Bilbao ferry; gd NH." ♦ € 14.60   2011*

SPAIN

⊞ **MONCOFA** *3D2* (2km E Coastal/Urban) *39.80861, -0.12805*
**Camping Monmar, Camino Serratelles s/n, 12593 Platja de
Moncófa (Castellón) [tel/fax 964-58 85 92; campingmonmar@
terra.es]** Exit 49 fr A7 or N340, foll sp Moncófa Platja passing
thro Moncófa & foll sp beach & tourist info thro 1-way system.
Site sp, adj Aqua Park. Lge, hdg pitch, hdstg, pt shd; htd wc;
chem disp; all serviced pitches; baby facs; shwrs inc; el pnts
(6A) inc; gas; lndtte (inc dryer); shop & 1km; tradsmn; rest;
snacks; bar; BBQ; playgrnd; pool; sand/shgl beach 200m;
entmnt; internet; 80% statics; no dogs; phone; bus 300m;
poss v cr; Eng spkn; adv bkg; quiet; ccard acc; red low ssn/
long stay; CCI. "Helpful owner & staff; rallies on site Dec-Apr;
mini-bus to stn & excursions; sunshades over pitches poss diff
high o'fits; excel clean, tidy site." ◆ € 26.00 SBS - W16
2010*

⊞ **MONCOFA** *3D2* (2km S Coastal) *39.78138, -0.14888*
**Camping Los Naranjos, Camino Cabres, Km 950.8, 12593
Moncófa (Castellón) [964-58 03 37; fax 964-76 62 37; info@
campinglosnaranjos.com]** Fr N340 at km post 950.8 turn L
at site sp, site 1km on R. Med, mkd pitch, hdstg, pt shd; wc;
chem disp; mv service pnt; shwrs inc; el pnts (10A) €5.35;
gas; lndtte; shop; tradsmn; rest; snacks; bar; playgrnd; pool;
paddling pool; beach 300m; games area; 20% statics; phone;
bus 1.5km; poss cr; adv bkg; quiet; red low ssn/long stay.
"Gd." € 26.96 2010*

MONTAGUT I OIX *3B3* (2km N Rural) *42.24538, 2.59943*
**Camping Montagut, Ctra de Sadernes, Km 2, 17855
Montagut I Oix (Gerona) [972-28 72 02; fax 972-28 72 01;
info@campingmontagut.com; www.campingmontagut.
com]** Exit AP7 junc 4 onto N260 W; join A26 & approx 10km
past Besalú at Sant Jaume turn R twd Montagut i Oix on
GIP5233. At end of vill turn L twd Sadernes on GIV5231, site
in 2km, sp. Med, hdg/mkd pitch, terr; shd; htd wc; chem
disp; mv service pnt; baby facs; shwrs inc; el pnts (6A) €3.90;
gas; lndtte; shop; tradsmn; rest (w/end); bar; playgrnd; pool;
paddling pool; no statics; quiet; red low ssn/long stay. "Excel,
peaceful, scenic site; high standard san facs; helpful staff; gd
walks nrby." ◆ 15 Mar-19 Oct. € 19.20 2008*

⊞ **MONTBLANC** *3C2* (1.5km NE Rural) *41.37743, 1.18511*
**Camping Montblanc Park, Ctra Prenafeta, Km 1.8, 43400
Montblanc (Tarragona) [977-86 25 44; fax 977-86 05 39;
info@montblancpark.com; www.montblancpark.com]**
Exit AP2 junc 9 sp Montblanc; foll sp Montblanc/Prenafeta/
TV2421; site on L on TV2421. Med, hdg pitch, pt sl, terr, pt
shd; htd wc; chem disp; mv service pnt; baby facs; shwrs inc;
el pnts (10A) inc; lndtte; shop; tradsmn; rest; snacks; bar;
BBQ; playgrnd; pool; paddling pool; wifi; entmnt; 50% statics;
dogs €4.50; phone; Eng spkn; adv bkg; ccard acc; red long
stay/snr citizens; CCI. "Excel site; excel facs; superb san facs;
lovely area; many static pitches only suitable for o'fits up to
7m; Cistercian monasteries nrby; conv NH Andorra." ◆
€ 34.50 2011*

MONTERROSO *1B2* (1km S Rural) *42.78720, -7.84414* **Camp
Municipal de Monterroso, A Pineda, 27569 Monterroso
(Lugo) [982-37 75 01; fax 982-37 74 16; aged@cinsl.es;
www.campingmonterroso.com]** Fr N540 turn W onto N640
to Monterroso. Fr town cent turn S on LU212. In 100m turn
sharp R then downhill for 1km; 2 sharp bends to site. Sm,
hdg/mkd pitch, pt sl, pt shd; wc; chem disp; shwrs inc;
el pnts (10A) €3.50; shop; tradsmn; rest, snacks, bar 500m;
pool adj; games area; internet; dogs; Eng spkn; quiet; CCI.
"Helpful staff; v quiet & ltd facs low ssn; vg." ◆ 1 Apr-30 Sep.
€ 15.00 2008*

MONTROIG see Cambrils *3C2*

⊞ **MORAIRA** *4F2* (1.5km SW Coastal) *38.68576, 0.11930*
**Camping Moraira, Camino del Paellero 50, 03724
Moraira-Teulada (Alicante) [965-74 52 49; fax 965-
74 53 15; campingmoraira@campingmoraira.com; www.
campingmoraira.com]** Fr A7 exit junc 63. Foll sp Teulada &
Moraira. Turn W 1km S of Moraira at km post 1.2, then site
500m up hill. Med, mkd pitch, hdstg, terr, shd; wc; chem
disp; 15% serviced pitches; baby facs; shwrs inc; el pnts (6A)
€4.28; lndtte (inc dryer); shop & 650m; tradsmn; rest; snacks;
bar; htd pool; sand beach 1km; internet; some statics; dogs;
phone; bus 500m; Eng spkn; adv bkg; poss noisy w/end high
ssn; red low ssn/long stay; ccard acc; CCI. "Coastal town with
harbour; modern site; gd touring base; ltd facs low ssn, san
facs stretched high ssn; pitching poss diff for lge o'fits due
trees & walls." ◆ € 31.00 2008*

I'll fill in a report
online and let the
Club know –
www.caravanclub.co.uk/
europereport

This is a wonderful site.

⊞ **MORATALLA** *4F1* (8km NW Rural) *38.21162, -1.94444*
**Camping La Puerta, Ctra del Canal, Paraje de la Puerta,
30440 Moratalla (Murcia) [tel/fax 968-73 00 08; info@
campinglapuerta.com; www.campinglapuerta.com]**
Fr Murcia take C415 dir Mula & Caravaca. Foll sp Moratalla &
site. Lge, mkd pitch, pt sl, terr, shd; htd wc; chem disp; shwrs
inc; el pnts (10A) €5.30; gas; lndtte (inc dryer); shop; tradsmn;
rest; snacks; bar; BBQ; playgrnd; pool; tennis; games area;
internet; TV rm; statics; dogs €1.20; adv bkg; quiet; ccard acc.
"Busy at w/ends." ◆ € 18.80 (CChq acc) 2011*

⊞ **MORELLA** *3D2* (2km NE Rural) *40.62401, -0.09141* **Motor
Caravan Parking, 12300 Morella (Castellón)** Exit N232 at sp
(m'van emptying). Sm, hdstg, pt shd; chem disp; mv service
pnt; water; quiet. "Free of charge; stay up to 72 hrs; clean;
superb location; lge m'vans acc." 2009*

MOSTEIRO CERVANTES see Becerreá *1B2*

⊞ **MOTILLA DEL PALANCAR** *4E1* (10km NW Rural) *39.61241, -2.10185* **Camping Pantapino, Paraje de Hontanar, s/n, 16115 Olmedilla de Alarcón (Cuenca) [969-33 92 33 or 676-47 86 11 (mob); fax 969-33 92 44; pantapina@ hotmail.com; www.paralelo40.net/pantapino]** Fr cent of Motilla foll NIII; turn NW onto rd CM2100 at sp for Valverde de Júcar; site on L just bef 12km marker - rough app rd. Med, mkd pitch, pt sl, pt shd; wc; chem disp; mv service pnt; serviced pitches; baby facs; shwrs inc; el pnts (10A) €4; gas; lndtte; shop; rest, bar high ssn; BBQ; playgrnd; pool; tennis; games area; horseriding; cycle hire; 40% statics; dogs €1.50; adv bkg; quiet; ltd facs low ssn; ccard acc; 10% red CCI. "Clean, attractive site but tatty statics; gd size pitches; resident owners hospitable; poss clsd in winter - phone ahead to check; vg." ♦ € 15.50　　　　　2010*

⊞ **MOTRIL** *2H4* (12km SE Coastal) *36.70066, -3.44032* **Camping Don Cactus, N340, Km 343, 18730 Carchuna (Granada) [958-62 31 09; fax 958-62 42 94; camping@ doncactus.com; www.doncactus.com]** On N340 SE fr Motril 1km W of Calahonda. Foll site sp. Lge, hdg/mkd pitch, hdstg, shd; wc; chem disp; mv service pnt; shwrs; el pnts (5A) €4.50; gas; lndtte; supmkt; rest; snacks; bar; BBQ; playgrnd; pool; shgl beach adj; tennis; archery; golf 6km; wifi; entmnt; TV rm; 60% statics; dogs €2.50 (not acc Jul & Aug); poss cr; no adv bkg; quiet; ccard acc; red long stay/low ssn; CCI. "Many greenhouses around site (unobtrusive); some sm pitches not rec lge o'fits; clean san facs; gd pool & rest; helpful staff; popular winter long stay; gd NH." ♦ € 28.50 SBS - W11　　2010*

⊞ **MOTRIL** *2H4* (3km SW Urban/Coastal) *36.71833, -3.54616* **Camping Playa de Poniente de Motril, 18600 Motril (Granada) [958-82 03 03; fax 958-60 41 91; camplapo@ infonegocio.com]** Turn off coast rd N340 to port bef flyover; at rndabt take rd for Motril. Turn R in town, site sp. Lge, pt shd; htd wc; chem disp; mv service pnt; baby facs; shwrs; el pnts (6-10) €3.35; gas; lndtte; shop; supmkt 4km; rest, bar in ssn; beach adj; pool; playgrnd; golf; tennis; horseriding; cycle hire; 70% statics; dogs €1.50; bus; Eng spkn; adv bkg; ccard acc; red low ssn/long stay. "Well-appointed site but surrounded by blocks of flats; gd, clean facs; helpful recep; gd shop; access diff for lge o'fits; poss lge flying beetles; excel long stay winter." ♦ € 23.50　　　　2008*

⊞ **MUNDAKA** *3A1* (1km N Coastal) *43.4094, -2.7003* **Camping Portuondo, Ctra Amorebieta-Bermeo, Km 43, 48360 Mundaka (Bilbao) [946-87 77 01; fax 946-87 78 28; recepcion@campingportuondo.com; www. campingportuondo.com]** Leave E70 E of Bilbao onto B1631 to Bermeo. Keep on coast rd dir Mundaka, site 1km on L. Ess to app fr Bermeo due to steep ent. Do not drive past recep until booked in due steep access. Med, terr, pt shd; wc; shwrs inc; el pnts (6A) €4.20; lndtte; rest; snacks; bar; playgrnd; pool; paddling pool; beach 500m; 30% statics; site clsd end Jan-mid Feb; dogs; train 800m; poss v cr w/ends; adv bkg rec; ccard acc. "Clean, modern facs; pitches tight; popular with surfers; conv Bilbao by train; site suitable sm m'vans only." € 28.20　　　　　2010*

⊞ **MURCIA** *4F1* (10km SW Rural) *37.95444, -1.26166* **Camping La Paz, Ctra 340 Murcia-Granada, Km 321, 30835 Sangonera La Seca (Murcia) [968-89 39 29; fax 968-80 13 37; horepa_@hotmail.com]** Tourist complex La Paz off A7 on W of junc 647; site sp visible both dirs. Med, hdg/mkd pitch, hdstg, unshd; htd wc; chem disp; serviced pitches; shwrs inc; el pnts inc (poss rev pol); lndtte; sm shop adj; tradsmn; rest; snacks; bar; BBQ; playgrnd; pool; tennis; games area; TV; 95% statics; dogs; phone; cash machine; bus 600m; Eng spkn; adv bkg; rd noise; red long stay/low ssn; ccard acc; CCI. "Gd NH but v ltd number touring pitches - rec walking to find pitch." ♦ € 17.36　　　　2008*

MUROS *1B1* (500m W Coastal/Rural) *42.76176, -9.07365* **Camping San Francisco, Camino de Convento 21, 15291 Louro-Muros (La Coruña) [981-82 61 48; fax 981-57 19 16; campinglouro@yahoo.es; www.campinglouro.com]** Fr Muros cont on C550 coast rd for 3km to San Francisco vill. Site sp to R up narr rd. Med, mkd pitch, pt shd; htd wc; chem disp; mv service pnt; shwrs; el pnts (5-8A) inc; gas; lndtte; rest; snacks; bar; sand beach 200m; playgrnd; dogs; phone; bus 300m; Eng spkn; adv bkg; quiet; ccard acc; CCI. "Pleasant site in walled monastery garden; gd, clean facs; vg sm rest; sh walk to lovely beach; excel security; unspoilt area." ♦ 22 Jun-7 Sep. € 27.60　　　　2009*

MUROS *1B1* (7km W Coastal) *42.76100, 9.11100* **Camping Ancoradoiro, Ctra Corcubión-Muros, Km.7.2, 15250 Louro (La Coruña) [981-87 88 97; fax 981-87 85 50; wolfgang@ mundo-r.com; www.rc-ancoradoiro.com/camping]** Foll AC550 W fr Muros. Site on L (S), well sp. Immed inside ent arch, to thro gate on L. Med, hdg/mkd pitch, terr, pt shd; wc; chem disp; shwrs inc; el pnts (6-15A) €3.50; lndtte; shop adj; rest; snacks, bar adj; playgrnd; sand beach 500m; watersports; entmnt; no statics; no dogs; bus 500m; phone; poss cr; adv bkg; quiet; CCI. "Excel, well-run, well-kept site; superb friendly site on headland bet 2 sandy beaches; welcoming owner; excel rest; excel san facs; poss diff for lge o'fits; beautiful beaches; scenic area." 15 Mar-15 Sep. € 22.00　　　　　2011*

MUTRIKU see Deba *3A1*

⊞ **MUXIA** *1A1* (10km E Coastal) *43.1164, -9.1583* **Camping Playa Barreira Leis, Playa Berreira, Leis, 15124 Camariñas-Muxia (La Coruña) [tel/fax 981-73 03 04]** Fr Ponte do Porto turn L sp Muxia; foll camp sp. Site is 1st after Leis vill on R. Med, hdg/mkd pitch, terr, pt shd; wc; chem disp; shwrs inc; el pnts €3.50; lndtte; shop; rest; bar; BBQ; playgrnd; sand beach 100m; dogs €1; TV; quiet; ccard acc; CCI. "Beautiful situation on wooded hillside; dir acces to gd beach; ltd, poorly maintained facs low ssn; mkt in Muxia Thurs." € 15.80　　2008*

NAJERA *3B1* (500m S Urban) *42.41183, -2.73168* **Camping El Ruedo, San Julián 24, 26300 Nájera (La Rioja) [941-36 01 02]** Take Nájera town dirs off N120. In town turn L bef x-ing bdge. Site sp. Sm, pt shd; htd wc; chem disp; shwrs inc; el pnts (10-16A) €3 (rev pol & poss no earth); gas; lndtte; shop; rest; snacks; bar; playgrnd; pool 1km; entmnt; TV; phone; bus 200m; poss cr; adv bkg; quiet; ccard acc; CCI. "Pleasant site in quiet location, don't be put off by 1st impression of town; monastery worth visit, some pitches in former bullring." 1 Apr-10 Sep. € 19.00　　　2011*

⊞ **NAVAJAS** *3D2* (1km W Rural) *39.87489, -0.51034* **Camping Altomira, Carretera, CV-213 Navajas Km. 1, E-12470 Navajas (Castellón)** [964-71 32 11; fax 964-71 35 12; reservas@campingaltomira.com; www.campingaltomira.com] Exit A23/N234 at junc 33 to rndabt & take CV214 dir Navajas. In approx 2km turn L onto CV213, site on L just past R turn into vill, sp. Med, hdstg, terr, pt shd; htd wc; chem disp; mv service pnt; serviced pitches; baby facs; shwrs; el pnts (3-6A) €3.80; gas; lndtte (inc dryer); shop; tradsmn; rest; snacks; bar; BBQ; playgrnd; pool; paddling pool; tennis; cycle hire; wifi; TV; 70% statics; dogs; phone; bus 500m; adv bkg; poss noisy w/end & public hols; ccard acc; red low ssn/long stay/CCI. "Friendly welcome; panoramic views fr upper level (steep approach) but not rec for lge o'fits due tight bends & ramped access/kerb to some pitches; gd birdwatching, walking, cycling; excel san facs; some sm pitches poss diff for lge o'fits without motor mover; poss clsd low ssn - phone ahead to check; useful NH & longer; excel." ♦ € 22.10 (CChq acc) 2011*

NAVALAFUENTE see Cabrera, La *1D4*

NAVARREDONDA DE GREDOS see Hoyos del Espino *1D3*

NAVARRETE see Logroño *3B1*

⊞ **NEGRAS, LAS** *4G1* (1km N Coastal) *36.87243, -2.00674* **Camping Náutico La Caleta, Parque Natural Cabo de Gata, 04116 Las Negras (Almería)** [tel/fax 950-52 52 37; campinglacaleta@gmail.com] Exit N344 at km stone 487 twd Las Negras. Site sp at ent to vill on R. Med, hdg pitch, hdstg, shd; wc; chem disp; shwrs inc; el pnts (10A) inc; gas; lndtte; shop & 1km; tradsmn; rest; snacks; bar; playgrnd; pool (high ssn); sand/shgl beach adj; cycle hire; dogs €3.20; phone; bus 300m; poss cr; quiet; red long ssn/low ssn; CCI. "Lge o'fits need care on steep app rd; vans over 2.50m take care sun shades on pitches; gd walking area; lovely site in lovely area." ♦ € 30.80 2010*

⊞ **NERJA** *2H4* (4km E Rural) *36.76035, -3.83490* **Nerja Camping, Ctra Vieja Almeria, Km 296.5, Camp de Maro, 29787 Nerja (Málaga)** [952-52 97 14; fax 952-52 96 96; nerjacamping5@hotmail.com] On N340, cont past sp on L for 200m around RH corner, bef turning round over broken white line. Foll partly surfaced rd to site on hillside. Fr Almuñécar on N340, site on R approx 20km. Med, pt sl, terr, pt shd; wc; chem disp; shwrs inc; el pnts (5A) €3.75 (check earth); gas; lndry rm; shops; tradsmn; rest; snacks; bar; playgrnd; sm pool; sand beach 2km; cycle hire; site clsd Oct; Eng spkn; adv bkg rec; rd noise; red long stay/low ssn/CCI. "5 mins to Nerja caves; mkt Tue; annual carnival 15 May; diff access lge o'fits; gd horseriding; site rds steep but gd surface; gd views; friendly owners." ♦ € 23.80 2011*

⊞ **NIJAR** *4G1* (23km SE Coastal) *36.80298, -2.07768* **Camping Los Escullos San José, Paraje de los Escullos s/n, 04118 Los Escullos (Almería)** [950-38 98 11; fax 950-38 98 10; info@ losescullossanjose.com; www.losescullossanjose.com] Fr E on E15/A7 exit 479 sp San Isidro; fr W exit junc 471 sp San José. Foll sp San José on AL3108 & after passing La Boca de los Frailes turn L onto AL4200 sp Los Escullos & site. After 3km turn R to site, ent on R in 1km - take care unmarked speed bumps. Lge, mkd pitch, hdstg, pt sl, shd; wc; chem disp; mv service pnt; baby facs; sauna; private san facs avail; shwrs inc; el pnts (10A) €5.10; gas; lndtte (inc dryer); shop; rest; snacks; bar; playgrnd; pool; beach 700m; watersports; diving; tennis; cycle hire; fitness rm; wifi; entmnt; TV rm; 40% statics; dogs €2.60; Eng spkn; adv bkg; ccard acc; red long stay/CCI. "Well-run, rustic, attractive site in National Park; many secluded beaches & walks; excel for watersports; vg pool & rest; clean facs; helpful staff; pitches poss flood in heavy rain." ♦ € 30.10 (CChq acc) 2010*

We can fill in site report forms on the Club's website – www.caravanclub.co.uk/ europereport

⊞ **NOIA** *1B2* (5km SW Coastal) *42.77198, -8.93761* **Camping Punta Batuda, Playa Hornanda, 15970 Porto do Son (La Coruña)** [981-76 65 42; camping@puntabatuda.com; www.puntabatuda.com] Fr Santiago take C543 twd Noia, then AC550 5km SW to Porto do Son. Site on R approx 1km after Boa. Lge, mkd pitch, terr, pt shd; htd wc; chem disp; shwrs inc; el pnts (3A) €3.74 (poss rev pol); gas; lndtte; shop; rest w/end only; snacks; bar; tradsmn; playgrnd; htd pool w/end only; sand beach adj; tennis; 50% statics; some Eng spkn; adv bkg; quiet; red long stay/low ssn; CCI. "Wonderful views; exposed to elements & poss windy; ltd facs low ssn; hot water to shwrs only; some pitches v steep &/or sm; gd facs for disabled; naturist beach 5km S." ♦ € 21.70 2011*

NOJA *1A4* (N Coastal) *43.48525, -3.53918* **Camping Los Molinos, Playa del Ris, 39180 Noja (Cantabria)** [942-63 04 26; fax 942-63 07 25; campinglosmolinos@campinglosmolinos.com; www.campinglosmolinos.com] Exit A8 at km 185. Go N & foll sp to Noja, then L at Playa del Ris. Site sp. V lge, hdg pitch, pt shd; wc; chem disp; mv service pnt; shwrs; baby facs; el pnts (3A) €3.60; gas; lndtte; shop; rest; snacks; bar; BBQ; playgrnd; pool; paddling pool; sand beach 500m; tennis; car wash; entmnt; 75% statics; dogs; poss cr; Eng spkn; adv bkg; ccard not acc; CCI. "Gd site; lovely beach; some noise fr karting circuit until late evening but noise levels strictly curtailed at midnight." ♦ 1 Jun-30 Sep. € 30.00 2010*

NOJA *1A4* (700m N Coastal) *43.49011, -3.53636* **Camping Playa Joyel, Playa del Ris, 39180 Noja (Cantabria) [942-63 00 81; fax 942-63 12 94; playajoyel@telefonica.net; www.playajoyel.com]** Fr Santander or Bilbao foll sp A8/E70 (toll-free). Approx 15km E of Solares exit m'way junc 185 at Beranga onto CA147 N twd Noja & coast. On o'skirts of Noja turn L sp Playa del Ris, (sm brown sp) foll rd approx 1.5km to rndabt, site sp to L, 500m fr rndabt. Fr Santander take S10 for approx 8km, then join A8/E70. V lge, mkd pitch, pt sl, pt shd; wc; chem disp; mv service pnt; baby facs; shwrs inc; el pnts (6A) inc; gas; lndtte (inc dryer); supmkt; tradsmn; rest; snacks; bar; BBQ (gas/charcoal); playgrnd; pool; paddling pool; jacuzzi; direct access to sand beach adj; windsurfing; sailing; tennis; hairdresser; car wash; cash dispenser; wifi; entmnt; games/TV rm; 15% statics; no dogs; no c'vans/m'vans over 8m high ssn; phone; recep 0800-2200; poss v cr w/end & high ssn; Eng spkn; adv bkg; ccard acc; quiet at night; red low ssn/snr citizens; CCI. "Well-organised site on sheltered bay; v busy high ssn; pleasant staff; gd, clean facs; superb pool & beach; some narr site rds with kerbs; midnight silence enforced; Wed mkt outside site; highly rec." ♦ 15 Apr-1 Oct. € 47.40 SBS - E05   2011*

⊞ **NOJA** *1A4* (1.9km NW Coastal) *43.49294, -3.5248* **Camping Playa de Ris, Paseo Maritimo 2, Avda de Ris, 39180 Noja [942-63 04 15]** Fr A8 take exit 185, at rdbt 3rd exit onto N634, at next rdbt take exit CA147, turn R CA452, turn R onto Barrio de Castillo San Pedro CA147, turn L onto Av de los Ris/CA451 turn R onto Paseo de Maritimo. Sm, pt shd; wc; chem disp (wc); shwr inc; lndry rm; shop 500m; snacks; bar; pool adj; sandy beach 200m; 50% statics; no dogs; poss cr; no twin-axles; CCI. "Conv for Santander ferry; poss tight for lge o'fits." € 24.34   2011*

NUEVALOS *3C1* (300m N Rural) *41.21846, -1.79211* **Camping Lago Park, Ctra De Alhama de Aragón a Cillas, Km 39, 50210 Nuévalos (Zaragoza) [tel/fax 976-84 90 38; info@campinglagopark.com; www.campinglagopark.com]** Fr E on A2/E90 exit junc 231 to Nuévalos, turn R sp Madrid. Site 1.5km on L when ent Nuévalos. Fr W exit junc 204, site well sp. Steep ent fr rd. V lge, hdg/mkd pitch, terr, pt shd; wc; chem disp; child/baby facs; shwrs inc; el pnts (10A) €5.40; gas; lndtte; shop 500m; rest, snacks high ssn; bar 500m; BBQ; playgrnd; pool; lake nrby; fishing; boating; games area; some statics; dogs free; bus 500m; poss cr; adv bkg; quiet but noisy w/end high ssn; red long stay; CCI. "Nr Monasterio de Piedra & Tranquera Lake; excel facs on top terr, but stretched high ssn & poss long, steepish walk; ltd facs low ssn; gd birdwatching; only site in area; gd." 1 Apr-30 Oct. € 27.50   2010*

⊞ **O GROVE** *1B2* (2km SW Coastal) *42.48305, -8.89083* Camping Moreiras, Reboredo 26, 36989 O Grove (Pontevedra) [986-73 16 91; campingmoreiras@campingmoreiras.com; www.campingmoreiras.com] Exit AP9 junc 119 W onto AG41 dir Sangenjo to Pedriñán; then foll sp N to O Grove, site sp, adj aquarium. Med, hdg/mkd pitch, shd; htd wc; chem disp; mv service pnt; baby facs; shwrs; el pnts €4.50; lndtte (inc dryer); shop; rest; snacks; bar; BBQ; playgrnd; sand beach adj; watersports; cycle hire; games area; golf 3km; wifi; some statics; no dogs; adv bkg; quiet. € 23.20   2010*

⊞ **OCHAGAVIA** *3A1* (500m S Rural) *42.90777, -1.08750* **Camping Osate, Ctra Salazar s/n, 31680 Ochagavia (Navarra) [tel/fax 948-89 01 84; info@campingsnavarra.com; www.campingsnavarra.com]** On N135 SE fr Auritz, turn L onto NA140 & cont for 24km bef turning L twd Ochagavia on NA140. Site sp in 2km on R, 500m bef vill. Lge, mkd pitch, pt shd; wc; chem disp; some serviced pitches; shwrs inc; el pnts (4A) €5.50; gas; lndtte; shop; rest high ssn; snacks; bar; BBQ; 50% statics; dogs €2; quiet but poss noise fr bar (open to public). "Attractive, remote vill; gd, well-maintained site; touring pitches under trees, sep fr statics; facs ltd & poss stretched high ssn; site clsd 3 Nov-15 Dec & rec phone ahead low ssn." € 19.40   2008*

There aren't many sites open at this time of year. We'd better phone ahead to check the one we're heading for is open.

⊞ **OLITE** *3B1* (2km S Rural) *42.48083, -1.67756* **Camping Ciudad de Olite, Ctra N115, Tafalla-Peralta, Km 2.3, 31390 Olite [948-74 10 14; fax 948-74 06 04; info@campingdeolite.com; www.campingdeolite.com]** Fr Pamplona S on AP15 exit 50 twd Olite. At rndabt turn L, then in 300m turn R onto NA115, site sp on L past Netto in 2km. Lge, mkd pitch, pt shd; wc; chem disp; mv service pnt; serviced pitches; baby facs; shwrs inc; el pnts (5A) inc; lndtte; shop 2km; rest; bar; playgrnd; htd pool (caps ess); tennis; entmnt; games area; 95% statics; dogs €1; poss cr; Eng spkn; phone; poss noisy at w/ends; ccard acc; CCI. "Close to m'way; ltd space & facs for tourers; site mostly used by Spanish for w/ends; site bleak in winter; narr site rds; Olite historic vill with fairytale castle; neglected facs (2009); ltd el pnts; 35 minute walk through fields to Olite; friendly owners." ♦ € 21.50   2011*

⊞ **OLIVA** *4E2* (2km E Coastal) *38.93250, -0.09750* **Camping Kiko Park, Calle Assagador de Carro 2, 46780 Playa de Oliva (València) [962-85 09 05; fax 962-85 43 20; kikopark@kikopark.com; www.kikopark.com]** Exit AP7/E15 junc 61; fr toll turn R at T-junc onto N332. Site sp on L (by iron monoliths) around seaboard side of town. Do not drive thro Oliva. Access poss diff on app rds due humps. Lge, hdg/mkd pitch, hdstg, shd; htd wc; chem disp; mv service pnt; some serviced pitches; baby facs; fam bthrm; shwrs inc; el pnts (16A) inc; gas; lndtte (inc dryer); supmkt; rest; snacks; bar; BBQ; playgrnd; 2 pools (1 covrd); paddling pool; whirlpool; spa; direct access to sand beach adj; watersports; windsurfing school; fishing; golf & horseriding nrby; tennis; games area; cycle hire; games rm; beauty centre; cash machine; wifi; entmnt; dogs €3; phone; pitch price variable (lge pitches avail); Eng spkn; adv bkg; quiet; ccard acc; red snr cititzens/long stay/low ssn; red CCI. "Gd, family-run site; v helpful staff; vg, clean san facs; excel rest in Michelin Guide; access tight to some pitches." ♦ € 50.10 SBS - E20   2011*

See advertisement on next page

OLIVA *4E2* (4km E Coastal) *38.90759, -0.06722* **Camping Azul,** 46780 Playa de Oliva (València) [962-85 41 06; fax 962-85 40 96; campingazul@ctv.es; www.campingazul.com] Exit A7/E15 junc 61; fr toll turn R at T-junc onto N332. Drive S thro Oliva, site sp, turn twds sea at km 209.8. Narr access rd. Med, mkd pitch, pt shd; wc; mv service pnt; shwrs inc; el pnts (10A) €3.20; gas; lndtte; shop; rest; bar; playgrnd; cycle hire; games area; golf 1km; wifi; entmnt; 20% statics; dogs free; no adv bkg; ccard acc; red long stay/low ssn. "Gd site but constant barking dogs fr adj houses; san facs tired." ◆ 1 Mar-1 Nov. € 25.60   2010*

I'll go online and tell the Club what we think of the campsites we've visited – www.caravanclub.co.uk/europereport

OLIVA *4E2* (3km SE Coastal) *38.90555, -0.06666* **Eurocamping, Ctra València-Oliva, Partida Rabdells s/n,** 46780 Playa de Oliva (València) [962-85 40 98; fax 962-85 17 53; info@eurocamping-es.com; www.eurocamping-es.com] Fr N exit AP7/E15 junc 61 onto N332 dir Alicante. Drive S thro Oliva & exit N332 km 209.9 sp 'urbanización'. At v lge hotel Oliva Nova Golf take 3rd exit at rndabt sp Oliva & foll camping sp to site. Fr S exit AP7 junc 62 onto N332 dir València, exit at km 209 sp 'urbanización', then as above. Lge, hdg/mkd pitch, hdstg, pt shd; htd wc; chem disp; mv service pnt; baby facs; shwrs inc; el pnts (6-10A) €4.64-6.70; gas; lndtte (inc dryer); shop; tradsmn; rest; snacks; bar; BBQ; playgrnd; sand beach adj; cycle hire; wifi; entmnt; TV; dogs €2.16; phone; poss cr; quiet but some noise fr adj bar; ccard acc; red long stay/low ssn/CCI. "Gd facs; busy, well-maintained, clean site adj housing development; helpful British owners; beautiful clean beach; gd rest; gd beach walks; cycle rte thro orange groves to town; pitch far fr recep if poss, night noise fr generators 1700-2400; recep clsd 1400-1600; highly rec." ◆ € 44.39 (CChq acc)   2010*

OLIVA *4E2* (3km S Coastal) *38.89444, -0.05361* **Camping Olé, Partida Aigua Morta s/n, 46780 Playa de Oliva** (València) [962-85 75 17; fax 962-85 75 16; campingole@hotmail.com; www.camping-ole.com] Exit AP7/E15 junc 61 onto N332 dir Valencia/Oliva. At km 209 (bef bdge) turn R sp 'Urbanización'. At 1st rndabt, take 2nd exit past golf club ent, then 1st exit at next rndabt, turn L sp ' Camping Olé' & others. Site down narr rd on L. Lge, hdg/mkd pitch, hdstg, pt shd; htd wc; chem disp; baby facs; shwrs inc; el pnts (6-10A) €5.42; gas; lndtte (inc dryer); supmkt; rest; snacks; bar; BBQ; playgrnd; pool; sand beach adj; fishing; tennis 600m; cycle hire; games rm; horseriding 2km; golf adj; wifi; entmnt; 15% statics; dogs €2.75; phone; Eng spkn; adv bkg; quiet; ccard acc; red long stay/low ssn; CCI. "Many sports & activities; direct access to beach; excel." ◆ € 28.54   2011*

See advertisement opposite

OLIVA *4E2* (5km S Coastal) *38.89503, -0.05422* **Camping Pepe, 46780 Playa de Oliva (València)** [962-85 75 19; fax 962-85 75 22; info@campingpepe.com; www.camping pepe.com] Exit A7 junc 61; fr toll turn R at T-junc onto N332 dir Valencia/Oliva. Drive S thro Oliva & in 3.5km at km 209, move R to service rd sp 'Urbanización'. Cont past service stn & across flyover. At 1st rndabt, take 2nd exit past golf club ent, then 1st exit at next rndabt, turn L sp ' Camping Pepe' & others. Site down narr rd on L. Lge, hdg/mkd pitch, hdstg, pt shd; wc; chem disp; baby facs; shwrs; el pnts (5A) €4.70; gas; lndtte; shop & 1km; tradmn; rest high ssn; snacks; bar; BBQ; playgrnd; sand beach adj; golf club nr; 30% statics; dogs €2; phone; poss cr; Eng spkn; quiet; red long stay/low ssn; CCI. "Well-managed, friendly, busy site; 5 san facs blocks; hot water avail all day for all needs; high kerb to some pitches; barrier locked at night; beautiful beach; vg for winter stay." ◆ € 25.50   2008*

⊞ **OLIVA** *4E2* (7km S Coastal) *38.88611, -0.03972* **Camping Rió Mar, Ctra N332, Km 207, 46780 Playa de Oliva (València) [962-85 40 97; fax 962-83 91 32; riomar@ campingriomar.com; www.campingriomar.com]** Exit A7/ E15 junc 61; fr toll turn R at T-junc onto N332. Drive S thro Oliva, site sp at km 207. Med, hdstg, shd; wc; chem disp; shwrs; el pnts (6A) €4.60; gas; lndtte; supmkt high ssn; rest, bar high ssn; playgrnd; sand beach adj; 20% statics; dogs €2.10; phone; poss cr; adv bkg; quiet; ccard acc; red snr citizens; CCI. "Friendly, clean, family-run site; facs in need of refurb; sm pitches but lge o'fits use sandy area bet site & beach; Fri mkt in Oliva." € 26.70   2008*

⊞ **OLOT** *3B3* (3km SE Rural) *42.15722, 2.51694* **Camping Fageda, Batet de la Serra, Ctra Olot-Santa Pau, Km 3.8, 17800 Olot (Gerona) [tel/fax 972-27 12 39; info@ campinglafageda.com; www.campinglafageda.com]** Fr Figueras exit A26 sp Olot E twd town cent. Pick up & foll so Santa Pau on rd GI524. Site in 3.8km. Med, mkd pitch, pt sl, terr, pt shd; htd wc; chem disp; shwrs inc; el pnts (10A) €3.50 (poss rev pol); gas; lndtte; shop; snacks; rest & bar high ssn; playgrnd; htd pool high ssn; wifi; 90% statics (sep area); dogs; phone; Eng spkn; adv bkg; quiet; ccard acc; CCI. "In beautiful area with extinct volcanoes & forests; isolated, pretty site; few visitors low ssn; friendly, helpful staff; diff access to water pnts for m'vans." ♦ € 21.05   2011*

ORGANYA *3B2* (500m NW Rural) *42.21527, 1.33222* **Camping Organyà, Calle Piscines s/n, Partida Lloredes, 25794 Organyà (Lleida) [973-38 20 39; fax 973-38 35 36]** Site sp to E of C14 adj sports cent/football pitch. Sharp rise off rd & narr access, not rec for lge o'fits. Med, pt shd; wc; shwrs; el pnts (3A) €4.30; shop, rest 1km; bar; playgrnd; pools adj; tennis; paragliding tuition avail; mainly statics; dogs €2; phone; some rd noise; CCI. "Excel mountain scenery & interesting vill; gd, clean san facs; pleasant pools adj; NH only - phone ahead low ssn to check site open." Holy Week & 22 Jun-11 Sep. € 17.65   2008*

⊞ **ORGIVA** *2G4* (2km S Rural) *36.88852, -3.41837* **Camping Órgiva, Ctra A348, Km 18.9, 18400 Órgiva (Granada) [tel/ fax 958-78 43 07; campingorgiva@descubrelaalpujarra. com; www.descubrelaalpujarra.com]** Fr N or S on Granada-Motril rd suggest avoid A348 via Lanjarón (narr & congested). Fr N323/A44 turn E nr km 179, 1km S of lge dam sp Vélez de Benaudalla, over multi-arch bdge, turn L sp Órgiva. Foll rd (easy climb) turn L after sh tunnel over rv bdge; site 2nd building on R. Sm, pt sl, pt shd; wc; chem disp; serviced pitches; baby facs; shwrs inc; el pnts (10A) €3.82 (rev pol); gas; lndtte; supmkt 2km; rest; snacks; bar; playgrnd; pool; shgl beach 30km; bus 2km; adv bkg; ccard acc; some Eng spkn; red low ssn/long stay; ccard acc; red long stay/CCI. "Immac san facs; excel, friendly site; some sm pitches; vg value rest open all yr; magnificent scenery; gd base for mountains & coast; Thurs mkt in town; fiesta 27 Sep-1 Oct; pleasant walk thro orange & almond groves to vill; loyalty discounts & gd red for longer stays." ♦ € 18.80   2011*

⊞ **ORGIVA** *2G4* (2km NW Rural) *36.90420, -3.43880* **Camping Puerta de la Alpujarra, Ctra Lanjarón-Órgiva (Las Barreras), 18418 Órgiva (Granada) [tel/fax 958-78 44 50; puertalpujarra@yahoo.es; www.campingpuertadela alpujarra.com]** Fr Órgiva take A348 to Lanjarón. Site on L in 2km. Lanjarón poss diff for long o'fits. Med, mkd pitch, hdstg, terr, pt shd; wc; chem disp; mv service pnt; shwrs inc; el pnts (16A) €3.50; gas 2km; lndtte; shop; rest; bar; playgrnd; pool, paddling pool high ssn; entmnt; few statics; dogs free; phone; bus adj; poss cr; Eng spkn; adv bkg; quiet; ccard acc; 10% red 7+ days. "Scenic area with gd views fr site; steepish access to pitches; excel walking; ltd facs & staff low ssn." ♦ € 30.00   2010*

ORIHUELA DEL TREMEDAL *3D1* (1km S Rural) *40.54784, -1.65095* **Camping Caimodorro, Camino Fuente de los Colladillos s/n, 44366 Orihuela del Tremedal (Teruel) [978-71 43 55 or 686-92 21 53 (mob); campingcaimodorro@ gmail.com; www.campingcaimodorro.com]** Fr Albarracin on A1512 head twd Orihuela. Turn R twd vill & R after petrol stn, sp. Sm, unshd; wc; shwrs; el pnts €3.30; lndtte (inc dryer); shop; snacks; bar; pool; paddling pool; wifi; dogs; some statics; phone; bus 600m; Eng spkn; ccard acc. "Elevated, breezy situation o'looking mountain vill; lovely scenery; gd touring base; friendly owner; v quiet low ssn." 1 Apr-31 Oct. € 13.40   2009*

SPAIN

ORINON

ORINON *1A4* (2km E Coastal) *43.40361, -3.31027* **Camping Playa Arenillas**, Ctra Santander-Bilbao, Km 64, 39798 Islares (Cantabria) [tel/fax 942-86 31 52 or 609-44-21-67 (mob); cueva@mundivia.es; www.campingplayaarenillas.com] Exit A8 at km 156 Islares. Turn W on N634. Site on R at W end of Islares. Steep ent & sharp turn into site, exit less steep. Lge, mkd pitch, pt shd; wc; chem disp; mv service pnt; baby facs; shwrs inc; el pnts (5A) €4.63 (poss no earth); gas; lndtte; shop; tradsmn; rest adj; snacks; bar; BBQ; playgrnd; sand beach 100m; horseriding; cycle hire; games area; TV; 40% statics; no dogs; phone; bus 500m; poss cr; adv bkg rec Jul/Aug; some rd noise; ccard acc; CCI. "Facs ltd low ssn & stretched in ssn; facs constantly cleaned; hot water to shwrs only; rec arr early for choice of own pitch; conv Guggenheim Museum; excel NH for Bilbao ferry." 1 Apr-30 Sep. € 24.21   2010*

ORINON *1A4* (500m NW Rural/Coastal) *43.39944, -3.32805* Camping Oriñón, 39797 Oriñón (Cantabria) [tel/fax 942-87 86 30; info@campingorinon.com; www.camping orinon.com] Exit A8/E70 at km 160 to Oriñón. Adj holiday vill. Med, mkd pitch, pt sl, unshd; wc; chem disp; mv service pnt; shwrs inc; el pnts (4A) €4; gas; lndtte (inc dryer); rest; snacks; bar; playgrnd; sand beach adj; internet; TV; 90% statics; dogs; phone; bus 1km; Eng spkn; quiet; red long stay. "Excel surfing beach adj; clean site; no hot water to wash basins; helpful staff; conv Bilbao ferry." ♦ Holy Week & 1 Jun-30 Sep. € 20.00   2009*

ORIO see Zarautz *3A1*

OROPESA *3D2* (3km NE Coastal) *40.12786, 0.16088* **Camping Torre La Sal 1**, Camí L'Atall s/n, 12595 Ribera de Cabanes (Castellón) [964-31 95 96; fax 964-31 96 29; info@ campingtorrelasal.com; www.campingtorrelasal.com] Leave AP7 at exit 44 or 45 & take N340 twd Tarragona. Foll camp sp fr km 1000.1 stone. Do not confuse with Torre La Sal 2 or Torre Maria. Lge, hdg/mkd pitch, hdstg, pt shd; htd wc; chem disp; mv service pnt; baby facs; shwrs inc; el pnts (10A) €4.20; gas; lndtte; shop adj; rest, snacks, bar; BBQ; playgrnd; htd, covrd pool; paddling pool; sand/shgl beach adj; tennis; games area; wifi; TV rm; 10% statics; dogs (except Jul/Aug); phone adj; bus 200m; poss cr; Eng spkn; adv bkg; quiet; ccard acc; red long stay/snr citizens; CCI. "Clean, well-maintained, peaceful site; elec metered for long stays; night security guard." ♦ € 24.00   2010*

OROPESA *3D2* (3.5km NE Coastal) *40.1275, 0.15972* **Camping Torre La Sal 2**, Cami L'Atall s/n, 12595 Ribera de Cabanes (Castellón) [964-31 95 67; fax 964-31 97 44; camping@torrelasal2.com; www.torrelasal2.com] Leave AP7 at exit 45 & take N340 twd Tarragona. Foll camp sp fr km 1000 stone. Site adj Torre La Sal 1. Lge, hdg/mkd pitch, hdstg, pt shd; htd wc; chem disp; sauna; serviced pitch; shwrs inc; el pnts (10A) €6.10; gas; lndtte; shop; tradsmn; supmkt adj & 1km; rest; snacks; bar; playgrnd; shgl beach adj; 4 pools (2 htd & covrd); tennis; games area; wifi; entmnt; library; wifi; TV rm; some statics; dogs free; Eng spkn; adv bkg; quiet; red long stay/low ssn/snr citizens; CCI. "Vg, clean, peaceful, well-run site; lger pitches nr pool; more mature c'vanners v welcome; many dogs; poss diff for lge o'fits & m'vans; excel rest; excel beach with dunes." ♦ € 31.05   2011*

OSSA DE MONTIEL *4E1* (10km SW Rural) *38.93717, -2.84744* **Camping Los Batanes**, Ctra Lagunas de Ruidera, Km 8, 02611 Ossa de Montiel (Albacete) [926-69 90 76; fax 926-69 91 71; camping@losbatanes.com; www.losbatanes. com] Fr Munera twd Ossa de Montiel on N430. In Ossa foll sp in vill to site in 10km. Fr Manzanares on N430 app to Ruidera, cross bdge; turn immed R alongside lagoon, camp at 12km. Lge, pt shd; htd wc; chem disp; mv service pnt; shwrs; el pnts (5A) €3.10; lndtte; shops 10km; tradsmn; rest 200m; snacks; bar; playgrnd; pool; paddling pool high ssn; lake sw adj; cycle hire; TV; 10% statics; dogs €2; phone; site clsd 28 Dec-2 Jan; Eng spkn; adv bkg; noisy at w/end; ccard acc; red CCI. "Lovely area of natural lakes; excel birdwatching & walking; friendly owners; low ssn phone to check open." ♦ € 23.90   2011*

OTURA see Granada *2G4*

PALAFRUGELL *3B3* (5km E Coastal) *41.9005, 3.1893* **Kim's Camping**, Calle Font d'en Xeco s/n, 17211 Llafranc (Gerona) [972-30 11 56; fax 972-61 08 94; info@campingkims.com; www.campingkims.com] Exit AP7 at junc 6 Gerona Nord if coming fr France, or junc 9 fr S dir Palamós. Foll sp for Palafrugell, Playa Llafranc. Site is 500m N of Llafranc. Lge, hdg/mkd pitch, hdstg, pl sl, terr, shd; wc; chem disp; baby facs; shwrs inc; el pnts (6A) inc; gas; lndtte; shop; rest; snacks; bar; BBQ (gas only); playgrnd; 2 pools; sand beach 500m; watersports; tennis 500m; games rm; games area; cycle hire 500m; golf 10km; wifi; entmnt; excursions; TV; 10% statics; dogs; phone; guarded; poss cr; Eng spkn; adv bkg; quiet; ccard acc; red low ssn/long stay; red CCI. "Excel, well-organised, friendly site; steep site rds & steps to rd to beach; discount in high ssn for stays over 1 wk; excel, modern san facs inc for disabled." ♦ 15 Apr-16 Oct. € 41.75   2011*

See advertisement

PALAFRUGELL *3B3* (5km SE Rural) *41.89694, 3.18250* **Camping La Siesta**, Chopitea 110, 17210 Calella de Palafrugell (Gerona) [972-61 51 16; fax 972-61 44 16; info@campinglasiesta.com; www.campingzodiac.com] Fr C66/C31 main rd Gerona-Palamós turn E at rndabt onto GI6546 & foll sp Calella - Avda del Mar. Site is 500m N of Calella dir Llafranc. V lge, mkd pitch, pt sl, pt shd; wc; chem disp; shwrs inc; el pnts (6A) inc; gas; lndtte (inc dryer); shops; rest; snacks; 2 bars; no BBQ; playgrnd; 2 lge pools; waterslide; beach 1.3km; tennis; horseriding; wifi; entmnt; 80% statics; no dogs; bus; site open w/ends Nov-March & clsd Xmas to 8 Jan; Eng spkn; adv bkg; noisy at w/end; red low ssn. "Excel beaches at Llafranc & Calella de Palafrugell; mkt at Palafrugell; many beaches & coves adj; narr, winding paths thro pines to pitches; most vans have to be manhandled onto pitches." ♦ Easter-31 Oct. € 52.70   2011*

188 ⊞Site open all year   Send in your site reports by mid September 2013

PALAFRUGELL *3B3* (5km S Coastal) *41.88831, 3.18013* **Camping Moby Dick, Carrer de la Costa Verda 16-28, 17210 Calella de Palafrugell (Gerona)** [972-61 43 07; fax 972-61 49 40; info@campingmobydick.com; www.campingmobydick.com] Fr Palafrugell foll sps to Calella. At rndabt just bef Calella turn R, then 4th L, site clearly sp on R. Med, hdstg, sl, terr, pt shd; wc; chem disp; mv service pnts; baby facs; shwrs inc; el pnts (6-10A); €4.05; lndtte; shop; supmkt 100m; rest 100m; snacks; bar; playgrnd; shgl beach 100m; TV; 15% statics; dogs €3.30; phone; bus 100m; poss cr; Eng spkn; adv bkg; quiet; ccard acc; CCI. ♦ 1 Apr-30 Sep. € 23.40   2009*

PALAMOS *3B3* (1km N Coastal) *41.85695, 3.13801* **Camping Internacional Palamós, Camí Cap de Planes s/n, 17230 Palamós (Gerona)** [972-31 47 36; fax 972-31 76 26; info@internacionalpalamos.com; www.internacionalpalamos.com] Fr N leave AP7 at junc 6 to Palamós on C66. Fr Palafrugell turn L 16m after o/head sp to Sant Feliu-Palamós at sm sp fr La Fosca & camp sites. Winding app thro La Fosca. Fr S, take exit 9 dir Sant Feliu & Lloret, then C65/C31 to Santa Christina-Palamós, then La Fosca. Lge, pt shd; wc (mainly cont); chem disp; mv service pnt; baby facs; serviced pitches; private bthrms avail; shwrs inc; el pnts; (5A) inc; lndtte; shop; rest; snacks; bar; playgrnd; pool; paddling pool; sand beach 300m; solarium; windsurfing, sailing & diving 1km; cycle hire; golf 15km; wifi; TV rm; car wash; 20% statics; phone; bus 600m; quiet. "Attractive site; superb san facs; some sm pitches on steep access rds - check bef pitching; highly rec; lovely area." ♦ 16 Apr-30 Nov. € 42.50 (CChq acc)   2011*

PALAMOS *3B3* (2km N Coastal) *41.87277, 3.15055* **Camping Benelux, Paratge Torre Mirona s/n, 17230 Palamós (Gerona)** [972-31 55 75; fax 972-60 19 01; cbenelux@cbenelux.com; www.cbenelux.com] Turn E off Palamós-La Bisbal rd (C66/C31) at junc 328. Site in 800m on minor metalled rd, twd sea at Playa del Castell. Lge, hdstg, pt sl, pt shd; wc; chem disp; mv service pnt; shwrs inc; el pnts (6A) €4.30; gas; lndtte; shop; tradsmn; supmkt; rest (w/end only low ssn); snacks; bar; playgrnd; pool; sand beach 1km; safe dep; car wash; currency exchange; TV; 50% statics; dogs; poss cr; Eng spkn; adv bkg; noisy at w/end; red low ssn/long stay; ccard acc; CCI. "In pine woods; many long stay British/Dutch; friendly owner; clean facs poss ltd low ssn; poss flooding in heavy rain; poss diff for disabled, rough ground." ♦ Easter-30 Sep. € 28.45   2008*

PALAMOS *3B3* (2km N Coastal) *41.86263, 3.14315* **Camping Caravanning Kings, Ctra de la Fosca, s/n 17230 Palamós (Gerona)** [972-31 75 11; fax 972-31 77 42; info@campingkings.com; www.campingkings.com] App Palamós on C66/C31 fr Gerona & Palafrugell, turn L immed after o'head sp Sant Felui-Palamós at sm sp La Fosca & campsites. Lge, pt sl, pt shd; wc; shwrs; el pnts (6A) inc; lndtte; supmkt; rest; bar; playgrnd; pool; spa; beach 200m; cycle hire; games rm; wifi; entmnt; dogs €2.70; adv bkg; quiet; ccard acc; red low ssn. "Upmarket recep building; helpful staff; clean modern san facs; super pool; gd walking & cycling; thoroughly rec; 2 Apr-18 Sep. € 48.40   2010*

PALAMOS *3B3* (3km N Coastal) *41.89194, 3.14388* **Camping Relax Ge, Barrio Roqueta s/n, 17253 Mont-Ràs (Gerona)** [972-30 15 49 or 972-31 42 06 (LS); fax 972-60 11 00; info@campingrelaxge.com; www.campingrelaxge.com] C31 Palafrugell-Palamós rd at km 38.7, site sp. Med, mkd pitch, pt shd; wc; chem disp; shwrs (5A) €3; gas; lndtte; shop; rest; snacks; bar; playgrnd; htd pool & paddling pool; sand beach 1km; 10% statics; dogs €2.50; adv bkg; quiet; ccard acc; CCI. "Friendly, family-run site; exceptional beaches; conv Gerona, Barcelona." 1 Jun-31 Aug. € 28.90   2008*

PALAMOS *3B3* (6.5km N Rural) *41.89166, 3.15583* **Camping Relax-Nat (Naturist), Barrio Roqueta s/n, 17253 Mont-Ràs (Gerona)** [972-30 08 18; fax 972-60 11 00; info@campingrelaxnat.com; www.campingrelaxnat.com] Exit C31 Palafrugell-Palamós rd at sp Mont-Ràs (exit 249), cross under carriageway to 2nd rndabt & take last exit. Lge, pt shd; wc; chem disp; shwrs; el pnts (2A) €3; lndtte; shop; rest; snacks; bar; playgrnd; sand beach 4km; pool; playgrnd; tennis; games area; entmnt; some statics; no dogs; adv bkg; quiet. "Naturist families & mixed groups min 2 people; diff pitch access for lge o'fits." ♦ 15 Mar-28 Sep. € 31.50   2008*

You could win a Sat Nav (see page 8)   *Last year of report   **189**

SPAIN

PALAMOS *3B3* (3km SW Coastal) *41.84598, 3.09460* **Camping Costa Brava, Avda Unió s/n, 17252 Sant Antoni de Calonge (Gerona) [tel/fax 972-65 02 22; campingcostabrava@ campingcostabrava.net; www.campingcostabrava.net]** Foll sp St Antoni de Calonge fr C31, site sp. Lge, mkd pitch, shd; wc; chem disp; baby facs; shwrs inc; el pnts (4A) €3.80; lndtte; shop adj; rest; snacks; bar; BBQ; playgrnd; pool & child pool; sand beach 300m; watersports; games rm; entmnt; car wash; dogs; phone; bus; poss cr; adv bkg; quiet; ccard acc. "Well-managed, family-run site; sm pitches; clean san facs; rec arr early high ssn to secure pitch; pleasant, helpful owners." ♦ 1 Jun-15 Sep. € 22.75   2011*

PALAMOS *3B3* (2.5km W Rural) *41.88194, 3.14083* **Camping Castell Park, Ctra C31 Palamós-Palafrugell, Km 328, 17253 Vall-Llobrega (Gerona) [tel/fax 972-31 52 63; info@ campingcastellpark.com; www.campingcastellpark.com]** Exit m'way at junc 6 & take C66/C31 to Palamós. Site on R sp after 40km marker. Lge, mkd pitch, terr, shd; wc (some cont); chem disp; baby facs; shwrs inc; el pnts (3A) inc; gas; lndtte; supmkt; rest; snacks; bar; BBQ; playgrnd; pool; paddling pool; sand beach 2.5km; cycle hire; golf 11km; games rm; internet; entmnt; TV rm; some statics; dogs; bus 700m; Eng spkn; adv bkg; quiet; red long stay/low ssn/snr citizens; CCI. "Pleasant, quiet family site with friendly atmosphere & gd welcome; rallies & single c'vanners welcome; c'van storage avail." ♦ 27 Mar-12 Sep. € 34.00   2009*

PALAMOS *3B3* (3km W Coastal) *41.84700, 3.09861* **Eurocamping, Avda de Catalunya 15, 17252 Sant Antoni de Calonge (Gerona) [972-65 08 79; fax 972-66 19 87; info@euro-camping.com; www.euro-camping.com]** Exit A7 junc 6 dir Palamós on C66 & Sant Feliu C31. Take exit Sant Antoni; on ent Sant Antoni turn R at 1st rndabt. Visible fr main rd at cent of Sant Antoni. V lge, hdg/mkd pitch, shd; wc; chem disp; mv service pnt; 20% serviced pitches; baby facs; shwrs inc; el pnts (5A) inc; lndtte; supmkt; rest; snacks; bar; BBQ; playgrnd; 2 pools & paddling pool; waterpark; sand beach 300m; waterpark 5km; tennis; golf 7km; games area; games rm; fitness rm; doctor Jul & Aug; car wash; entmnt high ssn; wifi; TV rm; 15% statics; dogs €4; phone; Eng spkn; adv bkg; quiet; ccard acc; red long stay/low ssn. "Excel facs for families; lots to do in area; excel." ♦ 16 Apr-18 Sep. € 48.25   2010*

PALS *3B3* (6km NE Coastal) *41.98132, 3.20125* **Camping Inter Pals, Avda Mediterránea s/n, Km 45, 17256 Playa de Pals (Gerona) [972-63 61 79; fax 972-66 74 76; interpals@ interpals.com; www.interpals.com]** Exit A7 junc 6 dir Palamós onto C66. Turn N sp Pals & foll sp Playa/Platja de Pals, site clearly sp. Lge, pt sl, terr, shd; htd wc; chem disp; mv service pnt; baby facs; shwrs inc; el pnts (5-10A) inc; lndtte (inc dryer); supmkt nr; rest; snacks; bar; playgrnd; pool; paddling pool; sand beach 600m (naturist beach 1km); watersports; tennis; cycle hire; games area; golf 1km; wifi; entmnt; TV; 20% statics; dogs €3.50; phone; adv bkg; quiet; red snr citizens/CCI. "Lovely, well-maintained site in pine forest; poss diff lge o'fits - lge pitches at lower end of site; modern, well-maintained facs." ♦ 1 Apr-25 Sep. € 48.90 (CChq acc)   2010*

⊞ PALS *3B3* (1km E Rural) *41.95541, 3.15780* **Camping Resort Mas Patoxas Bungalow Park, Ctra Torroella-Palafrugell, Km 339, 17256 Pals (Gerona) [972-63 69 28; fax 972-66 73 49; info@campingmaspatoxas.com; www. campingmaspatoxas.com]** AP7 exit 6 onto C66 Palamós/ La Bisbal, turn L via Torrent to Pals. Turn R & site on R almost opp old town of Pals on rd to Torroella de Montgri. Or fr Palafrugell on C31 turn at km 339. Lge, mkd pitch, terr, shd; htd wc; 30% serviced pitches; chem disp; mv service pnt; baby facs; shwrs inc; el pnts (5A) inc; gas; lndtte; supmkt; tradsmn; rest; snacks; bar; playgrnd; pool; sand beach 4km; games area; entmnt; tennis; cycle hire; golf 4km; TV; dogs €3.60; phone; site clsd 19 Dec-13 Jan; recep clsd Monday low ssn; Eng spkn; adv bkg ess high ssn; quiet; red long stay/low ssn; gd security; ccard acc; CCI. "Excel." ♦ € 47.00   2008*

PALS *3B3* (4km E Rural) *41.98555, 3.18194* **Camping Cypsela, Rodors 7, 17256 Playa de Pals (Gerona) [972-66 76 96; fax 972-66 73 00; info@cypsela.com; www.cypsela.com]** Exit AP7 junc 6, rd C66 dir Palamós. 7km fr La Bisbal take dir Pals & foll sp Playa/Platja de Pals, site sp. V lge, hdg/ mkd pitch, hdstg, shd; wc; chem disp; mv service pnt; 25% serviced pitches; child/baby facs; private bthrms avail; shwrs inc; el pnts (6-10A) inc; gas; lndtte; supmkt; rest; snacks; bar; BBQ; playgrnd; pool; sand beach 1.5km; tennis; mini-golf & other sports; cycle hire; golf 1km; games rm; wifi; entmnt; TV rm; free bus to beach; 30% statics; no dogs; Eng spkn; adv bkg; ccard acc; red long stay/low ssn/ CCI. "Noise levels controlled after midnight; excel san facs; 4 grades of pitch/price (highest price shown); vg site." ♦ 14 May-15 Sep. € 58.12   2011*

See advertisement

⊞ PAMPLONA *3B1* (7km N Rural) *42.85776, -1.62250* **Camping Ezcaba, Ctra N121, Km 7, 31194 Eusa-Oricain (Navarre) [948-33 03 15; fax 948-33 13 16; info@camping ezcaba.com; www.campingezcaba.com]** Fr N leave AP15 onto NA30 (N ring rd) to N121A sp Francia/Iruña. Pass Arre & Oricáin, turn L foll site sp 500m on R dir Berriosuso. Site on R in 500m - fairly steep ent. Or fr S leave AP15 onto NA32 (E by-pass) to N121A sp Francia/Iruña, then as above. Med, mkd pitch, pt sl, pt shd; wc; shwrs inc; el pnts (10A) €4.70; gas; lndtte (inc dryer); shop; rest; snacks; bar; playgrnd; pool; horseriding; tennis; wifi; dogs €2.70; phone; bus 1km; poss cr; adv bkg; rd noise; red low ssn. "Helpful, friendly staff; sm pitches unsuitable lge o'fits & poss diff due trees, esp when site full; attractive setting; gd pool, bar & rest; ltd facs low ssn & poss long walk to san facs; in winter use as NH only; phone to check open low ssn; cycle track to Pamplona." ♦ € 22.20   2010*

⊞ PANCORBO *1B4* (3km NE Rural) *42.63305, -3.11138* **Camping El Desfiladero, Ctra Madrid-Irún, Km 305, 09280 Pancorbo (Burgos) [tel/fax 947-35 40 27; hceldesfiladero@ teleline.es]** Fr AP1/E5 exit junc 4 onto N1 dir Vitoria/Gasteiz, site on L in 2km at hostel. Med, hdg pitch, some hdstg, terr, pt shd; wc; chem disp; shwrs; el pnts (8A) €3.40; lndtte; shop 3km; rest; snacks; bar; playgrnd; pool; tennis; 25% statics; dogs; train 3km; some rd & rlwy noise; ccard acc; red CCI. "Access diff lge o'fits due steep ent; recep in hostel rest low ssn; friendly, helpful owner; facs tired; sh stay/NH only." ♦ € 16.00   2008*

PEDROSILLO EL RALO see Salamanca *1C3*

PELIGROS see Granada *2G4*

PENAFIEL *1C4* (2km SW Rural) *41.59538, -4.12811* **Camping Riberduero, Avda Polideportivo 51, 47300 Peñafiel** [tel/fax 983-88 16 37; camping@campingpenafiel.com; www.campingpenafiel.com] Fr Valladolid 56km or Aranda de Duero 38km on N122. In Peñafiel take VA223 dir Cuéllar, foll sp to sports cent/camping. Med, mkd pitch, hdstg, shd; htd wc; chem disp; mv service pnt; baby facs; fam bthrm; shwrs inc; el pnts (5A) €3.50; gas; lndtte; shop; rest; snacks; bar; playgrnd; pool; rv 1km; cycle hire; TV; 20% statics; dogs €1.50; phone; bus 1km; site open w/end only low ssn; poss cr; Eng spkn; adv bkg; quiet; ccard acc; 10% red 15 days. "Excel, well-kept site; interesting, historical area; ideal for wheelchair users." ♦ Holy Week & 1 Apr-30 Sep. € 18.60   2008*

PENASCOSA see Alcaraz *4F1*

⊞ **PENISCOLA** *3D2* (500m N Coastal) *40.37694, 0.39222* **Camping El Cid, Azagador de la Cruz s/n, 12598 Peñíscola (Castellón)** [964-48 03 80; fax 964-46 76 02; info@campingelcid.com; www.campingelcid.com] Exit A7 at junc 43. Take N340 sp València for sh distance, turn L sp Peñíscola. Approx 2km look for yellow sp to site. Narr site ent - rec loop o'fit rnd in rd & ent thro R-hand site of security barrier. Med, mkd pitch, shd; wc; chem disp; shwrs inc; el pnts (10A) €4.50; gas; lndtte; shop; supmkt; rest; snacks; bar; playgrnd; pool; paddling pool; sand beach 500m; 50% statics; poss cr; ccard acc; red long stay/low ssn; CCI. "Vg, well-run site; popular with Spanish families; friendly staff." € 27.00   2009*

⊞ **PENISCOLA** *3D2* (500m N Coastal) *40.36222, 0.39583* **Camping Ferrer, Avda Estación 27, 12598 Peñíscola (Castellón)** [964-48 92 23; fax 964-48 91 44; campingferrer@campingferrer.com; www.campingferrer.com] Exit AP7 onto CV141 twd Peñíscola, site sp on R, adj Consum supmkt. Med, hdstg, terr, pt shd; htd wc; chem disp; mv service pnt; baby facs; shwrs inc; el pnts (6A) €3; lndry rm; shop adj; rest; snacks; bar; BBQ; playgrnd; pool; sand beach 500m; games rm; wifi; entmnt; some statics; dogs; bus 700m; adv bkg; poss rd noise; cc acc; red long stay; CCI. "Conv NH; vg, family run site; level pitches but access poss diff due trees." € 22.00   2010*

⊞ **PENISCOLA** *3D2* (1km N Coastal) *40.37152, 0.40269*
Camping El Edén, Ctra CS501 Benicarló-Peñíscola Km 6, 12598 Peñíscola (Castellón) [964-48 05 62; fax 964-48 98 28; camping@camping-eden.com; www.camping-eden.com] Exit AP7 junc 43 onto N340 & CV141 dir Peñíscola. Take 3rd exit off rndabt on seafront, L at mini-rndabt, L after Hotel del Mar. Rec avoid sat nav rte across marshes fr Peñíscola. Lge, hdg/mkd pitch, pt shd; htd wc; chem disp; mv service pnt; baby facs; shwrs inc; el pnts (10A) inc; gas; lndtte (inc dryer); shop 300m; rest, snacks; bar; playgrnd; pool; paddling pool; sand/shgl beach adj; wifi; 40% statics; dogs €0.75; bus adj; cash dispenser; poss cr; no adv bkg; rd noise in ssn; ccard acc; red long stay/low ssn. "San facs refurbished & v clean; beach adj cleaned daily; gd security; excel pool; easy access to sandy/gravel pitches but many sm trees poss diff for awnings or high m'vans; poss vicious mosquitoes at dusk; easy walk/cycle to town; 4 diff sizes of pitch (some with tap, sink & drain) with different prices; ltd facs low ssn; excel." ♦ € 60.00   2011*

When we get home I'm going to post all these site report forms to the Club for next year's guide. The deadline's mid September 2013

⊞ **PENISCOLA** *3D2* (2km W) *40.37916, 0.38833* **Camping Los Pinos, Calle Abellars s/n, 12598 Peñíscola (Castellón)** [tel/fax 964-48 03 79; info@campinglospinos.com; www.campinglospinos.com] Exit A7 junc 43 or N340 sp Peñíscola. Site sp on L. Med, pt shd; wc; chem disp; mv service pnt; baby facs; shwrs; el pnts €5.62; gas; lndtte; shop; rest; snacks; bar; BBQ; playgrnd; pool; phone; bus fr site; red low ssn. "Narr site rds, lots of trees; poss diff access some pitches." € 22.67   2008*

⊞ **PENISCOLA** *3D2* (2km NW Rural) *40.40158, 0.38116* **Camping Spa Natura Resort, Partida Villarroyos s/n, Playa Montana, 12598 Peñíscola-Benicarló (Castellón)** [964-47 54 80; fax 964-78 50 51; info@spanaturaresort.com; www.spanaturaresort.com] Exit AP7 junc 43, within 50m of toll booths turn R immed then immed L & foll site sp twd Benicarló (NB R turn is on slip rd). Fr N340 take CV141 to Peñíscola. Cross m'way bdge & immed turn L; site sp. Med, mkd pitch, hdstg, shd; htd wc; chem disp; mv service pnt; serviced pitches; sauna; baby facs; shwrs inc; el pnts (6A) inc; gas; lndtte (inc dryer); tradsmn; rest; snacks; bar; BBQ area; playgrnd; pool; htd pool; waterslide; paddling pool; spa; wellness centre; jacuzzi; sand beach 2.5km; tennis; cycle hire; gym; games area; games rm; wifi; entmnt; TV rm; 50% statics; dogs €3 (free low ssn); twin-axles acc (rec check in adv); phone; bus 600m; c'van storage; car wash; Eng spkn; adv bkg; some rd noise; ccard acc; red low ssn/long stay/snr citizens/ CCI. "Vg site; helpful, enthusiastic staff; gd clean san facs; wide range of facilities; gd cycling." ♦ € 48.50 (CChq acc) SBS - E23   2011*

⊞ **PILAR DE LA HORADADA** *4F2* (19.5km) *37.87916, -0.76555* **Lo Monte Camping & Caravaning, Avenida Comunidada Valenciana No 157 CP 03190** [00 34 966 766 782; fax 00 34 966 746 536; info@campinglomonte-alicante.es; www.campinglomonte-alicante.es] Exit 770 of AP7 dir Pilar de la Horadada; take the 1st L. Med, mkd/hdg pitch; htd wc; chem disp; serviced pitches; baby facs; shwrs inc; el pnts (16A) €2.50; lndtte; shop; rest; bar; BBQ; playgrnd; htd, covrd pool; beach 1km; bike hire; gym/wellness centre; entmnt; wifi; dogs €2.50; adv bkg; ccard acc; CCI. "New site; superb facs; great location - lots of golf & gd for walking; rec." ♦ € 47.84   2011*

See advertisement below

PINEDA DE MAR see Calella *3C3*

PINEDA, LA see Salou *3C2*

SPAIN

PITRES 2G4 (500m SW Rural) 36.93178, -3.33268 **Camping El Balcón de Pitres**, Ctra Órgiva-Ugijar, Km 51, 18414 Pitres (Granada) [958-76 61 11; fax 958-80 44 53; info@balcondepitres.com; www.balcondepitres.com] S fr Granada on A44/E902, turn E onto A348 for 22km. At Órgiva take A4132 dir Trevélez to Pitres to site. Ask at rest in vill for dirs. Sm, terr, shd; wc; chem disp; el pnts (10A) €4.28; gas; lndtte; shop; rest; snacks; bar; playgrnd; pool; cycle hire; some statics; bus 600m; poss cr Aug; adv bkg; quiet; red long stay; ccard acc; CCI. "Site in unspoilt Alpujarras region of Sierra Nevada mountains; fine scenery & wildlife; site on steep hillside, poss diff lge o'fits; san facs at top of hill - own san facs saves climb." 1 Mar-31 Oct. € 32.10 (3 persons) 2011*

PLASENCIA 1D3 (4km NE Urban) 40.04348, -6.05751 **Camping La Chopera**, Ctra N110, Km 401.3, Valle del Jerte, 10600 Plasencia (Caceres) [tel/fax 927-41 66 60; lachopera@campinglachopera.com; www.campinglachopera.com] In Plasencia on N630 turn E on N110 sp Ávila & foll sp indus est & sp to site. Med, shd; wc; serviced pitches; chem disp; baby facs; shwrs inc; el pnts (6A) inc; gas; lndtte; shop; rest; bar; BBQ; playgrnd; pool; paddling pool; tennis; cycle hire; wifi; dogs; quiet but w/end disco; ccard acc; CCI. "Peaceful & spacious; much birdsong; conv Manfragüe National Park (breeding of black/Egyptian vultures, black storks, imperial eagles); excel pool & modern facs; helpful owners." ♦ 1 Mar-30 Sep. € 29.95 2011*

⊞ **PLASENCIA** 1D3 (10km SE Rural) 39.94361, -6.08444 **Camping Parque Natural Monfragüe**, Ctra Plasencia-Trujillo, Km 10, 10680 Malpartida de Plasencia (Cáceres) [tel/fax 927-45 92 33; contacto@campingmonfrague.com; www.campingmonfrague.com] Fr N on A66/N630 by-pass town, 5km S of town at flyover junc take EXA1 (EX108) sp Navalmoral de la Mata. In 6km turn R onto EX208 dir Trujillo, site on L in 5km. Med, hdg pitch, pt sl, terr, pt shd; htd wc; chem disp; mv service pnt; baby facs; shwrs inc; el pnts (5-15A) €4; gas; lndtte (inc dryer); shop; tradsmn; rest; snacks; bar; BBQ; playgrnd; pool high ssn; tennis; games area; archery; cycle hire; rambling; 4x4 off-rd; horseriding; wifi; TV rm; 10% statics; dogs; phone; Eng spkn; no adv bkg; quiet; ccard acc; red long stay/cash/CCI. "Friendly staff; vg, clean facs; gd rest; clean, tidy, busy site but poss dusty - hoses avail; 10km to National Park (birdwatching trips)however, many birds on site; excel year round base." ♦ € 16.40 (CChq acc) 2011*

PLAYA DE ARO 3B3 (2km N Coastal) 41.83116, 3.08366 **Camping Cala Gogo**, Avda Andorra 13, 17251 Calonge (Gerona) [972-65 15 64; fax 972-65 05 53; calagogo@calagogo.es; www.calagogo.es] Exit AP7 junc 6 dir Palamós/Sant Feliu. Fr Palamós take C253 coast rd S twd Sant Antoni, site on R 2km fr Playa de Aro, sp. Lge, pt sl, pt terr, pt shd; wc; chem disp; mv service pnt; serviced pitch; baby facs; shwrs inc; el pnts (10A) inc; gas; lndtte (inc dryer); supmkt; rest; bar; snacks; bar; BBQ; playgrnds; htd pool; paddling pool; sand beach adj; boat hire; diving school; games area; games rm; tennis; cycle hire; golf 4km; wifi; entmnt; TV; no dogs 3/7-21/8 (otherwise €2); Eng spkn; adv bkg; quiet; red long stay/low ssn. "Clean & recently upgraded san facs; rest/bar with terrace; site terraced into pinewood on steep hillside; excel family site." ♦ 16 Apr-18 Sep. € 52.00 2011*
See advertisement above

⊞ **PLAYA DE ARO** 3B3 (2km N Coastal) 41.83333, 3.08416 **Camping Internacional Calonge**, Avda d'Andorra s/n, Ctra 253, Km 47, 17251 Calonge (Gerona) [972-65 12 33 or 972-65 14 64; fax 972-65 25 07; info@intercalonge.com; www.intercalonge.com] Fr A7 exit junc 6 onto C66 dir La Bisbal, Palamós & Playa de Aro; 3km bef Palamós foll sp St Antoni de Calonge. At 2nd rndbt bear R onto C253 dir Sant Feliu, site on R in 3km. V lge, mkd pitch, terr, shd; htd wc; chem disp; mv service pnt; some serviced pitches; baby facs; shwrs inc; el pnts (5A) inc; gas; lndtte; supmkt; rest; snacks; bar; BBQ; playgrnd; 2 pools; paddling pool; solarium; sand/shgl beach adj; tennis; extensive sports facs; wifi; entmnt; TV rm; 30% statics; phone; dogs €4.20; Eng spkn; adv bkg; poss noisy high ssn; ccard acc; red low ssn/long stay; CCI. "On side of steep hill - parking poss diff at times; conv Dali Museum; Roman ruins; gd security; superb facs; excel site." ♦ € 49.35 2011*
See advertisement on next page

SPAIN

PLAYA DE ARO 3B3 (2km N Coastal) 41.83666, 3.08722 Camping Treumal, Ctra Playa de Aro/Palamós, C253, Km 47.5, 17250 Playa de Arro (Gerona) [972-65 10 95; fax 972-65 16 71; info@campingtreumal.com; www. campingtreumal.com] Exit m'way at junc 6, 7 or 9 dir Sant Feliu de Guixols to Playa de Aro; site is sp at km 47.5 fr C253 coast rd SW of Palamós. Lge, mkd pitch, terr, shd; wc; baby facs; shwrs inc; chem disp; mv service pnt; el pnts (10A) inc; gas; lndtte; supmkt; tradsmn; rest; snacks; bar; playgrnd; sm pool; sand beach adj; fishing; tennis 1km; games rm; sports facs; cycle hire; golf 5km; wifi; entmnt; 25% statics; no dogs; phone; car wash; Eng spkn; adv bkg; quiet; ccard acc; red low ssn; CCI. "Peaceful site in pine trees; excel san facs; manhandling poss req onto terr pitches; gd beach." ♦ 31 Mar-30 Sep. € 49.30   2011*

See advertisement opposite (below)

PLAYA DE ARO 3B3 (2km N Rural) 41.81116, 3.01821 Yelloh! Village Mas Sant Josep, Ctra Santa Cristina-Playa de Aro, Km 2, 17246 Santa Cristina de Aro (Gerona) [972-83 51 08; fax 972-83 70 18; info@campingmassantjosep.com; www.campingmassantjosep.com or www.yellohvillage. co.uk] Fr A7/E15 take exit 7 dir Sant Feliu de Guixols to Santa Christina town. Take old rd dir Playa de Aro, site in 2km. V lge, mkd pitch, shd; htd wc; chem disp; mv service pnt; baby facs; serviced pitches; sauna; shwrs inc; el pnts (10A) inc; gas; lndtte (inc dryer); shop; rest; snacks; bar; BBQ; playgrnd; lge pools; sand beach 3.5km; tennis; games rm; games area; mini-golf & assorted sports; cycle hire; entmnt; golf 4km; internet; TV rm; 60% statics; dogs €4; Eng spkn; adv bkg; quiet; ccard acc; red low ssn; CCI. "Generous pitches; excel." ♦ 15 Apr-11 Sep. € 47.00   2010*

PLAYA DE ARO 3B3 (1km S Coastal) 41.81416, 3.04444 Camping Valldaro, Carrer del Camí Vell 63, 17250 Playa de Aro (Gerona) [972-81 75 15; fax 972-81 66 62; info@ valldaro.com; www.valldaro.com] Exit A7 junc 7 onto C65 dir Sant Feliu. Turn L onto C31 for Playa de Aro thro Castillo de Aro & site on R, 1km fr Playa at km 4.2. V lge, pt shd; htd wc; chem disp; mv service pnt; baby facs; shwrs inc; el pnts (5A) inc; gas; lndtte (inc dryer); shop; rest; snacks; bar; playgrnd; 2 pools; paddling pool; waterslides; beach 1km; watersports; tennis; horseriding 2km; golf 3km; games area; cycle hire; wifi; entmnt; 50% statics; dogs €2.90; phone; extra for lger pitch; adv bkg; red long stay. "Excel family site; some lge pitches; many facs." ♦ 1 Apr-25 Sep. € 48.00 (CChq acc)   2010*

PLAYA DE ARO 3B3 (2km S Coastal) 41.8098, 3.0466 Camping Riembau, Calle Santiago Rusiñol s/n, 17250 Playa de Aro (Gerona) [972-81 71 23; fax 972-82 52 10; camping@ riembau.com; www.riembau.com] Fr Gerona take C250 thro Llagostera, turn for Playa de Aro. Fr Playa de Aro take C253 twd Sant Feliu. Site access rd 2km on R. V lge, pt shd; wc; chem disp; baby facs; shwrs inc; el pnts (5A) inc; gas; lndtte; rest; snacks; bar; shop; beach 800m; 2 pools (1 indoor); playgrnd; tennis; fitness cent; games area; games rm; entmnt; internet; 40% statics; phone; adv bkg; some rd noise. ♦ Easter-30 Sep. € 35.90   2011*

PLAYA DE ARO 3B3 (2km S Urban/Coastal) 41.80472, 3.06333 Camping Vall d'Or, Avda Verona-Teruel s/n, 17250 Playa de Aro (Gerona) [972-81 75 85; fax 972-67 44 95; valldor@ betsa.es; www.betsa.es] Exit A7 junc 7 onto C65 dir Sant Feliu de Guixols, then C31 to Playa de Aro. V lge, pt shd; wc; chem disp; shwrs inc; el pnts (5A) €4.15; gas; lndtte; shop; rest; bar; playgrnd; sand beach adj; TV; 50% statics; dogs; phone; poss cr; adv bkg. "Gd family site." Easter-2 Nov. € 31.80   2008*

PLAYA DE OLIVA see Oliva 4E2

PLAYA DE PALS see Pals 3B3

PLAYA DE PINEDO see Valencia 4E2

PLAYA DE VIDIAGO see Llanes 1A4

PLAYA TAMARIT see Tarragona 3C3

POBLA DE SEGUR, LA 3B2 (3km NE Rural) 42.2602, 0.9862 Camping Collegats, Ctra N260, Km 306, 25500 La Pobla de Segur (Lleida) [973-68 07 14; fax 973-68 14 02; camping@ collegats.com; www.collegats.com] Fr Tremp N to La Pobla on N260. Site sp in town at traff lts, turn R onto N260 dir Sort. Ent by hairpin bend. Last section of rd narr & rough. Med, mkd pitch, shd; wc; chem disp; shwrs; el pnts €5; gas; lndtte; shop & 4km; tradsmn; snacks; bar; BBQ; playgrnd; pool; games area; some statics (sep area); dogs; poss cr; Eng spkn; quiet; CCI. "Clean facs; site not suitable lge o'fits; twin-axle vans not acc; conv NH." ♦ 1 Apr-31 Oct. € 20.00   2011*

SPAIN

⊞ **POBOLEDA** *3C2* (SW Rural) *41.23298, 0.84305* **Camping Poboleda, Plaça Les Casetes s/n, 43376 Poboleda (Tarragona)** [tel/fax 977-82 71 97; poboleda@campingsonline.com; www.campingpoboleda.com] By-pass Reus W of Tarragona on T11/N420 then turn N onto C242 sp Les Borges del Camp. Go thro Alforja over Col d'Alforja & turn L onto T207 to Poboleda & foll camping sp in vill. Alternative road 50m west called Calle Major though steep on exit from site. Med, mkd pitch, terr, pt shd; htd wc; chem disp; baby facs; fam bthrm; el pnts (4A) inc; lndry rm; shop, rest, snacks, bar in vill; pool; lake sw 8km; tennis; wifi; TV; no statics; dogs; phone; Eng spkn; quiet; ccard acc; CCI. "In heart of welcoming vill in mountain setting; friendly, helpful owner; not suitable lge o'fits as access thro vill." ♦ € 32.67   2011*

POLA DE SOMIEDO *1A3* (250m E Rural) *43.09222, -6.25222* **Camping La Pomerada de Somiedo, 33840 Pola de Somiedo (Asturias)** [985-76 34 04; csomiedo@infonegocio. com] W fr Oviedo on A63, turn S onto AS15/AS227 to Augasmestas & Pola de Somiedo. Site adj Hotel Alba, sp fr vill. Route on steep, winding, mountain rd - suitable sm, powerful o'fits only. Sm, mkd pitch, pt shd; wc; chem disp; mv service pnt; shwrs inc; el pnts €4.20; shop, rest bar in vill; quiet. "Mountain views; nr national park." 1 Apr-31 Dec. € 19.00   2009*

⊞ **PONFERRADA** *1B3* (10km W Rural) *42.56160, 6.74590* **Camping El Bierzo, 24550 Villamartín de la Abadia (León)** [tel/fax 987-56 25 15; info@campingbierzo.com; www. campingbierzo.com] Exit A6 junc 399 dir Carracedelo; after rndabt turn onto NV1 & foll sp Villamartín. Bef ent Villamartín turn L & foll site sp. Med, pt shd; wc; chem disp; mv service pnt (ltd); shwrs inc; el pnts (3A) €3.78; shops 2km; rest; bar; playgrnd; no statics; dogs €1.73; phone; bus 1km; adv bkg; quiet; ccard not acc; CCI. "Attractive, rvside site in pleasant area; gd facs; friendly, helpful owner takes pride in his site; Roman & medieval attractions nr." ♦ € 18.36   2010*

PONT D'ARROS see Vielha *3B2*

⊞ **PONT DE BAR, EL** *3B3* (2.6km E Rural) *42.37458, 1.63687* **Camping Pont d'Ardaix, N260, Km 210, 25723 El Pont de Bar (Lleida)** [973-38 40 98; fax 973-38 41 15; pontdardaix@ clior.es; www.pontdardaix.com] On Seo de Urgel-Puigcerdà rd, N260, at rear of bar/rest Pont d'Ardaix. Med, terr, pt shd; wc; mv service pnt; shwrs inc; el pnts (3-5A) €5.10-7.10; gas; lndtte; shop & 4km; rest; bar; playgrnd; pool; 80% statics; dogs €5.30; phone; Eng spkn; quiet; CCI. "In pleasant valley on bank of Rv Segre; touring pitches on rv bank; site poss scruffy & unkempt low ssn; gd NH." ♦ € 20.40   2008*

PONT DE SUERT *3B2* (4km N Rural) *42.43083, 0.73861* **Camping Can Roig, Ctra De Boí, Km 0.5, 25520 Pont de Suert (Lleida)** [973-69 05 02; fax 973-69 12 06; info@ campingcanroig.com; www.campingcanroig.com] N of Pont de Suert on N230 turn NE onto L500 dir Caldes de Boí. Site in 1km. App narr for 100m. Med, mkd pitch, hdstg, pt sl, pt shd; wc; chem disp; shwrs inc; el pnts (5A) €3.75; gas; lndtte; shop & 3km; snacks; bar; playgrnd; paddling pool; 5% statics; dogs €1.95; adv bkg; quiet; ccard acc. "NH en rte S; beautiful valley." 1 Mar-31 Oct. € 15.60   2011*

⊞ **PONT DE SUERT** *3B2* (5.5km N Rural) *42.44833, 0.71027* **Camping Alta Ribagorça, Ctra Les Bordes s/n, Km 131, 25520 Pont de Suert (Lleida)** [973-69 05 21; fax 973-69 06 97; ana.uma@hotmail.com] Fr N on N230 site sp S of Vilaller on L. Sm, mkd pitch, terr, pt shd; htd wc; chem disp; shwrs inc; el pnts (5A) inc; lndtte; rest; bar; playgrnd; pool; 10% statics; dogs; Eng spkn; rd noise. "Fair NH." € 19.50   2009*

⊞ **PONT DE SUERT** *3B2* (16km NE Rural) *42.51900, 8.84600* **Camping Taüll, Ctra Taüll s/n, 25528 Taüll (Lleida)** [973 69 61 74; www.campingtaull.com] Fr Pont de Suert 3km N on N230 then NE on L500 dir Caldes de Boí. In 13km turn R into Taüll. Site sp on R. Sm, pt sl, terr, pt shd; htd wc; chem disp; baby facs; shwrs inc; el pnts €6; lndry rm; shop, rest, bar 300m; 30% statics; dogs €3; clsd 15 Oct-15 Nov; poss cr; quiet; CCI. "Excel facs; taxis into National Park avail; ltd touring pitches; suitable sm m'vans only." € 21.50
                    2011*

⊞ **PONT DE SUERT** *3B2* (5km NW Rural) *42.43944, 0.69860* **Camping Baliera, Ctra N260, Km 355.5, Castejón de Sos, 22523 Bonansa (Huesca)** [974-55 40 16; fax 974-55 40 99; info@baliera.com; www.baliera.com] N fr Pont de Suert on N230 turn L opp petrol stn onto N260 sp Castejón de Sos. In 1km turn L onto A1605 sp Bonansa, site on L immed over rv bdge. Site sp fr N230. Lge, mkd pitch, pt sl, terr, shd; htd wc; chem disp; mv service pnt; baby facs; shwrs inc; el pnts (5-10A) €5; gas; lndtte (inc dryer); shop; tradsmn; rest snacks; bar; BBQ; playgrnd; pool; paddling pool; rv fishing; lake sw 10km; cycle hire; horseriding 4km; golf 4km; weights rm; wifi; sat TV; 50% statics; dogs €3.80; phone; site clsd Nov & Xmas; poss cr; Eng spkn; quiet; ccard acc; red low ssn; CCI. "Excel, well-run, peaceful site in parkland setting; walking in summer, skiing in winter; excel cent for touring; conv Vielha tunnel; all facs up steps; part of site v sl; helpful owner proud of his site; clean facs, some riverside pitches." ♦ € 30.00 (CChq acc) 2011*

PONTEAREAS *1B2* (1.5km N Rural) **Camping A Freixa, 36866 Ribadetea (Pontevedra)** [986-64 02 99] On N120 fr Vigo & Porriño, turn L at fountain bef bdge at ent to Ponteareas. In 1.5km at tall chimney on L, turn R & site in 200m adj Rv Tea. Med, sl, pt shd; wc; shwrs; el pnts €3.60; lndtte; shop; rest; bar; playgrnd; sand beach & rv sw; tennis; phone; bus 700m; quiet. Holy Week & 1 Jul-30 Aug. € 19.10 2008*

PORT DE LA SELVA, EL *3B3* (1km N Coastal) **Camping L'Arola, Ctra. Llança-El Port de la Selva, 17489 El Port de la Selva (Gerona)** [972-38 70 05; fax 972-12 60 81] Off N11 at Figueras, sp to Llançà on N260. In 20km turn R to El Port de la Selva. Site on L (N side of coast rd) bef town. Sm, hdstg, unshd; wc; chem disp; shwrs; el pnts (10A) €5; lndry rm; shops 1km; tradsmn; rest; snacks; bar; shgl beach adj; 5% statics; dogs €3.21; bus; poss cr; adv bkg; ccard acc; CCI. "Nr sm, pleasant town with gd shops, rests, harbour, amusements for all ages; scenic beauty; v friendly owner." ♦ 1 Jun-30 Sep. € 21.50 2010*

PORT DE LA SELVA, EL *3B3* (2km N Coastal) *42.34222, 3.18333* **Camping Port de la Vall, Ctra Port de Llançà, 17489 El Port de la Selva (Gerona)** [972-38 71 86; fax 972-12 63 08; portdelavall@terra.es] On coast rd fr French border at Llançà take GI612 twd El Port de la Selva. Site on L, easily seen. Lge, pt shd; wc; shwrs; el pnts (3-5A) €5.65; gas; lndtte; shop; rest; snacks; bar; playgrnd; shgl beach adj; internet; some statics; dogs €2.95; phone; poss cr; adv bkg; poss noisy; ccard acc; red low ssn. "Easy 1/2 hr walk to harbour; gd site; sm pitches & low branches poss diff - check bef siting." 1 Mar-15 Oct. € 43.00 (4 persons) 2011*

PORT DE LA SELVA, EL *3B3* (1km S Coastal) *42.32641, 3.20480* **Camping Port de la Selva, Ctra Cadaqués s/n, Km 1, 17489 El Port de la Selva (Gerona)** [972-38 72 87 or 972-38 73 86; info@campingselva.com; www.campingselva.com] Exit A7 junc 3 or 4 onto N260 to Llança, then take GI 612 to El Port de la Selva. On ent town turn R twd Cadaqués, site in R in 1km. Med, mkd pitch, pt shd; wc; chem disp (wc); shwrs inc; el pnts (4A) inc (poss no earth); lndtte; shop & 1km; rest, snacks, bar 1km; playgrnd; pool; sand/shgl beach 1km; games area; TV; 25% statics; dogs €2.50; poss cr; adv bkg; quiet; ccard not acc; red low ssn; CCI. "Excel for coastal & hill walking; well-run site; gd, clean facs; gd beach; pleasant, attractive vill; poss diff for lge m'vans due low branches." 1 Jun-15 Sep. € 37.00 2010*

POTES *1A4* (1km W Rural) *43.15527, -4.63694* **Camping La Viorna, Ctra Santo Toribio, Km 1, Mieses, 39570 Potes (Cantabria)** [942-73 20 21; fax 942-73 21 01; info@ campinglaviorna.com; www.campinglaviorna.com] Exit N634 at junc 272 onto N621 dir Panes & Potes - narr, winding rd (passable for c'vans). Fr Potes take rd to Fuente Dé sp Espinama; in 1km turn L sp Toribio. Site on R in 1km, sp fr Potes. Med, mkd pitch, terr, pt shd; htd wc; chem disp; mv service pnt; baby facs; shwrs inc; el pnts (6A) €3.40 (poss rev pol); lndtte (inc dryer); shop & 2km; tradsmn; rest; snacks; bar; BBQ; playgrnd; pool high ssn; paddling pool; cycle hire; wifi; bus 1km; poss cr; Eng spkn; adv bkg; quiet; ccard acc; CCI; "Lovely views; gd walks; friendly, family-run, clean, tidy site; gd pool; ideal Picos de Europa; conv cable car, 4x4 tours, trekking; mkt on Mon; festival mid-Sep v noisy; some pitches diff in wet & diff lge o'fits; excel." ♦ 1 Apr-31 Oct. € 21.70 2010*

POTES *1A4* (3km W Rural) *43.15742, -4.65617* **Camping La Isla-Picos de Europa, Ctra Potes-Fuente Dé, 39586 Turieno (Cantabria)** [tel/fax 942-73 08 96; campicoseuropa@ terra.es; www.liebanaypicosdeeuropa.com] Take N521 W fr Potes twd Espinama, site on R in 3km thro vill of Turieno (app Potes fr N). Med, mkd pitch, pt sl, shd; wc; chem disp; mv service pnt; shwrs inc; el pnts (6A) €3.60 (poss rev pol); gas; lndtte; shop; tradsmn; rest; bar; BBQ; playgrnd; pool; walking; horseriding; cycling; 4x4 touring; hang-gliding; mountain treks in area; wifi; some statics; phone; poss cr; Eng spkn; adv bkg; poss noisy high ssn; ccard acc; red long stay; CCI. "Delightful, family-run site; friendly, helpful owners; gd san facs; conv cable car & mountain walks (map fr recep); many trees & low branches; rec early am departure to avoid coaches on gorge rd; highly rec." Easter-31 Oct. € 20.50 2010*

POTES *1A4* (5km W Rural) *43.15527, -4.68333* **Camping San Pelayo, Ruta Potes-Fuente Dé, Km 5, 39587 San Pelayo (Cantabria)** [tel/fax 942-73 30 87; info@campingsanpelayo.com; www.campingsanpelayo.com] Take CA185 W fr Potes twd Espinama, site on R in 5km, 2km past Camping La Isla. Med, mkd pitch, pt sl, pt shd; wc; chem disp; shwrs inc; el pnts (6A) inc; lndtte (inc dryer); shop; rest; snacks; bar; playgrnd; pool; paddling pool; cycle hire; games rm; wifi; TV; bus; poss cr; adv bkg; quiet, but noise fr bar; ccard acc high ssn; red long stay; CCI. "Friendly, helpful owner; some sm pitches; conv mountain walking; excel pool." Easter-15 Oct. € 17.20 2010*

POZO ALCON *2G4* (7km N Rural) *37.75873, -2.91403* **Camping La Bolera, Ctra Castril, Km 8, Pantano Bolera, 23485 Pozo Alcón (Jaén)** [953-73 90 05] Fr Pozo Alcón take A326 N dir Castril. Site on L. Med, pt sl, pt shd; wc; chem disp; shwrs inc; el pnts (5A) €3; gas; lndtte; shop; rest; bar; BBQ; playgrnd; some statics; dogs €1.50; bus adj; quiet; ccard acc; CCI. "Excel scenery & wildlife." 1 Apr-14 Dec. € 14.40 2008*

PRADES see Vilanova de Prades *3C2*

PUEBLA DE CASTRO, LA see Graus *3B2*

PUEBLA DE SANABRIA *1B3* (500m S Rural) *42.04930, -6.63068* **Camping Isla de Puebla-DELETED, Pago de Barregas s/n, 49300 Puebla de Sanabria (Zamora) [980-56 79 54; fax 980-56 79 55; c.isladepuebla@hotmail.com; www. isladepuebla.com]** Fr Portugal border on C622, at ent to Puebla de Sanabria foll sp down short track twd rv. Fr N525 ent vill & foll sp Isla de Puebla. Med, mkd pitch, pt shd; wc; chem disp;mv service pnt; shwrs inc; el pnts (10-16A) €4.90-6; gas; lndtte (inc dryer); shop; rest; snacks; bar; BBQ; playgrnd; pool; trout-fishing; games area; some statics; dogs; bus 200m; adv bkg; quiet; red long stay; ccard acc; CCI. "Vg, modern san facs; interesting town; vg for nature lovers; friendly, helpful staff; vg rest in old mill; facs ltd low ssn." Holy Week-30 Sep.
€ 18.10   2010*

PUEBLA DE SANABRIA *1B3* (10km NW Rural) *42.13111, -6.70111* **Camping El Folgoso, Ctra Puebla de Sanabria-San Martin de Castañeda, Km 13, 49361 Vigo de Sanabria (Zamora) [980-62 67 74; fax 980-62 68 00; camping@ elfolgoso.com]** Exit A52 sp Puebla de Sanabria & foll sp for Lago/Vigo de Sanabria thro Puente de Sanabria & Galende; site 2km beyond vill of Galende; sp. Med, pt sl, terr, shd; wc; chem disp; shwrs €1; el pnts (5A) €2.50; gas; lndtte; shop high ssn; rest high ssn; snacks; bar; playgrnd; cycle hire; statics; phone; ccard acc. "Lovely setting beside lake; v cold in winter." ♦ 1 Apr-31 Oct. € 16.80   2008*

PUEBLA DE SANABRIA *1B3* (10km NW Rural) *42.11778, -6.69116* **Camping Peña Gullón, Ctra Puebla de Santabria-Ribadelago, Km 11.5, Lago de Sanabria, 49360 Galende (Zamora) [980-62 67 72]** Fr Puebla de Sanabria foll sp for Lago de Sanabria. Site 3km beyond vill of Galende clearly sp. Lge, pt shd; wc; shwrs inc; el pnts (15A) €2.51; gas; lndtte; shop in ssn; rest; playgrnd; lake adj; poss cr; quiet; red long stay; CCI. "Site in nature park 35km fr Portugal's Montesinho Park; rec arr by 1200; beautiful area; excel site." 28 Jun-31 Aug.
€ 17.00   2011*

⊞ **PUERTO DE MAZARRON** *4G1* (3km NE Rural/Coastal) *37.58981, -1.22881* **Camping Las Torres, Ctra N332, Cartagena-Mazarrón, Km 29, 30860 Puerto de Mazarrón (Murcia) [968-59 52 25; fax 968 59 55 16; info@camping lastorres.com; www.campinglastorres.com]** Fr N on A7/E15 exit junc 627 onto MU602, then MU603 to Mazarrón. At junc with N322 turn L to Puerto de Mazarrón & foll Cartagena sp until site sps. Lge, hdg/mkd pitch, terr, hdstg, pt shd; wc; chem disp; mv service pnt; 40% serviced pitch; baby facs; shwrs inc; el pnts (6A) inc; gas; lndtte; rest (w/end only); snacks; bar; sm shop & 3km; playgrnd; 2 pools (1 htd, covrd); sand/shgl beach 2km; tennis; cycle hire; wifi; entmnt; sat TV; 60% statics; dogs; phone; bus 1km; Eng spkn; adv bkg rec in winter; poss noisy; ccard acc; red low ssn/long stay; CCI. "Unspoilt coastline; busy at w/end; well-managed, family site; poss full in winter; excel pool; sm pitches." ♦ € 24.50
                                                                             2010*

⊞ **PUERTO DE MAZARRON** *4G1* (5km NE Coastal) *37.5800, -1.1950* **Camping Los Madriles, Ctra a la Azohía 60, Km 4.5, 30868 Isla Plana (Murcia) [968-15 21 51; fax 968-15 20 92; camplosmadriles@terra.es; www.campinglosmadriles. com]** Fr Cartegena on N332 dir Puerto de Mazarrón. Turn L at rd junc sp La Azohía (32km). Site in 4km sp. Fr Murcia on E15/N340 dir Lorca exit junc 627 onto MU603 to Mazarrón, then foll sp. (Do not use rd fr Cartegena unless powerful tow vehicle/gd weight differential - use rte fr m'way thro Mazarrón.) Lge, hdg/mkd pitch, hdstg, pt sl, pt shd; wc; chem disp; mv service pnt; serviced pitches; shwrs inc; el pnts (10A) €5; gas; lndtte; shop; rest high ssn; bar; playgrnd; 2 htd pools; jacuzzi; shgl beach 500m; games area; wifi; no dogs; bus; poss cr; Eng spkn; adv bkg (fr Oct for min 2 months only); quiet; ccard acc high ssn; red long stay/low ssn/CCI. "Clean, well-run, v popular winter site; adv bkg ess fr Oct; some sm pitches, some with sea views; poss not suitable for disabled due to sl bet terrs; 3 days min stay high ssn; v helpful staff; excel." ♦ € 30.50   2010*

⊞ **PUERTO DE MAZARRON** *4G1* (2km E Rural/Coastal) *37.56777, -1.2300* **Camping Los Delfines, Ctra Isla Plana-Playa El Mojon, 30860 Puerto de Mazarrón (Murcia) [tel/ fax 968-59 45 27; www.campinglosdelfines.com]** Fr N332 turn S sp La Azohía & Isla Plana. Site on L in 3km. Med, mkd pitch, hdstg, pt sl, pt shd; htd wc; chem disp; mv service pnt; serviced pitches; baby facs; private san facs avail; shwrs inc; el pnts (5A) €3; gas; lndtte; tradsmn; snacks & bar high ssn; BBQ; playgrnd; shgl beach adj; TV; 5% statics; dogs €3; quiet; poss cr; Eng spkn; phone; red long stay; CCI. "Gd sized pitches; popular low ssn." ♦ € 40.80   2009*

⊞ **PUERTO DE MAZARRON** *4G1* (5km SW Coastal) *37.56388, -1.30388* **Camping Playa de Mazarrón, Ctra Mazarrón-Bolnuevo, Bolnuevo, 30877 Mazarrón (Murcia) [968-15 06 60; fax 968-15 08 37; camping@playamazarron. com; www.playamazarron.com]** Take Bolnuevo rd fr Mazarrón, at rndabt go strt, site immed on L. Lge, mkd pitch, hdstg, pt shd; wc; 90% serviced pitches; chem disp; mv service pnt; shwrs inc; el pnts (5A) €4; gas; lndtte; shop, rest (high ssn); snacks, bar; playgrnd; sand beach adj; tennis; games area; internet; TV; dogs free; bus; phone; poss v cr; adv bkg; red long stay/low ssn; ccard acc. "Some lge pitches but tight turning for lge o'fits; friendly staff; metal-framed sunshades in ssn on most pitches but low for m'vans; poss poor daytime security; gd for wheelchair users; popular & v cr in winter - many long stay visitors." ♦ € 36.85   2011*

SPAIN

⊞ **PUERTO DE SANTA MARIA, EL** *2H3* (2km SW Coastal) *36.58768, -6.24092* **Camping Playa Las Dunas de San Antón, Paseo Maritimo La Puntilla s/n, 11500 El Puerto de Santa María (Cádiz) [956-87 22 10; fax 956-86 01 17; info@ lasdunascamping.com; www.lasdunascamping.com]** Fr N or S exit A4 at El Puerto de Sta María. Foll site sp carefully to avoid narr streets of town cent. Site 2-3km S of marina & leisure complex of Puerto Sherry. Alternatively, fr A4 take Rota rd & look for sp to site & Hotel Playa Las Dunas. Site better sp fr this dir & avoids town. Lge, pt sl, pt shd; wc; chem disp; mv service pnt; shwrs inc; el pnts (5-10A) €3.10-5.89; gas; lndtte; shop (high ssn); tradsmn; snacks; bar; playgrnd; pool adj; sand beach 50m; sports facs; internet; 30% statics; phone; guarded; poss cr; adv bkg rec; poss noisy disco w/ end; red facs low ssn; ccard acc; CCI. "Friendly staff; conv Cádiz & Jerez sherry region, birdwatching areas & beaches; conv ferry or catamaran to Cádiz; facs poss stretched high ssn; pitches quiet away fr rd; take care caterpillars in spring - poss dangerous to dogs; dusty site but staff water rds." ♦ € 22.18   2011*

⊞ **PUERTO DE SANTA MARIA, EL** *2H3* (12km W Coastal) *36.67111, -6.40611* **Camping Playa Aguadulce, Ctra Rota-Chipiona, Km 21, Pago Aguadulce, 11520 Rota (Cádiz) [956-84 70 78; fax 956-84 71 94; cpa@playaaguadulce. com; www.playaaguadulce.com]** W fr El Puerto on A491, twd Chipiona. Ignore sp Rota & take last exit rndabt sp Costa Ballena (camping sp). Foll site sp & narr track for 1km. Med, hdg pitch, hdstg, shd; wc; chem disp; mv service pnt; baby facs; shwrs inc; el pnts (6-10A) inc; gas; lndtte; shop & 7km; tradsmn; rest; snacks; bar; playgrnd; sand beach adj; wifi; 25% statics; dogs; noisy; adv bkg; Eng spkn; ccard acc; CCI. "Well-kept, attractive site; adj to excel beach; noisy at w/end & school holidays; helpful owners; sm pitches poss diff lge o'fits; site rds narr & restricted by trees/bushes." € 27.69

2008*

PUIGCERDA *3B3* (2km NE Rural) *42.44156, 1.94174* **Camping Stel, Ctra de Llívia s/n, 17520 Puigcerdà (Gerona) [972-88 23 61; fax 972-14 04 19; puigcerda@stel.es; www. stel.es]** Fr France head for Bourg-Madame on N820 (N20) or N116. Cross border dir Llívia on N154, site is 1km after rndabt on L. Lge, mkd pitch, terr, pt shd; htd wc; chem disp; mv service pnt; baby facs; shwrs; el pnts (7A) €4.50; lndtte (inc dryer); shop; rest; snacks; bar; BBQ; playgrnd; htd pool; paddling pool; canoeing; watersports; archery; cycle hire; games area; golf 4km; wifi; entmnt; TV rm; 10% statics; dogs; site open w/ends only in winter; Eng spkn; adv bkg; some rd noise; ccard acc. "Pitches upper terr quieter; superb scenery; sep area for campers with pets; gd walking, cycling." ♦ 3 Jun-11 Sep. € 36.40 (CChq acc)   2011*

PUYARRUEGO see Ainsa *3B2*

QUEVEDA see Santillana del Mar *1A4*

RIANO *1A3* (7km E Rural) *42.97361, -4.92000* **Camping Alto Esla, Ctra León-Santander, 24911 Boca de Huérgano (León) [987-74 01 39; camping@altoesla.eu; www.altoesla.eu]** SW on N621 fr Potes just past junc with LE241 at Boca de Huérgano. Site on L. (See Picos de Europa in Mountain Passes & Tunnels in the section Planning & Travelling at front of guide). Sm, pt sl, pt shd; wc; chem disp; mv service pnt; el pnts (5A) €2.68 (poss rev pol); lndtte; shops 500m; bus 300m; bar; phone; quiet; ccard acc; CCI. "Lovely setting; superb views; attractive site; ltd el pnts; excel san facs." ♦ 26 Jun-8 Sep. € 17.76   2011*

⊞ **RIAZA** *1C4* (1.5km W Rural) *41.26995, -3.49750* **Camping Riaza, Ctra de la Estación s/n, 40500 Riaza (Segovia) [tel/fax 921-55 05 80; info@camping-riaza.com; www.camping-riaza.com]** Fr N exit A1/E5 junc 104, fr S exit 103 onto N110 N. In 12km turn R at rndabt on ent to town, site on L. Lge, hdg pitch, unshd; htd wc; chem disp; mv service pnt; baby facs; shwrs inc; el pnts (15A) €4.70; lndtte (inc dryer); shop; rest; snacks; bar; BBQ; playgrnd; pool; paddling pool; games area; games rm; internet; some statics; dogs free; phone; bus 900m; Eng spkn; adv bkg; quiet. "Vg site; various pitch sizes - some lge; excel san facs; easy access to/fr Santander or Bilbao; beautiful little town." ♦ € 27.00   2010*

RIBADEO *1A2* (4km E Coastal) *43.55097, -6.99699* **Camping Playa Peñarronda, Playa de Peñarronda-Barres, 33794 Castropol (Asturias) [tel/fax 985-62 30 22; campingpenarrondacb@hotmail.com; www.camping playapenarronda.com]** Exit A8 at km 498 onto N640 dir Lugo/Barres; turn R approx 500m and then foll site sp for 2km. Med, mkd pitch, shd; wc; chem disp; mv service pnt; shwrs inc; el pnts (6A) €4 (poss rev pol); gas; lndtte; shop; rest; snacks; bar; BBQ; playgrnd; sand beach adj; games area; cycle hire; some statics; phone; Eng spkn; quiet; red long stay; CCI. "Beautifully-kept, delightful, clean, friendly, family-run site on 'Blue Flag' beach; rec arr early to get pitch; facs clean; gd cycling along coastal paths & to Ribadeo; ltd facs low ssn, sm pitches." Holy Week-25 Sep. € 23.60   2011*

⊞ **RIBADEO** *1A2* (4km E Coastal) *43.54587, -6.99613* **Camping Vegamar, Ctra Playa de Peñarronda-Barres, 33794 Castropol (Asturias) [985-62 39 48; rlopezo@terra. es]** Fr E on E70/N634 turn L at junc (rndabt) N640 & N634 dir Vegadeo. Immed take 1st R & immed R under main rd. Site sp 500m. Med, pt shd; wc; chem disp; mv service pnt; shwrs; el pnts €2.57; gas; lndtte; shop; rest; snacks; bar; playgrnd; pool; sand beach 400m; games are; 60% statics; dogs; bus 1km; adv bkg; quiet; CCI. "Excel facs; family-run site; unreliable opening low ssn; excel NH." ♦ € 15.10   2008*

RIBADEO *1A2* (3km W Rural) *43.53722, -7.08472* **Camping Ribadeo, Ctra Ribadeo-La Coruña, Km 2, 27700 Ribadeo (Lugo) [982-13 11 68; fax 982-13 11 67; www.camping ribadeo.com]** W fr Ribadeo on N634/E70 twd La Coruña, in 2km pass sp Camping Ribadeo. Ignore 1st camping sp, take next L in 1.4km. Lge, mkd pitch, pt shd; wc; chem disp; mv service pnt; shwrs inc; el pnts (3A) €3.20 (rev pol); gas 4km; lndtte; shop; tradsmn; rest; snacks; bar; BBQ; playgrnd; pool; sand beach 2km; no dogs; bus 500m; quiet; red for 10+ days; CCI. "Gd NH; friendly, family owners; request hot water for shwrs; everything immac; highly rec; many interesting local features." Holy Week & 1 Jun-30 Sep. € 19.10   2010*

SPAIN

RIBADESELLA *1A3* (4km W Rural) *43.46258, -5.08725* **Camping Ribadesella, Sebreño s/n, 33560 Ribadesella (Asturias)** [985-85 82 93; camping.reservas@fade.es; www.camping-ribadesella.com] W fr Ribadesella take N632. After 2km fork L up hill. Site on L after 2km. Poss diff for lge o'fits & alternative rte fr Ribadesella vill to site to avoid steep uphill turn can be used. Lge, mkd pitch, pt sl, pt terr, pt shd; wc; chem disp; baby facs; shwrs inc; el pnts (5A) €3.70; gas; lndtte; shop, rest, snacks, bar; BBQ; playgrnd; htd, covrd pool; sand beach 4km; tennis; games area; games rm; poss cr; adv bkg; quiet; ccard acc; red low ssn/long stay; CCI. "Clean san facs; some sm pitches; attractive fishing vill; prehistoric cave paintings nrby." ♦ Easter-26 Sep. € 23.40   2010*

⊞ **RIBADESELLA** *1A3* (8km W Coastal/Rural) *43.47472, -5.13416* **Camping Playa de Vega, Vega, 33345 Ribadesella (Asturias)** [985-86 04 06; fax 985-85 76 62; campingplaya devega@hotmail.com; www.campingplayadevega.com] Fr A8 exit junc 333 sp Ribadesella W, thro Bones. At rndabt cont W dir Caravia, turn R opp quarry sp Playa de Vega. Fr cent of Ribadesella (poss congestion) W on N632. Cont for 5km past turning to autovia. Turn R at sp Vega & site. Med, hdg pitch, pt terr, pt shd; wc; chem disp; serviced pitch; shwrs inc; el pnts €3.50; lndtte; shop; beach rest; snacks; bar; BBQ; sand beach 400m; TV; dogs; bus 700m; phone; quiet; ccard acc; CCI. "Sh walk to vg beach thro orchards; sm pitches not suitable lge o'fits; poss overgrown low ssn." € 19.10   2010*

⊞ **RIBEIRA** *1B2* (7km N Rural) *42.62100, -8.98600* **Camping Ría de Arosa II, Oleiros, 15993 Santa Eugenia (Uxía) de Ribeira (La Coruña)** [902-33 30 40; fax 981-86 55 55; info@ camping.riadearosa.com; www.campingriadearosa.com] Exit AP9 junc 93 Padrón & take N550 then AC305/VG11 to Ribeira. Then take AC550 to Oleiros to site, well sp. Med, hdg/ mkd pitch, shd; htd wc; chem disp; mv service pnt; baby facs; shwrs inc; el pnts (6A) inc; gas; lndtte; supmkt; rest; snacks; bar; BBQ; playgrnd; pool; sand beach 7km; fishing; tennis; games area; games rm; wifi; TV; some statics; dogs €2.50; phone; Eng spkn; adv bkg; quiet; ccard acc; red low ssn; CCI. "Beautiful area; helpful, friendly staff; excel." ♦ € 25.90   2008*

RIBEIRA *1B2* (8km NE Coastal) *42.58852, -8.92465* **Camping Ría de Arosa I, Playa de Cabío s/n, 15940 Puebla (Pobra) do Caramiñal (La Coruña)** [981-83 22 22; fax 981-83 32 93; playa@campingriadearosa.com; www.campingriadearosa. com] Exit AP9/E1 junc 93 or N550 at Padrón onto VG11 along N side of Ría de Arosa into Puebla do Caramiñal. Site is 1.5km S of Pobra, sp fr town. Lge, pt shd; wc; chem disp; mv service pnt; shwrs; el pnts (6A) €4.60; gas; lndtte; shop; rest; snacks; bar; playgrnd; sand beach adj; watersports; cycle hire; internet; TV; some statics; dogs €2.50; phone; poss cr; adv bkg; quiet; ccard acc. 13 Mar-15 Oct. € 24.00   2010*

RIBEIRA *1B2* (2km E Coastal) *42.5700, -8.97138* **Camping Coroso, Playa de Coroso, 15950 Santa Eugenia (Uxía) de Ribeira (La Coruña)** [981-83 80 02; fax 981-83 85 77; info@ campingcoroso.com; www.campingcoroso.com] Fr Padrón on N550 or AP9 6km S of Santiago de Compostela take VRG11 (fast rd) to Ribeira (approx 40km), then foll sp to site on L on ent Ribeira. Lge, some hdg/mkd pitch, hdstg, pt sl, terr, pt shd; wc; chem disp; baby facs; fam bthrm; shwrs inc; el pnts (10A) inc; gas; lndtte; shop in ssn; café in ssn; snacks; bar; BBQ; sandy beach; sailing; tennis; bus; Eng spkn; poss cr; adv bkg; fairly quiet; red long stay; ccard acc; CCI. "Marvellous views; gd coastal walks; friendly staff; gd rest." 1 Apr-30 Sep. € 25.10   2008*

RIBERA DE CARDOS see Llavorsí *3B2*

⊞ **RIBES DE FRESER** *3B3* (500m NE Rural) *42.31260, 2.17570* **Camping Vall de Ribes, Ctra de Pardines, Km 0.5, 17534 Ribes de Freser (Gerona)** [tel/fax 972-72 88 20; info@ campingvallderibes.com; www.campingvallderibes.com] N fr Ripoll on N152; turn E at Ribes de Freser; site beyond town dir Pardines. Site nr town but 1km by rd. App rd narr. Med, mkd pitch, terr, pt shd; htd wc; chem disp; shwrs inc; el pnts (6A) €4.20; lndry rm; shop 500m; rest; bar; playgrnd; pool; 50% statics; dogs €3; train 500m; quiet; CCI. "Gd, basic site; steep footpath fr site to town; 10-20 min walk to stn; cog rlwy train to Núria a 'must' - spectacular gorge, gd walking & interesting exhibitions; sm/med o'fits only; poss unkempt statics low ssn." € 20.00   2011*

RIOPAR *4F1* (7.6km E Rural) *38.48960, -2.34588* **Campsite Rio Mundo, Ctra Comarcal 412, km 205, 02449 Mesones (Albacete)** [967-43 32 30; fax 967-43 32 87; riomundo@ campingriomundo.com; www.campingriomundo.com] On N322 Albacete-Bailén, turn off at Reolid direction Ríopar. Camp site 7km past Ríopar on side rd on L (km-marker 205) (Mesones). Med, mkd pitch, hdstg; shd; wc; chem disp; mv service pnt; shwrs inc; lndry rm; gas; shop; rest; snacks; bar; BBQ; playgrnd; pool; cycle hire; fishing; games area; wifi; dogs €3.40; Eng spkn; adv bkg; quiet; ccard acc; red low ssn; CCI; "Well run site in mountainous nature reserve by Rv Mundo; gd dogs walks; spotless san facs." ♦ 20 Mar-13 Oct. € 35.55   2011*

⊞ **RIPOLL** *3B3* (2km N Rural) *42.21995, 2.17505* **Camping Ripollés, Ctra Barcelona/Puigcerdà, Km 109.3, 17500 Ripoll (Gerona)** [972-70 37 70; fax 972-70 35 54] At km 109.3 up hill N fr town; well sp. Steep access rd. Med, mkd pitch, pt sl, pt shd; htd wc; chem disp; mv service pnt; baby facs; shwrs inc; el pnts €4; lndtte; shop 2km; rest; snacks; bar; BBQ; playgrnd; pool; tennis; 20% statics; dogs €2.80; phone; adv bkg; quiet; ccard acc; CCI. "V pleasant; gd bar/rest; not suitable med/lge o'fits." ♦ € 19.00   2011*

RIPOLL *3B3* (1km S Rural) *42.18218, 2.19552* **Camping Solana del Ter, Ctra Barcelona-Puigcerdà, C17, Km 92.5, 17500 Ripoll (Gerona)** [972-70 10 62; fax 972-71 43 43; camping@ solanadelter.com; www.solanadelter.com] Site sp S of Ripoll on N152 behind hotel & rest. Med, mkd pitch, hdstg, pt shd; htd wc; chem disp; baby facs; shwrs inc; el pnts (4A) €5.90; lndtte; shop; rest; snacks; bar; playgrnd; pool high ssn only; paddling pool; tennis; TV; Eng spkn; phone; some rd & rlwy noise; ccard acc; CCI. "Historic monastery in town; scenic drives nr." Holy Week-15 Oct. € 27.30   2010*

⊞ **RIPOLL** *3B3* (6km NW Rural) *42.23522, 2.11797* **Camping Molí Serradell, 17530 Campdevànol (Gerona) [tel/fax 972-73 09 27; calrei@teleline.es]** Fr Ripoll N on N152; L onto GI401 dir Gombrèn; site on L in 4km. NB 2nd site. Sm, pt shd; htd wc; chem disp; mv service pnt; shwrs inc; el pnts €4.50; lndtte (in dryer); shop; tradsmn; rest; 75% statics; poss cr; quiet; red low ssn; CCI. € 25.40   2009*

⊞ **ROCIO, EL** *2G3* (1km N Rural) *37.14194, -6.49250* **Camping La Aldea, Ctra del Rocío, Km 25, 21750 El Rocío (Huelva) [959-44 26 77; fax 959-44 25 82; info@campinglaaldea. com; www.campinglaaldea.com]** Fr A49 turn S at junc 48 onto A483 by-passing Almonte, site sp just bef El Rocío rndabt. Fr W (Portugal) turn off at junc 60 to A484 to Almonte, then A483. Lge, hdg/mkd pitch, hdstg, pt shd; htd wc; chem disp; mv service pnt; baby facs; shwrs inc; el pnts (10A) €6; gas; lndtte (inc dryer); shop; tradsmn; rest; snacks; bar; BBQ; playgrnd; htd pool high ssn; sand beach 16km; horseriding nrby; van washing facs; wifi; 30% statics; dogs €3; phone; bus 500m; poss cr; Eng spkn; adv bkg; rd/motocross noise; red long stay/low ssn; ccard acc; CCI. "Well-appointed & maintained site; winter rallies; excel san facs; friendly, helpful staff; tight turns on site; most pitches have kerb or gully; pitches soft after rain; gd birdwatching (lagoon 1km); interesting town; avoid festival (2nd week May) when town cr & site charges higher; poss windy; excel birdwatching nrby." ♦ € 26.00   2011*

RODA DE BARA *3C3* (2km E Coastal) *41.17003, 1.46427* **Campsite Stel Cat 1., Ctra N340, Km 1182, 43883 Roda de Barà (Tarragona) [977-80 20 02; fax 977-80 05 25; rodadebara@stel.es; www.stel.es]** Exit AP7 junc 31, foll sps for Tarragona on N340. Site on L immed after Arco de Barà. Lge, mkd pitch, pt shd; wc; chem disp; mv service pnt; baby facs; htd private bthrms avail; shwrs inc; el pnts (5A) inc; gas; lndtte (inc dryer); shop; rest; snacks; bar; BBQ; playgrnd; htd pool; waterslides; sand beach adj; watersports; tennis; sports & entmnt; cycle hire; games area; golf 20km; wifi; TV; 10% statics; no dogs; phone; poss cr; adv bkg; some rd/rlwy noise; red long stay/low ssn; CCI. "Some sm pitches, exc well maintained site, first class san facs, 2 mins walk from sandy beach, more expensive than some but worth the money." ♦ 7 Apr-25 Sep. € 57.40 (CChq acc)   2011*

⊞ **RODA DE BARA** *3C3* (3km E Coastal/Rural) *41.17034, 1.46708* **Camping Arc de Barà, N340, Km 1182, 43883 Roda de Barà (Tarragona) [977-80 09 02; camping@camping arcdebara.com; www.campingarcdebara.com]** Exit AP7 junc 31 or 32, foll sp Arc de Barà on N340 dir Tarragona. Site on L after 5km shortly after Camping Park Playa Barà. NB When app fr N ess to use 'Cambia de Sentido' just after Arc de Barà (old arch). Lge, shd; htd wc; chem disp; baby facs; shwrs inc; el pnts (5A) €3.50; gas; lndtte (inc dryer); shop high ssn; supmkt 200m; rest; snacks; bar; BBQ; pool; paddling pool; sand beach adj; games area; 75% statics in sep area; dogs €2.80; phone; bus adj; site clsd Nov; poss cr; Eng spkn; rlwy noise; ccard acc; CCI. "Ltd number sm touring pitches; gd, clean NH in rte Alicante; phone ahead winter/low ssn to check open, minimum price in high season 01/07 - 31/08." ♦ € 28.00 (3 persons)   2011*

RONDA *2H3* (4km NE Rural) *36.76600, -5.11900* **Camping El Cortijo, Ctra Campillos, Km 4.5, 29400 Ronda (Málaga) [952-87 07 46; fax 952-87 30 82; elcortijo@ hermanosmacias.com; www.hermanosmacias.com]** Fr Ronda by-pass take A367 twd Campillos. Site on L after 4.5km opp new development 'Hacienda Los Pinos'. Med, mkd pitch, pt shd; wc; chem disp; mv service pnt; serviced pitches; baby facs; shwrs inc; el pnts inc; lndtte; shop; rest; bar; playgrnd; pool; tennis; games area; cycle hire; 5% statics; dogs; phone; Eng spkn; some rd noise; CCI. "Friendly, helpful owner; conv NH." ♦ 1 Apr-15 Oct. € 16.00   2011*

⊞ **RONDA** *2H3* (1km S Rural) *36.72111, -5.17166* **Camping El Sur, Ctra Ronda-Algeciras Km 1.5, 29400 Ronda (Málaga) [952-87 59 39; fax 952-87 70 54; info@campingelsur.com; www.campingelsur.com]** Site on W side of A369 dir Algeciras. Do not tow thro Ronda. Med, mkd pitch, hdstg, terr, sl, pt shd; htd wc; chem disp; mv service pnt; baby facs; shwrs inc; el pnts (5-10A) €4.30-5.35 (poss rev pol &/or no earth); lndtte; shop; rest adj; snacks; bar; playgrnd; pool high ssn; wifi; dogs €1.70; phone; poss cr; Eng spkn; adv bkg; quiet; red low stay/low ssn; CCI. "Gd rd fr coast with spectacular views; long haul for lge o'fits; busy family-run site in lovely setting; conv National Parks & Pileta Caves; poss diff access some pitches due trees & high kerbs; hard, rocky ground; san facs poss stretched high ssn; easy walk to town; friendly staff; vg rest; excel." ♦ € 22.50   2010*

ROQUETAS DE MAR see Almería *4G1*

ROSES *3B3* (200m SW Coastal) *42.26888, 3.1525* **Camping Rodas, Calle Punta Falconera 62,17480 Roses (Gerona) [972-25 76 17; fax 972-15 24 66; info@campingrodas. com; www.campingrodas.com]** On Figueras-Roses rd, at o'skts of Roses sp on R after supmkt. Lge, hdg/mkd pitch, pt shd; wc; chem disp; serviced pitches; shwrs inc; el pnts (6A) inc; gas; lndtte; shop adj; tradsmn; rest; snacks; bar; lndtte; sm playgrnd; htd pool; paddling pool; sand beach 600m; bus 1km; poss cr; Eng spkn; adv bkg; quiet; ccard acc; CCI. "Well-run site; site rds all tarmac; Roses gd cent for region." 1 Jun-30 Sep. € 31.50   2009*

ROSES *3B3* (1km W Urban/Coastal) *42.26638, 3.16305* **Camping Joncar Mar, Ctra Figueres s/n, 17480 Roses (Gerona) [tel/fax 972-25 67 02; info@campingjoncarmar. com; www.campingjoncarmar.com]** At Figueres take C260 W for Roses. On ent Roses turn sharp R at last rndabt at end of dual c'way. Site on both sides or rd - go to R (better) side, park & report to recep on L. Lge, pt sl, pt shd; htd wc; chem disp; baby facs; shwrs; el pnts (6-10A) €4.40 (poss no earth); gas; lndtte; shop; rest; bar; playgrnd; pool; sand beach 150m; golf 15km; entmnt; games rm; internet; 15% statics; dogs €2.40; phone; bus 500m; poss cr; Eng spkn; adv bkg; rd noise; ccard acc; red low ssn/long stay. "Conv walk into Roses; hotels & apartment blocks bet site & beach; poss cramped/ tight pitches; narr rds; vg value low ssn; new san facs under construction 2009." 1 Jan-31 Oct. € 27.75   2010*

ROSES *3B3* (2km W Coastal) *42.26638, 3.15611* **Camping Salatà, Port Reig s/n, 17480 Roses (Gerona) [972-25 60 86; fax 972-15 02 33; info@campingsalata.com; www. campingsalata.com]** App Roses on rd C260. On ent Roses take 1st R after Roses sp & Caprabo supmkt. Lge, mkd pitch, hdstg, pt shd; htd wc; chem disp; baby facs; shwrs inc; el pnts (6-10A) inc; gas; lndtte (inc dryer); shop; tradsmn; rest; snacks; bar; playgrnd; htd pool high ssn; sand beach 200m; wifi; 10% statics; dogs €2.80 (not acc Jul/Aug); phone; poss cr; Eng spkn; adv bkg; red long stay/low ssn; ccard acc; CCI. "Vg area for sub-aqua sports; vg clean facs; red facs low ssn; pleasant walk/cycle to town." ♦ 19 Feb-13 Nov. € 44.90   2011*

ROTA see Puerto de Santa María, El *2H3*

RUILOBA see Comillas *1A4*

⊞ **SABINANIGO** *3B2* (6km N Rural) *42.55694, -0.33722* **Camping Valle de Tena, Ctra N260, Km 512.6, 22600 Senegüe (Huesca). [974-48 09 77; correo@camping valledetena.com; www.campingvalledetena.com]** Fr Jaca take N330, in 12km turn L onto N260 dir Biescas. In 5km ignore site sp Sorripas, cont for 500m to site on L - new ent at far end. Lge, mkd pitch, terr, unshd; htd wc; chem disp; mv service pnt; serviced pitches; baby facs; shwrs inc; el pnts (6A) €6; lndtte; shop; rest; snacks; bar; playgrnd; pool; paddling pool; sports facs; hiking & rv rafting nr; entmnt; internet; TV rm; 60% statics; dogs €2.70; phone; Eng spkn; adv bkg; rd noise during day but quiet at night. "Helpful staff; steep, narr site rd; sm pitches; excel, busy NH to/fr France; beautiful area." € 20.00   2010*

⊞ **SABINANIGO** *3B2* (1km NE Urban) *42.52739, -0.35923* **Camping Aurín, Ctra C330, Circunvalación Sabiñánigo-Francia, s/n, 22600 Sabiñánigo (Huesca) [974-48 34 45; fax 974-48 32 80; recep.sabi@trhhoteles.com]** On Sabiñánigo by-pass (N330) 1km SE of junc with N260. Fr Jaca (S) site on L, go past to turning point in 800m. Site well sp behind & beside TRH Sabinanigo Hotel. Lge, mkd pitch, pt shd; htd wc; mv service pnt; chem disp; baby facs; shwrs inc; el pnts (5A) €6; gas; lndtte; shop 2km; supmkt opp; rest, bar in hotel; snacks; playgrnd; 2 pools; tennis; watersports; car wash; 95% statics; no dogs; bus 400m; site clsd 1 Nov-19 Dec; poss cr; Eng spkn; quiet excl w/end; ccard acc. "V sm, cr area for tourers; pitches poss soft; lge o'fits park adj pool low ssn; san facs gd - plenty hot water; site poss scruffy early ssn; mountain walking; skiing; all hotel facs avail to campers; conv NH." ♦ € 24.00   2009*

⊞ **SACEDON** *3D1* (500m E Rural) *40.48148, -2.72700* **Camp Municipal Ecomillans, Camino Sacedón 15, 19120 Sacedón (Guadalajara) [949-35 10 18; fax 949-35 10 73; ecomillans63@hotmail.com]** Fr E on N320 exit km220, foll Sacedón & site sp; site on L. Fr W exit km222. Med, mkd pitch, hdstg, pt sl, shd; wc (cont); shwrs; el pnts €5; lndry rm; shop 500m; lake sw 1km; quiet. "NH only in area of few sites; sm pitches; low ssn phone to check open." ♦ € 15.40   2009*

⊞ **SAGUNTO** *4E2* (7km NE Coastal) *39.72027, -0.19166* **Camping Malvarrosa de Corinto, Playa Malvarrosa de Corinto, 46500 Sagunto (València) [962-60 89 06; fax 962-60 89 43; camalva@live.com; www.malvacorinto.com]** Exit 49 fr A7 onto N340, foll dir Almenara-Casa Blanca. Turn E twd Port de Sagunto & Canet d'en Berenguer on CV320. Site poorly sp. Lge, pt shd; wc; chem disp; sauna; shwrs inc; el pnts (5-10A) €4.40; gas; lndtte; shop & 5km; rest; snacks; bar; BBQ; playgrnd; sand & shgl beach adj; tennis; horseriding; gym; 85% statics; dogs €2.70; phone; poss cr; Eng spkn; quiet; red ow ssn/long stay; CCI. "Lovely site under palm trees; friendly, helpful owners; gd facs; many feral cats & owners' dogs on site; excel pitches adj beach; ltd touring pitches but access to some poss diff; ltd facs & poss neglected low ssn; no local transport." € 19.10   2010*

SALAMANCA *1C3* (4km N Rural) *41.02805, -5.67472* **Camping La Capea, Ctra N630, Km 384, 37189 Aldeaseca de la Armuña (Salamanca) [923-25 10 66; campinglacapea@ hotmail.com]** Close to km post 333 on N630. Site sp fr both dirs. Ent on brow of a hill on W side of rd. Med, hdg/mkd pitch, hdstg, shd; wc; chem disp; mv service pnt; shwrs inc; el pnts (10A) €3.45; lndtte; shop; snacks; bar; playgrnd; pool; TV; 10% statics; dogs; some Eng spkn; some rd noise; CCI. "Friendly; variety of pitch sizes but most not suitable c'vans 6m & over; site poss untidy, unkempt low ssn; conv NH." 1 Apr-30 Sep. € 13.80   2008*

SALAMANCA *1C3* (4.5km NE Rural) *40.97611, -5.60472* **Camping Don Quijote, Ctra Salamanca-Aldealengua, Km 4, 37193 Cabrerizos (Salamanca) [tel/fax 923-20 90 52; info@ campingdonquijote.com; www.campingdonquijote.com]** Fr Madrid or fr S cross Rv Tormes by most easterly bdge to join inner ring rd. Foll Paseo de Canalejas for 800m to Plaza España. Turn R onto SA804 Avda de los Comuneros & strt on for 5km. Site ent 2km after town boundary sp. Fr other dirs, head into city & foll inner ring rd to Plaza España. Site well sp fr rv & ring rd. Med, hdg/mkd pitch, hdstg, pt shd; wc; chem disp; mv service pnt; baby facs; shwrs inc; el pnts (10A) €3.45 (poss earth fault, 2010); lndtte; shop; supmkt 3km; rest; snacks; bar; playgrnd; pool; paddling pool; beach 200m; rv fishing; wifi; 10% statics; dogs; bus; poss cr w/end; adv bkg; quiet; red CCI. "Gd rv walks; conv city cent - easy cycle ride; basic, clean facs." ♦ 1 Mar-31 Dec. € 20.50   2010*

⊞ **SALAMANCA** *1C3* (12km NE Rural) *41.05805, -5.54611* **Camping Olimpia, Ctra de Gomecello, Km 3.150, 37427 Pedrosillo el Ralo (Salamanca) [923-08 08 54 or 620-46 12 07; fax 923-35 44 26; info@campingolimpia.com; www.campingolimpia.com]** Exit A62 junc 225 dir Pedrosillo el Ralo & la Vellés, strt over rndabt, site sp. Sm, hdg pitch, pt shd; htd wc; chem disp; shwrs inc; el pnts €3; lndtte (inc dryer); tradsmn; rest; snacks; bar; no statics; dogs €1; phone; bus 300m; site clsed 8-16 Sep; Eng spkn; adv bkg; some rd nois; CCI. "Helpful & pleasant owner; really gd 2 course meal for €10 (2010); handy fr road & easy to park; poss open w/ends only low ssn; excel." € 16.50   2011*

⊞ **SALAMANCA** *1C3* (4km E Urban) *40.94722, -5.6150* **Camping Regio, Ctra Ávila-Madrid, Km 4, 37900 Santa Marta de Tormes (Salamanca)** [923-13 88 88; fax 923-13 80 44; recepcion@campingregio.com; www. campingregio.com] Fr E on SA20/N501 outer ring rd, pass hotel/camping sp visible on L & exit Sta Marta de Tormes, site directly behind Hotel Regio. Foll sp to hotel. Lge, mkd pitch, pt sl, pt shd; wc; chem disp; mv service pnt; baby facs; shwrs inc; el pnts (10A) €3.95 (no earth); gas; lndtte; shop & 1km; hypmkt 3km; rest, snacks in hotel; bar; playgrnd; hotel pool high ssn; cycle hire; wifi (at adj hotel); TV; 5% statics; dogs; phone; bus to Salamanca; car wash; poss cr; Eng spkn; quiet; ccard acc; CCI. "In low ssn stop at 24hr hotel recep; poss v cold in winter; poss no hdstg in wet conditions; conv en rte Portugal; refurbished facs to excel standard; site poss untidy low ssn; ltd security low ssn; spacious pitches but some poss tight for lge o'fits; take care lge brick markers when reversing; excel pool; vg." ♦ € 17.40   2011*

SALAMANCA *1C3* (3km NW Rural) *40.99945, -5.67916* **Camping Ruta de la Plata, Ctra de Villamayor, 37184 Villares de la Reina (Salamanca)** [tel/fax 923-28 95 74; recepcion@campingrutadelaplata.com; www.camping rutadelaplata.com] Fr N on A62/E80 Salamanca by-pass, exit junc 238 & foll sp Villamayor. Site on R about 800m after rndabt at stadium 'Helmántico'. Avoid SA300 - speed bumps. Fr S exit junc 240. Med, some hdg/mkd pitch, terr, pt sl, pt shd; htd wc; chem disp; mv service pnt; shwrs inc; el pnts (6A) €2.90; gas; lndtte; shop & 1km; tradsmn; snacks; bar; playgrnd; pool high ssn; golf 3km; TV rm; dogs €1.50; bus to city at gate; poss cr; rd noise; red snr citizen/CCI. "Family-owned site; some gd, modern san facs (poss unhtd in winter); ltd facs low ssn; less site care low ssn & probs with el pnts; conv NH." ♦ 1 Feb-30 Nov. € 12.40 (CChq acc)   2011*

⊞ **SALDES** *3B3* (3km E Rural) *42.2280, 1.7594* **Camping Repos del Pedraforca, Ctra B400, Km 13.5, 08697 Saldes (Barcelona)** [938-25 80 44; fax 938-25 80 61; pedra@ campingpedraforca.com; www.campingpedraforca.com] S fr Puigcerdà on C1411 for 35km, turn R at B400, site on L in 13.5km. Lge, mkd pitch, pt sl, shd; htd wc; chem disp; mv service pnt; baby facs; sauna; shwrs inc; el pnts (3-10A) €4.50-6.95; lndtte (inc dryer); shop; tradsmn; rest, snacks high ssn; bar; playgrnd; 2 htd pools (1 covrd); paddling pool; cycle hire; gym; wifi; entmnt; TV rm; 50% statics; dogs €2.50; phone; Eng spkn; some rd noise; adv bkg; red long stay; ccard acc; CCI. "Tow to pitches avail; vg walking; in heart of nature reserve; poss diff ent long o'fits; lger, sunnier pitches on R of site; excel." ♦ € 29.30 (CChq acc)   2010*

⊞ **SALOU** *3C2* (2km NE Coastal) *41.08840, 1.18270* **Camping La Pineda de Salou, Ctra Tarragona-Salou, Km 5, 43481 La Pineda-Vilaseca (Tarragona)** [977-37 30 80; fax 977-37 30 81; info@campinglapineda.com; www. campinglapineda.com] Exit A7 junc 35 dir Salou, Vilaseca & Port Aventura. Foll sp Port Aventura then La Pineda/Platjes on rd TV 3148. Med, mkd pitch, pt shd; wc; baby facs; chem disp; sauna; shwrs; el pnts (5A) €4.80; gas; lndtte; shop; rest; snacks; bar; playgrnd; pool & paddling pool; spa cent; beach 400m; watersports; fishing; tennis; horseriding; cycle hire; mini club; tourist info; entmnt; TV; some statics; dogs €4 (not acc mid-Jul to mid-Aug); phone; ccard acc; red low ssn. "Conv Port Aventura & Tarragona." € 45.30   2009*

SALOU *3C2* (1km S Urban/Coastal) *41.0752, 1.1176* **Camping Sangulí-Salou, Paseo Miramar-Plaza Venus, 43840 Salou (Tarragona)** [977-38 16 41; fax 977-38 46 16; mail@ sanguli.es; www.sanguli.es] Exit AP7/E15 junc 35. At 1st rndbt take dir to Salou (Plaça Europa), at 2nd rndabt foll site sp. V lge, mkd pitch, hdstg, pt sl, shd; htd wc; chem disp; mv service pnt; some serviced pitches; baby facs; shwrs inc; el pnts (10A) inc; gas; lndtte; shop; 2 supmkts; rest; snacks; bar; BBQ; playgrnd; 3 pools & 3 paddling pools; waterslide; jacuzzi; sand beach 50m; games area; tennis; games rm; fitness rm; entmnt; excursions; cinema; youth club; mini-club; amphitheatre; wifi; TV; dogs; 35% statics; phone; bus; car wash; Eng spkn; adv bkg rec Jul-Aug; some rlwy noise; red low ssn/long stay/snr citizens; ccard acc; CCI. "Quiet end of Salou nr Cambrils & 3km Port Aventura; site facs recently updated/upgraded; excel, well-maintained site." ♦ 1 Apr-1 Nov. € 58.00   2011*

See advertisement

SAN MIGUEL DE SALINAS see Torrevieja *4F2*

⊞ **SAN ROQUE** *2H3* (6km E Rural) *36.25055, -6.66166* **Camping La Casita, Ctra N340, Km 126.2, 11360 San Roque (Cádiz)** [tel/fax 956-78 00 31] Site sp 'Via de Servicio' parallel to AP7/E15. Access at km 119 fr S, km 127 fr N. Site visible fr rd. Med, pt sl, pt terr, pt shd; wc; chem disp; mv service pnt; shwrs; el pnts (10A) €4.54; shop; rest; bar; playgrnd; pool; sand beach 3km; horseriding; entmnt; 90% statics; dogs €2.67; bus 100m; phone; poss cr; Eng spkn; adv bkg ess; noisy; ccard acc; red long stay/low ssn; CCI. "Shwrs solar htd - water temp depends on weather (poss cold); san facs poss unclean; friendly staff; conv Gibraltar & Morocco; daily buses to La Línea & Algeciras; ferries to N Africa (secure parking at port)." ♦ € 39.50   2008*

⊞ **SAN SEBASTIAN/DONOSTIA** *3A1* (5km NW Rural) *43.30458, -2.04588* **Camping Igueldo, Paseo Padre Orkolaga 69, 20008 San Sebastián (Guipúzkoa)** [943-21 45 02; fax 943-28 04 11; info@campingigueldo.com; www. campingigueldo.com] Fr W on A8, leave m'way at junc 9 twd city cent, take 1st R & R at rndabt onto Avda de Tolosa sp Ondarreta. At sea front turn hard L at rndabt sp to site (Avda Satrústegui) & foll sp up steep hill 4km to site. Fr E exit junc 8 then as above. Site sp as Garoa Camping Bungalows. Steep app poss diff for lge o'fits. Lge, hdg/mkd pitch, terr, pt shd; 40% serviced pitches; wc; chem disp; baby facs; shwrs inc; el pnts (10A) inc; gas; lndtte; shop; rest, bar high ssn; playgrnd; pool 5km; sand beach 5km; TV; phone; bus to city adj; poss cr/noisy; Eng spkn; red long stay/low ssn; CCI. "Gd, clean facs; sm pitches poss diff; spectacular views; pitches muddy when wet; excel rest 1km (open in winter)." ♦ € 31.00   2010*

SAN VICENTE DE LA BARQUERA

SAN VICENTE DE LA BARQUERA *1A4* (1km E Coastal) *43.38901, -4.3853* **Camping El Rosal, Ctra de la Playa s/n, 39540 San Vicente de la Barquera (Cantabria)** [942-71 01 65; fax 942-71 00 11; info@campingelrosal.com; www.campingelrosal.com] Fr A8 km 264, foll sp San Vicente. Turn R over bdge then 1st L (site sp) immed at end of bdge; keep L & foll sp to site. Med, mkd pitch, pt sl, terr, pt shd; wc; chem disp; shwrs; el pnts (6A) €3.50; gas; lndtte; shop; rest; snacks; bar; sand beach adj; wifi; phone; poss cr; Eng spkn; adv bkg; quiet; ccard acc; red low ssn/long stay; CCI. "Lovely site in pine wood o'looking bay; surfing beach; some modern, clean facs; helpful staff; vg rest; easy walk or cycle ride to interesting town; Sat mkt." ♦ Easter-30 Sep. € 27.00
2011*

SAN VICENTE DE LA BARQUERA *1A4* (5km E Coastal) *43.38529, -4.33831* **Camping Playa de Oyambre, Finca Peña Gerra, 39540 San Vicente de la Barquera (Cantabria)** [942-71 14 61; fax 942-71 15 30; camping@oyambre.com; www.oyambre.com] Fr N634 foll sp to La Revilla. Site on L in 3km. Lge, mkd pitch, terr, pt sl, pt shd; wc; chem disp; mv service pnt; shwrs inc; el pnts (10A) €4.55; gas; lndtte; shop & 5km; tradsmn; rest; snacks; bar; pool; beach 800m; wifi; 40% statics; bus 200m; Eng spkn; adv bkg; ccard acc; CCI. "V well-kept site; clean, dated san facs; helpful owner; quiet week days low ssn; gd base for N coast & Picos de Europa; 4x4 avail to tow to pitch if wet; some sm pitches & rd noise some pitches; conv Santander ferry." 1 Apr-30 Sep. € 20.30
2009*

SANGONERA LA SECA see Murcia *4F1*

SANGUESA *3B1* (500m S Urban) *42.57087, -1.28403* **Camping Cantolagua, Camino de Cantolagua, 31400 Sangüesa (Navarra)** [948-43 04 49; fax 948-87 13 13; info@campingcantolagua.com; www.campingcantolagua.com] Turn off N240 fr Pamplona onto N127 to Sangüesa. Turn into town over bdge, site well sp in town. Med, hdg pitch, pt shd; wc; chem disp; mv service pnt; some serviced pitches; shwrs inc; el pnts (8A) €4; lndtte (inc dryer); shops 1km; tradsmn; rest; snacks; bar; BBQ; htd pool adj; playgrnd; tennis; horseriding; cycle hire; wifi; TV rm; 20% statics; dogs; phone; poss cr; Eng spkn; 10% statics; quiet; ccard acc; CCI. "Facs clean & modern; friendly staff; lovely historic unspoilt town; gd NH." ♦ 1 Feb-31 Oct. € 19.00
2010*

SANT ANTONI DE CALONGE see Palamós *3B3*

SANT FELIU DE GUIXOLS *3B3* (1km N Urban/Coastal) *41.78611, 3.04111* **Camping Sant Pol, Ctra Dr Fleming 1, 17220 Sant Feliu de Guixols (Gerona)** [972-32 72 69 or 972-20 86 67; fax 972-32 72 11 or 972-22 24 09; info@campingsantpol.cat; www.campingsantpol.cat] Exit AP7 junc 7 onto C31 dir Sant Feliu. At km 312 take dir S'Agaro; at rndabt foll sp to site. Med, hdg/mkd pitch, terr, shd; htd wc; chem disp; mv service pnt; some serviced pitches; baby facs; shwrs inc; el pnts (10A) €4; lndtte; shop; rest; bar; BBQ; playgrnd; 3 htd pools; sand beach 350m; games rm; cycle hire; wifi; 30% statics; dogs €2; sep car park; Eng spkn; adv bkg; quiet - some rd noise; ccard acc; red long stay/snr citizens/CCI. "Vg, well-run site; excel facs; lovely pool; cycle track to Gerona." ♦ 26 Mar-12 Dec. € 53.00
2009*

SANT JOAN DE LES ABADESSES see Sant Pau de Segúries *3B3*

⊞ **SANT JORDI** *3D2* (1.5km S Rural) **Camping Maestrat Park, 12320 Sant Jordi (Castellón) [964-41 22 62 or 679-29 87 95 (mob); info@maestratpark.es; www.maestratpark.es]** Exit AP7 junc 42 onto CV11 to Sant Rafel del Riu. At rndabt with fuel stn take CV11 to Traiguera; then at rndabt take 1st exit onto N232 dir Vinarós & at next rndabt take 2nd exit sp Calig. Site 2km on L. Med, hdg/mkd pitch, hdstg, pt sl, pt shd; wc; chem disp; mv service pnt; baby facs; shwrs inc; el pnts (10A) €4.50; lndtte (inc dryer); shop; snacks; bar; BBQ; pool; paddling pool; games rm; cycle hire; wifi; TV; 25% statics; dogs; phone; Eng spkn; adv bkg; quiet; red long stay/low ssn; CCI. "Excel." ♦ € 20.00   2010*

SANT LLORENC DE LA MUGA see Figueres *3B3*

⊞ **SANT PAU DE SEGURIES** *3B3* (500m S Rural) *42.26292, 2.36913* **Camping Els Roures, Avda del Mariner 34, 17864 Sant Pau de Segúries (Gerona) [972-74 70 00; fax 972-74 71 09; info@elsroures.com; www.elsroures.com]** On C38/C26 Camprodón S twd Ripoll for 6km. In Sant Pau turn L 50m after traff lts. Site on R after 400m. Lge, mkd pitch, terr, shd; wc; mv service pnt; baby facs; shwrs inc; el pnts (4-8A) €3.20-6.50; gas; lndtte; shop; rest; bar; playgrnd; 2 pools; tennis; cinema; games rm; gym; internet; 80% statics; dogs €3.50; phone; bus 200m; poss cr; some noise; CCI. "Gd." ♦ € 26.00   2011*

⊞ **SANT PAU DE SEGURIES** *3B3* (4km SW Rural) *42.25549, 2.35081* **Camping Abadesses, Ctra Camprodón, Km 14.6, 17860 Sant Joan de les Abadesses (Gerona) [630-14 36 06; fax 972-70 20 69; info@campingabadesses.com; www.campingabadesses.com]** Fr Ripoll take C26 in dir Sant Joan, site approx 4km on R after vill. Steep access. Sm, mkd pitch, terr, unshd; htd wc; baby facs; shwrs; el pnts (6A) €2.88; gas; lndtte; shop; snacks; bar; playgrnd; pool; games area; wifi; 70% statics; dogs €3.21; bus 150m; quiet; ccard acc. "Vg facs; gd views fr most pitches; steep access to recep; poss diff access around terraces." ♦ € 21.90   2011*

SANT PERE PESCADOR *3B3* (200m E Rural) *42.18747, 3.08891* **Camping Riu, Ctra de la Playa s/n, 17470 Sant Pere Pescador (Gerona) [972-52 02 16; fax 972-55 04 69; info@campingriu.com; www.campingriu.com]** Fr N exit AP7 junc 4 dir L'Escala & foll sp Sant Pere Pescador, then turn L twds coast, site on L. Fr S exit AP7 junc 5 dir L'Escala, then as above & turn R to beaches & site. Lge, mkd pitch, shd; wc; chem disp; baby facs; shwrs inc; el pnts (5A) €3.90; gas; lndtte; shop & 300m; rest; snacks; bar; BBQ; playgrnd; pool; sand beach 2km; rv fishing adj; kayak hire; games area; entmnt; internet; 5% statics; dogs €3.40; Eng spkn; adv bkg; quiet; ccard acc; red long stay; CCI. "Excel boating facs & fishing on site; gd situation; site rec." ♦ 4 Apr-19 Sep. € 38.00   2009*

SANT PERE PESCADOR *3B3* (1km E Coastal) *42.18908, 3.1080* **Camping La Gaviota, Ctra de la Playa s/n, 17470 Sant Pere Pescador (Gerona) [972-52 05 69; fax 972-55 03 48; info@lagaviota.com; www.lagaviota.com]** Exit 5 fr A7 dir Sant Martí d'Empúries, site at end of beach rd. Med, hdg/mkd pitch, pt shd; wc; chem disp; baby facs; shwrs inc; el pnts (5A) €3.70; gas; lndtte; shop; rest; bar; playgrnd; direct access sand beach 50m; games rm; internet; 20% statics; phone; dogs €4; poss cr; Eng spkn; adv bkg; quiet; ccard acc; red long stay; CCI. "V friendly owners; gd, clean site; excel facs & constant hot water; some sm pitches & narr site rds; poss ltd access for lge o'fits; take care o'hanging trees; poss mosquito problem." ♦ 19 Mar-24 Oct. € 38.00   2009*

SANT PERE PESCADOR *3B3* (1km SE Coastal) *42.18180, 3.10403* **Kawan Village Camping L'Àmfora, Avda Josep Tarradellas 2, 17470 Sant Pere Pescador (Gerona) [972-52 05 40; fax 972-52 05 39; info@campingamfora.com; www.campingamfora.com]** Fr N exit junc 3 fr AP7 onto N11 fro Figueres/Roses. At junc with C260 foll sp Castelló d'Empúries & Roses. At Castelló turn R at rndabt sp Sant Pere Pescador then foll sp to L'Amfora. Fr S exit junc 5 fr AP7 onto GI 623/GI 624 to Sant Pere Pescador. V lge, hdg/mkd pitch, pt shd; htd wc; chem disp; mv service pnt; serviced pitches; baby facs; private san facs avail; shwrs inc; el pnts (10A) inc; gas; lndtte (inc dryer); ice; supmkt; rest; snacks; bar; BBQ (charcoal/elec); playgrnd; 4 pools; waterslide; paddling pool; sand beach adj; windsurf school; fishing; tennis; horseriding 5km; cycle hire; entmnt; wifi; games/TV rm; 15% statics; dogs €4.95; no c'vans/m'vans over 10m Apr-Sep; phone; adv bkg; Eng spkn; quiet; ccard not acc; red long stay/low ssn/snr citizens/CCI. "Excel, well-run, clean site; helpful staff; immac san facs; gd rest; poss flooding on some pitches when wet; Parque Acuatico 18km." ♦ 16 Apr-30 Sep. € 56.20 (CChq acc) SBS - E22   2011*

See advertisement opposite

SANT PERE PESCADOR *3B3* (2km SE Coastal) *42.16194, 3.10888* **Camping Las Dunas, 17470 Sant Pere Pescador (Gerona) (Postal Address: Aptdo Correos 23, 17130 L'Escala) [972-52 17 17 or 01205 366856 (UK); fax 972-55 00 46; info@campinglasdunas.com; www.campinglasdunas.com]** Exit AP7 junc 5 dir Viladamat & L'Escala; 2km bef L'Escala turn L for Sant Martí d'Empúries, turn L bef ent vill for 2km, camp sp. V lge, mkd pitch, pt sl, pt shd; wc; chem disp; mv service pnt; baby facs; serviced pitches; shwrs inc; el pnts (6A) inc; gas; lndtte (inc dryer); kiosk; supmkt; souvenir shop; rest; snacks; bar; BBQ; playgrnd; pool; paddling pool; sand beach adj; watersports; tennis; games area; games rm; money exchange; cash machines; doctor; wifi; entmnt; TV; 5% statics; dogs €4.50; phone; quiet; adv bkg (ess high ssn); Eng spkn; red low ssn; CCI. "Greco-Roman ruins in Empúries; gd sized pitches - extra for serviced; busy, popular site; excel, clean facs; vg site." ♦ 20 May-16 Sep. € 53.00   2011*

See advertisement on inside back cover

SPAIN

SANT PERE PESCADOR *3B3* (3km SE Coastal) *42.17701, 3.10833* **Camping Aquarius, Camí Sant Martí d'Empúries, 17470 Sant Pere Pescador (Gerona)** [972-52 00 03; fax 972-55 02 16; camping@aquarius.es; www.aquarius.es] Fr AP7 m'way exit 3 on N11, foll sp to Figueres. Join C260, after 7km at rndabt at Castello d'Empúries turn R to Sant Pere Pescador. Cross rv bdge in vill, L at 1st rndabt & foll camp sp. Turn R at next rndabt, then 2nd L to site. Lge, pt shd; wc; chem disp; mv service pnt; serviced pitches; baby facs; fam bthrm; shwrs; el pnts (6A) €3.75; gas; lndtte; supmkt; rest; snacks; bar; 2 playgrnds; sand beach adj; nursery in ssn; games rm; games area; car wash; internet; some statics; dogs €3.95; phone; cash point; poss cr; Eng spkn; adv bkg (ess Jul/Aug); quiet; ccard not acc; red low ssn/long stay/snr citizens (except Jul/Aug)/CCI. "Immac, well-run site; helpful staff; vg rest; windsurfing; vast beach; recycling facs; excel." ♦ 15 Mar-5 Nov. € 53.50   2010*

SANT PERE PESCADOR *3B3* (1.3km S Coastal) *42.18816, 3.10265* **Camping Las Palmeras, Ctra de la Platja 9, 17470 Sant Pere Pescador (Gerona)** [972-52 05 06; fax 972-55 02 85; info@campinglaspalmeras.com; www.campinglaspalmeras.com] Exit AP7 junc 3 or 4 at Figueras onto C260 dir Roses/Cadaqués rd. After 8km at Castelló d'Empúries turn S for Sant Pere Pescador & cont twd beach. Site on R of rd. Lge, mkd pitch, shd; wc; chem disp; mv service pnt; some serviced pitches; baby facs; shwrs inc; el pnts (10A) €4; gas; lndtte (inc dryer); shop; rest; snacks; bar; playgrnd; htd pool; paddling pool; sand beach 200m; tennis; cycle hire; games area; games rm; wifi; entmnt; TV; dogs €4.50; phone; cash point; poss cr; Eng spkn; adv bkg; quiet; red low ssn/CCI. "Pleasant site; helpful, friendly staff; superb, clean san facs; gd cycle tracks; nature reserve nrby; excel." ♦ 15 Apr-5 Nov. € 49   2010*

See advertisement

SANT PERE PESCADOR *3B3* (4km S Rural/Coastal) *42.15222, 3.11166* **Camping La Ballena Alegre, Ctra Sant Martí d'Empúries, 17470 Sant Pere Pescador (Gerona)** [902-51 05 20; fax 902 51 05 21; info2@ballena-alegre.com; www.ballena-alegre.com] Fr A7 exit 5, dir L'Escala to rd GI 623, km 18.5. At 1st rndabt turn L dir Sant Martí d'Empúries, site on R in 1km. V lge, mkd pitch, hdstg, terr, unshd; htd wc; chem disp; mv service pnt; some serviced pitches; baby facs; shwrs inc; el pnts (10A) inc; gas; lndtte (inc dryer); supmkt; tradsmn; rest; snacks; bar; BBQ; playgrnd; 3 pools; sand beach adj; watersports; tennis; games area; games rm; fitness rm; cycle hire; money exchange; surf shop; doctor; wifi; entmnt; TV rm; 10% statics; dogs €4.75; poss cr; Eng spkn; adv bkg; quiet; ccard not acc; red low ssn/snr citizens/long stay; CCI. "Excel site; superb facs." ♦ 14 May-26 Sep. € 55.90   2010*

⊞ **SANT QUIRZE SAFAJA** *3C3* (2km E Rural) *41.72297, 2.16888* **Camping L'Illa, Ctra Sant Feliu de Codina-Centelles, Km 3.9, 08189 Sant Quirze Safaja (Barcelona)** [938-66 25 26; fax 935-72 96 21; info@campinglilla.com; www.campinglilla.com] N fr Sabadell on C1413 to Caldes de Montbui; then twds Moià on C59. Turn R at vill sp, cont thro vill to T-junc, site ent opp junc. Lge, mkd pitch, hdstg, terr, pt shd; htd wc; chem disp; shwrs inc; el pnts (6A) €5.50; gas; lndtte; rest; snacks; bar; sm shop; tradsmn; playgrnd; pool; paddling pool; games area; games rm; TV; 50% statics; dogs €5; phone; bus 100m; site clsd mid-Dec to mid-Jan; Eng spkn; adv bkg; CCI. "Easy drive to Barcelona; poss open w/end only low ssn." € 28.00   2010*

⊞ **SANTA CILIA DE JACA** *3B2* (3km W Rural) *42.55556, -0.75616* **Camping Los Pirineos, Ctra Pamplona N240, Km 300.5, 22791 Santa Cilia de Jaca (Huesca)** [tel/fax 974-37 73 51; info@campingpirineos.es; www.campingpirineos.es] Fr Jaca on N240 twd Pamplona. Site on R after Santa Cilia de Jaca, clearly sp. Lge, hdg/mkd pitch, hdstg, terr, shd; wc; chem disp; mv service pnt; baby facs; shwrs inc; el pnts (5A) €6 (check for earth); gas; lndtte; shop; rest; snacks; bar; playgrnd; pool in ssn; paddling pool; tennis; games area; 30% statics; dogs; phone; site clsd Nov & open w/ends only low ssn; Eng spkn; adv bkg; some rd noise; ccard acc; red low ssn; CCI. "Excel site in lovely area; ltd access for tourers & some pitches diff lge o'fits; gd bar/rest on site; on Caminho de Santiago pilgrim rte; conv NH." ♦ € 26.00   2009*

SANTA CRISTINA DE ARO see Playa de Aro *3B3*

SANTA CRUZ see Coruña, La *1A2*

⊞ **SANTA ELENA** *2F4* (N Rural) *38.34305, -3.53611* **Camping Despeñaperros, Calle Infanta Elena s/n, Junto a Autovia de Andulucia, Km 257, 23213 Santa Elena (Jaén)** [953-66 41 92; fax 953-66 19 93; info@campingdespenaperros. com; www.campingdespenaperros.com] Leave A4/E5 at junc 257 or 259, site well sp to N side of vill nr municipal leisure complex. Med, mkd pitch, hdstg, pt shd; wc; chem disp; mv service pnt; all serviced pitches; shwrs inc; el pnts (6A) €4.25 (poss rev pol); gas; lndtte; sm shop; tradsmn; rest high ssn; snacks; bar; playgrnd; pool; internet; TV & tel points all pitches; dogs free; many statics; phone; bus 500m; adv bkg; poss noisy w/end high ssn; ccard acc; red long stay/CCI. "Gd winter NH in wooded location; gd size pitches but muddy if wet; gd walking area; friendly, helpful staff; clean san facs; disabled facs (wc only) only useable with manual wheelchair; conv national park & m'way; gd rest; sh walk to vill & shops." ♦ € 21.35   2011*

The opening dates and prices on this campsite have changed. I'll send a site report form to the Club for the next edition of the guide.

SANTA MARINA DE VALDEON *1A3* (500m N Rural) *43.13638, -4.89472* **Camping El Cares, El Cardo, 24915 Santa Marina de Valdeón (León)** [tel/fax 987-74 26 76; campingelcares@ hotmail.com] Fr S take N621 to Portilla de la Reina. Turn L onto LE243 to Santa Marina. Turn L thro vill, just beyond vill turn L at camping sp. Vill street is narr & narr bdge 2.55m on app to site. Do not attempt to app fr N if towing - 4km of single track rd fr Posada. Med, terr, pt shd; wc; chem disp; shwrs; el pnts (5A) €3.20; lndtte (inc dryer); shop; tradsmn; rest; bar; 10% statics; dogs €2.10; phone; bus 1km; quiet; ccard acc; CCI. "Lovely, scenic site high in mountains; gd base for Cares Gorge; friendly, helpful staff; gd views; tight access - not rec if towing or lge m'van." ♦ Holy Week & 15 Jun-16 Sep. € 18.85   2010*

SANTA MARTA DE TORMES see Salamanca *1C3*

⊞ **SANTA PAU** *3B3* (2km E Rural) *42.15204, 2.54713* **Camping Ecológic Lava, Ctra Olot-Santa Pau, Km 7, 17811 Santa Pau (Gerona)** [972-68 03 58; fax 972-68 03 15; vacances@i-santapau.com; www.i-santapau.com] Take rd Gl 524 fr Olot, site at top of hill, well sp & visible fr rd. Lge, mkd pitch, pt shd; wc; chem disp (wc); shwrs inc; baby facs; el pnts €4.20; gas; lndtte; shop 2km; tradsmn; rest; snacks; bar; playgrnd; pool; horseriding adj; dogs; phone; Eng spkn; adv bkg; quiet; ccard acc. "V helpful staff; gd facs; v interesting, unspoilt area & town; in Garrotxa Parc Naturel volcanic region; v busy with tourists all ssn; walks sp fr site; Pyrenees museum in Olot; tourist train fr site to volcano; excel rests in medieval town." € 24.50   2011*

⊞ **SANTA POLA** *4F2* (1km NW Urban/Coastal) *38.20105, -0.56983* **Camping Bahía de Santa Pola, Ctra de Elche s/n, Km 38, 03130 Santa Pola (Alicante)** [965-41 10 12; fax 965-41 67 90; campingbahia@santapola.com] Exit A7 junc 72 dir airport, cont to N332 & turn R dir Cartagena. At rndabt take exit sp Elx/Elche onto CV865, site 100m on R. Lge, mkd pitch, hdstg, pt shd; htd wc; chem disp; mv service pnt; baby facs; shwrs inc; el pnts (10A) €2.50; gas; lndtte (inc dryer); shop; supmkt; rest; playgrnd; pool; sand beach 1km; sat TV; 50% statics; dogs; phone; bus adj; Eng spkn; adv bkg; rd noise; ccard acc; red long stay/low ssn/CCI. "Helpful, friendly manager; well-organised site; sm pitches; recep in red building facing ent; excel san facs; site rds steep; attractive coastal cycle path." ♦ € 21.00   2010*

⊞ **SANTAELLA** *2G3* (5km N Rural) *37.62263, -4.85950* **Camping La Campiña, La Guijarrosa-Santaella, 14547 Santaella (Córdoba)** [957-31 53 03; fax 957-31 51 58; info@campinglacampina.com; www.campinglacampina. com] Fr A4/E5 leave at km 441 onto A386 rd dir La Rambla to Santaella for 11km, turn L onto A379 for 5km & foll sp. Sm, mkd pitch, hdstg, pt sl, pt shd; wc; chem disp; baby facs; shwrs inc; el pnts (10A) €4; gas; lndtte; shop & 6km; rest; snacks; bar; BBQ; playgrnd; pool; TV; dogs €2; bus at gate to Córdoba; Eng spkn; adv bkg; rd noise; ccard acc; red long stay/low ssn; CCI. "Fine views; friendly, warm welcome; popular, family-run site; many pitches sm for lge o'fits; guided walks; poss clsd winter - phone to check." ♦ € 20.50   2009*

⊞ **SANTANDER** *1A4* (12km E Rural) *43.44777, -3.72861* **Camping Somo Parque, Ctra Somo-Suesa s/n, 39150 Suesa-Ribamontán al Mar (Cantabria)** [tel/fax 942-51 03 09; somoparque@somoparque.com; www.somoparque.com] Fr car ferry foll sp Bilbao. After approx 8km turn L over bdge sp Pontejos & Somo. After Pedreña climb hill at Somo Playa & take 1st R sp Suesa. Foll site sp. Med, pt shd; wc; chem disp; shwrs & bath; el pnts (6A) €3 (poss rev pol); gas; shop; snacks; bar; playgrnd; beach 1.5km; 99% statics; site clsd 16 Dec-31 Jan; some Eng spkn; quiet; CCI. "Friendly owners; peaceful rural setting; sm ferry bet Somo & Santander; poss unkempt low ssn & poss clsd; NH only." € 17.80   2009*

SANTANDER *1A4* (6km W Coastal) *43.47611, -3.95944* **Camping Virgen del Mar, Ctra Santander-Liencres, San Román-Corbán s/n, 39000 Santander (Cantabria)** [942-34 24 25; fax 942-32 24 90; cvirdmar@ceoecant.es; www. campingvirgenmar.com] Fr ferry turn R, then L up to football stadium, L again leads strt into San Román. If app fr W, take A67 (El Sardinero) then S20, leave at junc 2 dir Liencres, strt on. Site well sp. Lge, mkd pitch, pt shd; wc; chem disp; mv service pnt; shwrs; el pnts (4-10A) €4; lndtte; shop; supmkt 2km; rest; snacks; bar; playgrnd; pool; sand beach 300m; no dogs; bus 500m; adv bkg; quiet; red long stay; CCI. "Basic facs; poss ltd hot water; some sm pitches not suitable lge o'fits; site adj cemetary; phone in low ssn to check site open; expensive low ssn." ♦ 1 Mar-10 Dec. € 28.00   2009*

SPAIN

⊞ **SANTANDER** *1A4* (2km NW Coastal) *43.46762, -3.89925* Camping Costa San Juan, Avda San Juan de la Canal s/n, 39110 Soto de la Marina (Cantabria) [tel/fax 942-57 95 80 or 629-30 36 86; hotelcostasanjuan@yahoo.es; www. hotelcostasanjuan.com] Fr A67 exit junc 2 & foll sp Liencres. In 2km at Irish pub rndabt foll sp to hotel, site behind hotel on L. Sm, pt shd; wc; chem disp; shwrs €2; el pnts (3-6A) €3.20 (poss rev pol); lndtte; rest; bar; sand beach 400m;wifi; TV rm; 90% statics; no dogs; bus 600m; poss cr; quiet. "NH for ferry; muddy in wet; poss diff lge o'fits; gd coastal walks." € 28.70   2011*

SANTANDER *1A4* (6km NW Coastal) *43.48916, -3.79361* Camping Cabo Mayor, Avda. del Faro s/n, 39012 Santander (Cantabria) [tel/fax 942-39 15 42; info@cabomayor.com; www.cabomayor.com] Sp thro town but not v clearly. On waterfront (turn R if arr by ferry). At lge junc do not foll quayside, take uphill rd (resort type prom) & foll sp for Faro de Cabo Mayor. Site 200m bef lighthouse on L. Lge, mkd pitch, terr, unshd; wc; chem disp (wc); baby facs; shwrs inc; el pnts (5A) inc; gas; lndtte; shop; rest; snacks; bar; playgrnd; pool high ssn; many beaches adj; TV; 10% statics; no dogs; phone; poss cr; Eng spkn; no ccards; CCI. "San facs old but clean; sm pitches; site popular with lge youth groups high ssn; shwrs clsd 2230-0800; conv ferry; pitches priced by size, pleasant coastal walk to Sardinero beachs." ♦ 1 Apr-14 Oct. € 27.80   2011*

⊞ **SANTIAGO DE COMPOSTELA** *1A2* (2km E Urban) *42.88972, -8.52444* Camping As Cancelas, Rua 25 do Xullo 35, 15704 Santiago de Compostela (La Coruña) [981-58 02 66 or 981-58 04 76; fax 981-57 55 53; info@campingascancelas. com; www.campingascancelas.com] Exit AP9 junc 67 & foll sp Santiago. At rndabt wth lge service stn turn L sp 'camping' & foll sp to site turning L at McDonalds. Site adj Guardia Civil barracks - poorly sp. Lge, mkd pitch, terr, pt sl, shd; wc; chem disp; baby facs; shwrs inc; el pnts (5-10A) €4.60; gas; lndtte; shop, rest, snacks & bar in ssn; BBQ; playgrnd; pool & paddling pool high ssn; wifi; entmnt; TV; dogs; phone; bus 100m; poss v cr; Eng spkn; quiet; red low ssn; CCI. "Busy site - conv for pilgrims; rec arr early high ssn; some sm pitches poss diff c'vans & steep ascent; clean san facs but stretched when site busy; gd rest; bus 100m fr gate avoids steep 15 min walk back fr town (low ssn adequate car parks in town); poss interference with car/c'van electrics fr local transmitter - if problems report to site recep; in winter recep in bar." ♦ € 26.80   2011*

SANTIAGO DE COMPOSTELA *1A2* (4km E Urban) *42.88694, -8.49027* Camping Monte do Gozo, Ctra Aeropuerto, Km 2, 15820 Santiago de Compostela (La Coruña) [981-55 89 42 or 902-93 24 24; fax 981-56 28 92; info@cvacaciones-montedogozo.com; www.cvacaciones-montedogozo.com] Site sp on 'old' rd N634 (not new autovia) into town fr E, nr San Marcos. Do not confuse with pilgrim site nr to city. Foll sp 'Ciudad de Vacaciones'. Lge, pt sl, shd; wc; chem disp; shwrs; el pnts €5 (poss rev pol); gas; lndtte; shop; rest; bar; playgrnd; 2 pools; tennis; cycle hire; 20% statics; no dogs; phone; bus 1km; ccard acc. 1 Jul-31 Aug. € 21.95   2011*

SANTILLANA DEL MAR *1A4* (3km E Rural) *43.38222, -4.08305* Camping Altamira, Barrio Las Quintas s/n, 39314 Queveda (Cantabria) [942-84 01 81; fax 942-26 01 55; altamiracamping@yahoo.es] Clear sp to Santillana fr A67; site on R 3km bef vill. Med, mkd pitch, pt sl, terr, unshd; wc; shwrs; el pnts (3A)- (5A) inc (poss rev pol); gas; lndtte; sm shop; rest; bar; pool; sand beach 8km; horseriding; TV rm; 30% statics; no dogs; bus 100m; poss cr; Eng spkn; adv bkg ess high ssn; ccard acc in ssn; CCI. "Pleasant site; ltd facs low ssn; nr Altimira cave paintings; easy access Santander ferry on m'way; gd coastal walks; open w/end only Nov-Mar - rec phone ahead; excel." 10 Mar-7 Dec. € 23.50   2011*

⊞ **SANTILLANA DEL MAR** *1A4* (500m W Rural) *43.39333, -4.11222* Camping Santillana del Mar, Ctra de Comillas s/n, 39330 Santillana del Mar (Cantabria) [942-81 82 50; fax 942-84 01 83; www.campingsantillana.com] Fr W exit A8 junc 230 Santillana-Comillas, then foll sp Santillana & site on rd CA131. Fr E exit A67 junc 187 & foll sp Santillana. Turn R onto CA131, site on R up hill after vill. Lge, sl, terr, pt shd; wc; chem disp (wc); mv service pnt; baby facs; shwrs inc; el pnts (6A) inc (poss rev pol); gas; lndtte (inc dryer); shop; rest; snacks; bar; playgrnd; pool; paddling pool; beach 5km; tennis; cycle hire; horseriding; golf 15km; entmnt; internet; car wash; cash machine; 20% statics; dogs; bus 300m; phone; poss cr; Eng spkn; some rd noise; CCI. "Useful site in beautiful historic vill; gd san facs; hot water only in shwrs; diff access to fresh water & to mv disposal point; narr, winding access rds, projecting trees & kerbs to some pitches - not rec lge o'fits or twin-axles; poss muddy low ssn & pitches rutted; poss itinerants; gd views; lovely walk to town." ♦ € 30.00 (CChq acc)   2011*

SANXENXO *1B2* (2km E Coastal) *42.39638, -8.77777* Camping Airiños do Mar, Playa de Areas, O Grove, 36960 Sanxenxo (Pontevedra) [tel/fax 986-72 31 54] Fr Pontevedra take P0308 W twd Sanxenxo & O Grove. Turn L at km post 65; site sp on S side of rd. Access rd needs care in negotiation. Sm, mkd pitch, pt shd; wc; shwrs inc; el pnts (16A) €4.81; gas; lndtte; shop; rest; bar; beach adj; bus adj; poss cr; Eng spkn; adv bkg; quiet. "Not suitable for m'vans over 2.50m high; c'vans over 6m may need help of staff at ent; bar & rest o'look beach; lovely views." 1 Jun-30 Sep. € 24.60   2011*

SANXENXO *1B2* (4km W Rural/Coastal) *42.39944, -8.85472* Camping Suavila, Playa de Montalvo 76-77, 36970 Portonovo (Pontevedra) [tel/fax 986-72 37 60; suavila@ terra.es; www.campingzodiac.com] Fr Sanxenxo take P0308 W; at km 57.5 site sp on L. Med, mkd pitch, shd; wc; serviced pitches; baby facs; shwrs inc; el pnts (6A) €3.75; gas; lndtte; shop; tradsmn; rest; snacks; bar; BBQ; playgrnd; sand beach; TV rm; phone; adv bkg; ccard acc; red long stay; quiet; CCI. "Warm welcome; friendly owner; sm pitches in 1 part of site." ♦ Holy Week-30 Sep. € 19.00   2011*

SPAIN

⊞ **SANXENXO** *1B2* (3km NW Coastal) *42.41777, -8.87555*
**Camping Monte Cabo, Soutullo 174, 36990 Noalla
(Pontevedra) [tel/fax 986-74 41 41; info@montecabo.
com; www.montecabo.com]** Fr AP9 exit junc 119 onto
upgraded VRG4.1 dir Sanxenxo. Ignore sp for Sanxenxo until
rndabt sp A Toxa/La Toja, where turn L onto P308. Cont to
Fontenla supmkt on R - minor rd to site just bef supmkt. Rd
P308 fr AP9 junc 129 best avoided. Sm, mkd pitch, terr, pt
shd; wc; chem disp; mv service pnt; shwrs inc; el pnts €3.90;
lndtte (inc dryer); shop & 500m; tradsmn; rest; snacks; bar;
playgrnd; sand beach 250m; TV; 10% statics; phone; bus
600m; poss cr; Eng spkn; adv bkg; quiet; ccard acc; red long
stay/low ssn; CCI. "Peaceful, friendly site set above sm beach
(access via steep path) with views; sm pitches; beautiful
coastline & interesting historical sites; vg." € 23.20   2011*

SANXENXO *1B2* (3km NW Coastal) *42.39254, -8.84517*
**Camping Playa Paxariñas, Ctra C550, Km 2.3 Lanzada-
Portonovo, 36960 Sanxenxo (Pontevedra) [986-72 30 55;
fax 986-72 13 56; info@campingpaxarinas.com; www.
campingpaxarinas.com]** Fr Pontevedra W on P0308 coast rd;
3km after Sanxenxo. Site thro hotel on L at bend. Site poorly
sp. Fr AP9 fr N exit junc 119 onto VRG41 & exit for Sanxenxo.
Turn R at 3rd rndabt for Portonovo to site in dir O Grove. Do
not turn L to port area on ent Portonovo. Lge, mkd pitch,
pt sl, terr, shd; wc; chem disp; baby facs; shwrs inc; el pnts
(5A) €4.75; gas; lndtte (inc dryer); shop; snacks; bar; BBQ;
playgrnd; sand beach adj; wifi; TV; 25% statics; dogs; phone;
bus adj; Eng spkn; adv bkg; quiet; ccard acc; red long stay/
CCI. "Site in gd position; secluded beaches; views over estuary;
take care high kerbs on pitches; excel san facs - ltd facs low
ssn & poss clsd." ♦ Easter-15 Oct. € 27.00   2011*

SAVINAN see Calatayud *3C1*

SAX *4F2* (5km NW Rural) **Camping Gwen & Michael, Colonia
de Santa Eulalia 1, 03630 Sax (Alicante) [965-47 44 19 or
01202 291587 (UK)]** Exit A31 at junc 48 & foll sp for Santa
Eulalia, site on R just bef vill square. Rec phone prior to arr.
Sm, hdg pitch, hdstg, unshd; wc; chem disp; fam bthrm;
shwrs inc; el pnts (3A) €1; lndtte; shops 6km; bar 100m; no
statics; dogs; quiet. "Vg CL-type site; friendly British owners;
beautiful area; gd NH & touring base." 15 Mar-30 Nov.
€ 14.00   2009*

SEGOVIA *1C4* (3km SE Urban) *40.93138, -4.09250* **Camping El
Acueducto, Ctra de La Granja, 40004 Segovia [tel/fax 921-
42 50 00; informacion@campingacueducto.com; www.
campingacueducto.com]** Turn off Segovia by-pass N110/
SG20 at La Granja exit, but head twd Segovia on DL601. Site
in approx 500m off dual c'way just bef Restaurante Lago.
Lge, mkd pitch, pt sl, pt shd; wc; chem disp; mv service pnt;
shwrs inc; el pnts (6-10A) €5; gas; lndtte; sm shop; mkt 1km;
rest adj; bar; BBQ; playgrnd; pool & paddling pool high ssn;
cycle hire; wifi; some statics; dogs; phone; bus 150m; poss
cr; m'way noise; CCI. "Excel; helpful staff; lovely views; clean
facs; gates locked 0000-0800; gd bus service; some pitches
sm & diff for lge o'fits; city a 'must' to visit." ♦ 1 Apr-30 Sep.
€ 29.00   2010*

SENA DE LUNA *1A3* (1km S Rural) *42.92181, -5.96153*
**Camping Río Luna, Ctra de Abelgas s/n, 24145 Sena de
Luna (León) [987-59 77 14; lunacamp@telefonica.net;
www.campingrioluna.com]** S fr Oviedo on AP66, at junc 93
turn W onto CL626 to Sena de Luna in approx 5km. Site on L,
sp. Med, pt shd; htd wc; chem disp; mv service pnt; shwrs inc;
el pnts (5A) €3.50; lndtte; tradsmn; snacks; bar; BBQ; rv sw
adj; internet; TV; dogs; phone; adv bkg; quiet; ccard acc. "Vg,
scenic site; walking, climbing; cent for wild boar & wolves." ♦
Easter & 1 May-30 Sep. € 15.00   2010*

SENEGUE see Sabiñánigo *3B2*

⊞ **SEO DE URGEL** *3B3* (8km N Rural) *42.42777, 1.46333*
**Camping Frontera, Ctra de Andorra, Km 8, 25799 La Farga
de Moles (Lleida) [973-35 14 27; fax 973-35 33 40; info@
fronterapark.com; www.fronterapark.com]** Sp on N145
about 300m fr Spanish Customs sheds. Access poss diff.
Suggest app fr N - turn in front Customs sheds if coming fr S.
Lge, mkd pitch, hdstg, pt sl, pt shd; htd wc; chem disp; mv
service pnt; baby facs; shwrs inc; el pnts (10A) €5.40; gas;
lndtte (inc dryer); hypmkt 2km; tradsmn; rest; snacks; bar;
playgrnd; pool; paddling pool; internet; TV rm; 90% statics;
dogs €3.60; phone; car wash; poss cr; adv bkg; noisy; CCI.
"Ideal for shopping in Andorra; winter skiing; beautiful
situation but poss dusty; sm pitches; helpful owners." ♦
€ 23.00 (CChq acc)   2011*

⊞ **SEO DE URGEL** *3B3* (3km SW Urban) *42.34777, 1.43055*
**Camping Gran Sol, Ctra N260, Km 230, 25711 Montferrer
(Lleida) [973-35 13 32; fax 973-35 55 40; info@camping
ransol.com; www.campinggransol.com]** S fr Seo de Urgel on
N260/C1313 twds Lerida/Lleida. Site approx 3km on L fr town.
Med, pt shd; wc; chem disp (wc); shwrs inc; el pnts (6A) €5.85;
gas; lndtte; shop; rest; playgrnd; pool; some statics; dogs free;
bus 100m; some Eng spkn; adv bkg; some rd noise; CCI. "Gd
site & facs (poss stretched if full); conv for Andorra; beautiful
vills & mountain scenery; in low ssn phone to check site
open; gd NH." ♦ € 21.60   2010*

SEO DE URGEL *3B3* (8.5km NW Rural) *42.37388, 1.35777*
**Camping Buchaca, Ctra St Joan de l'Erm, 25712 Castellbò
(Lleida) [973-35 21 55]** Leave Seo de Urgel on N260/1313 twd
Lerida. In approx 3km turn N sp Castellbò. Thro vill & site
on L, well sp. Steep, narr, winding rd, partly unfenced - not
suitable car+c'van o'fits or lge m'vans. Sm, mkd pitch, pt sl, pt
shd; wc; chem disp (wc); shwrs inc; el pnts (5A) €5.85; lndtte;
shop; snacks; playgrnd; pool; dogs €3.60; phone; poss cr; adv
bkg; quiet. "CL-type site in beautiful surroundings; friendly
recep." 1 May-30 Sep. € 24.50   2010*

SEVILLA See site listed under Dos Hermanas.

SPAIN

⊞ **SITGES** *3C3* (2km SW Urban/Coastal) *41.23351, 1.78111* **Camping Bungalow Park El Garrofer, Ctra C246A, Km 39, 08870 Sitges (Barcelona)** [93 894 17 80; fax 93 811 06 23; info@garroferpark.com; www.garroferpark.com] Exit 26 on the C-32 dir St. Pere de Ribes, at 1st rndabt take 1st exit, at 2nd rndabt take 2nd exit, foll rd C-31 to campsite. V lge, hdg/mkd pitch, hdstg, pt shd; htd wc; chem disp; mv service pnt; baby facs; shwrs inc; serviced pitches; el pnts (5-10A) €4.10 (poss rev pol); gas; lndtte; shop; rest; snacks; bar; playgrnd; pool; shgl beach 900m; windsurfing; tennis 800m; horseriding; cycle hire; games area; games rm; car wash; wifi; entmnt; TV; 10% statics; dogs €2.65; phone; bus adj (to Barcelona); recep open 0800-2100; site clsd 19 Dec-27 Jan to tourers; poss cr; Eng spkn; adv bkg; ccard acc; red snr citizen/low ssn; CCI. "Great location, conv Barcelona; sep area for m'vans; pleasant staff." ♦ € 36.30   2011*

See advertisement

SITGES *3C3* (1.5km W Urban/Coastal) *41.2328, 1.78511* **Camping Sitges, Ctra Comarcal 246, Km 38, 08870 Sitges (Barcelona)** [938-94 10 80; fax 938-94 98 52; info@camping sitges.com; www.campingsitges.com] Fr AP7/E15 exit junc 28 or 29 dir Sitges. Site on R after El Garrofer, sp. If app fr Sitges go round rndabt 1 more exit than sp, & immed take slip rd - avoids a L turn. Lge, mkd pitch, hdstg, pt shd; htd wc; chem disp; baby facs; shwrs inc; el pnts (4A) €4.80; gas; lndtte; shop; rest; snacks; bar; BBQ; playgrnd; pool high ssn; paddling pool; sand beach 800m; wifi; 30% statics; dogs; phone; bus 300m; train 1.5km; poss cr; Eng spkn; quiet but some rlwy noise; ccard acc; red long stay/low ssn. "Well-maintained, clean site; friendly staff; excel, clean san facs; some pitches v sm; m'vans with trailers not acc; gd pool, rest & shop; rec arr early as v popular & busy, espec w/ends; gd security." ♦ 1 Mar-20 Oct. € 26.50   2010*

⊞ **SOLSONA** *3B3* (2km N Rural) *42.01271, 1.51571* **Camping El Solsonès, Ctra St Llorenç, Km 2, 25280 Solsona (Lleida)** [973-48 28 61; fax 973-48 13 00; info@campingsolsones. com; www.campingsolsones.com] Fr Solsona to St Llorenç site on R in 2km well sp. Ignore new rd sp St Llorenç. Lge, mkd pitch, pt sl, pt shd; wc; chem disp; shwrs; el pnts (4-10A) €3.65-6.75; lndtte; shops & 2km; snacks; pool; 25% statics; clsd mid- Dec to mid-Jan; no dogs; poss cr w/end; quiet off peak; ccard acc; red CCI. "Helpful staff." € 21.60   2007*

SOPELANA see Bilbao *1A4*

SORIA *3C1* (2km SW Rural) *41.74588, -2.48456* **Camping Fuente de la Teja, Ctra Madrid-Soria, Km 223, 42004 Soria** [tel/fax 975-22 29 67; camping@fuentedelateja. com; www.fuentedelateja.com] Fr N on N111 (Soria by-pass) 2km S of junc with N122 (500m S of Km 223) take exit for Quintana Redondo, site sp. Fr Soria on NIII dir Madrid sp just past km 223. Turn R into site app rd. Fr S on N111 stake exit for Quintana Redondo & foll site sp. Med, mkd pitch, pt sl, pt shd; wc; chem disp; baby facs; shwrs inc; el pnts (6A) €3 (poss no earth); gas; lndtte; hypmkt 3km; tradsmn; rest; snacks; bar; playgrnd; pool high ssn; TV rm; many statics; dogs; phone; poss cr; adv bkg; some rd noise; ccard acc; CCI. "Vg site; excel, busy NH; vg san facs; interesting town; phone ahead to check site poss open bet Oct & Easter; easy access to site; pitches around 100sqm, suits o'fits upto 10m." ♦ Holy Week-30 Sep. € 23.80   2011*

SOTO DEL REAL see Manzanares el Real *1D4*

SOTOSERRANO *1D3* (3km E Rural) *40.43138, -5.93138* **Camping Vega de Francia, Ctra Sotoserrano-Béjar, Paraje Vega de Francia, 37657 Sotoserrano (Salamanca)** [tel/ fax 923-16 11 04; info@vegadefrancia.com; www. vegadefrancia.com] Fr Sotoserrano take Ctra de Béjar E sp Colmenar de Montemayor. Bef Roman bdge turn L onto rd sp Camping Vega de Francia for 500m to site. Single track in places. Sm, hdg pitch, hdstg, terr, shd; wc; chem disp; mv service pnt; baby facs; shwrs inc; el pnts (3A) €3; lndtte inc dryer; shop; tradsmn; rest; snacks; bar; BBQ; playgrnd; rv sw adj; TV rm; 50% statics; dogs; phone; Eng spkn; adv bkg; quiet; 20% red 15+ days; ccard acc. "Friendly, family-run site; excel bar-rest popular with locals; gd walking & views; approach poss not suitable lge o'fits." ♦ 1 Mar-31 Oct. € 17.50   2008*

⊞ **SUECA** *4E2* (5km NE Coastal) *39.30354, -0.29270* **Camping Les Barraquetes, Playa de Sueca, Mareny Barraquetes, 46410 Sueca (València) [961-76 07 23; fax 963-20 93 63; info@barraquetes.com; www.barraquetes.com]** Exit AP7 junc 58 dir Sueca onto N332. In Sueca take CV500 to Mareny Barraquetes. Or S fr València on CV500 coast rd. Foll sp for Cullera & Sueca. Site on L. Lge, mkd pitch, shd; wc; chem disp; mv service pnt; baby facs; shwrs inc; el pnts (10A) €5.88; gas; lndtte; shop; bar; BBQ; playgrnd; pool; paddling pool; waterslide; sand beach 350m; windsurfing school; tennis; games area; entmnt; TV rm; 5% statics; dogs €4.28; phone; bus 500m; site clsd Dec to mid-Jan; poss cr; Eng spkn; ccard acc; red long stay/snr citizens; CCI. "Quiet, family atmosphere; conv touring base & València." ♦ € 28.35   2008*

⊞ **SUECA** *4E2* (6km SE Coastal) *39.17711, -0.24403* **Camping Santa Marta, Ctra Cullera-Faro, Km 2, Playa del Raço, 46400 Cullera (València) [961-72 14 40; fax 961-73 08 20; info@santamartacamping.com; www.santamartacamping. com]** On N332 ent Cullera & foll sp. Turn up steep lane beside bullring (white building). Lge, terr, pt sl, shd; wc; chem disp; baby facs; shwrs; el pnts (10A) €5.88; lndtte; shop; tradsmn; rest; bar; no BBQ; playgrnd; pool; sand beach 100m; windsurfing school; cycle hire; entmnt; 5% statics; dogs €4.28; phone; site clsd mid-Dec to mid-Jan; Eng spkn; quiet; ccard acc; red long stay; CCI. "Pleasant site amongst pine trees; pitching poss diff on steep terrs; beach across busy rd; vg." ♦ € 28.35   2008*

⊞ **TABERNAS** *4G1* (8km E Rural) **Camping Oro Verde, Piezas de Algarra s/n, 04200 Tabernas (Almería) [687-62 99 96]** Fr N340A turn S onto ALP112 sp Turrillas. Turn R in 100m into narr tarmac lane bet villas, site on L in 600m, not well sp. Sm, pt shd; wc; chem disp; shwrs inc; el pnts (6-10A) inc (poss long lead req); gas; lndtte; shop 1km; rest, bar nrby in hotel; BBQ; pool; sand beach 40km; dogs; adv bkg; quiet; red long stay; CCI. "In sm olive grove; beautiful views; pitches muddy in wet; basic san facs; friendly British owners; 'Mini-Hollywood' 7km where many Westerns filmed; conv Sorbas & Guadix caves; excel." ♦ € 16.00   2011*

TALARN see Tremp *3B2*

TAMARIT see Tarragona *3C3*

⊞ **TAPIA DE CASARIEGO** *1A3* (2km W Rural) *43.54870, -6.97436* **Camping El Carbayin, La Penela-Serantes, 33740 Tapia de Casariego (Asturias) [tel/fax 985-62 37 09; http:// campingelcarbayin.com/]** Foll N634/E70 E fr Ribadeo for 2km to Serantes. Site on R 400m fr rd, well sp. Sm, mkd pitch, pt sl, pt shd; wc; chem disp; baby facs; shwrs inc; el pnts (3A) €3; lndtte; shop; rest; bar; playgrnd; sand beach 1km; fishing; watersports; some statics; bus 400m; phone; adv bkg; quiet; ccard acc; CCI. "Gd for coastal walks & trips to mountains; gd." ♦ € 18.00   2010*

TAPIA DE CASARIEGO *1A3* (3km W Coastal) *43.56394, -6.95247* **Camping Playa de Tapia, La Reburdia, 33740 Tapia de Casariego (Asturias) [tel/fax 985-47 27 21]** Fr E on N634 go past 2 exits sp Tapia de Casariego; then 500m on R foll sp over x-rd to site on L. Med, hdg/mkd pitch, pt sl, wc; chem disp; shwrs inc; el pnts (16A) €4.06; gas; lndtte (inc dryer); shop; rest; bar; sand beach 500m; wifi; dogs; bus 800m; phone; Eng spkn; adv bkg; quiet; CCI. "Gd access; busy, well-maintained, friendly site; o'looking coast & harbour; poss ltd hot water; walking dist to delightful town." ♦ Holy Week & 1 Jun-15 Sep. € 23.00   2011*

TARAZONA *3B1* (8km SE Rural) *41.81890, -1.69230* **Camping Veruela Moncayo, Ctra Vera-Veruela, 50580 Vera de Moncayo (Zaragoza) [976-64 91 54 or 639-34 92 94 (mob); antoniogp@able.es]** Fr Zaragoza, take AP68 or N232 twd Tudela/Logroño; after approx. 50km, turn L to join N122 (km stone 75) twd Tarazona; cont 30km & turn L twd Vera de Moncayo; go thro town cent; site on R; well sp. Lge, hdg pitch, pt sl, unshd; wc; shwrs inc; el pnts €5.35; gas; rest, snacks, bar & shop 300m; playgrnd adj; pool 500m; cycle hire; dogs; adv bkg; CCI. "Quiet site adj monastery; NH only." ♦ Holy Week & 15 Jun-15 Oct. € 14.50   2008*

⊞ **TARIFA** *2H3* (11km W Coastal) *36.07027, -5.69305* **Camping El Jardín de las Dunas, Ctra N340, Km 74, 11380 Punta Paloma (Cádiz) [956-68 91 01; fax 956-69 91 06; recepcion@campingjdunas.com; www.campingjdunas. com]** W on N340 fr Tarifa, L at sp Punta Paloma. Turn L 300m after Camping Paloma, site in 500m. Lge, hdg pitch, pt shd; wc; chem disp; serviced pitches; baby facs; shwrs inc; el pnts (6A) €3.37; lndtte; shop; rest; snacks; bar; playgrnd; beach 50m; entmnt; TV rm; no dogs; phone; noisy; ccard acc; red low ssn. "Poss strong winds; unsuitable lge o'fits due tight turns & trees." ♦ € 30.38   2008*

⊞ **TARIFA** *2H3* (3km NW Coastal) *36.04277, -5.62972* **Camping Rió Jara, 11380 Tarifa (Cádiz) [tel/fax 956-68 05 70; campingriojara@terra.es]** Site on S of N340 Cádiz-Algeciras rd at km post 81.2; 3km after Tarifa; clearly visible & sp. Med, mkd pitch, pt shd; wc (some cont); chem disp; mv service pnt; shwrs inc; el pnts (10A) €4; gas; lndtte (inc dryer); shop; tradsmn; rest; snacks; bar; playgrnd; sand beach 200m; fishing; wifi; dogs €3.50; poss cr; adv bkg; rd noise; ccard acc; red low ssn; CCI. "Gd, clean, well-kept site; friendly recep; long, narr pitches diff for awnings; daily trips to N Africa; gd windsurfing nrby; poss strong winds; mosquitoes in summer." ♦ € 31.00   2010*

TARIFA *2H3* (6km NW Coastal) *36.05468, -5.64977* **Camping Tarifa, N340, Km 78.87, Los Lances, 11380 Tarifa (Cádiz) [tel/fax 956-68 47 78; info@campingtarifa.es; www. campingtarifa.es]** Site on R of Cádiz-Málaga rd N340. Med, mkd pitch, hdstg, shd; wc; chem disp; mv service pnt; serviced pitch; baby facs; shwrs inc; el pnts (5A) €3.50; gas; lndtte; shop; rest; snacks; bar; playgrnd; pool; sand beach adj; wifi; no dogs; phone; car wash; Eng spkn; adv bkg; quiet; red long stay & low ssn; ccard acc. "Vg; ideal for windsurfing; immed access to beach; lovely site with beautiful pool; v secure - fenced & locked at night; some pitches sm & poss diff access due bends, trees & kerbs; conv ferry to Morocco; poss strong winds." ♦ 1 Mar-31 Oct. € 33.20 (CChq acc)   2009*

⊞ **TARIFA** *2H3* (7km NW Coastal) *36.06055, -5.66083*
**Camping Torre de la Peña 1, Ctra Cádiz, 11380 Tarifa
(Cádiz)** [956-68 49 03; fax 956-68 14 73; informacion@
campingtp.com; www.campingtp.com] Site at km 79 on
both sides of N340, sp. Steep access fr fast main rd. Lge,
terr, pt sl, pt shd; wc; shwrs; el pnts (5A) €3.50; gas; lndtte;
shop; rest; bar; pool; sand beach adj (via tunnel under rd);
dogs €2.70 (Aug not acc); few statics; poss cr; adv bkg; quiet;
red long stay/low ssn. "Excel; upper level poss diff lge o'fits;
helpful staff; superb views to Africa; conv for Gibraltar &
Tangiers; poss strong winds." € 30.60   2008*

⊞ **TARIFA** *2H3* (11km NW Coastal) *36.07621, -5.69336*
**Camping Paloma, Ctra Cádiz-Málaga, Km 74, Punta
Paloma, 11380 Tarifa (Cádiz)** [956-68 42 03; fax
956-68 18 80; campingpaloma@yahoo.es; www.
campingpaloma.com] Fr Tarifa on N340, site on L at 74km
stone sp Punta Paloma, site on R. Lge, mkd pitch, hdstg, pt
sl, terr, pt shd; wc (some cont); chem disp; mv service pnt;
shwrs inc; el pnts (6A) €4.28; gas; lndtte; shop; rest; snacks;
bar; playgrnd; pool high ssn; sand beach 1km; waterspsorts;
windsurfing; horseriding; cycle hire; 20% statics; buses 200m;
poss cr; Eng spkn; no adv bkg; quiet; ccard acc; red long stay/
low ssn; CCI. "Well-run site; vg facs; peaceful away fr busy rds;
lge o'fits poss diff due low trees; trips to N Africa & whale-
watching; mountain views." ♦ € 21.47   2009*

TARRAGONA *3C3* (4km NE Coastal) *41.13082, 1.30345*
**Camping Las Salinas, Ctra N340, Km 1168, Playa Larga,
43007 Tarragona** [977-20 76 28] Access via N340 bet km
1167 & 1168. Med, shd; wc; shwrs; el pnts €3.74; gas; lndtte;
shop; snacks; bar; beach adj; some statics; bus 200m; poss cr;
rlwy noise. Holy Week & 15 May-30 Sep. € 29.20   2011*

TARRAGONA *3C3* (5km NE Coastal) *41.13019, 1.31170*
Camping Las Palmeras, N340, Km 1168, 43080 Tarragona
[977-20 80 81; fax 977-20 78 17; laspalmeras@laspalmeras.
com; www.laspalmeras.com] Exit AP7 at junc 32 (sp Altafulla).
After about 5km on N340 twd Tarragona take sp L turn at crest
of hill. Site sp. V lge, mkd pitch, pt shd; wc; chem disp; baby
facs; shwrs inc; el pnts (6A) inc; gas; lndtte (inc dryer); shop;
tradsmn; rest; snacks; bar; playgrnd; pool; paddling pool; sand
beach adj; naturist beach 1km; tennis; games area; games rm;
wifi; entmnt; some statics; dogs €5; phone; poss cr; rlwy noise;
ccard acc; red long stay/snr citizens/low ssn; CCI. "Gd beach,
ideal for families; poss mosquito prob; many sporting facs; gd,
clean san facs; friendly, helpful staff, supermarket 5km." ♦
2 Apr-12 Oct. € 45.00 (CChq acc)   2011*

TARRAGONA *3C3* (7km NE Coastal) *41.12887, 1.34415*
**Camping Torre de la Mora, Ctra N340, Km 1171, 43080
Tarragona-Tamarit** [977-65 02 77; fax 977-65 28 58; info@
torredelamora.com; www.torredelamora.com] Fr AP7 exit
junc 32 (sp Altafulla), at rndabt take La Mora rd. Then foll site
sp. After approx 1km turn R, L at T-junc, site on R. Lge, hdstg,
terr, pt shd; wc; chem disp; mv service pnt; baby facs; shwrs
inc; el pnts (6A) €4.30; gas; lndtte; shop & 1km; tradsmn;
rest; snacks; bar; playgrnd; pool; sand beach adj; tennis;
sports club adj; golf 2km; entmnt; internet; 50% statics; dogs
€2.90; bus 200m; Eng spkn; adv bkg; quiet away fr rd & rlwy;
ccard acc; red long stay; CCI. "Improved, clean site set in
attractive bay with fine beach; excel pool; conv Tarragona &
Port Aventura; sports club adj; various pitch sizes, some v sm;
private bthrms avail." ♦ 28 Mar-31 Oct. € 42.00   2011*

TARRAGONA *3C3* (7km NE Coastal) *41.1324, 1.3604* **Camping-
Caravaning Tamarit Park, Playa Tamarit, Ctra N340, Km
1172, 43008 Playa Tamarit (Tarragona)** [977-65 01 28; fax
977-65 04 51; tamaritpark@tamarit.com; www.tamarit.
com] Fr A7/E15 exit junc 32 sp Altafulla/Torredembarra, at
rndabt join N340 by-pass sp Tarragona. At rndabt foll sp
Altafulla, turn sharp R to cross rlwy bdge to site in 1.2km,
sp. V lge, hdg pitch, some hdstg, pt sl, shd; htd wc; chem
disp; mv service pnt; serviced pitches; baby facs; fam bthrm;
private bthrms avail; shwrs inc; el pnts (10A) inc; gas; lndtte;
supmkt; rest; snacks; bar; BBQ; playgrnd; htd pool; paddling
pool; sand/shgl beach adj; watersports; tennis; games area;
entmnt; internet; TV; 30% statics; dogs €4; phone; cash
machine; car wash; adv bkg (rec Jul/Aug); Eng spkn; ccard
acc; red long stay/snr citizens/low ssn; CCI. "Well-maintained,
secure site with family atmosphere; excel beach; superb pool;
best site in area but poss noisy at night & w/end; variable
pitch prices; beachside pitches avail; take care overhanging
trees; Altafulla sh walk along beach worth visit." ♦ 3 Apr-13 Oct.
€ 62.00   2008*

TAULL see Pont de Suert *3B2*

TAVASCAN *3B2* (5km NW Rural) *42.67021, 1.23501* **Camping
Masia Bordes de Graus, Ctra Pleta del Plat, Km 5, Pallars
Sobirà, 25577 Tavascan (Lleida)** [973-62 32 46; info@
bordesdegraus.com; www.bordesdegraus.com] N fr Llavorsí
on L504. In approx 20km at Tavascan foll site sp along single
track rd. Sm, mkd pitch, pt sl, pt shd; htd wc; chem disp;
shwrs inc; el pnts (6A) €5.15; lndtte; tradsmn; rest; snacks;
bar; BBQ; playgrnd; games area; games rm; some statics;
dogs €3.60; adv bkg; quiet; CCI. "Vg site at high altitude;
gd mountain walking & climbing; not rec towed c'vans/lge
m'vans." ♦ Holy Week & 24 Jun-11 Sep. € 20.60   2008*

TIEMBLO, EL *1D4* (8km W Rural) *40.40700, -4.57400* **Camping
Valle de Iruelas, Las Cruceras, 05110 Barraco (Ávila)**
[918-62 50 59; fax 918-62 53 95; iruelas@valledeiruelas.
com; www.valledeiruelas.com] Fr N403 turn off at sp
Reserva Natural Valle de Iruelas. After x-ing dam foll sp Las
Cruceras & camping. In 5km foll sp La Rinconada, site in 1km.
Med, hdg/mkd pitch, terr, shd; wc; chem disp; baby facs;
shwrs inc; el pnts €5; lndtte; supmkt; rest; bar; playgrnd;
pool; paddling pool; canoeing; horseriding; bird hide; quiet;
CCI. "Pleasant, woodland site with wildlife." ♦ Easter-31 Aug.
€ 26.00   2009*

⊞ **TOLEDO** *1D4* (2km W Rural) *39.86530, -4.04714* **Camping
El Greco, Ctra Pueblo Montalban, Km.97, 45004 Toledo**
[tel/fax 925-22 00 90; campingelgreco@telefonica.net;
www.campingelgreco.es] Site on CM4000 fr Toledo dir La
Puebla de Montalbán & Talavera. When app, avoid town
cent, keep to N outside of old town & watch for camping sp.
Or use outer ring rd. Diff to find. Med, hdg/mkd pitch, hdstg, pt
sl, pt shd; htd wc; chem disp; mv service pnt; shwrs inc; el pnts
(6A) €4.30 (poss rev pol); gas; lndtte; shop; tradsmn; bar;
BBQ; playgrnd; pool; paddling pool; games area; dogs; bus
to town; train to Madrid fr town; phone; Eng spkn; ccard acc;
CCI. "Clean, tidy, well-maintained; all pitches on gravel; easy
parking on o'skts - adj Puerta de San Martín rec - or bus; some
pitches poss tight; san facs clean; lovely, scenic situation;
excel rest; friendly, helpful owners." € 25.40   2011*

SPAIN

TORDESILLAS *1C3* (1km SW Urban) *41.49653, -5.00614* **Kawan Village El Astral, Camino de Pollos 8, 47100 Tordesillas (Valladolid)** [tel/fax 983-77 09 53; info@campingelastral. com; www.campingelastral.com] Fr NE on A62/E80 thro town turn L at rndabt over rv & immed after bdge turn R dir Salamanca & almost immed R again into narr gravel track (bef Parador) & foll rd to site; foll camping sp & Parador. Poorly sp. Fr A6 exit sp Tordesillas & take A62. Cross bdge out of town & foll site sp. Med, hdg/mkd pitch, hdstg, pt shd; htd wc; chem disp; mv service pnt; baby facs; shwrs inc; el pnts (5A-10A) €3.60-5 (rev pol); gas; lndtte (inc dryer); shop; supmkt in town; rest; snacks; bar; playgrnd; pool in ssn; rv fishing; tennis; cycle hire; wifi; TV rm; 10% statics; dogs €2.35; phone; site open w/end Mar & Oct; Eng spkn; quiet, but some traff noise; ccard acc; CCI. "V helpful owners & staff; easy walk to interesting town; pleasant site by rv; vg, modern san facs & excel facilities; vg rest; popular NH; excel site in every way, facilities superb.." ♦ 1 Apr-30 Sep. € 39.90 (CChq acc)
2011*

TORLA *3B2* (500m N Rural) *42.63194, -0.11194* **Camping Rió Ara, Ctra Ordesa s/n, 22376 Torla (Huesca)** [974-48 62 48; campingrioara@ordesa.com; www.ordesa.net/camping-rioara] Leave N260/A135 on bend approx 2km N of Broto sp Torla & Ordesa National Park. Drive thro Torla; as leaving vill turn R sp Rió Ara. Steep, narr rd down to & across narr bdge (worth it). Med, pt sl, pt shd; wc; chem disp; baby facs; shwrs inc; el pnts (5A) €4.39; lndtte; shop; tradsmn; rest 500m; bar; no statics; phone; bus; 500m; ccard not acc; CCI. "Attractive, well-kept, family-run site; mainly tents; conv for Torla; bus to Ordesa National Park (high ssn); not rec for lge o'fits due to steep app; gd walking & birdwatching; excel." Easter-31 Oct. € 19.10
2008*

TORLA *3B2* (2km N Rural) *42.63948, -0.10948* **Camping Ordesa, Ctra de Ordesa s/n, 22376 Torla (Huesca)** [974-48 61 25; fax 974-48 63 81; info@hotelordesa.com; www.campingordesa.es] Fr Ainsa on N260 twd Torla. Pass Torla turn R onto A135 (Valle de Ordesa twd Ordesa National Park). Site 2km N of Torla, adj Hotel Ordesa. Med, pt shd; wc; chem disp; serviced pitch; baby facs; shwrs; el pnts (6A) €5.50; gas 2km; lndtte; shop 2km; tradsmn; rest high ssn; bar; playgrnd; pool; tennis; wifi (in adj hotel); some statics (sep area); dogs €3; phone; bus 1km; poss cr; Eng spkn; adv bkg (ess Jul/Aug); quiet; red low ssn; ccard acc; CCI. "V scenic; recep in adj Hotel Ordesa; excel rest; helpful staff; facs poss stretched w/end; long, narr pitches & lge trees on access rd poss diff lge o'fits; ltd facs low ssn; no access to National Park by car Jul/Aug, shuttlebus fr Torla." Easter-13 Oct. € 22.00
2010*

TORLA *3B2* (8km N Rural) *42.67721, -0.12337* **Camping Valle de Bujaruelo, 22376 Torla (Huesca)** [974-48 63 48; info@ campingvalledebujaruelo.com; www.campingvallede bujaruelo.com] N fr Torla on A135, turn L at El Puente de los Navarros onto unmade rd for 3.8km. Unsuitable lge m'vans & c'vans. Med, mkd pitch, terr, pt shd; htd wc; chem disp; mv service pnt; shwrs inc; el pnts (6A) €4.50; gas; lndtte; shop (high ssn) & 8km; rest; snacks; bar; BBQ; some statics; dogs €2; poss cr; Eng spkn; adv bkg; quiet. "In beautiful, peaceful valley in Ordesa National Park; superb views & walking." ♦ Easter-15 Oct. € 18.70
2010*

⊞ **TORRE DEL MAR** *2H4* (1km SW Coastal) *36.7342, -4.1003* **Camping Torre del Mar, Paseo Maritimo s/n, 29740 Torre del Mar (Málaga)** [952-54 02 24; fax 952-54 04 31; info@ campingtorredelmar.com; www.campingtorredelmar.com] Fr N340 coast rd, at rndabt at W end of town with 'correos' on corner turn twds sea sp Faro, Torre del Mar. At rndabt with lighthouse adj turn R, then 2nd R, site adj big hotel, ent bet lge stone pillars (no name sp). Lge, hdg/mkd pitch, hdstg, shd; wc; chem disp; mv service pnt; serviced pitches; shwrs inc; el pnts (10A) €4 (long lead req); gas; lndtte; shop & 500m; rest, snacks, bar nrby in ssn; playgrnd; pool & paddling pool; sandy/shgl beach 50m; tennis; sat TV; 39% statics; phone; poss cr all year; quiet but noise fr adj football pitch; red low ssn/long stay; CCI. "Tidy, clean, friendly, well-run site; some sm pitches; site rds tight; gd san facs; popular low ssn." ♦ € 21.20
2011*

⊞ **TORRE DEL MAR** *2H4* (1km W Coastal) *36.72976, -4.10285* **Camping Laguna Playa, Prolongación Paseo Maritimo s/n, 29740 Torre del Mar (Málaga)** [952-54 06 31; fax 952-54 04 84; info@lagunaplaya.com; www.lagunaplaya.com] Fr N340 coast rd, at rndabt at W end of town with 'correos' on corner turn twds sea sp Faro, Torre del Mar. At rndabt with lighthouse adj turn R, then 2nd R, site sp in 400m. Med, pt shd; wc; chem disp; mv service pnt; shwrs inc; el pnts (5-10A) €3.70; gas; lndtte; shop; rest; snacks; bar; playgrnd; pool; sand beach 1km; 80% statics; dogs; poss cr; Eng spkn; adv bkg; quiet; red low ssn. "Popular low ssn; sm pitches; excel, clean san facs; gd location, easy walk to town; NH only." € 19.80
2008*

⊞ **TORRE DEL MAR** *2H4* (2km W Coastal) *36.72660, -4.11330* **Camping Naturista Almanat (Naturist), Ctra de la Torre Alta, Km 269, 29749 Almayate (Málaga)** [952-55 64 62; fax 952-55 62 71; info@almanat.de; www.almanat.de] Exit E15/N340 junc 274 sp Vélez Málaga for Torre del Mar. Exit Torre del Mar on coast rd sp Málaga. In 2km bef lge black bull on R on hill & bef water tower turn L at sp. If rd not clear cont to next turning point & return in dir Torre del Mar & turn R to site at km 269. Site well sp. Lge, hdg/mkd pitch, hdstg (gravel), pt shd; htd wc; chem disp; mv service pnt (on request); sauna; shwrs inc; el pnts (10-16A) €3.90; gas; lndtte; shop; rest; bar; BBQ; playgrnd; pool; jacuzzi; sand/shgl beach adj; tennis; wifi; entmnt; cinema; games area; gym; golf 10km; some statics; dogs €2.70; phone; bus 500m; poss cr; Eng spkn; adv bkg; quiet but poss noise fr birdscarer; ccard acc; red long stay/low ssn/snr citizens up to 50%; INF card. "Superb facs; popular & highly rec; reasonable dist Seville, Granada, Córdoba; easy walk/cycle to town; emergency exit poss kept locked; sm pitches & narr site rds diff for lge o'fits." ♦ € 21.00
2009*

⊞ **TORREMOLINOS** *2H4* (3km NE Coastal) *36.64666, -4.48888* **Camping Torremolinos, Loma del Paraíso 2, 29620 Torremolinos (Málaga)** [952-38 26 02; reservas@ campingtorremolinos.com; www.campingtorremolinos. com] Fr Málaga by-pass heading W take exit sp 'aeropuerto' & foll sp Torremolinos & site. Med, hdstg; terr, pt sl, pt shd; wc (some cont); shwrs; el pnts (5A) €3.90; gas; lndtte; shop; rest 200m; snacks; bar; sand beach 700m; golf 500m; no dogs; buses & trains nrby; no adv bkg; noise fr rd, rlwy & aircraft; red CCI. "V helpful staff; v clean site; gd san facs." € 44.00
2008*

TORREVIEJA

TORREVIEJA *4F2* (4.5km S Urban) *37.94762, -0.71500*
**Camping La Campana, Ctra Torrevieja-Cartagena, Km
4.5, 03180 Torrevieja (Alicante)** [965-71 21 52] Take N332
S fr Torrevieja. Site ent dir off rndabt for Rocío del Mar at
S end of Torrevieja by-pass. Med, mkd pitch, hdstg, pt shd;
wc; chem disp; shwrs; el pnts (6A) €3.20; gas; 500m; lndtte;
shop; rest; snacks; bar; playgrnd; pool; shgle beach 1km;
80% statics; dogs €2.15; phone adj; bus 50m; poss cr; Eng
spkn; noisy; red low ssn/CCI. "OK NH." ♦ 1 Apr-30 Sep.
€ 24.60   2008*

⊞ **TORREVIEJA** *4F2* (7km SW Rural) *37.97500, -0.75111*
**Camping Florantilles, Ctra San Miguel de Salinas-Torrevieja,
03193 San Miguel de Salinas (Alicante)** [965-72 04 56; fax
966-72 32 50; camping@campingflorantilles.com; www.
campingflorantilles.com] Exit AP7 junc 758 onto CV95, sp
Orihuela, Torrevieja Sud. Turn R at rndabt & after 300m
turn R again, site immed on L. Or if travelling on N332 S past
Alicante airport twd Torrevieja. Leave Torrevieja by-pass
sp Torrevieja, San Miguel. Turn R onto CV95 & foll for 3km
thro urbanisation 'Los Balcones', then cont for 500m, under
by-pass, round rndabt & up hill, site sp on R. Lge, hdg/
mkd, hdstg, terr, pt shd; wc; chem disp; mv service pnt;
shwrs inc; el pnts (10A) inc; gas; lndtte; supmkt; snacks;
bar; BBQ; playgrnd; pool & paddling pool (high ssn); 3 golf
courses nrby; sand beach 5km; horseriding 10km; fitness
studio/keep fit classes; workshops: calligraphy, card making,
drawing/painting, reiki, sound therapy etc; basic Spanish
classes; walking club; games/TV rm; 20% statics; no dogs; no
c'vans/m'vans over 10m; recep clsd 1330-1630; adv bkg; rd
noise; ccard acc; red low ssn; CCI. "Popular, British owned
site; friendly staff; many long-stay visitors & all year c'vans;
suitable mature couples; own transport ess; gd cyling, both
flat & hilly; conv hot spa baths at Fortuna & salt lakes." ♦
€ 30.05 SBS - E11   2011*

TORROELLA DE MONTGRI *3B3* (6km SE Coastal) *42.01111,
3.18833* **Camping El Delfin Verde, Ctra Torroella de
Montgrí-Palafrugell, Km 4, 17257 Torroella de Montgrí
(Gerona)** [972-75 84 54; fax 972-76 00 70; info@
eldelfinverde.com; www.eldelfinverde.com] Fr N leave
A7 at junc 5 dir L'Escala. At Viladamat turn R onto C31 sp La
Bisbal. After a few km turn L twd Torroella de Montgrí. At
rndabt foll sp for Pals (also sp El Delfin Verde). At the flags
turn L sp Els Mas Pinell. Foll site sp for 5km. V lge, mkd
pitch, pt sl, pt shd; wc; chem disp; mv service pnt; baby
facs; shwrs inc; el pnts (6A) inc; lndtte (inc dryer); supmkt;
rests; snacks; 3 bars; BBQ; playgrnd; pool; sand beach adj;
fishing; tennis; horseriding 4km; cycle hire; windsurfing;
sportsgrnd; hairdresser; money exchange; games rm; entmnt;
disco; wifi; TV; 40% statics (sep area); winter storage; no dogs
18/7-21/8, at low ssn €4; no c'vans/m'vans over 8m high ssn;
poss cr; quiet; ccard acc; red low ssn; CCI. "Superb, gd value
site; excel pool; wide range of facilities; clean, modern san
facs; all water de-salinated fr fresh water production plant;
bottled water rec for drinking & cooking; mkt Mon." ♦
28 Apr-16 Sep. € 58.00 SBS - E01   2011*

See advertisement opposite (below)

⊞ **TORROX COSTA** *2H4* (N Urban) *36.73944, -3.94972*
**Camping El Pino, Urbanización Torrox Park s/n, 29793
Torrox Costa (Málaga)** [952-53 00 06; fax 952-53 25 78;
info@campingelpino.com; www.campingelpino.com]
Exit A7 at km 285, turn S at 1st rndabt, turn L at 2nd rndabt
& foll sp Torrox Costa N340; in 1.5km at rndabt turn R to
Torrox Costa, then L onto rndabt sp Nerja, site well sp in
4km. App rd steep with S bends. Fr N340 fr Torrox Costa foll
sp Torrox Park, site sp. Lge, mkd pitch, terr, shd; wc; chem
disp; shwrs inc; el pnts €3.80 (long lead req); gas; lndtte (inc
dryer); shop; rest, snacks adj; bar; BBQ; playgrnd; 2 pools;
sand beach 800m; games area; golf 8km; wifi; 35% statics;
dogs €2.50; phone; car wash; Eng spkn; red low ssn/long
sta/CCI. "Gd size pitches but high kerbs; narr ent/exit; gd hill
walks; conv Malaga; Nerja caves, Ronda; gd touring base."
♦ € 18.00   2011*

See advertisement opposite (Above)

TOSSA DE MAR *3B3* (500m N Coastal) *41.72885, 2.92584*
**Camping Can Martí, Avda Pau Casals s/n, 17320 Tossa
de Mar (Gerona)** [972-34 08 51; fax 972-34 24 61;
campingcanmarti@terra.es; www.campingcanmarti.net]
Exit AP7 junc 9 dir Vidreras & take C35 dir Llagostera. Turn R
at rndabt onto GI681 to coast, then GI682 to site. Mountain
rd fr Sant Feliu not rec. V lge, mkd pitch, pt shd; wc; chem
disp; baby facs; shwrs inc; el pnts (10A) €3; gas; lndtte; shop;
rest; snacks; bar; playgrnd; pool & paddling pool; shgl beach
500m; fishing; tennis; horseriding; 10% statics; dogs free;
phone; car wash; sep car park; Eng spkn; no adv bkg; quiet;
red long stay/low ssn/CCI. "Helpful, friendly staff; facs clean."
♦ 15 May-15 Sep. € 32.00   2009*

TOSSA DE MAR *3B3* (4km NE Coastal) *41.73627, 2.94683*
**Camping Pola, Ctra Tossa-Sant Feliu, Km 4, 17320 Tossa
de Mar (Gerona)** [972-34 10 50; campingpola@giverola.
es; www.camping-pola.es] Exit AP7 junc 9 onto C35 dir Sant
Feliu de Guíxols. In approx 9km turn R onto GI681 dir Tossa
de Mar. In Tossa take GI GE682 dir Sant Feliu. Narr, winding rd
but gd. Site sp. Lge, pt sl, pt shd; wc; shwrs inc; el pnts (15A)
inc; gas; lndtte (inc dryer); shop; rest; bar; playgrnd; pool;
paddling pool; sand beach adj; tennis; games area; entmnt;
some statics; dogs €3.50; bus 500m; sep car park high ssn;
adv bkg; ccard acc. "Site deep in narr coastal inlet with excel
beach; few British visitors; san facs old but clean; gd."
1 Jun-30 Sep. € 44.80   2009*

⊞ **TOTANA** *4G1* (2km SW Rural) *37.74645, -1.51933* **Camping
Totana, Ctra N340, Km 614, 30850 Totana (Murcia)**
[tel/fax 968-42 48 64; info@campingtotana.es; www.
campingtotana.es] Fr N340/E15 exit at km 612 fr N. Fr S
exit km 609. Foll Totana rd, site 2km on R. Sl ent. Sm, hdg/
mkd pitch, hdstg, terr, pt shd; wc; chem disp; shwrs inc; el
pnts (6A) €3; shop & 4km; rest, bar high ssn; BBQ; playgrnd;
pool high ssn; games rm; entmnt; 90% statics; dogs €2; Eng
spkn; red long stay; CCI. "Access to sm pitches tight due
trees; helpful owners; tidy site; ltd privacy in shwrs; vg NH."
€ 16.00   2011*

TREMP *3B2* (4km N Rural) *42.18872, 0.92152* **Camping Gaset, Ctra C13, Km 91, 25630 Talarn (Lleida)** [973-65 07 37; fax 973-65 01 02; campingaset@pallarsjussa.net; www.pallarsjussa.net/gaset/] Fr Tremp, take C13/N260 N sp Talarn. Site clearly visible on R on lakeside. Lge, pt sl, terr, pt shd; wc; chem disp; shwrs; el pnts (4A) €5.30; lndtte; shop; rest 4km; snacks; bar; BBQ; playgrnd; pool; paddling pool; sand beach & lake sw; fishing; tennis; games area; wifi; 15% statics; dogs €3.60; phone; poss cr; quiet; ccard acc. "Picturesque setting; some sm pitches." 1 Apr-15 Oct. € 24.50   2010*

⊞ **TREVELEZ** *2G4* (1km E Rural) *36.99195, -3.27026* **Camping Trevélez, Ctra Órgiva-Trevélez, Km 1, 18417 Trevélez (Granada)** [tel/fax 958-85 87 35 or 625-50-27-69 (mob); info@campingtrevelez.net; www.campingtrevelez.net] Fr Granada on A44/E902 exit junc 164 onto A348 dir Lanjarón, Pampaneira. Cont for approx 50km to on A4132 to Trevélez, site sp. Med, mkd pitch, terr, pt shd; htd wc; chem disp; mv service pnt; shwrs inc; el pnts (9A) €3.50; gas; lndtte; shop; tradsmn; rest; snacks; bar; playgrnd; pool; rv 1km; entmnt; few statics; dogs; phone; bus adj; poss cr; Eng spkn; adv bkg; quiet; red long stay. "Excel site; helpful, welcoming owners; access to Mulhacén (highest mountain mainland Spain); lots of hiking Free Wi-Fi." ♦ € 27.30   2011*

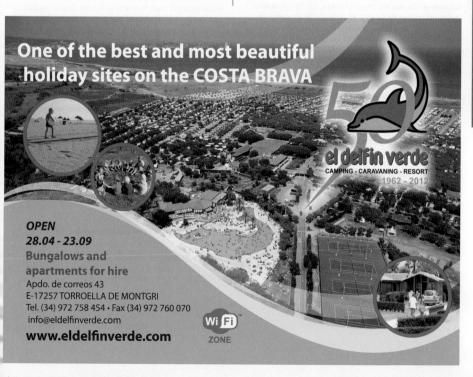
SPAIN

TURIENO see Potes *1A4*

UBRIQUE *2H3* (15km N Rural) *36.76898, -5.46043* **Camping Los Linares, Calle Nacimiento s/n, 11679 Benamahoma (Cádiz) [956-71 62 75; fax 956-71 64 73; parque@ campingloslinares.com; www.campingloslinares.com]** N fr Ubrique to El Bosque, turn E dir Benamahoma & Grazalema. Site well sp in vill. To avoid narr streets ent fr El Bosque end of vill. Med, mkd pitch, unshd; wc; chem disp; shwrs inc; el pnts inc; shop 500m; rest; snacks; bar; playgrnd; pool; some statics; no dogs; bus 300m; poss cr; CCI. "Gd walking/birdwatching area in National Park; narr vill streets poss diff lge o'fits; open w/end & public hols all year." ♦ 1 Mar-31 Oct. € 28.00   2008*

UCERO see Burgo de Osma, El *1C4*

UNQUERA *1A4* (3km N Coastal) *43.39127, -4.50986* **Camping Las Arenas, Ctra Unquera-Pechón, Km. 2, 39594 Pechón (Cantabria) [tel/fax 942-71 71 88; info@campinglasarenas. com; www.campinglasarenas.com]** Exit A8/E70 at km 272 sp Unquera. At rndabt foll CA380 dir Pechón, climb narr winding rd to site ent at top on L. Lge, pt sl, terr, pt shd; wc; chem disp; shwrs inc; el pnts (5A) €3.95 (poss rev pol); gas; lndtte (inc dryer); rest; shop & 3km; bar; playgrnd; pool; shgl beach adj; fishing; cycle hire; internet; no statics; dogs; poss cr & noisy; Eng spkn; quiet; ccard acc; CCI. "Magnificent position on terr cliffs; peaceful, well-kept & clean; immac, modern san facs; helpful staff." 1 Jun-30 Sep. € 30.40   2010*

UNQUERA *1A4* (3km S Rural) *43.3750, -4.56416* **Camping El Mirador de Llavandes, Vegas Grandes, 33590 Colombres (Asturias) [tel/fax 985-41 22 44; info@campingelmirador dellavandes.com; www.campingelmiradordellavandes. com]** Fr N634 12km W of San Vicente de la Barquera turn at km 283/284 dir Noriega, site in 1.3km. Med, mkd pitch, terr, unshd; wc; chem disp; shwrs inc; el pnts (3A) €3.20; lndtte; shop & 2km; sand beach 1km; TV; some statics; dogs €2.15; phone; no adv bkg; quiet; red CCI. "Peaceful setting; excel for touring Picos." ♦ Holy Week & 15 Jun-15 Sep. € 20.00   2008*

⊞ **VALDEAVELLANO DE TERA** *3B1* (1km NW Rural) *41.94523, -2.58837* **Camping Entrerrobles, Ctra de Molinos de Razón s/n, 42165 Valdeavellano de Tera (Soria) [975-18 08 00; fax 975-18 08 76; entrerobbles@hotmail.com; www. entrerrobles.freeservers.com]** S fr Logroño on N111, after Almarza turn R onto SO-820 to Valdeavellano. In 10km turn R at site sp, site on R in 1km. Med, mkd pitch, pt sl, pt shd; htd wc; chem disp; baby facs; shwrs inc; el pnts (6A) €5; lndtte (inc dryer); tradsmn; rest; snacks; bar; playgrnd; pool; games area; cycle hire; TV rm; 8% statics; dogs; phone; Eng spkn; adv bkg; quiet; ccard acc; red CCI. "Excel touring base; attractive area but isolated (come prepared); friendly staff; new san facs (2008)." ♦ € 19.00   2009*

VALDOVINO *1A2* (700m W Coastal) *43.61222, -8.14916* **Camping Valdoviño, Ctra Ferrol-Cedeira, Km 13, 15552 Valdoviño (La Coruña) [981-48 70 76; fax 981-48 61 31]** Fr Ortigueira on C642; turn W onto C646 sp Cadeira then Ferrol; turn R at camping sp, down hill R again, site on R almost on beach. Med, terr, pt shd; wc; chem disp; baby facs; shwrs inc; el pnts (15A) inc; gas; lndtte; shop; rest; bar; snacks; playgrnd; sand beach adj; playgrnd; wifi; TV; some statics; no dogs; bus adj; poss cr; quiet; Eng spkn; CCI. "Pleasant, busy site nr lge beach with lagoon & cliffs but poss windy; locality run down; vg rest." ♦ 10 Apr-30 Sep. € 28.50   2009*

VALENCIA *4E2* (9km S Coastal) *39.39638, -0.33250* **Camping Coll Vert, Ctra Nazaret-Oliva, Km 7.5, 46012 Playa de Pinedo (València) [961-83 00 36; fax 961-83 00 40; info@ collvertcamping.com; www.collvertcamping.com]** Fr S on V31 turn R onto V30 sp Pinedo. After approx 1km turn R onto V15/CV500 sp El Salar to exit El Salar Platjes. Turn L at rndabt, site on L in 1km. Fr N bypass València on A7/E15 & after junc 524 turn N twd València onto V31, then as above. Turn L at rndabt, site in 1km on L. Med, hdg/mkd pitch, shd; wc; shwrs inc; el pnts €4.81; gas; lndtte; shop; bar; BBQ; playgrnd; pool; paddling pool; sand beach 500m; games area; entmnt; 5% statics; dogs €4.28; phone; bus to city & marine park; car wash; poss cr; Eng spkn; adv bkg; quiet; some rd noise; ccard acc; red long stay. "Hourly bus service fr outside site to cent of València & marine park; helpful, friendly staff." ♦ 16 Feb-14 Dec. € 31.32   2009*

⊞ **VALENCIA** *4E2* (9.5km S Urban/Coastal) **Camping Park, Ctra del Riu 548, 46012 El Saler (València) [961-83 02 44]** Fr València foll coast rd or V15 to El Saler. Site adj rndabt just N of El Saler. Med, hdg/mkd pitch, hdstg, pt shd; wc; chem disp; shwrs inc; el pnts (6A) inc; lndtte; shop; rest; bar; pool; sand beach 300m; 50% statics; dogs; phone; bus at gate; poss cr; rd noise; CCI. "V conv València - hourly bus." € 25.00   2011*

⊞ **VALENCIA** *4E2* (16km S Rural) *39.32302, -0.30940* **Camping Devesa Gardens, Ctra El Saler, Km 13, 46012 València [961-61 11 36; fax 961-61 11 05; alojamiento@devesa gardens.com; www.devesagardens.com]** S fr València on CV500, site well sp on R 4km S of El Saler. Med, mkd pitch, hdstg, pt shd; htd wc; chem disp; mv service pnt; baby facs; el pnts (7-15A) €5; gas; lndtte; supmkt (high ssn) & 4km; rest; bar; BBQ; playgrnd; pool; beach 700m; tennis; lake canoeing; horseriding; 70% statics; no dogs; phone; bus to València; quiet; adv bkg; ccard acc. "Friendly staff; warden needed to connect to el pt; site has own zoo (clsd low ssn); excel." ♦ € 22.70   2011*

VALENCIA DE DON JUAN see Villamañán *1B3*

VALL LLOBREGA see Palamós *3B3*

⊞ **VALLE DE CABUERNIGA** *1A4* (1km NE Rural) *43.22800, 4.28900* **Camping El Molino de Cabuérniga, Sopeña, 39510 Cabuérniga (Cantabria)** [942-70 62 59; fax 942-70 62 78; cmcabuerniga@campingcabuerniga.com; www. campingcabuerniga.com] Fr A8/E70 take exit 249 onto N634 Cabezón de la Sal. Turn R onto CA180 sp Valle de Cabuérniga & Rionansa. After 11km turn L into vill of Sopeña. Foll sm green or blue sp to apartments & site - v narr rds. Med, shd; wc; shwrs inc; el pnts (3A) €2.67 (check earth); gas; lndtte; sm shop; snacks; bar; playgrnd; rv 200m; fishing; tennis; dogs €1.50; phone; bus 500m; adv bkg; quiet; ccard acc; CCI. "Excel site & facs on edge of vill; no shops in vicinity, but gd location, roads to site narrow in places." ♦ € 20.00   2011*

VECILLA, LA *1B3* (1km N Rural) *42.85806, -5.41155* **Camping La Cota, Ctra Valdelugueros, LE321, Km 19, 24840 La Vecilla (León)** [987-74 10 91; lacota@campinglacota.com; www.campinglacota.com] Fr N630 turn E onto CL626 at La Robla, 17km to La Vecilla. Site sp in vill. Med, mkd pitch, shd; wc; chem disp; baby facs; shwrs inc; el pnts €3.50; lndry rm; snacks; bar; games area; wifi; 50% statics; open w/ends out of ssn; train nr; quiet; ccard acc. "Pleasant site under poplar trees - poss diff to manoeuvre lge o'fits; gd walking, climbing nr; interesting mountain area." 1 Apr-30 Sep. € 17.50
                                                          2010*

VEJER DE LA FRONTERA *2H3* (4km SE) *36.25456, -5.93518* **Camping Vejer, 11150 Vejer de la Frontera (Cádiz)** [tel/fax 956-45 00 98; campingvejer@terra.es; www.campingvejer. com] App fr Málaga dir on N340, at km stone 39.5, exit to L, bet 2 rests, site in 100m. Do not take o'fit into Vejer. Sm, pt sl, terr, pt shd; wc; chem disp; shwrs; el pnts (10A) €3; lndtte; shop; snacks; bar; playgrnd; pool; sand beach 9km; golf 2km; cycle hire; internet; 10% statics; dogs €1; phone; adv bkg; quiet; ccard acc; red low ssn; CCI. "In wooded area away fr main rd; v ltd, neglected facs low ssn." 13 Apr-30 Sep. € 27.00   2008*

VEJER DE LA FRONTERA *2H3* (10km S Coastal) *36.20141, -6.03549* **Camping Caños de Meca, Ctra de Vejer-Los Caños de Meca, Km 10, 11160 Barbate (Cádiz)** [956-43 71 20; fax 956-43 71 37; info@camping-canos-de-meca.com; www.camping-canos-de-meca.com] Fr A48/N340 exit junc 36 onto A314 to Barbate, then foll dir Los Caños de Meca. Turn R at seashore rd dir Zahora. Site on L 2km beyond town. Med, mkd pitch, shd; wc; chem disp; shwrs inc; el pnts (5A) inc; gas; lndtte; shop; rest; snacks; bar; playgrnd; pool; sand beach 600m; watersports; cycle hire; 20% statics; no dogs Jul/Aug; phone; poss cr; adv bkg; ccard acc; red low ssn; CCI. "Vg." ♦ 26 Mar-12 Oct. € 39.60 (3 persons)   2008*

⊞ **VEJER DE LA FRONTERA** *2H3* (10km S Coastal) *36.20084, -6.03506* **Camping Pinar San José, Ctra de Vejer-Caños de Meca, Km 10.2, Zahora 17, 11159 Barbate (Cadiz)** [956-43 70 30; fax 956-43 71 74; info@campingpinarsanjose. com; www.campingpinarsanjose.com] Fr A48/N340 exit junc 36 onto A314 to Barbate, then foll dir Los Caños de Meca. Turn R at seashore rd dir Zahora. Site on L, 2km beyond town. Med, mkd pitch, shd; wc; chem disp; mv service pnt; fam bthrm; shwrs; el pnts inc; lndtte; shop; rest; playgrnd; pool; paddling pool; sand beach 700m; tennis; games area; wifi; sat TV; some statics; dogs €2 (low ssn only); adv bkg; quiet. "New site 2008; excel, modern facs." ♦ € 28.40   2010*

⊞ **VELEZ BLANCO** *4G1* (1km S Rural) *37.65394, -2.07845* **Camping El Pinar del Rey, Paseo de los Sauces 5, 04830 Vélez Blanco (Almería)** [950-41 55 00 or 649-90 16 80 (mob); camping@pinardelrey.es; www.pinardelrey.es] Fr A92N turn off at Vélez Rubio & foll sp Vélez Blanco on A317. Site on R bef vill. Sm, hdstg, pt shd; htd wc; chem disp (wc); mv service pnt; shwrs inc; el pnts (10A) inc; rest; snacks; bar; playgrnd; pool; TV rm; no statics; site open w/end only low ssn; poss cr; adv bkg; CCI. "Beautiful area; clean mountain air; friendly staff; site poss untidy; gd, clean facs." ♦ € 20.00
                                                          2008*

VENDRELL, EL *3C3* (2km S Coastal) *41.18312, 1.53593* **Camping Sant Salvador, Avda Palfuriana 68, 43880 Sant Salvador (Tarragona)** [tel/fax 977-68 08 04; camping santsalvador@troc.es; www.campingsantsalvador.com] Exit A7 junc 31 onto N340, after 1km turn L. Site bet Calafell & Coma-Ruga. Lge, pt shd; wc; chem disp; baby facs; shwrs inc; el pnts (4A) €5; gas; lndtte; shop; rest; bar; playgrnd; beach; 75% statics; dogs €2.50; bus adj; poss cr; ccard acc; red long stay/low ssn; CCI. "Secure site; not suitable lge o'fits; conv Safari Park & Port Aventura." ♦ 26 Mar-3 Oct. € 29.20
                                                          2010*

VENDRELL, EL *3C3* (7km SW Coastal) *41.17752, 1.50132* **Camping Francàs, Ctra N340, Km 1185.5, 43880 Coma-Ruga (Tarragona)** [977-68 07 25; fax 977-68 47 73; info@ campingfrancas.net; www.campingfrancas.net] Exit N340 at km stone 303 to Comarruga. Lge, mkd pitch, shd; wc; chem disp; baby facs; shwrs; el pnts €3.65; lndtte; shop; rest; snacks; bar; BBQ; playgrnd; sand beach adj; watersports; fishing; games area; car wash; wifi; entmnt; some statics; dogs; bus 100m; car wash; adv bkg; quiet. "Pleasant site." ♦ Easter-1 Sep. € 24.50   2010*

VIELHA *3B2* (6km N Rural) *42.73638, 0.76083* **Camping Artiganè, Ctra N230, Km 171, Val d'Arán, 25537 Pont d'Arròs (Lleida)** [tel/fax 973-64 03 38; info@camping artigane.com; www.campingartigane.com] Fr French border head S on N230 for 15km. Fr Vielha head N to France & turn L at Pont d'Arròs. Site on main rd by rv. Lge, pt sl, pt shd; wc; chem disp; baby facs; shwrs inc; el pnts (10A) €4.50; gas; lndry rm; shop; rest, snacks, bar in high ssn; BBQ; playgrnd; htd pool; games area; golf; 5% statics; dogs €3.25; bus adj; phone; poss cr; quiet; CCI. "Scenic area - wild flowers, butterflies; friendly warden; low ssn site yourself - warden calls; simple/v basic facs, poss stretched when site full." ♦ Holy Week-15 Oct. € 25.10   2011*

⊞ **VIELHA** *3B2* (7km N Rural) *42.73649, 0.74640* **Camping Verneda, Ctra Francia N230, Km 171, 25537 Pont d'Arròs (Lleida)** [973-64 10 24; fax 973-64 32 18; info@ campingverneda.com; www.campingverneda.com] Fr Lerida N on N230 twd Spain/France border, site on R adj N230, 2km W of Pont d'Arròs on rvside, 1km after Camping Artigane. Med, pt shd; wc; chem disp; baby facs; shwrs inc; el pnts (4A) €3.90; gas; lndtte; rest; snacks; bar; playgrnd; pool; horseriding; games rm; cycle hire; entmnt; TV; 10% statics; dogs €2.50; adv bkg; Eng spkn; ccard acc; CCI. "Gd area for walking; site open w/end rest of year; well-run site; gd facs." € 25.00   2011*

VIELHA

VIELHA *3B2* (6km SE Rural) *42.70005, 0.87060* **Camping Era Yerla D'Arties, Ctra C142, Vielha-Baquiera s/n, 25599 Arties (Lleida) [973-64 16 02; fax 973-64 30 53; yerla@coac.net; www.aranweb.com/yerla]** Fr Vielha take C28 dir Baquiera, site sp. Turn R at rndabt into Arties, site in 30m on R. Med, shd; htd wc; chem disp; baby facs; shwrs inc; el pnts (4-10A) €4.25-5.15; gas; lndtte; shop & rest nrby; snacks; bar; pool; skiing nr; some statics; bus 200m; phone; quiet; ccard acc; CCI. "Pleasant site & vill; ideal for ski resort; san facs variable; gd walking; OK for sh stay." 1 Dec-14 Sep. € 23.65   2010*

We can fill in site report forms on the Club's website – www.caravanclub.co.uk/europereport

VILAGARCIA DE AROUSA *1B2* (4km NE Coastal) *42.63527, -8.75555* **Camping Río Ulla, Bamio, 36612 Vilagarcía de Arousa (Pontevedra) [tel/fax 986-50 54 30; 986505430@telefonica.net; www.campingrioulla.com]** Fr N exit A9 at km 93 dir Pontecesures & take PO548 twd Vilagarcía de Arousa. Thro Catoira & in 5km turn R at traff lts at top of hill, site in 500m. Med, hdg/mkd pitch, pt shd; wc; chem disp; mv service pnt; baby facs; shwrs inc; el pnts (10A) €4; lndtte; shop; rest; snacks; bar; BBQ; playgrnd; pool; paddling pool; sand beach adj; games area; TV; 10% statics; bus 200m; Eng spkn; adv bkg; rd & rlwy noise; ccard acc; CCI. "Helpful owners; excel, clean facs." ♦ Holy Week & 1 Jun-15 Sep. € 20.00   2009*

VILALLONGA DE TER *3B3* (500m NW Rural) *42.33406, 2.30705* **Camping Conca de Ter, Ctra Setcases s/n, Km 5.4, 17869 Vilallonga de Ter (Gerona) [972-74 06 29; fax 972-13 01 71; concater@concater.com; www.concater.com]** Exit C38 at Camprodón; at Vilallonga de Ter do NOT turn off into vill but stay on main rd; site on L. Lge, mkd pitch, hdstg, pt shd; htd wc; chem disp; shwrs inc; el pnts (5-15A) €3.50-6.54; lndtte (inc dryer); shop; rest; bar; pool; paddling pool; games area; games rm; skilift 15km; entmnt; 95% statics; dogs €4.30; poss cr; Eng spkn; ccard acc; CCI. "Pitches sm & cr together; gd." ♦ € 31.00   2010*

VILANOVA DE PRADES *3C2* (500m NE Rural) *41.34890, 0.95860* **Camping Parc de Vacances Serra de Prades, Calle Sant Antoni s/n, 43439 Vilanova de Prades (Tarragona) [tel/fax 977-86 90 50; info@serradeprades.com; www.serradeprades.com]** Fr AP2 take exit 8 (L'Albi) or 9 (Montblanc), foll C240 to Vimbodi. At km 47.5 take TV7004 for 10km to Vilanova de Prades. Site ent on R immed after rndabt at ent to vill. Lge, some hdg/mkd pitch, terr, pt shd; wc; chem disp; mv service pnt; baby facs; shwrs inc; el pnts (6A) €5.80 (poss long lead req) gas; lndtte (inc dryer); basic shop & 8km; tradsmn; rest; snacks; bar; BBQ; playgrnd; htd pool; lake sw 20km; tennis; games area; games rm; wifi; TV rm; many statics; dogs; phone; Eng spkn; adv bkg high ssn; quiet; red long stay/CCI. "Well-maintained, well-run, scenic, friendly site; clean facs; sm pitches; access some pitches diff due steep, gravel site rds & storm gullies; conv Barcelona; vg touring base/NH." ♦ € 27.20 (CChq acc)   2009*

VILANOVA DE PRADES *3C2* (4km S Rural) *41.31129, 0.98020* **Camping Prades, Ctra T701, Km 6.850, 43364 Prades (Tarragona) [977-86 82 70; camping@campingprades.com; www.campingprades.com]** Fr S take N420 W fr Reus, C242 N to Albarca, T701 E to Prades. Fr N exit AP2/E90 junc 9 Montblanc; N240 to Vimbodi; TV7004 to Vilanova de Prades; L at rndabt to Prades; go thro town, site on R in 500m. Narr rds & hairpins fr both dirs. Lge, mkd pitch, pt shd; wc; chem disp; mv service pnt; baby facs; shwrs; el pnts (3A) €5.50; gas; lndtte; shop; tradsmn; rest; snacks; bar; playgrnd; pool; paddling pool; cycle hire; wifi; entmnt; TV rm; 60% statics; phone; bus 200m; poss cr; adv bkg; ccard acc; CCI. "Beautiful area; in walking dist of lovely, tranquil old town; excel, helpful staff" ♦ € 30.75   2011*

VILANOVA I LA GELTRU *3C3* (5km SW Coastal) *41.19988, 1.64339* **Camping La Rueda, Ctra C31, Km 146.2, 08880 Cubelles (Barcelona) [938-95 02 07; fax 938-95 03 47; larueda@la-rueda.com; www.la-rueda.com]** Exit A7 junc 29 then take C15 dir Vilanova onto autopista C32 & take exit 13 dir Cunit. Site is 2.5km S of Cubelles on C31 at km stone 146.2. Lge, mkd pitch, shd; htd wc; chem disp; mv service pnt; shwrs inc; el pnts (4A) €6.90; gas; lndtte; shop; rest; snacks; bar; sand beach 100m; playgrnd; pool; tennis; horseriding; watersports; fishing; entmnt; car wash; 12% statics; dogs €3.70; phone; bus; train; Eng spkn; adv bkg; quiet; red long stay/low ssn; ccard acc; red CCI. "Conv Port Aventura & Barcelona; vg family site." 16 Apr-11 Sep. € 34.50   2010*

VILANOVA I LA GELTRU *3C3* (3km NW Urban) *41.23190, 1.69075* **Camping Vilanova Park, Ctra Arboç, Km 2.5, 08800 Vilanova i la Geltru (Barcelona) [938-93 34 02; fax 938-93 55 28; info@vilanovapark.com or reservas@vilanovapark.com; www.vilanovapark.com]** Fr N on AP7 exit junc 29 onto C15 dir Vilanova; then take C31 dir Cubelles. Leave at 153km exit dir Vilanova Oeste/L'Arboç to site. Fr W on C32/A16 take Vilanova-Sant Pere de Ribes exit. Take C31 & at 153km exit take BV2115 dir L'Arboc to site. Fr AP7 W leave at exit 31 onto the C32 (A16); take exit 16 (Vilanova-L'Arboc exit) onto BV2115 to site. Parked cars may block loop & obscure site sp. V lge, hdg/mkd pitch, hdstg, terr, pt shd; htd wc; chem disp; mv service pnt; some serviced pitches; baby facs; fam bthrm; sauna; shwrs inc; el pnts (10A) inc (poss rev pol); gas; lndtte (inc dryer); supmkt; tradsmn; rest; snacks; bar; BBQ (gas/elec); playgrnd; 2 pools (1 htd covrd) & fountains; paddling pool; jacuzzi & spa; fitness cent; sand beach 3km; lake sw 2km; fishing; tennis; cycle hire; mini golf and jumping pillow for children due to open in 2012; horseriding 500m; golf 1km; games rm; wifi; entmnt; TV rm; 50% statics; dogs €12.50; phone; bus directly fr campsite to Barcelona; poss cr; Eng spkn; adv bkg ess high ssn; ccard acc; red snr citizens/low ssn/long stay; CCI. "Gd for children; excel san facs; gd rest & bar; gd winter facs; helpful staff; gd security; some sm pitches with diff access due trees or ramps; conv bus/train Barcelona, Tarragona, Port Aventura & coast; mkt Sat; excel site." ♦ € 48.60 (CChq acc) SBS - E08   2011*

See advertisement

VILLADANGOS DEL PARAMO see León *1B3*

218   ⊞Site open all year   Send in your site reports by mid September 2013

⊞ **VILLAFRANCA DE CORDOBA** *2F4* (1km W Rural) *37.95333, -4.54710* **Camping La Albolafia, Camino de la Vega s/n, 14420 Villafranca de Córdoba (Córdoba) [tel/fax 957- 19 08 35; informacion@campingalbolafia.com; www. campingalbolafia.com]** Exit A4/E5 junc 377, cross rv & at rndabt turn L & foll sp to site in 2km. Beware humps in app rd. Med, hdg/mkd pitch, hdstg, pt shd; wc; chem disp; mv service pnt; shwrs inc; el pnts (10A) €4.20 (long lead poss req); lndtte (inc dryer); shop; rest; snacks; bar; BBQ; playgrnd; pool; wifi; TV; some statics; dogs €2.80; bus to Córdoba 500m; phone; Eng spkn; quiet; CCI. "V pleasant, well-run, friendly, clean site; watersports park nrby." ♦ € 20.00
2010*

⊞ **VILLAJOYOSA** *4F2* (1km SW Coastal) *38.50000, -0.24888* **Camping Playa Paraíso, Ctra Valencia-Alicante, Km 136, 03570 Villajoyosa (Alicante) [966-85 18 38; fax 966- 85 07 98; info@campingplayaparaiso.com]** Exit AP7 junc 65A onto N332 & foll sp Villajoyosa Sud. Site on R in approx 1km, just past Campsa g'ge. Med, pt shd; htd wc; chem disp; baby facs; shwrs inc; el pnts (16A) €4.20; lndtte (inc dryer); shop; rest 500m; snacks; bar; BBQ; playgrnd; pool; beach adj; games area; games rm; wifi; 5% statics; dogs; phone; bus adj; Eng spkn; adv bkg; ccard acc; red long stay/low ssn; CCI. " Gd." € 29.50
2008*

⊞ **VILLAMANAN** *1B3* (1km SE Rural) *42.31403, -5.57290* **Camping Palazuelo, 24680 Villamañán (León) [tel/fax 987-76 82 10]** Fr N630 Salamanca-León turn SE at Villamañán onto C621 dir Valencia de Don Juan. Site on R in 1km behind hotel. Med, pt shd; wc; shwrs inc; el pnts (10A) €2.50; lndtte; shop 1km; rest; snacks; pool; quiet but some rd noise; ccard acc. "NH only; neglected & run down low ssn, poss unclean; ltd privacy in shwrs; Valencia de Don Juan worth visit." € 19.00
2009*

VILLAMANAN *1B3* (6km SE Rural) *42.29527, -5.53777* **Camping Pico Verde, Ctra Mayorga-Astorga, Km 27.6, 24200 Valencia de Don Juan (León) [tel/fax 987-75 05 25; campingpicoverd@terra.es]** Fr N630 S, turn E at km 32.2 onto C621 sp Valencia de Don Juan. Site in 4km on R. Med, mkd pitch, mkd pitch; wc; shwrs inc; el pnts (6A) inc; lndtte; shop & 1km; rest; snacks 1km; playgrnd; covrd pool; paddling pool; tennis; 25% statics; dogs free; quiet; red CCI. "Friendly, helpful staff; conv León; picturesque vill; phone ahead to check site open if travelling close to opening/closing dates." ♦ 15 Jun-8 Sep. € 17.60
2008*

VILLAMARTIN DE LA ABADIA see Ponferrada *1B3*

SPAIN

VILLANANE *1B4* (3km S Rural) *42.84221, -3.06867* **Camping Angosto, Ctra Villanañe-Angosto 2, 01425 Villanañe (Gipuzkoa) [945-35 32 71; fax 945-35 30 41; info@camping-angosto.com; www.camping-angosto.com]** S fr Bilbao on AP68 exit at vill of Pobes & take rd to W sp Espejo. Turn L 2.4km N of Espejo dir Villanañe, lane to site 400m on R. Med, some mkd pitch, pt shd; htd wc; chem disp; baby facs; shwrs inc; el pnts €4.15 (long cable poss req - supplied by site); lndtte; shop; rest; snacks; bar; BBQ; playgrnd; htd, covrd pool; entmnt; TV; 50% statics; dogs; phone; poss cr w/ends; Eng spkn; quiet. "Beautiful area; friendly staff; open site - mkd pitches rec if poss; gd rest; conv NH fr Bilbao; vultures!" ♦ 15 Feb-30 Nov. € 20.10   2009*

⊞ **VILLANUEVA DE TAPIA** *2G4* (2km S Rural) **Camping Cortijo La Alegria, Cortijo La Alegria 36, 29315 Villanueva de Tapia (Málaga) [952-75 04 19; cabinning@yahoo.co.uk]** Exit A92 junc 175 onto A333 to Villanueva de Tapia. Turn L into layby at 63km opp Hotel/Rest La Paloma. Sm, pt sl, unshd; fam bthrm; lndtte; tradsmn; lake sw & beach 11km; Eng spkn; quiet. "Vg CL-type site with superb mountain views; phone in advance; v steep ent suited m'vans & sm o'fits only; gd rest opp." € 10.00   2011*

⊞ **VILLARGORDO DEL CABRIEL** *4E1* (3km NW Rural) *39.5525, -1.47444* **Kiko Park Rural, Ctra Embalse Contreras, Km 3, 46317 Villargordo del Cabriel (València) [962-13 90 82; fax 962-13 93 37; kikoparkrural@kikopark.com; www.kikopark.com/rural]** A3/E901 València-Madrid, exit junc 255 to Villargordo del Cabriel, foll sp to site. Med, mkd pitch, hdstg, terr, pt shd; wc; chem disp; mv service pnt; some serviced pitches; shwrs inc; el pnts (6A) €3.60; gas; lndtte (inc dryer); shop; tradsmn; rest; snacks; bar; pool; lake sw 1km; canoeing; watersports; fishing; horseriding; white water rafting; cycle hire; TV; some statics; dogs €0.70; some rlwy noise; Eng spkn; adv bkg rec high ssn; ccard acc; red long stay/low ssn/snr citizens; red CCI. "Beautiful location; superb, well-run, peaceful site; lge pitches; gd walking; vg rest; many activities; helpful staff." ♦ € 28.40   2010*

VILLAVICIOSA *1A3* (8km NE Rural) *43.50900, -5.33600* **Camping La Rasa, Ctra La Busta-Selorio, 33316 Villaviciosa (Asturias) [985-89 15 29; info@campinglarase.com; www.campinglarasa.com]** Fr A8 exit km 353 sp Lastres/Venta del Pobre. In approx 500m foll site sp, cross bdge over m'way to site. Lge, hdg/mkd pitch, sl, unshd; wc; chem disp; mv service pnt; serviced pitches; shwrs inc; el pnts (6A) €3.10; lndtte; sm shop; snacks; bar; playgrnd; pool; sand beach 7km; 60% statics; dogs €2.80; phone; site open w/end low ssn/winter; Eng spkn; red low ssn; CCI. "Pleasant, friendly site; beautiful countryside; conv m'way & coast; tight access rds to sm pitches." ♦ 15 Jun-15 Sep. € 22.80   2009*

VILLAVICIOSA *1A3* (15km NW Rural) *43.5400, -5.52638* **Camping Playa España, Playa de España, Quintes, 33300 Villaviciosa (Asturias) [tel/fax 985-89 42 73; camping@campingplayaespana.es; www.campingplayaespana.es]** Exit A8 onto N632/AS256 dir Quintes then Villaverde. Site approx 12km fr Villaviciosa & 10km fr Gijón. Last 3km of app rd narr & steep with sharp bends. Med, pt shd; wc; chem disp; shwrs; el pnts €4.25 (poss rev pol); gas; lndtte; shop; snacks; bar; beach 200m; dogs €3; phone; quiet; ccard acc. "Gd site; lovely coast & scenery with mountains behind; clean; vg san facs." Holy Week & 16 May-19 Sep. € 24.60   2010*

⊞ **VILLAVICIOSA DE CORDOBA** *2F3* (8km E Rural) *38.08127, -4.92761* **Camping Puente Nuevo, Ctra A3075, Km 8.5, 14300 Villaviciosa de Córdoba (Córdoba) [tel/fax 957-36 07 27; info@campingpuentenuevo.com; www.camping puentenuevo.com]** Exit A4/E5 onto N432 dir Badajoz. In 32km turn L onto A3075, site in 8.5km. Med, hdg pitch, hdstg, sl, pt shd; wc; chem disp; shwrs inc; el pnts (16A) €4.28; lndtte; shop; tradsmn; rest; bar; BBQ; playgrnd; pool; lake sw 3km; games area; cycle hire; 40% statics; dogs €2; phone; bus 500m; poss cr; adv bkg; CCI. "Pitches poss tight lge o'fits; levellers needed all pitches; area well worth visit." ♦ € 19.92   2008*

⊞ **VINAROS** *3D2* (5km N Coastal) *40.49363, 0.48504* **Camping Vinarós, Ctra N340, Km 1054, 12500 Vinarós (Castellón) [tel/fax 964-40 24 24; info@campingvinaros.com; www.campingvinaros.com]** Fr N exit AP7 junc 42 onto N238 dir Vinarós. At junc with N340 turn L dir Tarragona, site on R at km 1054. Fr S exit AP7 junc 43. Lge, hdg/mkd pitch, hdstg, pt shd; htd wc; chem disp; mv service pnt; 85% serviced pitches; baby facs; shwrs inc; el pnts (6A) €6; gas; lndtte; shop 500m; tradsmn; rest adj; snacks; bar; playgrnd; pool; sand/shgl beach 1km; wifi; 15% statics; dogs €3; phone; bus adj; currency exchange; poss cr; Eng spkn; adv bkg - rec high ssn; quiet but some rd noise; ccard acc; red long stay/low ssn; CCI. "Excel gd value, busy, well-run site; many long-stay winter residents; spacious pitches; vg clean, modern san facs; el volts poss v low in evening; gd rest; friendly, helpful staff; rec use bottled water; Peñíscola Castle & Morello worth a visit; site set amongst orange groves; easy cycle to town." ♦ € 45.60   2011*

VINUESA *3B1* (2km N Rural) *41.9272, -2.7650* **Camping Cobijo, Ctra Laguna Negra, Km 2, 42150 Vinuesa (Soria) [tel/fax 975-37 83 31; recepcion@campingcobijo.com; www.campingcobijo.com]** Travelling W fr Soria to Burgos, at Abejar R on SO840. by-pass Abejar cont to Vinuesa. Well sp fr there. Lge, pt sl, pt shd; wc; chem disp; baby facs; shwrs inc; el pnts (3-6A) €4-5.70 (long lead poss req); gas; lndtte; shop; rest, snacks, bar high ssn; BBQ; playgrnd; pool; cycle hire; internet; 10% statics; dogs; phone; poss cr w/end; Eng spkn; phone; quiet; ccard acc; CCI. "Friendly staff; clean, attractive site; some pitches in wooded area poss diff lge o'fits; special elec connector supplied (deposit); ltd bar & rest low ssn, excel rests in town; gd walks." ♦ Holy Week-2 Nov. € 17.10   2009*

⊞ **VITORIA/GASTEIZ** *3B1* (3km W Rural) *42.8314, -2.7225* **Camping Ibaya, Arbolado de Acacias en la N102, Km 346.5, 01195 Zuazo de Vitoria/Gasteiz (Alava) [945-14 76 20]** Fr A1 take exit 343 sp N102/A3302. At rndabt foll sp N102 Vitoria/Gasteiz. At next rndabt take 3rd exit & immed turn L twd filling stn. Site ent on R in 100m, sp. Sm, mkd pitch, pt sl, pt shd; wc; chem disp; shwrs inc; el pnts (10A) €3.50; gas; lndry rm; sm shop; supmkt 2km; tradsmn; rest adj; bar; playgrnd; 5-10% statics; phone; poss cr; rd noise; CCI. "NH only; gd, modern san facs; phone ahead to check open low ssn." € 17.30   2010*

VIU DE LINAS see Broto *3B2*

VIVEIRO *1A2* (500m NW Coastal) *43.66812, -7.59998* **Camping Vivero, Cantarrana s/n, Covas, 27850 Viveiro (Lugo)** [982-56 00 04; fax 982-56 00 84; campingvivero@gmail.com] Fr E twd El Ferrol on rd LU862, turn R in town over rv bdge & bear R & foll yellow camping sp. Site in 500m adj football stadium in Covas, sp. Fr W go into town on 1-way system & re-cross rv on parallel bdge to access rd to site. Site not well sp - foll stadium sp. Med, shd; wc; chem disp; shwrs inc; el pnts (10A) €4.30; lndtte; shop & 1.5km; snacks; bar; beach 500m; wifi; phone; bus adj; o'night area for m'vans; ccard acc. "Sh walk to interesting old town, outstanding craft pottery at sharp RH bend on Lugo rd; vg clean site." Easter & 1 Jun-30 Sep. € 17.00   2011*

VIVER *3D2* (3.5km W Rural) *39.90944, -0.61833* **Camping Villa de Viver, Camino Benaval s/n, 12460 Viver (Castellón)** [964-14 13 34; info@campingviver.com; www.campingviver.com] Fr Sagunto on A23 dir Terual, approx 10km fr Segorbe turn L sp Jérica, Viver. Thro vill dir Teresa, site sp W of Viver at end of single track lane in approx 2.8km (yellow sp) - poss diff for car+c'van, OK m'vans. Med, hdg pitch, terr, pt shd; htd wc; chem disp; mv service pnt; some serviced pitches; shwrs inc; el pnts (6A) €3.80; lndtte; shop 3.5km; tradsmn; rest; snacks; bar; playgrnd; pool; TV; 10% statics; dogs €3; phone; Eng spkn; adv bkg; quiet; red long stay; ccard acc; CCI. "Improved site; lovely situation - worth the effort." ♦ 15 Feb-15 Dec. € 21.85   2009*

ZAMORA *1C3* (2.5km SE Urban) *41.48455, -5.72145* **Camping Ciudad de Zamora, Ctra Zamora-Fuentesaúco, Km 2.5, 49021 Zamora (Zamora)** [980-53 72 95; fax 980-52 14 29; info@campingzamora.com; www.campingzamora.com] Fr N630 fr N or S, turn onto C605 dir Fuentesaúco, site sp. Med, mkd pitch, pt shd; wc; chem disp; mv service pnt; baby facs; shwrs inc; el pnts (6A) inc; gas; lndry service; shop; tradsmn; rest high ssn; snacks; bar; BBQ; playgrnd; pool high ssn; rv & sand beach 3km; TV; dogs €1; phone; bus 2km; Eng spkn; adv bkg; quiet; ccard acc; red long stay/low ssn; ccard acc; red CCI. "Clean, well-run, conv site for town cent; excel san facs; friendly, helpful owners; gd cycling; ltd facs low ssn." ♦ Holy Week-15 Sep. € 27.20   2011*

⊞ **ZARAGOZA** *3C1* (3km S Urban) *41.63766, -0.94227* **Camping Ciudad de Zaragoza, Calle San Juan Bautista de la Salle s/n, 50112 Zaragoza** [876-24 14 95; fax 876-24 12 86; info@campingzaragoza.com; www.campingzaragoza.com] Fr S on A23 foll Adva Gómez Laguna, turn L at 2nd rndabt, in 500m bear R in order to turn L at rndabt, site on R in 750m, sp. Fr all other dirs take Z40 ring rd dir Teruel, then Adva Gómez Laguna twd city, then as above. Site well sp. Med, mkd pitch, hdstg, pt sl, unshd; htd wc; chem disp; mv service pnt; baby facs; shwrs inc; el pnts (10A) €4.71; lndtte (inc dryer); shop; rest; snacks; bar; BBQ; playgrnd; pool; tennis; games area; wifi; some statics; dogs €2.95; poss cr; Eng spkn; adv bkg; poss noisy (campers & daytime aircraft). "Modern san facs but poss unclean low ssn & pt htd; poss itinerants; unattractive, but conv site in suburbs." € 23.00   2011*

⊞ **ZARAUTZ** *3A1* (2.5km E Coastal) *43.28958, -2.14603* **Gran Camping Zarautz, Monte Talaimendi s/n, 20800 Zarautz (Guipúzkoa)** [943-83 12 38; fax 943-13 24 86; info@grancampingzarautz.com; www.grancampingzarautz.com] Exit A8 junc 11 Zarautz, strt on at 1st & 2nd rndabt after toll & foll site sp. On N634 fr San Sebastián to Zarautz, R at rndabt. On N634 fr Bilbao to Zarautz L at rndabt. Lge, hdg/mkd pitch, hdstg, pt sl, terr, pt shd; htd wc; chem disp; mv service pnt; shwrs inc; el pnts (6A) inc; gas; lndtte (inc dryer); shop; tradsmn; rest; bar; BBQ; playgrnd; beach 1km (steep walk); games rm; golf 1km; wifi; TV rm; 50% statics; phone; train/bus to Bilbao & San Sebastian; poss cr; Eng spkn; no adv bkg; ccard acc; CCI. "Site on cliff o'looking bay; excel beach, gd base for coast & mountains; helpful staff; some pitches sm with steep access & o'looked fr terr above; old san facs block in need of upgrade - new OK; excel disabled facs; excel rest; pitches poss muddy; NH for Bilbao ferry; rec arr early to secure pitch." ♦ € 26.10 (CChq acc)   2011*

We can fill in site report forms on the Club's website – www.caravanclub.co.uk/europereport

ZARAUTZ *3A1* (4km E Coastal) *43.27777, -2.12305* **Camping Playa de Orio, 20810 Orio (Guipúzkoa)** [943-83 48 01; fax 943-13 34 33; kanpina@terra.es; www.oriora.com] Fr E on A8 exit junc 33 & at rndabt foll sp Orio, Kanpin & Playa. Site on R. Or to avoid town cent cross bdge & foll N634 for 1km, turn L at sp Orio & camping, turn R at rndabt to site. Lge, mkd pitch, pt sl, pt shd; wc; chem disp; mv service pnt; baby facs; shwrs inc; el pnts (5A) inc; gas; lndtte (inc dryer); shop high ssn; tradsmn; rest adj; snacks; bar; playgrnd; pool high ssn; paddling pool; sand beach adj; tennis; 50% statics (sep area); no dogs; phone; car wash; poss cr at w/end; Eng spkn; adv bkg; quiet; red low ssn; ccard acc; CCI. "Busy site; flats now built bet site & beach & new marina adj - now no sea views; walks; gd facs; friendly staff; useful NH bef leaving Spain." ♦ 1 Mar-1 Nov. € 32.50   2009*

ZEANURI *3A1* (3km SE Rural) *43.08444, -2.72333* **Camping Zubizabala, Otxandio, 48144 Zeanuri** [944-47 92 06 or 660-42 30 17 (mob); zubizabala@gmail.com; www.zubizabala.com] E fr Bilbao on A8, exit at Galdakao junc 19 onto N240 dir Vitoria/Gasteiz. 2.5km S of Barazar Pass, turn L on minor rd B3542 to Otxandio. Site 300m on R, sp. Sm, mkd pitch, unshd; wc; chem disp; mv service pnt; baby facs; shwrs inc; el pnts €3.55; lndtte; shop; bar; tradsmn; playgrnd; pool 4km; lake sw 20km; games area; no statics; phone; bus at site ent; Eng spkn; adv bkg; quiet; CCI. "V pleasant, tranquil site in woods; superb countryside; conv Bilbao & Vitoria/Gasteiz." ♦ 15 Jun-15 Sep. € 22.10   2011*

ZUBIA, LA see Granada *2G4*

SPAIN

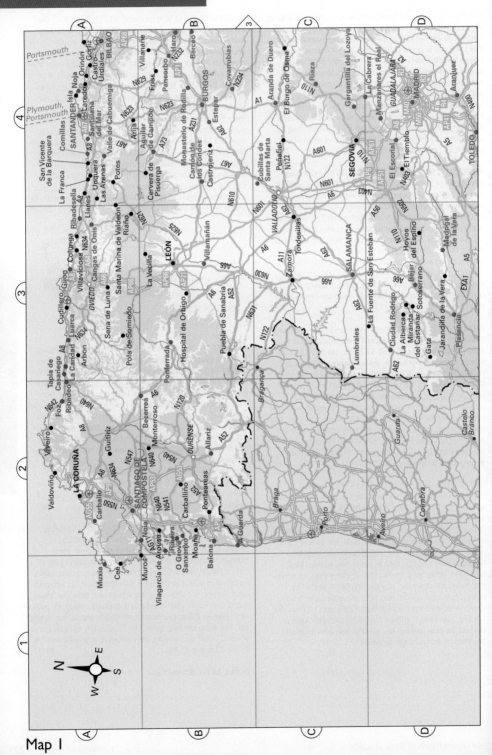

SPAIN

Map 1

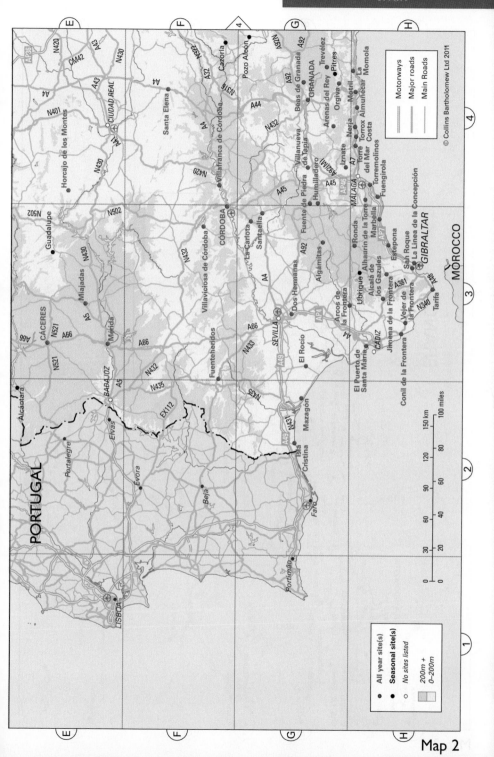

SPAIN

© Collins Bartholomew Ltd 2011

Map 2

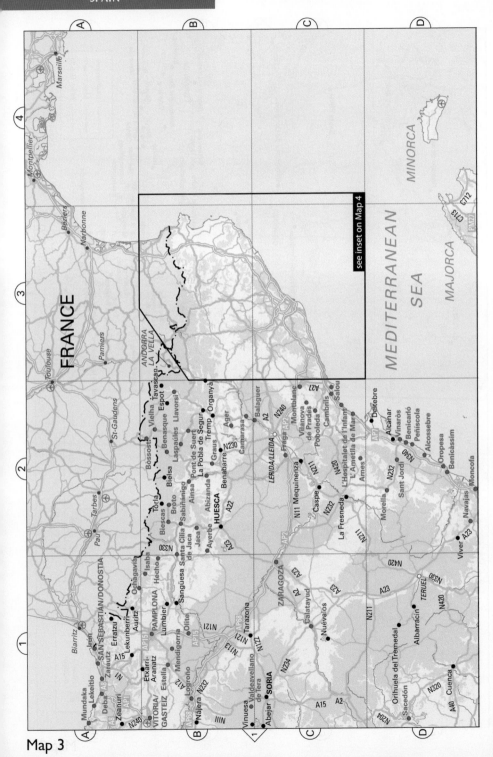

Map 3

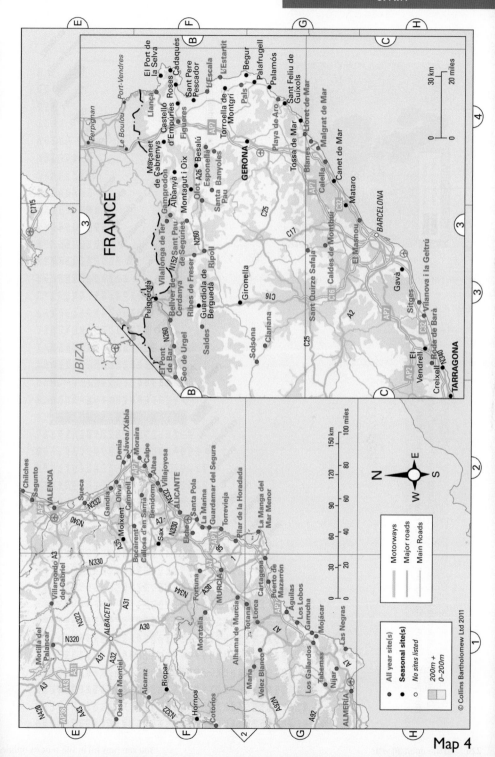

Map 4

© Collins Bartholomew Ltd 2011

Motorways
Major roads
Main Roads

• All year site(s)
• Seasonal site(s)
○ No sites listed
  200m +
  0–200m

Distances are shown in kilometres and are calculated from town/city centres along the most practical roads, although not necessarily taking the shortest route. 1km = 0.62miles

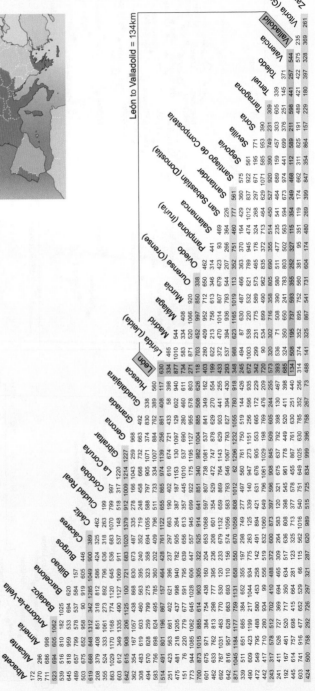

Mountain Passes and Tunnels

Passes/Tunnel Report Form

Name of Pass/Tunnel ....

To/From ....

Date Travelled..

Comments (eg gradients, traffic, road surface, width of road, hairpins, scenery)

....

....

....

..Year of Guide used:..

ARE YOU A Caravanner	Motorhome Owner	Trailer-tenter?

==

Passes/Tunnel Report Form

Name of Pass/Tunnel ....

To/From ....

Date Travelled..

Comments (eg gradients, traffic, road surface, width of road, hairpins, scenery)

....

....

Year of Guide used:...

ARE YOU A: Caravanner	Motohome Owner	Trailer-tenter?

CUT ALONG DOTTED LINE

Mountain Passes and Tunnels

Passes/Tunnel Report Form

Name of Pass/Tunnel ....

To/From ....

Date Travelled...

Comments (eg gradients, traffic, road surface, width of road, hairpins, scenery)

....

....

....

..Year of Guide used:...

ARE YOU A Caravanner	Motorhome Owner	Trailer-tenter?

==

Passes/Tunnel Report Form

Name of Pass/Tunnel ....

To/From ....

Date Travelled...

Comments (eg gradients, traffic, road surface, width of road, hairpins, scenery)

....

....

Year of Guide used:...

ARE YOU A: Caravanner	Motorhome Owner	Trailer-tenter?

Caravan Europe Site Report Form **

If campsite is already listed, complete only those sections of the form where changes apply

Please print, type or tick in the white areas

Sites not reported on for 5 years may be deleted from the guide

Year of guide used	20..........	Is site listed?	Listed on page no.	Unlisted	Date of visit	......../......../........

A – CAMPSITE NAME AND LOCATION

Country		Name of town/village site listed under *(see Sites Location Maps)*				
Distance & direction from centre of town site is listed under *(in a straight line)*		....................km	eg N, NE, S, SW	Urban	Rural	Coastal
Site open all year?	Y / N	Period site is open *(if not all year)*	................./............ to ..../...............			
Site name					Naturist site	Y / N
Site address						
Telephone			Fax			
E-mail			Website			

B – CAMPSITE CHARGES

Charge for car, caravan + 2 adults in local currency	PRICE		EL PNTS inc in this price?	Y / N	Amps ....

C – DIRECTIONS

Brief, specific directions to site (in km) *To convert miles to kilometres multiply by 8 and divide by 5 or use Conversion Table in guide*	
GPS	Latitude...(eg 12.34567) Longitude...(eg 1.23456 or -1.23456)

D – CAMPSITE DESCRIPTION

SITE size ie number of pitches	Small Max 50	SM	Medium 51-150	MED	Large 151-500	LGE	Very large 500+	V LGE	Unchanged
PITCH size	*eg small, medium, large, very large, various*								Unchanged
Pitch features if **NOT** open-plan/grassy		Hedged	HDG PITCH	Marked or numbered	MKD PITCH	Hardstanding or gravel	HDSTG	Unchanged	
If site is **NOT** level, is it		Part sloping	PT SL	Sloping	SL	Terraced	TERR	Unchanged	
Is site shaded?		Shaded	SHD	Part shaded	PT SHD	Unshaded	UNSHD	Unchanged	

E – CAMPSITE FACILITIES

WC	Heated	HTD WC	Continental	CONT	Own San recommended		OWN SAN REC	
Chemical disposal point		CHEM DISP		Dedicated point		WC only		
Motor caravan waste discharge and water refill point				MV SERVICE PNT				
Child / baby facilities (bathroom)		CHILD / BABY FACS		Family bathroom		FAM BTHRM		
Hot shower(s)		SHWR(S)		Inc in site fee?	Y / N	Price...................*(if not inc)*		
ELECTRIC HOOK UP *if not included in price above*		EL PNTS		Price...........................		Amps.............................		
Supplies of bottled gas		GAS		On site	Y / N	Or in .... Kms		
Launderette / Washing Machine		LNDTTE	Inc dryer Y / N		LNDRY RM *(if no washing machine)*			

** *You can also complete forms online: www.caravanclub.co.uk/europereport*

F – FOOD & DRINK

Shop(s) / supermarket	SHOP(S) / SUPMKT	On site		or		.... kms	
Bread / milk delivered	TRADSMN						
Restaurant / cafeteria	REST	On site		or		.... kms	
Snack bar / take-away	SNACKS	On site		or		.... kms	
Bar	BAR	On site		or		.... kms	
Barbecue allowed	BBQ	Charcoal		Gas		Elec	Sep area
Cooking facilities	COOKING FACS						

G – LEISURE FACILITIES

Playground	PLAYGRND						
Swimming pool	POOL	On site		or ....km		Heated	Covered
Beach	BEACH	Adj		or ....km		Sand	Shingle
Alternative swimming *(lake)*	SW	Adj		or ....km		Sand	Shingle
Games /sports area / Games room	GAMES AREA	GAMES ROOM					
Entertainment in high season	ENTMNT						
Internet use by visitors	INTERNET	Wifi Internet			WIFI		
Television room	TV RM	Satellite / Cable to pitches			TV CAB / SAT		

H – OTHER INFORMATION

% Static caravans / mobile homes / chalets / cottages / fixed tents on site				..............% STATICS
Dogs allowed	DOGS	Y / N	Price per night .... *(if allowed)*	
Phone	PHONE	On site	Adj	
Bus / tram / train	BUS / TRAM / TRAIN	Adj	or .... km	
Twin axles caravans allowed?	TWIN AXLES Y / N	Possibly crowded in high season		POSS CR
English spoken	ENG SPKN			
Advance bookings accepted	ADV BKG	Y / N		
Noise levels on site in season	NOISY	QUIET	If noisy, why?	
Credit card accepted	CCARD ACC	Reduction low season		RED LOW SSN
Camping Card International accepted in lieu of passport	CCI	INF card required *(If naturist site)*		Y / N
Facilities for disabled	Full wheelchair facilities	♦	Limited disabled facilities	♦ ltd

I – ADDITIONAL REMARKS AND/OR ITEMS OF INTEREST

Tourist attractions, unusual features or other facilities, eg waterslide, tennis, cycle hire, watersports, horseriding, separate car park, walking distance to shops etc	YOUR OPINION OF THE SITE:	
	EXCEL	
	VERY GOOD	
	GOOD	
	FAIR	POOR
	NIGHT HALT ONLY	
Your comments & opinions may be used in future editions of the guide, if you do not wish them to be used please tick		

J – MEMBER DETAILS

ARE YOU A:	Caravanner		Motor caravanner		Trailer-tenter?	
NAME:		CARAVAN CLUB MEMBERSHIP NO:				
		POST CODE:				
DO YOU NEED MORE BLANK SITE REPORT FORMS?			YES		NO	
Address *(Non-members only please complete this section)*						

Please use a separate form for each campsite and do not send receipts. Owing to the large number of site reports received, it is not possible to enter into correspondence. Please return completed form to:

The Editor, Caravan Europe, The Caravan Club
FREEPOST, PO Box 386, (RRZG-SXKK-UCUJ)
East Grinstead RH19 1FH

(This address to be used when mailing within the UK only)

Caravan Europe Site Report Form **

If campsite is already listed, complete only those sections of the form where changes apply

Please print, type or tick in the white areas

Sites not reported on for 5 years may be deleted from the guide

Year of guide used	20.........	Is site listed?	Listed on page no.	Unlisted	Date of visit	......../......../........

A – CAMPSITE NAME AND LOCATION

Country		Name of town/village site listed under *(see Sites Location Maps)*					
Distance & direction from centre of town site is listed under *(in a straight line)*	....................km		eg N, NE, S, SW		Urban	Rural	Coastal
Site open all year?	Y / N	Period site is open *(if not all year)*	................/................	to	................/................		
Site name						Naturist site	Y / N
Site address							
Telephone			Fax				
E-mail			Website				

B – CAMPSITE CHARGES

Charge for car, caravan + 2 adults in local currency	PRICE		EL PNTS inc in this price?	Y / N	Amps ....

C – DIRECTIONS

Brief, specific directions to site (in km) *To convert miles to kilometres multiply by 8 and divide by 5 or use Conversion Table in guide*	
GPS	Latitude...(eg 12.34567) Longitude..(eg 1.23456 or -1.23456)

D – CAMPSITE DESCRIPTION

SITE size ie number of pitches	Small Max 50	SM	Medium 51-150	MED	Large 151-500	LGE	Very large 500+	V LGE	Unchanged
PITCH size	*eg small, medium, large, very large, various*								Unchanged
Pitch features if NOT open-plan/grassy		Hedged	HDG PITCH	Marked or numbered	MKD PITCH	Hardstanding or gravel	HDSTG		Unchanged
If site is NOT level, is it		Part sloping	PT SL	Sloping	SL	Terraced	TERR		Unchanged
Is site shaded?		Shaded	SHD	Part shaded	PT SHD	Unshaded	UNSHD		Unchanged

E – CAMPSITE FACILITIES

WC		Heated	HTD WC	Continental	CONT	Own San recommended		OWN SAN REC	
Chemical disposal point			CHEM DISP		Dedicated point		WC only		
Motor caravan waste discharge and water refill point					MV SERVICE PNT				
Child / baby facilities (bathroom)			CHILD / BABY FACS		Family bathroom		FAM BTHRM		
Hot shower(s)			SHWR(S)		Inc in site fee?	Y / N	Price...................(if not inc)		
ELECTRIC HOOK UP *if not included in price above*			EL PNTS		Price..		Amps..		
Supplies of bottled gas			GAS		On site	Y / N	Or in .... Kms		
Launderette / Washing Machine			LNDTTE		Inc dryer Y / N		LNDRY RM *(if no washing machine)*		

*** You can also complete forms online at: www.caravanclub.co.uk/europereport*

F – FOOD & DRINK

Shop(s) / supermarket	SHOP(S) / SUPMKT	On site		or	.... kms
Bread / milk delivered	TRADSMN				
Restaurant / cafeteria	REST	On site		or	.... kms
Snack bar / take-away	SNACKS	On site		or	.... kms
Bar	BAR	On site		or	.... kms
Barbecue allowed	BBQ	Charcoal	Gas	Elec	Sep area
Cooking facilities	COOKING FACS				

G – LEISURE FACILITIES

Playground	PLAYGRND					
Swimming pool	POOL	On site	or ....km	Heated	Covered
Beach	BEACH	Adj	or ....km	Sand	Shingle
Alternative swimming (lake)	SW	Adj	or ....km	Sand	Shingle
Games /sports area / Games room	GAMES AREA	GAMES ROOM			
Entertainment in high season	ENTMNT				
Internet use by visitors	INTERNET	Wifi Internet		WIFI	
Television room	TV RM	Satellite / Cable to pitches		TV CAB / SAT	

H – OTHER INFORMATION

% Static caravans / mobile homes / chalets / cottages / fixed tents on site				................% STATICS
Dogs allowed	DOGS	Y / N	Price per night .... (if allowed)	
Phone	PHONE	On site	Adj	
Bus / tram / train	BUS / TRAM / TRAIN	Adj	or .... km	
Twin axles caravans allowed?	TWIN AXLES Y / N	Possibly crowded in high season		POSS CR
English spoken	ENG SPKN			
Advance bookings accepted	ADV BKG	Y / N		
Noise levels on site in season	NOISY	QUIET	If noisy, why?	
Credit card accepted	CCARD ACC	Reduction low season		RED LOW SSN
Camping Card International accepted in lieu of passport	CCI	INF card required (If naturist site)		Y / N
Facilities for disabled	Full wheelchair facilities	♦	Limited disabled facilities	♦ ltd

I – ADDITIONAL REMARKS AND/OR ITEMS OF INTEREST

Tourist attractions, unusual features or other facilities, eg waterslide, tennis, cycle hire, watersports, horseriding, separate car park, walking distance to shops etc	YOUR OPINION OF THE SITE:	
	EXCEL	
	VERY GOOD	
	GOOD	
	FAIR	POOR
	NIGHT HALT ONLY	

Your comments & opinions may be used in future editions of the guide, if you do not wish them to be used please tick ....

J – MEMBER DETAILS

ARE YOU A:	Caravanner		Motor caravanner		Trailer-tenter?	
NAME:		CARAVAN CLUB MEMBERSHIP NO:				
		POST CODE:				
DO YOU NEED MORE BLANK SITE REPORT FORMS?				YES		NO
Address (Non-members only please complete this section)						

Please use a separate form for each campsite and do not send receipts. Owing to the large number of site reports received, it is not possible to enter into correspondence. Please return completed form to:

The Editor, Caravan Europe, The Caravan Club
FREEPOST, PO Box 386, (RRZG-SXKK-UCUJ)
East Grinstead RH19 1FH

(This address to be used when mailing within the UK only)

Caravan Europe Site Report Form **

If campsite is already listed, complete only those sections of the form where changes apply

Please print, type or tick in the white areas

Sites not reported on for 5 years may be deleted from the guide

Year of guide used	20.........	Is site listed?	Listed on page no.		Unlisted	Date of visit	......./......./........

A – CAMPSITE NAME AND LOCATION

Country		Name of town/village site listed under *(see Sites Location Maps)*					
Distance & direction from centre of town site is listed under *(in a straight line)*		...................km	eg N, NE, S, SW		Urban	Rural	Coastal
Site open all year?	Y / N	Period site is open *(if not all year)*	................/................ to ..../................				
Site name					Naturist site		Y / N
Site address							
Telephone			Fax				
E-mail			Website				

B – CAMPSITE CHARGES

Charge for car, caravan + 2 adults in local currency	PRICE		EL PNTS inc in this price?	Y / N	Amps ....

C – DIRECTIONS

Brief, specific directions to site (in km) *To convert miles to kilometres multiply by 8 and divide by 5 or use Conversion Table in guide*	
GPS	Latitude...*(eg 12.34567)* Longitude...*(eg 1.23456 or -1.23456)*

D – CAMPSITE DESCRIPTION

SITE size ie number of pitches	Small Max 50	SM	Medium 51-150	MED	Large 151-500	LGE	Very large 500+	V LGE	Unchanged
PITCH size	*eg small, medium, large, very large, various*								Unchanged
Pitch features if **NOT** open-plan/grassy		Hedged	HDG PITCH	Marked or numbered	MKD PITCH	Hardstanding or gravel	HDSTG		Unchanged
If site is **NOT** level, is it		Part sloping	PT SL	Sloping	SL	Terraced	TERR		Unchanged
Is site shaded?		Shaded	SHD	Part shaded	PT SHD	Unshaded	UNSHD		Unchanged

E – CAMPSITE FACILITIES

WC	Heated	HTD WC	Continental	CONT	Own San recommended		OWN SAN REC	
Chemical disposal point		CHEM DISP		Dedicated point			WC only	
Motor caravan waste discharge and water refill point			MV SERVICE PNT					
Child / baby facilities (bathroom)		CHILD / BABY FACS		Family bathroom		FAM BTHRM		
Hot shower(s)		SHWR(S)		Inc in site fee?	Y / N	Price....................*(if not inc)*		
ELECTRIC HOOK UP *if not included in price above*		EL PNTS		Price............................		Amps..		
Supplies of bottled gas		GAS		On site	Y / N	Or in .... Kms		
Launderette / Washing Machine		LNDTTE		Inc dryer Y / N		LNDRY RM *(if no washing machine)*		

** *You can also complete forms online: www.caravanclub.co.uk/europereport*

F – FOOD & DRINK

Shop(s) / supermarket	SHOP(S) / SUPMKT	On site		or			.... kms
Bread / milk delivered	TRADSMN						
Restaurant / cafeteria	REST	On site		or			.... kms
Snack bar / take-away	SNACKS	On site		or			.... kms
Bar	BAR	On site		or			.... kms
Barbecue allowed	BBQ	Charcoal		Gas		Elec	Sep area
Cooking facilities	COOKING FACS						

G – LEISURE FACILITIES

Playground	PLAYGRND						
Swimming pool	POOL	On site		or ....km		Heated	Covered
Beach	BEACH	Adj		or ....km		Sand	Shingle
Alternative swimming *(lake)*	SW	Adj		or ....km		Sand	Shingle
Games /sports area / Games room	GAMES AREA	GAMES ROOM					
Entertainment in high season	ENTMNT						
Internet use by visitors	INTERNET	Wifi Internet			WIFI		
Television room	TV RM	Satellite / Cable to pitches			TV CAB / SAT		

H – OTHER INFORMATION

% Static caravans / mobile homes / chalets / cottages / fixed tents on site						.............% STATICS	
Dogs allowed	DOGS		Y / N	Price per night .... *(if allowed)*			
Phone	PHONE	On site		Adj			
Bus / tram / train	BUS / TRAM / TRAIN	Adj		or .... km			
Twin axles caravans allowed?	TWIN AXLES Y / N	Possibly crowded in high season				POSS CR	
English spoken	ENG SPKN						
Advance bookings accepted	ADV BKG		Y / N				
Noise levels on site in season	NOISY	QUIET	If noisy, why?				
Credit card accepted	CCARD ACC	Reduction low season				RED LOW SSN	
Camping Card International accepted in lieu of passport	CCI	INF card required *(If naturist site)*				Y / N	
Facilities for disabled	Full wheelchair facilities	♦		Limited disabled facilities		♦ ltd	

I – ADDITIONAL REMARKS AND/OR ITEMS OF INTEREST

Tourist attractions, unusual features or other facilities, eg waterslide, tennis, cycle hire, watersports, horseriding, separate car park, walking distance to shops etc	YOUR OPINION OF THE SITE:	
	EXCEL	
	VERY GOOD	
	GOOD	
	FAIR	POOR
	NIGHT HALT ONLY	

Your comments & opinions may be used in future editions of the guide, if you do not wish them to be used please tick ....

J – MEMBER DETAILS

ARE YOU A:	Caravanner		Motor caravanner		Trailer-tenter?	
NAME:		CARAVAN CLUB MEMBERSHIP NO:				
		POST CODE:				
DO YOU NEED MORE BLANK SITE REPORT FORMS?			YES		NO	
Address *(Non-members only please complete this section)*						

Please use a separate form for each campsite and do not send receipts. Owing to the large number of site reports received, it is not possible to enter into correspondence. Please return completed form to:

The Editor, Caravan Europe, The Caravan Club
FREEPOST, PO Box 386, (RRZG-SXKK-UCUJ)
East Grinstead RH19 1FH
(This address to be used when mailing within the UK only)

Caravan Europe **
Abbreviated Site Report Form

Use this abbreviated Site Report Form if you have visited a number of sites and there are no changes (or only insignificant changes) to their entries in the guide. If reporting on a new site, or reporting several changes, please use the full version of the report form. **If advising prices, these should be for a car, caravan and 2 adults for one night's stay. Please indicate high or low season prices and whether electricity is included.**

Remember, if you don't tell us about sites you have visited, they may eventually be deleted from the guide.

Year of guide used	20..........	Page No.	....	Name of town/village site listed under		
Site Name					Date of visit	.... /....... /........
GPS	Latitude...(eg 12.34567) Longitude...(eg 1.23456 or -1.23456)					

Site is in: Andorra / Austria / Belgium / Croatia / Czech Republic / Denmark / Finland / France / Germany / Greece / Hungary / Italy / Luxembourg / Netherlands / Norway / Poland / Portugal / Slovakia / Slovenia / Spain / Sweden / Switzerland

Charge for car, caravan & 2 adults in local currency	High Season	Low Season	Elec inc in price?	Y / N	............amps
			Price of elec (if not inc)		............amps

Year of guide used	20..........	Page No.	....	Name of town/village site listed under		
Site Name					Date of visit	.... /....... /........
GPS	Latitude...(eg 12.34567) Longitude...(eg 1.23456 or -1.23456)					

Site is in: Andorra / Austria / Belgium / Croatia / Czech Republic / Denmark / Finland / France / Germany / Greece / Hungary / Italy / Luxembourg / Netherlands / Norway / Poland / Portugal / Slovakia / Slovenia / Spain / Sweden / Switzerland

Charge for car, caravan & 2 adults in local currency	High Season	Low Season	Elec inc in price?	Y / N	............amps
			Price of elec (if not inc)		............amps

Year of guide used	20..........	Page No.	....	Name of town/village site listed under		
Site Name					Date of visit	.... /....... /........
GPS	Latitude...(eg 12.34567) Longitude...(eg 1.23456 or -1.23456)					

Site is in: Andorra / Austria / Belgium / Croatia / Czech Republic / Denmark / Finland / France / Germany / Greece / Hungary / Italy / Luxembourg / Netherlands / Norway / Poland / Portugal / Slovakia / Slovenia / Spain / Sweden / Switzerland

Charge for car, caravan & 2 adults in local currency	High Season	Low Season	Elec inc in price?	Y / N	............amps
			Price of elec (if not inc)		............amps

Your comments & opinions may be used in future editions of the guide, if you do not wish them to be used please tick ....

Please fill in NAME / MEMBERSHIP NUMBER etc
OVER PAGE

Please return completed form to:
The Editor, Caravan Europe, The Caravan Club
FREEPOST, PO Box 386 (RRZG-SXKK-UCUJ)
East Grinstead RH19 1FH
(This address to be used when mailing within UK only)

** You can also complete forms online: www.caravanclub.co.uk/europereport

CUT ALONG DOTTED LINE

Year of guide used	20.........	Page No.	....	Name of town/village site listed under			
Site Name						Date of visit	.... /....... /........
GPS	Latitude..(eg 12.34567) Longitude...(eg 1.23456 or -1.23456)						
Site is in: Andorra / Austria / Belgium / Croatia / Czech Republic / Denmark / Finland / France / Germany / Greece / Hungary / Italy / Luxembourg / Netherlands / Norway / Poland / Portugal / Slovakia / Slovenia / Spain / Sweden / Switzerland							

Charge for car, caravan & 2 adults in local currency	High Season	Low Season	Elec inc in price?	Y / N	............amps
			Price of elec (if not inc)		............amps

Year of guide used	20.........	Page No.	....	Name of town/village site listed under			
Site Name						Date of visit	.... /....... /........
GPS	Latitude..(eg 12.34567) Longitude...(eg 1.23456 or -1.23456)						
Site is in: Andorra / Austria / Belgium / Croatia / Czech Republic / Denmark / Finland / France / Germany / Greece / Hungary / Italy / Luxembourg / Netherlands / Norway / Poland / Portugal / Slovakia / Slovenia / Spain / Sweden / Switzerland							

Charge for car, caravan & 2 adults in local currency	High Season	Low Season	Elec inc in price?	Y / N	............amps
			Price of elec (if not inc)		............amps

Year of guide used	20.........	Page No.	....	Name of town/village site listed under			
Site Name						Date of visit	.... /....... /........
GPS	Latitude..(eg 12.34567) Longitude...(eg 1.23456 or -1.23456)						
Site is in: Andorra / Austria / Belgium / Croatia / Czech Republic / Denmark / Finland / France / Germany / Greece / Hungary / Italy / Luxembourg / Netherlands / Norway / Poland / Portugal / Slovakia / Slovenia / Spain / Sweden / Switzerland							

Charge for car, caravan & 2 adults in local currency	High Season	Low Season	Elec inc in price?	Y / N	............amps
			Price of elec (if not inc)		............amps

Name ....

Membership No. ....

Post Code ....

Address (if not a Caravan Club member)

Are you a Caravanner / Motor Caravanner / Trailer-Tenter?

Do you need more blank Site Report forms?   YES / NO

Caravan Europe **
Abbreviated Site Report Form

Use this abbreviated Site Report Form if you have visited a number of sites and there are no changes (or only insignificant changes) to their entries in the guide. If reporting on a new site, or reporting several changes, please use the full version of the report form. **If advising prices, these should be for a car, caravan and 2 adults for one night's stay. Please indicate high or low season prices and whether electricity is included.**

Remember, if you don't tell us about sites you have visited, they may eventually be deleted from the guide.

Year of guide used	20..........	Page No.	....	Name of town/village site listed under			
Site Name					Date of visit	.... /....... /........	
GPS	Latitude...(eg 12.34567) Longitude...(eg 1.23456 or -1.23456)						
Site is in: Andorra / Austria / Belgium / Croatia / Czech Republic / Denmark / Finland / France / Germany / Greece / Hungary / Italy / Luxembourg / Netherlands / Norway / Poland / Portugal / Slovakia / Slovenia / Spain / Sweden / Switzerland							
Charge for car, caravan & 2 adults in local currency	High Season	Low Season		Elec inc in price?	Y / N	............amps	
				Price of elec (if not inc)		............amps	

Year of guide used	20..........	Page No.	....	Name of town/village site listed under			
Site Name					Date of visit	.... /....... /........	
GPS	Latitude...(eg 12.34567) Longitude...(eg 1.23456 or -1.23456)						
Site is in: Andorra / Austria / Belgium / Croatia / Czech Republic / Denmark / Finland / France / Germany / Greece / Hungary / Italy / Luxembourg / Netherlands / Norway / Poland / Portugal / Slovakia / Slovenia / Spain / Sweden / Switzerland							
Charge for car, caravan & 2 adults in local currency	High Season	Low Season		Elec inc in price?	Y / N	............amps	
				Price of elec (if not inc)		............amps	

Year of guide used	20..........	Page No.	....	Name of town/village site listed under			
Site Name					Date of visit	.... /....... /........	
GPS	Latitude...(eg 12.34567) Longitude...(eg 1.23456 or -1.23456)						
Site is in: Andorra / Austria / Belgium / Croatia / Czech Republic / Denmark / Finland / France / Germany / Greece / Hungary / Italy / Luxembourg / Netherlands / Norway / Poland / Portugal / Slovakia / Slovenia / Spain / Sweden / Switzerland							
Charge for car, caravan & 2 adults in local currency	High Season	Low Season		Elec inc in price?	Y / N	............amps	
				Price of elec (if not inc)		............amps	

Your comments & opinions may be used in future editions of the guide, if you do not wish them to be used please tick ....

Please fill in NAME / MEMBERSHIP NUMBER etc
OVER PAGE

Please return completed form to:
The Editor, Caravan Europe, The Caravan Club
FREEPOST, PO Box 386 (RRZG-SXKK-UCUJ)
East Grinstead RH19 1FH
(This address to be used when mailing within UK only)

*** You can also complete forms online: www.caravanclub.co.uk/europereport*

Year of guide used	20..........	Page No.	....	Name of town/village site listed under	
Site Name				Date of visit	.... /....... /........
GPS	Latitude..(eg 12.34567) Longitude..(eg 1.23456 or -1.23456)				

Site is in: Andorra / Austria / Belgium / Croatia / Czech Republic / Denmark / Finland / France / Germany / Greece / Hungary / Italy / Luxembourg / Netherlands / Norway / Poland / Portugal / Slovakia / Slovenia / Spain / Sweden / Switzerland

Charge for car, caravan & 2 adults in local currency	High Season	Low Season	Elec inc in price?	Y / N	............amps
			Price of elec (if not inc)		............amps

Year of guide used	20..........	Page No.	....	Name of town/village site listed under	
Site Name				Date of visit	.... /....... /........
GPS	Latitude..(eg 12.34567) Longitude..(eg 1.23456 or -1.23456)				

Site is in: Andorra / Austria / Belgium / Croatia / Czech Republic / Denmark / Finland / France / Germany / Greece / Hungary / Italy / Luxembourg / Netherlands / Norway / Poland / Portugal / Slovakia / Slovenia / Spain / Sweden / Switzerland

Charge for car, caravan & 2 adults in local currency	High Season	Low Season	Elec inc in price?	Y / N	............amps
			Price of elec (if not inc)		............amps

Year of guide used	20..........	Page No.	....	Name of town/village site listed under	
Site Name				Date of visit	.... /....... /........
GPS	Latitude..(eg 12.34567) Longitude..(eg 1.23456 or -1.23456)				

Site is in: Andorra / Austria / Belgium / Croatia / Czech Republic / Denmark / Finland / France / Germany / Greece / Hungary / Italy / Luxembourg / Netherlands / Norway / Poland / Portugal / Slovakia / Slovenia / Spain / Sweden / Switzerland

Charge for car, caravan & 2 adults in local currency	High Season	Low Season	Elec inc in price?	Y / N	............amps
			Price of elec (if not inc)		............amps

Name ....

Membership No. ....

Post Code ....

Address (if not a Caravan Club member)

Are you a Caravanner / Motor Caravanner / Trailer-Tenter?

Do you need more blank Site Report forms?   YES / NO

Index

Index